DATE DUE

AP 23 '99		
Mar 20		
FEB 0		
AP 13 '01		
OCT 0 '01		
MY 23 '02		
JE 9 0		
AG 9 07		

DEMCO 38-296

HUMAN LEARNING

HUMAN LEARNING

THIRD EDITION

Jeanne Ellis Ormrod
University of Northern Colorado

Merrill,
an imprint of Prentice Hall
Upper Saddle River, New Jersey

Columbus, Ohio

blication Data

d.—3rd ed.

    p.   cm.
Includes bibliographical references and index.
ISBN 0-13-875684-8
   1. Learning, Psychology of. 2. Behaviorism (Psychology)
I. Title.
BF318.O76 1999
153.1'5—dc21   98–21670
                                        CIP

Cover art: © Superstock
Editor: Kevin M. Davis
Production Editor: Julie Peters
Production Coordination: Carlisle Publishers Services
Cover Design Coordinator: Diane C. Lorenzo
Cover Designer: Janoski Advertising
Production Manager: Laura Messerly
Director of Marketing: Kevin Flanagan
Marketing Manager: Suzanne Stanton
Advertising/Marketing Coordinator: Krista Groshong

This book was set in Garamond by Carlisle Communications, Ltd. and was printed and bound by Courier/Westford, Inc. The cover was printed by Phoenix Color Corp.

© 1999, 1995 by Prentice-Hall, Inc.
Simon & Schuster/A Viacom Company
Upper Saddle River, New Jersey 07458

Earlier edition © 1990 by Merrill, an imprint of Macmillan Publishing Company.

Printed in the United States of America

10 9 8 7 6 5 4 3 2 1

ISBN: 0-13-875684-8

Prentice-Hall International (UK) Limited, *London*
Prentice-Hall of Australia Pty. Limited, *Sydney*
Prentice-Hall of Canada, Inc., *Toronto*
Prentice-Hall Hispanoamericana, S.A., *Mexico*
Prentice-Hall of India Private Limited, *New Delhi*
Prentice-Hall of Japan, Inc., *Tokyo*
Simon & Schuster Asia Pte. Ltd., *Singapore*
Editora Prentice-Hall do Brasil, Ltda., *Rio de Janeiro*

Preface

Human learning is a complex and fascinating process. I have been excited about how much psychologists have learned about learning since the turn of the century. Yet I have been discouraged about how little their knowledge of the learning process has been used to help people learn more efficiently and effectively. For many years I searched for a textbook that explained principles and theories of human learning in a readable and down-to-earth fashion and also applied those theories and principles to educational practice. I continued to hope someone would write such a book but finally realized that the "someone" would have to be me.

I have written this book with particular students in mind: students who would like to learn about learning but often do not have much background in psychology. Such students may benefit from studying the historical roots of learning theories but prefer to focus their energies on studying contemporary perspectives and ideas. These students might find learning theories fascinating but lose patience when they cannot see the relevance of those theories to everyday practice. These students are capable of reading a dry, terse textbook but probably learn more effectively from a book that shows how different concepts relate to one another, provides numerous examples, and, especially, emphasizes meaningful learning—true *understanding*—of the material it presents.

In This Editon

This third edition of *Human Learning* is different in several ways from the second edition of 1995. The old chapter entitled "Perception and Attention" is gone; attention is now treated in Chapter 9, and the constructive nature of perception appears near the beginning of Chapter 10. The old chapter "Learning Concepts" has also disappeared; the nature of concepts and concept learning is now included in Chapter 11, and strategies for teaching concepts are discussed in Chapter 13. Treatment of long-term memory has been expanded from two chapters to three, with the second one, Chapter 11, describing the nature of knowledge. Furthermore, a new Chapter 16 addresses interactive methods of instruction, including class discussions, reciprocal teaching, cooperative learning, peer tutoring, apprenticeships, authentic activities, and communities of learners. Many other new topics appear throughout the book, including chaining (Chapter 4); cognitive aspects of applied behavior analysis (Chapter 5); constructivist and contextual views of learning (Chapter 8); effects of verbalization and enactment (Chapter 10); dichotomies in long-term memory, mental theories, and development of expertise (Chapter 11); effects of alternative forms of assessment (Chapter 13); self-regulated learning and epistemological beliefs (Chapter 14); self-worth theory (Chapter 17); and internalized motivation (Chapter 18). And of course I have rewritten every chapter to reflect the latest developments in learning theory and research.

Acknowledgments

Although I am listed as the sole author, I have certainly not written this book alone. Many people have helped me along the way:

- Frank Di Vesta, my adviser and mentor at Penn State, who taught me a great deal about learning and who absolutely refused to let me graduate until I also learned a great deal about writing.
- Kevin Davis, acquisitions editor for the second and third editions, and Dave Faherty, editor for the first edition, both of whom provided me with guidance when I needed it but trusted my instincts about how best to present the field of human learning to my readers.
- My colleagues across the nation who read earlier drafts most thoroughly and conscientiously and whose suggestions have greatly improved the final product: Livingston Alexander, Western Kentucky University; Martha B. Bronson, Boston College; Margaret W. Cohen, University of Missouri at St. Louis; Ralph F. Darr, Jr., The University of Akron; Jean C. Faieta, Edinboro University of Pennsylvania; Sarah Huyvaert, Eastern Michigan University; Janina Jolley, Clarion University of Pennsylvania; Joseph Kersting, Western Illinois University; Mary Lou Koran, University of Florida; Gerald Larson, Kent State University; Mark Lewis, University of Texas at Tyler; Michael S. Meloth, University of Colorado; John Newell, University of Florida at Gainesville; Jim O'Connor, California State University at Bakersfield; Sarah Peterson, Northern Illinois University; Steven Pulos, University of Northern Colorado; and Karen Zabrucky, Georgia State University.
- My husband, Richard, and my children, Christina, Alex, and Jeffrey, who have been eternally supportive of my writing endeavors and who have provided me with numerous examples of human learning in action.
- My parents, James and Nancy Ellis, who long ago taught me the value of higher education.
- My students, who urged me to write the book in the first place and continue to give me feedback about how I can make it better.

Jeanne Ellis Ormrod

Contents

CHAPTER 3

Classical Conditioning   21

CHAPTER 4

Operant Conditioning   35

Contents

CHAPTER 5

Applications of Operant Conditioning   67

CHAPTER 6

Effects of Aversive Stimuli   94

PART THREE

SOCIAL LEARNING THEORY

CHAPTER 7

Social Learning Theory   114

PART FOUR

COGNITIVE VIEWS OF LEARNING

CHAPTER 8

Antecedents and Assumptions of Cognitivism   145

CHAPTER 11

Long-Term Memory II: The Nature of Knowledge   230

CHAPTER 12

Long-Term Memory III: Retrieval, Forgetting, and Classroom Practice   264

CHAPTER 15

Transfer and Problem Solving   347

CHAPTER 16

Applications of Cognitivism II: Learning through Interactions with Others   385

CHAPTER 1

Definitions and Perspectives of Learning

When my son Alex was in kindergarten, his teacher asked me *please* to do something about his shoes. I had been sending Alex off to school every morning with his shoelaces carefully and lovingly tied, yet by the time he arrived at his classroom door, the laces were untied and flopping every which way—a state to which they invariably returned within 10 minutes of his teacher's retying them. I tried a series of shoe-tying lessons with Alex, but with little success. As an alternative, I proposed that we double-knot the laces when we tied them each morning, but Alex rejected my suggestion as being too babyish. I purchased a couple of pairs of shoes that had Velcro straps instead of laces, but Alex gave the shoes such a workout that the Velcro quickly separated itself from the leather. By March, the teacher, justifiably irritated that she had to tie Alex's shoes so many times each day, insisted that Alex learn to tie them himself. So I sat down with my son and demonstrated, for the umpteenth time, how to put two laces together to make a presentable bow. This time, however, I accompanied my explanation with a magical statement: "Alex, when you learn to tie your shoes, I will give you a quarter." Alex had shoe tying perfected in five minutes, and we haven't had a complaint from school since—at least not about his shoes.

When my daughter Tina was in fourth grade, she experienced considerable difficulty with a series of homework assignments in subtraction. She had never learned the basic subtraction facts, despite my continual nagging her to do so, with the result being that she could not solve two- and three-digit subtraction problems successfully. One night, after her typical half-hour tantrum about "these stupid problems," my husband explained to Tina that subtraction was nothing more than reversed addition and that her knowledge of addition facts could help her with subtraction. Something must have clicked in Tina's head, because we weren't subjected to any more tantrums about subtraction. Multiplication, yes, but not subtraction.

Human learning takes many different forms, some of which are easily seen and some of which are not. Some instances of learning are readily observable, such as when a child learns to tie shoes. But other instances of learning are more subtle, such as when a child gains a new understanding of mathematical principles. And people learn for many different reasons. Some learn for the rewards their achievements bring—for example, for good grades, recognition, or money (consider my mercenary son). But others learn for less obvious reasons—perhaps for a sense of accomplishment or simply to make life easier.

In this book, I will describe human learning from the various perspectives that have evolved in psychological theory throughout the twentieth century. As you will soon discover, learning is a complicated process, and psychologists disagree even about such basic issues as what learning is, how it occurs, and which factors are necessary for it to occur at all.

IMPORTANCE OF LEARNING

Many species have things easy compared with humans, or at least so it would seem. Birds, for example, are born with a wealth of knowledge that we humans must learn. Birds instinctively know how to build their houses; we either have to be taught something about framing, roofing, and drywalling or else have to hire someone to do these things for us. Birds know, without being told, exactly when to fly south and how to get there; we have to look at our calendars and road maps. Birds instinctively know how to care for their young; meanwhile, we attend prenatal classes, read child-care books, and watch others demonstrate how to change diapers.

On the other hand, it is the humans, not the birds, who are getting ahead in this world. Over the years, human beings have learned to make increasingly stronger and more comfortable homes for themselves, while birds are still making the same flimsy, drafty nests they have been living in for thousands of years. Humans have developed fast, dependable modes of transportation for themselves and their goods, while birds are still winging it. And humans are learning how better to feed and care for themselves and their young, so that each generation grows taller, stronger, and healthier than the previous one. Birds, meanwhile, are still eating worms.

The learning process allows the human race a greater degree of flexibility and adaptability than is true for any other species on the planet. Because so little of our behavior is instinctive and so much of it is learned, we are able to benefit from our experiences. We know which actions are likely to lead to successful outcomes and which are not, and we modify our behavior accordingly. And as adults pass on to children the wisdom gleaned from their ancestors and from their own experiences, each generation is just that much more capable of behaving intelligently. Let's face it: We can get from New York to Miami in two hours, but how long does it take the birds?

DEFINING LEARNING

My son Alex's learning to tie his shoes and my daughter Tina's learning how subtraction relates to addition are both examples of learning. Consider these instances of learning as well:

- The mother of a five-year-old boy insists that her son assume some household chores, for which he earns a small weekly allowance. The allowance, when saved for two or three weeks, enables the boy to purchase small toys of his own choosing. As a result, he develops an appreciation for the value of money.
- A college freshman from a small town is, for the first time, exposed to political viewpoints different from her own. After engaging in heated political debates with her classmates, she evaluates and modifies her own political philosophy.
- A toddler is overly affectionate with a neighborhood dog, and the dog responds by biting the boy's hand. After that, the child cries and runs quickly to his mother every time he sees a dog.

Learning is the means through which we acquire not only skills and knowledge but values, attitudes, and emotional reactions as well.

Just what do we mean by the term **learning?** Different psychologists conceptualize and define learning differently. Here are two definitions that reflect two common, yet quite different, conceptions of learning:

1. Learning is a relatively permanent change in behavior due to experience.
2. Learning is a relatively permanent change in mental associations due to experience.

What things do these definitions have in common? Both speak of learning as involving a "relatively permanent" *change*—a change that will last for some time, although not necessarily forever. And both definitions attribute that change to *experience;* in other words, learning takes place as a result of one or more events in the learner's life. Other changes, such as those due to maturational changes in the body, organic damage, or temporary body states (e.g., fatigue or drugs), are not attributable to experience and so do not reflect learning.

The two definitions I have just given you differ primarily in terms of *what* changes when learning occurs. The first definition refers to a change in *behavior*—an external change that we can observe—and reflects the perspective of a group of theories collectively known as **behaviorism.** Behaviorist theories focus on the learning of tangible, observable behaviors or *responses,* such as tying shoes, solving a subtraction problem correctly, or complaining about a stomachache to avoid going to school.

In contrast, the second definition focuses on a change in *mental associations*—an internal change that we *cannot* observe—reflecting the perspective of a group of theories collectively known as **cognitivism.** Cognitive theories focus not on behavioral outcomes but on the *thought processes* (sometimes called *mental events*) involved in human learning. Examples of such processes include finding relationships between addition and subtraction facts, using memory gimmicks to remember French vocabulary words, or deriving idiosyncratic and highly personalized meanings from classic works of literature.

In this book, I will describe both the behaviorist and cognitive views of learning in considerable detail; I will also describe perspectives that lie somewhere between the two extremes. Most psychologists tend to align themselves with one perspective or the other, and I, whose graduate training and research program have been rooted firmly in cognitive traditions, am no exception. Yet I firmly believe that both the behaviorist and cognitive perspectives have something important to say about human learning and that both provide useful suggestions for helping people learn more effectively.

NATURE OF PRINCIPLES AND THEORIES

The systematic study of human behavior, including human and animal learning processes, has emerged only within the last century, making psychology a relative newcomer to scientific inquiry. But in a century's time, thousands of experiments have investigated how people and animals learn, and the patterns in the results of these experiments have led psychologists to generalize about the learning process through the formulation of both principles and theories of learning.

Principles of learning identify specific factors that consistently influence learning and describe the particular effects of these factors. For example, consider this learning principle:

> *A behavior that is followed by a satisfying state of affairs (a reward) is more likely to be learned than a behavior not followed by such a reward.*

In this principle, a particular factor (a reward that follows a behavior) is identified as having a particular effect on learning (an increase in the frequency of the behavior). The principle can be observed in many different situations, including the following:

- A pigeon is given a small pellet of food every time it turns its body in a complete circle. It begins turning more and more frequently.
- Dolphins who are given fish for "speaking" in Dolphinese quickly become quite chatty.
- A boy who completes a perfect spelling paper and is praised for it by a favorite teacher works diligently for future success in spelling assignments.
- A high school girl who receives compliments on her new hairstyle continues to style her hair in the same way.

Principles are most useful when they can be applied to a wide variety of situations. The reward principle is an example of such broad applicability: it applies to both animals and humans and holds true for different types of learning and for different rewards. When a principle such as this one is observed over and over again—when it stands the test of time—it is sometimes called a **law.**

Theories of learning provide explanations about the underlying mechanisms involved in the learning process. Whereas principles tell us *what* factors are important for learning, theories tell us *why* these factors are important. For example, consider one aspect of social learning theory (described in Chapter 7):

> *People learn what they pay attention to. Reward increases learning when it makes people pay attention to the information to be learned.*

Here we have one possible explanation of why a reward affects learning. Attention is identified as the underlying process responsible for the observed effect of reward on learning.

Advantages of Theories

Theories have several advantages over principles. First, theories allow us to summarize the results of many research studies and integrate numerous principles of learning. In that sense, theories are often very concise (psychologists use the term **parsimonious**).

Second, theories provide starting points for conducting new research; they suggest research questions worthy of study. For example, the theory that attention is more important than reward leads to the following prediction:

> *When instruction draws an individual's attention to the information to be learned, learning occurs in the absence of a reward.*

In fact, this prediction has frequently been supported by research (e.g., Faust & Anderson, 1967; Hyde & Jenkins, 1969).

Third, theories help us to make sense of research findings. Research conducted outside of the context of a particular theoretical perspective frequently yields results that are trivial and nongeneralizable. Interpreted from a theoretical perspective, however, those same results become significant. For example, consider an experiment by Seligman and Maier (1967). In this classic study, dogs were placed in individual cages and given a number of painful and unpredictable shocks. Some dogs were able to escape the shocks by pressing a panel in the cage, whereas others were unable to escape. The following day, the dogs were placed in different cages, and again shocks were administered. This time, however, each shock was preceded by a signal (a tone) that the shock was coming, and the dogs could escape the shocks by jumping over a barrier as soon as they heard the tone. The dogs that had been able to escape the shocks on the preceding day learned to escape in this new situation, but the dogs that had been unable to escape previously did *not* learn to escape the shocks now that they could do so. On the surface, this experiment, although interesting, might not seem especially relevant to human learning. Yet Seligman and his colleagues used this and other experiments to develop their theory of *learned helplessness:* People who learn that they have no control over unpleasant or painful events in one situation are unlikely, in later situations, to try to escape or avoid those aversive events even when it is possible for them to do so.

Theories have a fourth advantage as well: By giving us ideas about the mechanisms that underlie human learning and performance, theories can ultimately help us to design learning environments that facilitate human learning to the greatest possible degree. For example, consider the teacher who is familiar with the theory that attention is an essential ingredient in the learning process. That teacher may identify and use a variety of approaches—perhaps providing interesting reading materials, presenting intriguing problems, and praising good performance—that are likely to increase students' attention to academic subject matter. In contrast, consider the teacher who is familiar only with the principle that rewarded behaviors are learned. That teacher may use certain rewards—perhaps small toys or trinkets—that are counterproductive because they distract students' attention from the academic tasks at hand.

Disadvantages of Theories

Despite their advantages, theories also have at least two disadvantages. First, no single theory explains everything that researchers have discovered about learning. Current theories of learning tend to focus on specific aspects of learning. Behaviorist theories, for example, limit themselves to situations in which learning involves a behavior change. Cognitive theories tend to focus instead on how people organize and remember the information they receive. Observed phenomena that do not fit comfortably within a particular theoretical perspective are usually excluded from that perspective.

Second, theories affect what new information is published, therefore biasing the knowledge that we have about learning. For example, imagine that several researchers propose a particular theory of learning and conduct a research study to support their idea. However, the results of their research are exactly the opposite of what they had expected and so cast doubt on their theory. If these researchers are fully committed to demonstrating that their theory is correct, they are unlikely to publish results that will indicate otherwise. In this way, theories may sometimes impede progress toward a truly accurate understanding of the learning process.

A Perspective on Theories and Principles

You should probably think of the learning theories I describe in this book as dynamic, changing models of the learning process. Each theory is based on several decades of research results, and each has some validity. However, as research continues in the decades ahead, our theories of learning will undoubtedly be revised to account for the new evidence that emerges. In this sense, no single theory can be considered "fact."

At the same time, you might think of learning principles as relatively enduring conclusions about cause-effect relationships in the learning process. Principles generally maintain their validity longer than theories do. The reward principle was introduced by Edward Thorndike in 1898 and has remained with us in one form or another ever since. Thorndike's theory of *why* reward affects learning, however, has been largely replaced by other explanations.

Both principles and theories provide a means to predict the conditions under which learning is likely to occur. To the extent that principles and theories are useful in this way, we are better off with them—imperfect and temporary as they may be—than without them.

APPLYING PRINCIPLES AND THEORIES TO INSTRUCTIONAL PRACTICE

A great deal of learning takes place in a classroom context, and most of it is undoubtedly beneficial. For example, it is in the classroom that most students learn how to read and how to subtract one number from another. Unfortunately, students may also learn things at school that are *not* in their best interest over the long run. For example, although students may learn to read, they may also learn that the "best" way to remember what they read is to memorize it, word for word, without necessarily trying to understand it. And although students may learn their subtraction facts, they may also learn that mathematics is a boring and often frustrating endeavor.

The learning that takes place in our schools cannot be left to chance. The better we understand the factors that influence learning (principles) and the processes that underlie it (theories), the more effectively we can promote the kinds of learning that will facilitate students' long-term success rather than the kinds of learning that might actually interfere with it.

The theories I have included in the chapters ahead portray human learning from different perspectives; sometimes they even contradict one another. Yet I hope you will take an eclectic perspective as you read the book, resisting the temptation to choose one theory over others as being the "right" one. Different theories are applicable in different situations, depending on the environmental factors under consideration, the specific content being learned, and the objectives of instruction. At the same time, each theory provides unique insights into how and why human beings learn and how instruction might be designed to enhance student learning (e.g., see Catania, 1985; Epstein, 1991; Reynolds, Sinatra, & Jetton, 1996). It is probably more helpful to think of theories in terms of their *usefulness* than in terms of their correctness.

As theories of learning continue to be revised and refined in the years to come, so, too, will instructional practices be revised and refined. In the meantime, we can use current theories to help people of all ages learn more effectively and less painfully than they seem to be learning now.

OVERVIEW OF THE BOOK

In Part II of the book, we will explore principles and theories of learning from the behaviorist perspective, focusing on relationships between environmental events (stimuli) and the behaviors (responses) that people acquire as a result of those events. We will begin with an introduction and historical overview of behaviorism (Chapter 2) and then examine in depth the two most commonly used models of learning within the behaviorist perspective: classical conditioning (Chapter 3) and operant conditioning (Chapters 4 and 5). We will also look at the role of unpleasant events, such as punishment, in the learning process (Chapter 6).

In Part III (Chapter 7), we will make the transition from behaviorism to cognitivism as we examine social learning theory, a theory that has evolved over the years from its behaviorist roots into a blend of behaviorist and cognitive ideas regarding how and what people learn by observing those around them.

In Part IV, we will turn to theories of learning that are almost entirely cognitive in nature. We will first look at a variety of cognitive perspectives, both old and new, that have contributed to our understanding of how people think and learn (Chapter 8). We will then examine in depth the internal mental processes involved in learning and memory (Chapters 9, 10, and 12) and the nature of the "knowledge" that such processes yield (Chapter 11). We will also consider several specific educational applications of cognitive theories (Chapter 13).

As we proceed to Part V, we will continue our exploration of cognitive theories by examining more complex aspects of human learning and cognition. More specifically, we will look at how well people understand and regulate their own thinking processes—a phenomenon known as *metacognition*—and how effectively they can apply what they have learned in one situation to new tasks and problems (Chapters 14 and 15). We will then identify additional educational applications of cognitivism that can facilitate such complex cognitive processes (Chapter 16).

Finally, in Part VI, we will consider the role that motivation plays in human learning. We will look at the effects of motivation on learning and behavior and examine several theoretical perspectives regarding the nature of motivation (Chapter 17). We will also discover that, in many respects, learning and motivation are closely interrelated phenomena (Chapter 18).

Throughout the book, we will stop frequently to identify the educational implications of the principles and theories we are studying. I hope that, once you have finished the final chapter, you will be convinced, as I am, that psychology has a great deal to say about how we can enhance teaching and learning both inside and outside of the classroom.

SUMMARY

Learning allows human beings a greater degree of flexibility and adaptability than is true for any other species. Currently, two major theoretical perspectives help us to understand how people learn. The behaviorist perspective emphasizes relationships among observable stimuli and responses. The cognitive perspective emphasizes the role of internal mental processes involved in learning. Principles (descriptions of what factors affect learning) and theories (explanations of why those factors have the effects they do) from both behaviorism and cognitivism can help educators optimize learning environments and facilitate student achievement.

CHAPTER 2

Overview of Behaviorism

Behaviorism, the first psychological perspective to have a significant impact on our understanding of how human beings learn, is the topic of Chapters 2 through 6. In this chapter, I will describe the major assumptions of the behaviorist approach to learning, provide a historical overview of some of the key theorists who have contributed to the behaviorist movement, give you a brief glimpse of how behaviorism has changed in recent years, and discuss some general implications of behaviorist theories for educational practice. In the chapters that follow, I will cover more specific aspects of behaviorism, including classical conditioning (Chapter 3), operant conditioning and its applications (Chapters 4 and 5), and the effects of aversive stimuli on learning and behavior (Chapter 6).

ASSUMPTIONS OF BEHAVIORISM

Before the twentieth century, the two dominant perspectives in psychology were **structuralism** (e.g., Wilhelm Wundt's work) and **functionalism** (e.g., John Dewey's writings). Although these two perspectives differed considerably in their underlying assumptions and topics of study, they shared a common weakness: They lacked a precise, carefully defined research methodology. The primary means of investigating learning and other psychological phenomena, especially for the structuralists, was a method called **introspection:** People were simply asked to "look" inside their minds and describe what they were "thinking."

Beginning with the efforts of the Russian physiologist Ivan Pavlov and the American psychologist Edward Thorndike, however, a more objective approach to the study of learning—one that focused on observable phenomena rather than on nonobservable mental events—emerged. These researchers looked primarily at *behavior*—something that they could easily see and objectively describe—and so the behaviorist movement was born.

As will become clear later in the chapter, behaviorists have not always agreed on the specific processes that account for learning. Yet most of them have historically shared certain basic assumptions about learning:

- *Principles of learning apply equally to different behaviors and to different species of animals.* Behaviorists typically assume that human beings and other animals learn in similar ways—an assumption known as **equipotentiality.** (Behaviorists often use the term **organism** to refer generically to a member of any species, human and nonhuman alike.) As a result of this assumption, behaviorists often apply to human learning situations the principles that they have derived primarily from research with such animals as rats and pigeons.

- *Learning processes can be studied most objectively when the focus of study is on stimuli and responses.* Behaviorists believe that psychologists must study learning through objective scientific inquiry, in much the same way that chemists and physicists study phenomena in the physical world. By focusing on two things that they can observe and measure—more specifically, by focusing on **stimuli** in the environment and **responses** that organisms make to those stimuli—psychologists can maintain such objectivity. A behaviorist principle of learning typically describes a relationship between a stimulus **(S)** and a response **(R)**; hence, behaviorism is sometimes called **S-R psychology.**

- *Internal cognitive processes are largely excluded from scientific study.* Many behaviorists believe that because we cannot directly observe and measure internal mental processes (e.g., thoughts, motives, and emotions), we should exclude such processes from our explanations of how learning occurs. These behaviorists describe an organism as a "black box," with stimuli impinging on the box and responses emerging from it, but with the things going on inside of it forever remaining a mystery.

- *Learning involves a behavior change.* As noted in Chapter 1, behaviorists define learning as a change in behavior; after all, we cannot observe any internal, mental changes that might be happening at the same time as a behavior changes. In fact, some behaviorists have proposed that if no behavior change occurs, then learning cannot possibly be taking place at all.

- *Organisms are born as blank slates.* Aside from certain species-specific instincts (such as the nest-building and migratory behaviors that many birds exhibit), organisms are not born with any predispositions to behave in particular ways. Instead, organisms enter the world as "blank slates" (an idea often referred to by the Latin equivalent, **tabula rasa**) upon which environmental experiences gradually "write." Because each organism has a unique set of environmental experiences, so, too, will it acquire its own unique set of behaviors.

- *Learning is largely the result of environmental events.* Rather than using the term *learning,* behaviorists often speak of **conditioning:** An organism *is conditioned* by environmental events. The passive form of this verb connotes many behaviorists' belief that because learning is the result of one's experiences, learning happens *to* an organism in a way that is often beyond the organism's control.

- *The most useful theories tend to be parsimonious ones.* According to behaviorists, we should explain the learning of all behaviors, from the most simple to the most complex, by as few learning principles as possible; this assumption reflects a preference for **parsimony** (conciseness) in explaining learning and behavior. As you will discover in the pages ahead, behaviorists have been quite successful in using just a few simple principles to explain a great deal of human and animal behavior.

Not all behaviorists would agree with all of the assumptions I have just listed. For instance, many theorists disagree with the "black box" assumption, believing that internal factors—those within the organism (O)—are also important in understanding learning and behavior. Such **neobehaviorist** theorists are sometimes called S-O-R (stimulus-organism-response) theorists rather than S-R theorists.

EARLY THEORISTS IN THE BEHAVIORIST TRADITION

Numerous theorists contributed to the rise of behaviorism during the early decades of the twentieth century. The contributions of six of them—Ivan Pavlov, Edward L. Thorndike, John B. Watson, Edwin R. Guthrie, Clark. L. Hull, and B. F. Skinner—are described briefly in this chapter. Two of these six, Pavlov and Skinner, have had such a significant impact that we will look at their theories again in more detail in Chapters 3 and 4.

Ivan Pavlov

The Russian physiologist Ivan Pavlov, while investigating salivation reflexes in dogs, discovered that a dog would salivate not only to food but also to other environmental events that it associated with food—for example, to the laboratory assistant who often delivered the dog's meals. Through a systematic study of how dogs learn to salivate to different stimuli, Pavlov developed a theory of learning now commonly known as *classical conditioning* (e.g., Pavlov, 1927).

From Pavlov's perspective, learning begins with a stimulus-response connection in which a particular stimulus (e.g., meat) leads to a particular response (e.g., salivation).

When that stimulus is repeatedly presented in association with one or more other stimuli (e.g., with the laboratory assistant or the sound of his footsteps in the hall), those other stimuli begin to elicit a similar response. This process of classical conditioning, which I will describe in greater detail in Chapter 3, appeared in the work of other early psychologists (e.g., Watson and Skinner) as well. We now realize that classical conditioning is a powerful force in learning, especially in the learning of emotional responses.

Edward L. Thorndike

In 1898 Edward Thorndike introduced a theory of learning that emphasized the role of experience in the strengthening and weakening of stimulus-response connections; this perspective is now known as **connectionism** (Thorndike, 1898, 1911, 1913). In his classic first experiment (his doctoral dissertation), Thorndike placed a cat in a "puzzle box" with a door that opened when some device (e.g., a wire loop) was appropriately manipulated. Thorndike observed the cat initiating numerous, apparently random movements in its attempts to get out of the box; eventually, by chance, the cat triggered the mechanism that opened the door and allowed escape. When returned to the box a second time, the cat again engaged in trial-and-error movements but managed to escape in less time than it had previously. With successive trials in the box, the cat, although continuing to demonstrate trial-and-error behavior, managed to escape within shorter and shorter time periods.

From his observations of cats in the puzzle box, Thorndike concluded that the learning of a behavior is affected by the consequence of that behavior (e.g., escape from a confining situation). We can sum up Thorndike's *law of effect* as follows:

> *Responses to a situation that are followed by satisfaction are strengthened; responses that are followed by discomfort are weakened.*

According to Thorndike, learning consists of trial-and-error behavior and a gradual "stamping in" of some behaviors (those leading to satisfaction) and "stamping out" of other behaviors (those leading to discomfort). In other words, rewarded responses increase, and punished responses diminish and disappear.

In addition to his law of effect, Thorndike proposed that practice influences S-R connections as well. His *law of exercise* can be paraphrased as follows:

> *Stimulus-response connections that are repeated are strengthened; stimulus-response connections that are not used are weakened.*

In other words, practice facilitates the learning of responses. Responses that are not practiced gradually disappear.

Thorndike eventually revised his law of effect and discarded his law of exercise (Thorndike, 1935). The original law of effect implied that reward and punishment have opposite but equal effects on behavior: One strengthens and the other weakens. But Thorndike's later research (1932a, 1932b) indicated that punishment may not be effective in weakening responses. For example, in one experiment (Thorndike, 1932a), college students completed a multiple-choice Spanish vocabulary test in which they were to choose the English translation for each of a long list of Spanish words. Every time a student chose the correct English word out of five alternatives, the experimenter said

"Right!" (presumably rewarding the response); every time a student chose an incorrect alternative, the experimenter said "Wrong!" (presumably punishing the response). In responding to the same multiple-choice questions over a series of trials, the students increased the responses for which they had been rewarded but did not necessarily decrease those for which they had been punished. In his *revised law of effect,* Thorndike continued to maintain that rewards strengthen the behaviors they follow, but he deemphasized the role of punishment. Instead, he proposed that punishment has an *indirect* effect on learning: As a result of an annoying state of affairs, an organism may engage in certain other behaviors (e.g., crying or running away) that interfere with performance of the punished response.

Thorndike also conducted research (described by Trowbridge & Cason, 1932) that casts doubt on the effect of practice alone on learning. For example, in one experiment, people were blindfolded and asked to draw a series of four-inch lines. They could not see the results of their efforts, and they received no information from the experimenter about the correctness of their drawings. Without feedback, they did not improve in accuracy despite their practice, a result that led Thorndike to repudiate his law of exercise.

Although not all of Thorndike's original ideas have stood the test of time, his belief that satisfying consequences bring about changes in behavior—in other words, that rewards promote learning—continues to be a key component of behaviorist perspectives today.

John B. Watson

Although Pavlov and Thorndike are considered to be among the earliest contributors to the behaviorist tradition, it was actually John Watson (1913) who introduced the term *behaviorism* and served as the most vocal advocate for the behaviorist perspective in the early part of the twentieth century.

In his major writings (Watson, 1914, 1919, 1925), Watson adamantly called for the introduction of scientific objectivity and experimentation into the study of psychological phenomena. He emphasized the need for focusing scientific inquiry on observable behaviors rather than on such nonobservable phenomena as "thinking." Not only did Watson oppose the study of internal mental events, he denied any existence of the mind at all! Thought, he proposed, was nothing more than tiny movements of the tongue and larynx and thus was a behavior just like any other.

Greatly influenced by the work of both Pavlov and another Russian, Vladimir Bechterev (Bechterev, 1913), Watson adopted the classically conditioned S-R **habit** as the basic unit of learning and extended it to human learning (Watson, 1916; Watson & Rayner, 1920). Watson proposed two laws that described how such habits developed. First, his *law of frequency* (similar to Thorndike's law of exercise) stressed the importance of repetition:

> *The more frequently a stimulus and response occur in association with each other, the stronger that S-R habit will become.*

Second, Watson's *law of recency* stressed the importance of timing:

> *The response that has most recently occurred after a particular stimulus is the response most likely to be associated with that stimulus.*

In other words, the last response that an organism has made to a stimulus is the one most likely to occur the next time the stimulus is presented. Through his law of recency, Watson rejected Thorndike's law of effect. According to Watson, reward has only an indirect effect on learning in that the most *recent* response is the one rewarded. For example, when a cat is in a puzzle box, the last response is the one that leads to escape and so is most likely to be connected to that stimulus situation.

Watson believed that past experience accounts for virtually all behavior. His extreme environmentalism, which denied that hereditary factors had any effect on behavior whatsoever, was reflected in the following infamous quote:

> Give me a dozen healthy infants, well-formed, and my own specified world to bring them up in and I'll guarantee to take any one at random and train him to become any type of specialist I might select—doctor, lawyer, artist, merchant-chief, and yes, even beggar-man and thief, regardless of his talents, penchants, tendencies, abilities, vocations and race of his ancestors. (Watson, 1925, p. 82)

Watson's influence continued to be felt long after he retired from academia in 1920. His strong advocacy of psychology as an objective and precise science and his insistence that environment plays a key role in human behavior led to a behaviorist tradition that dominated psychological research and theory in the western hemisphere until the 1960s.

Edwin R. Guthrie

Edwin Guthrie's **contiguity theory** (Guthrie, 1935, 1942) was similar to John Watson's perspective in that it emphasized S-R connections and rejected the role of reward in developing these connections. Guthrie's basic principle of learning was as follows:

> *A stimulus that is followed by a particular response will, upon its recurrence, tend to be followed by the same response again. This S-R connection gains its full strength on one trial.*

In other words, if an organism responds to a particular stimulus in a particular way on one occasion, the organism will make the same response the next time it encounters the same stimulus; in this manner, a habit is formed. Guthrie contended that the critical factor in learning is the **contiguity**—the more or less simultaneous occurrence—of a stimulus and a response.

Guthrie also shared Watson's belief that *recency* is critical in learning: An organism will respond to a stimulus in the way that it has most recently responded to that stimulus. A reward facilitates learning only to the extent that it removes the organism from the stimulus, thus preventing subsequent responses from being associated with that stimulus.

Guthrie's notion of **one-trial learning**—that an S-R connection is fully formed on one pairing—was quite different from Thorndike's idea that responses are gradually "stamped in." Guthrie explained the gradual learning of complex behavior by proposing that complex behavior is actually composed of many tiny S-R connections; with each practice trial, more and more appropriate S-R connections are formed, thus leading to the gradual changes observed in overall behavior.

The parsimony of Guthrie's theory--his proposal that the contiguity of stimuli and responses is the basis of all learning—is definitely appealing. Guthrie conducted little research to support his views, however, and later research has cast doubt on the notion that learning is as simple as Guthrie described it (Bower & Hilgard, 1981). Nevertheless, three techniques for breaking S-R habits that Guthrie derived from his theory continue to be used in educational and therapeutic practice. We will look at these techniques later in this chapter.

Clark L. Hull

It was primarily the work of Clark Hull (1943, 1951, 1952) that introduced "organismic" characteristics—characteristics unique to different organisms—into behaviorist learning theory. Like many of his predecessors, Hull maintained that learned S-R habits form the basis of behavior. Furthermore, he agreed with Thorndike about the importance of rewards in the learning process. However, he believed that the presence of a particular stimulus and one's past experiences with that stimulus are not the only determinants of whether a particular response will occur or how strongly it will be made. Hull proposed that a number of other factors (**intervening variables**) unique to each organism and each occasion must be considered in order to predict the likelihood and strength of a response's occurrence. Hull's theory was therefore the first major theory of the S-O-R genre.

According to Hull, one intervening variable influencing the occurrence of a response is **habit strength,** the degree to which a particular stimulus and a particular response are associated. The more often a response has previously been rewarded in the presence of the stimulus, the greater is the habit strength and the more likely the response is to occur.

A second intervening variable critical for a response to occur is the organism's **drive,** an internal state of arousal that motivates its behavior. Hull suggested that some drives (e.g., hunger and thirst) are directly related to an organism's survival. Other drives (called *acquired drives*) serve no apparent biological purpose; they develop over time when initially "unexciting" stimuli are associated with such drive-reducing stimuli as food or drink. To illustrate, one might become "driven" by a need for approval if approval has previously been associated with a candy bar. From Hull's perspective, rewards increase the strength of an S-R habit by reducing the organism's drive (e.g., food reduces hunger).

Hull proposed that intervening variables such as habit strength, drive, stimulus intensity (with an intense stimulus bringing about a stronger response than a weak stimulus), and incentive (based on the amount and immediacy of reward) all work together to increase the likelihood and relative strength of a particular response. At the same time, **inhibitory factors** (e.g., fatigue) decrease the likelihood and strength of the response.

According to Hull, an organism might learn several different responses to the same stimulus, each with a different degree of habit strength. The combination of the various S-R habits for a given stimulus, with their respective habit strengths, is known as a **habit-family hierarchy.** When a stimulus is presented, an organism will, if possible, make the response for which the habit strength is the strongest. If the organism is somehow prevented from making that response, however, it will try to make the second response, or, if again foiled, the third response, and so on down the hierarchy.

As an illustration of this concept of habit-family hierarchy, consider George, who faces a homework assignment involving the multiplication of fractions. George may first try to complete the assignment using the technique his teacher taught him for multiplying fractions. If he finds that he cannot remember the technique, he may instead ask his friend Angela if he may copy her answers. If Angela refuses his request, he may resort to a third response in his hierarchy: telling his teacher that the family dog ate his homework.

Hull developed a series of mathematical formulas through which the occurrence and strength of responses might be predicted once the various intervening variables were measured and their values entered. The precision of Hull's formulas permitted a careful testing of his theory through research, and many specifics of the theory were found to be incorrect (Bower & Hilgard, 1981; Klein, 1987). For example, learning apparently can take place in the absence of drive; you will see some examples of such learning in Chapters 7 and 8. In addition, Hull proposed that a reward is a stimulus that reduces drive, yet, as you will discover when you read Chapter 17, some rewards actually appear to *increase* drive (Olds & Milner, 1954).

Hull's theory was a predominant force in behaviorism throughout the 1940s and 1950s. Although many details of the theory did not hold up under empirical scrutiny, Hull's emphasis on intervening variables made such notions as *motivation* and *incentive* prominent concepts in learning research. And his many productive students—among them Kenneth Spence, Neil Miller, John Dollard, and O. H. Mowrer—have continued to advance and modify Hullian ideas.

Burrhus Frederic Skinner

B. F. Skinner (1938, 1953, 1958, 1966b, 1971, 1989; Skinner & Epstein, 1982) is unquestionably the best-known psychologist in the behaviorist tradition. Originally a fiction writer, Skinner was lured into psychology by the ideas of Pavlov and Watson (Skinner, 1967). His principles of *operant conditioning*, first proposed in 1938, underwent little change in the five decades before his death in 1990. Operant conditioning principles have served as the basis for thousands of research studies and have been applied extensively in both educational and therapeutic settings. I will present an overview of Skinner's ideas here and then describe operant conditioning again in more detail in Chapter 4.

Skinner, like Thorndike and Hull, proposed that we learn behaviors that are followed by certain consequences. Unlike his predecessors, however, Skinner spoke only about the strengthening of responses, not the strengthening of S-R habits. Skinner's use of the term *reinforcer* instead of *reward* reflects his concern that psychologists remain objective in their examination of behavior and not try to guess what people or other organisms find pleasing (rewarding) or why the reinforcer has a particular effect on behavior.

To study the effects of reinforcers using precise measurement of responses in a carefully controlled environment, Skinner developed a piece of equipment, now known as the Skinner box, that has gained widespread popularity in animal learning research. As shown in Figure 2-1, the Skinner box used in studying rat behavior includes a metal bar that, when pushed down, causes a food tray to swing into reach long enough for the

Figure 2–1

A prototypic Skinner box: The food tray
swings into reach to provide reinforcement.

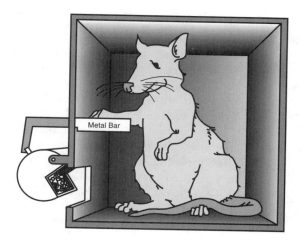

rat to grab a food pellet. In the pigeon version of the box, instead of a metal bar, a
lighted plastic disk (a "key") is located on one wall; when the pigeon pecks the key, the
food tray swings into reach for a short time. By observing rats and pigeons in their
respective Skinner boxes under varying conditions of reinforcement, Skinner developed
a set of principles that focuses on a *description* of learning rather than an explanation
of it; hence, some psychologists view Skinner's perspective more as a "nontheory" than a
theory of learning.

Skinner's most fundamental principle of operant conditioning, his *law of conditioning,* can be paraphrased as follows:

> *A response followed by a reinforcing stimulus is strengthened and therefore
> more likely to occur again.*

A corollary to this principle, Skinner's *law of extinction,* is as follows:

> *A response that is not followed by a reinforcing stimulus is weakened and
> therefore less likely to occur again.*

Unlike Watson, Skinner acknowledged the existence of thought, particularly as it is
reflected in verbal behavior (e.g., Skinner, 1963, 1989). Nevertheless, he contended that
the *causes* of mental events (including thoughts) lie in the environment and so argued
that a stimulus-response approach to the study of learning, which emphasizes the impact
of environment on behavior, is still quite appropriate.

Although Skinner focused his research almost exclusively on how animals acquire
such simple responses as pressing a bar or pecking a key, he used his principles of operant conditioning to explain a variety of complex human behaviors (e.g., Skinner, 1948b,
1957, 1971) and to recommend instructional strategies that teachers might use in the
classroom (e.g., Skinner, 1954, 1958, 1968, 1973). In Chapter 5 we will consider several
educational strategies that Skinner and others have derived from concepts and principles
of operant conditioning.

CONTEMPORARY BEHAVIORISM

Although much of the work in human learning has shifted toward a cognitive perspective in recent years, the behaviorist movement is still very much alive and well. Pavlov's classical conditioning and Skinner's operant conditioning remain as major theoretical perspectives that are continually refined by ongoing research (still conducted primarily with animals) and applied successfully to educational and clinical settings.

Several trends characterize the gradual evolution of early behaviorist theories into contemporary behaviorism. One trend is an increased focus on motivation as a major factor affecting learning and performance (e.g., Herrnstein, 1977). A second change subsequent to early theories is increased attention to the role of aversive consequences (punishment) in learning. Early theorists such as Thorndike, Guthrie, and Skinner maintained that punishment had little or no effect on behavior; however, a growing body of research (some of which I will present in Chapter 6) indicates that aversive consequences do influence behavior (e.g., Rachlin, 1991). A third trend is an increasing recognition that learning and performance must be considered as separate, albeit related, entities. A number of psychologists (e.g., Brown & Herrnstein, 1975; Estes, 1969a; Herrnstein, 1977; Schwartz & Reisberg, 1991) have proposed that many behaviorist laws are more appropriately applied to an understanding of what influences the *performance* of learned behaviors rather than what influences learning itself. But perhaps the most dramatic (and certainly the most surprising) change in recent years is the growing belief among traditionally behaviorist psychologists that they can more effectively understand both human and animal behavior when they consider *cognitive factors* as well as environmental events (Church, 1993; Hulse, 1993; Rachlin, 1991; Rescorla, 1988; Schwartz & Reisberg, 1991; Wasserman, 1993). We will get the flavor of some of these cognitive factors as we examine contemporary perspectives on classical and operant conditioning in Chapters 3 and 4.

GENERAL EDUCATIONAL IMPLICATIONS OF BEHAVIORISM

From what we have learned about behaviorist ideas so far, we can derive several implications for teaching practice: an emphasis on behavior, drill and practice, methods for breaking habits, and rewards (reinforcement) for desirable behavior.

Emphasis on Behavior

As we have already noted, behaviorists define learning as a change in behavior due to experience. This emphasis on behavior has at least two implications for education. First, students should be *active respondents* throughout the learning process rather than just passive recipients of whatever information is being taught. From a behaviorist perspective, people are more likely to learn when they actually have a chance to *behave*—for example, when they can talk, write, experiment, or demonstrate (e.g., see Drevno et al., 1994).

A second implication of the behaviorist perspective relates to the *assessment* of student learning. Regardless of how effective teachers think a certain lecture or a particular set of curriculum materials might be, they should never assume that students are learning anything unless they actually observe students' behaviors changing as a result of instruction. Only behavior changes—such as higher test scores, improved athletic performance, more appropriate social interaction skills, or better study habits—can ultimately confirm that learning has taken place.

Drill and Practice

Many behaviorists have stressed the principle that repetition of stimulus-response habits strengthens those habits. If people need to learn responses to particular stimuli thoroughly, then *practice* is essential. For example, students learn basic addition and subtraction facts better and recall them more quickly if they repeat those facts numerous times (e.g., through the use of flash cards). In a similar way, many reading teachers believe that the best way for students to improve their reading level is simply to read, read, read.

Breaking Habits

Guthrie's notion of recency—the idea that an organism will respond to a stimulus in the same way that it responded on the most recent previous encounter with that stimulus—implies that habits, once formed, are difficult to break. The trick in breaking a habit, from the perspective of the recency principle, is to lead an individual, in one way or another, to make a new response to the same old stimulus.

As an example, Guthrie (1935) described a girl who, upon entering the house after school each day, had the nasty habit of throwing her hat and coat on the floor rather than hanging up her garments. Despite repeated entreaties by the child's mother to change the sloppy behavior, the habit continued. One day, however, rather than admonishing the girl, the mother insisted that her daughter put her hat and coat back on, go outside, reenter the house, and hang up her clothes. The hanging-up response, being the one most recently exhibited, now became a new habit for the girl, and the throwing-on-the-floor response disappeared.

Guthrie proposed three ingenious techniques specifically designed to break habits: the exhaustion method, the threshold method, and the incompatible stimulus method.

Exhaustion Method

One way to break a stimulus-response habit is to continue to present the stimulus until the individual is too tired to respond in the habitual way. At that point, a new response will occur and a new S-R habit will form. For example, when breaking a bucking bronco, the persistent rider (the stimulus) stays on the horse's back until the horse is too exhausted to continue bucking; a new response (behavior reflecting acceptance of the rider, such as standing still) then becomes associated with the "rider" stimulus. Similarly, a teacher might eliminate a child's spitball-throwing behavior by having that child stay after school to make and throw spitballs until the child is too tired to continue.

Threshold Method

Another way of breaking a habit is to begin by presenting the stimulus so faintly that the individual does not respond to it in the habitual manner. The intensity of the stimulus is then increased so gradually that the individual continues *not* to respond to it. For example, when a student has test anxiety (in other words, when a test stimulus leads to an anxiety response), a teacher might eliminate that child's anxiety by first presenting tasks that are enjoyable to the child and only remotely resemble a test. Over time, the teacher can present a series of tasks that increasingly (but gradually) begin to take on testlike qualities.

Incompatible Stimulus Method

A third method for breaking a S-R connection is to present the stimulus when the habitual response cannot occur and when an opposite, or *incompatible*, response will occur. For example, Guthrie recommended tying a dead chicken around a dog's neck to teach the dog not to catch and eat chickens. The dog will struggle to get rid of the annoying chicken, thereby making a response that is incompatible with catching and eating the chicken. Similarly, imagine a classroom of highly achievement-motivated students who are overly competitive with one another. To reduce the competition among students, the teacher might divide the class into small groups and assign each group an academic task that requires cooperation rather than competition (e.g., developing an argument for one side of an issue in a class debate). Assigning grades on the basis of group performance rather than individual performance should increase the likelihood that students will cooperate. Hence, cooperative behavior will replace competitive behavior in that classroom environment.

Rewards (Reinforcement) for Desirable Behavior

Many behaviorists, Thorndike and Skinner among them, have emphasized the importance of rewards or reinforcement for learning. Students are most likely to learn and exhibit behaviors that lead to desired results. The kinds of reinforcers that are effective, and the many ways in which reinforcement principles can be incorporated into classroom practice, will be addressed in greater detail in Chapters 4 and 5.

SUMMARY

Behaviorism encompasses a group of theories that share several common assumptions, including the generalizability of learning principles across species, the importance of focusing on external, observable events (i.e., on stimuli and responses), and the "blank slate" nature of organisms. Early learning theorists—Pavlov, Thorndike, Watson, Guthrie, Hull, and Skinner—all viewed learning somewhat differently, but each made a unique contribution to our understanding of how human beings learn. For example, Pavlov outlined the basic components of classical conditioning; Watson and Guthrie described the importance of contiguity between a stimulus and a response; and Thorndike, Skinner, and Hull documented how the consequences that follow responses bring about behavior change. All of these theorists made us cognizant of the fact that past and present events have a strong influence on the behaviors we exhibit.

Contemporary behaviorists do not always adhere to traditional behaviorist assumptions; for example, they may make a distinction between learning and performance or they may believe that relationships between stimuli and responses can be better understood when cognitive factors are also taken into account. Educational implications of behaviorism include an emphasis on observable behavior, the use of drill and practice for teaching basic skills, several methods for breaking habits, and attention to the consequences of student behaviors.

CHAPTER 3

Classical Conditioning

I have a "thing" about bees. Whenever a bee flies near me, I scream, wave my arms frantically, and run around like a wild woman. Yes, yes, I know, I will be better off if I remain perfectly still, but somehow I just can't control myself. My overreaction to bees is probably due to the several painful bee stings I received as a small child.

One way to explain how people develop involuntary responses to particular stimuli, such as my fearful reaction to bees, is a theory of learning known as **classical conditioning.** This theory originated with the work of Ivan Pavlov, so we will begin this chapter by reviewing his classic research with dogs. We will then consider how we can apply Pavlov's learning paradigm to help us understand human learning and behavior. We will survey several phenomena associated with classical conditioning: extinction, spontaneous recovery, stimulus generalization and discrimination, higher-order conditioning, and sensory preconditioning. We will also see how the behaviorist perspective on classical conditioning has changed in recent years. Finally, we will look at ways of eliminating undesirable responses using the classical conditioning model and at some specific implications of the model for educational practice.

PAVLOV'S EXPERIMENT

Pavlov, a Russian physiologist whose work on digestion earned him a Nobel Prize in 1904, was conducting a series of experiments related to salivation in dogs. To study a dog's salivation responses, he would make a surgical incision in the dog's mouth, thus enabling him to collect and measure its saliva. After strapping the dog into an immobile position, he would give it some powdered meat and observe its resulting salivation. Pavlov noticed that the dog soon began to salivate before it saw or smelled the meat—in fact, it salivated as soon as the laboratory assistant entered the room with the meat. Apparently, the dog had learned that the lab assistant meant food was on the way and responded accordingly. Pavlov devoted a good part of his later years to a systematic study of this learning process upon which he had so inadvertently stumbled, and he eventually summarized his research in his book *Conditioned Reflexes* (Pavlov, 1927).

Pavlov's original studies of classical conditioning went something like this:

1. He first observed whether the dog salivated in response to a particular stimulus— perhaps to a flash of light, the sound of a tuning fork, or the ringing of a bell. For simplicity's sake, we will continue with our discussion using a bell as the stimulus in question. As you might imagine, the dog did not find a bell especially appetizing and so did not salivate.
2. Pavlov then rang the bell again and this time followed it immediately with the presentation of some powdered meat. The dog, of course, salivated. Pavlov rang the bell several more times, always presenting meat immediately afterward. The dog salivated on each occasion.
3. Pavlov then rang the bell again *without* presenting any meat. Nevertheless, the dog salivated. The bell, to which the dog had previously been unresponsive (in step one), now led to a salivation response. There had been *a change in behavior due to experience*; from the behaviorist perspective, then, *learning* had taken place.

Let's analyze the three steps in Pavlov's experiment in much the same way as he did:

1. A **neutral stimulus (NS)** is a stimulus to which the organism does not respond. In the case of Pavlov's dog, the bell was originally a neutral stimulus that did not elicit a salivation response.
2. The neutral stimulus is presented just before another stimulus, one that *does* lead to a response. This second stimulus is called an **unconditioned stimulus (UCS),** and the response to it is called an **unconditioned response (UCR),** because the organism responds to the stimulus unconditionally, without having had to learn to do so. (Pavlov's original term was actually uncondition*al,* but the mistranslation to uncondition*ed* remains in most classical conditioning literature.) For Pavlov's

Figure 3–1

A classical conditioning analysis of Pavlov's dog.

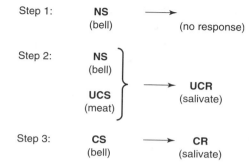

Step 1: **NS** (bell) ⟶ (no response)

Step 2: **NS** (bell) \ **UCS** (meat) ⟶ **UCR** (salivate)

Step 3: **CS** (bell) ⟶ **CR** (salivate)

dog, meat powder was an unconditioned stimulus to which it responded with the unconditioned response of salivation.

3. After being paired with an unconditioned stimulus, the previously neutral stimulus now elicits a response, so it is no longer neutral. The NS has become a **conditioned stimulus (CS)** to which the organism has learned a **conditioned response (CR).** In Pavlov's experiment, the bell, after being paired with the meat (the unconditioned stimulus) became a conditioned stimulus that led to the conditioned response of salivation. The diagram in Figure 3-1 shows graphically what happened from a classical conditioning perspective.

Pavlov's studies of classical conditioning continued long after this initial experiment, and many of his findings have been replicated with other responses and in other species, including humans. Let's take a closer look at the process of classical conditioning and at some examples of how it occurs in human learning.

THE CLASSICAL CONDITIONING MODEL

Classical conditioning has been demonstrated in many species—not only in dogs and laboratory rats but also in newborn human infants (Lipsitt & Kaye, 1964; Reese & Lipsitt, 1970), human fetuses still in the womb (Macfarlane, 1978), and even organisms as simple as flatworms (Thompson & McConnell, 1955). The applicability of classical conditioning clearly extends widely across the animal kingdom.

As Pavlov's experiments illustrated, classical conditioning occurs when two stimuli are presented at approximately the same time. One of these stimuli is an unconditioned stimulus: It has previously been shown to elicit an unconditioned response. The second stimulus, through its association with the unconditioned stimulus, begins to elicit a response as well: It becomes a conditioned stimulus that brings about a conditioned response. In many cases, conditioning occurs relatively quickly; it is not unusual for an organism to show a conditioned response after the two stimuli have been presented together only five or six times, and sometimes after only one pairing (Rescorla, 1988).

Classical conditioning is most likely to occur when the conditioned stimulus is presented just *before* (perhaps by half of a second) the unconditioned stimulus. For this reason, some psychologists describe classical conditioning as a form of **signal learning.** By

The conditioned stimulus may serve as a signal that the unconditioned stimulus is coming.

being presented first, the conditioned stimulus serves as a signal that the unconditioned stimulus is coming, much as Pavlov's dog might have learned that the sound of a bell indicated that yummy meat powder was on its way.

Classical conditioning usually involves the learning of *involuntary* responses—responses over which the learner has no control. When we say that a stimulus **elicits** a response, we mean that the stimulus brings about a response automatically, without the individual having much control over the occurrence of that response. In most cases, the conditioned response is similar to the unconditioned response (but see Hergenhahn & Olson, 1997; Hollis, 1997; or Rachlin, 1991, for exceptions), with the two responses differing primarily in terms of which stimulus elicits the response and sometimes in terms of the strength of the response.

CLASSICAL CONDITIONING IN HUMAN LEARNING

We can use classical conditioning theory to help us understand how people learn a variety of involuntary responses. For example, many people develop aversions to particular foods as a result of associating those foods with an upset stomach (Garb & Stunkard, 1974; Logue, 1979). To illustrate, after associating the taste of creamy cucumber salad dressing (CS) with the nausea I experienced during pregnancy (UCS), I developed an aversion (CR) to cucumber dressing that lasted for several years.

For many people, darkness is a conditioned stimulus for going to sleep, perhaps in part because it has frequently been associated with fatigue. I once became uncomfortably aware of how conditioned I was when I attended my daughter Tina's "astronomy night" at school. We parents were ushered into a classroom and asked to sit down. Then the lights were turned off, and we watched a half-hour filmstrip describing a NASA space museum. Although I am usually quite alert during the early evening hours, I found myself growing increasingly drowsy, and probably only my upright position in an uncomfortable metal chair kept me from losing consciousness altogether. In that situation, the darkness elicited a go-to-sleep response, and there were no stimuli (certainly not the filmstrip) to elicit a stay-awake response.

Classical conditioning is also a useful model for explaining some of the fears and phobias that people develop. For example, my bee phobia can probably be explained by the fact that bees (CS) were previously associated with a painful sting (UCS), such that I became increasingly fearful (CR) of the nasty insects. In a similar way, people who are bitten by a particular breed of dog sometimes become afraid of that breed, or even of all dogs.

Probably the best-known example of a classically conditioned fear of an animal is the case of "Little Albert," an infant who learned to fear white rats through procedures used by John Watson and Rosalie Rayner (1920). Albert was an even-tempered, 11-month-old child who rarely cried or displayed fearful reactions. One day, Albert was shown a white rat. As he reached out and touched the rat, a large steel bar behind him was struck, producing a loud, unpleasant noise. Albert jumped, obviously very upset by the startling noise. Nevertheless, he reached forward to touch the rat with his other hand, but the steel bar was struck once again. After five more pairings of the rat (CS) and the loud noise (UCS), Albert was truly rat phobic: Whenever he saw the rat he cried hysterically and crawled away as quickly as his hands and knees would allow. Watson and Rayner reported that Albert responded in a similarly fearful manner to a rabbit, a dog, a sealskin coat, cotton wool, and a Santa Claus mask with a fuzzy beard, although none of these had ever been paired with the startling noise. (Watson and Rayner never "undid" their conditioning of poor Albert. Fortunately, the ethical standards of the American Psychological Association would now prohibit such negligence.)

When I was growing up, my mother had an effective means of keeping my behavior within reasonable limits. Whenever I began to step out of bounds, she simply gave me The Look, a scowl accompanied by a wrinkled brow and sinister, piercing eyes. I suspect that this facial expression must have been paired with physical punishment sometime in my early childhood years, because The Look alone was eventually sufficient to send me to my bedroom in quick retreat. A threat of punishment such as The Look can arouse sufficient anxiety to control a child's behavior without one's actually having to resort to the punishment threatened. However, a threat can become a conditioned stimulus only if it has in fact been associated with punishment at one time or another, with that punishment following the threat in close proximity (Klein, 1987).

The use of punishment itself is controversial because any stimulus that is frequently associated with it—perhaps the home or school environment or a child's parent or teacher—can become a conditioned stimulus that also elicits fear and anxiety responses. We examine punishment in more detail in Chapter 6; at that time, we consider guidelines for minimizing the likelihood that negative side effects, such as the classical conditioning that I've just described, will occur.

Fear of failure is still another example of a response that may be classically conditioned. In some cases, people who are unusually afraid of failing may have previously associated failure with unpleasant circumstances; perhaps they've associated failure with painful punishment from an angry parent or ridicule by insensitive classmates. Yet occasional failure is a natural consequence of attempting new tasks, whether in school, at home, or elsewhere. Teachers and parents must be careful that failure does not become such a strong conditioned stimulus for children that they resist engaging in new activities and attempting challenging but possibly risky problems.

These examples of classical conditioning at work will, I hope, help you to recognize a classically conditioned response when you see one. We now turn to several phenomena associated with classical conditioning.

BASIC CONCEPTS IN CLASSICAL CONDITIONING

Pavlov described a number of phenomena characteristic of classical conditioning. Here we examine several of them: extinction, spontaneous recovery, stimulus generalization, stimulus discrimination, higher-order conditioning, and sensory preconditioning.

Extinction

Let's return for a moment to Pavlov's dog. Remember that the dog learned to salivate at the sound of a bell alone after that bell had rung in conjunction with meat powder on several occasions. But what would happen if the bell continued to ring over and over without the meat powder's ever again being presented along with it? Pavlov discovered that repeated presentations of the conditioned stimulus alone led to successively weaker and weaker conditioned responses. Eventually, the dog no longer salivated at the sound of the bell; in other words, the conditioned response disappeared.

The disappearance of a conditioned response when a conditioned stimulus is repeatedly presented *without* the unconditioned stimulus is a phenomenon Pavlov called **extinction.** For example, The Look from my mother no longer has the effect it used to. Whatever punishment was once associated with it has long since disappeared (and besides, now I'm bigger than she is).

Sometimes conditioned responses will extinguish, and sometimes they will not. The unpredictability of extinction is a source of frustration to anyone working with people who have acquired inappropriate, yet involuntary, conditioned responses. Later in the chapter, we identify some reasons why extinction does not always occur.

Spontaneous Recovery

Even though Pavlov quickly extinguished his dog's conditioned salivation response by repeatedly presenting the bell in the absence of meat powder, when he entered his laboratory the following day he discovered that the bell once again elicited salivation in the dog, almost as if extinction had never taken place. This reappearance of the salivation response after it had previously been extinguished is something Pavlov called **spontaneous recovery.**

In more general terms, spontaneous recovery is a recurrence of a conditioned response when a period of extinction is followed by a rest period. For example, if I am near lots of bees for a period of time, I eventually settle down and regain my composure.

However, my first response on a later encounter with a bee is to fly off the handle once again.

Pavlov found that when a conditioned response appears in spontaneous recovery, it is typically weaker than the original conditioned response and extinguishes more quickly. In situations in which a CR spontaneously recovers several times, each time after a period of rest has elapsed, the response appears in a weaker form than it had previously and disappears more rapidly.

Stimulus Generalization

You may recall that Little Albert, after being conditioned to fear a white rat, also became afraid of a rabbit, a dog, a fur coat, cotton wool, and a fuzzy-bearded Santa Claus mask. When individuals respond to other stimuli in the same way that they respond to conditioned stimuli, **stimulus generalization** is occurring. The more similar a stimulus is to the conditioned stimulus, the greater the probability of stimulus generalization. Albert exhibited fear of all objects that were white and fuzzy like the rat, but he was not afraid of his nonwhite, nonfuzzy toy blocks. In a similar way, a child who fears an abusive father may generalize that fear to other men but not to women.

Generalization of conditioned responses to new stimuli is a common phenomenon (Bouton, 1994). In some cases, generalization of conditioned fear responses may actually increase over time; that is, as time goes on, an individual may become fearful of an increasing number of objects (McAllister & McAllister, 1965). Thus, conditioned responses that do not quickly extinguish may actually become more frequent as the years go by because they are being elicited by an increasingly greater number of stimuli.

Stimulus Discrimination

Pavlov observed that when he conditioned a dog to salivate in response to a high-pitched tone, the dog would generalize that conditioned response to a low-pitched tone. To teach the dog the difference between the two tones, Pavlov repeatedly presented the high tone in conjunction with meat powder and presented the low tone without meat. After several such presentations of the two tones, the dog eventually learned to salivate only to the high tone. In Pavlov's terminology, *differentiation* between the two tones had taken place. Psychologists today more frequently use the term **stimulus discrimination** for this phenomenon.

Stimulus discrimination occurs when one stimulus (the CS+) is presented in conjunction with an unconditioned stimulus, and another stimulus (the CS−) is presented without that UCS. The individual learns a conditioned response to the CS+ but does not generalize the response to the CS−. For example, if a child who is abused by her father simultaneously has positive interactions with other adult men, she is not as likely to generalize her fear of her father to those other individuals.

Higher-Order Conditioning

Pavlov also described a phenomenon known as **second-order conditioning,** or more generally **higher-order conditioning.** When a dog had been conditioned to salivate to the sound of a bell, and the bell was later presented in conjunction with a neutral stimulus

Figure 3–2
An example of higher-order conditioning.

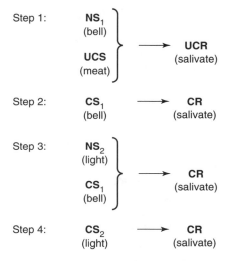

Step 1:   **NS₁** (bell)

UCS (meat)   ⟶   **UCR** (salivate)

Step 2:   **CS₁** (bell)   ⟶   **CR** (salivate)

Step 3:   **NS₂** (light)

CS₁ (bell)   ⟶   **CR** (salivate)

Step 4:   **CS₂** (light)   ⟶   **CR** (salivate)

such as a flash of light, that neutral stimulus would also begin to elicit a salivation response, even though it had never been directly associated with meat. In other words, the light flash became a conditioned stimulus through its pairing not with the unconditioned stimulus, but with another conditioned stimulus.

Higher-order conditioning works like this: First, a neutral stimulus (NS_1) becomes a conditioned stimulus (CS_1) by being paired with an unconditioned stimulus (UCS) and therefore elicits a conditioned response (CR). Next, a second neutral stimulus (NS_2) is paired with CS_1 and then independently elicits a similar conditioned response; that second stimulus has also become a conditioned stimulus (CS_2).

A diagram of higher-order conditioning appears in Figure 3-2. Steps 1 and 2 depict the original conditioning; steps 3 and 4 depict higher-order conditioning, in which a second neutral stimulus becomes a CS_2 by virtue of its being paired with the CS_1.

Higher-order conditioning is a possible explanation for some of the fears that students exhibit in the classroom (e.g., Klein, 1987). Let's say, first of all, that failure has previously been associated with painful physical punishment. Then another situation—perhaps a test, an oral presentation in front of classmates, or even school itself—becomes associated with failure. The painful punishment is the UCS. Failure, originally a neutral stimulus (NS_1), becomes a CS_1 after its association with the UCS. Some other aspect of school (e.g., a test), while first a neutral stimulus (NS_2), becomes an additional conditioned stimulus (CS_2) through its association with CS_1. In this way, a student may develop test anxiety, fear of public speaking, or even school phobia—fear of school itself.

Sensory Preconditioning

Higher-order conditioning is one way an individual can develop a conditioned response to a stimulus that has never been directly paired with an unconditioned stimulus. **Sensory preconditioning** is very similar to higher-order conditioning except that the steps occur in a different order. Let me first illustrate the process by once again conditioning Pavlov's

Figure 3–3
An example of sensory
preconditioning.

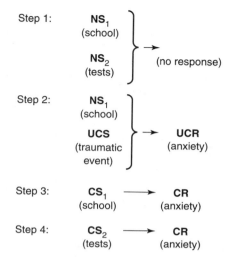

poor, overworked dog. Suppose that we first present the sound of a bell and a flash of
light simultaneously. Then we pair the bell with meat powder. Not only does the dog salivate in response to the sound of a bell, we discover that it also salivates in response to the
flash of light.

In more general terms, sensory preconditioning occurs like this: First, two neutral
stimuli (NS_1 and NS_2) are presented simultaneously. Then one of these neutral stimuli
(NS_1) is associated with an unconditioned stimulus (UCS), thus becoming a conditioned
stimulus (CS_1) and eliciting a conditioned response (CR). In cases of sensory preconditioning, the second neutral stimulus (NS_2) *also* elicits the conditioned response (i.e., NS_2 has
become CS_2) by virtue of its prior association with CS_1.

Klein (1987) has suggested that sensory preconditioning may be an alternative explanation for some cases of test anxiety. School (NS_1) is first associated with tests (NS_2). If
school is later associated with some traumatic event (UCS), then not only will school
become a conditioned stimulus (CS_1) eliciting anxiety (CR), but tests may become a conditioned stimulus (CS_2) as well. A diagram of how test anxiety might develop through sensory preconditioning is presented in Figure 3-3.

CONTEMPORARY PERSPECTIVES ON CLASSICAL CONDITIONING

Numerous psychologists have followed up on Pavlov's original studies of the classical conditioning phenomenon. Their research has led to several recent developments in our
understanding of when and how classical conditioning occurs:

• *Contingency between the conditioned and unconditioned stimuli is probably
more important than their contiguity.* Pavlov proposed that classical conditioning occurs
when the unconditioned stimulus and the would-be conditioned stimulus are presented at

approximately the same time; in other words, there must be *contiguity* between the two stimuli. In fact, as we noted earlier, classical conditioning is most likely to occur when the conditioned stimulus is presented just before the unconditioned stimulus. Conditioning is less likely to occur when the CS and UCS are presented at *exactly* the same time, and it rarely occurs when the CS is presented *after* the UCS (e.g., Miller & Barnet, 1993). Furthermore, people sometimes develop an aversion to certain foods (remember my aversion to creamy cucumber dressing) when the delay between the conditioned stimulus (food) and the unconditioned stimulus (nausea) is as much as 24 hours (Logue, 1979). As you can see, contiguity between the two stimuli is an overly simplistic explanation of how a conditioned response is acquired.

More recent theorists (e.g., Granger & Schlimmer, 1986; Rachlin, 1991; Rescorla, 1967, 1988) have proposed that *contingency* is the essential condition: The potential conditioned stimulus must occur *only* when the unconditioned stimulus is about to follow—in other words, when the CS serves as a signal that the UCS is coming (remember my reference to classical conditioning as "signal learning" earlier in the chapter). When two stimuli that are usually presented separately occur together a few times by coincidence, classical conditioning is unlikely to occur.

• *Characteristics of the would-be conditioned stimulus affect the degree to which conditioning occurs.* The more noticeable *(salient)* a neutral stimulus—in other words, the extent to which it is bright, loud, or otherwise intense—the more likely it is to become a conditioned stimulus when presented in conjunction with an unconditioned stimulus (Rachlin, 1991; Schwartz & Reisberg, 1991). Furthermore, some stimuli are especially likely to become associated with certain unconditioned stimuli; for example, food is more likely to become a conditioned stimulus associated with nausea (a UCS) than, say, a light or the sound of a tuning fork. In other words, associations between certain stimuli are more likely to be made than are associations between others—a phenomenon known as **associative bias** (Garcia & Koelling, 1966; Hollis, 1997; Schwartz & Reisberg, 1991).

• *Classical conditioning involves cognition as well as responding.* Some theorists now believe that classical conditioning involves the formation of associations not between two stimuli but between internal *mental representations* of those stimuli (Bouton, 1994; Furedy & Riley, 1987; Miller & Barnet, 1993; Rachlin, 1991; Rescorla, 1988; Schwartz & Reisberg, 1991; Wagner, 1976, 1978, 1979, 1981). Furthermore, the conditioned stimulus may enable an organism to *predict* (in a decidedly mental fashion) that the unconditioned stimulus is coming (Hollis, 1997; Martin & Levey, 1987; Rescorla, 1967, 1988; Rescorla & Wagner, 1972; Schwartz & Reisberg, 1991; Wagner & Rescorla, 1972). As you can see, then, some behaviorists are now beginning to talk about the thinking processes that they so deliberately steered clear of in earlier years.

CHANGING INAPPROPRIATE CONDITIONED RESPONSES

Conditioned responses are often difficult to eliminate because they are involuntary: People have little or no control over them. Yet some classically conditioned responses (e.g., some irrational fears) may be detrimental to an individual's functioning. How can we get rid of counterproductive conditioned responses? Extinction and counterconditioning are two possible methods.

Extinguishing Undesirable Responses

One obvious way to eliminate a conditioned response is through the process of extinction. If the conditioned stimulus is presented in the absence of the unconditioned stimulus frequently enough, the conditioned response should disappear—which is often exactly what happens.

Unfortunately, however, extinction is notoriously unpredictable as a means of eliminating conditioned responses: It simply doesn't always work. There are at least three reasons why:

1. The speed at which extinction occurs is unpredictable. If, during the conditioning process, the conditioned stimulus was sometimes presented in conjunction with the unconditioned stimulus but sometimes alone (i.e., the stimulus pairings were inconsistent), extinction is likely to be especially slow (Humphreys, 1939).
2. People tend to avoid a stimulus they have learned to fear, thus reducing the chances that they might eventually encounter the conditioned stimulus in the absence of the unconditioned stimulus. For example, a student who has learned to fear mathematics after a history of failing the subject typically avoids math as much as possible, thus minimizing any chance of experiencing math *without* failure.
3. Even when a response has been extinguished, it may reappear through spontaneous recovery. We can never be totally sure when a response will spontaneously recover and when it will not. Spontaneous recovery is especially likely if extinction has occurred in only one context; the conditioned response is apt to reappear in contexts in which extinction has not taken place (Bouton, 1994).

Counterconditioning More Desirable Responses

In an alternative procedure to extinction, called **counterconditioning,** one conditioned response is replaced with a new, more beneficial conditioned response. Counterconditioning tends to be more effective than extinction in eliminating undesirable conditioned responses; it also decreases the chances that those responses will recur through spontaneous recovery.

Mary Cover Jones's (1924) classic work with "Little Peter" provides an excellent example of counterconditioning. Peter was a two-year-old boy who had somehow acquired a fear of rabbits. To rid Peter of his fear, Jones placed him in a high chair and gave him some candy. As he ate, she brought the rabbit into the far side of the same room. Under different circumstances the rabbit might have elicited anxiety; however, the pleasure Peter felt as he ate the candy was a stronger response and essentially overpowered any anxiety he might have felt about the rabbit's presence. Jones repeated the same procedure every day over a two-month period, each time sitting Peter in a high chair with candy and bringing the rabbit slightly closer than she had the time before, and Peter's anxiety about rabbits eventually disappeared.

In general, counterconditioning involves the following components:

1. A new response that is **incompatible** with the existing conditioned response is chosen. Two responses are incompatible with each other when they cannot be performed at the same time. Because classically conditioned responses are often emotional in nature, an incompatible response is often some sort of opposite emotional reaction. For example, in the case of Little Peter, happiness was used as an incompatible response for fear. Since fear and anxiety create bodily tension, any response involving relaxation would be incompatible.

2. A stimulus that elicits the incompatible response must be identified; for example, candy elicited a "happy" response for Peter. If we want to help someone develop a happy response to a stimulus that has previously elicited displeasure, we need to find a stimulus that already elicits pleasure—perhaps a friend, a party, or a favorite food. If we want someone to acquire a relaxation response, we might ask that person to imagine lying in a cool, fragrant meadow or on a lawn chair by a swimming pool.

3. The stimulus that elicits the new response is presented to the individual, and the conditioned stimulus eliciting the undesirable conditioned response is *gradually* introduced into the situation. In treating Peter's fear of rabbits, Jones first gave Peter some candy; she then presented the rabbit at some distance from Peter, only gradually bringing it closer and closer in successive sessions. The trick in counterconditioning is to ensure that the stimulus eliciting the positive response is always *stronger* than the stimulus eliciting the negative response; otherwise, the negative response might prevail.[1]

Counterconditioning provides a means for decreasing or eliminating many conditioned anxiety responses. For example, **systematic desensitization** (Wolpe, 1958, 1969; Wolpe & Plaud, 1997), a therapeutic technique designed to replace anxiety with a relaxation response, is now widely used as a means of treating such difficulties as test anxiety and fear of public speaking (Hughes, 1988; Morris, Kratochwill, & Aldridge, 1988; Silverman & Kearney, 1991). I should point out, however, that treating test anxiety alone, without remediating possible academic sources of a student's poor test performance as well, may reduce test anxiety without any concurrent improvement in test scores (Covington, 1992; Naveh-Benjamin, 1991; Tryon, 1980).

A technique I recommend to many graduate students who dread their required statistics course because of mathematics anxiety is to find a math textbook that begins well below their own skill level—at the level of basic number facts, if necessary—so that the

---

[1]In counterconditioning, we see similarities with two of Guthrie's methods for breaking habits—methods discussed in Chapter 2. In Guthrie's *incompatible stimulus method,* a stimulus is presented in such a way that the usual response cannot occur and a more desirable response is likely to occur (remember his example of tying a dead chicken around a dog's neck as a way of teaching it not to catch and eat chickens). In Guthrie's *threshold method,* a stimulus is presented very faintly at first, so that it does not elicit the usual response, and then is so gradually increased in intensity that the organism continues not to respond to it.

problems are not anxiety arousing. As they work through the text, the students begin to associate mathematics with success rather than failure. Programmed instruction (described in Chapter 5) is another technique that can be useful in reducing anxiety about a given subject matter, because it allows a student to progress through potentially difficult material in small, easy steps.

EDUCATIONAL IMPLICATIONS OF CLASSICAL CONDITIONING

The durability and generalizability of some classically conditioned responses point to the need for a positive classroom climate for our students beginning with day one. Students should experience academic tasks in contexts that elicit pleasant emotions—feelings of enjoyment, enthusiasm, or excitement, for instance—rather than in contexts that elicit anxiety, disappointment, or anger. When students associate academic subject matter with positive feelings, they are more likely to pursue it of their own accord. For example, when children's early experiences with books are enjoyable ones, they are more likely to read frequently and widely in later years (Baker, Scher, & Mackler, 1997).

When schoolwork, a teacher, or even the school environment itself is associated with punishment, humiliation, failure, or frustration, school and its curriculum can become sources of excessive anxiety. Some classroom activities—for example, tests, oral presentations, and difficult subject matter—are especially likely to be associated with unpleasant circumstances such as failure or embarrassment, and many students may soon become anxious when involved in them. Teachers should therefore take special precautions when asking students to engage in any such "risky" activities. For example, I suspect that many students have early unpleasant experiences in public speaking because they receive little if any instruction about how to prepare and deliver an effective oral presentation. If students are asked to speak in front of a group, they should be given specific suggestions regarding what material to present and how to present it in such a way that classmates will react favorably rather than derisively.

Mathematics is a difficult and anxiety-arousing subject for many students, and students often dislike it because they find it so frustrating (Stodolsky, Salk, & Glaessner, 1991). I firmly believe that mathematics anxiety is so prevalent because most schools teach too much, too fast, and too soon, so that students quickly begin to associate mathematics with frustration and failure. Part of the problem may lie in the tendency to teach mathematical concepts before children are cognitively ready to deal with them. For instance, many developmental psychologists have proposed that the ability to understand the concept of *proportion,* which underlies fractions and decimals, does not appear until age 11 or 12 at the earliest (Schliemann & Carraher, 1993; Tourniaire & Pulos, 1985; also see the discussion of Piaget's theory in Chapter 8). Yet schools typically introduce fractions and decimals sometime around fourth grade, when students are only 9 or 10 years of age.

Educators have often argued that school should be a place where a student encounters more success than failure, and classical conditioning provides a justification for their argument. This is not to say that students should never encounter failure; people need feedback about what they are doing wrong as well as what they are doing right.[2] However, when students experience failure too frequently, either in their schoolwork or in their social relationships, school may quickly become a conditioned stimulus that leads to such counterproductive conditioned responses as fear and anxiety. These responses, once conditioned, may be very resistant to extinction and may interfere with a student's ability to learn effectively for years to come.

SUMMARY

Through a systematic study of salivation responses in dogs, Ivan Pavlov developed his theory of classical conditioning—an explanation of how certain involuntary responses develop. Classical conditioning occurs when two stimuli are presented at approximately the same time. One is an unconditioned stimulus that already elicits an unconditioned response. The second stimulus, through its association with the unconditioned stimulus, begins to elicit a response as well: It becomes a conditioned stimulus that brings about a conditioned response. If the conditioned stimulus is then presented numerous times in the absence of the unconditioned stimulus, however, the conditioned response decreases and may eventually disappear (extinction); nevertheless, it may reappear after a period of rest (spontaneous recovery).

Once an organism has learned to make a conditioned response in the presence of one conditioned stimulus, it may respond in the same way to a similar stimulus (stimulus generalization) unless that stimulus has repeatedly been experienced in the absence of the unconditioned stimulus (stimulus discrimination). Classically conditioned associations can build on one another through the processes of higher-order conditioning and sensory preconditioning; in both cases, a stimulus may become a conditioned stimulus (eliciting a conditioned response) not directly by its association with the unconditioned stimulus but indirectly by its association with a stimulus that either has been or will be experienced in conjunction with that UCS.

Contemporary psychologists propose that a contingent relationship between the conditioned and unconditioned stimuli is more critical than a contiguous one. Many of them speculate that the classical conditioning phenomenon involves the formation of associations between internal, mental representations of stimuli rather than associations between the stimuli themselves.

The classical conditioning paradigm is frequently used to explain human fears such as test anxiety, fear of failure, and school phobia, and it points to the importance of helping students experience academic subject matter in contexts that elicit pleasant rather than unpleasant emotions. Undesirable conditioned responses can sometimes be eliminated by either extinction or counterconditioning.

[2]In Chapter 18, we consider strategies for giving students negative feedback in ways that don't make them feel anxious or upset.

CHAPTER 4

Operant Conditioning

Different individuals work for different rewards. When my son Alex needs money to buy something he wants desperately, he engages in behaviors he never does otherwise—for example, mowing the lawn or scrubbing the bathtub. In contrast, financial incentives rarely entice my son Jeff into doing household chores, yet he will readily clean up the disaster area he calls his bedroom if doing so enables him to have a friend spend the night.

The idea that rewards affect behavior has influenced psychologists' thinking for at least 100 years; for example, Edward Thorndike's *law of effect* (see Chapter 2) dates back to 1898. The importance of rewards (or *reinforcers,* as many psychologists now prefer to call them) provides the foundation for B. F. Skinner's principles of **operant conditioning.**

In this chapter, we will examine operant conditioning in depth. We will first look at the basic operant conditioning model and see how it differs from the classical conditioning model that we studied in Chapter 3. We will then examine concepts central to our understanding of operant conditioning—concepts such as extinction, shaping, positive versus negative reinforcement, and continuous versus intermittent reinforcement. As we consider the topic of stimulus control, we will find that, although reinforcers are stimuli that follow responses, stimuli that *precede* responses can influence behavior as well. Toward the end of the chapter, we will discuss several ways in which contemporary views of operant conditioning differ somewhat from Skinner's original ideas, and we will apply operant conditioning principles to educational practice.

THE OPERANT CONDITIONING MODEL

We can paraphrase Skinner's (1938) basic principle of operant conditioning as follows:

> *A response followed by a reinforcer is strengthened and is therefore more likely to occur again.*

In other words, responses that are reinforced tend to increase in frequency. Because a response increase is a change in behavior, then, from a behaviorist viewpoint, reinforcement brings about learning. For example, Skinner found that rats will learn to press metal bars, and pigeons will learn to peck at round plastic disks, to get pellets of food. Likewise, my son Jeff will increase his housekeeping behavior if it allows him to see a friend, and my son Alex will do just about anything if the price is right.

Defining Reinforcers and Reinforcement

Skinner intentionally used the term *reinforcer* instead of *reward* to describe a consequence that increases the frequency of a behavior. The word *reward* implies that the stimulus following a behavior is somehow both pleasant and desirable, an implication that Skinner tried to avoid for two reasons. First, some individuals will work for what others see as unpleasant consequences; for example, my daughter Tina occasionally does something she knows will irritate me because she enjoys watching me blow my stack. Second, "pleasantness" and "desirability" are subjective judgments, and behaviorists such as Skinner prefer that psychological principles be restricted to the domain of objectively observable events. A reinforcer can be defined without any allusion to either pleasantness or desirability in this way:

> A **reinforcer** *is a stimulus that increases the frequency of a response it follows.*
> *(The act of following a response with a reinforcer is called **reinforcement**.)*

Notice how I have just defined a reinforcer totally in terms of observable phenomena, without reliance on any subjective judgment.

Now that I have given you definitions of both operant conditioning and a reinforcer, I need to point out a major problem with my definitions: Taken together, they constitute circular reasoning. I have said that operant conditioning is an increase in a behavior when it is followed by a reinforcer, but I cannot seem to define a reinforcer in any other way except to say that it increases behavior. I am therefore using reinforcement to explain a behavior increase, and a behavior increase to explain reinforcement! Fortunately, a paper by Meehl (1950) has enabled learning theorists to get out of this circular mess by pointing out the **transituational generality** of a reinforcer: The same reinforcer will increase many different behaviors in many different situations.

Three Important Conditions for Operant Conditioning

Three important conditions are necessary for operant conditioning to occur:

• *The reinforcer must follow the response.* "Reinforcers" that precede a response rarely have an effect on that response. For example, many years ago, a couple of instructors at my university were concerned that grades, because they were "threatening," interfered with student learning; therefore, they announced on the first day of class that everyone would receive an A for the course. Many students never attended class after that first day, so there was little learning for any grade to interfere with. Reinforcers must always, always *follow* the desired behavior.

• *The reinforcer must follow immediately.* A reinforcer tends to reinforce the response that has occurred just before it. Thus, reinforcement is less effective when its presentation is delayed: In the meantime, an organism may have made one or more responses that are reinforced instead. Once, when I was teaching a pigeon named Ethel to peck a lighted plastic disk, I made a serious mistake: I waited too long after she had pecked the disk before reinforcing her, and in the meantime she had begun to turn around. After eating her food pellet, Ethel began to spin frantically in counterclockwise circles, and it was several minutes before I could get her back to the pecking response I had in mind for her.

Our schools are notorious for delayed reinforcement. How many times have you completed an exam or turned in a written assignment, only to receive your grade days or even weeks later? Immediate reinforcers are typically more effective than delayed reinforcers in classroom situations (Kulik & Kulik, 1988). Furthermore, immediate reinforcers are probably the *only* effective reinforcers for animals and young children.

• *The reinforcer must be contingent on the response.* A reinforcer should never be presented unless the desired response has occurred. For example, teachers often specify certain conditions that children must meet before going on a field trip: They must bring their permission slips, they must complete previous assignments, and so on. When these teachers feel badly for children who have not met the stated conditions and allow them to go on the field trip anyway, the reinforcement is not contingent on the response, and the children are not learning acceptable behavior. If anything, they are learning that rules can be broken.

What Behaviors Can Be Reinforced?

Virtually any behavior—academic, social, or psychomotor—can be learned or modified through operant conditioning. As a teacher, I keep reminding myself of what student behaviors I want to increase and try to follow those behaviors with positive consequences. For example, when typically quiet students raise their hands to answer a question or make a comment, I call on them and give them whatever positive feedback I can. I also try to make my classes lively, interesting, and humorous, as well as informative, so that students are reinforced for coming to class in the first place.

Unfortunately, undesirable behaviors can be reinforced just as easily as desirable ones. Aggression and criminal activity often lead to successful outcomes: Crime usually *does* pay. Disruptive behavior in the classroom may get the teacher's attention in a way that no other behavior can (e.g., Taylor & Romanczyk, 1994). Getting "sick" allows the school-phobic child to stay home from school. Students sometimes appear at my office at the end of the semester pleading for a higher grade than their class performance has warranted or for the chance of completing an extra-credit project. I almost invariably turn them down, for a simple reason: I want good grades to be contingent on good study habits throughout the semester, not on begging behavior at my office door. Teachers must be extremely careful about what they reinforce and what they do not.

CONTRASTING OPERANT CONDITIONING AND CLASSICAL CONDITIONING

Skinner suggested that there are really two different kinds of learning: classical conditioning (he used the term *respondent conditioning*) and operant conditioning. The two forms of conditioning are different in several major respects; these differences are summarized in Figure 4–1.

	Classical Conditioning	**Operant Conditioning**
Occurs when:	Two stimuli (UCS and CS) are paired	A response (R) is followed by a reinforcing stimulus (S_{Rf})
Nature of response:	Involuntary: elicited by a stimulus	Voluntary: emitted by the organism
Model:	CS → CR	R → S_{Rf}

Figure 4–1
Differences between classical and operant conditioning.

Classical conditioning results from the pairing of two stimuli, the UCS and the CS. The learned response is a direct and immediate reaction to the stimulus that precedes it; that is, the conditioned stimulus brings about, or *elicits,* the conditioned response. The conditioned response is automatic and involuntary, such that the organism has virtually no control over what it is doing. Skinner's term *respondent* reflects the fact that the organism's behavior is an involuntary response to a stimulus.

In contrast, operant conditioning results when a response is followed by a reinforcing stimulus. The response is a voluntary one *emitted* by the organism, with the organism having complete control over whether the response occurs. Skinner's term **operant** reflects the fact that the organism voluntarily *operates* on, and thereby has some effect on, the environment. Because operant conditioning reflects a R → S_{Rf} model, where S_{Rf} symbolizes a reinforcing stimulus, Skinner was not really an S-R psychologist at all—he was actually an R-S psychologist.

Some theorists have suggested that both classical and operant conditioning are based on the same underlying learning processes (e.g., see Bower & Hilgard, 1981). In most situations, however, the classical and operant conditioning models are differentially useful in explaining different learning phenomena, so many psychologists continue to treat them as two distinct forms of learning.

BASIC CONCEPTS IN OPERANT CONDITIONING

Several concepts are central to our understanding of operant conditioning, including free operant level, terminal behavior, extinction, superstitious behavior, shaping, and chaining. Let's look briefly at each of them.

Free Operant Level (Baseline)

As we noted earlier, an *operant* is a voluntary response that has a particular effect on the environment. The **free operant level** is the frequency of an operant in the absence of reinforcement; in other words, it is the prereinforcement, or **baseline,** frequency of that response. People vary in their free operant levels for different responses. For example, for some students, getting-out-of-seat behavior is quite frequent, whereas for others it is rare. Similarly, some students read frequently without being asked to do so, whereas others seldom read on their own initiative.

Terminal Behavior

The **terminal behavior** is the form and frequency of a desired response at the end of a planned reinforcement program. Let's say, for example, that a second-grade boy rarely stays in his seat for more than five minutes at a time, and when he does sit down, he slouches so low in the chair that his head is barely level with the desk. A teacher who plans to alter this child's classroom behavior through reinforcement might specify the terminal behavior as "sitting up straight for a 10-minute period."

When we use reinforcement to change behavior, it is essential that we describe the terminal behavior in concrete terms ahead of time. Specifying the exact form of the desired behavior (e.g., sitting up straight) and the frequency or duration of the behavior (e.g., 10 minutes at a stretch) enables us to determine objectively whether our reinforcement program has been effective.

Extinction

In classical conditioning, when the CS is repeatedly presented in the absence of the UCS, the CR decreases and eventually disappears—that is, the response is extinguished. In operant conditioning, **extinction** occurs when a response is no longer followed by a reinforcer. A nonreinforced response gradually decreases and eventually returns to its baseline rate. For example, class clowns who find that no one laughs at their jokes anymore are likely to decrease their joke telling. Students who are never called on when they raise their hands may stop trying to participate in class discussions. Students who continue to fail exams despite hours of studying may eventually stop studying.

We should note here that in the initial stages of the extinction process we may sometimes see a brief *increase* in the behavior being extinguished—a phenomenon known as an **extinction burst** (Lerman & Iwata, 1995). We may also see increased variability in the kinds of responses exhibited (Rachlin, 1991). For example, students who find themselves doing poorly on exams may try studying more or studying differently; if such efforts continue to meet with failure, however, their studying behavior will eventually decrease and perhaps disappear altogether.

Although we want to extinguish undesirable behaviors such as disruptive joke telling, we need to take precautions that *desirable* behaviors are reinforced frequently enough that they *don't* extinguish. For example, if we see students failing classroom exams time after time despite their best efforts, we should look for the root of the problem. If only one student is failing, perhaps that student needs help in developing more appropriate study techniques, more individualized instruction, or placement in a situation better matched to his or her current knowledge and skills. If many other students find the same exams too difficult to pass, something may be wrong with those tests or with classroom instruction.

Superstitious Behavior

What happens when reinforcement is random and not contingent on any particular behavior? Skinner once left eight pigeons in their cages overnight with the food tray mechanism adjusted to present reinforcement at regular intervals, regardless of what responses the pigeons were making at the time. By morning, six of the pigeons were acting bizarrely. For example, one repeatedly thrust its head into an upper corner of the cage, and two others were swinging their heads and bodies in rhythmic pendulum movements (Skinner, 1948a).

Randomly administered reinforcement tends to reinforce whatever response has occurred immediately beforehand, and an organism will increase that response, thus displaying what Skinner called **superstitious behavior.** A nonbehaviorist way of describing the learning of a superstitious behavior is that the organism thinks that the response and reinforcement are related, when in fact they are not. For example, a student may have a "lucky sweater" to wear on exam days, or a football player may, before every game, perform a ritual totally unrelated to successful football play.

Superstitious behavior in the classroom can occur either when reinforcement is not contingent on behavior or when students do not know which of their many responses are responsible for bringing about reinforcement. It behooves teachers to ensure that classroom reinforcers such as praise, attention, and grades *are* contingent on desired behaviors and that response-reinforcement contingencies are clearly specified.

Shaping

Before we can reinforce someone for exhibiting a particular response, he or she must first *make* that response. But sometimes an individual's free operant level of a response is so low that it rarely, if ever, occurs. What should we do then?

To handle such a situation, Skinner introduced a method called **shaping,** a technique also known as **successive approximations.** Shaping is a means of teaching a behavior when the free operant level for that behavior is very low or when the desired terminal behavior is different in form from any responses that the organism exhibits.

To shape a particular behavior, we begin by reinforcing the first response that in any way approximates the desired behavior and then continue to reinforce it until the organism is emitting it fairly frequently. At that point, we reinforce only those responses that more closely resemble the desired behavior, then those that resemble it more closely still, until eventually only the desired behavior itself is being reinforced. In other words, shaping is a process of reinforcing successively closer and closer approximations to the terminal behavior until the terminal behavior is exhibited.

To illustrate, when I taught my pigeon Ethel to peck a lighted disk in her Skinner box, I began by reinforcing her every time she faced the wall on which the disk was located. Once this response was occurring frequently, I began to reinforce her only when she moved her beak near the wall, then only when she touched the wall with her beak, then only when she pecked within a two-inch radius of the disk, and so on. Within an hour, I had Ethel happily pecking the lighted disk and eating the food pellets that followed each correct peck.

Legend has it that a group of students once shaped a professor of mine a few days after he had given a lecture on shaping. Every time the professor stood on the side of the classroom near the door, the students all appeared interested in what he was saying, sitting forward in their seats and taking notes feverishly. Every time he walked away from the door, they acted bored, slouching back in their seats and looking anxiously at their watches. As the class went on, they reinforced the professor only as he moved closer and closer to the door until, by the end of class, he was lecturing from the hallway!

In much the same way, teachers gradually shape such behaviors as handwriting, sedentary behavior, and mathematical problem solving as children move through the grade levels. For example, kindergarten children are taught to print their letters on wide-lined paper; they are praised for making well-formed letters and for letters whose bottoms rest on one line and whose tops touch the line above. As children progress through the primary grades, the spaces between the lines become smaller, and teachers are more particular about how well the letters are written. Gradually children begin to write consistently sized and carefully shaped letters with the benefit of only a lower line, and eventually with no line at all. Teachers also shape the sedentary behavior of their students: As students grow older, teachers expect them to sit quietly in their seats for longer and longer periods. We can think of mathematics as a shaped behavior, too: Teachers introduce complex problem solving only after students have mastered more basic skills, such as counting, number recognition, and addition.

In a similar manner, teachers may inadvertently shape undesirable behavior as well. For example, let's say that Molly frequently exhibits such disruptive responses as talking out of turn and physically annoying other students. Molly's teacher, Mr. Smith, realizes that, because he has been reprimanding her for these responses, he has actually been giving her the attention that he knows she craves and so in essence has been reinforcing her for her disruptiveness. Mr. Smith decides to eliminate Molly's disruptive behavior by ignoring it—in other words, by using extinction. Unfortunately, although Mr. Smith can easily ignore minor infractions, he finds himself unable to ignore more extreme disruptions and so reprimands Molly for them. Rather than extinguishing Molly's disruptive behavior, then, Mr. Smith is actually shaping it: He is insisting that Molly be *very* disruptive, rather than just a little disruptive, in order to get reinforcement.

Chaining

In many cases, organisms can learn a sequence, or *chain,* of responses through shaping. For example, when visiting a tourist trap many years ago, I watched a chicken play a solitary game of "baseball": As soon as the chicken heard the appropriate signal (triggered by the quarter I deposited in the side of its cage), it hit a ball with a horizontal bar (a bat of sorts) that it could swivel at home plate, then ran counterclockwise around a three-foot-square baseball diamond back to home plate again (at which point it found some food in its feeding tray). The chicken's trainer had probably taught the chicken this complex chain of responses by first reinforcing only the last response in the sequence (running to home plate), then reinforcing the last two responses (running to third base and then to home plate), then reinforcing the last three (running to second base, third base, and then home plate), and so on, eventually reinforcing only the entire sequence.

This process of teaching a chain of responses by first reinforcing just one response, then reinforcing two responses in a row, then reinforcing a sequence of three, and so on is known as **chaining.**[1] Just as a chicken can learn to play baseball, so, too, can people learn lengthy, fairly complex behaviors through chaining. For example, students in a tennis class might learn to hold their rackets a certain way, then stand with their feet apart facing the net as they watch for the ball, then move toward an approaching ball and adjust their position appropriately, and then swing their rackets to meet the ball. Similarly, students in a first-grade classroom might learn to put their work materials away, sit quietly at their desks, and then line up single file at the classroom door before going to lunch. Such complex actions are often acquired more easily one step at a time—in other words, through chaining.

THE NATURE OF REINFORCERS

We have talked at length about how reinforcers can be used to change behavior. It is time now to talk more about reinforcers themselves. Let's first distinguish between primary and secondary reinforcers and between positive and negative reinforcement (which we will also contrast with punishment). We will then consider the different kinds of reinforcers teachers can use to change student behavior.

Primary and Secondary Reinforcers

A **primary reinforcer** is one that satisfies a biological need. Food, water, oxygen, and warmth are all examples of possible primary reinforcers. Physical affection and cuddling may also address biological needs (Harlow & Zimmerman, 1959), thus serving as primary reinforcers. Individual differences may exist regarding the consequences that serve as primary reinforcers; for example, sex is reinforcing to some individuals but not to others, and a particular drug is a primary reinforcer for a drug addict but not necessarily for a nonaddicted individual.

A **secondary reinforcer,** also known as a **conditioned reinforcer,** is a previously neutral stimulus that has become reinforcing to an organism through repeated association with another reinforcer (e.g., Wolfe, 1936). Examples of secondary reinforcers, which do not satisfy any obvious biological necessities, are praise, grades, money, and feelings of success.

Why do secondary reinforcers become reinforcing? An early explanation was that some stimuli become secondary reinforcers through the process of classical conditioning. A neutral stimulus is paired with an existing reinforcer (UCS) that elicits some form of biological satisfaction (UCR). That neutral stimulus becomes a CS (i.e., it becomes a

---

[1]When teaching the chicken to play baseball, the trainer probably used *backward chaining,* starting with the final response in the sequence and then adding, one by one, the responses that needed to precede it. In other situations, trainers or teachers might use *forward chaining,* reinforcing the first response in the sequence and then adding subsequent responses to the sequence that is reinforced. Research yields mixed results regarding the relative effectiveness of these two approaches with human beings (Zirpoli & Melloy, 1993).

Primary versus
secondary reinforcers.

secondary reinforcer) that elicits the same satisfaction (CR). For example, my daughter Tina learned very early that she could use money (CS) to buy candy (UCS) to satisfy her sweet tooth. The more often a secondary reinforcer has been associated with another reinforcer and the stronger that other reinforcer is, the more powerful the secondary reinforcer will be (Bersh, 1951; D'Amato, 1955).

More recently, some theorists have proposed that secondary reinforcers are effective to the extent that they give an organism information that a primary reinforcer is coming (Bower, McLean, & Meachem, 1966; Green & Rachlin, 1977; Mazur, 1993; Perone & Baron, 1980). This explanation has a decidedly cognitive flavor to it: An organism is *seeking information* about the environment rather than just responding to that environment in a "thoughtless" manner.

The relative influences of primary and secondary reinforcers on our lives probably depend a great deal on economic circumstances. When such biological necessities as food and warmth are scarce, these primary reinforcers, as well as the secondary reinforcers closely associated with them (e.g., money), may be major factors in reinforcing behavior. But in times of economic well-being, when cupboards are full and houses are warm, such secondary reinforcers as praise, grades, and feelings of success are more likely to play a major role in the learning process.

Positive Reinforcement, Negative Reinforcement, and Punishment

In addition to distinguishing between primary and secondary reinforcers, we can also distinguish between positive and negative reinforcement. Let's examine these two forms of reinforcement and look at how they differ from punishment.

Positive Reinforcement

Up to this point, the reinforcers I have mentioned have all been positive reinforcers. **Positive reinforcement** involves the *presentation* of a stimulus after the response. Food, praise, a smile, and success are all positive reinforcers.

Negative Reinforcement

In contrast to positive reinforcement, **negative reinforcement** increases a response through the *removal* of a stimulus, usually an aversive or unpleasant one.[2] For example, when rats learn to press a bar to terminate an electric shock, removal of the aversive shock is negative reinforcement that increases bar pressing. As another example, many cars sound a loud buzzer if the keys are still in the ignition when the driver's door is opened; removal of the keys from the ignition is negatively reinforced (so will presumably increase in frequency) because the buzzer stops.

The removal of guilt or anxiety can be an extremely powerful negative reinforcer. A child may confess to a crime committed days or even weeks earlier because she has been feeling guilty about the transgression all that time and needs to get it off her chest. Anxiety may drive one student to complete a term paper early, thereby removing an item from his things-to-do list. Another student confronted with the same term paper might procrastinate until the last minute, thereby removing anxiety—although only temporarily—about the more difficult aspects of researching and writing that paper.

We must keep in mind that negative reinforcement can affect the behavior of teachers as well as that of students. Teachers may often behave in ways that remove aversive stimuli; for example, they may use classroom discipline strategies (responses such as yelling at students or promising less homework) that eliminate unpleasant stimuli (disorderly conduct in the classroom) over the short run but that are ineffective over the long run. As an illustration, if Ms. Jones yells at Marvin for talking too much, Marvin may temporarily stop talking, which negatively reinforces Ms. Jones's yelling behavior.[3] But if Marvin likes getting Ms. Jones's attention (a positive reinforcer for him), he will be chattering again before very long.

Punishment

Both positive reinforcement and negative reinforcement increase the responses that they follow. **Punishment,** on the other hand, is likely to *decrease* those responses. We will consider the effects of punishment in more detail in Chapter 6, but let's briefly define punishment here so you can see how it differs from negative reinforcement.

Punishment takes one of two forms, frequently referred to as Punishment I and Punishment II. **Punishment I** involves the *presentation* of a stimulus, usually an aversive one. Scolding and spanking are examples of this form of punishment. **Punishment II** involves the *removal* of a stimulus, usually a pleasant one. Examples include fines for misbehaviors (because money is being taken away) and loss of privileges. Figure 4–2 illustrates the differences among positive reinforcement, negative reinforcement, Punishment I, and Punishment II.

Many people mistakenly use the term *negative reinforcement* when they are really talking about punishment. Although both phenomena involve aversive stimuli, they differ

---

[2]Don't let the word *negative* in *negative reinforcement* lead you astray here. It is not a value judgment but simply refers to the fact that something is being *taken away* from the situation.

[3]Note that, although behaving in a disruptive fashion is a response that Marvin makes, in this situation it serves as a *stimulus* that Ms. Jones wants to eliminate.

Nature of Stimulus

Stimulus is	Pleasant	Aversive
Presented after the response	Positive Reinforcement (response increases)	Punishment I (response decreases)
Removed after the response	Punishment II (response decreases)	Negative Reinforcement (response increases)

Figure 4–2
Positive reinforcement, negative reinforcement, and punishment.

in two critical respects. First, as we just noted, they have opposite effects: Negative reinforcement *increases* the frequency of a response, whereas punishment often *decreases* the frequency of a response. A second crucial difference concerns the order of events. With negative reinforcement, the aversive stimulus *stops* when the response is emitted. With Punishment I, on the other hand, the aversive stimulus *begins* when the response is emitted. Figure 4–3 illustrates this difference graphically. The termination of an aversive stimulus negatively reinforces a response; the initiation of an aversive stimulus punishes a response.

Different Kinds of Reinforcing Stimuli

When using reinforcement in the classroom, teachers often unnecessarily limit themselves to just a handful of reinforcers. In fact, a wide variety of events can be reinforcing to students. Let's look at several possibilities.

Material Reinforcers
A **material reinforcer**, or tangible reinforcer, is an actual object; food and toys are examples. For many people, the word *reinforcer* brings to mind such tangible consequences for good behavior. But in school situations at least, most psychologists recommend that we use material reinforcers only as a last resort, when absolutely no other reinforcer works. Food, toys, trinkets, and similar items have a tendency to distract

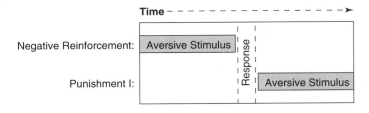

Figure 4–3
Negative reinforcement and punishment differ in terms of which occurs first—the aversive stimulus or the response.

students' attention from the things they should be doing in class and so may be counter-productive over the long run.

Social Reinforcers

A **social reinforcer** is a gesture or sign from one person to another that communicates positive regard. Praise, a smile, a pat on the back, and a hug are all social reinforcers. Social reinforcement is a common occurrence in the classroom and can be quite effective. Teacher attention, approval, praise, and appreciation are powerful classroom reinforcers (Becker, Madsen, Arnold, & Thomas, 1967; Drabman, 1976; Katz, 1993; Madsen, Becker, & Thomas, 1968; Schepis, Reid, & Fitzgerald, 1987; Ward & Baker, 1968).[4] The approval of peers can be effective as well (Evans & Oswalt, 1968; Lovitt, Guppy, & Blattner, 1969).

Activity Reinforcers

Speaking nonbehavioristically, an **activity reinforcer** is an opportunity to engage in a favorite activity. (A quick quiz: Which word is the nonbehaviorist part of my definition, and why?) David Premack (1959, 1963) discovered that people will often perform one activity if doing so enables them to perform another. His **Premack principle** for activity reinforcers is as follows:

> *A normally high-frequency response, when it follows a normally low-frequency response, will increase the frequency of the low-frequency response.*

A high-frequency response is, in essence, a response that an organism enjoys doing, whereas a low-frequency response is one that the organism does not enjoy. Another way of stating the Premack principle, then, is that organisms will perform less-preferred tasks so that they can subsequently engage in more-preferred tasks.

To illustrate, my own free operant level for housework is extremely low. I have found that I am more likely to do household chores if I make a higher-frequency behavior, such as reading a mystery novel or having a party, contingent on doing the housework. In a similar way, appropriate classroom behavior can be improved through the Premack principle. Young children can quickly be taught to sit quietly and pay attention if they are allowed to engage in higher-frequency "active" behaviors (e.g., talking and running around the room) only after they have been quiet and attentive for a certain period of time (Homme, deBaca, Devine, Steinhorst, & Rickert, 1963).

Although psychologists agree that the Premack principle works, they disagree as to *why* it works. If you are interested in exploring the theoretical underpinnings of the Premack principle, see the discussions by Bower and Hilgard (1981) and Timberlake and Allison (1974).

Intrinsic Reinforcers

In many situations, individuals engage in certain responses not because of any external reinforcers but because of the internal good feelings—the **intrinsic reinforcers**—that such responses bring. Feeling successful after solving a difficult puzzle, feeling proud after

---

[4]We should note here that praise has a potential downside, depending on the specific message that it contains and the context in which it is given. We will consider the possible negative side effects of praise in Chapter 18.

returning a valuable item to its rightful owner, and feeling relieved after completing a difficult assignment are all examples of intrinsic reinforcers. People who continue to engage in responses for a long time without any obvious external reinforcers for their efforts are probably working for intrinsic sources of satisfaction.

Positive Feedback

In some instances, material and social reinforcers may improve classroom behavior and lead to better learning of academic skills because they provide **feedback** to students about which responses are desirable and which are not (Butler, 1987; Gagné & Driscoll, 1988). Positive feedback is clearly effective in bringing about desired behavior changes (Lhyle & Kulhavy, 1987; Smith & Smoll, 1997).

I once spent a half hour each day for several weeks working with Michael, a nine-year-old boy with a learning disability who was having difficulty learning his cursive letters. Over the first three weeks, neither Michael nor I could see any improvement, and we were both becoming increasingly frustrated. To give ourselves more concrete feedback on the results of our sessions together, I decided to start graphing Michael's daily performance. I explained to Michael how we would chart his progress on a piece of graph paper by marking off the number of cursive letters he could remember each day. I also told him that as soon as he had reached a dotted line near the top of the page (a line indicating that he had written all 26 letters correctly) for three days in a row, he could have a special treat (his choice was a purple felt-tip pen).

At the beginning of each subsequent work session, I tested Michael on his cursive letters, and together we counted the number that he had correctly remembered. We entered his performance on the chart in the form of a bar of the appropriate height, and then Michael practiced the letters he had missed. Michael's daily performance began to improve dramatically. He was not only making noticeable progress but also looking forward to charting his performance and seeing a higher bar each day. Within two weeks, Michael had successfully met the criterion for his felt-tip pen: He had written all 26 cursive letters for three days in succession. As it turns out, the pen was probably not the key ingredient for our success: Michael lost it within 24 hours of receiving it. Instead, I suspect that the concrete positive feedback about his own improvement was the true reinforcer that helped Michael to learn.

Feedback is especially likely to be effective when it communicates what students have and have not learned and when it gives them guidance about how they might improve their performance (Butler & Winne, 1995; Lhyle & Kulhavy, 1987). Under such circumstances, even *negative* feedback can lead to enhanced performance (e.g., Barbetta, Heward, Bradley, & Miller, 1994). Interpreting such findings within a strictly behaviorist framework is difficult, however; it appears that students must be *thinking* about the specific meaning of the feedback they receive and using it to adjust their future behavior.

For many students, the true reinforcers for learning are probably the internal reinforcers—the feelings of success, competence, mastery, and pride—that their accomplishments bring. For such students, other reinforcers are more helpful if they provide feedback that academic tasks have been performed well. Grades are probably also reinforcing for the same reason: good grades reflect high achievement—a reason to feel proud.

From a teacher's perspective, positive feedback and the intrinsic reinforcement that such feedback brings are probably the most desirable forms of classroom reinforcement.

Keep in mind, however, that consistent positive feedback and resulting feelings of success and mastery can occur only when instruction has been carefully tailored to individual skill levels and abilities and only when students have learned to value academic achievement. When, for whatever reasons, children are not motivated to achieve academic success, then other reinforcers, such as social and activity reinforcers, can be helpful.

Always remember that what is reinforcing for one individual may not be reinforcing for another. Reinforcement, like beauty, is in the eyes of the beholder. And even for the same individual, a reinforcer on one occasion may not be a reinforcer on another. Several other factors influence the effectiveness of reinforcers, as we shall now see.

FACTORS INFLUENCING THE EFFECTIVENESS OF REINFORCEMENT

At least three factors influence the effectiveness of reinforcement in operant conditioning: timing, magnitude and appeal, and consistency.

Timing

Earlier in the chapter, I stressed the importance of *immediate* reinforcement for operant conditioning. In most cases, greater delays in reinforcement lead to slower acquisition of responses (e.g., Hockman & Lipsitt, 1961; Lett, 1973, 1975; Terrell & Ware, 1961). Fortunately, in situations in which immediate reinforcement is impossible, environmental cues that indicate that reinforcement, although delayed, will come eventually may be helpful (Fowler & Baer, 1981; Perin, 1943). For example, a teacher who wants to reinforce her students' persistence through a difficult lesson might say, "Because we have all worked so hard this morning, we will spend this afternoon practicing the class play that you all have been enjoying so much."

Magnitude and Appeal

The larger and more appealing the reinforcer, the faster a response will be learned and the more frequently it will be exhibited (e.g., Atkinson, 1958; Siegel & Andrews, 1962). For example, in a study by Siegel and Andrews (1962), three- to five-year-old boys learned more quickly when they were reinforced with such treats as candy, coins, balloons, and small toys than when the reinforcers were unexciting buttons. In fact, for older children and adults, large, *delayed* rewards are often more effective than small, immediate ones, provided that the individuals know that those delayed rewards will in fact be coming (e.g., Green, Fry, & Myerson, 1994).

Interestingly enough, it is not always the absolute magnitude of reinforcement that affects behavior as much as it is the *relative* magnitude compared with prior experience. For example, in a classic study by Crespi (1942), rats ran a runway to reach a food reinforcer at the far end. When rats accustomed to a small quantity of food were suddenly reinforced with a greater amount, they ran faster than rats who had always received that same large amount. Similarly, rats accustomed to a large amount of reinforcement who then began receiving less food ran more slowly than rats who had always had that smaller amount. Crespi's results have been replicated in other rat studies (e.g., McHale, Brooks, &

Wolach, 1982), although the results of analogous studies with infants have been inconsistent (e.g., Fagen & Rovee, 1976; Lipsitt & Kaye, 1965).

The changes in behavior observed when quantities of reinforcement increase or decrease are commonly known as **contrast effects.** One contrast effect—the **elation effect**—occurs when the amount of reinforcement is increased: The response rate becomes *faster* than it would be if the reinforcement had always been at that higher level. The opposite contrast effect—the **depression effect**—occurs when the amount of reinforcement is decreased: The result is that the response rate becomes *slower* than it would be if reinforcement had always been that low. The depression effect may be at least partly due to negative emotions associated with a reduction in reinforcement (Flaherty, 1985).

Consistency

One of the most critical factors affecting both the rate at which responses are learned and the rate at which they can be extinguished is the consistency of reinforcement (e.g., Staddon & Higa, 1991). To illustrate how consistency plays a role, consider this fantasy I have for the handful of students in my classes each semester who don't read their textbook:

> The student is locked in a small room. The assigned textbook lies on a nearby table. Every time the student opens the book to one of the assigned pages and looks at the page, a small piece of delicious junk food falls from a hole in the ceiling.

Essentially, I would like to put unmotivated students into my own version of a Skinner box—the Ormrod box!

Now imagine 20 students in 20 Ormrod boxes. Ten of these students, randomly selected, are in group A: They receive a piece of junk food every time they open the textbook and look at it. The other 10 are in group B: They get junk food for some of their book-reading responses (perhaps one response out of every four) but receive nothing for their efforts the rest of the time. Group A is receiving **continuous reinforcement:** Every response is reinforced. Group B is receiving **intermittent reinforcement:** Some of the responses are reinforced and some are not. Which group is going to increase its textbook-reading behavior faster? The answer, of course, is group A, the group with continuous reinforcement. Continuously reinforced responses are acquired faster than intermittently reinforced responses.

Now suppose that, after a few hours in their respective Ormrod boxes, all 20 students have begun to show a high frequency of textbook-reading responses, so I turn off the junk-food-dropping mechanisms. Which students are first going to notice that they are no longer being reinforced? The answer again is group A. Students who have been reinforced for every single response will notice rather quickly that reinforcement has stopped, and their textbook reading should extinguish rapidly (unless, of course, they find such behavior intrinsically reinforcing). Group B students, on the other hand, have been receiving reinforcement for only 25% of their responses, so they are accustomed to nonreinforcement; these students will probably continue to read their textbooks for some time before they realize that reinforcement has ceased. Intermittently reinforced responses are extinguished more slowly than continuously reinforced responses.

Psychologists usually recommend reinforcing a response continuously until the terminal behavior is reached and then maintaining the response through intermittent reinforcement so that it does not extinguish. Intermittent reinforcement can follow a variety of **reinforcement schedules,** each of them having different effects on resistance to extinction and on the frequency and pattern of the response being reinforced. Let's take a look at several different schedules and the behavior patterns that result from each one.

SCHEDULES OF REINFORCEMENT

In this section I describe three different groups of intermittent reinforcement schedules: ratio schedules (those in which reinforcement occurs after a certain number of responses), interval schedules (those in which reinforcement occurs for the first response after a certain time interval has elapsed), and differential schedules (those in which reinforcement is contingent on a certain rate of responding).

Ratio Schedules: Reinforcing a Certain Number of Responses

A **ratio schedule** is one in which reinforcement occurs after a certain number of responses have been emitted. That certain number can either be constant (a fixed-ratio schedule) or vary from one reinforcement to the next (a variable-ratio schedule).

Fixed Ratio (FR)

In a **fixed-ratio** reinforcement schedule, a reinforcer is presented after a certain constant number of responses have occurred. For example, reinforcement might occur after every third response (a 1:3 ratio schedule) or after every fiftieth response (a 1:50 schedule). Such a reinforcement schedule can lead to a high and consistent response rate over an indefinite period of time; for example, pigeons whose pecking is maintained on a high ratio schedule will peck as often as 10 times per second (Ferster & Skinner, 1957).

Whitlock (1966) has described the use of a series of ratio schedules with a six-year-old boy who had been unable to acquire basic reading skills. At first, the boy was asked to read words presented to him on flash cards. Every time he read a word correctly, he received a plastic poker chip as a reinforcer, reflecting a continuous reinforcement schedule. He could then trade jars of 36 poker chips for a variety of activities; for example, with two jars he could play a game, and with seven jars he could watch a cartoon. Once the boy was able to read from beginning reader storybooks, he was reinforced on a 1:2 fixed-ratio schedule; that is, he received one chip for every two words he read correctly. Eventually he was reinforced for every four words (a 1:4 schedule), then for every page (one reinforcer for every 10 to 25 words), then for every story (one reinforcer for every 50 to 70 words), and finally for every four stories. After 15 sessions of such individualized instruction, reinforcement was phased out altogether, and the boy was placed in his classroom's regular reading program; three months later, he was still reading at grade level. (One thing has always struck me about this study: Because so many poker chips were required to make a "purchase," the boy must have actually bought very few activities. I suspect that his increasing success in reading was the true reinforcer in this case.)

Ratio schedules even as high as 1:1000, when introduced through a series of successively higher ratios (as was done in the Whitlock study), have been found to maintain a response (Ferster & Skinner, 1957). In fact, high ratios typically lead to higher rates of responding than low ratios (Collier, Hirsh, & Hamlin, 1972; Stephens, Pear, Wray, & Jackson, 1975), although organisms operating under high ratio schedules tend to exhibit a **post-reinforcement pause** (a temporary decrease in responding) after each reinforced response (Ferster & Skinner, 1957).

Variable Ratio (VR)

A **variable-ratio** reinforcement schedule is one in which reinforcement is presented after a particular, yet *changing,* number of responses have been emitted; this kind of schedule is described by the average number of responses needed to obtain reinforcement. For example, in a 1:5 VR schedule, reinforcement might first take place after four responses, then after seven more, then after three, and so on. As you can see, the occurrence of reinforcement in a VR schedule is somewhat unpredictable.

Playing a Las Vegas slot machine is an example of a response that is reinforced on a variable-ratio schedule. The more times you put a quarter into the machine, the more times you will be reinforced by having quarters come back out again, but those quarters do not come out after any predictable number of quarters have gone in. In a similar way, telephone solicitation is also reinforced on a VR schedule. The greater the number of calls made, the greater the number of sales, but the soliciting caller never knows just which call will lead to reinforcement.

Margaret, one of my daughter Tina's friends, has always been very persistent when she wants something; she seldom takes no for an answer. The source of her persistence

Telephone solicitation is reinforced on a variable-ratio schedule.

became clear to me one evening many years ago when Tina and I had dinner at a restaurant with Margaret and her mother. The girls gobbled their food quickly and went off to explore the restaurant while we ladies nursed our coffee. Margaret quickly returned to the table to make a request of her mother:

"Mom, can I have a quarter for a video game?"

"No."

"Please, mom?"

"I said no, Margaret."

"But Tina has one." (I look absentmindedly into space.)

"No."

"I'll pay you back as soon as we get home."

"*No,* Margaret."

"*Pretty please*?!" (Margaret puts on a desperate face.)

"Oh, all right, here's a quarter."

Margaret's asking behaviors were probably on a variable-ratio reinforcement schedule: She had learned that persistence eventually paid off.

Variable-ratio schedules result in higher response rates than fixed-ratio schedules. Furthermore, responses reinforced on a VR schedule are highly resistant to extinction. In fact, pigeons working on very high VR schedules may expend more energy responding than they gain in food reinforcement, thus eventually working themselves to death (Swenson, 1980).

Interval Schedules: Reinforcing the First Response after a Time Period

An **interval schedule** is one in which reinforcement is contingent on the first response emitted after a certain time interval has elapsed. The time interval can either be constant (a fixed-interval schedule) or vary from one reinforcement to the next (a variable-interval schedule).

Fixed Interval (FI)

With a **fixed-interval** reinforcement schedule, reinforcement is contingent on the first response emitted after a certain fixed time interval has elapsed. For example, the organism may be reinforced for the first response emitted after five minutes have elapsed, regardless of how many responses may or may not have been made during those five minutes. Following reinforcement, another five-minute interval must elapse before a response is again reinforced.

A fixed-interval schedule produces a unique response pattern: Following reinforcement, the response rate tapers way off in a post-reinforcement pause until the end of the time interval approaches, at which point responding picks up again (e.g., Ferster & Skinner, 1957; Shimoff, Catania, & Matthews, 1981). To illustrate, when my daughter Tina was in fifth grade, she had a spelling test every Friday. She got the week's list of spelling words each Monday and so had four evenings on which to study the list. Occasionally she began on Wednesday, but she more often waited until Thursday night to study her spelling. If we

Figure 4–4
Responses reinforced on a fixed-interval schedule show a "scallop" pattern.

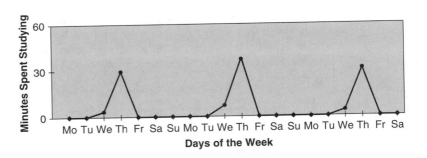

were to graph Tina's studying behavior, it might look something like the graph in Figure 4-4. This "scallop" pattern is typical of behaviors reinforced on a fixed-interval schedule. We do not see the high rate of responding with an FI schedule that is observed for fixed- and variable-ratio schedules, nor do we see as much resistance to extinction.

Variable Interval (VI)

In a **variable-interval** reinforcement schedule, reinforcement is contingent on the first response emitted after a certain time interval has elapsed, but the length of that interval keeps changing from one occasion to the next. For example, the organism may be reinforced for the first response after five minutes, then the first response after eight minutes, then the first response after two minutes, and so on, with the VI schedule being identified by the average time interval.

As an illustration, you may have a friend who really enjoys talking on the telephone, so that when you try to call this individual, you often hear a busy signal. If you have an urgent need to get in touch with your friend, you may continue to dial the phone number once every few minutes until eventually your call goes through. In a similar way, students who have been told that there is always the possibility of an unannounced ("pop") quiz in class are likely to study a little bit every night. They never know on exactly which day their studying will pay off. Your pattern of dialing your gabby friend and students' pattern of studying for pop quizzes are typical of the response pattern observed for variable-interval schedules: a slow, steady rate of responding. The longer the average time interval until reinforcement, the slower the response rate will be (e.g., Catania & Reynolds, 1968). (We should note here that for other reasons pop quizzes are generally not recommended; see Sax, 1989, or Ormrod, 1995, for their downside.)

For both ratio and interval schedules, then, variable schedules lead to steadier response rates than fixed schedules do, probably because of the unpredictability of reinforcement after a correct response. With a variable schedule, there is always the possibility that the next correct response will pay off. Variable schedules also appear to lead to greater resistance to extinction, again possibly because of their unpredictable nature.

When using ratio or interval schedules of reinforcement to prevent the extinction of a previously acquired response, the best schedule to use depends on the rate of response desired. In most cases, a variable ratio is recommended for a high rate of responding, with a variable-interval schedule being better for a slow yet steady rate. Ideally, when continuous reinforcement is first replaced by intermittent reinforcement, the ratio should be small (e.g., 1:2 or 1:3) or the time interval short. The ratio or interval can then gradually be extended until the response continues with very little reinforcement at all.

Differential Schedules: Reinforcing Rates of Responding

When a particular *rate* of responding is required, a **differential schedule of reinforcement** is appropriate: A specific number of responses occurring within a specific length of time leads to reinforcement. There are at least three such schedules:

* Reinforcement of a differential rate of high responding
* Reinforcement of a differential rate of low responding
* Reinforcement of the *non*occurrence of the response (differential reinforcement of other behaviors)

Differential Rate of High Responding (DRH)

A **DRH schedule** provides reinforcement only when a specific, *large* number of responses (or even more responses than that specified) have occurred within a particular period of time. For example, consider Tina's friend Margaret, the girl who persistently asked her mother for money to play a video game. Margaret may actually have been on a DRH schedule rather than a variable-ratio schedule, in that she had to ask for a quarter several times *all at once* to get reinforcement. With a ratio schedule, the time it takes to emit the necessary number of responses is irrelevant, but with a DRH schedule, this time period is critical. Because a DRH schedule requires many responses in a short amount of time, a high response rate is typical.

Theoretically, studying for regularly scheduled tests is really on a DRH schedule: The more studying that occurs, the greater the probability of reinforcement at exam time. However, as Klein (1987) has pointed out, too many students instead treat exams as fixed-interval schedules, thus showing the "goof off now, cram later" study pattern.

Differential Rate of Low Responding (DRL)

A **DRL schedule** reinforces the first response after a certain time interval has elapsed in which the organism has *not* made the response at all. This might sound like a fixed-interval schedule, but remember that in an FI schedule, responses during the time interval, although not reinforced, are otherwise acceptable. One example of a response on a DRL schedule is trying to start a car with a flooded engine. Repeated attempts at starting it will fail; you must wait for a few minutes, then try again, before you are likely to succeed.

Students' requests for their teacher's assistance are an example of responses that might be most appropriately reinforced on a DRL schedule. Reinforcing students continuously when they ask for the teacher's help might lead to a high rate of such requests and a resulting overdependence on the teacher. On the other hand, reinforcing students who ask for help only after they have been working independently for a period of time will teach them that independence with occasional questions is more acceptable.

We should note here that learning the appropriate response pattern for a DRL schedule often takes time, because it requires one *not* to perform a behavior that has previously been reinforced (Reynolds, 1975).

Differential Reinforcement of Other Behaviors (DRO)

In a **DRO schedule,** the organism is reinforced for doing anything *except* for making a certain response during a certain time period; in this situation, the organism must never make that particular response at all. As an example, consider the teacher who says, "I am going to write on the chalkboard the name of every student who speaks out of turn today. If your name is not on the board by three o'clock, you may have a half hour of free time." That teacher is using a DRO schedule, because she is reinforcing children for *not* talking without permission.

Continuous reinforcement is clearly the most effective way of teaching a new response. Once the terminal behavior has been reached, however, the various intermittent reinforcement schedules—ratio, interval, and differential—can be beneficial both in preventing extinction (the DRO schedule excepted) and in controlling the frequency and pattern of that response.

STIMULUS CONTROL

Earlier in the chapter, I described Skinner's operant conditioning as an $R \rightarrow S_{Rf}$ model (where S_{Rf} is reinforcement) rather than the $S \rightarrow R$ model more typical of other early behaviorists. Actually, a stimulus that precedes a response *can* influence the likelihood that the response will occur again, although the role of this **antecedent stimulus** in operant conditioning is different from the role it plays in other behaviorist models such as classical conditioning.

To illustrate, here is a typical scenario in a high school class: The teacher begins to describe the evening's homework assignment to a class of quiet and attentive students but is interrupted by a bell marking the end of the class period. Immediately the students, no longer interested in hearing their assignment, slam their notebooks shut and begin to push and shove their way toward the classroom door. These students are under **stimulus control:** They have learned that a particular response (leaving class) is acceptable under certain stimulus conditions (when the bell rings). A wise teacher would stand in front of the door while giving the homework assignment and not let the students leave their seats—bell or no bell. In that way, students would learn that leaving class is permissible only after a different stimulus—the teacher's movement away from the door—has occurred.

In operant conditioning, the antecedent stimulus does not directly elicit the response as it does in classical conditioning. Instead, the stimulus *sets the occasion* for a response to be reinforced. When an antecedent stimulus influences the likelihood that a response will occur, we call that stimulus a **discriminative stimulus,** often symbolized as **S+**,[5] and say

[5]If you read any of Skinner's writings on this topic, you should note that he used the symbol S^D instead of S+.

that the response is under stimulus control. Responses to stimuli in operant conditioning often show stimulus generalization and stimulus discrimination—phenomena similar to the generalization and discrimination observed in classical conditioning.

Stimulus Generalization

When an organism has learned to respond in a certain way in the presence of one stimulus (the S+), it is likely to respond in the same way in the presence of similar stimuli; this operant conditioning phenomenon is known as **stimulus generalization.** Just as is true in classical conditioning, stimulus generalization is more likely to occur when stimuli are similar to the discriminative stimulus. For example, students in a kindergarten classroom (the classroom being the S+) may learn such appropriate classroom behaviors as raising their hands and waiting to be called on before speaking. Such behaviors are more likely to generalize to a similar situation (such as first grade) than to a dissimilar situation (such as the family dinner table). This tendency of organisms to generalize more readily as stimuli become more similar to the discriminative stimulus is known as a **generalization gradient.**

Stimulus Discrimination

In classical conditioning, stimulus discrimination occurs when one stimulus (the CS+) is presented in conjunction with an unconditioned stimulus, and another stimulus (the CS−) is presented in the absence of the UCS. A similar phenomenon happens in operant conditioning: A response may be reinforced in the presence of one stimulus (S+) but not in the presence of another stimulus, symbolized as **S−**:[6]

$$(S+) \ R \rightarrow S_{Rf}$$

$$(S-) \ R \rightarrow (\text{nothing})$$

Learning under what circumstances a response will and will not be reinforced is operant conditioning's form of **stimulus discrimination.** Stimulus discrimination is essentially a process of learning that a conditioned response made in the presence of S+ should not be generalized to S−.

Consider the preschooler who has learned to say "bee" whenever she sees this symbol:

b

She then sees a similar stimulus:

d

and responds "bee" once again—that is, she generalizes. (Anyone who has worked with young children who are learning their alphabet letters has probably observed that, consistent with the generalization gradient, children are much more likely to generalize the

---

[6]Note that Skinner used the symbol S^{Δ} instead of S−.

"bee" response to the letter *d* than to less similar letters, such as *s* or *y*.) If the teacher does not reinforce the child for the "bee" response to the symbol *d,* the student should eventually learn to discriminate between the letters *b* and *d.*

Stimulus Control in the Classroom

At school, as in most other situations, different responses are desirable at different times. For example, it is perfectly appropriate, and in fact quite desirable, to talk with classmates at some times (e.g., during a classroom discussion) but not at others (e.g., during the weekly spelling test). Likewise, running may be appropriate in the gymnasium but can be dangerous in the school corridors. How can teachers encourage their students to exhibit different behaviors on different occasions? Psychologists have suggested two strategies: cueing and setting events.

Cueing

In the classroom, the discriminative stimuli that set the occasion for certain desired behaviors are not always obvious ones; for example, the only naturally occurring stimulus that sets the occasion for cleaning up work materials and getting ready to go to lunch might be a clock on the wall that says 11:55. Under such circumstances, teachers can provide additional discriminative stimuli that let students know how to behave—a strategy often called **cueing**[7] (e.g., Good & Brophy, 1994; Krumboltz & Krumboltz, 1972; Zirpoli & Melloy, 1993).

In some situations, teachers can provide nonverbal cues to indicate desired responses. For example, during a cooperative learning activity, they might quickly flash the overhead light on and off a few times to remind students to talk quietly rather than loudly. In other situations, teachers can give verbal cues to encourage appropriate behavior. For example, an elementary teacher whose students are preparing to go to the lunchroom might cue students by saying, "Walk quietly and in single file." The teacher can then reinforce the desired behavior by allowing students to proceed only when they behave as they have been instructed. A teacher who wants to give students a subtle reminder about the necessity for accomplishing a reading assignment quickly might say, "After you have all finished reading about recycling on pages 69 and 70 of your geography book, I will tell you about tomorrow's field trip to a recycling plant."

Setting Events

Thus far, we have focused our discussion of stimulus control on specific stimuli (e.g., the letter *b* or a teacher's cue to "walk quietly") that encourage students to behave in particular ways. Some psychologists talk not about specific stimuli but instead about complex environmental conditions—**setting events**—under which certain behaviors are most likely to occur (Brown, Bryson-Brockmann, & Fox, 1986; Brown, Fox, & Brady, 1987; Kantor, 1959; Martin, Brady, & Williams, 1991; Morris, 1982; Wahler & Fox, 1981). For example, preschoolers are more likely to interact with their classmates during free play time if they have a relatively small area in which to play and if the toys available to

---

[7]Some theorists instead use the term *prompting.*

them (balls, puppets, toy housekeeping materials) encourage group activity (Brown et al., 1987; Martin et al., 1991). Similarly, the nature of the games that children are asked to play influences the behaviors they exhibit: Cooperative games promote increases in cooperative behavior, whereas competitive games promote increases in aggressive behavior (Bay-Hinitz, Peterson, & Quilitch, 1994). Teachers are well advised, then, to create the kinds of environments that are likely to encourage the very behaviors they want their students to exhibit.

CONTEMPORARY PERSPECTIVES ON OPERANT CONDITIONING

As we noted in Chapter 2, B. F. Skinner's ideas about operant conditioning underwent little change from 1938 until his death in 1990. The views of other behaviorists have evolved considerably over time, however. Here are some examples of how contemporary perspectives of operant conditioning differ from Skinner's original notions:

• *Behavior is better understood by looking at a larger context and longer time frame than has traditionally been the case.* Early behaviorists tended to think in terms of specific S-R relationships within a relatively short time period; for example, a researcher might look at the immediate consequence of a particular response. In contrast, many behaviorists are now looking at larger and longer environment-behavior relationships (e.g., see Herrnstein, 1990; Rachlin, 1990, 1991). The *setting events* that we just discussed illustrate this trend, in that they are relatively complex environmental conditions rather than specific stimuli. Some psychologists look at the choices that organisms make in situations in which several different behaviors—each leading to a different reinforcer—are possible (de Villiers, 1977; Rachlin, 1991). Others examine the conditions under which certain behaviors are likely to persist despite *changes* in environmental stimuli—a phenomenon sometimes known as **behavioral momentum** (Belfiore, Lee, Vargas, & Skinner, 1997; Mace et al., 1988; Nevin, Mandell, & Atak, 1983).

A study by Belfiore and colleagues (1997) illustrates behavioral momentum nicely. Two girls (Allison, who was 14, and Roberta, who was 15) had a history of refusing to do the academic tasks that their teachers assigned. The researchers found that they could encourage the two students to work on difficult three-digit multiplication problems if they first gave the girls some simple one-digit problems. More generally, teachers can promote behavioral momentum by assigning easy or enjoyable tasks that lead naturally into more complex and potentially frustrating ones.

• *Operant conditioning involves cognition as well as behavior.* Many theorists now propose that operant conditioning can best be understood when we consider nonobservable mental processes as well as observable stimuli and responses (Colwill, 1993; Rachlin, 1991; Schwartz & Reisberg, 1991; Vaughan, 1988; Wasserman, 1993). For example, they talk about an organism forming *expectations* as to what reinforcer is likely to follow a particular response (Colwill, 1993; Rachlin, 1991; Schwartz & Reisberg, 1991). They find that humans and nonhumans alike develop *categories* of stimuli to which they respond; to illustrate, pigeons can be trained to discriminate (by making different responses) between members of different categories, including cats versus flowers, cars versus trucks, pictures of Charlie Brown versus those of other Peanuts characters, and even different lengths of time (Killeen, 1991; Rachlin, 1991; Vaughan, 1988; Wasserman, 1993). And behaviorists are beginning to use such phrases as *paying attention* to discriminative stimuli, mentally *encoding* response-reinforcement relationships, and *seeking information* about the environment—phrases with definite cognitive overtones (Colwill, 1993; Colwill & Rescorla, 1986; Rachlin, 1991; Rescorla, 1987; Schwartz & Reisberg, 1991).

- *Operant and classical conditioning, taken together, do not completely determine the behaviors that an organism will exhibit on any given occasion.* B. F. Skinner was a **determinist:** He proposed that if we were to have complete knowledge of an organism's past reinforcement history and present environmental circumstances, as well as knowledge of any genetic predispositions that the organism might have to behave in certain ways, we would be able to predict the organism's next response with total accuracy. The views of some contemporary behaviorists are not so deterministic in nature: They propose that any organism's behavior reflects a certain degree of variability that S-R relationships cannot explain (Epstein, 1991; Rachlin, 1991). For example, if you think about it, shaping behavior—refining it through successively "fussier" reinforcement contingencies—would not be possible unless an organism varied its responses somewhat from one occasion to another. Ultimately, it is only by making changes in responses (however small those changes may be) and experiencing their consequences that new and perhaps more adaptive behaviors can emerge over time (Epstein, 1991).

- *Just as reinforcement increases the frequency of a response, punishment can be an effective means of decreasing a response.* Early research by Thorndike (1932a, 1932b) and Skinner (1938) indicated that punishment was unlikely to reduce the behavior that it followed. But later research studies have shown that punishment *can* be effective in many situations. As a result, some theorists have revived the "punishment" part of Thorndike's original law of effect, asserting that responses followed by discomfort are in fact weakened (e.g., Aronfreed, 1968; Aronfreed & Reber, 1965; Lentz, 1988; Parke, 1972, 1977; Rachlin, 1991). We should note that when behaviorists describe the effects of both reinforcement and punishment in learning and behavior, they typically use the term **instrumental conditioning** rather than Skinner's *operant conditioning.*

We discuss punishment, including its effects and guidelines for its use, in Chapter 6. In the meantime, we turn to the three methods for eliminating undesirable behavior within the traditional, reinforcement-based operant conditioning paradigm.

ELIMINATING UNDESIRABLE BEHAVIORS

We have talked at length about how new responses are learned, modified, and maintained through operant conditioning. But sometimes we may instead want to get rid of a behavior that has previously been acquired through reinforcement. Three methods of reducing and eliminating misbehavior derived from Skinner's model of operant conditioning are extinction, differential reinforcement of other behaviors, and reinforcement of incompatible behaviors.

Extinguishing Responses

A psychologist was once consulted about Jimmy, a child who had been hospitalized for an extended period. Nurses in the children's ward were very concerned because Jimmy kept banging his head on the side of his crib; whenever they heard him doing so, they would rush to his room and stop the behavior, thereby inadvertently reinforcing and maintaining the head-banging behavior. The psychologist successfully eliminated Jimmy's head banging through a process of extinction: A protective helmet was strapped on Jimmy's head to prevent injury, and the nurses were instructed to ignore Jimmy during his head-banging episodes. At the same time, because Jimmy clearly craved attention, the nurses *did* attend to him on other occasions.

Extinction—making sure that a particular response no longer leads to reinforcement—is sometimes an effective means of eliminating inappropriate behavior. Students who engage in disruptive behavior in class may stop if such behavior no longer results in the teacher attention they seek (i.e., if the teacher ignores them). Cheating on classroom assignments may soon disappear if students never receive credit for the scores they obtain on those assignments. We don't necessarily want to eliminate the particular reinforcers (e.g., attention, class credit) that have been operating in such circumstances, but we need to make sure that those reinforcers are *not* contingent on the responses we are trying to eliminate (e.g., Fischer, Iwata, & Mazaleski, 1997).

Unfortunately, extinction is often not the most reliable method of eliminating unwanted behavior, for several reasons. First, it is not always possible to identify the specific consequence that is actually reinforcing a response; for example, children who, like Jimmy, engage in head-banging behavior do so for different reasons—perhaps to gain adult attention, to escape from academic tasks (a form of negative reinforcement), or to provide self-stimulation (Iwata, Pace, Cowdery, & Miltenberger, 1994). Second, there may often be several reinforcers involved in maintaining a response, including some that are difficult to remove; for example, although a teacher may be able to ignore the comments of a class clown, other students in the class may continue to reinforce those comments. Third, extinguished behaviors sometimes show spontaneous recovery: A response that has been extinguished one day may pop up again at a later date, perhaps in a different context (Alberto & Troutman, 1990; Skinner, 1953). And fourth, some responses may be particularly resistant to extinction because they have previously been reinforced on an intermittent schedule. When responses cannot be extinguished for any of these reasons, other methods may be more useful.

Reinforcing Other Behaviors

As noted earlier, the differential reinforcement of other behaviors—a DRO reinforcement schedule—is a procedure whereby an organism is reinforced for *not*-exhibiting a particular behavior during a specified time interval. For example, when a teacher praises a student who manages to get through an entire recess without fighting with any of his classmates, that teacher is using a DRO schedule. The differential reinforcement of other behaviors tends to be a more effective and long-lasting technique than extinction (Uhl, 1973; Uhl & Garcia, 1969; Zeiler, 1971) and has been shown to be effective in reducing a variety of inappropriate classroom behaviors (Parrish, Cataldo, Kolko, Neef, & Egel, 1986; Pinkston, Reese, LeBlanc, & Baer, 1973; Repp & Deitz, 1974; Repp, Barton, & Brulle, 1983).

Reinforcing Incompatible Behaviors

We have previously encountered the use of incompatible responses in Chapter 2's discussion of breaking habits and Chapter 3's discussion of counterconditioning. Within the operant conditioning model, the notion of incompatibility is equally useful. The first step is to identify a response that is incompatible with the undesirable response—a response that cannot be performed at the same time as the undesirable response. That incompatible behavior is then reinforced. For example, a child's inappropriate out-of-seat behavior may be reduced by reinforcing the child whenever she is sitting down. Similarly, an aggressive student can be reinforced whenever he is interacting in a prosocial manner with his classmates. Krumboltz and Krumboltz (1972) have described how reinforcing an incompatible behavior was effective in handling the chronic litterbug at a junior high school: The student was put in charge of his school's antilitter campaign and given considerable recognition and praise for his efforts.

The reinforcement of incompatible behaviors sounds similar to the DRO schedule, but a subtle difference exists between the two methods. The DRO schedule involves the reinforcement of *nonoccurrence* of a particular response. Reinforcing incompatible behaviors involves the reinforcement of a *specific, opposite* response. Like a DRO schedule, it is typically more effective than extinction in eliminating undesirable behaviors (Lentz, 1988; Zirpoli & Melloy, 1993).

When none of the techniques I've just listed—extinction, differential reinforcement of other behaviors, or reinforcement of incompatible behaviors—proves effective, punishment may be a viable alternative for eliminating an inappropriate behavior. In Chapter 6 we will consider some guidelines for using punishment effectively.

WHEN REINFORCEMENT DOESN'T WORK

The basic principle of operant conditioning—that a response increases in frequency when it is followed by reinforcement—has been used successfully in many different situations to change a wide variety of behaviors. When reinforcement doesn't work, the source of difficulty can often be traced to one of four circumstances: (1) the "reinforcer" is not reinforcing; (2) reinforcement isn't consistent; (3) the individual loses too much, or gains too little, by changing a behavior; or (4) too much is expected too soon.

The "Reinforcer" Doesn't Reinforce

A first-grade teacher once consulted me about one of her students, a boy so disruptive that he was only able to spend a half day in the classroom. In an effort to modify the disruptive behavior, the teacher had attached to the boy's desk a large sheet of heavy cardboard that was cut and painted to look like a clown, with a small red lightbulb for a nose. When the boy exhibited appropriate classroom behaviors, such as sitting quietly or attending to an assigned task, the teacher would push a button on a remote control that lit up the red nose. "I don't understand why his behavior isn't changing," she told me. "Maybe

The "reinforcer" must be
reinforcing.

Why Henry, honey,
let your old Auntie Audrey
give you a big kiss!

this clown isn't reinforcing to the boy," I suggested. "Nonsense!" exclaimed the teacher.
"The clown has always worked with *other* children!"

One of the most common mistakes that teachers make in using operant conditioning
techniques is to assume that certain consequences will be reinforcing for all students. Not
everyone will work for the same reinforcers; a consequence that increases desired behaviors for one child may not increase such behaviors for another. For example, although
most students find their teacher's praise reinforcing, some students do not (e.g., Pfiffner,
Rosén, & O'Leary, 1985). Some students may be afraid of being labeled "teacher's pet,"
especially if they value the friendship of peers who shun high achievers. Many Native
American students, although they appreciate praise for group achievements, may feel
uncomfortable when their own individual efforts are singled out as being noteworthy
(Grant & Gomez, 1996).

How can teachers determine what events will be reinforcing for different students?
One way is to watch the students to see what kinds of consequences seem to affect their
behavior. Another approach is to ask the students' parents, or even the students themselves. The one thing *not* to do is guess.

We should note here that any single reinforcer will not necessarily maintain its reinforcing value indefinitely, especially if it occurs with high frequency (Viken & McFall,
1994). For example, as much as you probably enjoy good food, you can only eat so much,
and as much as you enjoy the praise of people you respect, constant praise gets tiresome
after a while. It's certainly possible to get too much of a good thing.

Reinforcement Is Inconsistent

Sometimes it is inconvenient to reinforce a behavior every time it occurs. But remember, continuous reinforcement brings about more rapid behavior change than intermittent reinforcement. If a student's behavior has been particularly disruptive and
time-consuming, a little extra time devoted *now* to the continuous reinforcement of

appropriate behaviors, inconvenient as that may occasionally be, will probably save time over the long run.

Change Isn't Worthwhile

An individual may lose too much, or else gain too little, by changing a behavior. Consider the teenager who shies away from teacher praise because his peer group does not approve of academic achievement. It may be that teacher praise *is* a reinforcer to this student, but he risks losing his status in the group if he is praised too frequently or profusely. Praise given privately, out of the earshot of peers, will probably be much more reinforcing than public praise in this case.

Sometimes the desired behavior simply requires too much effort to be worth the payoff (e.g., Friman & Poling, 1995). For example, people in the workplace often recycle office paper when recycling boxes are placed on their desks; they are much less likely to do so when they have to walk across the room to find such boxes (Brothers, Krantz, & McClannahan, 1994). And consider the college student who estimates that she will have to study at least 20 hours a week to get an A in a history class. Although the A may be an effective reinforcer, it may not be worth the amount of time she will have to spend to earn it.

Consciously or otherwise, people may sometimes engage in a cost-benefit analysis when looking at the consequences of different behaviors (e.g., Eccles & Wigfield, 1985; Feather, 1982). Although they may have learned that a certain response will be reinforced, they will nevertheless not respond in that way if they have too much to lose, or too little to gain, by doing so. For people to respond positively to reinforcement, it must be worth their while.

Shaping Proceeds Too Rapidly

Reinforcement is ineffective when too much is expected too soon. In many situations, establishing a desirable behavior requires a process of *shaping* that behavior. Remember that shaping involves the reinforcement of a series of responses that more and more closely approximate the terminal behavior. Each response should be well learned before reinforcement proceeds to a closer approximation. If an attempt at shaping moves too quickly, such that each response is not well established before a more sophisticated one is expected, the reinforcement program will be ineffective in bringing about behavior change.

To illustrate, let's say that Ms. Garcia, a third-grade teacher, wants to reinforce Jack, an especially hyperactive student, for sitting quietly in his seat; her goal (the terminal behavior) is for him to sit quietly for 20 minutes. On the first morning of the intervention program, Jack sits quietly for one minute, and so Ms. Garcia reinforces him. She probably does *not* want to move on to a two-minute criterion just because he has met the one-minute criterion once. Instead, she should continue reinforcing Jack for one-minute "sits" until it is clear, from the frequency of his sitting behavior, that she can begin to expect that behavior for a longer period of time.

SKINNER ON EDUCATION

B. F. Skinner wrote prolifically on the weaknesses of schools from an operant conditioning perspective (Skinner, 1953, 1954, 1958, 1968, 1973). He contended that reinforcement in the classroom usually occurs inconsistently and too long after a desired response has occurred. Although "natural" reinforcers (e.g., the opportunity to control one's environment or the intrinsically rewarding value of the subject matter) can sometimes reinforce (and therefore increase) appropriate academic behaviors, in fact most classroom reinforcers are artificially imposed. A problem inherent in our educational system is that teachers must teach behaviors that will be useful to students in the *future* rather than in the present, so these behaviors are not likely to lead to the naturally positive consequences now that they might later on (e.g., although a student might find algebra useful when she becomes a mechanical engineer, she does not find it particularly useful in her current life). As a result, teachers resort to artificial reinforcers such as teacher approval, grades, stickers, or free time to foster academic achievement. These reinforcers are often ineffective, however, in part because their relationships to the responses that students make are often unclear.

In desperation, teachers often find themselves punishing *mis*behaviors, through such aversive consequences as displeasure, ridicule, and failing grades, rather than reinforcing appropriate responses; as Skinner puts it, teachers "induce students to learn by threatening them for not learning" (Skinner, 1968, p. 57). Not only is such aversive control of behavior ineffective, it may also encourage students to engage in behaviors that allow them to escape school tasks or avoid them altogether.

Skinner urged educators to focus on reinforcing student successes rather than on punishing student failures. He proposed a "technology of teaching" whereby instruction is individualized, complex verbal behaviors are gradually shaped, reinforcement for appropriate responses is consistent and immediate, and learned behaviors are maintained through intermittent reinforcement schedules. Skinner's suggestions for how operant conditioning might be successfully applied to classroom situations, and the suggestions of other psychologists and educators as well, are the subject of the next chapter.

SUMMARY

The basic principle of operant conditioning is that responses followed by reinforcement increase in frequency. For operant conditioning to occur, a reinforcer must follow immediately after a response and also be contingent on that response. Operant conditioning is different from classical conditioning in at least three ways: (1) it occurs as a result of a response being followed by a reinforcing stimulus rather than as a result of two stimuli being paired, (2) it involves voluntary rather than involuntary responses, and (3) it is better described as an $R \rightarrow S$ relationship than as an $S \rightarrow R$ relationship.

The free operant level, or baseline, of a response is its frequency in the absence of reinforcement; the terminal behavior is the form and frequency of the desired response at the end of a reinforcement program. Even when a response-reinforcer sequence occurs by coincidence rather than by design, an increase in the frequency of that response is observed (superstitious behavior). A response that has previously been reinforced but is no longer being reinforced tends to decrease in frequency to its baseline rate (extinction). Complex behaviors can be taught by reinforcing successive approximations to the desired terminal behavior (shaping) or by reinforcing an increasingly longer series of responses (chaining).

Reinforcement takes a variety of forms. A primary reinforcer is one that satisfies a biological need; a secondary reinforcer is one that becomes reinforcing through repeated association with another reinforcer. Whereas positive reinforcement involves the presentation of a (presumably pleasant) stimulus, negative reinforcement involves the removal of a (presumably aversive) stimulus; because negative reinforcement increases behavior just as positive reinforcement does, it is *not* a form of punishment. A reinforcer is not always a material object; for instance, it can also be a social event, a favorite activity, an intrinsic feeling of satisfaction, or positive feedback.

Timing, magnitude, and consistency of reinforcement affect the rate at which new behaviors are learned. Different schedules of reinforcement influence the frequency with which responses occur, as well as the rates at which those responses are acquired and extinguished.

Antecedent stimuli also affect the occurrence of a response. For example, when an organism has learned to respond in a certain way in the presence of one stimulus, it is likely to respond in the same way in the presence of similar stimuli (stimulus generalization). However, if a particular response has been reinforced in the presence of one stimulus but not in the presence of another, the organism will exhibit the response only when the former stimulus is presented (stimulus discrimination). Teachers can use a variety of antecedent stimuli, perhaps taking the form of cues or setting events, that encourage appropriate classroom behaviors.

Contemporary perspectives of operant conditioning differ somewhat from Skinner's original notions. For example, some theorists propose that behavior is better understood by looking beyond specific S-R relationships to a larger context and longer time frame. In addition, some current explanations of why operant conditioning takes place include a discussion of the cognitive factors that underlie conditioning. And many theorists now believe that behavior may never be totally predictable—that human and nonhuman behavior is somewhat variable even when reinforcement histories and stimulus conditions remain constant.

In addition to punishment (which, according to many contemporary behaviorists, *does* lead to a response decrease), three techniques based on a traditional, reinforcement-based model of operant conditioning—extinction, the differential reinforcement of other behaviors, and the reinforcement of incompatible behaviors—serve as viable means of eliminating undesirable behaviors. B. F. Skinner contended that, in classroom situations, appropriate behaviors are usually reinforced inconsistently and undesirable behaviors are often unintentionally reinforced.

CHAPTER 5

Applications of Operant Conditioning

Over the past 40 years, operant conditioning has influenced educational practice significantly. At least five educational innovations can be attributed either directly or indirectly to operant conditioning principles: (1) instructional objectives; (2) programmed instruction and its offspring, computer-assisted instruction; (3) mastery learning; (4) contingency contracts; and (5) applied behavior analysis. In this chapter we will look at the basic components of these innovations and consider empirical evidence concerning their effectiveness. We will then address frequently expressed concerns regarding the use of reinforcement in the classroom.

INSTRUCTIONAL OBJECTIVES

In its 1947 report, the President's Commission on Higher Education described the primary goal of the U.S. educational system as "the full, rounded, and continuing development of the person" (cited in Dyer, 1967, p. 14). At first glance, this might seem to be a worthwhile and appropriate goal for education, but on closer inspection, the statement provides very little *specific* information regarding what an educated person should be like. The President's Commission report is a good example of "word magic": It sounds nice, but we eventually realize that we don't have a clue as to what the words really mean (Dyer, 1967). When we don't know exactly what our educational objectives are, we don't know what or how to teach, nor do we know whether instruction is effectively accomplishing its goals.

As we noted in the preceding chapter, a standard practice in using operant conditioning is to specify the terminal behavior in precise, observable terms before conditioning begins, thereby allowing us to develop appropriate methods of shaping the desired behavior and of determining when that behavior has been acquired. This principle of a priori specification of the terminal behavior in observable, measurable terms has been applied to classroom instruction in the form of instructional objectives, and often more specifically in the form of behavioral objectives.

Behavioral Objectives

Ideally, a **behavioral objective** has three components (Mager, 1962, 1984; Schloss & Smith, 1994). First, the outcome is stated in terms of an observable and measurable behavior. Consider this objective:

> *The student will be aware of current events.*

A student's "awareness" is not easily observable. The same objective can be stated in terms of one or more specific behaviors that a student should exhibit; consider this one as an example:

> *The student will describe the major cause of political unrest in South Africa.*

Some verbs (e.g., *understand, appreciate, know, be aware of,* and *remember*) tell us little, if anything, about what students should actually be able to do, but others (e.g., *write, compute, list, describe,* and *select*) clearly communicate observable responses. We can probably conceptualize almost any objective in behavioral terms if we think about the specific things people would have to do to convince someone that they had met the objective (Mager, 1972).

Second, a behavioral objective specifies the conditions under which the behavior should be exhibited. Sometimes we expect desired behaviors to occur in specific situations (stimulus conditions). For example, one of my objectives for my graduate course in educational assessment is as follows:

> *The student will correctly compute test-retest reliability.*

I do not expect students to memorize the formula for calculating test-retest reliability, however. Hence, there is a condition under which I expect the behavior to occur:

> *Given the formula for a correlation coefficient, the student will correctly compute test-retest reliability.*

Finally, the objective includes a criterion for judging the acceptable performance of the behavior. Many behaviors are not strictly right or wrong; instead, they vary on a continuum of relative "rightness" and "wrongness." In cases where right and wrong behaviors are not obvious, a behavioral objective should specify the criterion for acceptable performance, perhaps in terms of a certain percentage of correct answers, a certain time limit, or the degree of acceptable deviation from the correct response (Mager, 1962, 1984). Here are some examples to illustrate this point:

> *On weekly written spelling tests, the student will correctly spell at least 85% of the year's 500 spelling words.*

> *Given a sheet of 100 addition problems involving the addition of two single-digit numbers, including all possible combinations of the digits 0 through 9, the student will correctly write the answers to these problems within five minutes.*

> *Given the formula for a correlation coefficient, the student will correctly compute test-retest reliability, with differences from a computer-calculated coefficient being attributable to rounding-off errors.*

The Current Perspective on Instructional Objectives

Behavioral objectives have frequently been criticized for focusing on concrete, picayune details rather than on more central, but probably more abstract, educational goals. For example, many lists of behavioral objectives emphasize behaviors that depend on the rote memorization of facts rather than on behaviors that reflect more complex and sophisticated learning (Trachtenberg, 1974); in other words, they focus on **lower-level skills** rather than **higher-level skills.** Such lower-level objectives may be prevalent simply because they are the easiest ones to conceptualize and write.

School personnel have many goals in mind for each classroom in any given year; these goals typically encompass both lower-level and higher-level skills. Writing behavioral objectives that cover each and every goal can sometimes become a burdensome, if not impossible, task. As a result, many educators have proposed that a smaller number of general, nonbehavioral objectives provide an acceptable alternative (e.g., Dressel, 1977; Gronlund, 1995; Popham, 1995; Posner & Rudnitsky, 1986). But in such situations, it is helpful to list examples of behaviors that reflect each abstract objective. To illustrate, imagine that we want high school students to understand, evaluate, and critique the things that they read—an objective that certainly involves higher-level thinking skills. We might list behavioral manifestations of critical reading such as the following:

1. Distinguishing between main ideas and supporting details
2. Distinguishing between facts and opinions
3. Distinguishing between facts and inferences
4. Identifying cause-effect relations
5. Identifying errors in reasoning
6. Distinguishing between valid and invalid conclusions
7. Identifying assumptions underlying conclusions (Adapted from Gronlund, 1995, p. 52)

This is hardly an exhaustive list of what critical reading entails, but it gives us an idea of the terminal behaviors we want to see.

Formulating Different Levels of Objectives

Sometimes objectives that reflect basic knowledge and skills are appropriate. But in many circumstances, objectives reflecting relatively sophisticated levels of learning are desired, especially as students get older (e.g., see Cole, 1990). In such situations, **taxonomies** of objectives—the various behaviors we might want to see students demonstrate, often listed in order of increasing complexity—are helpful (e.g., see Bloom, Englehart, Furst, Hill, & Krathwohl, 1956; Harrow, 1972; Krathwohl, Bloom, & Masia, 1964; Stiggins, 1994). As an example, Bloom's Taxonomy of Educational Objectives (Bloom et al., 1956) describes six general levels of knowing and using information—that is, six possible objectives in the **cognitive domain.** An overview of this taxonomy is presented in Figure 5–1.

Bloom and his colleagues originally presented the six levels as a hierarchy, with each one depending on those preceding it in the list. Although the hierarchical nature of Bloom's cognitive domain is in doubt (Furst, 1981; Krathwohl, 1994; Seddon, 1978), the taxonomy nevertheless provides a useful reminder that instructional objectives should often encompass higher-level cognitive skills as well as the knowledge of simple, discrete facts (Gronlund, 1995; Hastings, 1977; Popham, 1988).

Usefulness and Effectiveness of Objectives

From a teacher's perspective, objectives serve several useful functions (Gronlund, 1995; Mager, 1962, 1984; Stiggins, 1994). First, specification of a lesson's objectives in precise terms helps a teacher choose the most effective method of teaching that lesson. For example, when teaching a unit on basic addition, a teacher might use flash cards if the objective is *knowledge* of number facts but might instead use word problems if the objective is the *application* of those number facts. A second advantage is that objectives, especially when described in behavioral terms, are easily communicated from one teacher to another. For example, although teachers may differ in their conception of what "application of addition principles" means, they will be likely to interpret "correct solution of addition word problems" similarly. Finally, objectives facilitate the evaluation of both the

1. **Knowledge:** rote memorizing of information in a basically word-for-word fashion; for example, reciting definitions of terms or remembering lists of items.
2. **Comprehension:** translating information into one's own words; for example, rewording a definition or paraphrasing a rule.
3. **Application:** using information in a new situation; for example, applying mathematical principles to the solution of word problems or applying psychological theories of learning to educational practice.
4. **Analysis:** breaking information down into its constituent parts; for example, discovering the assumptions underlying a philosophical essay or identifying fallacies in a logical argument.
5. **Synthesis:** constructing something new by integrating several pieces of information; for example, developing a theory or presenting a logical defense for a particular point of view.
6. **Evaluation:** placing a value judgment on data; for example, critiquing a theory or determining the appropriateness of conclusions drawn from a research study.

Figure 5–1

Bloom's Taxonomy of Educational Objectives (Bloom, Englehart, Furst, Hill, & Krathwohl, 1956).

student and the instructional program: Student accomplishment and program effectiveness can be evaluated on the basis of whether manifestations of the desired behaviors are observed.[1] From a student's perspective, instructional objectives have an additional advantage: Students who are told what they should be able to do at the conclusion of an instructional unit have tangible goals to strive for and are better able to judge correctly how successfully they have learned (Gronlund, 1995; McAshan, 1979; Stiggins, 1994).

Because instructional objectives often specify the outcomes of instruction so explicitly, students usually view them favorably. However, research studies investigating the effectiveness of objectives for improving academic performance have yielded mixed results (Melton, 1978). Objectives tend to focus teachers' and students' attention toward certain information and skills (those things that are included in the objectives) and away from other subject matter (e.g., Slavin, 1990b). If the stated objectives encompass *everything* that students should learn, the use of objectives in the classroom will enhance learning. But if the objectives include only a portion of what the teacher deems to be important, while excluding other, equally important, material, some critical information and skills are not as likely to be learned as completely as they might otherwise be.

---

[1] For example, some schools use an approach called *outcomes-based education,* in which the desired objectives ("outcomes") of instruction are clearly delineated in advance; decisions about students' grades, promotion to higher grade levels, and high school graduation are based on whether students have achieved those objectives (e.g., Boschee & Baron, 1993; Guskey, 1994).

PROGRAMMED INSTRUCTION AND COMPUTER-ASSISTED INSTRUCTION

From the perspective of operant conditioning, reinforcement must occur immediately after a response to have a significant impact on that behavior. Yet many reinforcers of classroom learning are delayed by hours, days, or, in the case of a high school diploma or college degree, even years. To provide a means by which responses can be reinforced immediately, Skinner (1954) developed a technique most frequently known as **programmed instruction,** or **PI.**

In its earliest form, programmed instruction involved an adaptation of Pressey's (1926, 1927) **teaching machine.** This "machine" was a box enclosing a long roll of printed material that a student could advance past a display window, thereby viewing small portions of information successively and systematically. Since the teaching machine, programmed instruction has evolved into programmed textbooks and, more recently, computer-assisted instruction.

Regardless of the form it takes, programmed instruction consists of several standard features. First, the material to be learned is presented through a series of discrete segments, or **frames.** The first frame presents a small piece of information and poses a question about it. The student responds to the question, then turns to the next frame; that frame provides the correct answer to the question posed in the previous frame, presents more information, and asks another question. The student continues through the frames, encountering new information, responding to questions, and checking his or her answers against those provided by the program.

To illustrate the PI process, I have developed some possible frames for a unit on writing behavioral objectives, as follows:

FRAME 1

An *objective* is a goal for an instructional unit. **(information)**

Another name for the goal of an instructional unit is an
_____ . **(question)**

FRAME 2

objective **(answer to previous question)**

A behavioral *objective* is an objective that specifies the goals of an instructional unit in terms of the *behaviors* that the student should be able to demonstrate at the completion of the unit.

An objective that specifies instructional goals in terms of behaviors that the student can demonstrate is called a
_____ objective.

FRAME 3

behavioral

A behavioral objective should describe the desired behavior in such a way that the behavior is both *observable* and *measurable*.

A behavioral objective is an instructional goal in which an observable and _____ behavior is described.

FRAME 4

measurable

The student will write the correct answer to the problem "2 + 2 = ?" In this objective, the word *write* describes an observable behavior.

Which one of the following verbs is an example of an observable behavior: *think, appreciate, write,* or *learn?* _____

Intrinsic to programmed instruction are several concepts and principles based on operant conditioning, including the following:

1. **Terminal behavior.** The goals of instruction are specified before the instructional program is developed in terms of the terminal behaviors (the behavioral objectives) to be demonstrated upon completion of instruction.
2. **Active responding.** The student is required to make a response in each frame.
3. **Shaping.** Instruction begins with information that the student already knows. The new information to be learned is broken into tiny pieces, and instruction proceeds through a gradual presentation of increasingly more difficult pieces. As the successive pieces are presented and questions of increasing difficulty are answered, the terminal behavior is gradually shaped.
4. **Immediate reinforcement.** Because instruction involves a gradual shaping process, the probability is quite high that a student will give correct answers to the questions asked. Each correct answer is reinforced immediately in the form of feedback that it is correct.[2]

---

[2] We should note here that, in one study with undergraduate students, occasional 10-second delays in feedback actually *enhanced* students' learning, apparently because the delays gave students more time to study the material in front of them (Crosbie & Kelly, 1994).

5. **Individual differences in learning rate.** Programmed instruction is self-paced, allowing students to progress through an instructional unit at their own rate of speed.

The earliest form of programmed instruction was the **linear program:** All students proceeded through exactly the same sequence of frames in exactly the same order. A more recent trend is to use a **branching program,** a technique introduced by Norman Crowder (Crowder & Martin, 1961). Branching programs typically progress in larger steps than linear programs (each frame presents more information), so that error rates in responding are somewhat higher. A student who responds incorrectly is directed to one or more "remedial" frames for further practice on that part of the lesson before being allowed to continue with new information. To illustrate, let's resume our lesson on behavioral objectives (beginning where we left off, with frame 4) but now using a branching format.

FRAME 4

measurable

The student will write the correct answer to the problem "2 + 2 = ?" In this objective, the word *write* describes an observable behavior.

Which one of the following verbs is an example of an observable behavior: *think, appreciate, write,* or *learn?* _____

FRAME 5

If you answered *think, appreciate,* or *learn,* go to frame 6.
If you answered *write,* go to frame 7.

FRAME 6

The verbs *think, appreciate,* and *learn* all describe internal mental events; they are not observable behaviors. Only the verb *write* describes an observable behavior. Return to frame 4 and try again.

FRAME 7

Yes, the verb *write* is the only one of the four that describes an observable behavior. The other verbs—*think, appreciate,* and *learn*—cannot be directly observed.

The student will learn the alphabet. This is not a behavioral objective because the verb *learn* does not describe an observable behavior.

The above objective could be changed into a behavioral objective by replacing the verb *learn* with which one of the following: *remember, memorize,* or *recite?* _____

FRAME 8

If you answered *remember* or *memorize,* go to frame 9.
If you answered *recite,* go to frame 13.

FRAME 9

The verbs *remember* and *memorize* do not reflect observable behaviors. Only *recite* is a directly observable response.

The student will _____ Hamlet's soliloquy. One of the following verbs would make this objective a behavioral objective: *know, say, memorize,* or *learn.*

Which one of the four verbs can be used to make the statement a behavioral objective? _____

FRAME 10

If you answered *know, memorize,* or *learn,* go to frame 11.
If you answered *say,* go to frame 12.

FRAME 11

No. *Knowing, memorizing,* and *learning* cannot be directly observed. Only *saying* is an observable behavior. Return to frame 7 and review this section again.

FRAME 12

Yes. Only the verb *say* describes an observable behavior.

[*The lesson continues with new information.*]

The major advantage of a branching program is that it provides remedial instructional frames only for students who have difficulty with a particular concept; other students can move on to new information without having to spend time on practice they don't need. Unfortunately, however, a branching program can be cumbersome, at least in its textbook form. Students are referred to different frames, and often to different pages, for each response they make, so progression through the program is rarely smooth. Fortunately, this drawback of the branching program has been virtually eliminated by the advent of computer-assisted instruction.

Computer-assisted instruction, or **CAI,** is programmed instruction presented by means of a computer. It has several advantages not characteristic of paper-pencil forms of programmed instruction. First, branching programs can be used without having to instruct students to proceed to one frame or another; the computer automatically presents the appropriate frame for any response the student has given. Second, because of the graphics capabilities of computers (e.g., complex moving visual displays can be included in lessons), CAI can present information in a way that traditional programmed instruction cannot. A good example is the use of simulation programs, programs that give students practice in performing skilled operations (such as flying an airplane) without the risk or expense that would be associated with performing those operations in real-life situations. Third, the computer can record and maintain ongoing data for each student, including information such as how far a student has progressed in the program, how often he or she is right and wrong, how quickly he or she responds, and so on. With such data, a teacher can monitor each student's progress through the program and identify students who are having particular difficulty with the material. And, finally, a computer can be used to provide instruction when flesh-and-blood teachers are not available; for example, CAI is often used to deliver college instruction in rural areas far removed from university settings. (We should note here that, as cognitivism increasingly dominates theories of human learning, computer instruction is no longer restricted to the traditional, behaviorism-based CAI approach; hence, you may sometimes see reference to such terms as *computer-assisted learning* [CAL] or *computer-based instruction* [CBI] rather than CAI.)

Effectiveness of PI and CAI

Most research indicates that traditional (i.e., noncomputer-based) programmed instruction is no more effective than traditional instructional methods (Feldhusen, 1963; Lange, 1972; Reese & Parnes, 1970; Schramm, 1964). In contrast, CAI is frequently shown to be superior to traditional instruction in terms of both increased academic achievement and improved student attitudes toward schoolwork (Hativa & Shorer, 1989; Kulik, Kulik, and Cohen, 1980; Lepper & Gurtner, 1989; Tudor, 1995).

A cautionary note regarding the use of PI and CAI is in order, however. Some programmed instruction packages may be poorly conceived (Bell-Gredler, 1986; O'Leary & O'Leary, 1972); for example, they may not always adequately incorporate such principles as active responding, immediate reinforcement of responses, or gradual shaping of the terminal behavior. Programmed instruction is less likely to be effective when such principles of operant conditioning are violated.

MASTERY LEARNING

Inherent in the behaviorist perspective, and especially in the operant conditioning model, is the belief that, given appropriate environmental conditions (e.g., consistent reinforcement of desirable behaviors and gradual shaping of responses over time), people are capable of acquiring many complex behaviors. As an example of such optimism, you may remember John Watson's famous quote presented in Chapter 2: "Give me a dozen healthy infants, well-formed, and my own specified world to bring them up in and I'll guarantee to take any one at random and train him to become any type of specialist I might select. . . ."

The optimism of behaviorism is reflected in **mastery learning**—an approach to instruction in which students must learn one lesson well (i.e., *master* the content) before proceeding to the next lesson. Underlying this approach is the assumption that most students *can* learn school subject matter if they are given sufficient time and instruction to do so.

Mastery learning is based, in part, on the operant conditioning concept of *shaping:* At first, a relatively simple response is reinforced until it is emitted frequently (i.e., until it is mastered), then a slightly more difficult response is reinforced, and so on until eventually the desired terminal behavior is acquired. Consistent with shaping, mastery learning usually includes the following components:

1. **Small, discrete units.** Course content is broken up into a number of separate units or lessons, with each unit covering a small amount of material.
2. **A logical sequence.** Units are sequenced such that basic concepts and procedures—those that provide the foundation for later units—are learned first. More complex concepts and procedures, including those that build on basic units, are learned later. For example, a unit in which students learn what a fraction *is* would obviously come before a unit in which they learn how to add two fractions together. The process through which the component parts of course content are identified and sequenced, going from simpler to more complex, is called **task analysis.**

3. **Demonstration of mastery at the completion of each unit.** Before "graduating" from one unit to the next, students must show that they have mastered the current unit—for example, by taking a test on the content of that unit.

4. **A concrete, observable criterion for mastery of each unit.** Mastery of a topic is defined in specific, concrete terms. For example, to "pass" a unit on adding fractions with the same denominator, students might have to answer at least 90% of test items correctly.

5. **Additional "remedial" activities for students needing extra help or practice.** Students do not always demonstrate mastery on the first try. Additional support and resources—perhaps alternative approaches to instruction, different materials, workbooks, study groups, and individual tutoring—are provided for students who need them (e.g., Guskey, 1985).

Mastery learning gained prominence during the 1960s, and many educators still advocate it in one form or another (Block, 1980; Bloom, 1968, 1974, 1976, 1981, 1984; Boschee & Baron, 1993; Carroll, 1963, 1989; Guskey, 1985, 1994; Hunter, 1982; Keller, 1968; Lee & Pruitt, 1984). A particular form of mastery learning—Fred Keller's personalized system of instruction—has been used extensively at the college level. Let's take a closer look at what this approach entails.

Keller's Personalized System of Instruction (PSI)

As Michael (1974) has pointed out, traditional college instruction has definite weaknesses when viewed from the perspective of operant conditioning principles. For example, students may not learn what grades they've earned for their work until days or weeks after they've submitted the work; hence, achievement is not immediately reinforced. Furthermore, students must frequently proceed to advanced material before they have mastered the more basic information necessary to understand it.

To remedy such weaknesses of college instruction, Keller (1968, 1974) developed the **personalized system of instruction** (also known as **PSI**, or the **Keller Plan**) as an alternative approach to teaching college students. In addition to the discrete modules, logical sequence, and frequent measures of mastery characteristic of other mastery learning approaches, PSI encompasses the following features:

1. **Emphasis on individual study.** Most learning occurs through students' independent study of such written materials as textbooks and study guides. One-on-one tutoring provides additional assistance when necessary.

2. **Unit exams.** An examination on each module assesses students' mastery of the material. Students receive immediate feedback about how well they have performed on unit exams.

3. **Self-pacing.** Students report to class to take exams when they are ready to do so; in this sense, learning is self-paced. Some students proceed through the course very quickly, and others progress more slowly. (Note that self-pacing is sometimes, but not always, a component of other mastery approaches as well.)

4. **Supplementary instructional techniques.** Traditional group instructional methods (e.g., lectures, demonstrations, and discussions) are occasionally

provided as supplementary presentations of the same material that also appears in the textbook or other assigned readings. These group classes are optional but serve to motivate and stimulate students.

5. **Use of proctors.** Proctors, usually more advanced students, administer and score exams and tutor students on topics with which they are having difficulty.

The teacher of a PSI course plays a different role from that of someone using a more conventional approach to instruction. The PSI teacher is less of a lecturer and more of a curriculum developer, exam writer, proctor coordinator, and record keeper. Rather than leading students through course content, the PSI teacher instead provides an elaborate system whereby students, with the assistance of study guides and tutors, find their own way through.

Effectiveness of Mastery Learning and PSI

Several reviews of research findings (Arlin, 1984; Block & Burns, 1976; Kulik, Kulik, & Bangert-Drowns, 1990; Kulik, Kulik, & Cohen, 1979; Shuell, 1996) indicate that mastery learning (including PSI) facilitates student learning and often leads to higher achievement than more traditional approaches (although note that Slavin [1987, 1990b] found no substantial differences). Furthermore, students in mastery learning programs often retain the things they have learned for longer periods of time (DuNann & Weber, 1976; Kulik, et al., 1979); to illustrate, in one study, college students in mastery-based psychology classes remembered 75 to 85% of the material after four months and 70 to 80% after 11 months (Semb, Ellis, & Araujo, 1993). And PSI, at least, facilitates better study habits: Although PSI students don't appear to study more than other students, they study regularly rather than procrastinating and cramming the way students in traditional courses often do (Born & Davis, 1974; Kulik et al., 1979). Low-achieving students in particular seem to benefit from a mastery learning approach (DuNann & Weber, 1976; Kulik et al., 1990).

Mastery learning and PSI are not without their problems, however. In many cases, students who learn quickly receive less instruction than their classmates, raising a concern about possibly inequitable treatment of these students (Arlin, 1984). Furthermore, for logistical reasons, fast-learning students must sometimes wait until their slower classmates have also mastered the material before they can proceed to the next unit; as a result, they learn less than they might otherwise (Arlin, 1984). Yet when all students are allowed to work at their own pace, teachers must assist and keep track of perhaps 25 or 30 students working on different tasks and succeeding at different rates; hence, they may do more "managing" (e.g., distributing materials and grading tests) than actual teaching (Berliner, 1989; Prawat, 1992).

Additional weaknesses have been noted for PSI in particular. One difficulty lies in the required mastery of material; some students are unable to meet the criterion for passing exams, despite repeated testings (Sussman, 1981). A second weakness is the lack of interaction among students—interaction that many students see as beneficial to their learning (Gasper, 1980). A third problem is related to the self-paced nature of a PSI course, which is sometimes compromised if university policy requires that students complete a course within one quarter or semester (Sussman, 1981). Poorly motivated students are likely to procrastinate until finally they must withdraw from the course (Sussman, 1981; Swenson, 1980), although withdrawal rates from PSI courses do not appear to be appreciably higher than withdrawal rates from traditional courses (Kulik et al., 1979, 1990). Several techniques have been shown to reduce procrastination and withdrawal from PSI, among them setting target dates for the completion of different modules (Reiser & Sullivan, 1977), giving bonus points for early completion of modules (Bufford, 1976), and eliminating the necessity for completing the course within one college term (Sussman, 1981).

Mastery learning is probably most appropriately used when a teacher's main objective is for students to learn specific skills or a specified body of information. In such situations, the immediate feedback and emphasis on mastery of course material may well be reasons why mastery learning increases student achievement, particularly for low-achieving students. When the objective is something other than acquiring information or skills, however—for example, when it is to wrestle with controversial and unresolved issues—a mastery approach may not be the method of choice.

CONTINGENCY CONTRACTS

Programmed instruction and mastery learning are instances of operant conditioning principles applied to the education of large groups of students. The amount of time needed to prepare materials for both of these techniques makes their use for only one or two students virtually impossible. When the learning or behavior of a single student is of concern, a **contingency contract** is often more practical.

A contingency contract is an agreement between a student and a teacher that specifies certain expectations for the student (the terminal behavior) and the consequences of the student's meeting those expectations (the reinforcer). For example, a student and teacher may agree that the student should turn in all homework assignments, on time and with at least 80% accuracy, every day for a week. If the student accomplishes this task, the contract might specify that the student will have some time to engage in a favorite activity, or that the teacher and student will spend time after school studying a topic of particular interest to the student. Although a contingency contract can be as simple as a verbal agreement, more often it is an actual written contract. The student and teacher negotiate the conditions of the contract in one or more meetings; both individuals then sign and date the contract.

A contingency contract can be used to reward academic accomplishment; it can also be used to modify classroom behavior. For example, a teacher might help a student spend more class time attending to assigned work, or to engage in more prosocial behaviors on the playground, by contracting with the student that certain behaviors will lead to desired consequences. Contingency contracting has been shown to be effective for addressing such diverse problems as poor study habits (Brooke & Ruthren, 1984; Miller & Kelley, 1994), juvenile delinquency (Rueger & Liberman, 1984; Welch, 1985), and drug addiction (Anker & Crowley, 1982; Crowley, 1984; Rueger & Liberman, 1984). It can also be a useful supplement to Keller's personalized system of instruction (Brooke and Ruthren, 1984).

Guidelines for Writing Contingency Contracts

Teachers should keep several guidelines in mind when developing contingency contracts:

- *The contract should specify the desired behavior of the student and the consequence (reinforcer) that will be contingent on that behavior.* Both the desired behavior and the reinforcer should be specified in clear, precise terminology (Homme, Csanyi, Gonzales, & Rechs, 1970).

- *Early contracts should require small tasks that a student can accomplish within a short period of time* (Walker & Shea, 1995). Remember the problem with delayed reinforcement: Contracts that provide reinforcement only after the desired behavior has been exhibited for a lengthy period simply may not work.

- *Reinforcement should be contingent on accomplishment of the desired behavior* (Homme et al., 1970). Students occasionally tell their teacher that they *tried* to do a task but for one reason or another could not. Teachers who reinforce students only for successful completion of the task specified in the contract, *not* for their self-described unsuccessful efforts, will give students a clear message that task completion is essential for school success.

- *A criterion for judging the quality of the desired behavior should be specified.* When the task to be accomplished can differ considerably in quality from one student to another, as is true for an exam or a written composition, a criterion of successful completion of that task should be included in the contract. In the case of an exam, the criterion might be a percentage of correct items. For written work, some subjective judgment is almost inevitably involved in assessing the work; however, criteria that will be considered in the evaluation—specific content to be included, organization, clarity, grammar, and so on—should be clearly stated as a part of the contract.

A former colleague of mine once overlooked this critical principle when he used contingency contracts to assign grades in his college classes. For example, some contracts stated that students would take exams on assigned readings without specifying acceptable scores for those exams. Other contracts read something like this: "For an A, the student will write a 10-page paper about operant conditioning," without describing how well the paper was to be written or what topics should be included. My colleague found himself obligated to award As for multiple-choice exams with scores of 25% and for papers along the lines of "How I Shaped My Kid Brother at the Beach Last Summer."

- *When different contingency contracts are used with different students as a way of individualizing requirements for students, all contracts should nevertheless be equivalent in scope.* Unless there are compelling reasons to do otherwise, contracts should require tasks that are equal in difficulty and reflect equal levels of competence for

```
+----------------------------------+    +----------------------------------+
| For an A, ___Mary Lamb___        |    | For an A, ___John Goat___        |
| will read one book somehow       |    | will write a 500-page            |
| related to education.            |    | treatise on the use of           |
|                                  |    | computer-assisted                |
|                                  |    | instruction for teaching         |
|                                  |    | Chinese calligraphy to           |
|                                  |    | dysgraphic children.             |
|                                  |    |                                  |
| Signed:                          |    | Signed:                          |
|    ___Mary L___                  |    |    ___John G___                  |
|    ___Dr Schmoe___               |    |    ___Dr Schmoe___               |
+----------------------------------+    +----------------------------------+
```

When used to address individual students' instructional needs, contingency contracts should be equivalent in scope.

all students. The need for equivalence across contracts is particularly critical when the reinforcers used are course grades: Assigning grades based on student behaviors differing radically in difficulty level and quality typically renders those grades uninterpretable.

Contingency contracts are often used within the context of *applied behavior analysis*—a group of strategies for bringing about behavior change that are based on behaviorist principles. We turn to a discussion of such strategies now.

APPLIED BEHAVIOR ANALYSIS

Applied behavior analysis (ABA), sometimes known as *behavior modification, behavior therapy,* or *contingency management,* is probably the most straightforward application of operant conditioning principles. Based on the assumption that behavior problems are the result of past and present environmental circumstances, applied behavior analysis encompasses a number of procedures whereby an individual's present environment is modified to promote the reinforcement of acceptable behaviors and the nonreinforcement of inappropriate ones. Central to ABA techniques are such operant conditioning concepts as reinforcement, extinction, shaping, stimulus control, and the reinforcement of incompatible behaviors. The concepts of punishment and modeling, though not components of Skinner's model of operant conditioning, are also frequently used in ABA programs; these two aspects of ABA are addressed in Chapters 6 and 7, respectively.

Components of Applied Behavior Analysis

Although ABA encompasses a number of different techniques, some strategies are common to many of them:

- *Both the present behaviors and the desired behaviors are specified in observable, measurable terms.* Consistent with behaviorist tradition, users of ABA focus their attention on specific, concrete responses. The actual behaviors to be increased or decreased are called **target behaviors.** For example, in a program designed to decrease a child's aggressiveness, such target behaviors as screaming, hitting other people, and throwing objects might be identified (Morris, 1985).

- *An effective reinforcer is identified.* As we noted in the preceding chapter, we should never assume that particular consequences will be reinforcing to particular students. Instead, we can identify one or more reinforcers that are likely to change students' behavior by observing what they will work for or even by asking them outright. When an ABA program is instituted in a school setting, social reinforcers (such as praise) or activity reinforcers (such as special privileges or the opportunity to spend time with a classmate of one's choice) are often effective (Bates, 1979; Brophy, 1981; Northup et al., 1995; Piersel, 1987). In some cases, immediate feedback that a student has done something correctly is all the reinforcement a student needs, especially when it is not otherwise clear that the student has been successful (Bangert-Drowns, Kulik, Kulik, & Morgan, 1991; Harris & Rosenthal, 1985; Kulik & Kulik, 1988). If material reinforcers are called for (primarily because other reinforcers don't work), having parents provide those reinforcers at home for behaviors exhibited at school often works quite well (Barth, 1979; Kelley & Carper, 1988; Miller & Kelley, 1994; Wielkiewicz, 1986).

- *A specific intervention or treatment plan is developed.* Developing a treatment plan involves determining the method by which the target behavior is to be modified. Sometimes a behavior's frequency can be increased simply by reinforcing that behavior every time it occurs. When the free operant level (baseline) of a desired response is very low, however, that response may have to be shaped through the reinforcement of successively closer and closer approximations. An undesirable behavior can be eliminated through such methods as extinction, the differential reinforcement of other behaviors (a DRO schedule), the reinforcement of incompatible behaviors, or stimulus control (i.e., limiting the situations in which the behavior is allowed).

- *Behavior is measured both before and during treatment.* Only through the objective measurement of the target behavior during both baseline and treatment can we determine whether a particular ABA procedure is effectively changing the target behavior. One way of measuring the target behavior is simply to count the overall *frequency* of a given response; for example, if we have designed a program to modify Johnny's hitting-others behavior, we would count each instance of hitting. A second method of behavior measurement is to examine the *rate* of responding by counting the number of responses occurring within a specified time interval; for example, we might count the number of times Johnny hits in each hour of the day. Still a third method, called **time sampling,** involves dividing the time period during which the individual is being observed into equal intervals and then checking whether the target behavior occurred in each interval. For example, we might measure Johnny's hitting behavior by dividing his school day into five-minute intervals and then identifying those intervals in which hitting was observed.

Behaviors frequently persist because they are either intentionally or unintentionally reinforced, so it is often helpful to record the consequences of the behavior as well as the behavior itself. In addition, many behaviorists (e.g., Rimm & Masters, 1974; Schloss & Smith,

Antecedent		student teased him	none observed		student hit him
Target Behavior (hitting)	no	yes	yes	no	yes
Consequence		scolded	scolded		none

9:00   9:05   9:10   9:15   9:20
(Times indicate start of each five-minute interval.)

Figure 5–2
A time sample of target behaviors in conjunction with antecedent and consequent events.

1994; Sulzer-Azaroff, 1981) believe that antecedent events should also be noted to determine whether a behavior is under stimulus control. Figure 5–2 illustrates a time sample of Johnny's hitting responses, with events antecedent and consequent to those responses also recorded.

Behaviorists urge that target behaviors be observed and recorded as objectively as possible. Ideally, they recommend that one person (e.g., a teacher or therapist) administer the ABA intervention and at least two other individuals trained in observation techniques observe and record occurrences of the target behavior. If the method of behavior measurement is such that the behavior is being objectively and accurately recorded, the agreement between the recordings of the two observers (the **interrater reliability**) should be very high.

• *The treatment is monitored for effectiveness as it progresses and modified if necessary.* When a desired behavior increases or an unwanted behavior decreases during the treatment program (compared with the baseline rate), the logical conclusion is that the ABA program is effective. When little change is observed from baseline to treatment, however, a modification of the program is warranted. Perhaps the teacher or therapist is trying to shape behavior too quickly. Perhaps the "reinforcer" is not really reinforcing, and a different reinforcer should be substituted. Perhaps an undesired behavior that the teacher or therapist is attempting to eliminate through extinction is being maintained by reinforcers beyond his or her control. An unsuccessful treatment program should be carefully examined for these and other possible explanations for its ineffectiveness and then modified accordingly.

• *Measures are taken to promote generalization of newly acquired behaviors.* Although people often generalize the responses they learn in one situation to other situations (Hall, Cristler, Cranston, & Tucker, 1970; Walker, Mattsen, & Buckley, 1971), there is no guarantee that they will do so. In fact, many ABA programs have limited success precisely because responses that are learned under some stimulus conditions do not generalize to others (Alberto & Troutman, 1990; Hughes, 1988; Schloss & Smith, 1994). Psychologists have suggested several strategies for promoting generalization during an ABA program:

• Teach the desired behavior in a wide variety of contexts, including many realistic ones; if possible, teach the behavior in the actual situations in which it is ultimately desired (Anderson-Inman, Walker, & Purcell, 1984; Emshoff, Redd, & Davidson, 1976; Hall et al., 1970; Haring & Liberty, 1990; Stokes & Baer, 1977).

- Teach many different versions of the behavior; for example, when teaching interpersonal skills, teach a variety of ways to interact appropriately with others (Stokes & Baer, 1977).
- Teach the relationship of the desired behavior to reinforcers that occur naturally in the environment; for example, point out that better personal hygiene leads to positive attention from others (Bourbeau, Sowers, & Close, 1986; Stokes & Baer, 1977).
- Reinforce the behavior when it spontaneously occurs in new situations; in other words, specifically reinforce generalization (Stokes & Baer, 1977).

- *Treatment is phased out after the desired behavior is acquired.* Once the terminal behavior has been reached, the ABA program should be gradually phased out. In many instances, the newly learned behaviors begin to have their own rewards; for example, the aggressive student who learns more acceptable social behaviors begins to acquire new friends, and the student who has finally learned to read begins to feel successful and enjoy reading. In other situations, maintaining the target behavior may require intermittent reinforcement, such as a series of successively higher variable-ratio reinforcement schedules.

Using Applied Behavior Analysis with Large Groups

Our emphasis up until now has been on the use of applied behavior analysis with individuals. But ABA techniques can also be used to change the behavior of *groups* of people (e.g., the behavior of an entire class of students). Two methods are particularly effective in working with groups: the group contingency and the token economy.

Group Contingency

In a **group contingency,** the entire group must perform a desired behavior for reinforcement to occur. For example, in one study (Lovitt, Guppy, & Blattner, 1969), the performance of a class of 32 fourth graders on their weekly spelling tests improved with a group contingency. In phase 1 of the study, baseline data indicated that about 12 students (38%) had perfect spelling tests in any given week. In phase 2, spelling tests were administered each of four days during the week; any student who obtained a perfect test score one day had free time on any successive days that the same test was repeated. During this individually based contingency period, the average number of perfect spelling tests a week more than doubled to 25.5 (80%). In phase 3, the individual contingencies of phase 2 continued to apply; in addition, when the entire class achieved perfect spelling tests by Friday, the class could listen to the radio for 15 minutes. The group contingency of phase 3 led to 30 perfect spelling tests (94% of the class) a week!

The "good behavior game" is an example of how a group contingency can reduce classroom misbehaviors. In research conducted by Barrish, Saunders, and Wolf (1969), a class of particularly unruly fourth graders (seven of the students had repeatedly been referred to the principal for problem behaviors) was divided into two teams whose behaviors were carefully observed during reading and mathematics lessons. Every time a team member engaged in out-of-seat or talking-out behavior, that team received a mark on its

Figure 5–3

Percentage of one-minute intervals in which talking-out and out-of-seat behaviors occurred during math and reading periods.

From "Good Behavior Game: Effects of Individual Contingencies for Group Consequences on Disruptive Behavior in a Classroom" by H. H. Barrish, M. Saunders, & M. M. Wolf, 1969, *Journal of Applied Behavior Analysis, 2,* p. 122. Copyright 1969 by *Journal of Applied Behavior Analysis.* Reprinted by permission.

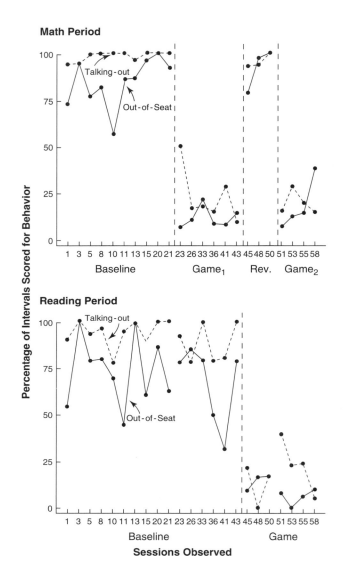

designated part of the chalkboard. The team that had fewer marks during the lesson received special privileges (e.g., first in the lunch line or free time at the end of the day); if both teams had five marks or fewer, both won privileges.

Figure 5–3 shows the results of Barrish and colleagues' study. Notice how baseline data were first collected for both math and reading periods. The good behavior game was instituted in the mathematics period on day 23; out-of-seat and talking-out behaviors decreased sharply during mathematics instruction while continuing at a high frequency during reading. On day 45, the game was initiated during reading instruction and stopped during math instruction; notice how the frequencies of misbehaviors changed accordingly. On day 51, the game was reinstated in the math period, and again the misbehavior decreased to a low level in that class. By the way, collecting data from two different situations (**multiple baseline** data) and switching from reinforcement to nonreinforcement and then back again (a technique called **reversal**) are common techniques in ABA research for ruling out coincidence as the reason for observed behavior changes.

Numerous other studies support the effectiveness of group contingencies, particularly when they are used within the context of cooperative learning activities (Barbetta, 1990; Johnson & Johnson, 1987; Pigott, Fantuzzo, & Clement, 1986; Slavin, 1983a, 1983b). Peer pressure and social reinforcement are clearly among the reasons that group contingencies are effective (O'Leary & O'Leary, 1972; Swenson, 1980). Misbehaving students are encouraged by other students to change their behaviors and are frequently praised when those changes occur (Johnson & Johnson, 1987; Slavin, 1983b). In addition, when increased academic achievement is the desired behavior, high-achieving students often assist their lower-achieving classmates by tutoring and providing extra practice in their academic work (Bronfenbrenner, 1970; Johnson & Johnson, 1987; Pigott, Fantuzzo, & Clement, 1986).

Token Economy

The **token economy,** undoubtedly the most prevalent ABA technique in group settings, is a situation in which individuals who behave appropriately are reinforced with **tokens**—items that can later be traded in for **backup reinforcers,** which are objects or privileges of each individual's choice. For example, a teacher using a token economy in the classroom might reinforce students with one poker chip for each completed assignment. Just before lunch, students can use their poker chips to "buy" small treats, free time in the reading center, or a prime position in the lunch line.

A token economy typically includes the following components:

1. *A set of rules* describing the responses that will be reinforced. The rules should be relatively few in number, so that they can be remembered easily.
2. *Token reinforcers* that can be awarded immediately when appropriate behaviors are exhibited. Such items as poker chips, checkmarks on a grid sheet, play money, or points can be used. Even class grades have been successfully used as tokens (McKenzie, Clark, Wolf, Kothera, & Benson, 1968).
3. *A variety of backup reinforcers* (objects, activities, and privileges) for which tokens can be exchanged. Examples of backup reinforcers that have been shown to be effective in classroom token economies are free time (Osborne, 1969), participation in special events (Bushell, Wrobel, & Michaelis, 1968), and parent-awarded allowance (McKenzie et al., 1968).
4. *A "store" at which the backup reinforcers can be "purchased."* Young children should be allowed at least one purchase opportunity a day; for older children, one or two opportunities a week may be sufficient.

Token reinforcers are advantageous because teachers can use them to reward individual behaviors immediately and conveniently within a group setting. The fact that students can trade tokens for many different backup reinforcers is another advantage; every individual can probably find at least one desirable item. The tokens themselves often become effective reinforcers (Hundert, 1976); perhaps they become secondary reinforcers through repeated association with other reinforcing objects and events, or perhaps they are effective simply because they provide feedback that students are doing something right.

Adding a Cognitive Component to ABA

In recent years, many practitioners have added a cognitive element to ABA techniques, using such terms as *cognitive behavior modification, cognitive behavior therapy,* or *cognitive-behavioral intervention* to describe their approach (Elliott & Busse, 1991; Hughes, 1988; Yell, 1993; Zirpoli & Melloy, 1993). In such approaches, the teacher or therapist frequently models the desired behavior, the assumption being that such modeling helps the student understand the particular behavior that is desired and so facilitates the learning process. Another common strategy is **coaching,** whereby the teacher or therapist verbally instructs and guides the student as the latter practices appropriate behaviors. Cognitive approaches also focus on problem solving; for example, the teacher or therapist might ask the student to think carefully about the effects that various behaviors may have in problem situations and to choose those behaviors that are likely to bring about desired consequences.

Effectiveness of ABA

Applied behavior analysis has often been shown to bring about behavior change, and it frequently works where other techniques fail (e.g., O'Leary & O'Leary, 1972). Numerous studies point to its effectiveness in improving academic performance and study habits (Braukmann, Ramp, & Wolf, 1981; Glover & Gary, 1976; Harris & Sherman, 1973; Iwata, 1987; Lovitt et al., 1969; McLaughlin & Malaby, 1972; McLaughlin & Williams, 1988; McNamara, 1987; Piersel, 1987; Rapport & Bostow, 1976). It is also useful in improving such behaviors as attention (Packard, 1970), social skills (Braukmann et al., 1981; Iwata, 1987; McLaughlin & Williams, 1988; Schloss & Smith, 1994), and cleanliness (Taylor & Kratochwill, 1978). Furthermore, it can effectively reduce such undesirable behaviors as hyperactivity, impulsivity, aggression, and violence (Ayllon, Layman, & Kandel, 1975; Braukmann et al., 1981; Frankel & Simmons, 1985; Mayer & Butterworth, 1979; Northup et al., 1995; Plummer, Baer, & LeBlanc, 1977; Shafto & Sulzbacher, 1977; Wulbert & Dries, 1977).

Applied behavior analysis is particularly beneficial for students who must be continually motivated to engage in appropriate academic and social behaviors. It is therefore used frequently in the education and therapy of students with special needs, especially those with either learning difficulties or behavioral problems (Braukmann et al., 1981; Haring, Roger, Lee, Breen, & Gaylord-Ross, 1986; Hobbs & Holt, 1976; McLaughlin & Williams, 1988; Northup et al., 1995; O'Leary & Becker, 1967; Plummer et al., 1977; Witt, Elliott, & Gresham, 1988; Wolf, Braukmann, & Ramp, 1987).

Although we know that ABA techniques work, we don't always know just *why* they work. One likely factor underlying their effectiveness is the use of clearly specified response-reinforcement contingencies. Because desired behaviors are described in specific, concrete terms, students know exactly what is expected of them. And the immediate feedback that students receive through reinforcement provides them with clear guidance as to when their behaviors are on target and when they are not.

CRITICISMS OF USING REINFORCEMENT IN THE CLASSROOM

Although instructional techniques based on operant conditioning principles are clearly effective, such techniques are not without their critics. Some criticisms are probably ill founded, while others should be considered more seriously. We first examine some of the common bogus complaints and then turn to more genuine concerns.

Bogus Complaints

Many criticisms directed toward the use of reinforcement in the classroom reflect either a misunderstanding of operant conditioning principles or an ignorance of empirical findings. Following are some typical examples of such criticisms:

• *Reinforcement is bribery.* The bribery argument is probably the most frequent complaint leveled against the use of reinforcement in the classroom. However, the word *bribery* implies that the behavior being reinforced is somehow illegal or unethical. On the contrary, the appropriate use of reinforcement in the classroom can facilitate the attainment of educational objectives, all of which involve academically and socially desirable behaviors.

• *Reinforcement develops dependence on concrete, external rewards for appropriate behavior.* Some critics propose that students should engage in learning simply for learning's sake; by reinforcing leaning, they argue, teachers foster the expectation that students will always receive rewards for their accomplishments. This argument can be countered in two ways. First of all, ABA techniques do not necessarily involve material reinforcers. Social reinforcers, activities, feedback, and intrinsic reinforcers (e.g., feelings of success or accomplishment) are also effective in changing behavior, and the sensible teacher will use them instead of material reinforcers whenever possible.

Reinforcement as bribery.

Second, even when a teacher must use material reinforcers to change behavior, these reinforcers bring about desired changes in a student—changes that apparently *will not occur any other way*. Reinforcement is often used when more traditional methods of changing behavior have failed to increase important academic and social skills or to decrease counterproductive behaviors. If the choice comes down to either teaching Mary to read by reinforcing her for reading or else not teaching her to read at all, obviously Mary must learn to read through whatever means possible. We must remember, too, that when material reinforcers are used, social events (e.g., praise) that are paired with them should eventually become secondary reinforcers and so can be used instead.

• *Reinforcing one student for being good teaches other students to be bad.* "Hmmm," Leslie thinks. "Linda has been such a loudmouth the past few weeks that the teacher is now giving her raisins so she'll keep quiet. Maybe if I start shooting my mouth off, I'll start getting some raisins, too." If students are thinking along these lines, then something is clearly wrong with the way reinforcement is being administered in the classroom. All students should be reinforced for their appropriate behaviors. Praise and positive feedback should not be limited to a handful of chronic misbehavers but should be awarded consistently to all students. If the behavior of a particular student can be modified *only* with material reinforcers such as raisins, such reinforcement should be administered discretely and in private.

• *Changing a problem behavior does not change the underlying cause of that behavior; other behavioral manifestations of that underlying cause will appear.* Reflected in this criticism is Sigmund Freud's notion of *symptom substitution*: Problem behaviors are a function of deep-rooted psychological conflicts, so that when a behavior is eliminated without treatment of its underlying cause, another problem behavior will emerge in its place. The best rebuttal to the symptom substitution criticism is an empirical one: When problem behaviors are treated through applied behavior analysis, symptom substitution rarely occurs (e.g., Rimm & Masters, 1974).

One likely reason for this finding is that changing an individual's behavior may indirectly address its underlying causes as well. For example, consider the girl who is inappropriately aggressive on the playground. This girl might truly want to interact with her classmates, but aggression is the only way she knows of initiating that interaction. Reinforcing the girl for more appropriate methods of social interaction not only helps her develop friendships but also addresses the underlying cause for her aggression—her desire for companionship.

Genuine Concerns

The bogus complaints just listed can be easily rebutted. Three major criticisms of operant conditioning techniques should be taken more seriously, however:

• *Attempts at changing behaviors ignore cognitive factors that may be interfering with learning.* When students are capable of learning a new skill but are not motivated to do so, the use of reinforcement may be all that is needed to bring about the desired behavior change. But when cognitive deficiencies (e.g., specific learning disabilities) exist that interfere with the acquisition of a new skill, reinforcement alone may be insufficient. In the latter situation, teachers may need to employ teaching techniques based more on cognitive learning theories—theories that we explore in later chapters.

• *Reinforcement of particular predetermined behaviors sometimes interferes with maximal learning and performance over the long run.* Reinforcement for accomplishing a certain task focuses students' attention and effort more on getting that task done quickly, perhaps at a minimally acceptable level, than on *learning* from that task (Brophy, 1986; Clifford, 1990; Lepper & Hodell, 1989; McCaslin & Good, 1996). When teachers want their students to engage in complex, higher-level thinking—for example, to think flexibly and creatively about the subject matter—then extrinsic reinforcement simply for task accomplishment may sometimes be counterproductive (Brophy, 1986; Deci & Ryan, 1985; Hennessey & Amabile, 1987; Lepper & Hodell, 1989).

• *Extrinsic reinforcement of a behavior already motivated by intrinsic reinforcement may undermine the intrinsically reinforcing value of that behavior.* Individuals often engage in activities because of the intrinsic rewards—for example, pleasure or feelings of success—that those activities bring. A number of research studies indicate that enjoyable activities can be increased by extrinsic reinforcers but will then *decrease* to a below-baseline frequency once the extrinsic reinforcers are removed (Bates, 1979; Lepper & Greene, 1978; Lepper & Hodell, 1989). For example, in one study, preschool children who had previously been reinforced for certain drawing activities were actually *less* likely to engage in drawing in a free-play situation than children who had not been reinforced (Lepper, Greene, & Nisbett, 1973). Similar results have been obtained in a study with college students: Students who received a dollar for each correct solution of a series of block puzzles were less likely to continue to work at such puzzles in the absence of reinforcement than students who had not been paid for their correct solutions (Deci, 1971). It appears, then, that externally reinforcing a behavior that is already occurring because of intrinsic motivation may actually undermine that intrinsic motivation (deCharms, 1968, 1984; Deci, 1992; Deci & Ryan, 1985, 1987; Fabes, Fultz, Eisenberg, May-Plumlee, & Christopher, 1989; Gottfried, Fleming, & Gottfried, 1994; Lepper & Hodell, 1989; Spaulding, 1992). We will identify a possible reason for this puzzling finding in our discussion of motivation in Chapter 18.

WHEN OPERANT CONDITIONING TECHNIQUES ARE MOST APPROPRIATE

Instructional methods based on principles of operant conditioning are probably more appropriate for certain groups of students than for others. Among the students who appear to benefit the most from the structure and clearly specified response-reinforcement contingencies of operant conditioning techniques are students with a history of academic failure, poorly motivated students, anxious students, and students for whom nothing else works.

Frequent success experiences and reinforcements, such as those provided by programmed instruction, are particularly beneficial to students who have previously had little success in their academic careers (e.g., Gustafsson & Undheim, 1996; Snow, 1989).

Children officially identified as "developmentally delayed" or "learning disabled" fall into this category, as do many juvenile delinquents and "slow learners" (children with below-normal intelligence whose test scores are not sufficiently low to qualify them for special educational services). Academic success is exactly what such students need to bolster the poor self-esteem that has resulted from a long string of academic failures.

Students with little motivation to engage in academic tasks can also benefit from operant conditioning techniques. Although some students thrive on the feelings that academic success can bring, others do not value academic achievement. The introduction of extrinsic reinforcers (material, social, or activity reinforcers) contingent on academic accomplishments may be helpful in motivating seemingly "uninterested" students to master essential skills (Covington, 1992; Lepper, 1981).

Highly anxious students appear to need structure in their curriculum to perform well on academic tasks (Dowaliby & Schumer, 1973; Grimes & Allinsmith, 1961; Helmke, 1988, 1989). Such students need a classroom environment that specifies expectations for behavior and clearly lays out response-reinforcement contingencies. They also seem to require frequent success experiences and positive feedback. Many of the methods derived from operant conditioning principles address the needs of anxious children particularly well: Instructional objectives spell out desired behaviors in concrete terms, programmed instruction provides success and positive feedback, and ABA techniques clearly communicate which behaviors will yield the reinforcers the students seek.

Finally, there are some students for whom nothing else works. Techniques based on operant conditioning principles have been shown to be effective methods of changing even the most resilient of problem behaviors (Greer, 1983; Rimm & Masters, 1974). Such stubborn problems as childhood autism and juvenile delinquency have been dealt with more successfully by applied behavior analysis than by any other method currently available.

Yet methods based on operant conditioning are probably not well suited for everyone. Bright students may find the gradual, inch-by-inch approach of programmed instruction slow and tedious. A token economy in a classroom of highly motivated college-bound students may undermine the intrinsic desire of these students to achieve at a high level. Other learning theories, notably cognitive theories, are probably more useful for helping these students learn.

SUMMARY

Instructional objectives, and especially behavioral objectives (which express educational goals in terms of precise, observable responses), are a direct outgrowth of the concept of terminal behavior. Objectives facilitate communication among students and teachers; they also help in the selection of appropriate instructional strategies and evaluation techniques. Objectives tend to focus teachers' and students' attention toward the information and skills they identify (an advantage) and away from other information and skills (a possible disadvantage).

Programmed instruction, computer-assisted instruction, and mastery learning incorporate such operant conditioning principles as active responding, shaping, and immediate reinforcement. Although noncomputer-based programmed instruction is probably no more effective than traditional instructional methods, computer-assisted instruction and mastery learning have frequently been shown to facilitate student achievement.

A contingency contract provides a means through which a teacher and student can specify the behavior expected of the student and the consequence (reinforcer) that will follow such behavior. Reinforcement is also a key ingredient of applied behavior analysis, which can be used with students either individually or on a group basis. Contingency contracts and applied behavior analysis have been shown to improve both academic and social behavior.

Use of reinforcement in the classroom has drawn a number of criticisms; some reflect a misunderstanding of common behaviorist practices, but others are legitimate. Operant conditioning techniques are probably best used with certain kinds of students (e.g., those with high anxiety, poor motivation, or a history of academic failure) rather than as a matter of course with all students.

CHAPTER 6

Effects of Aversive Stimuli

In our discussion of operant conditioning in Chapters 4 and 5, we focused on the role that desirable consequences (reinforcers) play in learning and behavior. In this chapter, we will look at the impact of *aversive* events on learning and behavior, with particular attention to three different situations. We will first examine how people and animals learn to escape and avoid unpleasant situations and then look at the effects of punishing consequences on learning and behavior. Finally, we will examine a phenomenon that occurs when people and animals are exposed to aversive stimuli that they can neither avoid nor escape—a phenomenon known as learned helplessness.

ESCAPE AND AVOIDANCE LEARNING

My university, like most others, abounds in faculty committees. When I first joined the faculty as an assistant professor, I eagerly agreed to serve on committees whenever I could, perceiving them to be a means of meeting other faculty members and having input into university decision making. Before long, however, I discovered that most faculty committees spend years chewing on the same old issues without ever arriving at consensus or otherwise accomplishing very much. Frustrated by the amount of time I was wasting, I soon found myself inventing excuses to leave committee meetings early ("I'm *so* sorry, but I have to take my son to the dentist"). Eventually, I stopped volunteering to join committees in the first place, thus avoiding them altogether.

Committee meetings had become an aversive event for me. My learning to make excuses so I could leave meetings early and then learning not to serve on committees at all is typical of what happens when an aversive stimulus is presented: Organisms learn to *escape* and eventually to *avoid* that stimulus if they possibly can.

Escape Learning

Escape learning is the process of acquiring a response that terminates an aversive stimulus. For example, in Neal Miller's (1948) classic study of escape learning, rats were placed in one compartment of a two-compartment cage and then given a series of electric shocks. The rats quickly learned to turn a wheel that enabled them to run to the other compartment, thereby escaping the aversive shocks. In an analogous study with humans (Hiroto, 1974), people readily learned to move a knob to turn off an unpleasantly loud noise.

Just as in the laboratory, students learn various ways of escaping unpleasant tasks or situations in the classroom. Making excuses ("My dog ate my homework!") and engaging in inappropriate classroom behaviors provide means of escaping tedious or frustrating academic assignments (e.g., Taylor & Romanczyk, 1994). Lying about one's own behaviors ("I didn't do it—*he* did!") is a way of escaping the playground supervisor's evil eye. Chronic truancy and hypochondria are ways of escaping the school environment altogether.

Because escape from an aversive stimulus terminates that stimulus, the escape response is *negatively reinforced.* When rats make a response that stops an electric shock, when children make a response that terminates the evil eye,[1] and when I make an excuse to leave a committee meeting, we are all reinforced by virtue of the fact that an unpleasant event is removed.

Common escape and avoidance responses.

---

[1]The evil eye may remind you of The Look described in Chapter 3's discussion of classical conditioning. Although some stimuli (e.g., those that cause physical pain) are naturally aversive, others (e.g., certain facial expressions) may become aversive over time through their association with other unpleasant stimuli—in other words, through classical conditioning.

The more aversive a stimulus is, the more likely people are to learn to escape that stimulus (Piliavin, Dovidio, Gaertner, & Clark, 1981; Piliavin, Piliavin, & Rodin, 1975). For example, children who have particular difficulty with assignments are more likely to have dogs who have allegedly eaten their homework. And truancy is most likely to occur when school is a very unpleasant environment for a student; chronic truants are often those students who have encountered repeated failures both in their academic work and in their relationships with teachers and peers.

Avoidance Learning

Avoidance learning is the process of learning to stay away from an aversive stimulus altogether. For avoidance learning to occur, an organism must have some sort of **pre-aversive stimulus,** a cue signaling the advent of the aversive stimulus. For example, rats who hear a buzzer (the pre-aversive stimulus) and are then given an electric shock easily learn to jump a hurdle as soon as the buzzer sounds, thereby avoiding the painful shock (Mowrer, 1938, 1939). Similarly, children quickly learn to pull a brass handle as soon as a light flashes so that they can avoid an unpleasantly loud noise (Robinson & Robinson, 1961).

Avoidance learning appears in two forms: active avoidance learning and passive avoidance learning. In **active avoidance learning,** the organism must actively make a particular response to avoid an aversive event. To illustrate, studying behavior is, in many cases, an instance of active avoidance learning. Ideally, studying should be an enjoyable activity in its own right (thereby providing intrinsic reinforcement), but unfortunately many people do not enjoy it in the least (I, for example, would much rather read a mystery novel or watch a television game show). Yet by studying fairly frequently, most students are able to avoid an aversive stimulus—a failing grade. But notice how rarely studying behavior occurs when there is no signal of possible impending doom (i.e., no pre-aversive stimulus), such as an assigned research report or an upcoming exam.

In other situations, organisms learn that *not* making a particular response allows them to avoid an aversive event (e.g., Lewis & Maher, 1965; Seligman & Campbell, 1965); this form of learning is called **passive avoidance learning.** For example, people who feel awkward and uncomfortable in social situations tend not to go to parties or other social events. Likewise, students who have difficulty with mathematics rarely sign up for advanced math classes if they can help it.

What learning processes underlie avoidance learning? An early and widely cited theory of avoidance learning is Mowrer's two-factor theory (Mowrer, 1956; Mowrer & Lamoreaux, 1942). According to Mowrer's theory, avoidance learning is a two-step process that involves both classical conditioning and operant conditioning. In the first step, because the pre-aversive stimulus and the aversive stimulus are presented close together in time, the organism learns to fear the pre-aversive stimulus through a process of classical conditioning, as illustrated in Figure 6-1. In the second step, an avoidance response results in negative reinforcement, because it leads to escape from the fear-inducing pre-aversive stimulus.

Logical as Mowrer's proposal may appear, research does not completely support it. For example, rats can learn to avoid an aversive stimulus even when they are unable to escape the pre-aversive stimulus (Kamin, 1956); this finding refutes Mowrer's notion that escape from the pre-aversive stimulus negatively reinforces the avoidance response.

Figure 6–1

Learning to fear a pre-aversive stimulus
through classical conditioning.

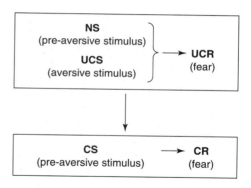

Furthermore, once an avoidance response has been well learned, organisms may exhibit little if any fear of the pre-aversive stimulus; thus, the avoidance response can no longer be negatively reinforced by a reduction of that fear (e.g., Kamin, Brimer, & Black, 1963).

Since Mowrer's time, several other theories of avoidance learning have been advanced (e.g., Bolles, 1975; D'Amato, 1970; Herrnstein, 1969; Seligman & Johnston, 1973). For example, some theorists postulate that the actual reinforcer of an avoidance response is a feeling of relief (D'Amato, 1970; Denny & Weisman, 1964). However, because avoidance behavior can occur in the absence of fear, other theorists (e.g., Bolles, 1975; Seligman & Johnston, 1973) have abandoned behaviorism for a cognitive explanation of avoidance learning: Organisms form *expectations* about what situations are aversive and what behaviors enable them to avoid those situations.

Extinguishing Avoidance Responses

Although disagreement exists about the best theoretical explanation of avoidance learning, there is general agreement about one thing: Avoidance responses are difficult to extinguish. When a previously aversive situation loses all sources of unpleasantness, organisms nevertheless continue to avoid it. For example, dogs will continue to escape from a box that has been previously associated with shock long after the shock has been eliminated (Solomon & Wynne, 1954).

One likely reason for the high resistance of avoidance responses to extinction is that when an organism avoids a formerly aversive situation, it has no opportunity to learn that the situation is no longer aversive. Let's consider students' avoidance of mathematics as an example. As I suggested in Chapter 3, mathematics anxiety may be a conditioned response acquired at a time when children are not cognitively ready to learn abstract mathematical concepts. Students with math anxiety may avoid math classes indefinitely, even though they may eventually develop the cognitive maturity necessary for comprehending previously troublesome concepts. If students never again enroll in another math class, they will never learn that they have nothing to fear.

Many psychologists believe that the best way to get rid of an avoidance response is to extinguish the fear that leads to the avoidance behavior in the first place. One way of extinguishing this fear is through *systematic desensitization,* a technique I mentioned in Chapter 3: Having someone relax while imagining a series of increasingly anxiety-arousing scenarios can reduce fear of certain situations, such as mathematics or public speaking engagements. Another approach is to prevent a person from making the avoidance response; by doing so, we create an occasion in which the person experiences the conditioned stimulus *without* the fear-eliciting unconditioned stimulus (and so we promote the extinction of a classically conditioned fear response). For example, if we have a math-anxious student who we know possesses adequate cognitive skills to succeed in mathematics, we might require that student to enroll in a math class; once in class, the student can discover that mathematics is a rewarding experience rather than a frustrating one. In some circumstances, it is probably true that students don't always know what is best for them!

Undoubtedly, the best way to deal with both escape and avoidance behaviors in the classroom is to *prevent* such behaviors from being learned in the first place—something we can accomplish only by minimizing aversive classroom stimuli. For example, teachers should have students' existing knowledge, skills, and cognitive maturity in mind when they develop instructional objectives, and they should then provide the resources and assistance that students need to accomplish those objectives successfully. When students achieve success at classroom tasks (a positive reinforcer), rather than experiencing frustration and failure at every turn, they are more likely to seek out those tasks than to avoid them.

In escape learning and avoidance learning, an organism makes a response that allows it to either terminate or avoid an aversive stimulus—a stimulus that, especially in the case of escape learning, is already present in the environment. But when an aversive stimulus occurs only *after* the organism makes a response, we have an instance of punishment instead. We turn to an examination of this phenomenon now.

PUNISHMENT

Punishment actually takes two forms. **Punishment I** (also called *positive punishment*) is the more commonly recognized form; it decreases the strength of a response when it is *presented* after that response. Typically, Punishment I involves the presentation of an aversive stimulus (e.g., a spanking or a failing grade). **Punishment II** (sometimes called *negative punishment*) decreases the strength of a response by virtue of the *removal* of a stimulus, usually a pleasant one. Losing a privilege and being fined (in which case money is lost) are examples of Punishment II. Punishment is a common occurrence in our daily lives; some psychologists believe that even the absence of reinforcement can be punishing (we will explore this idea in Chapter 7).

Views on the effectiveness of punishment have changed considerably over the past 60 years. Early research indicated that punishment was a very *in*effective means of changing behavior. For example, Thorndike (1932b) found that, although positive feedback facilitated students' learning of correct responses, negative feedback did not reduce *in*correct responses. Similarly, Skinner (1938) found that when rats were punished for a response that had previously been reinforced, the response was temporarily suppressed but soon returned to its prepunishment frequency. As a result, many early behaviorists discouraged the use of punishment.

Probably because of the negative views of punishment held by prominent learning theorists during the first half of the century, punishment as a means of behavior control was largely ignored until the 1960s. Until that time, concern centered more on disadvantages than on any possible advantages of punishment. More recently, however, research evidence has emerged to indicate that punishment *can* be effective in many situations.

In the following pages, we will explore the many-faceted topic of punishment. We will begin by examining punishment's numerous disadvantages. We will then look at evidence supporting the use of punishment as an effective means of behavior change and consider various theoretical explanations for its effect on behavior. Finally, we will discuss some guidelines for using punishment effectively in classroom contexts.

Disadvantages of Punishment

Over the years, psychologists have cited a number of disadvantages associated with the use of punishment:

• *A punished behavior is not eliminated; it is only suppressed.* Punishment *suppresses* a response, making it less likely to occur. However, this suppression effect is often only temporary: The punished behavior may eventually reappear, perhaps when the punishment stops or when the punisher is absent (Appel & Peterson, 1965; Azrin, 1960; Griffore, 1981; Holz & Azrin, 1962; Skinner, 1938).

• *Punishment sometimes leads to an increase in the punished behavior.* In some cases, this effect may be due to the fact that the "punishment" is actually reinforcing. For example, a teacher's reprimands may be reinforcing to the girl who craves her teacher's attention or to the boy who wants to look "cool" in front of his classmates. Yet even in situations in which the punishment is truly punishing, it may nevertheless lead to an increase in the response that it follows. More specifically, when a behavior is punished in one situation, it may decrease in that situation but *increase* in a situation in which it has *not* been punished—an effect known as **behavioral contrast** (e.g., Reynolds, 1975; Swenson, 1980). For example, some children who behave badly at school may be described by their parents as being little angels at home. Such children are possibly being held to strict behavioral rules on the home front, with severe punishment following any infractions; if so, they may engage in the forbidden behaviors at school, where they can do so with milder consequences.

• *The response-punishment contingency may not be recognized.* Punishment, particularly physical punishment, can distract an individual's attention away from the behavior that was punished. People are often less aware of the response that was punished than they are of the punishment itself (Maurer, 1974). Punishment is clearly ineffective if people do not know what they are being punished for.

• *Punishment often elicits undesirable emotional responses and may lead to escape and avoidance behaviors.* When punishment involves a particularly aversive stimulus, the association of that stimulus with other stimuli (e.g., with the punisher or with the situation in which punishment occurred) can, through classical conditioning, lead to undesirable emotional responses to those other stimuli (Skinner, 1938). For example, when a teacher punishes a student at school, that punishment (the UCS) may be associated with the teacher, the task, or the classroom, any of which may then become conditioned stimuli (CSs) that elicit conditioned responses (CRs) such as fear and anxiety. In a similar manner, when a baseball coach continually yells at children for their poor performance during a game, negative attitudes toward baseball are likely to result (Smith & Smoll, 1997).

Furthermore, a stimulus that has become fear inducing because of its association with punishment may lead to escape or avoidance behavior (e.g., Redd, Morris, & Martin, 1975). Escape and avoidance responses at school take many forms, including inattention, cheating, lying, refusal to participate in classroom activities, and truancy (e.g., Becker, 1971; Skinner, 1938; Taylor & Romanczyk, 1994).

• *Punishment may lead to aggression.* When punishment produces pain, it evokes emotional arousal in an individual—arousal that may result in anger and aggression, especially in characteristically aggressive individuals (Azrin, 1967; Berkowitz & LePage, 1967; Walters & Grusec, 1977). Aggressive behavior appears to reduce such emotional arousal and, more generally, to "feel good," the result being that aggression is reinforced (Bramel, Taub, & Blum, 1968; Hokanson & Burgess, 1962).

Furthermore, some forms of punishment provide a model of aggression, thus communicating the message that aggression is acceptable. I am reminded of the many hypocritical interactions I have witnessed in the grocery store. A mother yells, "How many times have I told you not to hit your sister?!" and gives her child a solid whack. Children who observe others being aggressive are more likely to be aggressive themselves (Bandura, Ross, & Ross, 1961, 1963; Mischel & Grusec, 1966; Steuer, Applefield, & Smith, 1971). Particularly aggressive children (i.e., juvenile delinquents) are likely to come from homes where severe punishment has been frequent (Welsh, 1976).

• *Punishment does not illustrate the correct behavior.* As Skinner (1938) pointed out, punishment tells an individual what *not* to do but not what should be done instead. Consider the boy who is consistently aggressive on the playground; perhaps aggression is the only way he knows of interacting with other children. Punishing this child for aggressive behavior without simultaneously teaching him more appropriate social skills does little to help him develop friendly relationships with his classmates.

• *Severe punishment may cause physical or psychological harm.* Obviously, severe physical punishment can lead to bodily injury. Severe psychological punishment, such as

Physical punishment models aggression.

How many times have I told you: Don't hit other people!

extreme embarrassment or deflation of one's self-esteem, can be equally harmful. The mother of a college friend of mine constantly degraded my friend with such remarks as "How can you be so *stupid!*" and "Can't you ever do *anything* right?" Throughout our four years in college, my friend fought numerous bouts with depression and was in and out of mental institutions. The line between punishment and abuse is often a very fuzzy one.

Despite these many potential disadvantages, punishment *can* be an effective method of bringing about desired behavior change. In the next few pages, we will look at some instances in which punishment *does* work. A bit later in the chapter, I will offer some guidelines for using punishment that can help avert the disadvantages I have just listed.

Effectiveness of Punishment

Although early research cast doubt on the idea that punishment decreases the responses it follows, researchers have more recently reported evidence that punishment can success- fully reduce or eliminate undesirable behaviors (Azrin & Holz, 1966; Dinsmoor, 1954, 1955; Rachlin, 1991; Tanner & Zeiler, 1975; Walters & Grusec, 1977). Punishment is often used when methods such as extinction, the differential reinforcement of other behaviors (DRO schedule), or the reinforcement of an incompatible response are ineffective or impractical; furthermore, it appears that punishment may often be more effective than any of these other techniques (Boe & Church, 1967; Corte, Wolf, & Locke, 1971; Frankel & Simmons, 1985; Pfiffner & O'Leary, 1987; Walters & Grusec, 1977). Punishment is especially advised when a behavior might harm either oneself or others; in such cases, using punishment to eliminate such behavior rapidly may actually be the most humane course of action.

In a series of studies, Vance Hall and his colleagues (Hall, Axelrod, Foundopoulos, Shellman, Campbell, & Cranston, 1971) have demonstrated the speed with which punish- ment can bring about behavior change. For example, in one study, consistent punishment virtually eliminated the aggressive behavior of a seven-year-old deaf girl named Andrea. Ini- tially, this girl pinched and bit both herself and anybody else with whom she came into contact; the frequency of such responses (an average of 72 per school day) was so high that normal academic instruction was impossible. Following a baseline period, punish- ment for each aggressive act began: Whenever Andrea pinched or bit, her teacher pointed at her sternly and shouted "No!" Figure 6-2 shows the changes in Andrea's behavior (the brief *reversal* to nonreinforcement for a few days was used to rule out coincidence as an explanation for the behavior changes). Even though Andrea was deaf, the shouting and pointing virtually eliminated her aggressiveness.

In a second study, Hall and his colleagues modified the whining and complaining behaviors of a boy named Billy. Billy frequently cried, whined, and complained of stom- achaches whenever he was given a reading or arithmetic assignment, while apparently being quite healthy the rest of the day. The treatment program consisted of giving Billy five slips of colored paper bearing his name at the beginning of reading and arithmetic periods every day and then removing one slip of paper (Punishment II) each time Billy cried, whined, or complained. Treatment was instituted on day 6 for Billy's reading period and on day 11 for his math period (this *multiple baseline* approach was used to rule out the coincidence factor). Figure 6-3 shows the effectiveness of such obviously mild pun- ishment (note the temporary reversal to nonpunished baseline similar to that shown in Figure 6-2).

Figure 6–2

Number of bites and pinches by Andrea during the school day.

Reprinted with permission from "The Effective Use of Punishment to Modify Behavior in the Classroom" by R.V. Hall, S.Axelrod, M. Foundopoulos, J. Shellman, R.A. Campbell, & S.S. Cranston, 1972, in K. D. O'Leary & S. O'Leary (Eds.), *Classroom Management: The Successful Use of Behavior Modification,* p. 175. Copyright 1972 by Pergamon Press, Ltd.

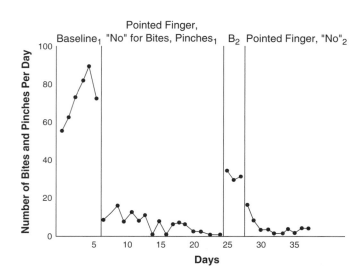

Figure 6–3

Frequency of Billy's cries (C), whines (W), and complaints (C_1) during reading and arithmetic periods.

Reprinted with permission from "The Effective Use of Punishment to Modify Behavior in the Classroom" by R.V. Hall, S.Axelrod, M. Foundopoulos, J. Shellman, R.A. Campbell, & S.S. Cranston, 1972, in K. D. O'Leary & S. O'Leary (Eds.), *Classroom Management: The Successful Use of Behavior Modification,* p. 177. Copyright 1972 by Pergamon Press, Ltd.

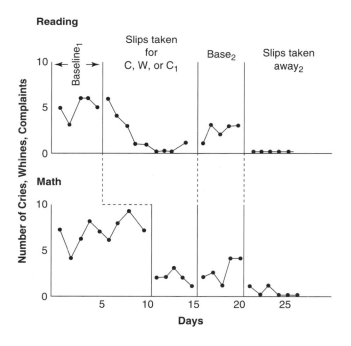

In yet another study by Hall and his colleagues, three 10th-grade students enrolled in a French class earned higher grades when after-school tutoring was the "punishment" for low grades. These students—Dave, Roy, and Debbie—had been consistently earning Ds and Fs on daily quizzes. Their teacher informed them that because they were obviously having difficulty with their French, they would have to come in for a half hour of tutoring after school whenever they received a grade lower than C. Quiz grades during

Figure 6–4

Quiz grades for three high school French class students.

Reprinted with permission from "The Effective Use of Punishment to Modify Behavior in the Classroom" by R. V. Hall, S. Axelrod, M. Foundopoulos, J. Shellman, R. A. Campbell, & S. S. Cranston, 1972, in K. D. O'Leary & S. O'Leary (Eds.), *Classroom Management: The Successful Use of Behavior Modification,* p. 180. Copyright 1972 by Pergamon Press, Ltd.

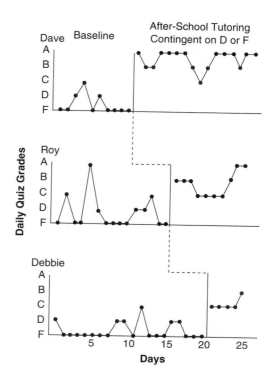

baseline and during the time when poor quiz performance would be punished are shown in Figure 6-4 (note the multiple baseline approach once again). As you can see, none of the students ever needed to report for after-school tutoring. Apparently, the threat of punishment alone was sufficient to bring about desired study behaviors.

What is unique about the studies by Hall and his colleagues is that none of the punishments could be construed as being either physically or psychologically harmful. Yet all of them—pointing and yelling "No," taking away colored slips of paper, and requiring after-school tutoring—were clearly effective in bringing about dramatic behavior changes in different students. But just why does punishment work? Let's explore some possible explanations.

Theoretical Perspectives on Punishment

Several theories have been advanced to explain why punishment decreases the behavior that precedes it. Guthrie (1935) and Skinner (1953) offered two early theories based on the notion of incompatibility: Punishment reduces a response only when it leads to a behavior (such as escape from the situation) that is incompatible with the punished response. Thus, Guthrie and Skinner argued that punishment affects the punished behavior indirectly (by bringing about a new response) rather than directly. An alternative theory (Estes, 1969b; Walters & Grusec, 1977) is also based on the notion of incompatibility, albeit the incompatibility of motives rather than behaviors. According to this explanation, punishment leads to motives (e.g., fear) incompatible with the motives that originally led to the behavior being punished. For example, when a rat that has learned to press a bar to obtain food is then punished for pressing the bar, the fear induced by the punishment may lower the rat's appetite.

Mowrer (1960) proposed a two-stage theory of punishment similar to his theory of avoidance learning. First, when an organism is punished for a particular behavior, fear of the environment in which punishment occurred is established through a process of classical conditioning. Second, escape from that environment is reinforced because such escape reduces that fear (negative reinforcement). Punishment is effective to the extent that the escape response is incompatible with the punished response. In contrast, Aronfreed (1968; Aronfreed & Reber, 1965) proposed that anxiety is associated not with stimuli in the environment but with the initiation of the punished response and perhaps also with the thoughts that precede the response; suppressing the response—*not* emitting it—is negatively reinforced by anxiety reduction.

Still other theorists (e.g., Azrin & Holz, 1966; Fantino, 1973; Rachlin, 1991; Rachlin & Herrnstein, 1969) have reverted to Thorndike's original law of effect and view punishment in the same way they view reinforcement—as a consequence that alters the frequency of future behaviors. Many of these researchers advocate an atheoretical approach to punishment; they focus more on the factors influencing the effectiveness of punishment than on the reasons underlying its effectiveness (Walters & Grusec, 1977).

Using Punishment in Classroom Settings

The use of punishment as a means of behavior control is widespread in both child rearing and educational practice (Sears, Maccoby, & Levin, 1957; Wielkiewicz, 1986). One likely reason for the prevalence of punishment as a disciplinary measure is that, because it tends to decrease or eliminate an undesirable behavior fairly quickly, the punisher is *negatively reinforced*: By using punishment, he or she gets rid of an unwanted state of affairs.

Two particular forms of punishment—time-out and response cost—are frequently used in classroom situations. Both involve the withdrawal of reinforcers and so are examples of Punishment II. Three other types of punishment—verbal reprimands, restitution, and overcorrection—are also useful in some instances; these involve imposing unpleasant consequences and so are examples of Punishment I. Let's examine the evidence for each of these.

Time-Out

Time-out (Alberto & Troutman, 1990; Ullmann & Krasner, 1969; Walters & Grusec, 1977; Zirpoli & Melloy, 1993) involves placing the misbehaving individual in an environment with no reinforcers—in other words, in a dull, boring situation. Often, this time-out environment is a separate room, furnished sparsely or not at all, in which the individual cannot interact with others. At other times, it may be a corner of the classroom screened from the rest of the room by partitions or tall furniture. In any event, the time-out environment should be neither reinforcing, as the hall or the principal's office is likely to be, nor frightening, as a dark closet might be (Walker & Shea, 1995; Wielkiewicz, 1986). Foxx and Shapiro (1978) have developed a procedure that easily incorporates time-out into a classroom context without requiring any special facilities. Students wear ribbons that make them eligible to participate in rewarding classroom activities. Students who misbehave remain in the classroom, but their ribbons are removed, making them ineligible to receive the reinforcers available to their classmates.

Time-out effectively reduces a variety of disruptive, aggressive, and dangerous behaviors (Frankel & Simmons, 1985; Lentz, 1988; Mace, Page, Ivancic, & O'Brien, 1986; MacPherson, Candee, & Hohman, 1974; Mathews, Friman, Barone, Ross, & Christophersen, 1987; Rolider & Van Houten, 1985; Rortvedt & Miltenberger, 1994). Short time-outs that do not significantly interfere with students' academic learning are often quite effective (Skiba & Raison, 1990); many psychologists argue that durations of 10 minutes (even as few as 2 minutes for preschool children) are sufficient. A key to using time-out effectively is that the inappropriate behavior must *stop* before the child is released from the time-out situation; release from time-out (a negative reinforcer) is therefore contingent on appropriate behavior.

Response Cost

Response cost involves the withdrawal of a previously earned reinforcer; a ticket for speeding (resulting in the payment of a fine) and the loss of previously earned privileges are examples. Response cost has been shown to reduce such misbehaviors as aggression, inappropriate speech, disruptiveness, hyperactivity, and tardiness (Iwata & Bailey, 1974; Kazdin, 1972; McLaughlin & Malaby, 1972; Rapport, Murphy, & Bailey, 1982) and appears to be particularly effective when combined with reinforcement of appropriate behavior (Phillips, Phillips, Fixsen, & Wolf, 1971).

Verbal Reprimand

Although some students find teacher attention of any kind to be reinforcing, most probably regard a **verbal reprimand**—a scolding or admonishment—as punishment (O'Leary, Kaufman, Kass, & Drabman, 1970; Van Houten, Nau, MacKenzie-Keating, Sameoto, & Colavecchia, 1982). In addition to suppressing undesirable behavior, occasional reprimands also appear to enhance the positive reinforcement value of praise (Pfiffner & O'Leary, 1987).

Reprimands are often more effective when they are accompanied by eye contact (e.g., The Look) or a firm grip (Van Houten et al., 1982). They may also be more effective when spoken quietly and in close proximity to the child being punished (O'Leary et al., 1970; Van Houten et al., 1982); such unobtrusive reprimands are less likely to attract the (potentially reinforcing) attention of other individuals in the room.

Restitution and Overcorrection

Restitution and overcorrection involve requiring people to take actions that correct the results of their misdeeds. In **restitution,** a misbehaving individual must return the environment to the same state of affairs it was in before the misbehavior. As examples, a child who breaks a window must pay for a new one, and a child who makes a mess must clean it up. Restitution is a good example of a logical consequence, whereby the punishment fits the crime.

In the case of **restitutional overcorrection,** the punished individual must make things *better* than they were before the inappropriate behavior (Foxx & Azrin, 1973; Foxx & Bechtel, 1983; Rusch & Close, 1976). For example, a student who throws food in the lunchroom might be asked to mop the entire lunchroom floor, or the student who offends a classmate might be asked to apologize to the entire class.

Positive-practice overcorrection involves having an individual repeat an action, but this time doing it correctly, perhaps in an exaggerated fashion. For example, a student who runs dangerously down the school corridor might be asked to back up and then *walk* (perhaps at a normal pace, or perhaps very slowly) down the hall. Similarly, a student in a drivers' education class who neglects to stop at a stop sign might be asked to drive around the block, return to the same intersection, and come to a complete stop (perhaps counting aloud to five) before proceeding.

Practitioners have mixed views regarding the value of restitutional overcorrection and positive-practice overcorrection as methods of bringing about behavior improvement in school settings; in some cases, these techniques may be overly time-consuming and draw unnecessary attention to the punished behavior (Schloss & Smith, 1994; Zirpoli & Melloy, 1993). When such approaches *are* used, however, teachers should portray them more as means for helping students acquire appropriate behavior than as punishment per se (Alberto & Troutman, 1990; Carey & Bucher, 1986; Zirpoli & Melloy, 1993).

The punishments I've just described appear to have fewer negative side effects than either physical punishment (e.g., spanking) or psychological punishment (e.g., withdrawal of love) (Walters & Grusec, 1977). Yet teachers who use recommended forms of punishment to reduce inappropriate behavior must nevertheless monitor their effects on the behaviors being punished. For example, some individuals find time-out to be reinforcing rather than punishing (Alberto & Troutman, 1990; Solnick, Rincover, & Peterson, 1977), and thus their "punished" behaviors will increase rather than diminish.

In Chapter 4 I discussed the importance of reinforcement as a means of providing feedback about what constitutes appropriate behavior. In much the same way, punishment is probably effective to the extent that it gives feedback about inappropriate behavior. Sometimes students are truly unaware of how frequently they misbehave (e.g., Krumboltz & Krumboltz, 1972), and the occasional punishment of inappropriate responses can provide reminders that keep these students on task. But how do we avoid such negative side effects as aggression, escape responses, and negative emotional reactions? Let's turn to some guidelines for using punishment in the classroom.

Guidelines for Using Punishment Effectively

Psychologists and educators have offered numerous suggestions on how to use punishment effectively, many of which decrease the chances of negative side effects. The guidelines that follow are among those most commonly cited:

• *The "punishment" must be punishing.* Punishment, like reinforcement, is defined by its effect on behavior: True punishment decreases the response it follows. If a given consequence does not decrease the response it is meant to punish, that consequence may not be aversive to the individual being "punished"; in fact, it may even be reinforcing.

Teachers and parents too often make assumptions about what consequences will be punishing for children. For example, a common "punishment" around our house is to be sent to one's room. For my two sons, such a consequence is truly aversive, because they

Tina is "punished."

would much rather socialize with the family in the kitchen or living room than be isolated in their rooms for any length of time. But when my daughter Tina is banished to her bedroom, she is probably being reinforced: She rearranges her furniture, listens to her radio, or settles under the covers with a good book. And the behaviors for which she has been most often punished in this way—behaviors related in one way or another to annoying and teasing her brothers—seem to have increased rather than decreased.

• *The punishment must be strong enough to be effective but not overly severe.* Punishment that is too short or mild is not effective (e.g., Parke & Walters, 1967). For example, fines for such behaviors as speeding and drunken driving are obviously insufficient deterrents for some individuals. Similarly, grades in many college classrooms may be too lenient to discourage a student from academically unproductive behaviors. A college teacher may believe that by giving some students a C, she is punishing those students for their lack of class attendance and poor exam performance. Yet a C average is quite acceptable at most institutions, so the students may not be sufficiently "punished" to reduce their frequency of party going and Frisbee throwing at times when they should be attending classes or reading their textbooks.

At the same time, punishment must not be overly severe, or it might lead to such undesirable side effects as resentment, hostility, aggression, or escape behavior. Furthermore, although severe punishment may quickly suppress a response, that response may reappear at its original level once the punisher has left the scene (Appel & Peterson, 1965; Azrin, 1960). The ultimate purpose of administering punishment is to communicate that the limits of acceptable behavior have been exceeded; it should not be so excessive that it undermines the personal relationship between the punisher and the person being punished (Spaulding, 1992).

• *Punishment should be threatened once before it is administered.* (My use of the term *threaten* here means only that people should be warned ahead of time, not that they should be intimidated.) Punishment is most likely to deter behavior when an individual *knows* that the behavior will lead to punishment (e.g., Aronfreed, 1968). Therefore, people should know ahead of time that a particular behavior will be punished and what the punishment will be. I remember an incident, when I was about four years old, in which I was punished without warning. Sitting at lunch one day, apparently considering the old adage "Waste not, want not," I proceeded to lick a large quantity of peanut butter off my butter knife. An adult scolded me sternly for my behavior, and I was devastated. Being the Miss Goody Two-shoes that I was at the time, I would never have engaged in knife-licking behavior if I had known it was an unacceptable response.

One common mistake many teachers and parents make is to continue to threaten punishment without ever following through. One threat is advisable, but repeated threats are not. The mother who continually says to her son, "If you hit your sister again, Tommy, I'll send you to your room for the rest of the week," but never does send Tommy to his room, is giving her son the message that no response-punishment contingency really exists.

One of the reasons that teachers and parents often fail to follow through with threatened punishment is that they too often *bluff,* proposing punishment that is impractical or unrealistically extreme. Tommy's mother does not punish her son because forcing Tommy to spend "the rest of the week" in his room would be a major inconvenience for both of them. A teacher who threatens that certain behaviors will result in students not going on a promised field trip should do so only if he or she knows that leaving some students behind at school is logistically possible.

• *The behavior to be punished should be described in clear, concrete terms.* Students should understand exactly which responses are unacceptable. A student who is told, "If you disrupt the class again this morning, you will lose your free time," may not understand exactly what the teacher means by "disrupt" and so may continue to engage in inappropriate classroom behavior. The teacher should instead take the student aside and say something like this: "Sharon, two behaviors are unacceptable in this classroom. When you talk without permission and when you get out of your seat during quiet reading time, you keep other children from getting their work done. This morning I expect you to talk and get out of your seat only when I give you permission to do so. Otherwise, you will have to sit quietly at your desk this afternoon when the other children have their free time."

• *Punishment should be consistent.* Just as is true for reinforcement, punishment is much more effective when it is a consistent consequence of a particular response (Leff, 1969; Parke & Deur, 1972; Rachlin, 1991). When a response is punished only occasionally, with other occurrences of that response being either reinforced or ignored, the response disappears slowly, if at all. Consistent with this principle is the fact that many juvenile delinquents come from home environments in which parental discipline has been administered inconsistently (Glueck & Glueck, 1950; McCord, McCord, & Zola, 1959).

Unfortunately, people can only be punished when they have been caught in the act. Thieves are rarely apprehended, and speeders are ticketed only when the highways on which they drive are patrolled. Many undesirable classroom behaviors, such as talking out, getting out of one's seat, being aggressive, and cheating, may be reinforced as frequently as they are punished. To deal with the difficulty of detecting some undesirable student behaviors, the next two guidelines—changing the situation so the misbehavior is less likely to occur and providing a positively reinforceable alternative behavior—are especially critical.

- *Whenever possible, the environment should be modified so that the misbehavior is less likely to occur.* In other words, the temptation to engage in a misbehavior should be reduced or, if possible, eliminated. People on diets should not stock their kitchens with junk food. Troublemaking friends should be placed on opposite sides of the classroom or in separate classrooms. Cheating on an exam can be reduced by having students sit apart from one another or by administering two different forms of the exam (perhaps the same test items in two different orders).

- *Desirable alternative behaviors should be taught and reinforced.* Punishment of misbehavior is typically more effective when it is combined with reinforcement of appropriate behavior (Carey & Bucher, 1986; Rimm & Masters, 1974; Walters & Grusec, 1977). A misbehavior is more likely to be suppressed permanently when alternative behaviors are reinforced, especially when those behaviors are incompatible with the punished behavior. For example, when punishing aggression on the playground, teachers should remember also to reinforce appropriate social behavior. Teachers can punish a student for cheating, but they should also reinforce that student for demonstrating good study habits and for working well independently.

- *Whenever possible, punishment should immediately follow the inappropriate behavior.* As is true for reinforcement, the effectiveness of punishment decreases dramatically when it is delayed (Trenholme & Baron, 1975; Walters, 1964; Walters & Grusec, 1977). The more closely punishment follows a misbehavior, the more effective it will be. Punishment is particularly effective when it is administered as soon as the misbehavior *begins* (Aronfreed, 1968; Aronfreed & Reber, 1965). When, for whatever reason, punishment cannot be administered immediately, delayed punishment may be effective provided that the punished behavior is clearly described (Aronfreed & Reber, 1965).

- *An explanation of why the behavior is unacceptable should be given.* Although behaviorists tend to focus their attention on responses and their consequences, a growing body of research indicates that punishment is more effective when reasons why certain behaviors cannot be tolerated are given (Baumrind, 1983; Hess & McDevitt, 1984; Parke, 1972, 1974, 1977; Perry & Perry, 1983). For example, notice how Sharon's teacher incorporated reasoning into her description of Sharon's inappropriate behaviors: "When you talk without permission and when you get out of your seat during quiet reading time, *you keep other children from getting their work done.*"

Providing reasons as to why behaviors are unacceptable has at least four advantages:

1. When punishment is accompanied by reasoning, it appears to make the immediacy of punishment a less critical factor in its effectiveness (Walters & Grusec, 1977).
2. Reasoning increases the likelihood that when one behavior is punished, similar misbehaviors are also suppressed; that is, the effect of the punishment generalizes to other misbehaviors (Walters & Grusec, 1977).
3. If reasons are given, misbehaviors are likely to be suppressed even when the punisher is absent (Walters & Grusec, 1977).
4. Older children apparently expect to be told why they cannot engage in certain behaviors and are likely to be defiant when reasons are not provided (Cheyne & Walters, 1970).

• *Some punishments are particularly ineffective and should be avoided.* Among the punishments generally *not* recommended are physical punishment, psychological punishment, extra classwork, and suspension from school.

Physical punishment may be the only means of keeping very young children from engaging in potentially harmful behaviors. For example, the toddler who takes delight in sticking metal objects into electrical outlets must be quickly discouraged from such behavior, and a slap on the hand may be the only way of doing so. However, the use of physical punishment with older children is likely to provide a model of aggression for those children: Consider as evidence the finding that the great majority of abusive parents have been themselves abused as children (Steele & Pollack, 1968; Steinmetz, 1977; Strauss, Gelles, & Steinmetz, 1980).

Psychological punishment, such as embarrassing or insulting a child, also is not recommended (Davis & Thomas, 1989; Walker & Shea, 1995). Children who are consistently made to feel inferior or inadequate are likely to develop low self-esteem, which will interfere with their engaging in appropriate and constructive behaviors on future occasions.

Extra classwork is appropriate when it is a logical consequence of the misbehavior (e.g., when students are failing at academic tasks because of their inattentiveness in class), but in other situations it transmits the message that schoolwork is not fun. When Marcus is punished for his disruptive classroom behaviors by being assigned an additional 100 mathematics problems, he is unlikely to continue to regard mathematics in a positive light.

Finally, suspension from school is typically an ineffective remedy for misbehavior (Doyle, 1990; Moles, 1990). Many chronically misbehaving students are students who have difficulty with their academic work; many high school troublemakers, for example,

Suspension is not an effective punishment.

are students with poor reading skills. Suspending such students from school puts these students at an even greater disadvantage and decreases still further the likelihood of academic success. Additionally, when students find school to be an aversive situation, removal from that environment is negatively reinforcing rather than punishing. (It is also negatively reinforcing to the administrators who have gotten rid of their troublemakers!)

An alternative, more effective punishment for chronic misbehavers is **in-house suspension** (e.g., see anecdotal reports by DiSciullo, 1984; Huff, 1988; Short & Noblit, 1985; Sullivan, 1989; and Weiss, 1983). In-house suspension is similar to a time-out in that punished students are placed in a quiet, boring room within the school building. In-house suspension typically lasts one or more days rather than just a few minutes, however, and students suspended in this manner are continually monitored by a member of the school staff. Students bring their schoolwork with them and must keep up with their classroom assignments. In-house suspension tends to be effective because it does not allow students to escape the school environment yet prevents the social interactions with peers that most students find reinforcing.

• *Punishment should be used sparingly.* The studies by Hall and his colleagues (1971) that I depicted earlier in Figures 6-2, 6-3, and 6-4 provide several illustrations of how quickly punishment can reduce inappropriate behavior. An effective punishment is one that does not need to be administered very often to be effective. Only when punishment is a frequent occurrence (in which case it is obviously not effective anyway) are the numerous disadvantages of punishment likely to appear.

When used properly, punishment is the quickest way of reducing or eliminating unacceptable behaviors. Remember, behaviorists define punishment as a consequence that decreases the response it follows. A "punishment" that clearly is not suppressing an undesirable behavior very quickly should be replaced by a different consequence.

LEARNED HELPLESSNESS

Imagine that you are a student who is continually failing assignments and exams. You try all kinds of strategies to improve your grades—studying longer, memorizing your textbooks word for word, having a friend drill you on key points, and even sleeping with your books open over your head (hoping that the information will sink in)—and still you get F after F after F. Eventually, you would probably just stop trying to achieve academic success and accept the "fact" that you have no control over the grades you receive.

When aversive stimuli are presented repeatedly, and when an organism cannot avoid, escape from, or otherwise terminate them, the organism will eventually give up and passively accept those stimuli. This passive acceptance of uncontrollable aversive events is a phenomenon known as **learned helplessness.**

Let me illustrate the phenomenon by describing research conducted by Seligman and Maier (1967). In the first phase of this classic experiment, dogs received numerous painful and unpredictable shocks. Some dogs were able to escape the shocks by pushing a panel in the cage, whereas other dogs could not escape the shocks regardless of what they did. The following day, each dog was placed in a box divided into two compartments by a barrier.

While in this box, the dog was presented with a series of tone-shock combinations, with a tone always preceding a shock; the dog could avoid the shock by jumping over the barrier into the other compartment as soon as it heard the tone. Dogs that had been able to escape the shocks on the previous day quickly learned to escape the shocks on the second day. In contrast, dogs that previously had been unable to escape displayed learned helplessness: They made few attempts to escape, instead simply sitting still and whining as the shocks were presented.

People, too, begin to exhibit symptoms of learned helplessness when they cannot control the occurrence of aversive events (Hiroto, 1974; Hiroto & Seligman, 1975; Peterson, Maier, & Seligman, 1993). According to Maier and Seligman (1976), learned helplessness is manifested in three ways. First, there is a *motivational* effect: The individual is slow to exhibit responses that will yield reinforcement or allow escape from punishment. Second is a *cognitive* effect: The individual has difficulty learning in future situations in which control of consequences *is* possible. Even when the individual's responses lead to reinforcement or escape from an aversive stimulus, the individual tends not to learn from those experiences. The third effect is an *emotional* one: The individual tends to be passive, withdrawn, fearful, and depressed.

Learned helplessness has been offered as an explanation of clinical depression (Seligman, 1975, 1991): Depressed people typically perceive that they have less control over their lives than nondepressed people. It may also be characteristic of some school children, particularly those who experience consistent difficulty completing academic tasks (Dweck, 1986; Eccles & Wigfield, 1985; Fennema, 1987; Holliday, 1985; Jacobsen, Lowery, & DuCette, 1986; Stipek & Kowalski, 1989; Wood, Schau, & Fiedler, 1990). Consider the child with a learning disability as an example. Often unidentified as a student with special educational needs, the child may encounter repeated failure in academic work, despite reasonable efforts to succeed, and so may eventually stop trying. I have also seen the learned helplessness phenomenon in presumably nondisabled students when I talk with them about certain subject areas. Many students, for example, attribute their mathematics anxiety to the fact that, as elementary school students, they could not comprehend how to solve certain problems no matter what they did or how hard they tried. Others show learned helplessness in the area of spelling: Even when they know they have spelled a word incorrectly, they do not try to correct the spelling, excusing their behavior by such statements as "I'm just a bad speller" or "I never could spell very well" (Ormrod & Wagner, 1987).

Learned helplessness is clearly a situation in which aversive consequences occur unpredictably rather than being contingent on certain behaviors. Ultimately, individuals experiencing such seemingly random consequences may begin to believe, perhaps justifiably, that they have little or no control over the things that happen to them. We will look in more detail at the effects of perceived control (or lack thereof) as we discuss the cognitive side of learned helplessness in Chapter 18.

In the last three chapters, we have seen how response-reinforcement contingencies increase certain responses and how response-punishment contingencies decrease others. To succeed in the school environment, students must be aware of those contingencies and be able to exhibit the responses that lead to positive outcomes. When students are unable to learn despite clearly specified contingencies and a slow, carefully designed curricular sequence, they may have cognitive problems that teachers cannot address from a strictly behaviorist perspective. In such situations, cognitive learning theories, which I will describe in Part Four of the book, may provide a more useful framework.

We will make a gradual transition to the study of cognition in Part Three (Chapter 7). There we will look at social learning theory, a theory that originated within the behaviorist perspective (especially operant conditioning) but has more recently begun to use cognitive ideas in its explanation of human behavior.

SUMMARY

Escape learning is the process of learning to terminate an aversive stimulus. Avoidance learning is the process of learning to avoid an aversive stimulus altogether. Unfortunately, when organisms avoid a particular situation, they never have the opportunity to discover when the situation is no longer aversive; hence, avoidance responses, once learned, are difficult to extinguish.

Views on punishment have changed considerably over the past 60 years: Early researchers found that punishment did little to reduce behaviors and cited numerous disadvantages of its use. More recently, however, some forms of punishment (e.g., time-outs, response cost, and reprimands) have been found to be effective in decreasing a variety of inappropriate behaviors. A number of guidelines in the use of punishment promote its effectiveness.

When aversive stimuli are repeatedly presented regardless of how a person behaves, he or she may develop a sense of learned helplessness—a sense of having little control over the environment—with motivational, cognitive, and emotional side effects.

Social Learning Theory

One summer, my sons Alex and Jeff spent quite a bit of time with their Uncle Pete, a large man who could pick them both up at the same time and carry them around on his shoulders. Uncle Pete's feats of strength were quite a contrast to Mom's and Dad's difficulties in lifting either boy alone, or even in opening pickle jars. For several years after that summer, Alex and Jeff spoke often of wanting to be like Uncle Pete, and I found that I could talk them into eating many foods they had previously shunned simply by saying, "This is what helps Uncle Pete get big and strong." The ploy never did work for broccoli, however.

When my daughter Tina was in junior high school, some of her friends got in the habit of calling her every morning to find out what she would be wearing to school that day. Tina was apparently somewhat of a fashion trendsetter at school, and several other girls were mimicking her attire. Given the apparel in which Tina left for school most mornings, I shudder at the thought of what her cronies must have looked like.

Almost daily, we see instances of people watching others and learning from them. Little boys often emulate hero figures such as Superman, Batman, and Uncle Pete. Through watching and copying one another, preadolescent girls often begin to behave in similar ways, dressing alike, wearing their hair in faddish styles, and poking fun at the same boys. Children imitate their parents by developing similar hobbies and interests, by expressing similar political and religious beliefs, and by eventually raising their own children using the same disciplinary techniques with which they were raised. Students in the classroom learn many academic skills, including reading, writing, adding, and subtracting, at least partly through watching and imitating what their teachers and classmates do.

Such learning by observation and modeling is the focus of **social learning theory** (e.g., Bandura, 1977b, 1986; Rosenthal & Zimmerman, 1978; Schunk, 1989c). Social learning theory originally evolved from behaviorism but now includes many of the ideas that cognitivists also hold; as a result, it is sometimes called **social cognitive theory.** In this chapter we will consider social learning theory's perspective on how both environmental and cognitive factors interact to influence human learning and behavior. We will explore

My daughter the trendsetter.

the phenomenon of *modeling,* examining the mental processes involved, the effects of modeling on behavior, and the characteristics of effective models. We will find that people's beliefs about their own ability to execute various behaviors successfully (their *self-efficacy*) play a role in the responses they choose to make and the effort they exert in making those responses. And we will discover how, through the process of *self-regulation,* people become less and less influenced by environmental conditions as time goes on. At the end of the chapter, we will examine a number of implications that social learning theory has for educational practice.

THE SOCIAL LEARNING MODEL

Social learning theory focuses on the learning that occurs within a social context. It considers how people learn from one another, encompassing such concepts as observational learning, imitation, and modeling. Although many species of animals can probably learn by imitation (Hayes & Hayes, 1952; Herbert & Harsh, 1944; Zentall, Sutton, & Sherburne, 1996), social learning theory deals primarily with human learning, and so we will be leaving research involving rats and pigeons behind us at this point.

The study of learning through imitation was launched by two of Clark Hull's students, Neal Miller and John Dollard (1941). It was not until the early 1960s, however, that a theory of imitation and modeling separate from its behaviorist roots began to take shape. Development of this theory, originally called *observational learning,* was due in large part to the research and writings of Albert Bandura of Stanford University (e.g., Bandura, 1969, 1973, 1977b, 1986, 1989; Bandura & Walters, 1963). Bandura's perspective has evolved considerably over the years and continues to be the driving force in studies of imitation and modeling.

General Principles of Social Learning Theory

Several general principles underlie social learning theory. Let's consider some of the key ideas that have shaped the evolution of the social learning perspective:

- *People can learn by observing the behaviors of others and the outcomes of those behaviors.* Many early behaviorists viewed learning largely as a matter of trial and error: People learn by making a variety of responses and then modifying their behavior based on the consequences (e.g., the reinforcement) that their responses bring. In contrast, social learning theorists propose that most learning takes place not through trial and error but instead through watching the behavior of other individuals (**models**).

- *Learning can occur without a change in behavior.* As we noted in Chapter 1, behaviorists define learning as a relatively permanent change in behavior due to experience; thus, no learning can occur without a behavior change. In contrast, social learning theorists argue that because people can learn through observation alone, their learning will not necessarily be reflected in their performance. In other words, learning may or may not result in a behavior change. Something learned at one time may be reflected in behavior exhibited at the same time, at a later time, or never.

- *The consequences of behavior play a role in learning.* The role of consequences in social learning theory has evolved as the theory itself has evolved. In Miller and Dollard's (1941) early theoretical analysis of learning new behaviors through imitation, reinforcement of those behaviors was a critical factor. Operant conditioning continued to be a major component of Albert Bandura's early work as well (e.g., see Bandura & Walters, 1963). More recently, however, the role of consequences has been reconceptualized (Bandura, 1977b, 1986; Rosenthal & Zimmerman, 1978). Contemporary social learning theorists propose that both reinforcement and punishment have less critical, *indirect* effects on learning—effects that we shall examine shortly.

- *Cognition plays a role in learning.* Over the past 30 years, social learning theory has become increasingly "cognitive" in its analysis of human learning. For example, contemporary social learning theorists such as Bandura maintain that an individual's *awareness* of response-reinforcement and response-punishment contingencies is an essential component of the learning process. They also assert that *expectations* of future reinforcements and punishments can have a major impact on the behaviors that people exhibit. Finally, as you will soon see, social learning theorists incorporate such cognitive processes as *attention* and *retention* (memory) into their explanations of how learning occurs.

Let's turn now to the ways in which environmental factors—reinforcement and punishment in particular—play a role in learning by observation. We will then look at how cognition is also involved.

ENVIRONMENTAL FACTORS IN SOCIAL LEARNING: REINFORCEMENT AND PUNISHMENT

If we were to explain imitation from an operant conditioning perspective, we might propose that people imitate others because they are reinforced for doing so. In fact, this explanation is exactly what Miller and Dollard proposed back in 1941. According to these theorists, an individual uses another person's behavior as a discriminative stimulus for an imitative response. The observer is then reinforced in some way for displaying imitation. For example, let's say that a French teacher carefully enunciates:

Comment allez vous?   (Discriminative stimulus)

Students repeat the phrase in more or less the same way:

Comma tally voo?   (Response)

The teacher then praises them for their efforts:

Trés bien! Very good!   (Reinforcement)

From an operant conditioning perspective, imitation of other people's behavior is maintained by an intermittent reinforcement schedule: Individuals are not *always* reinforced for mimicking the responses of others, but they are reinforced often enough that they continue to copy those around them. Eventually imitation itself becomes a habit, a phenomenon Miller and Dollard called **generalized imitation.**

How the Environment Reinforces and Punishes Modeling

People are often reinforced for modeling the behaviors of others. Bandura has suggested that the environment reinforces modeling and also may occasionally punish modeling in several possible ways:

- *The observer is reinforced by the model.* People often reinforce others who copy what they themselves do. For example, a group of teenage girls is more likely to welcome another girl into the group if she dresses as they do. A gang of delinquent boys will probably accept a new member only if he acts "tough."

    In the French lesson I described earlier, the model—the teacher—reinforced students for imitative behavior. Teachers and parents often reinforce children for copying appropriate behaviors. For example, when my children were young, I would occasionally hear one of them use polite, "adult" language on the telephone, perhaps along this line: "I'm sorry, but my mother is busy right now. If you will give me your name and number, I'll have her call you back in a few minutes." Such a statement was similar to what I myself would tell callers, and I was likely to praise the child profusely. On the other hand, a statement such as, "Ma! Telephone! Hurry up and get off the potty!" was definitely *not* learned through observation of the adults in the house, and I certainly never reinforced it.

- *The observer is reinforced by a third person.* On some occasions an individual is reinforced by a third person rather than by the model. For example, children are often reinforced by parents and teachers when they imitate other children. Something I used to tell my youngest child, Jeff, was this: "Oh, you're such a big boy now! You're getting dressed all by yourself, just like Alex does!"

    During the Beatlemania of the 1960s, many teenage boys began sporting "moppet" haircuts like those of the Beatles. Such haircuts were "in," at least in my high school, and none of us girls would have ever been caught dead with a boy who had hair shorter than John Lennon's. My friends and I were, in essence, reinforcing boys who modeled themselves after the Beatles. In earlier days, we would have reinforced anyone who could play the guitar and bat his eyelashes in a come-hither fashion, just as Ricky Nelson used to do in the television show *Ozzie and Harriet.*

- *The imitated behavior itself leads to reinforcing consequences.* Many behaviors that we learn through observing others produce satisfying (reinforcing) results. For example, a French student who pronounces his *Comment allez vous?* correctly will have greater success communicating with a Parisian. An individual who can closely model a tennis instructor's body positions and arm movements is more likely to get the ball over the net.

- *Consequences of the model's behavior affect the observer's behavior vicariously.* When people observe a model making a particular response, they may also observe the consequence of that response. If a model is reinforced for a response, then the *observer* may show an increase in that response; this phenomenon is known as **vicarious reinforcement.** For example, if Andy sees Adam gain popularity among the girls because he can play the guitar and bat his eyelashes in a come-hither fashion, Andy may very well buy a guitar and take a few guitar lessons; he may also stand in front of the mirror practicing eyelash batting.

Reinforcement of the model affects the observer's behavior as well.

The power of vicarious reinforcement (and of **vicarious punishment** as well) was dramatically illustrated in an early study by Bandura (1965b). Children watched a film of a model hitting and kicking an inflated punching doll. One group of children saw the model reinforced for such aggressive behavior, a second group saw the model punished, and a third group saw the model receive no consequences for the aggression. When the children were then placed in a room with the doll, those who had seen the model being reinforced for aggression displayed the most aggressive behavior toward the doll: They had been vicariously reinforced for aggression. Conversely, those who had seen the model punished for aggression were the least aggressive of the three groups: They had been vicariously punished for such behavior.

Vicarious punishment indicates to the observer that a particular behavior will not be tolerated; vicarious reinforcement indicates that a behavior is acceptable. Apparently, a *lack* of punishment to the model may also be a form of vicarious reinforcement in that it conveys the message that a behavior will be tolerated (Bandura, 1973, 1977b, 1986; Walters & Parke, 1964; Walters, Parke, & Cane, 1965). For example, in a study by Walters and Parke (1964), children in three different experimental groups watched a film in which a boy (the model) was told by a female experimenter not to play with a number of toys that lay on the table in front of him but instead to read a book that she had given him. Yet as soon as the woman left the room, the boy began to play with the toys. At this point, the film was different for the three experimental groups, as follows:

1. *Reward.* The woman returned, handed the boy some toys, and played with him affectionately.
2. *Punishment.* The woman returned, snatched away the toys the boy was playing with, shook him vigorously, and sat him back down with the book.
3. *No consequence.* The woman did not return to the room.

Children in these three groups, and children in a control group who did not view a film, were then taken to a room full of toys, told not to touch them, given a book to read, and left alone for 15 minutes. Children in the no-consequence group played with the toys (thus disobeying the experimenter's instructions) just as much as the reward group did. Children in the punishment group were more obedient, but the most obedient children were those in the control group, who had not watched the disobedient model at all.

When people see others misbehave without negative consequences, they are more likely to misbehave themselves. For example, when my daughter was in elementary school, she came home almost daily with complaints about who had gotten away with what on the playground that day. When playground supervisors ignore transgressions day after day, their inaction not only perpetuates those misbehaviors but may even increase them. In the same way, I often wonder whether individuals who see others quite literally get away with murder are not more likely to engage in criminal activities themselves.

Problems with a Strict Operant Conditioning Analysis of Social Learning

Although early social learning theorists tried to explain imitative behavior from the perspective of operant conditioning, they encountered several problems in doing so. For one thing, operant conditioning does not address the effects of punishment, yet, as we saw in Bandura's (1965b) study of children watching a boy playing with prohibited toys, punishment *can* influence behavior.

A second problem is that completely new behaviors can be learned simply by watching others perform them (Bandura, 1977b, 1986; Rosenthal, Alford, & Rasp, 1972). As you should recall, operant conditioning must start with an emitted response, a response that can then be modified through shaping. The learning of entirely novel responses— responses that an individual has seen but never previously emitted in any form—is difficult to explain from a strictly Skinnerian perspective.

A third difficulty in explaining modeling as an instance of operant conditioning is the phenomenon of **delayed imitation:** Some behaviors that are learned through observing others do not appear until a later point in time. The operant conditioning paradigm, if we consider the role of the antecedent stimulus, looks like this:

$$(S+) \; R \rightarrow S_{Rf}$$

These three parts of the model—discriminative stimulus (S+), response (R), and reinforcement (S_{Rf})—follow one right after the other, with the response occurring in the presence of the discriminative stimulus. Yet as Bandura (1977b) has pointed out, the response and resulting reinforcement do not always appear immediately after the discriminative stimulus but instead occur at a later time. For such delayed imitation to be exhibited, learning must actually take place when the discriminative stimulus is presented, despite the absence of reinforcement at that time.

Still a fourth problem lies in the powerful effect of vicarious reinforcement: Individuals sometimes exhibit behaviors for which they themselves are *never* reinforced.

A Contemporary Social Learning Perspective of Reinforcement and Punishment

Contemporary social learning theorists (e.g., Bandura, 1977b, 1986; Rosenthal & Zimmerman, 1978) do not view direct consequences of behavior as being essential for learning to occur. They do believe, however, that consequences play at least two roles in learning and performance:

• *Reinforcement and punishment influence the extent to which an individual exhibits a behavior that has been learned.* Social learning theorists believe that, although people may learn new behaviors, they will not demonstrate those behaviors unless there is a reason (i.e., reinforcement) for doing so. For example, I learned many years ago that the capital of Alaska is Juneau. Yet I have never had a reason to demonstrate that knowledge, because I have never been tested on the capital of Alaska, nor have I ever been in Alaska desperately seeking the state capital. Now, of course, I do have a reason: I want to impress you with the fact that I know the capital of at least one of the 50 states.

Bandura (1977b, 1986) has proposed that an individual forms *hypotheses* about what responses are most appropriate in different situations. These hypotheses are formed and modified with the feedback that reinforcement and punishment, either of one's own actions or those of others, provide. Although an individual may learn both appropriate and inappropriate behaviors equally well, the appropriate behaviors—those that will lead to reinforcement—are the ones more likely to occur.

• *The expectation of reinforcement influences cognitive processes that promote learning.* As an example of a cognitive process involved in learning, social learning theorists (e.g., Bandura, 1977b, 1986) maintain that *attention* plays a critical role in learning. And attention is influenced by the expectation of reinforcement: People are more likely to pay attention to someone else's behavior when they think they will be reinforced for modeling that behavior.

I have learned the hard way that when I tell my students they will not be held responsible for certain information, I am making a BIG MISTAKE. All I have to do is say something like, "Now I want you to listen carefully to what I have to say for the next five minutes, but *it won't be on the next test*," and students put their pens down, settle back in their seats, and start to nod off. People are less likely to pay attention to information when they do not anticipate a payoff for learning it.

As you can see, social learning theorists stress the role of environmental factors in learning, but they acknowledge the importance of cognitive factors as well. Let's now turn our attention to those cognitive factors.

COGNITIVE FACTORS IN SOCIAL LEARNING

The cognitive side of social learning theory is evident in many aspects of the theory; examples include learning without performance, cognitive processing during learning, expectations, and the awareness of response-consequence contingencies.

Learning without Performance

Bandura makes a distinction between learning through observation (something he calls **vicarious acquisition**) and the actual imitation of what has been learned. As we noted earlier, people can learn by watching others without necessarily imitating the behaviors they have seen (Bandura, 1977b, 1986; Rosenthal & Zimmerman, 1978). At least two sources of evidence indicate that this is true. For one thing, people can verbally describe a behavior they have observed without actually performing it (Bandura, 1965a). Second, people who observe a model perform a behavior may not demonstrate that behavior until some later time when they have a reason for doing so. For example, I previously described a study by Bandura (1965b) in which children watched a film of a model acting aggressively toward an inflated punching doll. As you may recall, the consequences of the aggression to the model (reinforcement, punishment, or no consequence) influenced the extent to which children themselves engaged in aggressive acts toward the doll. Later in the study, however, all of the children were promised rewards (stickers and fruit juices) if they could imitate the model's behavior. At that point, differences among the three groups of children disappeared. Clearly they had all *learned* the model's behavior equally well; the consequences to the model apparently affected their earlier performance but not their learning.

Cognitive Processing during Learning

Social learning theorists describe the cognitive processes (i.e., thinking) that occur when people are learning. For example, they contend that *attention* is a critical factor in learning. Furthermore, they propose that people are more likely to remember information when they mentally repeat *(rehearse)* it and when they develop verbal and visual mental representations *(memory codes)* of this information. I will illustrate each of these processes when, later in the chapter, I describe Bandura's four conditions for successful modeling to occur.

Expectations

Social learning theorists believe that, as a result of being reinforced for some behaviors and punished for others, people form expectations about the consequences that future behaviors are likely to bring (Bandura, 1977b, 1986, 1989; Rosenthal & Zimmerman, 1978). People often have expectations of what is likely to happen in different situations; they expect certain behaviors to lead to reinforcement and others to lead to punishment. The concept of **incentive**—anticipating that a particular reinforcement will occur if a particular behavior is performed—reflects this idea of expectation. Obviously, when people expect to be rewarded for imitating a behavior, they will be more likely to pay attention to that behavior and try to remember how it is performed. Furthermore, they will be motivated to demonstrate the behavior they have learned. You should notice a critical difference here between the role of reinforcement in operant conditioning and in social learning. In operant conditioning, reinforcement influences learning of the behavior it *follows*. In social learning, on the other hand, an *expectation* of reinforcement influences the learning of a behavior it *precedes* (Bandura, 1977b, 1986).

As we discovered earlier, the nonoccurrence of expected punishment can be reinforcing. Conversely, the nonoccurrence of expected reinforcement is often a form of punishment (Bandura, 1977b, 1986). Both of these principles involve situations in which expectations are not being met. For example, imagine yourself as a student in a class in which the teacher has clearly described the criteria necessary to earn an A. You work hard, and your performance meets the specified criteria, so you are naturally expecting an A. But at the last minute, your teacher adds an additional requirement: To earn an A, students must write a 20-page term paper. You are probably angry and frustrated (in a sense, you feel punished), because you had expected reinforcement based on the work you had already completed and that reinforcement is now being withheld.

Awareness of Response-Consequence Contingencies

According to social learning theorists, reinforcement and punishment have little effect on learning and behavior unless people are *aware* of the response-reinforcement and response-punishment contingencies (Bandura, 1977b, 1986; Spielberger & DeNike, 1966). Reinforcement increases a response only when an individual realizes which particular response has led to the reinforcement. Similarly, an individual must recognize what particular behavior is being punished before that behavior is likely to decrease. For example, consider a situation in which a student receives an F on a writing assignment, with such comments as "Poorly written" and "Disorganized" noted in the margins. For many students, such feedback is insufficient to bring about an improvement in writing because, among other things, it does not identify the specific parts of the assignment that are poorly written and disorganized.

It should be clear by now that social learning theory incorporates elements of both behaviorism and cognitivism. We have examined some of the environmental and cognitive factors that, from a social learning perspective, are involved in the learning process. We must also consider how environment and cognition *interact* with one another. Let's turn next to that topic—in particular, to Bandura's concept of reciprocal causation.

RECIPROCAL CAUSATION

We have already seen how the environment influences behavior and how a person's characteristics (e.g., cognitive processes and expectations) influence behavior. Bandura (1989) has proposed that, in a reciprocal fashion, behavior can also influence both the environment and the person. In fact, each of these three variables—environment, person, and behavior—influences the other two, a phenomenon Bandura calls **reciprocal causation.**[1] The interaction of environment (E), person (P), and behavior (B) can be depicted like this:

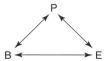

Certainly the environment influences a person's behavior. For example, the occurrence of a desirable or undesirable consequence as a result of a particular response influences the probability that an individual will make that response again. But an individual's *perception* of the environment (a "person" variable) can be equally influential on behavior. For example, I mentioned earlier that awareness of response-reinforcement contingencies influences the extent to which those contingencies affect behavior. Consider an experiment by Kaufman, Baron, and Kopp (1966) as a case in point. Participants in the experiment were all placed on a variable-interval reinforcement schedule, with the average interval before reinforcement being one minute, and told one of three different things about the schedule they were on. People in group 1 were told that they were on a one-minute variable-interval schedule (i.e., they were told the truth). People in group 2 were told that they were on a one-minute *fixed*-interval schedule. People in group 3 were told that they were on a variable-ratio (1:150) schedule. People's response patterns corresponded to the reinforcement schedules they *believed* they were on: Group 3 showed the fastest response rate, and group 2 showed the slowest response rate, consistent with the response patterns that are actually observed for these different reinforcement schedules. Baron, Kaufman, and Stauber (1969) have reported similar results.

Yet behavior affects both the environment that individuals encounter and the personal characteristics that they develop. The responses people make (e.g., the academic courses they choose, the extracurricular activities they pursue, and the company they keep) determine the situations they find themselves in and the consequences they experience (environmental variables). For example, individuals typically behave in ways that increase reinforcement and decrease punishment. Furthermore, the pattern of one's responses over time affects one's self-confidence and expectations for future performance (person variables). For example, a boy who stumbles and falls frequently may begin to think that he is a klutz. By consistently performing well on mathematics assignments, a girl may begin to believe that she is a mathematics whiz.

Finally, person variables and environmental variables affect each other. For example, by directing attention (a person variable) to one stimulus and not to another, certain aspects of the environment will be experienced and others will not. And we have already seen how the consequences of past behaviors (an environmental variable) affect the expectations that people have (a person variable) regarding the outcomes of future behaviors.

One prime example of the interplay among environment, person, and behavior variables is modeling. Let's now look more closely at the modeling process.

---

[1]Before 1989, Bandura used the term *reciprocal determinism.*

MODELING

According to Bandura (1977b, 1986), many of the behaviors people exhibit have been acquired through observing and modeling what others do. In this section, we will explore several topics related to modeling. We will first consider the different types of models we may see and the kinds of behaviors that can be modeled. We will then look at four conditions essential for learning to occur through modeling and at the various ways in which models can affect behavior. Finally, we will identify several characteristics of effective models. Before we proceed, however, I should point out that social learning theorists sometimes use the term *modeling* to describe what a model does (i.e., demonstrate a behavior) and at other times to describe what the observer does (i.e., copy that behavior). I have tried to write this section in such a way that the term's meaning is always readily discernible from the context in which it is used.

Types of Models

Bandura identifies three different types of models. When we think of modeling, we most frequently think of a **live model**—an actual person demonstrating a particular behavior. But we can also learn by observing a **symbolic model**—a person or character portrayed in a film, television show, book, or other medium. For example, many children model their behavior after football players, rock singers, or such fictional characters as Superman, G.I. Joe, or Pippi Longstocking. And finally, we can learn from **verbal instructions**—descriptions of how to behave—without another human being, either live or symbolic, being present at all.

Behaviors That Can Be Learned through Modeling

Many behaviors are learned, at least in part, through modeling. For example, students:

- Are better readers when their parents read frequently at home (Hess & McDevitt, 1989).
- Solve mathematics problems more successfully when they see others demonstrate the appropriate procedure (Schunk & Hanson, 1985).
- Are more likely to resist the enticements of a stranger when a peer has modeled techniques for resisting such enticements (Poche, Yoder, & Miltenberger, 1988).
- Begin to deal with a fear-inducing situation with little or no fear after seeing a model behave fearlessly in that situation (Bandura, Grusec, & Menlove, 1967; Bandura & Menlove, 1968; Silverman & Kearney, 1991).
- Are more likely to show intolerance of racist statements made by others when those around them refuse to tolerate such statements (Blanchard, Lilly, & Vaughn, 1991).
- Are more likely to violate traditional gender stereotypes—that is, to behave without regard to what is "appropriate" behavior for males and females—when they see others behaving in a nonstereotypic manner (Carlson, 1984; Hoffman, 1984; Ruble & Ruble, 1982; Selkow, 1984; Weinraub, Clemens, Sockloff, Ethridge, Gracely, & Myers, 1984).

Considerable research has been conducted concerning the impact of modeling on two kinds of behavior in particular: aggression and morality.

Aggression

Numerous research studies indicate that children become more aggressive when they observe aggressive or violent models (Bandura, 1965b; Bandura, Ross, & Ross, 1961, 1963; Mischel & Grusec, 1966; Steuer, Applefield, & Smith, 1971; Walters & Thomas, 1963; Walters, Thomas, & Acker, 1962). In the classic study in this area (Bandura, Ross, & Ross, 1961), preschoolers were taken one at a time to a playroom containing a variety of toys and were seated at a table where they could draw pictures. Some of these children then observed an adult (an aggressive model) enter the room and engage in numerous aggressive behaviors toward an inflatable punching doll, including kicking the doll in the air, straddling it and hitting it over the head with a wooden mallet, and making statements like "Pow!" "Kick him," and "Punch him in the nose." Other children instead observed an adult (a nonaggressive model) come in and play in a constructive way with building blocks. Still other children saw no model while they were in the playroom. The children were then led to another room where they were mildly frustrated: Just as they began to play with some very attractive, entertaining toys, the toys were taken away from them. Finally, the children were taken to a third room in which both nonaggressive and aggressive toys (including the inflatable punching doll and wooden mallet) were present; their behaviors were recorded and coded for aggressive content by observers on the other side of a one-way mirror. Children who had seen the aggressive model were clearly the most aggressive of the three groups, and in fact they mimicked many of the same behaviors that they had seen the aggressive model display (e.g., straddling the doll and hitting it with the mallet). Children who had seen a nonaggressive model were even less aggressive than the no-model group. With regard to aggression, then, models can have an impact either way: Aggressive models will lead to increased aggression in children, and nonaggressive models will lead to decreased aggression.

Children can also learn aggression from observing it in films or on television (Rushton, 1980). In another study by Bandura and his colleagues (1963), preschool children who had seen a film of either an adult or a cartoon character being aggressive exhibited just as much aggression toward an inflatable doll as did children who had seen a live adult model; all of these children were significantly more aggressive than children who had not observed a model at all. But modeled aggression is not limited to toys: In a study by Steuer, Applefield, and Smith (1971), children who watched cartoons depicting aggressive and violent behavior were significantly more aggressive toward other children than children who had not seen the cartoons.

The fact that children model aggressive behavior depicted in the media has obvious implications for television and movie violence. Children not only model aggression but also tend to model the same *forms* of aggression that they observe (Bandura et al., 1963; Mischel & Grusec, 1966). Even cartoons that display violent behaviors, including such classics as *Tom* and *Jerry* and *Roadrunner,* may not be as harmless as they appear.

Morality

Many aspects of moral thinking and moral behavior are apparently influenced by observation and modeling. Research has demonstrated the importance of modeling for such behaviors as generosity (Elliott & Vasta, 1970; Radke-Yarrow, Zahn-Waxler, & Chapman, 1983; Rushton, 1975, 1982), self-control (Harter, 1983; Stevenson & Fantuzzo, 1986), and resistance to temptation (Wolf & Cheyne, 1972). Consider the study by Rushton (1975) as an example: Children first observed a model playing a bowling game and reinforcing himself with tokens for high performance. Some children saw the model donate half of the earned tokens to a poor boy named Bobby pictured on a poster in the room; other children observed the model keep all of his winnings for himself despite the presence of the poster. The children then had the opportunity to play the game and to reward themselves with tokens. The more tokens they earned, the better prize they could purchase (therefore, donating to Bobby meant that they would have to purchase a lesser prize for themselves). Children who had watched generous models were more likely to donate some of their own tokens to Bobby than were children who had watched selfish models. This difference was true not only in the initial experimental session but also in a follow-up session two months later.

Moral judgments regarding right and wrong may also develop, at least in part, through modeling (Bandura & McDonald, 1963; Prentice, 1972; Schliefer & Douglas, 1973). For example, in a study by Bandura and McDonald (1963), experimenters presented children with pairs of stories such as these:

1. John was in his room when his mother called him to dinner. John goes down, and opens the door to the dining room. But behind the door was a chair, and on the chair was a tray with fifteen cups on it. John did not know the cups were behind the door. He opens the door, the door hits the tray, bang go the fifteen cups, and they all get broken.
2. One day when Henry's mother was out, Henry tried to get some cookies out of the cupboard. He climbed up on a chair, but the cookie jar was still too high, and he couldn't reach it. But while he was trying to get the cookie jar, he knocked over a cup. The cup fell and broke. (Bandura & McDonald, 1963, p. 276)

In each pair, stories portrayed one well-intended child (such as John) who caused major damage and another child with malicious intent (such as Henry) who did minor damage. For each pair of stories, the children were asked which child was naughtier. Some children consistently picked the child with the bad intentions as being naughtier; these children were then exposed to a model who used amount of damage as the criterion for naughtiness. Other children had a pattern of judging the well-meaning but more destructive child as being naughtier; they were exposed to a model who used bad intentions as the criterion for naughtiness. Observing the model had a profound effect on the children's later moral judgments: Children began to make moral decisions similar to those the model had made and opposite to their own previous judgments.

We have already seen that when models on film depict aggressive behavior, that behavior is often imitated. But visual media can model appropriate social responses as well, often quite effectively (Huston, Watkins, & Kunkel, 1989; Rushton, 1980). For example, in a study by Friedrich and Stein (1973), a group of preschool children watched *Mister Rogers' Neighborhood*—a television show that stresses such prosocial behaviors as cooperation, sympathy, and sharing—for 30 minutes each day over a four-week period. These children displayed more socially appropriate behavior and less aggression than children who instead watched shows with aggressive content (e.g., *Batman* and *Superman*) during the same time period.

What about situations in which a model preaches one set of moral values and practices another? A review of research by Bryan (1975) leads to a clear conclusion: When children hear a model say one thing and do something else, they are more likely to imitate what the model *does* than what the model *says*. In other words, to be effective, models must practice what they preach.

Conditions Necessary for Effective Modeling to Occur

According to Bandura (1969, 1973, 1977b, 1986), four conditions are necessary before an individual can successfully model the behavior of someone else: attention, retention, motor reproduction, and motivation.

Attention

To imitate a behavior accurately, a person must first pay attention to the model and especially to the significant aspects of the modeled behavior. For example, if Martha wishes to learn how to swing a golf club, she should watch how the golf pro stands, how her legs are placed, how her hands hold the club, and so on. Paying attention to the irrelevant parts of the model or her behavior—how the pro clears her throat or how her socks don't quite match—will of course not be helpful.

I still remember my first French teacher, a woman who came to my fifth-grade class for an hour one day each week. This woman always wore the same dark green wool dress, which, unfortunately, turned to a turquoise color in places where she perspired. I remember focusing on those turquoise spots, fascinated that a wool dress could actually change color just because of a little human sweat. Yes, I was paying attention to my model, but, no, I did not learn much French, because I did not pay attention to the important aspect of the model's behavior—her voice.

Retention

The second step in learning from a model is to remember the behavior that has been observed. One simple way to remember what one has seen is **rehearsal**—repeating whatever needs to be remembered over and over again. For example, in a study by Weiss and Klint (1987), elementary school students were asked to remember a sequence of actions (do a crabwalk, pick up a beanbag, gallop, do a log roll, and skip) that they needed to perform on mats on the gymnasium floor. Students remembered the sequence more successfully if they were instructed to repeat, or *rehearse,* it to themselves while they executed it.

According to Bandura, people store both verbal representations (such as step-by-step instructions or labels that describe the actions to be performed) and visual images of the behaviors they have seen. These verbal and visual **memory codes** serve as guides when people perform the observed behavior, whether they perform it immediately after the model has illustrated it or at some time in the future. To illustrate such memory codes, my son Jeff's swimming teacher used the words *chicken, airplane,* and *soldier* to describe the three arm movements of the elementary backstroke (see Figure 7–1). The words provided Jeff with verbal codes for these actions; the teacher's demonstration of them facilitated the formation of visual images.

Arm Movements for the Elementary Back Stroke

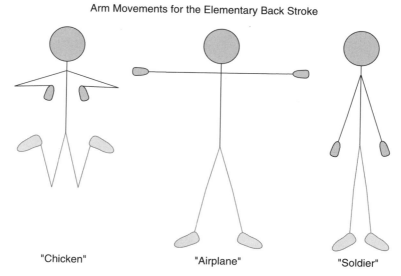

"Chicken"   "Airplane"   "Soldier"

Figure 7–1
Students often remember a model's behaviors more easily when those behaviors have verbal labels.

Considerable evidence indicates that learning from a model is easier if learners have assistance in forming memory codes for the behaviors they observe (Alford & Rosenthal, 1973; Bandura & Jeffery, 1973; Bandura, Jeffery, & Bachicha, 1974; Coates & Hartup, 1969; Cohen, 1989; Gerst, 1971; Rosenthal, Alford, & Rasp, 1972). For example, in a study by Gerst (1971), college students studied a number of words (hand signals) in sign language for the deaf. Students who were instructed either to describe the signals verbally or to form mental images of them remembered the signals more successfully than an uninstructed control group; students who were instructed to develop verbal labels descriptive of the hand movements remembered the signals most accurately. Teachers, too, can provide codes for learners. For example, in a study by Rosenthal, Alford, and Rasp (1972), second graders more effectively remembered the actions that an adult model demonstrated when she simultaneously described what she was doing.

The storage of information in memory and the different forms that such stored information can take are topics that have been studied more extensively by cognitive theorists than by social learning theorists. So we will return to this topic of memory storage again, and in much greater detail, in Chapters 10 and 11.

Motor Reproduction

The third condition for modeling to occur is the ability to replicate the behavior that the model has demonstrated. When an individual cannot reproduce an observed behavior, perhaps because of physical immaturity, lack of strength, or disability, this third condition obviously does not exist. For example, a child with a speech impediment may never be

Modeling cannot occur without the physical capability.

Ready, and — one, two, one, two...

able to pronounce *sassafras* correctly, no matter how many times she has heard the word spoken. And a toddler who watches his teenage brother throw a football does not possess the muscular coordination to mimic that throw.

In my never-ending battle with the bulge, I turn on Jane Fonda's physical workout videocassette tape religiously every night (well, at least twice a month). Jane performs exercises in various pretzel-like contortions that I, even in my wildest dreams, would never be able to do. My body is not built to be folded in that many ways. Motor reproduction of everything I watch Model Jane do is simply not possible.

Reproduction of an observed behavior at the same time it is observed facilitates learning for at least two reasons. For one thing, it enables learners to encode that behavior not only in verbal and visual forms but perhaps in a *motoric* form as well—that is, in terms of the specific actions it encompasses (Cohen, 1989). Furthermore, by modeling a behavior in the presence of the model, learners can get feedback about how to improve their performance (Bandura, 1977b; Schunk, 1981).[2] For example, when teaching division to children having difficulty with mathematics, instruction that includes an opportunity for practice and immediate feedback about the quality of performance is clearly superior to instruction that provides no opportunity for such practice and feedback (Schunk, 1981).

Motivation

The final necessary ingredient for modeling to occur is motivation: Learners must want to demonstrate what they have learned. For example, many people who have grown up in

---

[2]We should note, however, that some children may prefer to practice newly learned behaviors in private before showing an adult what they have learned; for example, this may be the case for many Native American children (Grant & Gomez, 1996; Suina & Smolkin, 1994).

our society have seen models on television point a gun in someone's ribs and say "Reach for the sky" (or at least something to that effect). Fortunately, very few people are motivated to model that behavior, at least with a real gun.

Although parents and teachers are often models for children, children do not model *all* of the behaviors they observe their parents and teachers perform. For example, although my children model my ways of speaking to people on the telephone and my cookie-baking techniques, for some reason they don't seem to copy my broccoli-cooking or floor-scrubbing behaviors. Children model behaviors only when they are motivated to do so.

To review, Bandura's four conditions essential for modeling to occur are attention, retention, motor reproduction, and motivation. Because these conditions vary among individuals, different people will model the same behavior differently. For example, Martha and Mary might pay attention to different aspects of their tennis instructor's tennis swing: Martha may focus on how the instructor is standing while Mary attends more to the way the instructor grips her racket. Or the two girls might store different visual images of the swing, Martha remembering that the instructor was facing the net and Mary remembering her standing with the left shoulder toward the net. Martha may be stronger, but Mary may be more motivated to play tennis well. The end result is that Martha and Mary will model the same tennis swing differently. Not only will the four essential conditions for modeling lead to individual differences in modeled behaviors, the absence of any one of these conditions will make modeling unlikely to occur at all.

Effects of Modeling on Behavior

In what ways do models influence behavior? Social learning theorists (e.g., Bandura, 1969, 1973, 1977b, 1986; Bandura & Walters, 1963; Rosenthal & Zimmerman, 1978) have proposed that modeling has several effects:

• *Modeling teaches new behaviors.* People can learn entirely new behaviors by observing others perform those behaviors. For example, by listening to and imitating the sounds made by others, a person learns to speak new words. And by watching how a parent swings a baseball bat and following the parent's verbal instructions ("Keep your eye on the ball!"), a child learns to hit a baseball.

• *Modeling influences the frequency of previously learned behaviors.* As we noted earlier, people are more likely to exhibit behaviors they have previously learned when they see others being reinforced for such behaviors; in other words, vicarious reinforcement has a **facilitation** effect. By the same token, people are less likely to perform behaviors for which they have seen others being punished; in other words, vicarious punishment has an **inhibition** effect.

• *Modeling may encourage previously forbidden behaviors.* In some situations, when people observe a model engaging in behavior that has previously been described as forbidden or "wrong," and especially when the model is reinforced for engaging in that behavior, they themselves are more likely to display the behavior. On these occasions, vicarious reinforcement has a ***dis***inhibition effect (because previously inhibited behavior is now reoccurring). For example, in studies by Walters and his colleagues (Walters & Thomas, 1963; Walters, Thomas, & Acker, 1962), adults viewed either a film depicting aggression and violence (*Rebel without a Cause*) or a neutral film (*Picture Making by Teenagers*) and then were asked to administer "shocks" to other individuals. (These other individuals were confederates of the experimenter who did not really receive any shocks but behaved as if they did.) People who had watched the violent, aggressive film administered more frequent and more intense "shocks" to the confederates. The film had apparently disinhibited previously learned aggressive behavior.

• *Modeling increases the frequency of similar behaviors.* When a person observes a model performing a particular behavior, that person may display similar rather than identical behavior. For example, a boy who sees his older brother excel at basketball, but who lacks his brother's height advantage, may instead try to become a successful soccer player. As a high school student, I would have liked to become a "cool" cheerleader but did not have the gymnastic skills necessary for cheerleading. Instead, I became a majorette in the marching band, an activity that was almost as cool.

Characteristics of Effective Models

People who are most likely to serve as live or symbolic models for others tend to have one or more characteristic traits:

• *The model is competent.* People demonstrating a particular behavior are more likely to be imitated by others if they are viewed as being competent, capable individuals (Bandura, 1986; Schunk, 1987). For example, a person trying to learn tennis is more likely to model the techniques of a successful tennis player than those of a friend who cannot even get the ball over the net. And a student trying to learn how to write a good term paper is more likely to look at the work of someone who has consistently received high grades on term papers than at the work of a student who has historically done poorly on such assignments.

• *The model has prestige and power.* Individuals that have high status, respect, and power, either within a small group or within society as a whole, are more likely to serve as models for others (Bandura, 1986). A child is more likely to imitate the behaviors of a student leader or a famous rock star than the behaviors of a class dunce or a rock-and-roll "has-been." To illustrate, Sasso and Rude (1987) taught a number of nondisabled children (some of whom were popular with their peers and some of whom were not) methods of initiating appropriate social interactions with children who had physical disabilities. Other children who saw their popular classmates interacting with disabled children were likely to do so as well, but children who saw unpopular students modeling the same behavior were unlikely to follow suit.

• *The model behaves in stereotypical "gender-appropriate" ways.* Males are more likely to model behavior that is consistent with male stereotypes; similarly, females are more likely to model behaviors that follow traditional female patterns (Schunk, 1987). For example, in studies in which children watched adult models of both genders being aggressive (Bandura, Ross, & Ross, 1961, 1963), boys were more likely than girls to imitate the aggressive behaviors, presumably because aggression is a trait more frequently associated with males than with females.

• *The model's behavior is relevant to the observer's situation.* Individuals are more likely to model behaviors that have functional value in their own circumstances (Rosenthal & Bandura, 1978; Schunk, 1987). For example, my daughter models many of

Models are often competent, prestigious, and powerful.

my behaviors, but she definitely does not model the way I dress. She has told me, in so many words, that she would be laughed out of town if she dressed the way I do.

Parents and teachers are among the people whom children most often model, particularly when those parents and teachers are seen as competent, respected, and powerful. Children also frequently model their behavior after famous personalities and fictional heroes. And children's peer groups—other children of the same gender and age—can be a source of powerful and influential models as well.

Yet characteristics of the model are not the only variables determining whether modeling takes place. Another important variable is the observer's self-efficacy, the topic to which we now turn.

SELF-EFFICACY

People are more likely to engage in certain behaviors when they believe they are capable of executing those behaviors successfully—that is, when they have high **self-efficacy** (Bandura, 1977a, 1982, 1986, 1989; Schunk, 1989b). For example, I hope you believe that you are capable of understanding and remembering the ideas I present in this book; in other words, I hope you have high self-efficacy for learning about learning. You may or may not believe that with instruction and practice you will eventually be able to perform a passable swan dive; in other words, you may have high or low self-efficacy about learning to dive. You are probably quite skeptical that you could ever walk barefoot over hot coals, so my guess is that you have low self-efficacy regarding this activity.

Self-efficacy is a concept similar to *self-esteem* but with one important difference. One's self-esteem tends to pervade a wide variety of activities; thus, people are described as having generally high or low self-esteem. Self-efficacy is more situation specific. For example, people may have high self-efficacy about reading a textbook about human learning but not about reading a textbook on neurosurgery. They may have high self-efficacy about learning to perform a swan dive but not about swimming the entire length of a swimming pool underwater. In one recent study, fifth graders had significantly higher self-efficacy about learning social studies than about learning mathematics (Stodolsky, Salk, & Glaessner, 1991).

How Self-Efficacy Affects Behavior

According to social learning theorists (e.g., Bandura, 1977a, 1982, 1986, 1989; Phillips & Zimmerman, 1990; Schunk, 1989c; Zimmerman, Bandura, & Martinez-Pons, 1992), people's feelings of self-efficacy affect several aspects of their behavior, including their choice of activities, their effort and persistence, and ultimately their learning and achievement.

Choice of Activities
People tend to choose tasks and activities at which they believe they can succeed; they also tend to avoid those at which they think they will fail. For example, students who believe they can succeed at mathematics are more likely to take math courses than students who believe they are mathematically incompetent. Those who believe they can win a role in the school play are more likely to try out for the play than students with little faith in their acting or singing abilities.

Effort and Persistence
People with a high sense of self-efficacy are more likely to exert effort in attempting to accomplish a task; they are also more likely to persist when they encounter obstacles. Students with low self-efficacy about a particular task put less effort into it and give up more quickly in the face of difficulty.

Learning and Achievement
Students with high self-efficacy tend to learn and achieve more than students with low self-efficacy, even when actual ability levels are the same (Assor & Connell, 1992; Bandura, 1986; Collins, 1982; Pajares, 1996; Schunk, 1989a; Zimmerman, Bandura, & Martinez-Pons, 1992). In other words, when several students have equal ability, students who *believe* they can do a task are more likely to accomplish it successfully than those who do not believe they are capable of success.

Factors in the Development of Self-Efficacy

Students usually hold fairly accurate opinions about their own self-efficacy: They typically have a good sense of what they can and cannot do (Bandura, 1986). But sometimes students seriously underestimate their chances of success, perhaps because of a few bad experiences (Phillips & Zimmerman, 1990). For example, a girl who gets a C in science from a teacher with exceptionally strict grading criteria may erroneously believe that she is "no good" in science. A new boy at school whose attempts at being friendly are rejected by two or three thoughtless classmates may erroneously believe that no one likes him.

According to social learning theorists (e.g., Bandura, 1986, 1989; Schunk, 1989a; Schunk, Hanson, & Cox, 1987), at least three factors affect the development of self-efficacy: one's own previous successes and failures, the messages that others communicate, and the successes and failures of others.

Previous Successes and Failures

Students feel more confident that they can succeed at a task—that is, they have greater self-efficacy—when they have succeeded at that task or at similar ones in the past (Bandura, 1986; Klein, 1990; Nicholls, 1984). For example, a student is more likely to believe he can learn to divide fractions if he has successfully mastered the process of multiplying fractions. Similarly, a student will be more confident about her ability to play field hockey if she has already developed skills in soccer.

Once students have developed a high sense of self-efficacy, an occasional failure is unlikely to have much effect on their optimism. In fact, when people encounter small setbacks on the way to achieving success, they learn that sustained effort and perseverance are key ingredients for that success; in other words, they develop what Bandura (1989) calls **resilient self-efficacy.** When students meet with *consistent* failure in performing a particular task, however, they tend to have little confidence in their ability to succeed at that task in the future. Each new failure confirms what they already "know" about the task—they can't do it.

It is not surprising, then, that students with a history of academic success have higher self-efficacy for academic tasks than students with lower school performance. For example, students with learning disabilities—students who typically have encountered failure after failure in classroom activities—often have low self-efficacy with regard to the things they study in school (Schunk, 1989c).

Messages from Others

To some extent, students' self-efficacy beliefs are enhanced when others provide assurances that success is possible. Statements such as "You can do this problem if you work at it" or "I'll bet Judy will play with you if you just ask her" give students a slight boost in self-confidence. This boost is short-lived, however, unless students' efforts at a task ultimately meet with success (Schunk, 1989a).

We should note, too, that the messages students receive are sometimes implied rather than directly stated, yet they can influence self-efficacy nonetheless. For example, by giving constructive criticism about how to improve a poorly written research paper—criticism that indirectly communicates the message that "I know you can do better, and here are some suggestions how"—a teacher may boost students' self-confidence about writing such research papers (Pintrich & Schunk, 1996). In some cases, actions speak louder than words. For example, the teacher who provides a great deal of assistance to a struggling student—more assistance than the student really needs—is communicating the message that "I don't think you can do this on your own" (Schunk, 1989b).

Successes and Failures of Others

People often acquire information about their own self-efficacy by observing the successes and failures of other individuals, especially those who seem to be similar to themselves (Schunk, 1983b, 1989c). As an example, students often consider the successes and failures of other students, especially those of similar ability, when appraising their own chances of success on academic tasks. Thus, seeing a classmate model a behavior successfully is often more effective than seeing an adult teacher do it. In one situation (Schunk & Hanson, 1985), elementary school children having difficulty with subtraction were given 25 subtraction problems to complete. Those who had seen another student successfully complete the problems got an average of 19 correct, whereas those who saw a teacher complete the problems got only 13 correct, and those who saw no model at all solved only 8!

At the same time, students should not become excessively dependent on other people as they strive to learn new things. Teachers cannot always be looking over students' shoulders to see what they are doing or to goad them into engaging in more appropriate and productive behaviors. Ultimately, students must begin to rely primarily on *themselves* for their own learning. Social learning theorists believe that people can and should ultimately regulate their own behavior. We therefore turn to a topic gaining increasing prominence in psychological and educational literature—the topic of *self-regulation.*

SELF-REGULATION

As social learning theory has evolved over the years, it has increasingly emphasized the role of **self-regulation** of behavior (Bandura, 1977b, 1982, 1986; Zimmerman, 1989). Through both direct and vicarious reinforcement and punishment, growing children gradually learn which behaviors are acceptable to the people around them and which are not. Eventually, they develop their *own* ideas about appropriate and inappropriate behavior, and they choose their actions accordingly. For example, my son Alex's bedroom used to be a disaster area; getting from the door to the bed was a matter of wading through several layers of toy trucks, building blocks, and little plastic people. Now, however, Alex keeps his bedroom immaculate even without any parental nagging, and he prides himself on his tidiness. (Tina's and Jeff's rooms still resemble the city landfill, but that's another story.)

Aspects of Self-Regulation

From the perspective of social learning theorists, self-regulation entails at least four components: setting standards and goals, self-observation, self-judgment, and self-reaction (Bandura, 1986; Schunk, 1989c, 1996b).

Setting Standards and Goals
As human beings, we tend to set standards for our own behavior; in other words, we establish criteria regarding what constitutes acceptable performance. We also establish certain goals that we value and toward which we direct many of our behaviors.

The kinds of performance standards that people establish for their own behavior depend to some degree on the standards they see other people adopt (Bandura, 1977b, 1986). In a study by Bandura and Kupers (1964), for example, children watched adult or child models reward themselves with candy and self-praise for their performance in a bowling game. Some of the children watched the models reward themselves only after achieving 20 points or more (reflecting very high performance); these models admonished themselves for lower performance. Other children observed models reward themselves after achieving as few as 10 points. All of the children then had the opportunity to play the game themselves and to help themselves to candy whenever they chose. Bandura and Kupers found that the children tended to reinforce themselves using performance standards very similar to those they had seen the models use.

People are most apt to adopt the kinds of standards that models similar to themselves in ability adopt (Bandura, 1977b). They are unlikely to adopt the standards of models who are much more competent (Bandura & Whalen, 1966) or who apply performance standards inconsistently (Bandura, 1977b).

Self-Observation

An important part of self-regulation is to observe oneself in action. To make progress toward important goals, people must be aware of how well they are doing at present; in other words, they must know what parts of their performance are working well and what parts need improvement.

Self-Judgment

People's behaviors are frequently judged by others, such as relatives, teachers, classmates, friends, and the general public. Eventually, people begin to judge and evaluate their *own* behaviors based on the standards they hold for themselves.

Self-Reaction

As people become increasingly self-regulated, they begin to reinforce themselves—perhaps by feeling proud or telling themselves that they did a good job—when they accomplish their goals. They also begin to punish themselves—perhaps by feeling sorry, guilty, or ashamed—when they do something that does not meet their own performance standards. Such self-praise and self-criticism can be as influential in altering behavior as the reinforcements and punishments that others administer (Bandura, 1977b, 1986).

To illustrate, consider Jason, a student who perceives himself to have average intelligence. Jason is likely to form standards for his own academic achievement that match the achievement of other "average" students; he is therefore likely to pat himself on the back for "B" work and to maintain a similar level of effort on future tasks. In contrast, consider Joanna, a student whose close friends are the high achievers of the class. If Joanna believes that her ability is similar to that of her friends, she is likely to adopt high standards for herself and to admonish herself for the same B-level achievement of which Jason is so proud. Provided that the B does not appreciably undermine her self-efficacy, Joanna is likely to try harder on the same task the next time around (Bandura, 1989).

Promoting Self-Regulation

Writing a textbook is a major undertaking. As I sit here in my basement tapping at the keys of my word processor day after day, I sometimes wonder why in the world I ever committed myself to such a project when I could instead be upstairs in my warm, comfortable living room reading mystery novels or watching television game shows. Yet each day I drag myself down to the basement to produce a few more pages. How do I do it? I do it by reinforcing myself every time I finish a small section of the book. For example, as soon as I finished the section on self-efficacy that you just read, I gave myself permission

The author engages in
self-regulation.

to go upstairs to watch my favorite game show. Before I can watch another one, though, I
need to finish this section on self-regulation.

A growing body of research provides several techniques for promoting self-regulation.
These techniques (sometimes called *self-control*[3] or *self-management*) include self-
instructions, self-monitoring, self-reinforcement, and self-imposed stimulus control.

Self-Instructions

One effective strategy is to teach learners to give themselves instructions that guide their
behavior (Mace, Belfiore, & Shea, 1989; Meichenbaum, 1985; Schunk, 1989c; Shaffer, 1988).
As one simple illustration, beginning tennis students improve the accuracy of their returns
when they give themselves these four verbal cues:

- "Ball" (to remind them to keep their eyes on the ball).
- "Bounce" (to continue tracking the path of the ball).
- "Hit" (to focus on contacting the ball with the racket).
- "Ready" (to get into position for the next ball) (Ziegler, 1987).

Other studies show self-instructions to be effective in helping students acquire more
effective approaches to academic tasks, develop better social skills, and keep their impul-
sive and aggressive behavior in check (Alberto & Troutman, 1990; Guevremont, Osnes, &
Stokes, 1988; Hughes, 1988; Leon & Pepe, 1983; Meichenbaum, 1977; Yell, 1993).

Meichenbaum (1977) has successfully used five steps in teaching children how to
give themselves instructions to guide their behavior:

1. *Cognitive modeling:* An adult model performs the desired task while verbalizing
   instructions that guide performance.

---

[3]Díaz, Neal, and Amaya-Williams (1990) distinguish between the terms *self-control* and *self-regulation*.
From their perspective, self-control involves complying with someone else's standards for appropriate
behavior even when the latter individual is absent. In contrast, self-regulation involves setting one's
own standards for appropriate behavior. Not all theorists make this distinction, however.

2. *Overt, external guidance:* The child performs the task while listening to the adult verbalize the instructions.

3. *Overt self-guidance:* The child repeats the instructions aloud while performing the task.

4. *Faded, overt self-guidance:* The child whispers the instructions while performing the task.

5. *Covert self-instruction:* The child silently thinks about the instructions while performing the task.

As you can see, then, the adult initially serves as a model not only for the behavior itself but also for self-instructions. Responsibility for performing the task *and* for guidance about how to perform the task is gradually turned over to the child.

Self-Monitoring

Another method that can help people control their own behavior is simply to have them observe and measure their own responses, just as someone else might measure those responses in traditional applied behavior analysis. The mere recording of responses is often enough to alter the frequency of a behavior. For example, my family was once part of a research project in which randomly selected households recorded their television-watching habits over a period of several weeks. We were instructed to mark down every instance of television viewing—including the date, time of day, length of time, and programs watched—on a specially designed record sheet. Each time I thought about turning on the television set, I remembered all of the work I would have to go through to record my viewing, and, as often as not, I found something else to do instead. Thus, the simple process of having to record my television-watching behavior altered that behavior.

Self-monitoring can be instituted in a classroom setting as well. For example, in one study (Harris, 1986) students having difficulty keeping their minds on their spelling assignments were given tape recorders that emitted a small beep at random intervals about 45 seconds apart. Whenever students heard a beep, they asked themselves, "Was I paying attention?" This simple technique doubled their time on task and tripled their productivity on spelling assignments. Other studies have obtained similar results in terms of increased on-task behavior and assignment completion (Hallahan, Marshall, & Lloyd, 1981; Harris, 1986; Heins, Lloyd, & Hallahan, 1986; Mace et al., 1989; Mace & Kratochwill, 1988; Webber et al., 1993; Yell, 1993).

Just as desirable behaviors can be increased, undesirable behaviors can be *de*creased through self-monitoring. For example, self-recording of a target behavior has been found to reduce such disruptive classroom behaviors as talking out of turn, leaving one's seat without permission, and hitting classmates (Bolstad & Johnson, 1972; Mace et al., 1989; Moletzsky, 1974; Webber et al., 1993; Yell, 1993).

Self-Reinforcement

People are often able to change their behavior by reinforcing themselves when they behave in a desired fashion and withholding reinforcement when they do not (Mace et al., 1989; Mahoney & Thoresen, 1974; O'Leary & O'Leary, 1972; Rimm & Masters, 1974). For example, I am able to maintain my book-writing behavior by applying the Premack principle with myself: I let myself engage in enjoyable activities only after I have completed less enjoyable ones.

When students learn to reinforce themselves for their accomplishments—perhaps by giving themselves some free time, helping themselves to a small treat, or simply praising themselves—their study habits and academic performance improve (Beneke & Harris, 1972; Greiner & Karoly, 1976; Hayes, Rosenfarb, Wulfert, Munt, Korn, & Zettle, 1985; Stevenson & Fantuzzo, 1986). In one research study (Stevenson & Fantuzzo, 1986), students who had been performing poorly in arithmetic were taught to give themselves points when they did well on their assignments; they could later use these points to "buy" a variety of items and privileges. Within a few weeks, these students were doing as well as their classmates on both in-class assignments and homework. In another study (Bandura & Perloff, 1967), self-reinforcement was just as effective in modifying student behaviors as reinforcement administered by a teacher.

Self-Imposed Stimulus Control

As you should recall from Chapter 4's discussion of operant conditioning, a response is under stimulus control when it is emitted in the presence of some stimuli but not in the presence of others. This idea can be translated into an effective means of promoting self-regulation (Mahoney & Thoresen, 1974); I call it self-imposed stimulus control. To increase a particular desired behavior, an individual might be instructed to seek out an environment in which that behavior is most likely to occur. For example, a student who wishes to increase the time actually spent studying each day should sit down at a table in the library rather than on a bed at home. Conversely, to decrease an undesired behavior, an individual should engage in that behavior only in certain situations. For example, I once knew a professor who, in an effort to stop smoking, gradually reduced the number of situations in which he permitted himself to smoke. Eventually, he was able to smoke in only one situation, facing a back corner of his office; at that point, he successfully stopped smoking.

We should note here that techniques designed to promote self-regulation work only when learners are motivated to change their own behavior. Under these circumstances, such techniques can help learners discover that they have some control, not only over their behavior, but over their environment as well (Heward, 1996). Two precautions must be taken, however. First, people being trained in self-regulation strategies must have the capability for performing the desired behaviors; for example, students who wish to modify their study habits will only achieve higher grades if they possess adequate academic skills to ensure success. Second, people must be cautioned not to expect too much of themselves too quickly. Many individuals would prefer overnight success, but shaping, either of oneself or of another, is usually a slow, gradual process. Just as the dieter will not lose 40 pounds in one week, it is equally unlikely that a habitually poor student will achieve honor roll status immediately. For self-regulation techniques to be effective, one's expectations for oneself must be practical and realistic.

Self-Regulation from a Cognitive Perspective

We have seen numerous indications that self-regulation involves cognitive processes as well as behavior. As a concrete example, in Meichenbaum's final step for teaching self-instructions, the learner does not verbalize, but merely *thinks* about, the instructions that a model has provided. More generally, such elements of self-regulation as setting standards for performance, self-judgment, and self-reaction (e.g., feeling proud or ashamed) are probably more cognitive than behavioral in nature.

In recent years psychologists have applied the concept of self-regulation more explicitly to the control of one's mental processes; in particular, they now talk about *self-regulated learning* as well as self-regulated behavior. For example, self-regulated learners set goals for a learning activity, choose study strategies that are likely to help them accomplish the goals, monitor their progress toward the goals, and change their study strategies if necessary (Winne, 1995a). We will talk more about self-regulated learning when we discuss metacognition and study strategies in Chapter 14.

EDUCATIONAL IMPLICATIONS OF SOCIAL LEARNING THEORY

Social learning theory has numerous implications for classroom practice. Let's look at some of the most important ones:

* *Students often learn a great deal simply by observing other people.* According to many behaviorists (B. F. Skinner as an example), people must make active responses for learning to occur. But in this chapter, I have presented examples of how learning can also occur through observations of what other people do. For instance, we have seen that children can acquire new skills, make moral judgments, and develop standards for their own behavior in large part by observing those around them.

Furthermore, people may learn what behaviors are and are not acceptable through their vicarious experiences—more specifically, by seeing others receive reinforcement or punishment for various responses. Teachers and other school personnel must therefore be consistent in the rewards and punishments they administer—not only from time to time but also from student to student.

* *Describing the consequences of behaviors can effectively increase appropriate behaviors and decrease inappropriate ones.* As you should recall, social learning theorists propose that reinforcement and punishment affect behavior only when people are consciously aware of response-consequence contingencies. Promises of rewards for good behaviors and warnings of punishments for misdeeds can therefore be effective means of improving student behavior. But administering reinforcement or punishment when students do not recognize the relationship between a particular response they have made and its consequence is unlikely to bring about behavior change.

* *Modeling provides an alternative to shaping for teaching new behaviors.* Operant conditioning provides one means—shaping—for teaching a new response. Remember, however, that to shape a particular behavior, one must begin by reinforcing an existing behavior and then gradually modifying that behavior through differential reinforcement; for complex behaviors, this process can be quite time-consuming. Social learning theory offers a faster, more efficient means for teaching new behavior: the modeling process.

To promote effective modeling, a teacher must make sure that four essential conditions exist: attention, retention, motor reproduction, and motivation. First of all, the teacher must make sure that students pay attention to the model and particularly to the relevant aspects of the model's behavior. Second, the teacher can facilitate students' retention of what they observe by helping them form appropriate memory codes (perhaps verbal labels or visual images) for their observations. Third, giving students opportunities to practice the behaviors they see and providing corrective feedback about their efforts will aid their motor reproduction of the responses they are modeling. Finally, the teacher must remember that students will display behaviors they have learned only if they have the motivation to do so. Many children are intrinsically motivated to perform, but others may require external incentives and reinforcers. (We will consider additional motivational strategies in Chapters 17 and 18.)

• *Teachers and parents must model appropriate behaviors and take care that they don't model inappropriate ones.* Teachers and parents often possess characteristics (e.g., competence, prestige, and power) that make them influential models for children. Adults must therefore be careful that they model appropriate behaviors for the children with whom they interact. I am delighted when I see teachers and other adults show characteristics such as open-mindedness, empathy, and concern for physical fitness; I cringe when I see them express disdain for particular points of view, disregard the needs and concerns of other human beings, or smoke cigarettes.

A child I know once tried out for a role in a school Christmas pageant. Lisa went off to school on the morning of pageant tryouts, aware that students could each try out for one part only and thinking that she had a good chance of winning the role of Mrs. Claus. Lisa was convinced that the teacher would award the leading role of Santa Claus to a girl named Ann; however, because Ann was late that morning and the teacher had announced that latecomers would not be allowed to try out, Lisa instead tried out for Santa himself. When Ann arrived 10 minutes late, the teacher disregarded her rule about latecomers being ineligible, allowed Ann to try out for Santa Claus, and ultimately awarded the role to Ann. In doing so, this teacher, one of the school's most visible role models, modeled both hypocrisy and favoritism.

As an educational psychologist who helps future teachers learn how to teach, my job is particularly difficult because I must practice what I preach. If I tell my students that immediate feedback, organization of information, vivid examples, hands-on experiences, and assessment practices that match instructional objectives are all important components of effective teaching, my students' learning will obviously be enhanced when I model all of those things as well. To say one thing but do another would not only be hypocritical, but also counterproductive.

• *Teachers should expose students to a variety of other models.* Adult models need not be limited to children's teachers and parents. Other adults can be invited to visit classrooms on occasion; for example, police officers, prominent city officials, business people, and nurses might demonstrate appropriate behaviors and attitudes related to safety, good citizenship, responsibility, and health. Symbolic models can also be effective; for example, studying the lives of such individuals as Helen Keller, Martin Luther King Jr., and Eleanor Roosevelt is a viable method of illustrating many desirable behaviors.

Models don't just demonstrate appropriate behaviors. Carefully chosen ones can also help break down traditional stereotypes regarding what different groups of people can and cannot do. For example, teachers might introduce students to male nurses, female engineers, African-American physicians, Hispanic business executives, or athletes who are wheelchair bound. By exposing students to successful individuals of both genders, from many cultural and socioeconomic backgrounds, and with a variety of physical disabilities, teachers can help students realize that they themselves may also have the potential to accomplish great things.

• *Students must believe that they are capable of accomplishing school tasks.* As we have seen, students' self-efficacy affects their learning and academic achievement. Yet students are likely to differ widely in their confidence about performing tasks successfully. For example, at the adolescent level, boys are likely to have higher self-efficacy than girls with regard to mathematics and sports; meanwhile, girls are likely to have higher self-efficacy than boys for assignments in an English class (Wigfield, Eccles, & Pintrich, 1996).

To enhance students' self-efficacy related to school activities, teachers can make use of three circumstances that appear to promote greater self-efficacy: receiving confidence-building messages from others, watching others be successful, and experiencing success oneself. For instance, teachers can tell students that children similar to themselves have mastered the things they are learning. They might also have students actually observe their peers successfully accomplishing tasks; it may be especially beneficial for students to see a peer struggling with a task or problem at first—something they themselves are likely to do—and then eventually mastering it (Hughes, 1988; Schunk et al., 1987). But teachers best help students develop high self-efficacy when they enable the students to be successful themselves, such as by teaching important basic skills to mastery and providing guidance and support for complex, challenging tasks.

• *Teachers should help students set realistic expectations for their academic accomplishments.* As growing children become increasingly self-regulating, they begin to adopt standards for their own behavior. Such standards are often based on those that people around them have adopted, and so they may in some cases be either overly optimistic or overly pessimistic (Paris & Cunningham, 1996; Phillips & Zimmerman, 1990; Pintrich & Schunk, 1996). When a student's standards for performance are unrealistically high, as might be true for a perfectionist, continual disappointment and frustration are likely to result. Yet when a student's standards are too low, underachievement will be the outcome. Teachers can facilitate students' academic and social progress by helping them form self-expectations commensurate with their current skills and ability levels.

• *Self-regulation techniques provide effective methods for improving student behavior.* Earlier in the chapter, I described four techniques for promoting self-regulation: self-instructions, self-monitoring, self-reinforcement, and self-imposed stimulus control. When students are intrinsically motivated to change their own behaviors, such techniques can provide a viable alternative to behaviorist approaches.

As social learning theorists have so clearly shown, we cannot ignore the social context of the classroom. Students can and do learn from the models—parents, teachers, and peers—they see every day. Social learning theorists have also made it clear that we must consider cognitive as well as environmental factors when trying to explain how human beings learn and behave. As we move into cognitivism in the next chapter, we will begin to focus on such cognitive factors even more closely.

SUMMARY

Social learning theory focuses on the ways in which individuals learn from observing one another. This perspective reflects a blending of behaviorist concepts (e.g., reinforcement and punishment) and cognitive notions (e.g., awareness and expectations). Environmental and cognitive variables interact with one another and with behavior in a manner referred to as reciprocal causation.

Many behaviors, beliefs, and attitudes are acquired through modeling; aggression and morality are but two examples. Four conditions are necessary for modeling to occur: attention, retention, motor reproduction, and motivation. Effective models are likely to be competent, prestigious, and powerful and to exhibit behaviors that are "gender appropriate" and relevant to the observer's own situation.

Individuals with high self-efficacy—those who believe they can successfully accomplish a particular task—are more likely to choose challenging activities, exert effort and persist at those activities, and show higher learning and achievement over the long run. Self-efficacy can be enhanced through encouraging messages, successes of others, and, most importantly, one's *own* successes.

Social learning theorists propose that, although the environment influences behavior, over time people begin to regulate their own behavior; they do so by developing their own standards for performance, observing and judging themselves on the basis of those standards, and reinforcing or punishing themselves (even if just mentally and emotionally) for what they have or have not done. Teachers can help their students become more self-regulating by teaching such techniques as self-instructions, self-monitoring, self-reinforcement, and self-imposed stimulus control.

Social learning theory has numerous implications for educational practice. For example, when instruction involves teaching new skills, modeling provides an effective alternative to operant conditioning techniques. Describing response-reinforcement and response-punishment contingencies makes students aware of what those contingencies are; hence, such descriptions can affect behavior before any consequences are ever imposed. And promoting high self-efficacy is one means through which teachers can promote students' school success.

CHAPTER 8

Antecedents and Assumptions of Cognitivism

Since the 1960s cognitivism (also known as *cognitive psychology*) has provided the predominant perspective within which learning research has been conducted and theories of learning have evolved. As we begin to explore this perspective, you will undoubtedly notice a change in emphasis. In earlier chapters, we focused largely on the roles of environmental conditions (stimuli) and observable behaviors (responses) in learning, although social learning theory also provided a brief window into such mental phenomena as attention, expectations, and self-efficacy. At this point, we begin to look more directly at **cognitive processes,** considering how people perceive, interpret, remember, and otherwise think about the environmental events they experience.

As you should recall, early behaviorists chose not to incorporate mental events into their learning theories, arguing that such events were impossible to observe and measure and so could not be studied objectively. During the 1950s and 1960s, however, many psychologists became increasingly dissatisfied with such a "thoughtless" approach to human learning. Major works with a distinctly cognitive flavor began to emerge; publications by Noam Chomsky (1957) in psycholinguistics and by Bruner, Goodnow, and Austin (1956) in concept learning are examples. Ulric Neisser's *Cognitive Psychology,* published in 1967, was a landmark book that helped to legitimize cognitive theory as a major alternative to behaviorism (Calfee, 1981). Increasingly, cognitivism began appearing in educational psychology literature as well, with Jerome Bruner (1961a, 1961b, 1966) and David Ausubel (1963, 1968; Ausubel & Robinson, 1969) being two well-known early proponents. By the 1970s the great majority of learning theorists had joined the cognitive bandwagon.

Yet the roots of cognitive psychology preceded the mass discontentment with strict S-R psychology by several decades. Some cognitive learning theories appeared in the 1920s and 1930s, notably those of the American psychologist Edward Tolman, the Gestalt psychologists of Germany, the Swiss developmentalist Jean Piaget, and the Russian developmentalist Lev Vygotsky. These early theories have had considerable influence on contemporary cognitivism, and Piaget's and Vygotsky's theories in particular continue to provide dominant perspectives for developmental research.

Equally important to the cognitive movement was research conducted during the 1930s to 1960s in an area known as *verbal learning.* Verbal learning theorists originally attempted to apply a stimulus-response analysis to human language and verbal behavior, but they soon discovered that the complexities of human language–based learning were sometimes difficult to explain from the behaviorist perspective. Increasingly, verbal learning theorists began to incorporate cognitive processes into their explanations of research results.

In this chapter, we will consider some of the contributions of Tolman, the Gestaltists, Piaget, Vygotsky, and the verbal learning theorists. We will then look at the basic assumptions of contemporary cognitivism and at several specific theoretical perspectives that cognitivists advocate. Finally, we will identify some general educational implications of the cognitive perspective.

EDWARD TOLMAN'S PURPOSIVE BEHAVIORISM

Edward Chace Tolman (1932, 1938, 1942, 1959) was a prominent learning theorist during the heyday of behaviorism, yet his work had a distinctly cognitive flair. Like his behaviorist contemporaries, Tolman valued the importance of objectivity in conducting research and used nonhuman species (especially rats) as the subjects of his research. Unlike his contemporaries, however, Tolman included internal mental phenomena in his explanations of how learning occurs and adopted a more holistic view of learning than was true of S-R theorists.

Tolman developed his mentalistic view of learning by using some rather ingenious adaptations of traditional behaviorist research methods. We will see some examples of his approach as, in the next few pages, we consider the central ideas of his theory.

• *Behavior should be studied at a molar level.* Early theorists in the behaviorist tradition, such as Pavlov, Thorndike, and Watson, attempted to reduce behavior to simple stimulus-response connections. In contrast, Tolman was adamant in his position that more global (molar) behaviors are the appropriate objects of study. Tolman argued that breaking behavior down into isolated S-R reflexes, rather than looking at it in its totality, obscures the meaning and purpose of that behavior.

• *Learning can occur without reinforcement.* Tolman opposed the behaviorist idea that reinforcement is necessary for learning to occur, and he conducted several experiments to support his contention. As an example, let's look at a study by Tolman and Honzik (1930) in which three groups of rats ran a difficult maze under different reinforcement conditions. Group 1 rats were reinforced with food each time they successfully completed the maze. Group 2 rats received no reinforcement for successful performance. Group 3 rats were not reinforced during the first 10 days in the maze but began receiving reinforcement on the 11th day.

Before we examine the results of this experiment, let's predict what should have happened in this situation if reinforcement was an essential condition for learning to occur. Because group 1 rats were continuously reinforced, we would expect their performance to improve over time. Because group 2 rats were *not* reinforced, we would expect their performance to stay at a constant low level. And we would expect the rats in group 3 to show no improvement in performance until after day 11, at which point they should show a pattern of behavior similar to the group 1 rats' first few days of performance.

The actual results of the Tolman and Honzik experiment appear in Figure 8-1. Notice that the performance of groups 2 and 3 improved somewhat even when they were not receiving reinforcement. Notice also that once the rats in group 3 began receiving reinforcement, their performance in the maze equaled (in fact, it surpassed!) group 1's performance. Apparently, group 3 rats had learned as much as group 1 rats despite their lack of

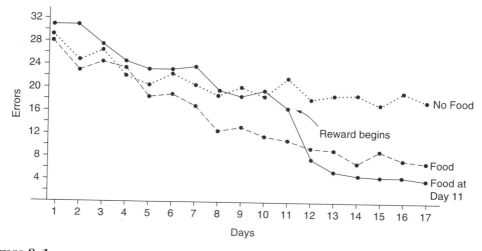

Figure 8–1

Maze performance of rats receiving food, no food, or food at day 11.

Adapted from "Introduction and Removal of Reward, and Maze Performance in Rats" by E. C. Tolman & C. H. Honzik, 1930, *University of California Publications in Psychology, 4,* p. 267. Copyright 1930 by University of California Press. Adapted with permission.

reinforcement during the first 10 days. Such results cast doubt on Thorndike's law of effect: Perhaps reinforcement is not as critical a factor in learning as behaviorists have suggested.

• *Learning can occur without a change in behavior.* While behaviorists have historically equated learning with behavior changes, Tolman argued that learning can occur *without* being reflected in a change in behavior, using the term **latent learning** for such unobservable learning. The Tolman and Honzik study just described provides an example of latent learning: Group 3 rats must have been learning just as much as group 1 rats during the first 10 days, even though their behavior did not reflect such learning. (Presumably, group 2 rats were also learning more than they let on.) Tolman proposed that reinforcement influences *performance* rather than learning, in that it increases the likelihood that a learned behavior will be exhibited. (As we noted in the preceding chapter, social learning theorists have more recently come to conclusions similar to those of Tolman, proposing that learning can occur without a change in behavior and that reinforcement increases the likelihood that people will demonstrate what they have learned.)

• *Intervening variables must be considered.* As you may recall from Chapter 2, Clark Hull incorporated **intervening variables** into his theory of learning, arguing that such variables as drive, habit strength, and incentive play critical roles. The concept of intervening variables did not originate with Hull, however; as early as 1932, Tolman proposed that variables within the organism (e.g., cognitions and physiological states) affect the behaviors observed. Thus, with Tolman's work, we have an early concern for *individual differences* in the learning process, a concern that continues in contemporary cognitivism.

• *Behavior is purposive.* Tolman believed that learning should be viewed not as the formation of S-R connections but as a process of learning that certain events lead to other events (e.g., that following a particular path through a maze leads to reinforcement). He proposed that once an organism has learned that a behavior produces a certain goal, the organism behaves in order to achieve that goal. In other words, behavior has a *purpose,* that of goal attainment. Because Tolman stressed the goal-directed nature of behavior, his theory of learning is often referred to as **purposive behaviorism.**

• *Expectations affect behavior.* According to Tolman, once an organism learns that certain behaviors produce certain kinds of results, it begins to form expectations about the outcomes of its behaviors. Rather than reinforcement affecting the response that it follows, the organism's *expectation* of reinforcement affects the response that it *precedes.* (Once again, we see a similarity with social learning theory.)

When an organism's expectations are not met, its behavior may be adversely affected. For example, in an experiment by Elliott (cited in Tolman, 1932), rats received one of two different reinforcers for running a maze: An experimental group received a favorite rat delicacy—bran mash—whereas a control group received relatively unenticing sunflower seeds. The experimental group ran the maze faster than the control group, apparently because they were expecting a yummier treat at the end of the maze. On the 10th day, the experimental group rats were switched to the sunflower seed reinforcement that the control group rats had been getting all along. After discovering the change in reinforcement, these rats began to move through the maze more slowly than they had previously, and even more slowly than the control rats. Since both groups were being reinforced identically at this point (i.e., with boring sunflower seeds), the inferior performance of the rats in the experimental group was apparently due to the change in reinforcement, resulting in a *depression effect* similar to what I described in Chapter 4. As Tolman might put it, the rats' expectation of reinforcement was no longer being confirmed. As you or I might say, the rats were very disappointed with the treat awaiting them.

• *Learning results in an organized body of information.* Through a series of studies, Tolman demonstrated that rats who run a maze learn more than just a set of independent responses. It appears that they also learn how the maze is arranged—the lay of the land, so to speak. For example, in a classic study by Tolman, Ritchie, and Kalish (1946), rats ran numerous times through a maze that looked like maze 1 of Figure 8–2. They were then put in a situation similar to maze 2 of Figure 8–2. Since the alley that had previously led to food was now blocked, the rats had to choose among 18 other alleys. Using S-R theory's notion of stimulus generalization, we would expect the rats to make their running response to a stimulus very similar to the blocked alley. We would therefore predict that the rats would choose alleys near the blocked one—particularly alley 9 or alley 10. However, few of the rats chose either of these routes. By far the most common choice was alley 6, the one that presumably would provide a shortcut to the location in which the rats had come to expect food.

Based on such research, Tolman proposed that rats (and other organisms as well) develop **cognitive maps** of their environments: They learn where different parts of the environment are situated in relation to one another. Knowing how things are organized in space enables an organism to get from one place to another quickly and easily, often by the shortest possible route. The concept of a cognitive map (sometimes called a mental

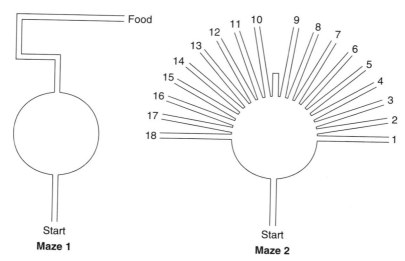

Figure 8–2
Mazes used by Tolman, Ritchie, and Kalish (1946).

map) has continued to be a focus of research for contemporary researchers—psychologists and geographers alike (e.g., Downs & Stea, 1977).

Tolman's notion of a cognitive map reflects his belief that learning is *organized:* Rats integrate their experiences into an organized body of information from which they can then draw inferences (e.g., about shortest routes). In developing his views about the organized nature of what organisms learn, Tolman was influenced by the ideas of the Gestalt psychologists of Germany. It is to Gestalt psychology that we now turn.

GESTALT PSYCHOLOGY

During the early decades of the twentieth century, a perspective emerged in German psychology that was largely independent of behaviorism-dominated American psychology. This perspective, known as **Gestalt psychology,** was advanced by such theorists as Max Wertheimer (1912, 1945, 1959), Wolfgang Köhler (1925, 1929, 1938, 1940, 1947, 1959, 1969), and Kurt Koffka (1935). Gestalt psychologists emphasized the importance of organizational processes in perception, learning, and problem solving and believed that individuals were predisposed to organize information in particular ways. Following are some of the most basic ideas of Gestalt psychology:

• *Perception is often different from reality.* The origin of Gestalt psychology is usually attributed to Wertheimer's (1912) description and analysis of an optical illusion known as the **phi phenomenon.** Wertheimer observed that when two lights blink on and off sequentially at a particular rate, they often appear to be only one light moving quickly back and forth. (This effect can be observed in the blinking lights of many roadside signs.) The fact that an individual "sees" motion when observing stationary objects led Wertheimer to conclude that perception of an experience is sometimes different from the experience itself.

• *The whole is more than the sum of its parts.* Gestaltists believed that human experience cannot be successfully understood when various aspects of experience are studied in isolation from one another. For example, the illusion of movement in the *phi* phenomenon is perceived only when two or more lights are present; no motion is perceived in a single light. A combination of elements may show a pattern not evident in any of the elements alone; to use a Gestaltist expression, the whole is more than the sum of its parts.

The importance of the interrelationships among elements in a situation can be seen in Köhler's (1929) **transposition** experiments with chickens. Hens were shown two sheets of gray paper, one a darker shade of gray than the other. Grain was placed on both sheets, but the hens were only allowed to feed from the darker one. On a subsequent occasion, the hens were shown a sheet of paper the same shade as that on which they had previously been fed, along with a sheet of an even darker shade. In this second situation, the hens tended to go to the darker of the two sheets—in other words, to one on which they had *not* previously been reinforced. The hens had apparently learned something about the relationship between the two sheets of paper; in a sense, they learned that darker is better.

• *The organism structures and organizes experience.* The German word *Gestalt,* roughly translated, means "structured whole." Structure is not necessarily inherent in a

Figure 8–3

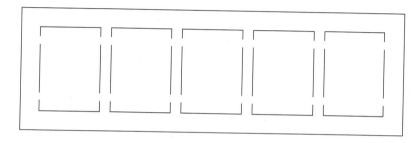

Figure 8–4

situation; instead, the organism imposes structure and organization on that situation. For example, the *phi* phenomenon represents a person's synthesis of two flashing lights into the perception of a single moving light.

Figure 8-3 provides another example of how experiences are organized. As you look at this figure, you probably perceive four pairs of lines with individual lines at each end. Yet turn your attention to Figure 8-4, in which the same lines appear within a particular context. You probably now see the lines differently—as five pairs forming the sides of five rectangles. The lines themselves are identical in both cases, but the way in which you organize them (i.e., which lines you group together) is different. The "structure" of the lines is something that you yourself impose on the figure.

• *The organism is predisposed to organize experience in particular ways.* Gestaltists believed that organisms are predisposed to structure their experiences in similar, and therefore predictable, ways. They proposed several principles to describe how people organize their experiences. One of the dominant principles affecting how people organize information is the **law of proximity**: People tend to perceive as a unit those things that are close together in space. For example, look at the following dots:

Not only do you see nine dots, you probably also perceive an arrangement of three groups of three dots each; that is, you see those dots that are in closer proximity to one another as somehow belonging together. In the same way, when you looked at Figure 8-3, you perceived lines that were close together as forming pairs. And notice how you read this phrase:

One very high way

Figure 8–5   ○ ○ ● ○ ○   **Figure 8–6**   ● ○ ○ ○ ●
                 ○ ● ○ ○ ○   ○ ● ○ ● ○
                 ○ ○ ○ ○ ●   ○ ○ ● ○ ○
                 ● ○ ● ○ ○   ○ ○ ● ○ ○
                 ○ ○ ● ○ ●   ○ ○ ● ○ ○

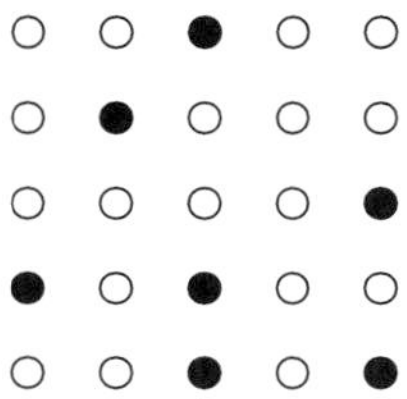

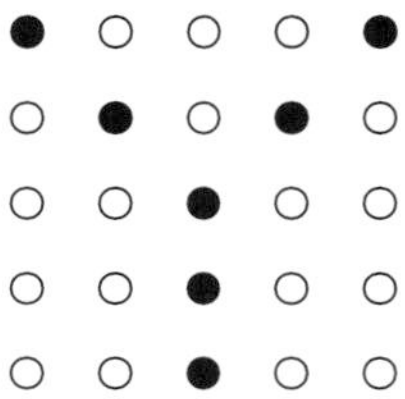

and this one:

On every highway

In both phrases, the same letters appear in exactly the same sequence:

Oneveryhighway

Yet because of the different ways the letters are grouped together, you read the phrases differently.

Another organizational principle from Gestalt psychology is the **law of similarity:** People tend to perceive as a unit those things that are similar to one another. For example, look at the dots in Figure 8-5. Can you see the letter *Y* among them? Perhaps not. But now look at the dots in Figure 8-6. This time a letter *Y* is obvious. The arrangement of the dots in both cases is the same, but in the second case the dots forming the *Y* are all black, and you tend to perceive those similar black dots as a unit. Yet you probably haven't noticed other letters, such as the letter *E,* that are also formed by some of the dots.

Still another Gestaltist principle is the **law of closure:** People tend to fill in missing pieces to form a complete picture. For example, when you looked at Figure 8-4, you filled in missing segments of what appeared to be continuous straight lines to perceive five rectangles. Similarly, when you look at Figure 8-7, you are probably able to read "Singing in the rain," even though 50% of the print is missing. You simply fill in what isn't there.

Gestaltists further proposed that individuals always organize their experience as simply, concisely, symmetrically, and completely as possible, a principle known as the **law of Prägnanz** ("terseness" or "preciseness") (Koffka, 1935). For example, you are likely to see rectangles in Figure 8-4 because rectangles are simple, symmetric figures. It is unlikely that you would mentally fill in the missing pieces of that figure in a wild and crazy fashion such as that shown in Figure 8-8. People are very simple folks, after all!

• *Learning follows the law of Prägnanz.* According to Gestalt psychologists, learning involves the formation of **memory traces.** These memory traces are subject to the law of Prägnanz, so that over time they tend to become simpler, more concise, and more complete than the actual input. For example, after seeing the somewhat irregular objects in Figure 8-9, people are likely to remember them later as being a "circle" and a "square." As another example, consider a study by Tversky (1981), in which people studied maps and then drew them from memory. Distortions in people's reproductions often followed the law of Prägnanz: Curvy, irregular lines were straightened, slanted lines were represented as north-south or east-west lines, and map features were placed in better alignment with one another than they had been in the original maps.

Figure 8–7

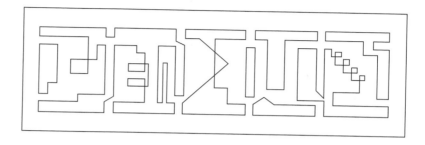

Figure 8–8

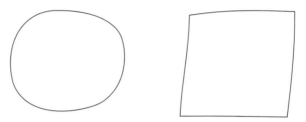

Figure 8–9
Irregularly shaped
objects may later be
remembered as
"circles" or "squares."

• *Problem solving involves restructuring and insight.* As we noted in Chapter 2, the American psychologist Edward Thorndike (1898) had previously described problem solving (such as that exhibited by cats in puzzle boxes) as a process of trial and error. Gestaltists proposed a very different view of how organisms solve problems. Köhler (1925), for instance, suggested that problem solving involves mentally combining and recombining the various elements of a problem until a structure that solves the problem is achieved. He described numerous observations of chimpanzees solving problems through what he perceived to be the mental manipulation of the problem situation. In one situation, a chimpanzee named Sultan was faced with a dilemma: Some fruit was placed far enough outside his cage that he could not reach it. Sultan had had earlier experiences in which he had successfully used sticks to rake in fruit; however, the only stick inside the cage was too short. A longer stick was outside the cage, but, like the fruit, was beyond Sultan's reach. The following scenario ensued:

> Sultan tries to reach the fruit with the smaller of the two sticks. Not succeeding, he tears at a piece of wire that projects from the netting of his cage, but that, too, in vain. Then he gazes about him (there are always in the course of these tests some long pauses during which the animals scrutinize the whole visible area). He suddenly picks up the little stick, once more goes up to the bars, directly opposite to the long stick, scratches it towards him with the [short stick], seizes it, and goes with it to the point opposite the [fruit],

which he secures. From the moment that his eyes fall upon the long stick, his procedure forms one consecutive whole, without hiatus.... (Köhler, 1925, p. 180)

In another situation, Sultan, again confronted with fruit placed outside the cage beyond his reach, had two hollow bamboo rods, one somewhat thinner than the other, and both too short to reach the fruit. After numerous "fruitless" attempts, he seemingly gave up and resorted to playing indifferently with the sticks. At one serendipitous point, Sultan found himself holding the two sticks end to end in such a way that they appeared to form a long, straight line. Immediately he pushed the end of the thinner stick into the end of the thicker one (thus making a single long stick), ran over to the edge of the cage, and successfully obtained the elusive bananas.

In neither of the situations I have just described did Sultan engage in the random trial-and-error learning that Thorndike had observed for cats. Instead, it appeared to Köhler as if Sultan thought about possible solutions to the problem, arranging the problem elements in various ways, until he arrived at a sudden **insight** as to a problem solution.

Gestalt psychology continues to influence how cognitive psychologists conceptualize learning and cognition (e.g., Henle, 1985). For example, we will see *closure* at work when we examine constructive processes in perception and memory in Chapters 10 and 12. We will revisit the Gestaltist idea of *insight* in our exploration of problem solving in Chapter 15. And the general idea that people organize the things that they learn will come up repeatedly in our discussion of learning and cognition in the chapters to come.

JEAN PIAGET'S DEVELOPMENTAL THEORY

Independent of Tolman's work in the United States and of the Gestalt movement in Germany, the Swiss biologist Jean Piaget began a research program during the 1920s that has probably had a greater impact on contemporary theories of cognitive development than that of any other single researcher. Piaget had interests in philosophy as well as biology and was particularly curious about the origins of knowledge, a branch of philosophy known as *epistemology*. To discover where knowledge comes from and the forms it takes as it develops, Piaget and his colleagues undertook a series of studies that provided some unique insights into how children think and learn about the world around them (Inhelder & Piaget, 1958; Piaget, 1928, 1952, 1959, 1970, 1971, 1972, 1980; Piaget & Inhelder, 1969).

Although Piaget's theory dates from the 1920s, its impact on psychological thought in the western hemisphere was not widely felt until the 1960s, probably for several reasons. One likely reason is that Piaget, being Swiss, wrote in French, making his early work less accessible to English-speaking psychologists. Although his writings were eventually translated into English, Piaget's ideas gained widespread prominence and visibility largely through a summary of his early work written by the American psychologist John Flavell (1963).

A second reason that the Geneva research program was largely overlooked for more than three decades was Piaget's unconventional research methodology. Piaget employed what he called the **clinical method:** He gave children a variety of tasks and problems, asking a series of questions about each one. He tailored his interviews to the particular responses that the children gave, with follow-up questions varying from one child to the next. Such a procedure was radically different from the standardized, tightly controlled conditions typical of behaviorist animal research and was therefore unacceptable to many of Piaget's contemporaries in North America.

But perhaps the most critical reason that Piaget's theory did not immediately become part of the mainstream of psychological thought was its philosophical incompatibility with the behaviorist perspective that dominated the study of learning until the 1960s. Piaget focused on mental events—for example, on logical reasoning processes and the structure of knowledge—at a time when such mentalism was still being rejected by most other learning theorists. The cognitivism that began to emerge in the 1960s was more receptive to Piagetian ideas.

Piaget's work is probably so popular today because it is the single most global theory of intellectual development; it incorporates such diverse topics as language, logical reasoning, moral judgments, and conceptions of time, space, and number. In addition, Piaget's unique studies with children, often involving cleverly designed problem situations, reveal a great deal about the nature of children's thought. In the next few pages, we will look at Piagetian ideas that are especially relevant to our understanding of human learning and cognition.

• *People are active processors of information.* Whereas behaviorists portrayed organisms, including humans, as passive respondents to environmental conditions, Piaget portrayed human beings as being *actively involved* in interpreting and learning from the events around them. Rather than just responding to the stimuli around them, people manipulate those stimuli and observe the effects of their actions. For example, consider Piaget's observation of his son Laurent at 16 months of age:

> Laurent is seated before a table and I place a bread crust in front of him, out of reach. Also, to the right of the child I place a stick about 25 cm. long. At first Laurent tries to grasp the bread without paying attention to the instrument, and then he gives up. I then put the stick between him and the bread. . . . Laurent again looks at the bread, without moving, looks very briefly at the stick, then suddenly grasps it and directs it toward the bread. But he grasped it toward the middle and not at one of its ends so that it is too short to attain the objective. Laurent then puts it down and resumes stretching out his hand toward the bread. Then, without spending much time on this movement, he takes up the stick again, this time at one of its ends . . . and draws the bread to him.
>
> An hour later I place a toy in front of Laurent (out of his reach) and a new stick next to him. He does not even try to catch the objective with his hand; he immediately grasps the stick and draws the toy to him. (Piaget, 1952, p. 335)

In this situation, Laurent is acting on his environment; he is obviously experimenting with the elements of the situation to see what outcomes he can achieve. (You may have noticed a similarity between Laurent's behavior and that of the chimpanzee Sultan that I described earlier in the chapter. Sultan, too, was an active problem solver rather than a passive respondent to environmental events.)

• *Knowledge can be described in terms of structures that change with development.* Piaget proposed the concept of **scheme** as being the basic structure through which an individual's knowledge is mentally represented. Although Piaget's notion of scheme is somewhat abstract, it can be roughly defined as a mental unit that represents a class of similar actions or thoughts. For example, an infant might have a scheme for grasping and use it for grabbing everything from bottles to rubber ducks. A teenager may have certain schemes related to logical thinking that might be applied to reasoning about a variety of social, political, or moral issues. As children develop, new schemes emerge, and existing schemes are modified and sometimes integrated with one another into **cognitive structures.** A good deal of Piaget's theory focused on the development of the cognitive structures that govern logical reasoning—structures that Piaget called **operations.**

• *Cognitive development results from the interactions that children have with their physical and social environments.* By interacting with the environment, growing children develop and modify schemes. For example, in the anecdote involving Laurent that I presented earlier, we see a toddler actively manipulating parts of his physical environment—more specifically, manipulating the stick and bread—and presumably learning that some objects can be used as tools to obtain other objects. Equally essential to children's development is their interaction with other people. For example, Piaget described young children as being **egocentric**—as having difficulty understanding that others don't share their perspective of the world. Through social interactions, both positive (e.g., conversations) and negative (e.g., conflicts over such issues as sharing and fair play), children begin to discover that they hold a perspective of the world uniquely their own.

• *The processes through which people interact with the environment remain constant.* According to Piaget, people interact with their environment through two unchanging processes (**functions**) known as assimilation and accommodation. In **assimilation,** an individual interacts with an object or event in a way that is consistent with an existing scheme. For example, the infant who sees Mama's flashy, dangling earrings may assimilate those earrings to his grasping scheme, clutching and pulling at them in much the same way that he grasps bottles. A second grader who has developed a scheme for adding two apples and three apples to make five apples may apply this scheme to the addition of two dollars and three dollars. In **accommodation,** an individual either modifies an existing scheme or forms a new one to account for a new event. For example, an infant who has learned to crawl must adjust her style of crawling somewhat when she meets a flight of stairs. A boy who calls a spider an "insect" must revise his thinking when he learns that insects have six legs but spiders have eight.

Assimilation and accommodation are complementary processes: Assimilation involves modifying one's perception of the environment to fit a scheme, and accommodation involves modifying a scheme to fit the environment. According to Piaget, these two processes typically go hand in hand, with individuals interpreting new events within the context of their existing knowledge (assimilation) but also modifying their knowledge as a result of those events (accommodation).

Learning results from the conjoint processes of assimilation and accommodation. Learning is especially reflected in the process of accommodation, because it is through accommodation that major cognitive changes occur. An environmental event cannot lead to accommodation of schemes, however, unless that event can be related (assimilated) to those schemes in the first place. For example, consider this sentence:

> *D.O. Hebb proposed that learning is a process of developing cell assemblies and phase sequences.*

Unless you know who D.O. Hebb is, and unless you are familiar with the concepts of *cell assembly* and *phase sequence,* you can learn very little from the sentence. Assimilation is almost always a necessary condition for accommodation to occur: You must be able to relate a new experience to what you already know before you can learn from it. This necessity for overlap between prior knowledge and the material to be learned is an important principle not only in Piagetian theory but in contemporary cognitive views of learning as well.

• *People are intrinsically motivated to try to make sense of the world around them.* According to Piaget, people are sometimes in a state of **equilibrium**; they can comfortably explain new events in terms of their existing schemes. But this equilibrium doesn't continue indefinitely, because people sometimes encounter new events that they cannot adequately explain in terms of their current understanding of the world. Such inexplicable events create **disequilibrium,** a "mental discomfort" of sorts. Only through replacing, reorganizing, or better integrating their schemes (in other words, through accommodation) do people become able to understand and explain previously puzzling phenomena. The movement from equilibrium to disequilibrium and back to equilibrium again is known as **equilibration**—a process that promotes increasingly more complex levels of thought and knowledge.

• *Cognitive development occurs in distinct stages, with thought processes at each stage being qualitatively different from those at other stages.* A major feature of Piaget's theory is the identification of four distinct stages of cognitive development, each with its own unique patterns of thought. The schemes of each stage are modified and incorporated into the schemes of the following stage, thereby providing a foundation for that next stage. As a result, children progress through the four stages in the same, invariant sequence. The characteristics of Piaget's four stages are more completely described in other secondary sources (e.g., see Flavell, 1963; Flavell, Miller, & Miller, 1993; Sund, 1976; Wadsworth, 1989), but I will discuss them briefly here.

The first stage, the **sensorimotor stage,** is evident from birth until about two years of age (the exact ages of each stage vary from child to child). Much of the sensorimotor stage is characterized by behavior- and perception-based schemes, rather than by internal, mental schemes that we might think of as being "thought." According to Piaget, infants do not yet possess schemes that enable them to think about objects other than those directly in front of them; in other words, the expression "out of sight, out of mind" definitely applies. Near the end of the sensorimotor stage, however, **symbolic thinking**—the ability to represent external objects and events in terms of internal, mental symbols— emerges, marking the beginning of true thought as Piaget defined it.

The second stage, which Piaget called the **preoperational stage,** emerges when children are about two years old and continues until they are about six or seven. Language skills virtually explode during this stage; the words in children's rapidly increasing vocabularies reflect the many new mental schemes that they are developing. However, the preoperational stage is characterized by thinking that is often illogical by adult standards. For example, young children tend to confuse psychological phenomena (e.g., thoughts and emotions) with physical reality, a confusion manifested by such actions as attributing feelings to inanimate objects and insisting that monsters and bogeymen are lurking under the bed.

A commonly cited example of the illogical thinking of preoperational children is their reaction to a **conservation of liquid** problem. Imagine three glasses: Glasses A and B are tall, thin, and filled to equal heights with water, while glass C is short, fat, and empty, as is shown in the "before" part of Figure 8-10. Clearly glasses A and B contain the same amount of water. But now the contents of glass B are poured into glass C, thereby creating the situation shown in the "after" part of Figure 8-10. Do glass A and glass C contain the same amount of water, or does one contain more?

Being a logical adult, you would probably conclude that the two glasses hold identical amounts of water (excluding a drop or two that might have been lost in the process of pouring). The preoperational child, however, is likely to say that the glasses hold different amounts of water: Most will say that glass A has more because it is taller, although a few will say that glass C has more because it is fatter. The child's thinking depends more on perception than logic during the preoperational stage and is therefore susceptible to outward appearances: The glasses *look* different and so must *be* different.

According to Piaget, the third stage of cognitive development, **concrete operations,** appears when children are about 6 or 7 years old and continues until they are about 11 or

Figure 8–10

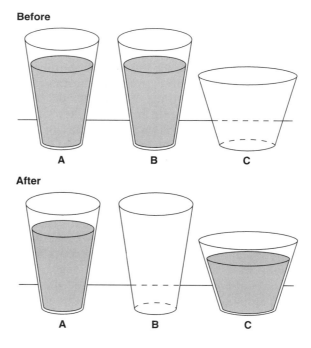

Before

A   B   C

After

A   B   C

12. Children at this stage begin to think logically about conservation problems and other situations as well. Concrete operational children are limited in one very important respect, however: They can apply their logical operations only to concrete, observable objects and events. They have difficulty dealing with abstract information and with hypothetical ideas contrary to their own reality. For example, the concrete operational child should readily agree with the logic that

If all first graders are children

And if all children are people

Then all first graders are people

yet will have trouble recognizing the logical validity of a similar problem that includes a contrary-to-fact premise:

If all first graders are children

And if all children are hippopotamuses

Then all first graders are hippopotamuses

Concrete operational children, although generally very logical, cannot readily distinguish between logic and reality, and, after all, first graders are *not* hippopotamuses!

The fourth and final stage, **formal operations,** rarely appears before children are 11 or 12 years of age and continues to evolve for at least several years after that. During formal operations, the child develops the ability to reason with abstract, hypothetical, and contrary-to-fact information. Other abilities essential to mathematical and scientific reasoning emerge as well. For example, proportional thinking develops, through which the child truly begins to understand the concept of *proportion,* as reflected in such mathematical entities as fractions and decimals. The child also begins to separate and control variables: In testing a hypothesis about which factor among many may bring about a particular result, the child tests one variable at a time while holding all others constant. In addition, with the onset of formal operations children are able to examine their own thought processes and evaluate the quality and logic of those thoughts; for example, a child may notice a logical fallacy in something that he or she has said.

It is important to note here that recent research, though sometimes confirming Piaget's assertions regarding characteristics of the different stages (Flavell, 1996), does not support Piaget's proposed stage characteristics in their entirety. For example, it appears that infants and young children are cognitively more sophisticated than Piaget's descriptions of the sensorimotor and preoperational stages would indicate (Baillargeon, 1987; Carey, 1985; Donaldson, 1978; Flavell et al., 1993; Metz, 1995; Rosser, 1994; Trawick-Smith, 1997). At the same time, Piaget may have overestimated the capabilities of adolescents and even adults; for instance, many adults (including many college students) show behavior more characteristic of concrete operations than of formal operational thought (Pascarella & Terenzini, 1991; Siegler, 1991).

A second problem with Piaget's notion of stage-related logical thinking skills is that children often use a given logical thinking skill in one situation while being unable to use what is presumably the same skill in another situation (Case, 1985; Ceci & Roazzi, 1994;

Flavell et al., 1993; Girotto & Light, 1993; Siegler & Ellis, 1996). Children's knowledge about the specific topics under consideration appears to be critical here (Carey, 1985; Metz, 1995; Pulos & Linn, 1981). For example, in one study (Pulos & Linn, 1981), many seventh graders living in a rural area demonstrated the formal operational ability to separate and control variables on a problem related to fishing but not on Piaget's traditional laboratory methods for assessing the same ability.

• *The rate of cognitive development is controlled to some extent by maturation.* One unique aspect of Piaget's theory is his assertion that children's progression through the four stages is limited by maturation—that is, by genetically controlled physiological changes. Piaget contended that a necessary prerequisite for the transition to each successive stage is the occurrence of certain neurological changes that allow more sophisticated cognitive structures to develop. Because of physiological limitations, it would be virtually impossible for a two-year-old child to think logically like a concrete operations child or for a seven-year-old to deal successfully with abstract ideas. In support of Piaget's proposal, research by Epstein (1978) and Hudspeth (1985) indicates that significant neurological changes occur at the typical transition ages for progression from one of Piaget's cognitive stages to the next. On the other hand, researchers often find that, with proper training, children become capable of thinking in ways that Piaget suggested were possible only for older individuals; such findings cast doubt on maturation as a limiting factor in cognitive development (Case, 1985; Field, 1987; Mayer, 1992; Murray, 1978; Siegler, 1978).

Many of Piaget's ideas are evident in contemporary cognitivism. The current notion that knowledge is structured and organized can be seen in Piaget's work as well as in that of Tolman and the Gestaltists. Also important in contemporary theories of learning is Piaget's proposal that for learning to occur, an individual must be able to assimilate new information into existing cognitive structures; in other words, a new experience and prior knowledge must overlap. Finally, although many psychologists now question the idea that cognitive development can be characterized as a series of distinct stages (Flavell et al., 1993; Rosser, 1994; Siegler & Ellis, 1996), Piaget's analyses of how children think about a variety of tasks and problems have provided the impetus for many studies of the development of cognition. Although not all of Piaget's ideas have been validated by research, his theory continues to be a dominant force in both the thinking and methodology of cognitive psychology.

While Piaget was conducting his early, groundbreaking research, another psychologist had ideas of his own about the factors that facilitate cognitive development. We turn to Lev Vygotsky's ideas now.

LEV VYGOTSKY'S DEVELOPMENTAL THEORY

The Russian psychologist Lev Vygotsky conducted numerous studies of children's thinking from the 1920s until his premature death from tuberculosis in 1934. Western psychologists did not fully appreciate the value and usefulness of his work until several decades later, when his major writings were translated into English (Vygotsky, 1962, 1978, 1987,

1997). Although Vygotsky never had the chance to develop his theory fully, his views are clearly evident in our views of learning and instruction today. Here we will look at some of his most influential ideas:

• *Complex mental processes begin as social activities; as children develop, they gradually internalize these processes and can use them independently of those around them.* Vygotsky believed that many thinking processes have their roots in social interactions with other people; the process through which social activities evolve into internal mental activities is called **internalization.** As an example, children frequently argue with one another about a variety of matters—how best to carry out an activity, what games to play, who did what to whom, and so on. Childhood arguments serve a purpose: They help children discover that there are often several points of view about the same situation. Eventually, children can, in essence, internalize the "arguing" process, developing the ability to look at a situation from several different angles *on their own.*

• *Thought and language initially develop independently of each other; the two become interdependent when children are about two years old.* For us as adults, thought and language are closely interconnected. For one thing, we often think in terms of the specific words that our language provides; for example, when we think about household pets, words such as *dog* and *cat* are likely to pop up repeatedly in our heads. In addition, we usually express our thoughts when we converse with others; as we often like to put it, we "speak our minds."

Vygotsky proposed that, in contrast to the state of affairs for adults, thought and language are distinctly separate functions for infants and young toddlers. In these early years of life, thinking occurs independently of language, and when language appears, it is first used primarily as a means of communication rather than as a mechanism of thought. But sometime around two years of age, thought and language become intertwined: Children begin to express their thoughts when they speak, and they begin to think in terms of words.

When thought and language merge, we begin to see **self-talk** (whereby children talk to themselves out loud) and eventually **inner speech** (whereby children "talk" to themselves mentally rather than orally). According to Vygotsky, both self-talk and inner speech have a similar purpose: By talking to themselves, children learn to guide and direct their own behaviors through difficult tasks and complex maneuvers in much the same way that adults have previously guided them (also see Berk, 1994). Self-talk and inner speech, then, are examples of the internalization process I described earlier: Children gradually internalize the directions that they have initially received from those around them, so that they eventually give *themselves* such directions.

• *Children can accomplish more difficult tasks when they have the assistance of people more advanced and competent than themselves.* Vygotsky distinguished between two kinds of "abilities" that children are likely to have at any particular point in their development. A child's **actual developmental level** is the extent to which he or she can perform tasks independently, without help from anyone else. A child's **level of potential development** is the extent to which he or she can perform tasks with the assistance of a more competent individual.

Children can typically do more difficult things in collaboration with adults than they can do on their own. For example, children just learning how to use a baseball bat can hit a baseball more successfully when adults are present to guide their swings. Children can play more difficult piano pieces when adults assist them in locating some of the notes on the keyboard. Students can solve more difficult mathematics problems when their teacher helps them identify critical problem components and potentially fruitful problem-solving strategies. And students can often read more complex prose within a reading group at school than they are likely to read independently at home.[1]

• *Tasks within the zone of proximal development promote maximum cognitive growth.* The range of tasks that children cannot yet perform independently, but *can* perform with the help and guidance of others, is known as the **zone of proximal development (ZPD)**. A child's zone of proximal development includes learning and problem-solving abilities that are just beginning to develop within that child—abilities that are in an immature, "embryonic" form. Naturally, any child's ZPD will change over time; as some tasks are mastered, more complex ones will appear to provide new challenges.

Vygotsky proposed that children learn very little from performing tasks they can already do independently. Instead, they develop primarily by attempting tasks they can accomplish only in collaboration with a more competent individual—that is, when they attempt tasks within their zone of proximal development. In a nutshell, it is the challenges in life, rather than the easy successes, that promote cognitive development.

In the past two decades, learning theorists and educators alike have made considerable use of Vygotsky's ideas. For example, as we saw in the preceding chapter on social learning theory, self-instructions (in other words, self-talk) are a recommended strategy for helping children regulate their own behavior. If you look back at Meichenbaum's five steps for teaching self-instructions (described in Chapter 7), you should notice how each step promotes increasing internalization of what is initially a social interaction between the teacher and student.

In addition, we are seeing an increasing interest in teaching methods that involve social interaction. Some methods, such as classroom discussions and cooperative learning, involve frequent interaction among students themselves. Others, such as reciprocal teaching and apprenticeships, involve ongoing interactions between students and their teachers. I will describe each of these approaches in more detail in Chapter 16.

Finally, theorists and educators have given considerable thought to the kinds of assistance that can help students complete challenging assignments. The term **scaffolding** is often used here: Adults and other more competent individuals provide some form of guidance or structure that enables students to engage in activities and perform tasks that are in their zone of proximal development. For example, adults might make a task simpler than it would otherwise be, give hints about how to proceed, demonstrate parts of the activity that students have trouble remembering on their own, and give frequent feedback about how students are progressing (Gallimore & Tharp, 1990; Good, McCaslin, & Reys, 1992; Wood, Bruner, & Ross, 1976). As the children become more adept at performing tasks, scaffolding is gradually phased out, and the children eventually perform those tasks on their own.

---

[1]Reading specialists often distinguish between a student's instructional and independent reading levels; for example, see Burron and Claybaugh (1992).

The perspectives that we've examined so far—those of Tolman, the Gestalt psychologists, Piaget, and Vygotsky—had a cognitivist flavor from their inception. At about the same time, certain other theorists began with the best of behaviorist intentions, but over time, they found it increasingly difficult to explain their research results using stimulus-response principles alone. Let's turn now to the work of these verbal learning theorists—psychologists who helped pave the way for a wider acceptance of cognitive views of learning.

VERBAL LEARNING RESEARCH

A logical outgrowth of the behaviorist movement was an extension of behaviorist principles to a uniquely human behavior—language. In the middle of the twentieth century (especially the 1930s through the 1960s), many researchers attempted to study verbal behavior and the learning of verbal material by applying an S-R approach to these phenomena. The results of this research program are collectively known as **verbal learning** research.

Central to verbal learning research were two learning tasks, serial learning and paired associate learning, that could easily be analyzed in terms of an S-R perspective. **Serial learning** involves learning a sequence of items in their correct order; the alphabet, the days of the week, and the nine planets of our solar system are all examples. Verbal learning theorists explained serial learning in this way: The first item in the list is a stimulus to which the second item is learned as a response, the second item then serves as a stimulus to which the third item is the learned response, and so on.

Paired associate learning involves learning pairs of items. Learning foreign language vocabulary words and their English equivalents (e.g., *le papier* is French for *paper*) and learning state capitals (e.g., Juneau is the capital of Alaska) are two examples. Verbal learning theorists described paired associates as being distinct stimulus-response associations: The first item in each pair is the stimulus, and the second item is the response.

Increasingly, verbal learning studies yielded results that could not be easily explained in terms of S-R connections, and theorists began to introduce a variety of mental phenomena into their discussions of learning processes. In this section, I will describe some general learning principles that emerged from verbal learning research. Some of the findings are relatively easy to explain from a behaviorist perspective; others are not so easily explained.

• *Serial learning is characterized by a particular pattern.* In a serial learning task, a **serial learning curve** is usually observed: People learn the first few items and last few items more quickly and easily than they learn the middle items (Hall, 1971; McCrary & Hunter, 1953; Roediger & Crowder, 1976). If we were to graph the speed with which the various items in a serial list are learned, we might obtain results similar to what you see in Figure 8–11. An example of the serial learning curve is the way in which most children learn the alphabet: They learn the first letters (*A, B, C, D*) and the last letters (*X, Y, Z*) before they learn the middle letters (e.g., *H, I, J, K*).

Figure 8–11
A typical serial learning curve.

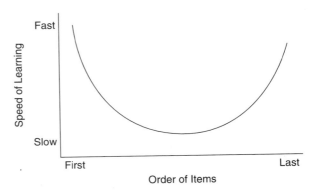

The tendency for the first items in a serial learning curve to be learned quickly is called the **primacy effect.** The tendency for the last items to be learned quickly is called the **recency effect.** Verbal learning theorists explained both effects by proposing that the end points of the list (i.e., the first and last items) served as *anchors* to which the other items would then be attached in a stimulus-response fashion.

• *Overlearned material is more easily recalled at a later time.* What happens when you learn information perfectly and then continue to study it? This process of **overlearning,** in which you learn material to mastery and then practice the material for additional study trials, enables you to remember the information much more accurately at a later time (Bahrick, Bahrick, Bahrick, & Bahrick, 1993; Krueger, 1929; Underwood, 1954). For example, Krueger (1929) found that overlearning of a list of words enhanced recall for up to a month after the learning session. As you may recall from Chapter 2, many early behaviorists also emphasized the importance of practice for learning.

• *Distributed practice is usually more effective than massed practice.* Imagine that you have to study for a test. You estimate that you need six hours to master the test material. Would you do better on the test if you studied for six hours all at once or if you broke your study time into smaller chunks of time—say, six one-hour sessions? Research has indicated that **distributed practice,** spreading study time out over several occasions, usually leads to better learning than **massed practice,** in which study time occurs all at once (Dempster, 1991; Glenberg, 1976; Underwood, 1961; Underwood, Kapelak, & Malmi, 1976). Thus, studying for a test over several short sessions is more likely to be effective than one long cram session. Furthermore, the further apart the study sessions are, the better one's recall for the learned information is likely to be over the long run (Bahrick et al., 1993).

• *Learning in one situation often affects learning and recall in another situation.* Imagine yourself having to learn two sets of paired associates. The first set looks like this:

Set 1
house – dragon
plant – sled
lamp – music
onion – pillow

The second one looks like this:

Set 2
house – paper
plant – clock
lamp – turkey
onion – chair

After you have first learned set 1 and then learned set 2, you are asked to remember the responses to each of the stimulus words in set 1. Will you have difficulty? You probably will, because you learned different responses to those same words when you learned set 2. You would have an easier time remembering the correct responses you learned in set 1 if you had *not* had to learn the set 2 responses as well.

Verbal learning theorists observed that when individuals learn two sets of paired associates in succession, their learning of the second set often diminishes their ability to recall the first set (Hall, 1971), a phenomenon known as **retroactive inhibition.** They further observed that individuals in this situation often have difficulty remembering the second set as well as the first (Hall, 1971), a phenomenon known as **proactive inhibition.** The tendency for a set of paired associates learned at one time to interfere with the recall of a set learned either earlier or later is particularly likely to occur when the two sets have the same or similar stimulus words but different response words (Osgood, 1949).

Under different circumstances, learning one set of information may actually improve the recall of information learned at another time, a phenomenon that verbal learning theorists called either **retroactive facilitation** or **proactive facilitation,** depending on the order in which the two sets of information were learned (Hall, 1971). Facilitation is most likely to occur when two situations have similar or identical stimuli and when they have similar responses as well (Osgood, 1949). As an example, after learning the stimulus-response pair "house–dragon," you would probably learn "house–monster" rather easily.

Verbal learning theorists (e.g., McGeoch, 1942; Melton & Irwin, 1940; Underwood, 1948) proposed that retroactive and proactive inhibition were major factors in *forgetting* verbal information; they were therefore among the first to discuss theoretical ideas related to *memory.* Although their explanations were based primarily on stimulus-response analyses, many cognitive psychologists also consider inhibition to play a significant role in memory and forgetting.

• *Characteristics of the material affect the speed with which people can learn it.* Verbal learning researchers discovered a number of characteristics that affect the ease of learning verbal material:

1. Items are more quickly learned when they are *meaningful*—that is, when they can be easily associated with other ideas (Cofer, 1971; Paivio, 1971). This principle was discovered very early by the German psychologist Hermann Ebbinghaus (1913). Ebbinghaus, who served as his own subject of study for a number of experiments in serial learning, observed that the associations he could make with words helped him to learn those words. He attempted to eliminate the influence of associations by using presumably meaningless **nonsense syllables** ("words" such as JAD, MON, and ZIV). Yet even many nonsense syllables often have

Some items are
more meaningful
than others.

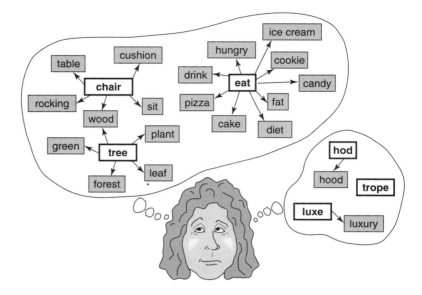

meaningfulness and evoke associations, thus making them relatively easy to learn (Hall, 1971). For example, the nonsense syllable JAD might make you think of jade, and the syllable MON might remind you of money.

2. Items are easier to learn when they are *pronounceable* (Di Vesta & Ingersoll, 1969; Underwood & Schulz, 1960). For example, the nonsense syllable DNK should be learned faster than BPX because most people can pronounce it more easily.

3. *Concrete* items are easier to learn than abstract items (Gorman, 1961; Paivio, 1963); for example, items such as

   turtle, hammer, sandwich

   are learned faster than items such as

   truth, joy, experience

4. One probable reason that the concreteness of items makes them easier to learn is that concrete items can be *mentally visualized.* The extent to which we form visual images of items appears to influence the ease with which those items can be learned (Clark & Paivio, 1991; Paivio, 1971; Sadoski, Goetz, & Fritz, 1993). For example, it is easier to form a mental image of a turtle than it is to form an image of truth. Notice how, in discussing visual imagery, verbal learning theorists were beginning to talk about mental events. This phenomenon of visual imagery is particularly difficult to explain from an S-R perspective.

• *People often impose meaning when learning new information.* The effect of meaningfulness on learning can be explained from an S-R perspective: When a stimulus word has many other words associated with it, one of those associations may in turn be associated with the response to be learned. What is more troublesome for an S-R approach is the fact that people will go out of their way to *make* information meaningful when they are trying to learn it. For example, when Bugelski (1962) asked adults to learn paired associates involving nonsense syllables, they invariably reported that they imposed meanings to help them learn the pairs. To illustrate, when given this pair:

DUP - TEZ

one person used the word *deputize* to help form the connection. Cognitive theories have emerged that probably better explain this tendency for human beings to search for meaning.

• *People organize what they learn.* When people are allowed to recall items of a serial learning task in any order (a task known as **free recall**), they typically do *not* recall those items in their original presentation order. Instead, the order in which they recall items often reflects an organizational scheme of some kind (Bousfield, 1953; Buschke, 1977; Jenkins & Russell, 1952). In a classic experiment by Bousfield (1953), college students were given a list of 60 words, 15 from each of four categories: animals, names, vegetables, and professions. Although the words were presented in a random order, the students tended to recall them in category clusters. For example, a typical recall order might have been something like the following:

camel, giraffe, zebra, donkey, Jason, Adam, Howard, pumpkin, cabbage, carrot, lettuce, radish, milkman, baker, dentist

People even try to organize seemingly unorganized material (Tulving, 1962). This tendency people have to insist on organizing the information they learn is difficult to explain from behaviorist principles. As you will see in later chapters, however, it lends itself quite easily to an explanation based on cognitive learning theories.

• *People often use coding strategies to help them learn.* People often change, or *encode,* information in some way to make it easier to learn (Bugelski, 1962; Dallett, 1964; Underwood & Erlebacher, 1965). Furthermore, when experimenters specifically tell people to use a certain encoding strategy to help them learn information, learning improves (Bugelski, Kidd, & Segmen, 1968; Hall, 1971). For example, when people are instructed in techniques for forming mental visual images, they are able to remember a list of words more accurately than individuals who have not been given such instructions (Bugelski et al., 1968).

• *People are more likely to learn general ideas than to learn words verbatim.* In fact, when people focus on learning ideas rather than on learning information word for word, their learning is faster and their recall more accurate (Briggs & Reed, 1943; English, Welborn, & Killian, 1934; Jones & English, 1926). Verbal learning research focused on the learning of verbatim information. In doing so, it may very well have ignored the way in which human beings actually learn most verbal material.

Clearly, verbal learning research provided us with a number of useful learning principles. It also provided us with two learning tasks, serial and paired associate learning, that continue to be used in learning research. At the same time, in trying to stretch S-R models of learning to explain human verbal behavior, it began to demonstrate some weaknesses of the behaviorist perspective.

In more recent years, the focus of verbal learning research has been on how people learn meaningful verbal material (e.g., prose passages) rather than artificially constructed serial lists or paired associates. In fact, the term *verbal learning* was largely abandoned (e.g., the *Journal of Verbal Learning and Verbal Behavior* became the *Journal of Memory and Language* in 1985) as verbal learning researchers began to embrace cognitivist ideas.

INTRODUCTION TO CONTEMPORARY COGNITIVISM

We have just seen how, even during the heyday of behaviorism, the work of Tolman, the Gestalt psychologists, Piaget, Vygotsky, and the verbal learning researchers was laying a foundation for cognitive learning theories. During the 1960s discontent with the inadequacies of behaviorism became more widespread. The behaviorist perspective could not easily explain why people attempt to organize and make sense of the information they learn or sometimes even alter the form of that information (e.g., by remembering general meanings rather than verbatim input). Among learning psychologists grew the realization that mental events—cognition—could no longer be ignored (e.g., see Kendler, 1985).

In this section of the chapter, we will examine some of the major assumptions that underlie most cognitive explanations of learning. We will also look at three different approaches to understanding learning—human information processing theory, constructivism, and contextual views—that fall within the larger theoretical perspective we call cognitivism.

General Assumptions of Cognitive Theories

The assumptions underlying contemporary cognitive theories of learning are radically different from those underlying behaviorism. What follow are some of the most central assumptions:

• *Some learning processes may be unique to human beings.* Because people possess abilities unique to the species (complex language is an example), the processes involved in learning may be different for human beings than they are for other animals. Accordingly, almost all research within the cognitivist perspective is conducted with human beings, and theories formulated from this research are typically not generalized to other species.

• *Cognitive processes are the focus of study.* Mental events are centrally involved in human learning and must therefore be incorporated into theories of learning processes. To the extent that individuals think about the same situation differently, they will learn different things from that situation.

• *Objective, systematic observations of people's behavior should be the focus of scientific inquiry; however, inferences about unobservable mental processes can often be drawn from such behavior.* Cognitive psychologists share with behaviorists the beliefs that the study of learning must be objective and that learning theories should be based on the results of empirical research. Cognitivists differ from behaviorists in one critical respect, however: By observing the responses that individuals make to different stimulus conditions, they believe that they can draw inferences about the nature of the internal mental events that produce those responses. In fact, researchers have become increasingly more ingenious in designing research studies that enable them to draw conclusions about specific cognitive processes.

A classic study by Bransford and Franks (1971) provides an example of inference drawing in cognitive research. In this experiment, undergraduate students listened to 24 sentences and answered simple questions about each one. The sentences were variations on four general ideas: a rock rolling down a hill, a man reading a newspaper, a breeze blowing, and ants eating jelly. To illustrate, the six sentences about the ants eating jelly were as follows:

The ants ate the sweet jelly which was on the table.

The ants in the kitchen ate the jelly which was on the table.

The ants in the kitchen ate the jelly.

The ants ate the sweet jelly.

The ants were in the kitchen.

The jelly was on the table.

The students then listened to a second set of 28 sentences (variations on the same themes as before) and were asked to indicate whether or not each had been in the first set. Most of the sentences (24 out of 28) were *new* sentences; here are some examples:

The ants in the kitchen ate the sweet jelly which was on the table.

The ants in the kitchen ate the sweet jelly.

The ants ate the jelly which was on the table.

The jelly was sweet.

The students erroneously "recognized" most of these new sentences as being "old" ones. Sentences that contained a lot of information were particularly likely to be recognized as having been heard before; for instance, "The ants in the kitchen ate the sweet jelly which was on the table" was more likely to be recognized than "The jelly was sweet." From such results, Bransford and Franks concluded that people abstract ideas from the verbal information they receive (rather than learning it verbatim) and organize similar ideas together in their memories. Sentences in the experiment that included most or all of the information related to a single theme may have more closely resembled the students' organized memories and therefore seemed familiar to them.

Obviously, we cannot directly see the cognitive processes about which Bransford and Franks theorized. Yet such processes seem to be reasonable explanations of the behaviors that we *do* see.

• *Individuals are actively involved in the learning process.* Rather than being passive victims of environmental conditions, people are active participants in the learning process and in fact *control* their own learning. Individuals themselves determine how they mentally process the information they receive, and these cognitive processes in turn determine what, if anything, will be learned in a given situation.

• *Learning involves the formation of mental associations that are not necessarily reflected in overt behavior changes.* Like Tolman, who advanced the concept of *latent learning,* contemporary cognitive psychologists believe that learning involves an internal, mental change rather than the external behavior change that many behaviorists propose. Learning can therefore occur without being reflected in an individual's observed performance. (Of course, other people have no way of knowing that learning has taken place until there *is* a behavior change of some sort.)

• *Knowledge is organized.* An individual's knowledge, beliefs, attitudes, and emotions are not isolated from one another but are instead all associated and interconnected. This emphasis on organization is one that we saw in several early cognitive theories, notably those of Tolman, the Gestaltists, and Piaget.

• *Learning is a process of relating new information to previously learned information.* Similar to Piaget's assertion that accommodation almost always involves assimilation, contemporary cognitive theorists believe that learning is most likely to occur when individuals can relate a new experience to the information they have acquired from earlier experiences.

Despite sharing certain common assumptions, cognitivists take somewhat different approaches in their attempts to portray how learning occurs. The predominant approach to the study of human learning, as reflected in ongoing research and journal space, is a group of theories known collectively as *information processing theory.* In recent years, however, two other perspectives—*constructivism* and *contextual views*—have also gained popularity, especially among psychologists who concern themselves with instructional practice and other educational issues. Let's look briefly at each of these three perspectives.

Information Processing Theory

Many cognitive theories focus on how people process the information they receive from the environment—how they perceive the stimuli around them, how they "put" what they've perceived into their memories, how they "find" what they've learned when they need to use it, and so on. Such theories are collectively known as **information processing theory.**

Many early information processing theories (e.g., those that emerged in the 1960s) portrayed human learning as being similar to how computers process information. To illustrate, theorists talked about "storing" information in and "retrieving" it from memory, borrowing the terms *storage* and *retrieval* so often used in reference to computer memory. It soon became clear, however, that the computer analogy was overly simplistic—that people often think about and interpret information in ways that are difficult to explain in the rigid, algorithmic ways that computers process information (e.g., see Bransford & Franks, 1971; Mayer, 1996a; Reisberg, 1997). At this point, the general perspective known as information processing theory includes a variety of specific theories about how people mentally think about the information they receive; some of these theories are computer-like in nature, but many others are not.[2]

Constructivism

Within the past three decades, it has become increasingly apparent that learners don't just "absorb" information at face value. Instead, people do a great deal with the information they acquire, actively trying to organize and make sense of it, often in unique, idiosyncratic ways. Most cognitive theorists now portray learning more as *constructing* knowledge from the information one receives rather than directly receiving that information from the outside world (e.g., see Collins & Green, 1992; De Corte, Greer, & Verschaffel, 1996; Driver, 1995; Hiebert & Raphael, 1996; Leinhardt, 1994; Marshall, 1992; Mayer, 1996a, 1996b; Prawat, 1993; Spivey, 1997; Stanovich & Cunningham, 1991). In some (although not all) cases, such theorists refer to their perspective as **constructivism** rather than information processing theory.

In this chapter, we have already seen several theoretical perspectives that are distinctly constructivist in flavor. For example, Tolman's concept of *cognitive map,* the Gestaltist concept of *closure,* and Piaget's concept of *cognitive structure* all involve constructing knowledge for oneself rather than absorbing it exactly as it has been presented. In these situations, we see the process of construction occurring separately within each learner, reflecting a perspective known as *individual constructivism.*

In other situations, people work together to make sense of their world. For example, several students may form a study group when they have a difficult and confusing textbook; helping one another, they may be able to interpret and understand the book in ways that they may not have been able to do on their own. As another example, over the course of several centuries astronomers have made increasingly better sense of the phenomena they observe through their telescopes; the discipline of astronomy provides a view of the universe that innumerable scientists have pieced together over many centuries. Theories of learning that focus on how people work together, whether at a single sitting or over the course of many years, reflect a perspective known as *social constructivism.*

Contextual Views

Within the past few years, several cognitive theories have emerged that place considerable emphasis on the importance of the immediate environment—the *context*—in learning and behavior. As an example of this perspective, we noted earlier in the chapter that, contrary to Piaget's belief that different forms of logic are associated with different developmental stages, children of a particular age actually show considerable variability in their

---

[2]In the first and second editions of this book, I used the term *information processing theory* to encompass most of the ideas that I presented relative to cognitive views of learning. In the meantime, however, I have discovered that some people continue to associate information processing theory with the computer metaphor. In the interest of minimizing any confusion about this issue, I have adopted the terms *cognitivism* and *cognitive psychology* (terms with less "baggage" attached to them) in this edition.

logical thinking skills, depending on the specific situation. As another example, people can often think more "intelligently" when they have calculators, computers, diagrams, equations, or even things as simple as, say, paper and pencil to help them (Greeno, Collins, & Resnick, 1996; Pea, 1993; Perkins, 1995; Sternberg & Wagner, 1994). As a third example, consider Vygotsky's concepts of *actual developmental level* (the extent to which some-one can perform a task independently), *level of potential development* (the extent to which the same person can perform a task with someone else's help), and *zone of proxi-mal development* (the range of tasks that the person can perform with assistance). As Vygotsky pointed out, one's level of potential development will always be higher than one's actual developmental level; in other words, people can always accomplish more dif-ficult tasks when they have the assistance of those around them. Furthermore, they can advance cognitively *only* when they work on tasks that they cannot do alone—tasks that are in their zone of proximal development.

Contextual views of learning have a variety of labels attached to them. Terms such as *situated learning, situated cognition,* and *distributed intelligence* all refer to situations in which learning and thinking are influenced by the physical and social contexts in which people are immersed; for example, the term *distributed intelligence* refers, in part, to the notion that we often think more" intelligently" when we think about and discuss ideas with others than when we think alone. (Social constructivist theories, because they involve cognition within a social context, can often be classified as contextual views as well.)

Integrating Cognitive Perspectives

It is important to note that complete consensus does not exist, even among cognitivists, as to how different cognitive theories can best be categorized (for different possibilities, see Bredo, 1997; Case, 1996; Derry, 1996; Greeno, et al., 1996; Mayer, 1996a, 1996b; Reynolds et al., 1996). As one simple example of this point, some theorists portray contemporary information processing theory as being decidedly constructivist in nature (Derry, 1996; Mayer, 1996a, 1996b; Phye, 1997b; Prawat, 1996; Pressley et al., 1997).

In my own mind, ideas from information processing theory, constructivism, and con-textual views all make significant contributions to our understanding of how human beings think and learn. Accordingly, we will be pulling from all three perspectives as we explore how people think and learn in the next few chapters.

GENERAL EDUCATIONAL IMPLICATIONS OF COGNITIVE THEORIES

Theories of human cognition give us many ideas about how we can best help others learn. We will derive some very specific educational applications in later chapters. At this point, however, let's identify some of the more general educational implications of the cognitive perspective, including those of early cognitive theories:

- *Cognitive processes influence learning.* If learning is a function of how informa-tion is mentally processed, then students' cognitive processes should be a major concern to educators. Students' learning difficulties often indicate ineffective or inappropriate cognitive processes; for example, children with learning disabilities tend to process information less effectively than other children (e.g., Swanson, 1987). Teachers must be aware not only of *what* students are trying to learn but also of *how* they are trying to learn it.

• *As children grow, they become capable of increasingly more sophisticated thought.* Both Piaget and Vygotsky have pointed out that children acquire more complex reasoning processes over time. Piaget described such development in terms of four qualitatively different stages, whereas Vygotsky spoke more in terms of a continually advancing zone of proximal development. Regardless of whose perspective we take, we come to the same conclusion: Teachers must take their students' current level of cognitive functioning into account when planning topics and methods of instruction. For example, children in the elementary school grades are likely to have difficulty with abstract ideas that don't tie in with their own experiences (using Piaget's terms, they are in either the preoperational or concrete operational stage rather than in the formal operational stage) and so will learn more effectively if information is presented through concrete, hands-on activities. Even high school and college students, if they have not completely acquired formal operational characteristics, may benefit from having concrete experiences before studying abstract material.

• *People organize the things they learn.* Teachers can facilitate students' learning by presenting information in an organized fashion and by helping students see how one thing relates to another. We will identify some strategies for promoting such organization in Chapter 13.

• *New information is most easily acquired when people can associate it with things they have already learned.* Teachers can therefore help students learn by showing them how new ideas relate to old ones (once again, we will identify more specific strategies in Chapter 13). When students are unable to relate new information to anything with which they are familiar, learning is likely to be slow and ineffective.

• *People control their own learning.* B. F. Skinner (1954, 1968) argued from an operant conditioning perspective that students must actively respond if they are to learn. Cognitivists share Skinner's view; however, they emphasize *mental* activity rather than physical activity. If students control their own cognitive processes, it is ultimately they themselves, not their teachers, who determine what things will be learned, and how.

OVERVIEW OF UPCOMING CHAPTERS

In the next eight chapters, we will explore cognitivist views of learning in greater detail. In Part IV, we will examine the nature of human memory, looking at the basic components of memory (Chapter 9), the various ways in which people store information in memory (Chapter 10), the nature of the knowledge that they create (Chapter 11), and the factors that promote long-term retention of the things that they've learned (Chapter 12). Throughout these chapters, we will identify specific implications of memory theory for classroom instruction; in addition, we will examine several teaching practices that facilitate effective memory processes in Chapter 13.

We will continue our discussion of cognitivist ideas in Part V as well, where we will focus on some of the more complex aspects of learning and cognition. In Chapters 14 and 15 we will look at how people think about their own thinking (a phenomenon known as *metacognition*) and at how they apply what they've learned to new situations (phenomena known as *transfer* and *problem solving*). In Chapter 16 we will consider several specific teaching methods that are likely to promote such complex phenomena.

SUMMARY

Cognitivism is currently the predominant perspective within which human learning is described and explained. The roots of cognitive theory can be found in research and theories dating back to the 1920s and 1930s. For example, Edward Tolman, while conducting animal laboratory studies similar to those of behaviorists, included mental phenomena in his perspective of how learning occurs and adopted a more holistic view of learning than was true of S-R theorists. Gestalt psychologists emphasized the importance of organizational processes in perception, learning, and problem solving, proposing that people are predisposed to organize information in particular ways. Jean Piaget described a variety of cognitive abilities that appear at different stages of development. Lev Vygotsky stressed the importance of social activities for promoting more complex thought. And midcentury verbal learning theorists, who initially attempted to apply an S-R analysis to the study of human language–based learning, increasingly began to incorporate mental events into explanations of their research results.

Contemporary cognitivism emphasizes mental processes and proposes that many aspects of learning may be unique to the human species. Cognitivists share behaviorists' belief that the study of learning must be objective and that learning theories should be based on empirical research; however, they also believe that by observing the responses people make to different stimulus conditions, they can draw inferences about the cognitive processes that lead to those responses. Cognitivism encompasses several perspectives—information processing theory, constructivism, and contextual views—that all contribute to our understanding of how human beings think and learn. Teachers must take students' cognitive processes into account when considering how best to help students be successful in the classroom.

CHAPTER 9

Basic Components of Memory

Imagine yourself studying for an upcoming exam that will cover a lengthy and somewhat confusing reading assignment. You understand most of the material you have read and are confident that you will remember it. But you have trouble learning one section of the assignment, mainly because it doesn't make much sense to you. In desperation, you try to memorize this section word for word, but your learning becomes slow and painful.

Now imagine yourself taking the exam. It was not as difficult as you had anticipated it would be, but you cannot remember the answer to a particularly trivial question: "What was Edward C. Tolman's middle name?" You know you studied the relevant section in the book, but you simply cannot remember the information called for. After considering all of the names you can think of that begin with *C*, you finally give up and turn in your exam paper with the question unanswered.

Immediately afterward, you congregate with your classmates in the hall and rehash the questions. "What was Tolman's middle name?" you ask. Your friend Harry responds smugly, "It was Chace. I can remember that easily because my sister married a guy named Marvin Chace." And then your friend Carol adds, "I learned the name by imagining Tolman *chacing* his rats down their mazes." You grit your teeth, thinking it ridiculous that Harry and Carol would do better than you on a question because of a coincidental brother-in-law or a silly visual image. But let's face it, your classmates remembered and you did not.

Learning a piece of information at one point in time does not guarantee that you will remember it later on. Many variables determine what information gets into memory in the first place and what information stays there long enough for you to recall it when you need it. In this chapter, we will begin our examination of how human memory seems to work and how various factors influence its effectiveness.

The study of human cognition takes two major approaches (Calfee, 1981). One approach focuses on the *structures* of the human mind—that is, on its different components and their interrelationships. The second focuses on *functions*—that is, on how the mind operates to process information. Most of this chapter describes a dual-store model of memory, one that focuses primarily on structure. Later in the chapter, we will turn to alternative views of memory that focus more on how memory functions and how information is processed. Before we look at memory from either perspective, let's define some basic terminology.

BASIC TERMINOLOGY IN MEMORY THEORY

Memory theorists make a distinction between *learning* and *memory*. They also refer frequently to the processes of *storage, encoding,* and *retrieval.*

Learning versus Memory

Up to this point, we have not really separated learning and memory, but memory theorists do draw a distinction between the two terms. **Learning** is viewed, quite simply, as the acquisition of new information; as we defined it in Chapter 1, learning involves a relatively permanent change in mental associations due to experience. **Memory,** on the other hand, is related to the ability to recall information that has previously been learned. In some instances, the word *memory* is used to refer to the process of retaining information. In other instances, it is used to refer to the "location" where learned information is placed; for example, we will be talking about *working memory* and *long-term memory.* The distinction between learning and memory is an important one; for a number of reasons that you will discover in later chapters, not everything that is learned is necessarily remembered over the long run.

Storage

Storage is the process of "putting" new information in memory. For example, if you can put the following fact in your head:

Jeanne Ormrod's birthday is August 22.

then you are *storing* the information. We will be talking at length about the processes that people use to store information in memory.

Encoding

As people store information in memory, they often modify it in some way; this process of **encoding**[1] often helps people store information more easily. Encoding sometimes involves *changing the form* of the information. For example, I once had a combination lock for which the first two numbers of the combination were 22 and 8. I quickly learned these two numbers by encoding them as "the day and month of my birthday." In this case, I encoded numerical information into a verbal form. Encoding may also involve *adding to* new information using one's existing knowledge of the world. For example, consider this information:

Jeanne Ormrod was born in Providence, Rhode Island.

Upon reading this, you might conclude that I am a native New Englander or that I am a U.S. citizen—inferences that you might store along with the information I actually gave you. Yet another encoding process is one of *simplifying* information that has been presented, perhaps by remembering the overall meaning or gist of a situation rather than the specific details of what happened. For example, you might remember that the author of one of your textbooks talked about her birthday without remembering the actual date.

Retrieval

Retrieval is the process by which people "find" information they have previously stored in memory so that they can use it again. For example, I am hoping that, come mid-August, you will retrieve the date of my birthday and send me a tasteful card. Because I get cards from few of my readers (and primarily from students in my own classes), we can conclude

---

[1] In our discussion of modeling in Chapter 7, we noted that people can often remember a model's behavior more accurately when they form verbal or visual *memory codes* to help them remember the specific actions that the model has demonstrated. Such memory codes are examples of encoding in action.

that retrieval is quite easy in some cases but more difficult in others. (An alternative hypothesis, of course, is that information retrieval is occurring but is not resulting in a behavior change.)

A DUAL-STORE MODEL OF MEMORY

In the latter part of the nineteenth century, the Harvard psychologist William James (1890) proposed that human memory has three components: an after-image, a primary memory, and a secondary memory. James's model was largely ignored during the behaviorism-dominated early decades of the twentieth century, but the advent of cognitivism in the 1960s brought a renewed interest in human memory, and in 1968 Richard Atkinson and Richard Shiffrin (1968, 1971) proposed a model of memory similar to that of James. This model laid the groundwork for what has become the most prevalent view of human memory today—a **dual-store model** of memory, depicted in simplified form in Figure 9–1.

Like William James, Atkinson and Shiffrin proposed that memory has three components: a sensory register (SR), short-term memory (STM), and long-term memory (LTM). (The model is called *dual*-store in reference to the distinction between short-term memory and long-term memory.) Information from the environment—input—first enters the sensory register, where it is held for a very short time (a few seconds at the most). If the information is processed in a particular way, it moves on to short-term memory. Information is held in short-term memory for less than a minute, however, and must be processed further if it is to move on to long-term memory. Processing of information in short-term memory frequently involves the use of information from long-term memory as well (hence the two-way arrows between short-term and long-term memory in Figure 9–1). If a piece of information reaches the sensory register or short-term memory but is not then processed sufficiently for its transference to the next component of the memory system, that information is assumed to be lost from the memory system—in other words, it is forgotten. Whether information can be lost from long-term memory as well (note the dotted arrow and question mark) is still an open question, one that we will address in Chapter 12.

A dual-store model of human memory can be likened to an information selection and storage system similar to what you might use to store important documents at home. You undoubtedly acquire numerous pieces of paper in your home over the course of a few months; among this mass of paper may be such items as newspapers, personal letters, bills,

Figure 9–1
A simplified dual-store
model of memory.

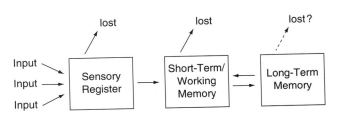

a driver's license, university transcripts, junk mail, and grocery store receipts. You probably discard some items (such as junk mail and grocery receipts) almost as soon as you get them; these things get no further than the "sensory register" of your storage system. You need to deal with others (such as bills) briefly (e.g., you need to pay them), and then you can more or less forget them; they are processed for a short time in your system's "short-term storage." Still others (such as a driver's license and transcripts) may be important enough to require storage in a safe, organized place where you will be able to find them later; they end up in a "long-term storage" compartment such as a wallet, desk drawer, or safe-deposit box.

Learning theorists have continued to modify the dual-store model over the years. For example, they have theorized about the forms in which information is stored and the processes through which it is moved from short-term memory to long-term memory. But perhaps the most noticeable change is an increasing reference to short-term memory as a "working" memory that processes information in addition to storing it (hence, the term *working* in the second box of Figure 9–1). To be consistent with contemporary theorists, we will use the term *working memory* from this point on.

In the pages that follow, we examine the three components of the dual-store model; we also look at the various **control processes** that affect the movement of information from one component to another. As we proceed, however, we must remember that the language we use in our discussion of human memory is largely metaphorical in nature (Roediger, 1980; Rosenfield, 1988). For example, the three components of memory are not necessarily three separate "places" in the brain. Furthermore, when we talk about memory processes, we are not necessarily saying anything about neurological events. Psychologists still have much to learn about how memory processes occur physiologically and how brain structure relates to psychological models of human memory.

SENSORY REGISTER

The first component of the dual-store model, the **sensory register** (also called sensory memory, sensory store, iconic memory, or echoic memory) holds incoming information long enough for it to undergo preliminary cognitive processing. All of the environmental information that we are capable of sensing probably stays with us in the sensory register for a very brief time. For example, if you have ever waved a flashlight or sparkler in the air on a dark night, you have probably noticed that the light leaves a trail behind it. This trail is not present in the air itself; it is the result of your sensory register holding the light you have seen for a short time after you saw it. As another example, when you sit in a classroom for an hour or more, your attention will almost inevitably wander away from the instructor at some point. You may have noticed that when you tune back in to what the instructor is saying, you can often recall two or three words that the instructor has said *before* you tuned in. Virtually everything the instructor has uttered has probably been recorded in your sensory register despite your mental absence from class, but, alas, only those last two or three words are still there when you decide to be present again.

Characteristics of the Sensory Register

Let's look specifically at three characteristics of the sensory register: capacity, form of storage, and duration.

Capacity

The capacity of the sensory register, as far as psychologists can tell, is unlimited. All of the environmental information that human beings are capable of sensing is probably stored briefly in the sensory register.

Form of Storage

Information appears to be stored in the sensory register basically in the form in which it has been sensed: visual input is stored in a visual form, auditory input in an auditory form, and so on (Coltheart, Lea, & Thompson, 1974; Cowan, 1995; Howard, 1983; Turvey & Kravetz, 1970). At this point, information has not yet been understood or interpreted by the individual. In other words, the sensory register holds information *before* it is processed.

Duration

Information remains in the sensory register for only a very brief time, but measuring its exact duration is difficult. One problem in studying the characteristics of information in the sensory register is that when we ask people to think about or otherwise process something that they've stored there, the information automatically moves on to working memory and so is no longer in the place where we want to study it!

The classic experiment designed to assess the duration of the sensory register was conducted by George Sperling (1960). Recruiting adults to participate in his experiment, Sperling presented displays of three rows of four letters and digits each; following is a typical display:

7	1	V	F
X	L	5	3
B	4	W	7

Each display was presented for a fraction of a second, then participants were asked to recall either one particular row of symbols or all 12 symbols. When asked to recall a single row, people were able to do so with 76% accuracy; because they were not told *which* row they would need to recall until after the display had disappeared, they apparently remembered approximately 76% of the symbols they had seen. Yet when asked to recall all 12 symbols, they could do so with only 36% accuracy! Sperling's explanation of this result was that most of the symbols were stored initially but faded from memory before the participants had a chance to write them all down. In a follow-up experiment, Sperling (1960) varied the amount of time that elapsed between the display and the signal indicating which row was to be remembered. People could recall little of a display after a delay of more than a quarter of a second.

From the results of research studies such as Sperling's, it appears that the duration of visual information in the sensory register is probably less than a second (Loftus & Loftus,

1976; Wingfield & Byrnes, 1981). Auditory information probably lasts longer, with a duration of two to four seconds (Conrad & Hull, 1964; Darwin, Turvey, & Crowder, 1972; Moray, Bates, & Barnett, 1965).

Why does auditory input last longer than visual input? One possible explanation (Wingfield & Byrnes, 1981) is that a major source of auditory input—human speech—can be understood only within its sequential context. For example, consider this sentence:

I scream for ice cream.

You can interpret the first two words as either *I scream* or *ice cream*. Only when you hear the third word—*for*—can you begin to interpret the first two words accurately. The task of understanding speech, which is frequently filled with temporarily ambiguous sounds, is often easier if you can hold those sounds in memory in an uninterpreted form until you receive additional, clarifying information.

Two reasons probably account for the rapid disappearance of information from the sensory register. First of all, *interference* may be a factor: New information coming in effectively replaces (and thereby erases) the information already there (e.g., Breitmeyer & Ganz, 1976). Many psychologists also believe that, even without new input, existing information in the sensory register simply fades away, or *decays,* over time (e.g., Loftus & Loftus, 1976; Wingfield & Byrnes, 1981). Regardless of the reasons for the sensory register's short duration, in most instances people don't need to store information there for very long. Important information is probably going to be processed so that it enters working memory. Unimportant information, like junk mail, is probably best dealt with by throwing it away.

MOVING INFORMATION ON TO WORKING MEMORY: THE ROLE OF ATTENTION

If we want to move information from the sensory register into working memory, it appears that, at least in most cases, we must *pay attention* to it (Atkinson & Shiffrin, 1968; Cowan, 1995; Kulhavy, Peterson, & Schwartz, 1986). For example, as you read this book, you are probably attending to only a small part of the visual input that your eyes sense right now (I hope you are attending to the words on this page!). In the same way, you do not worry about all of the sounds you hear at any particular time; you select only certain sounds to pay attention to. In essence, information that an individual pays attention to advances to working memory, whereas information that is not attended to may be lost from the memory system.

One reason that people don't remember something that they've seen or heard, then, is that they never really paid attention to it. If you are sitting in class with your mind a thousand miles away from the professor's lecture, you might say that you forgot what the instructor said or that you never heard it in the first place. The reality of the situation is somewhere in between: the lecture reached your sensory register but was not sufficiently processed to move on to working memory.

Factors Influencing Attention

What kinds of stimuli are likely to capture one's attention? Certain kinds of stimuli tend to draw attention, whereas other kinds do not (e.g., Cowan, 1995; Sergeant, 1996). Following are some important factors affecting what people pay attention to and therefore what they store in working memory.

Size
Which of the following letters first draw your eye?

A B *c* D *E* F G

You probably noticed the *B* and *E* before the other letters because of their larger size. Attention tends to be drawn to large objects, a fact that newspaper publishers employ when they typeset front-page headlines in large letters and that advertisers use when they put potentially unenticing information in fine print.

Intensity
More intense stimuli—bright colors and loud noises, for instance—attract attention. Teachers frequently speak more loudly than usual—**"Be quiet!"**—when they want to get their students' attention. Similarly, toy manufacturers emphasize bright colors in the toys they produce, knowing that children browsing store shelves will be more attracted to vivid reds and yellows than to muted pastels.

Novelty
Stimuli that are novel or unusual in some way tend to draw people's attention. For example, look at the women in Figure 9-2. You probably find yourself attending more to the woman on the right than to the other three. A woman with two heads and three legs is not someone you see every day.

Figure 9–2
Novelty draws attention.

Incongruity

Objects that are incongruous—those that don't make sense within their context—tend to capture people's attention. For example, read this sentence:

I took a walk to the rabbit this morning.

Did you spend more time looking at the word *rabbit* than at the other words? If so, it may have been because *rabbit* does not make much sense within the context of the sentence.

Emotion

Stimuli with strong emotional associations attract attention. A nude body flashing through a crowded room usually draws the attention (and astonished expressions) of just about everyone present. Words such as *blood* and *murder* also are attention getters because of their emotional overtones.

Personal Significance

Individuals tend to pay attention to stimuli that are important to them at a given point in time (Gibson & Rader, 1979; Voss & Schauble, 1992; Vurpillot & Ball, 1979). When a student sits in front of a television set with an open textbook, the stimulus that the student attends to—the television or the book—depends in large part on which stimulus is more closely related to the student's motives at that particular time. If the textbook is interesting or if an important examination is scheduled for the next day, the student will attend to the book. But if a popular situation comedy or a cliff-hanging soap opera is on, or if the textbook is dry and unenticing, the student may very well forget that the text is even in the same room!

Think, for a moment, about curriculum materials, including textbooks, that you have seen recently. Do they possess characteristics that are likely to catch a student's eye? Do important words and concepts stand out, perhaps because they are larger or **more intense** or *unusual*? Are certain topics likely to grab a student's interest because they are interesting and relevant to the age group? If your answer to these questions is no, then students are likely to have difficulty attending to and learning from those materials.

Nominal versus Effective Stimuli

Even when several people are all paying attention to the same stimulus, they may all be attending to different *aspects* of that stimulus. For example, suppose that a first-grade teacher shows his students a picture of a girl and asks them to shout out the first letter of the word that the picture represents. Most students will probably shout out "G" for *girl*. But if Louise is focusing on the girl's dress rather than on the entire picture, she may instead shout "D." The stimulus that appears to us, as outsiders, to be present (sometimes called the **nominal stimulus**) is not necessarily the stimulus that people are actually attending to (the **effective stimulus**).

Once, when I was teaching introductory psychology to college freshmen, a student who had failed my first two examinations came to my office and expressed frustration about her lack of success in my class. When I asked her to describe how she went about completing the assigned readings in the textbook, she told me, "Well, I start looking through the chapter, and when I get to a page that looks important, I read it." With further probing, I discovered that this young woman had been reading approximately one out of every three pages assigned! In this case, the effective stimulus was only one-third of the nominal stimulus.

As another example of how differences in attention can lead to differences in learning, let's look at an experiment by Faust and Anderson (1967) in which students studied Russian vocabulary words under one of two conditions. Some students read single statements presenting an English word and its Russian equivalent and then were required to write the Russian word. Following is an example of the materials that these students received:

A table is a stohl.

A table is a _____.

Other students were shown short paragraphs, each containing several Russian words and their English equivalents, following which they wrote one of the Russian words. An example follows:

A rag is a tryapka. A bridge is a mohst.
A table is a stohl. A college is a vooz.
An onion is a look.

A table is a _____.

Faust and Anderson found that students who were given the paragraphs learned the English meanings of more Russian words than students who were given the single sentences; they reasoned that differences in attention explained the differences in achievement. To understand how attention might differ in the two situations, pretend for a moment that you are a student who wants to complete the Russian vocabulary task with a minimum of time and effort. Now look at the first set of stimulus materials. You don't have to read (attend to) the English word to answer correctly with *stohl*. If you know that the Russian word consistently appears as the last word of the sentence, then you only need to attend to that last word and copy it on the blank line. As a result, you may learn the Russian word but not connect it to its English meaning.

Now look at the second set of stimulus materials. Because several Russian words appear in the paragraph, you must determine which of them is the correct answer. At the very least, you must look at the English word *table* in the incomplete statement at the bottom and then locate that word in the paragraph above. You find "A table is a stohl" and so write *stohl* in the blank. You may or may not have paid attention to other sentences in the paragraph, but at least you have attended to both the English word and its Russian equivalent. Hence you are more likely to learn that *stohl* means *table*. Clearly, then, characteristics of the task at hand influence what you must pay attention to in order to perform that task successfully and therefore what you ultimately learn from completing the task.

Nature of Attention

What cognitive processes underlie people's ability to attend to certain aspects of the environment and to ignore others? On the surface, the answer might appear simple: They just focus their eyes directly on what they want to pay attention to. Yet you can probably think of many times when you have directed your eyes toward a specific object yet not paid attention to it at all: Perhaps you were listening intently to a piece of music or were deep in thought about something that wasn't anywhere in sight.

Furthermore, people are able to focus the attention of senses other than vision without having to physically orient themselves in a particular direction. Consider the case of auditory attention: You can go to a party at which numerous conversations are going on simultaneously and successfully attend to one conversation over the din of others, regardless of where your ears are "aimed." You may be listening to the person standing directly in front of you, or, if that person has been rambling on for more than an hour about the difficulty he has had cultivating rhubarb in his backyard, you may instead tune in to a more interesting conversation a few feet to your right or left. Even though you may be looking directly at the rhubarb grower and nodding in mock agreement, your attention is somewhere else altogether.

The ability to attend to one spoken message while ignoring others—aptly called the **cocktail party phenomenon**—has been studied using a technique called **shadowing**: A person participating in a research study is asked to listen through earphones to two simultaneously spoken messages and to repeat the message presented by one of the speakers. By assessing the accuracy of the person's repetition, researchers have been able to speculate about cognitive processes underlying attention.

In pioneering research by Cherry (1953), people who listened simultaneously to two speeches (each consisting of numerous clichés strung together) spoken by the same individual were unable to attend to just one of the speeches: Although these people were able to repeat entire clichés accurately, they sampled these clichés equally from the two speeches. On the other hand, when they heard two messages on different topics by different speakers with different voices coming from different directions, repetition of one of the messages was much more accurate.

People who shadow one of two messages notice very little of the other message. They can seldom report any of the words included in the unattended message and typically do not even notice whether the language spoken is their native tongue. Superficial characteristics, such as a change from a man's voice to a woman's voice, are noticed, but the content of the message is not (Cherry, 1953). Because of Cherry's findings, an early theory of attention (Broadbent, 1958) likened auditory attention to a filter that allowed the selection of one message on the basis of physical characteristics and the screening out of others, much as a television tuner tunes in to one broadcast and shuts out the rest.

Yet research subsequent to this proposed filter theory has indicated that people do not totally filter out information from a supposedly unattended message. People who participate in shadowing experiments notice particularly meaningful words (such as their own names) in the unattended message (Treisman, 1964). They also hear words from that message if those words fit meaningfully into the attended message (Gray & Wedderburn, 1960; Treisman, 1964). For example, suppose you hear these two sentences simultaneously and are asked to shadow only the first one:

Speaker 1: I bought candy at the plate today.
Speaker 2: Put the rhubarb on my store, please.

You might very well "hear" the first speaker say, "I bought candy at the store today" (borrowing the word *store* from the second speaker) because such a sentence makes more sense than what the speaker really said.

Figure 9–3
The Peter-Paul goblet.

Although most psychologists now reject the idea that attention is like a filter, they continue to have difficulty pinning down its precise nature. Generally speaking, you might think of attention as being focused cognitive processing of particular aspects of the environment (Barkley, 1996a; Cowan, 1995; Johnston, McCann, & Remington, 1995). Such processing does not necessarily exclude other parts of the environment, however. For example, at a cocktail party, people might select the sounds that resemble a particular person's voice and that seem to fit into a meaningfully constructed sentence. If a word from another speaker also fits the meaning, however, it might very well be incorporated into what is heard.

Attention as a Limited Capacity

Perhaps life would be much simpler if people didn't have to choose certain stimuli to pay attention to but could instead attend to *everything* that they record in their sensory registers. Unfortunately, it turns out that people are incapable of attending to everything at once. For example, look at Figure 9–3. At first glance, you probably see a white goblet. But if you look at the black spaces on either side of the goblet, you should also be able to see two silhouettes ("Peter" and "Paul") staring at each other.

Now try this little exercise: See if you can focus on both the goblet and the two silhouettes at *exactly* the same time, so that you can clearly see the details of both. Can you do it? Most people are unable to attend to the goblet and the faces at exactly the same time, although they may be able to shift their focus from the goblet to the faces and back again very quickly.

The Peter-Paul goblet illustrates a phenomenon that early Gestalt psychologists called **figure-ground**: An individual can attend to one object (the **figure**) and notice the details of that object. Whatever the individual is not paying attention to (i.e., the background, or **ground**) is not carefully inspected: The individual may notice a few salient characteristics, such as color, but is likely to overlook more specific information about unattended objects.[2]

Gestalt psychologists proposed that people can pay attention to only one thing at a time—hence the difficulty most folks have in attending to both the goblet and the faces simultaneously. More recently, other theorists (e.g., Broadbent, 1958; Cherry, 1953; Shapiro, 1994; Treisman, 1964; Welford, 1977) have proposed something similar: People can attend to only one *complex* source of information at a time. In situations in which more than one stimulus requires attention, one's attention must be switched quickly back and forth from one to another.

But now consider a situation in which you are driving your car while also carrying on a conversation with a friend. Are you not attending to two things, the road and the conversation, at once? To account for such a situation, some theorists (e.g., Anderson, 1990; Cowan, 1995; Kahneman, 1973; Norman & Bobrow, 1975; Pashler, 1992) have begun to describe attention as involving a **limited processing capacity,** with the number of stimuli being attended to depending on how much cognitive processing is required for each stimulus. If you are engaging in a difficult task, such as learning to drive a car with a standard transmission, you may very well need to devote your full attention to that task and therefore not hear a thing that your friend is telling you. However, if you are doing something more habitual or automatic, such as driving a standard transmission after years of driving experience, you can easily devote some attention to what your friend is saying. (Many tasks, such as driving, become increasingly automatic over time, therefore requiring less and less of our attention; we will address this phenomenon, known as *automaticity,* in Chapter 12.)

Regardless of how we view attention, one thing is clear: People's ability to attend to the stimuli around them is limited, such that they usually cannot attend to or otherwise learn from two complex situations at the same time (see Reisberg, 1997, for an exception). Thus, people must be quite selective about the information they choose to process and must ignore (and so lose) a lot of the information they receive. Frustrating as it may seem, people simply cannot attend to, learn, and remember everything they encounter.

WORKING MEMORY

Atkinson and Shiffrin (1968) used the term **short-term memory** to refer to a storage mechanism that holds information for a brief time after it is attended to so that it can be mentally processed. But as I mentioned earlier, most theorists now believe that this component of memory is also where cognitive processing itself takes place, hence their more frequent use of the term **working memory** (Baddeley, 1978, 1986; Baddeley & Hitch, 1974; Cowan, 1995; Daneman & Carpenter, 1980).

---

[2]For a contemporary analysis of the figure-ground phenomenon, see Peterson (1994) or Peterson and Gibson (1994).

As an example of the storage and processing functions of working memory, try solving this long division problem in your head, without referring back to the page until you have solved it:

$$37\overline{)4281}$$

Almost impossible, isn't it? You may have found that while you were dividing 37 into 42, you forgot what the last two digits of the dividend were. Although you probably had no trouble holding six numbers in your working memory, you may not have been able to hold all six and also process those numbers at the same time.

Working memory is that component of memory in which the active processing of information takes place. It determines what information will be attended to in the sensory register, saves that information for a longer period of time, and processes it further. It may also hold and think about information that it retrieves from long-term memory—information that will help in interpreting newly received environmental input. Many theorists portray working memory as playing a *central executive* role, in essence controlling and monitoring an individual's overall memory processes (Baddeley, 1986; Barkley, 1996b; Cowan, 1995; Haberlandt, 1997). In a nutshell, working memory is the component in which "thinking" occurs; therefore, you might think of it as the "awareness" or "consciousness" of the memory system (Bellezza, 1986).

Characteristics of Working Memory

The exact nature of working memory is beyond the scope of this book; for theoretical analyses of its possible structure, I refer you to Baddeley (1986) and to Schneider and Detweiler (1987). Here we will focus on the same three characteristics we examined for the sensory register: capacity, form of storage, and duration.

Capacity

Unlike the sensory register, working memory appears to have a very limited capacity for storing information. After reviewing a number of early studies, George Miller (1956) proposed that its capacity can be characterized as the *magical number seven, plus or minus two*: Individuals can hold from five to nine units of information in working memory at one time, with the average number of memorable units being about seven.

Miller further proposed that although the *number* of information units in working memory cannot be increased beyond 7 ± 2, the *amount* of information in each unit can be increased. For example, consider this nine-digit string:

6 3 1 9 8 0 2 5 7

People are more successful in learning long strings of digits if they group the digits into larger numbers, perhaps storing them something like this:

6-3-1   9-8-0   2-5-7

This process of combining pieces of information, called **chunking,** increases the amount of information that the limited space of working memory can hold. To use Miller's analogy, if you can hold only seven coins, you are far richer holding seven quarters, or even seven gold pieces, than seven pennies.

Current theorists believe that Miller's original assessment of 7 ± 2 is probably overly simplistic (Anderson, 1990; Schneider & Detweiler, 1987). It now appears that the number of chunks that can be stored depends on how much information each chunk includes. For example, Simon (1974) found that, although he himself could remember a list of seven one- or two-syllable words, he could remember only six three-syllable words, four two-word phrases, and even fewer phrases of more than two words. In other words, the larger the chunks, the fewer of them working memory can hold at any one time. Therefore, as Anderson (1990) has pointed out, it may be difficult to identify the true capacity of working memory, at least in terms of a specific number of discrete items that can be stored there at any given time. Furthermore, there may be a trade-off between how much processing is necessary and how much information can be held in working memory: Cognitive processing may take up some of its capacity, leaving less room for information storage. Nonetheless, one thing is clear: Working memory can hold only a small amount of information at any one time.

Form of Storage

Regardless of the form in which information is received, it appears that much of the information stored in working memory is stored in an *auditory* form, particularly when the information is language based (Baddeley, 1986; Baddeley & Hitch, 1974; Baddeley & Logie, 1992; Conrad, 1962, 1964, 1971). For example, in a study by Conrad (1964), adults were shown six-letter sequences, with letters being presented visually, one at a time, at intervals of three-fourths of a second. As soon as the last letter of each sequence had been presented, participants in the study wrote the letters down, guessing at any letters that they could not easily recall. When people recalled letters incorrectly, the letters they said they had seen were more likely to resemble the actual stimuli in terms of how they sounded than how they looked. For example, the letter *F* was "remembered" as the auditorially similar letter *S* 131 times but as the visually similar letter *P* only 14 times. Similarly, the letter *V* was remembered as *B* 56 times but as *X* only 5 times.

Working memory probably includes a means of storing information in a visual form as well (Baddeley, 1986; Baddeley & Hitch, 1974; Hitch, 1984). For example, deaf children probably store information in a visual form (Conrad, 1972). And young children (e.g., 5-year-olds) are less likely to use an auditory code than older children (e.g., 11-year-olds) (Conrad, 1971). Nevertheless, the auditory encoding of information provides a distinct advantage: It appears to improve the memory of information, at least over the short term (Conrad, 1971).

Duration

Working memory is just what its alternative name *short-term memory* implies: short. An experiment by Peterson and Peterson (1959) gives us some idea of how long information in working memory lasts. In this experiment, adults were told three consonant letters (e.g., *D X P*) and then immediately asked to count backward by threes from a three-digit number, which was different in each trial. At a signal that occurred anywhere from 3 to 18 seconds after the three consonants had been presented, the participants were asked to recall those consonants. When recall was delayed only 3 seconds, people were able to remember the letters with 80% accuracy; after an 18-second interval, however, their accuracy was only about 10%.

Considering research results such as those of Peterson and Peterson, psychologists believe that the duration of working memory is probably somewhere between 5 and 20 seconds. As is true for the sensory register, both decay and interference have been offered as explanations for the short time span of working memory. Some information stored in working memory may simply fade away (i.e., decay) if it is not processed further (Peterson & Peterson, 1959; Reitman, 1974; Shiffrin & Cook, 1978). Other information may be replaced ("bumped out," as one of my professors used to put it) by new input (Cowan, Wood, Nugent, & Treisman, 1997; Keppel & Underwood, 1962; Melton, 1963; Reitman, 1974). For example, with a husband and three children in the house, I find myself frequently interrupted in the middle of tasks. If I have a batch of cookies in the oven, and Jeff asks me to make him a snack and Tina asks me to help her find something she's misplaced, my cookies are very likely to be pushed from my working memory until I am confronted with new environmental input: The smell of something burning. My husband calls me absentminded, but I know better. My mind is definitely present, but the working component of it has a limited capacity, and new input interferes with the information already stored there.

Control Processes in Working Memory

Some of the control processes in working memory relate *only* to working memory; others help move information on to long-term memory. At this point, we will consider only the former processes, focusing on three in particular: organization, retrieval, and maintenance rehearsal. We will consider processes that promote long-term memory storage later in the chapter and again in Chapter 10.

Organization

Earlier, I described Miller's (1956) proposal that the process of chunking helps increase the amount of information that can be stored in working memory. As they develop, children show an increasing tendency to chunk information, thereby enhancing the capacity of their working memories (Farnham-Diggory, 1972).

Chunking is an organizational process, in that two or more pieces of information are combined. Information can be organized in a variety of ways. For example, consider again the nine-digit string I presented earlier:

6 3 1 9 8 0 2 5 7

I have already described one way of chunking this string: grouping it into three groups of three digits each. Another frequently observed organizational strategy is to impose a rhythm, or even a melody, on the numbers (Bower & Springston, 1970). Still another way of organizing the digits is to attach some meaning to them—a process that involves retrieving information that has previously been stored in long-term memory. For example, I can store the numbers as three meaningful pieces of information: My son Alex's birthday (the *6*th month and *3*rd day of *1980*), a quarter (*25* cents), and a week (*7* days). (We should note here that by attaching meaning to the numbers, we will also facilitate their storage in long-term memory; we will look at such meaningful learning as a means of long-term memory storage in Chapter 10.)

Retrieval

Retrieval of information from working memory depends largely on how much information is stored there, a point illustrated in a study by Sternberg (1966). In this experiment, college students were given a set of from one to six numbers, which the students presumably stored in working memory. An additional number was then presented, and the students were asked whether that number had been among the original set. The time it took for students to answer the question depended almost entirely on the size of number set already stored in working memory, with each successively larger set yielding a reaction time of about 40 milliseconds longer. Apparently, retrieval of information from working memory is simply a process of scanning all of the contents of working memory, successively and exhaustively, until the desired information is found.

Maintenance Rehearsal

You look up a friend's telephone number and store that number in your working memory; its seven digits are about the limit of what your working memory can hold. But then you find that someone else is using the telephone, and so you must wait to place your call. How do you keep your friend's number in working memory? If you are like most people, you probably repeat it to yourself over and over again.

Repeating information to keep it alive in working memory is a process known as **maintenance rehearsal,** which may be a form of subvocal speech (Landauer, 1962; Sperling, 1967). Maintenance rehearsal provides a means for saving information from the forgetting processes of decay and interference; when such rehearsal isn't possible, information in working memory disappears quickly. As an example, recall Peterson and Peterson's (1959) examination of the duration of working memory that I described earlier. After participants in the experiment were given the three consonants that they needed to remember, they were asked to count backward by threes until the signal for recall. Such backward counting kept them from rehearsing the three letters; otherwise, they might have kept them in working memory indefinitely simply by repeating them over and over as long as necessary.

Maintenance rehearsal is observed more frequently in older children and adults than in younger children (Conrad, 1971; Gathercole & Hitch, 1993; Rosser, 1994), so it may be a learned skill. I myself used rehearsal frequently in high school and college whenever I had difficulty remembering something I would be tested on—perhaps when I needed to know a complicated formula, a verbatim definition, or a lengthy list of items. I would continue to repeat the information to myself as test papers were distributed, then immediately write it in the margin so it would be there for me if and when I needed it.

Although maintenance rehearsal can indeed be a useful strategy for keeping information in working memory, teachers must remember that information in working memory will disappear once rehearsal stops. If students are using maintenance rehearsal frequently, their teachers might suspect that they are having trouble storing that information in their long-term memories. Yet long-term memory is where important information *should* be stored. Let's turn now to this final component of the dual-store model.

LONG-TERM MEMORY

Long-term memory is the part of the memory system that retains information for a relatively long period of time. It includes both memory for specific events and general knowledge that has been gleaned from those events over the years (Tulving, 1991, 1993). Some of the things stored in long-term memory may be easily retrievable, whereas others, even though they may ultimately affect our behavior, may be difficult or even impossible to bring into conscious awareness (Ellis, 1994; Gabrieli, Keane, Zarella, & Poldrack, 1997; Graf & Masson, 1993; Jacoby & Hayman, 1987; Schacter, 1993).

Long-term memory is clearly the most complex component of the human memory system. As such, it has been studied more extensively than either the sensory register or working memory, and theories about its characteristics and control processes abound. I will summarize the major characteristics of long-term memory here and then describe them in more depth in the following three chapters.

Characteristics of Long-Term Memory

As we did for both the sensory register and working memory, we will look at the capacity, form of storage, and duration of long-term memory; we will then turn to control processes.

Capacity
As far as theorists can determine, the capacity of long-term memory is unlimited. In fact, as you will discover in Chapter 10, the more information that is already stored in long-term memory, the easier it is to store additional information there.

Form of Storage
Information is probably stored in long-term memory in a number of different ways. For example, language provides one basis of storing information, and visual imagery may provide another. However, most psychologists agree that the bulk of information in long-term memory is probably stored *semantically*—in terms of meanings.

Two characteristics of long-term memory storage should be mentioned here. First, information is rarely stored in long-term memory exactly as it was received. Individuals tend to remember the gist of what they see and hear, rather than word-for-word sentences or precise mental images. Second, information stored in long-term memory is organized: Related pieces of information tend to be associated together. Ultimately, probably every piece of information is either directly or indirectly connected with every other piece.

Duration
As you will learn in Chapter 12, theorists disagree regarding the duration of long-term memory. Some theorists believe that information, once stored in long-term memory, remains there permanently. Others, however, believe that information can disappear from

long-term memory through a variety of forgetting processes. In fact, although some information may remain in long-term memory for long periods, there is probably no way to show conclusively that *all* information stored there remains permanently. The question about the duration of long-term memory is still open, and the best we can say is that long-term memory's duration is indefinitely *long*.

Control Processes in Long-Term Memory

In Chapters 10 and 12 we will examine long-term memory storage and retrieval processes in depth. At this point, let's get a general idea of what these processes entail.

Storage

Storage processes in the first two components of memory are fairly straightforward; anything sensed is stored in the sensory register, and anything attended to is stored in working memory. However, as we shall see in the next chapter, storage of information in long-term memory is not so simple. Although some information may be stored easily (visual images are an example), most information must be consciously and actively processed before it is stored. People store information in long-term memory most successfully when they understand it, organize it, and integrate it with information that they already have.

Remember, the processing necessary for storing information in long-term memory is accomplished in working memory. Remember, too, that working memory has a limited capacity and can handle only so much information at one time.[3] The result is that long-term memory storage occurs slowly, and a great deal is lost from working memory along the way. In essence, working memory is the bottleneck in the memory system: It prevents most information from ever getting into long-term memory.

Retrieval

Retrieval of information from either the sensory register or working memory is simple and easy: If the information is still there, it will probably be found. Retrieval of information from long-term memory is more difficult: Long-term memory has much more information than an individual can realistically search through at one time, so the success of retrieval depends largely on whether the individual searches in the right "location." Furthermore, retrieval from long-term memory is closely tied to storage processes: The more completely information has been understood, the better it has been organized; and the more closely it has been integrated with previously stored concepts, the more easily that information can be remembered.

Speaking of retrieval from long-term memory, what was Edward C. Tolman's middle name? Did you perhaps remember your friend Harry's brother-in-law, Marvin *Chace*? Or

---

[3]Some advocates for *speed-reading* programs claim that speed-reading greatly increases the amount of information that a person can learn and remember within a certain time period. Contemporary views of memory indicate that such results are highly unlikely. In fact, research tells us that people's comprehension of text is significantly lower when they speed-read than when they read at a normal rate (Carver, 1990; Crowder & Wagner, 1992).

did you think of Tolman *chacing* his rats down their mazes? The more ways that people store a piece of information in long-term memory, the better their chances of retrieving the information when they need it.

ARE WORKING MEMORY AND LONG-TERM MEMORY REALLY DIFFERENT?

Up to this point, we have been talking about working memory and long-term memory as two distinctly different components of memory. Some psychologists have proposed, however, that working and long-term memory are really a single entity. Let's look at the evidence both in favor of and against the working memory/long-term memory distinction.

Evidence Supporting the Distinction

Several research findings have been cited as evidence for the distinction between working and long-term memory. For one thing, the major form of storage in the two memories appears to be different, working memory being primarily acoustic and long-term memory being primarily semantic.

As another source of evidence, let's reconsider the serial learning curve described in Chapter 8 (to refresh your memory, refer back to Figure 8–12). Given a list of items to remember, individuals more often remember the first few items in the list (the **primacy effect**) and the last few items (the **recency effect**) than they remember the middle items. Some theorists have explained the serial learning curve in terms of a dual-store model of memory (Glanzer & Cunitz, 1966; Norman, 1969). From this perspective, people can process the first few items in a list sufficiently to store them in long-term memory, and they continue to hold the last few items in working memory after the entire list has been presented. They lose many of the middle items, however, because they don't have enough time to process them adequately for long-term memory storage and lose them from working memory as later items are presented. In support of the view that early items in a serial learning list are stored in long-term memory is the finding that when the presentation rate is slowed down (thus allowing for more processing), the primacy effect is increased (Glanzer & Cunitz, 1966). Conversely, when processing of list items is prevented, the primacy effect disappears; that is, items early in the list are remembered no better than items in the middle of the list (Peterson & Peterson, 1962). On the other hand, the recency effect seems to be more affected by the recall interval: The longer recall of the list is delayed, the less individuals are able to remember items at the end of the list, a finding consistent with the notion that these items are stored in the short-lived working memory (Glanzer & Cunitz, 1966; Postman & Phillips, 1965).

Third, studies of individuals who have undergone certain brain injuries or neurosurgical procedures sometimes show an impairment of one kind of memory without a corresponding loss of function in the other (Atkinson & Shiffrin, 1968; Eysenck & Keane, 1990; Scoville & Milner, 1957). For example, some individuals can recall events experienced before the brain trauma but are unable to retain new experiences, indicating a possible problem with working memory while long-term memory remains intact. Other individuals can recall new experiences long enough to talk briefly about them but cannot remember them a few minutes later; these are cases in which working memory is functioning, but new information seemingly cannot be transferred into long-term memory. Consistent with such findings, some evidence indicates that working memory and long-term memory processes may occur in different parts of the brain (Zola-Morgan & Squire, 1990).

Evidence against the Distinction

Other research findings indicate that working memory and long-term memory may not be as distinctly different as I have portrayed them. For example, although information is frequently stored acoustically in working memory and semantically in long-term memory, there is also evidence for *semantic* storage in working memory (Shulman, 1971, 1972) and for *acoustic* storage in long-term memory (Nelson & Rothbart, 1972).

Furthermore, some research studies have poked holes in the idea that the recency effect in serial learning necessarily reflects the use of a working memory separate from long-term memory (Crowder, 1993; Greene, 1986; Reisberg, 1997; Wickelgren, 1973). For example, in a study by Thapar and Greene (1993), undergraduate students viewed a list of words presented two words at a time on a computer screen; they also performed a 20-second "distractor" task (mentally adding a series of digits) after each pair of words. The students remembered the last few words in the list much better than the middle words, even though, thanks to the distractor task, *none* of the words could possibly have still been in working memory. Considering results such as these, theorists have suggested that the serial learning curve can be explained as easily by a single-store model as by a dual-store model. One possible explanation is simply that forgetting occurs rapidly at first and then slowly tapers off—a pattern that holds true for many different species and many different tasks (Wickelgren, 1973; Wixted & Ebbesen, 1991). From this perspective, the recency effect may simply be due to the fact that the last items of a list have not yet undergone that rapid decay. Another possibility is that items in a list are easier to remember if they are distinctive in some way; items near the end of the list have more memorable positions (e.g., a word may be "the last one" or "the next-to-last one") and so may be more memorable as a result (Greene, 1986; Reisberg, 1997).

Alternative explanations also exist for the impairments in memory observed in individuals who have undergone brain traumas (Eysenck & Keane, 1990; Glass, Holyoak, & Santa, 1979; Zechmeister & Nyberg, 1982). These impairments may reflect specific difficulties in storage or retrieval processes rather than in working memory or long-term memory per se.

The debate regarding dual-store and single-store models is by no means resolved; more complete discussions of the issue are presented elsewhere (Cowan, 1994, 1995; Crowder, 1993; Eysenck & Keane, 1990). In the meantime, many theorists are more concerned about how information is processed than about how many separate components human memory might have. The alternative views of memory I present next are examples of such functional theories.

FUNCTIONAL THEORIES OF HUMAN MEMORY

At least two alternatives to the dual-store model of memory have been proposed: a levels-of-processing model and an activation model. These theories emphasize the cognitive processes involved in human memory rather than its structure. Let's look briefly at each theory.

Levels of Processing

The **levels-of-processing** model of human memory (Cermak & Craik, 1979; Craik & Lockhart, 1972) was the first major theoretical alternative to the dual-store model. According to this view, incoming information is processed by a **central processor** (something similar to the *central executive* aspect of working memory) at any one of a number of different levels of complexity. This central processor has a limited capacity, in that it can hold only so much at one time; the information temporarily held there is what we are aware of at any given point in time.

How long and how well information is remembered after it leaves the central processor depends on how thoroughly it is processed initially. Information that isn't processed at all leaves only a very brief impression (much as it does in the sensory register of the dual-store model). Information processed superficially, such that only surface characteristics (e.g., appearance and brightness) are attended to, may last a few seconds (much as it does in the dual-store model's working memory). Only when information undergoes "deep" processing—that is, when it is interpreted, understood, and related to previously learned information—do we remember it for any length of time.

An experiment by Turnure, Buium, and Thurlow (1976) illustrates how different levels of processing lead to different degrees of information recall. Children 4 and 5 years old were asked to remember pairs of common objects (e.g., remembering that *soap* and *jacket* go together). Children processed the information in one of five different ways, as follows:

1. *Labels.* They repeated the names of the objects.
2. *Sentence generation.* They made up sentences that included both objects in a pair.
3. *Sentence repetition.* They repeated experimenter-generated sentences that stated a relationship between the two objects (e.g., "The soap is hiding in the jacket").
4. *"What" question.* They answered a question about a relationship between the objects (e.g., "What is the soap doing in the jacket?").
5. *"Why" question.* They answered a question concerning why a particular relationship existed between the objects (e.g., "Why is the soap hiding in the jacket?").

In this experiment, children learned most effectively when they were forced to think about (i.e., process) a relationship between the objects: the question-answering conditions (conditions 4 and 5) led to the greatest recall of the word pairs. Repeating a sentence that expressed such a relationship (condition 3) led to some recall; presumably repetition promoted some processing of the association between each pair. Least effective for learning were the first two conditions. In the labeling condition (condition 1), no relationship between objects was processed, and children in the sentence-generation condition (condition 2) often constructed sentences that did not effectively connect the two objects (e.g., "I have some soap and a jacket").

One element that frequently arises as being important in learning is **intention to learn**: people who intend to learn something are more likely to learn and remember it than people who do not specifically try to learn that information. Proponents of the levels-of-processing model have argued that people process information more thoroughly when they are intending to learn it and that the depth of processing, rather than the intention to learn per se, affects the success of learning. In fact, research supports this point: When individuals process material deeply, they often learn it successfully even when they are not specifically *trying* to learn it (Postman, 1964). In other words, nonintentional learning (often called **incidental learning**) is just as effective as intentional learning if the degree of processing is equal in the two situations.

A study by Hyde and Jenkins (1969) provides an example of successful incidental learning due to deep processing. College students were shown a list of 24 words presented at a rate of one word every two seconds. Some students (a control group) were merely told to learn the words; thus, they would be intentionally learning the words. Different experimental groups received different instructions, as follows:

1. *Pleasantness rating.* Students were told to rate each word for its degree of pleasantness; for example, a word such as *love* might be rated as relatively pleasant, whereas *hate* might be rated as less pleasant.
2. *Counting letters.* Students were told to count the number of letters in each word.
3. *Counting letter Es.* Students were told to count the number of letter *E*s in each word.

At the same time, some of the students receiving each of the different instructions were told to learn the words as they went along; these students were presumably engaged in intentional learning of the words. Other students were not told to learn the words; for these students, any recall of the words would presumably be the result of incidental learning.

The different tasks used in the Hyde and Jenkins study should lead to different levels of processing. In counting all of the letters in a word or the number of *E*s, one would need to look only at the superficial characteristics of the word and not have to interpret the word's meaning; thus, a counting task should lead to relatively shallow processing. In rating a word's pleasantness, one must examine the word's meaning; hence, deeper, semantic processing of the word should result. Consistent with levels-of-processing theory, students who rated words for their pleasantness remembered more words than students who counted letters. More interesting, however, is the fact that incidental learning students who rated the words for their pleasantness generally remembered as many words as any of the intentional learning groups (in fact, they did *better* than the intentional counting groups). Here was a case where learning was facilitated simply by virtue of the fact that students had to focus on the underlying meaning of the material to be learned. Depth of processing, not intention to learn, was the critical factor affecting the degree of learning.

Despite such convincing evidence, weaknesses of the levels-of-processing model have surfaced. For one thing, the idea of *depth* of processing is a vague notion that is difficult to define or measure in precise terms (Baddeley, 1978). Furthermore, some research indicates that degree of learning is not always a function of the degree of processing in the way that the model predicts. For example, the more frequently information is repeated, the better it can be remembered *regardless* of the depth of processing it has undergone (Nelson, 1977). Even more damaging, however, is the finding that, in some cases, superficial processing actually leads to *better* recall than deeper processing. In an experiment by Morris, Bransford, and Franks (1977), college students were given a series of words and asked (1) whether each word fit appropriately into a sentence (a task involving "deep" semantic processing) or (2) whether the word rhymed with another word (a task involving "superficial" phonetic processing). Students recalled more words on an unexpected recall test when they had processed them semantically; however, they were more successful at identifying rhymes of the original words when they had processed them phonetically. Stein (1978) has reported similar results.

More recent thinking related to the levels-of-processing approach is that information processing is most effective not necessarily when it is semantic but rather when it is *elaborative*—that is, when the learner adds information to the material to be learned in such a way that the new material is encoded more precisely, more meaningfully, and more completely (Craik & Tulving, 1975; Ellis & Hunt, 1983). We will examine the process of elaboration in more detail in the next chapter.

Memory Activation

Some psychologists (e.g., J. Anderson, 1983b, 1984, 1990, 1995; Collins & Loftus, 1975) have proposed that working and long-term memory are not separate components but instead simply reflect different **activation** states of a single memory. According to this view, all information stored in memory is in either an active or inactive state. Information

The author activates part of her memory.

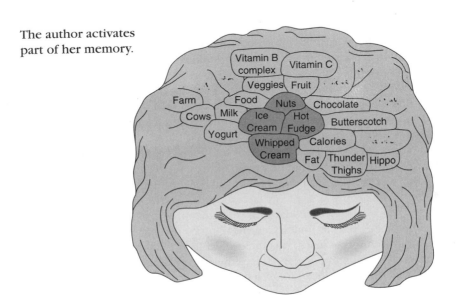

that is currently active, which may include both incoming information and information previously stored in memory, is the information that individuals are paying attention to and processing—information I have previously described as being in working memory. As attention shifts, other pieces of information in memory become activated, and the previously activated information gradually becomes inactive. The bulk of the information stored in memory is in an inactive state, so that we are not consciously aware of it—I have previously described this information as being in long-term memory. The activation theory of memory is particularly useful in understanding how individuals retrieve information from long-term memory. Accordingly, we will encounter this theory again in Chapter 12.

GENERALIZATIONS ABOUT MEMORY AND THEIR EDUCATIONAL IMPLICATIONS

Clearly, not all theorists agree about exactly how memory is structured or how it functions. But regardless of how we conceptualize the human memory system, there are several things we can conclude about how memory operates. At this point, let's make a few generalizations and consider their implications for educational practice:

- *Attention is essential for learning.* Regardless of which model of memory we use, we know that attention is critical for long-term retention of information. People will *not* learn the things that they don't process in some way, and paying attention is the first step that they must take.

There is an old saying, "You can lead a horse to water, but you can't make him drink." Ormrod's corollary is "The horse can't possibly drink if you don't at least lead him to the water." Helping students to focus their attention on important information is the first step in helping them learn it: It gets them to the water trough.

Yet classrooms are usually lively environments, with many stimuli competing for students' attention. For example, think of yourself in one of your college classes. Sometimes you pay attention to what the teacher is saying, but at other times your attention drifts to such things as the shape of the instructor's nose, the style of another student's clothes, the doodles on your notebook, or the plans you've made for the upcoming weekend. If adults cannot pay attention during every minute of a class session, how can we reasonably expect younger students to do so?

Actually, the things that teachers do in the classroom make a big difference in the extent to which students pay attention to the tasks at hand. Following are several effective strategies for capturing and holding students' attention:

- *Include variety in topics and presentation styles.* Repetition of the same topics and the same procedures day after day can lead to boredom and reduced attention (Zirin, 1974). Variety and novelty in the subject matter and the mode of presentation will help keep students' attention focused on a lesson (Berlyne, 1960; Good & Brophy, 1994; Keele, 1973; Keller, 1987).
- *Provide frequent breaks, especially when working with young children.* After prolonged periods of sitting quietly and attentively, even adults are likely to become restless and distracted. Frequent breaks are particularly

important for students in the early and middle elementary grades. For example, children are often more attentive after recess than before, even when they have been playing quietly in the classroom rather than running around the schoolyard (Pellegrini & Bjorklund, 1997; Pellegrini, Huberty, & Jones, 1995).

- *Ask questions.* Questions are an excellent way of maintaining students' attention when it might otherwise wander away from the topic at hand (Grabe, 1986; Piontkowski & Calfee, 1979; Samuels & Turnure, 1974). By asking questions periodically, and perhaps by occasionally addressing questions to particular students, teachers can help students keep their attention where it should be. (We will consider additional benefits of teacher questions in Chapter 13.)

- *Minimize distractions when independent work is assigned.* Most students are better able to concentrate on challenging independent assignments when their work environment is relatively quiet and subdued.

- *Seat students near the teacher if they have difficulty paying attention.* Students are more likely to pay attention when they are placed at the front of the room and near the teacher (Schwebel & Cherlin, 1972). Front row seats may be particularly appropriate for students with a history of being easily distracted.

- *Monitor students' attention.* Behaviors often provide a clue to whether students are paying attention. For example, students should be directing their eyes at the teacher, textbook, or other appropriate stimulus and should be clearly working on the task at hand (Grabe, 1986; Piontkowski & Calfee, 1979; Samuels & Turnure, 1974).

- *Different people may attend differently to the same stimulus.* As we discovered in our discussion of nominal versus effective stimuli, even when teachers successfully draw students' attention to instructional events or materials, they cannot always control *how* students attend to them. The Faust and Anderson (1967) study that I described earlier in the chapter (the one in which students studied Russian vocabulary words by reading either single sentences or several-sentence paragraphs) points to one important strategy for helping students attend effectively: Teachers should design classroom tasks in such a way that students can perform the tasks successfully *only* by paying attention to the things that are most important for them to learn.

- *People can process only a limited amount of information at a time.* We have characterized both attention and the "working" aspect of memory as having a limited capacity; in other words, people can pay attention to and think about only a small amount of information at any one time. Accordingly, getting information into long-term memory will be a slow process. Educators must remember this point in pacing their lectures and choosing their instructional materials. When too much information is presented too fast, students will simply not be able to remember it all.

- *Memory is selective.* Because learners usually receive much more information than they can possibly process and remember, they must continually make choices about what things to focus on and what things to ignore. Unfortunately, teachers and textbooks often load students up with more details than any normal person can possibly remember

(Calfee, 1981). In such situations, students must inevitably select some information to the exclusion of other information, but they aren't always the best judges of what material is most important for them to learn.

Details are often important means of illustrating, clarifying, and elaborating upon the main points of a lecture or textbook. In this sense, they are indispensable. At the same time, teachers must help their students sort through essential and nonessential information so that the students don't lose sight of the forest because of the trees.

• *The limited capacity of working memory is not necessarily a bad thing.* The working memory bottleneck forces learners to condense, organize, and synthesize the information they receive (e.g., Gagné & Driscoll, 1988). These processes may be in learners' best interest over the long run, as you will discover in our discussion of long-term memory storage in the following chapter.

SUMMARY

Memory theorists use some terminology that is uniquely their own. *Storage* means "putting" information in memory, *encoding* involves changing information to store it more effectively, and *retrieval* is the process of "finding" information already stored in memory.

Currently the most prevalent view of human memory—a *dual-store model*—maintains that memory has three distinct components. The first component, the sensory register, holds virtually all of the information that has been sensed for a very short period of time (a fraction of a second for visual information, two to four seconds for auditory information). If the information held in the sensory register is not processed in some fashion—at a minimum, by being paid attention to—it appears to disappear from memory.

Attention involves the selection of certain stimuli in the environment for further processing. Attention is influenced by several stimulus characteristics (size, intensity, novelty, incongruity, emotion, and personal significance), and what people actually pay attention to (the effective stimulus) is not always what outside observers *think* they are paying attention to (the nominal stimulus). Attentional capacity is limited: People usually cannot pay attention to more than one demanding task at any given time.

Information that is attended to moves on to working memory (also called short-term memory), where it is actively processed; in essence, working memory is the "thinking" center of the memory system. Working memory has a limited capacity; for example, most people can hold no more than five to nine digits there at a single time. Furthermore, information stored in working memory lasts only about 5 to 20 seconds unless it is processed further.

Information that undergoes further processing (e.g., integration with previously stored information) moves on to the third component—long-term memory. Long-term memory appears to have the capacity to hold a great deal of information for a relatively long period of time.

Theorists disagree as to whether working memory and long-term memory are distinctly different entities, and research investigating this issue has yielded mixed results. At least two alternatives to the dual-store model have been proposed: a *levels-of-processing* model, in which information processed in depth is retained longer than is information processed only superficially, and an *activation* model, in which the information stored in memory is either in an "active," conscious state or in an "inactive," unconscious state.

Despite differing perspectives regarding the exact nature of the human memory system, we can make several generalizations about how memory operates. For one thing, attention is essential for effective learning. Also, people can process only a limited amount of information at any one time, so they must be selective about the things they study. Finally, the processing bottleneck of the memory system is not necessarily a bad thing; it forces people to condense and integrate information in ways that are often beneficial over the long run.

Long-Term Memory I: Storage

A t least once a semester, a student will appear at my office door after receiving a low score on one of my exams. "But I studied so *hard*!" the student will whine, displaying a look of frustrated desperation. "I studied twice as long as my roommate did, yet my roommate only missed 1 question while I missed 17!"

Storing information in long-term memory and retrieving it later can be a tricky business. If the two roommates are equally motivated to achieve in my class, the difference between them may be due to their storage and retrieval processes. After more than 20 years of talking with students about how they typically study, I have come to the conclusion that most students are sadly uninformed about how best to learn and remember information.

Even when students do store information in their long-term memories, they don't always learn what their teachers *think* they are learning. For example, when my daughter

Tina was in fourth grade, she came home one day complaining about a song she was learning in the school choir. "It has bad words in it, Mom," she told me. I was quite surprised to learn that she was talking about "America the Beautiful," but then she recited the guilty line from the second verse:

All the bastard cities gleam.

After shuddering about the richness of my daughter's vocabulary, I patiently explained to her that the line in question was actually "Alabaster cities gleam." Two weeks later the rest of the family went to hear Tina's choir performing in concert. As the children began to sing "America the Beautiful," 6-year-old Alex turned to me and whispered, "Why are they singing about *spaceship* skies?"

Long-term memory provides a mechanism for saving information over a relatively long period of time. It also provides a knowledge base from which to interpret new information. As we shall see, people frequently store incoming information in long-term memory by relating it to things they already know—in other words, to things already existing in long-term memory. Different people are likely to store the same information differently, then, because they have previously stored different kinds of information in their respective long-term memories. Alex had never heard the word *spacious* before, but *spaceship* was a frequent word in his world of science fiction cartoons. Similarly, Tina was unfamiliar with *alabaster,* but . . . well, never mind.

In this chapter we will explore the multifaceted nature of long-term memory storage. We will first consider how storage is often constructive in nature and look at numerous examples of construction in action. We will then examine six control processes that are sometimes involved in long-term memory storage: selection, rehearsal, meaningful learning, internal organization, elaboration, and visual imagery. Later in the chapter, we will examine several factors that affect what people store in their long-term memories and how effectively they store it. In the following two chapters, we will look at the nature of the knowledge that people store and at the processes involved in retrieving that knowledge from long-term memory.

CONSTRUCTION IN STORAGE

Imagine, for a minute, that your mind worked like a videocassette recorder, such that you recorded everything you saw and heard. Your memory of an event would involve a simple process of finding and replaying the appropriate cassette, and you would be able to remember the event as completely and accurately as if you were reliving it. Studying for an exam would be easy, you might think—no need for reading the textbook more than once or for mindless repetition of meaningless facts over and over again.

Unfortunately, our minds are not accurate recorders of life events. As we discovered in the preceding chapter, we can process only a small amount of information in working memory at any one time, and so we quickly lose most of what we've stored in our sensory registers. In a manner of speaking, most of the information we receive from the environment is in one ear (or eye) and out the other.

Perhaps because we can save so little information for any length of time, many learning theorists believe that long-term memory storage often involves a process of *construction,* whereby we use the bits and pieces of information we do retain to build a reasonable understanding of the world around us. Let's look at several examples.

Examples of Construction in Action

At any given point in time, our interpretation of the environment (**perception**) is usually both less and more than the information we actually receive from the environment (**sensation**). Perception is *less* than sensation because people cannot possibly interpret all of the information that bombards their sensory receptors at any given moment. Right now, as you are looking at this book, light waves are bouncing off of the page and hitting the light-sensitive cells in the retinas of your eyes. At the same time, you may also be receiving light waves from a table on which your book is resting, the carpet on the floor, and the pictures on the walls. Your ears are probably receiving numerous sound waves, perhaps from a radio, a nearby conversation, an air conditioner, or traffic outside of your window. Perhaps a certain smell is drifting through the air, or a certain taste from your last meal lingers in your mouth. It is neither necessary nor possible for you to interpret *all* of these sensations, so you will attend to some of them and ignore the others.

But perception is also much *more* than sensation, because sensation alone provides insufficient information for an adequate interpretation of ongoing events. It appears that people use the data they receive from their sensory receptors to put together, or construct, an overall perception of any given situation (Neisser, 1967; Ornstein, 1972). As an example, consider the fact that our eyes do not provide a continual report of visual stimulation; rather, they jump from one focal point to another, taking periodic "snapshots" of the visual field. These jumps in focus, or **saccades,** occur four or five times a second, with

People often make assumptions about what they don't see and are often surprised when such assumptions are inaccurate.

visual sensation occurring primarily during the rest periods between them (Abrams, 1994; Irwin, 1996). If we receive only four or five snapshots of visual information each second, our visual world should appear jerky and erratic, much as an old-time movie does. The fact that we instead see smooth-flowing motion is due in large part to the mental "filling in" that occurs as our minds interpret visual sensations.

Even if human eyes functioned 100% of the time, they would typically provide an incomplete picture of the environment, and we would have to fill in mentally the information that we did not sense. For example, imagine walking into a bookstore and seeing the store clerk behind the counter. You probably sense only the clerk's head and upper torso, yet you perceive an entire person. You assume that the clerk has a lower torso and two legs, and in fact you would be quite surprised if the clerk's lower body looked any other way.

As another example of construction in perception, look at the three pictures in Figure 10–1. Most people perceive the picture on the left as being that of a woman, even though many of her features are missing. Enough features are visible—an eye and parts of the nose, mouth, chin, and hair—that you can construct a meaningful perception from them. Do the other two figures provide enough information for you to construct two more faces? Construction of a face from the figure on the right may take you a while, but it can be done.

Consider, too, how much is missing from the spoken language that we hear. For example, let's say that you are in a noisy room and hear someone say:

I -an't -ear a thing in this -lace!

Although you haven't heard everything the person said, you may have enough information to perceive the sentence:

I can't hear a thing in this place!

Figure 10–1
Can you construct a person from each of these pictures?
Reprinted from "Age in the Development of Closure Ability in Children" by C. M. Mooney, 1957, *Canadian Journal of Psychology, 11,* p. 220. Copyright 1957 by Canadian Psychological Association. Reprinted with permission.

Even when you do hear everything the speaker says, what you *really* hear is a continu-ousstreamofsoundwaves rather than . . . separate . . . words . . . spoken . . . like . . . this. Only when you are familiar with the particular language being spoken can you mentally divide the one long sound you actually sense into separate words. For instance, you could easily understand the following sentence when you heard it:

> *I read a book*

even though the identical sentence in Chinese would give you trouble:

> *Wŏkànshū.*

To an individual fluent in Mandarin Chinese rather than English, the situation would be reversed; that person would "hear" this:

> *Ireadabook*

and this:

> *Wŏ kàn shū.*

Curiously, once you have constructed meaning from what you have seen or heard, that meaning then seems quite obvious to you. Furthermore, you tend to perceive the same sensory information in the same way at a future time; a particular construction of sensory input tends to stick. For example, if you were to close this book now and not pick it up again for a week or more, you would see the three faces in Figure 10–1 almost imme-diately, even if you had had difficulty perceiving them originally.

We should note here that people don't always construct the same interpretation of any given event. For example, consider Tina's and Alex's rather unconventional interpreta-tions of "America the Beautiful." As another example, take a close look at the picture in Fig-ure 10–2. Describe to yourself what you see. Notice the shape of the head, the eye, the nose, the mouth, the chin. But just what is it that you *do* see? Is this a picture of a man? Or is it, perhaps, a picture of a rat or a mouse?

The man-rat picture in Figure 10–2 is an example of an **ambiguous stimulus,** some-thing that readily lends itself to more than one possible construction. Some people per-ceive the figure as a bald man with an overbite and a backward tilt to his head. Others instead perceive a rat or mouse with a very short front leg and a long tail curling beneath its body (Bugelski & Alampay, 1961).

Figure 10–2

Reprinted from "The Role of Fre-quency in Developing Perceptual Sets" by B. R. Bugelski & D. A. Alam-pay, 1961, *Canadian Journal of Psy-chology, 15,* p. 206. Copyright 1961 by Canadian Psychological Associa-tion. Reprinted with permission.

As you can see, then, people often perceive the world in their own unique ways, and all may arrive at different conclusions about what they have seen and heard. As a result, several people witnessing the same event often store very different things in their long-term memories. Let's now look more closely at the processes involved in long-term memory storage.

LONG-TERM MEMORY STORAGE PROCESSES

Before we begin our discussion of long-term memory storage processes, try this exercise. Following is a short story entitled "The War of the Ghosts." Read it silently *one time only;* then cover the page and write down as much of the story as you can remember.

The War of the Ghosts

One night two young men from Egulac went down to the river to hunt seals, and while they were there it became foggy and calm. Then they heard war-cries, and they thought, "Maybe this is a war-party." They escaped to the shore, and hid behind a log. Now canoes came up, and they heard the noise of paddles, and saw one canoe coming up to them. There were five men in the canoe, and they said:

"What do you think? We wish to take you along. We are going up the river to make war on the people."

One of the young men said: "I have no arrows."

"Arrows are in the canoe," they said.

"I will not go along. I might be killed. My relatives do not know where I have gone. But you," he said, turning to the other, "may go with them."

So one of the young men went, but the other returned home.

And the warriors went on up the river to a town on the other side of Kalama. The people came down to the water, and they began to fight, and many were killed. But presently the young man heard one of the warriors say, "Quick, let us go home: that Indian has been hit." Now he thought: "Oh, they are ghosts." He did not feel sick, but they said he had been shot.

So the canoes went back to Egulac, and the young man went ashore to his house, and made a fire. And he told everybody and said, "Behold I accompanied the ghosts, and we went to fight. Many of our fellows were killed, and many of those who attacked us were killed. They said I was hit, and I did not feel sick."

He told it all, and then he became quiet. When the sun rose he fell down. Something black came out of his mouth. His face became contorted. The people jumped up and cried.

He was dead. (Bartlett, 1932, p. 65)

Now cover the story and write down everything you can remember of it.

Once you have finished, compare your reproduction with the original. What differences do you notice? Your reproduction is probably shorter than the original. Some details are almost certainly omitted. Perhaps you even added some things. But you probably maintained the gist of the story: You included its main ideas and events, mostly in their proper sequence.

Using this Native American ghost story, Frederic Bartlett (1932) conducted one of the earliest studies of the long-term memory of meaningful verbal information. Bartlett asked his students at Cambridge University to read the story two times, then to recall it at various times later on. Students' recalled stories differed from the actual story in a number of ways:

1. *The words themselves were changed.* In other words, recall was not verbatim.
2. *The gist of the story, including the major sequence of events, was usually retained.* Some details, especially ones that were either essential to the story or particularly striking, were retained. Unimportant details and meaningless information, however, were omitted. For example, such details as "something black came out of his mouth" and "he was dead" were likely to be remembered; such details as "the young man . . . made a fire" and "a town on the other side of Kalama" were frequently forgotten.
3. *Parts of the story were distorted and other information was added to make the story more logical and consistent with English culture.* For example, people rarely go "to the river to hunt seals," because seals are saltwater animals. Students might therefore say that the men went to the river to *fish.* Similarly, the supernatural element did not fit comfortably with the religious beliefs of most Cambridge students and was often altered. In the following recollection, written by a student six months after he had read the original story, several additions and distortions are evident:

> Four men came down to the water. They were told to get into a boat and to take arms with them. They inquired, "What arms?" and were answered "Arms for battle." When they came to the battle-field they heard a great noise and shouting, and a voice said: "The black man is dead." And he was brought to the place where they were, and laid on the ground. And he foamed at the mouth. (Bartlett, 1932, pp. 71–72)

The main idea of the story—a battle—is retained. But after six months, the story has been so distorted that it is barely recognizable!

4. *There was a tendency to explain the story's events in addition to describing them.* For example, one student insisted on explaining events in parentheses:

> The young man did not feel sick (i.e., wounded), but nevertheless they proceeded home (evidently the opposing forces were quite willing to stop fighting). (Bartlett, 1932, p. 86)

Bartlett's findings illustrate several general principles of long-term memory storage. First, individuals select some pieces of information to store and exclude others. Second, they are more likely to store underlying meanings than verbatim input. Third, they use their existing knowledge about the world (i.e., things they have already stored in long-term memory) to help them understand new information. And fourth, some of that existing knowledge may be added to the new information, such that what is learned may be more than, and perhaps different from, the information actually presented.

In this section of the chapter, we will look at six processes related to long-term memory storage. We will first look at *selection,* the process of determining which information is stored in long-term memory and which is not. We will also examine *rehearsal,* a means of processing information in a relatively nonmeaningful, rote manner. Next, we will turn to *meaningful learning, internal organization,* and *elaboration*—three processes that involve encoding information in terms of its meanings. Finally, we will consider *visual imagery,* whereby information is encoded in a manner that reflects its physical appearance.

Selection

As you learned in the previous chapter, working memory is a bottleneck in the human memory system. It can hold only a fraction of what enters the sensory register. Furthermore, information in working memory must undergo additional processing before it can be stored in long-term memory. People must be extremely selective about the information they choose to process and must therefore have a means of determining what is important and what is not.

Long-term memory plays a critical role in selecting information for processing through the memory system. Individuals' knowledge about the world, their priorities, and their predictions about what environmental input is likely to be useful affect what they pay attention to and hence also affect what information moves from the sensory register into working memory (Schwartz & Reisberg, 1991; Voss & Schauble, 1992). A student who has learned that a teacher's lecture content will probably reappear on an upcoming exam is likely to pay attention to what the teacher is saying. A student who has learned that a teacher's exam questions are based entirely on outside reading assignments or has decided that an active social life is more important than classroom achievement may instead attend to something more relevant or interesting—perhaps the flattering sweater worn by the student on her right.

In some cases, once information has been attended to, it is automatically stored in long-term memory (Hasher & Zacks, 1984; Zacks, Hasher, & Hock, 1986). For example, consider the following question:

Which word occurs more frequently in English—bacon *or* pastrami?

You probably had no difficulty answering correctly that *bacon* is the more frequent word. Hasher and Zacks (1984) found that people could easily answer such questions about the frequency of events even though they had never bothered to count them. Similarly, they could answer questions about the spatial and temporal locations of events without having intentionally processed such information.

However, more meaningful information apparently must be encoded as well as attended to if it is to be stored effectively in long-term memory. Such encoding takes time. For example, Simon (1974) has estimated that each new piece of information takes about 10 seconds to encode. Using this estimate and her own estimate that 30 new pieces of information may be presented in a minute of a typical classroom lecture, one theorist (E. Gagné, 1985) has estimated that students can process only six pieces of information per minute—*one-fifth* of the lecture content.

Given the capacity and time constraints of human memory, how can teachers help students select important information? An obvious way is simply to tell students what information is important and what is not; when students are told *not* to remember certain information, that information is less likely to go beyond working memory (Bjork, 1972). Another way is to build redundancy into lectures and instructional materials by repeating important points several times. For example, when I am presenting an important idea to my students, I typically present it several different times. I state the idea once and then state it again using different words. I then illustrate it with at least two examples (often as many as five), and I present the idea itself once again. Notice the redundancy in the last four sentences—it should have been very difficult not to process my meaning at least once!

Rehearsal

You should recall from the preceding chapter that rehearsal provides a means of maintaining information in working memory indefinitely. Atkinson and Shiffrin (1971) proposed that rehearsal is also a method of storing information in long-term memory, and there is some evidence that they were right. Several studies have shown that people remember frequently rehearsed items better than less frequently rehearsed ones (Nelson, 1977; Rundus, 1971; Rundus & Atkinson, 1971).

Yet a number of theorists have argued that rehearsal leads to storage in long-term memory only if, in the process, the learner associates the new information with existing knowledge (Craik & Watkins, 1973; Klatzky, 1975; Watkins & Watkins, 1974). From their perspective, mere repetition of information—maintenance rehearsal—is sufficient to keep the information in working memory but *in*sufficient to move it into long-term memory. Rehearsal that in some way helps learners make associations between the new information and things they already know—**elaborative rehearsal**—does facilitate storage in long-term memory. For example, in a study by Craik and Watkins (1973), college students were asked to perform two tasks simultaneously: They had to keep one word in their working memories (by rehearsing it) while at the same time examining additional words to see if they met certain criteria. In this situation, the amount of rehearsal did *not* influence the extent to which the students were able to recall the words they had rehearsed; apparently the second task kept them busy enough that they were unable to make associations with the rehearsed words. When the additional words were presented at a slower rate, however, recall of the rehearsed words improved, presumably because the students could devote more working memory capacity to forming associations with those words.

Learning information primarily through repetition is sometimes called **rote learning** (Ausubel, Novak, & Hanesian, 1978; Ausubel & Robinson, 1969; Hiebert & Lefevre, 1986; Mayer, 1996b). In rote learning, there is little or no attempt to make the information meaningful or to understand it in terms of things one already knows. If such information is stored in long-term memory at all, it is stored in relative isolation from other information. As you will discover when you read Chapter 12, information stored in this unconnected fashion becomes difficult to retrieve.

So many times I have seen students engage in simple repetition as a means of trying to learn new information. This process, often referred to as memorizing, emphasizes the learning of verbatim information rather than the learning of underlying meanings. Although young children (e.g., elementary school students) are especially likely to use this strategy when trying to learn new information (Cuvo, 1975; Gathercole & Hitch, 1993; Rosser, 1994), I have observed high school and college students using it as well. Teachers must help students understand that mere repetition is an inefficient means of storing information for the long run, if in fact it works at all. The four processes we turn to now—meaningful learning, internal organization, elaboration, and visual imagery—are clearly more effective methods of long-term memory storage.

Meaningful Learning

Look at this list of 15 letters:

MAIGUWRSENNFLOD

And now look at this list:

MEANINGFULWORDS

Both lists are the same length, and both contain exactly the same letters. Which list is easier to learn? No doubt you will agree that the second list is easier, because you can relate it to words you already know. In the same way, my daughter Tina related a phrase from "America the Beautiful" to her existing knowledge about the world (which unfortunately included *bastard* but not *alabaster*), as did my son Alex, who heard *spaceship skies* instead of *spacious skies.* By relating new information to knowledge already stored in their long-term memories, people find *meaning* in that information. Hence, this process is frequently known as **meaningful learning;** it is also what we are referring to when we talk about understanding or comprehension.

We learn information meaningfully by storing it in long-term memory in association with similar, related pieces of information. Meaningful learning appears to facilitate both storage and retrieval: The information goes in more quickly and is remembered more easily (Ausubel et al., 1978; Mayer, 1996b). To illustrate, consider the following passage from an experiment by Bransford and Johnson (1972):

> The procedure is actually quite simple. First you arrange things into different groups. Of course, one pile may be sufficient depending on how much there is to do. If you have to go somewhere else due to lack of facilities that is the next step, otherwise you are pretty well set. It is important not to overdo things. That is, it is better to do too few things at once than too many. In the short run this may not seem important, but complications can easily arise. A mistake can be expensive as well. At first the whole procedure will seem complicated. Soon, however, it will become just another facet of life. It is difficult to foresee any end to the necessity for this task in the immediate future, but then one never can tell. After the procedure is completed one arranges the materials into different groups again. Then they can be put into their appropriate places. Eventually they will be used once more and the whole cycle will then have to be repeated. However, that is part of life. (p. 722)

All of the words in this passage were undoubtedly familiar to you, yet you may have had some difficulty understanding what you were reading. If you didn't know what the passage was about, you would have been unable to relate it to things in your long-term memory. But now try reading the passage again, this time thinking of it as a description of washing clothes. Bransford and Johnson found that college students who knew the topic of the passage remembered twice as much as those who had no topic with which to connect things.

People can also store nonverbal material more easily when it has meaning to them. For example, in a study by Bower, Karlin, and Dueck (1975), students were asked to remember somewhat meaningless line drawings; examples of these "droodles" appear in Figure 10–3. Students who were given meaningful labels for such pictures, such as "a midget playing a trombone in a telephone booth" or "an early bird who caught a very

Figure 10–3

Droodles from Bower, Karlin, and Dueck (1975).

From "Comprehension and Memory for Pictures" by G. H. Bower, M. B. Karlin, and A. Dueck, 1975, *Memory and Cognition, 3,* p. 217. Reprinted by permission of Psychonomic Society, Inc.

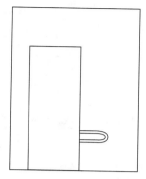
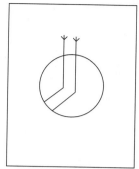

strong worm" were more likely to remember them correctly a week later than students who weren't given such labels.

Relating new information to one's *self* can have a particularly dramatic effect on learning. This point was clearly illustrated in a study by Rogers, Kuiper, and Kirker (1977). College students were given a list of 40 adjectives (some words were presented in large type and some in small type) and asked to respond to one of four questions about each word. They were then unexpectedly asked to remember as many of the 40 adjectives as they could. Following are the four questions asked about different adjectives and the amount of incidental learning that resulted from answering each of them:

Question	Percentage Recalled
1. Does it have big letters?	3%
2. Does it rhyme with _____?	7%
3. Does it mean the same as _____?	13%
4. Does it describe you?	30%

When the students were required to relate the word to something they already knew (question 3), they remembered more than when they were asked to deal with superficial characteristics of the word (questions 1 and 2). But when they were asked to relate the word to themselves (question 4), incidental learning was more than *twice* what it was for meaningful but not self-related processing.

Because meaningful learning allows new information to be organized with previously learned information, it is sometimes referred to as **external organization** (E. Gagné, 1985). Another equally important process is the organization of a new body of information within itself—a process known as **internal organization.**

Internal Organization

A body of new information to be learned is stored more effectively and remembered more completely when it is organized—in other words, when the various pieces are interconnected in some way. In fact, people seem to have a natural tendency to organize and integrate the information they receive. For example, in our discussion of verbal learning research in Chapter 8, we noted that people who are asked to remember a list of words

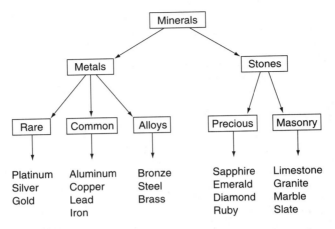

Figure 10–4
Example of a conceptual hierarchy from Bower et al. (1969).
From "Hierarchical Retrieval Schemes in Recall of Categorized Word Lists" by G. H. Bower, M. C. Clark, A. M. Lesgold, and D. Winzenz, 1969, *Journal of Verbal Learning and Verbal Behavior, 8,* p. 324. Copyright 1969 by Academic Press. Reprinted by permission.

often put those words into categories as they learn them (e.g., remembering all of the animals together, all of the vegetables together, and so on). You may also recall the Bransford and Franks (1971) study described in Chapter 8, in which students learned that "The ants in the kitchen ate the sweet jelly which was on the table" by integrating the content of several shorter sentences.

You have undoubtedly had teachers whose lectures were unorganized, with one point following another in an unpredictable sequence. As you might expect, material presented in such an unorganized fashion is more difficult to learn than clearly organized material. An experiment by Bower, Clark, Lesgold, and Winzenz (1969) demonstrates just how significant internal organization can be. College students were given four study trials in which to learn 112 words that fell into four categories (e.g., minerals, plants, etc.). Some students had words arranged randomly, whereas other students had words arranged in four conceptual hierarchies (the minerals hierarchy in Figure 10-4 is an example). After one study trial, students who had studied the organized words could remember more than three times as many words as those who had studied the randomized words. After four study trials, the students in the organized group remembered all 112, whereas those in the random group remembered only 70.

Many good students organize information spontaneously as they learn it, and such student-generated organization can in fact be very effective (Buschke, 1977; Mandler & Pearlstone, 1966; McDaniel & Einstein, 1989; Tulving, 1962). Furthermore, providing students with specific organizational schemes can dramatically affect student learning and retrieval (DuBois, 1987; DuBois, Kiewra, & Fraley, 1988; DuBois, Staley, Guzy, & DiNardo, 1995; Kiewra, DuBois, Christian, McShane, Meyerhoffer, & Roskelly, 1988). We will explore ways of facilitating students' organizational processes when we examine metacognition and study strategies in Chapter 14.

Elaboration

Suffering from cold symptoms? Consider the following:

> Aren't you tired of sniffles and runny noses all winter? Tired of always feeling less than your best? Get through a whole winter without colds. Take Eradicold Pills as directed. (Harris, 1977, p. 605)

Do Eradicold Pills prevent colds? If you believe that they do, then you were the unwitting victim of **elaboration:** You added your own information to the passage you read and "learned" that information along with what you had actually read. In a study by Harris (1977), people who read the preceding passage asserted that Eradicold Pills prevented colds almost as frequently as those who read an explicit statement to that effect.

When people receive new information, they often impose their own interpretations on it—perhaps making assumptions, drawing inferences, and so on—and learn those interpretations right along with the information they've actually received. Elaboration, then, is a process of learning *more* than the material actually presented; I like to think of it as *learning between the lines.* As an example, my son Jeff tells me that when he first heard the expression "losing one's voice" when he was in first or second grade, he concluded that people eventually lose their voices permanently. From this, he deduced that people are born with a finite amount of "voice" that they eventually use up. So as not to waste his own supply, he would mouth the words, rather than actually singing them, in his class's weekly music sessions.

Numerous studies lead to the same conclusion: People frequently elaborate on the information they receive and later have difficulty distinguishing between the actual "truth" and their elaborations of it (Bower, Black, & Turner, 1979; Graesser & Bower, 1990; Harris, 1977; Johnson, Bransford, & Solomon, 1973; Owens, Bower, & Black, 1979; Reder, 1982; Reder & Ross, 1983). To illustrate, the following is a passage from an experiment by Owens et al. (1979). Read it *one time only*:

> Nancy woke up feeling sick again and she wondered if she really were pregnant. How would she tell the professor she had been seeing? And the money was another problem.
>
> Nancy went to the doctor. She arrived at the office and checked in with the receptionist. She went to see the nurse, who went through the usual procedures. Then Nancy stepped on the scale and the nurse recorded her weight. The doctor entered the room and examined the results. He smiled at Nancy and said, "Well, it seems my expectations have been confirmed." When the examination was finished, Nancy left the office. (Owens et al., 1979, pp. 185–186)

Did the doctor tell Nancy she was pregnant? The fact is, he did not. Yet in the study conducted by Owens and his colleagues, when students read the passage and then were asked a day later to recall information about it, they "remembered" considerably more than they had actually read. Many of their recalled elaborations were directly related to Nancy's suspected condition. Other students in the experiment read only the second paragraph of the passage and so were unaware that Nancy thought she was pregnant; these students added far fewer elaborations.

As was the case for my son Jeff when he heard the expression "losing one's voice," and as may also have been the case for you when you read about Eradicold Pills, elaboration sometimes leads to distortions and errors in what is learned. But most of the time, elaboration is a highly effective means of long-term memory storage: Elaborated information is typically learned and remembered far more easily than nonelaborated information (Anderson, 1990, 1995; Bobrow & Bower, 1969; Craik & Tulving, 1975; Greeno, Collins, & Resnick, 1996; McDaniel & Einstein, 1989; Myers & Duffy, 1990; Pressley, 1982; Stein & Bransford, 1979; van der Broek, 1990). As Anderson (1990) has pointed out, most elaborations reflect correct assumptions and interpretations of an event, not incorrect ones.

Elaboration appears to be especially effective when it helps to tie new information together. For example, in studies by Stein, Bransford, and their colleagues (Stein & Bransford, 1979; Stein, Bransford, Franks, Owings, Vye, & McGraw, 1982), fifth graders and college students were instructed to learn a series of sentences. Each sentence involved a particular kind of man and a particular activity; following are some examples:

The fat man read the sign.

The hungry man got into the car.

The sentences were elaborated with phrases added on to them—elaborations generated either by the experimenters or by the students themselves. Some of the elaborative phrases (*precise* elaborations) explained the connection between a man's characteristic and his activity:

The fat man read the sign warning about the thin ice.

The hungry man got into the car to go to the restaurant.

Other elaborative phrases (*imprecise* elaborations) did not tie the characteristic and activity together:

The fat man read the sign that was two feet high.

The hungry man got into the car and drove away.

Precise elaborations were much more effective than imprecise ones in helping the students learn the sentences.

Elaboration probably facilitates long-term memory for several reasons. First, elaborated information is less likely to be confused with other similar information stored in long-term memory (Ellis & Hunt, 1983). Second, elaboration provides additional means through which the information can later be retrieved (Anderson, 1990, 1995); in a sense, it provides more places to "look" for the information. And third, elaboration may help with inferences about what the information was *likely* to have been when the information itself cannot be accurately recalled (Anderson, 1990).

Unfortunately, many students try to learn information strictly at face value, without trying to understand it, organize it, or elaborate on it (Linn, Songer, & Eylon, 1996; Snow, Corno, & Jackson, 1996). (As we shall discover in Chapter 13, teachers' frequent overreliance on assessment techniques that require verbatim knowledge may encourage such an ineffective approach to learning.) Students should instead develop study strategies that involve meaningful learning, internal organization, and elaboration processes. For instance, they can be encouraged to state ideas in their own words, generate their own examples of ideas, make connections between new concepts and their own past experiences, and draw logical inferences from the data they receive. We will identify several ways to help them acquire such strategies in our discussion of metacognition in Chapter 14.

Visual Imagery

Without looking back at Figure 10-3, can you remember what the "midget playing a trombone in a telephone booth" looked like? Can you remember the "early bird who caught a very strong worm"? If so, then you may have stored these things not only as the verbal labels that I gave them but also in terms of **visual imagery**—that is, in terms of mental "pictures" that capture how the figures actually looked.

As we shall discover in the next chapter, theorists disagree regarding the exact nature of visual imagery. Nevertheless, research indicates that forming visual images can be a powerful means of storing information in long-term memory. Numerous studies have shown that people have a remarkably accurate memory for visual information (Bower, 1972; Bruck, Cavanagh, & Ceci, 1991; Levin & Mayer, 1993; Standing, 1973; Standing, Conezio, & Haber, 1970). For example, in an experiment by Shepard (1967), college students looked at more than 600 pictures (color photos and illustrations from magazines), with an average inspection time of less than six seconds per picture. The students were then given pairs of dissimilar pictures and asked to identify which picture in each pair they had seen; they were able to do so with 98% accuracy. (Their accuracy on a similar task using words was only 88%.) Furthermore, images may be relatively enduring. For instance, in a study by Mandler and Ritchey (1977), people's memory for meaningfully organized pictures showed little decline over a four-month period.

We should note, however, that visual imagery does not always provide a complete, accurate representation of the information that has been received. Images tend to be fuzzy and less detailed than the original environmental input (Anderson, 1990; Loftus & Bell, 1975). They can also be distorted by an individual's general knowledge, as an early study by Carmichael, Hogan, and Walters (1932) illustrates. The experimenter asked adults to remember simple pictures like the ones shown on the left side of Figure 10-5. Two different groups were given two different sets of labels for these pictures, and the participants tended to remember the pictures in ways that more closely fit the specific labels they were given. For example, as you can see in Figure 10-5, the first picture was reproduced differently depending on whether it had been labeled as eyeglasses or dumbbells. Similarly, recall of the second picture was influenced by its identity as a kidney bean or a canoe.

Because images tend to be incomplete and inaccurate, they may not be helpful when precise, detailed information must be stored. For example, many educators have advocated the use of visual imagery in learning to spell (e.g., Harris, 1985; Radebaugh, 1985), and some research has provided support for this practice (Kernaghan & Woloshyn, 1994;

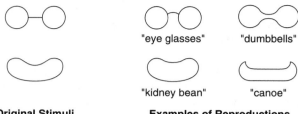

Original Stimuli   **Examples of Reproductions**

Figure 10–5
Experimental stimuli and examples of participants' reproductions, from Carmichael,
Hogan, and Walters (1932).

Adapted from "An Experimental Study of the Effect of Language on the Reproduction of Visually Perceived Form" by L. Carmichael, H. P. Hogan, & A. A. Walters, 1932, *Journal of Experimental Psychology, 15,* p. 80.

Roberts & Ehri, 1983). Although imagery may help spelling, we should remember that
one's visual image of a word will not necessarily include *all* of its letters (Ormrod & Jenkins, 1988). To illustrate, my mental image of the word *silhouette,* until I looked it up in
the dictionary just now, was something along these lines:

$$\text{sil} \text{ʔ} \text{ɔɪ̣ɛ} \text{ette}$$

I had an image of the word that was sufficient to recognize it when I read it but not sufficiently detailed for spelling it correctly.

Despite this drawback of visual imagery, its increased use in the classroom has been
widely recommended. Visual images can be stored quickly and retained over long periods
of time. Thus, students tend to learn more and remember it longer when the material they
are studying is concrete and easily visualizable (Clark & Paivio, 1991; Mastropieri, Scruggs,
McLoone, & Levin, 1985; Rice, Hauerwas, Ruggiero, & Carlisle, 1996; Sadoski et al., 1993;
Thrailkill & Ormrod, 1994). They also benefit when pictures and diagrams are provided to
support and supplement the ideas presented verbally (Clark & Paivio, 1991; Denis, 1984;
Kulhavy, Lee, & Caterino, 1985; Kulhavy, Schwartz, & Shaha, 1983; Mayer, 1983a, 1989a;
Small, Lovett, & Scher, 1993; Waddill, McDaniel, & Einstein, 1988; Wagner, 1989).

Encouraging students to form their own mental images of information can be an
effective instructional technique (Clark & Paivio, 1991; Gambrell & Bales, 1986; Sadoski &
Quast, 1990). For example, when students form visual images while reading stories or listening to explanations of school subject matter, they more effectively understand and
remember what they have read or heard (Cothern, Konopak, & Willis, 1990; Dewhurst &
Conway, 1994). Imagery can even help students form simple associations. For example,
when students are instructed to form visual images connecting pairs of objects, memory
for those pairs is enhanced (Bower, 1972). Accordingly, imagery provides the foundation
for a number of memory strategies called *mnemonics,* strategies that we will consider in
Chapter 13.

Of the six long-term memory storage processes we have just examined, the last three—internal organization, elaboration, and visual imagery—are clearly constructive in nature. Each of these processes involves combining new information with things that we already know. When we organize information, we often use a familiar framework (perhaps a hierarchy of well-known categories) to give new material a meaningful structure. When we elaborate, we use both new information and our existing knowledge to construct a reasonable interpretation of an event. When we use visual imagery, we often create those images for ourselves based on what we know about how objects typically appear.

FACTORS AFFECTING LONG-TERM MEMORY STORAGE

Several factors influence the specific ways in which learners store information in long-term memory and the idiosyncratic interpretations that they may construct from that information. In this section we will consider five factors influencing long-term memory storage: activities that occur during learning, working memory, prior knowledge, prior misconceptions, and expectations.

Activities That Occur during Learning

Some kinds of activities appear to facilitate long-term memory storage. One of these activities is **verbalization**—talking or writing about an experience that either has happened or is happening (Benton, 1997; Drevno et al., 1994; Hemphill & Snow, 1996; Konopak, Martin, & Martin, 1990; Nelson, 1993b; Tessler & Nelson, 1994). Children often talk with their parents or teachers about events they have experienced together. As an example, consider the following dialogue, in which 6-year-old Kerry and her mother talk about a recent whale-watching expedition:

Mother:	And we went with, who'd we go with?
Kerry:	David.
Mother:	David. Who else?
Kerry:	And Nana and Papa.
Mother:	And who else? Daddy went too, didn't he?
Kerry:	Yeah.
Mother:	Yeah. Who else?
Kerry:	That's all.
Mother:	Oh, and Auntie Karen and Uncle Pete, right?
Kerry:	Yeah.
Mother:	And David's two brothers.
Kerry:	Mmhm.
Mother:	We went whale watching and um I think it turned out to be a disaster because it was rough out there and we got kind of seasick. We did see whales, but not as good as we wanted to.
Kerry:	I saw one.
Mother:	Yeah, we saw them. They're big, huh?

Kerry:	[Nods.]
Mother:	How many were there?
Kerry:	About thirteen.
Mother:	About thirteen! There were only two or three!
Kerry:	No, there wasn't, because they were runnin' back and forth like fifty times! (Hemphill & Snow, 1996, p. 182)

Such discussions, which Hemphill and Snow (1996) call **co-constructed narratives,** can help the participants make better sense of an event and therefore encode it more effectively.

Writing provides an alternative form of verbalization that can facilitate long-term memory storage. For instance, when students write about what they are reading in their textbooks—answering study questions, relating the material to things they already know, analyzing various points of view, and so on—they are more likely to engage in such storage processes as meaningful learning, organization, and elaboration (Benton, 1997; Burnett & Kastman, 1997; Durst & Newell, 1989; Greene & Ackerman, 1995; Konopak, Martin, & Martin, 1990; Marshall, 1987).

Another activity that helps people encode what they are learning is **enactment**—performing physical actions related to the material to be learned. For example, young children more easily remember geometric shapes when they can actually draw those shapes (Heindel & Kose, 1990). Seventh graders better understand concepts related to map interpretation (e.g., latitude, longitude, scale, and map symbols) when they use such concepts to construct their *own* maps rather than when they simply answer questions about existing maps (Gregg & Leinhardt, 1994a). Undergraduate students studying physics can better apply the things they learn about how pulley systems work when they can experiment with actual pulleys rather than when they just look at diagrams of various pulley systems (Ferguson & Hegarty, 1995). We should note here that the importance of enactment has popped up in previous chapters under different guises: In our early discussion of behaviorism (Chapter 2) we noted the necessity for *active responding* in learning, and in our discussion of social learning theory (Chapter 7) we noted the importance of *motor reproduction* in modeling.

Working Memory

As we have seen, long-term memory storage is most likely to be effective when new material has numerous connections with existing knowledge. For learners to make a connection between a new piece of information and a piece of information that they already possess, they must be *aware* of the relationship between the two; in other words, both pieces of information must be in working memory at the same time (Bellezza, 1986; Daneman, 1987; Gagné & Driscoll, 1988; Glanzer & Nolan, 1986; Kintsch & van Dijk, 1978; Sweller & Chandler, 1994).

An experiment by Hayes-Roth and Thorndyke (1979) illustrates this idea. In this experiment, students read one of two passages describing a fictional country. The same pieces of information appeared in both passages but in a different order: In one passage related pieces of information appeared in sequential sentences, whereas in the other they appeared in separate paragraphs. Students more frequently made the connection between the two related pieces of information (and thus could draw an inference from them) when those pieces of information were presented one right after the other, presumably because both pieces were more likely to be stored in working memory at the same time.

People don't necessarily have to experience two things in sequence to make connections between them, however. In many cases, new information reminds learners of something they already know, leading them to retrieve that knowledge to working memory. In other cases, a wise teacher might point out the relationships between the new information and previously learned material, thus encouraging retrieval of relevant ideas.

Prior Knowledge

People can connect new information to prior knowledge only when they actually *have* knowledge that relates to the things they are learning. One of the most important factors affecting long-term memory storage, then, is what a person *already knows* (e.g., Ausubel et al., 1978). Learners who have a large body of information already stored in long-term memory have more ideas to which they can relate their new experiences and so can more easily engage in such processes as meaningful learning and elaboration. Learners who lack relevant knowledge must resort to inefficient rote-learning strategies. To put it bluntly, the rich (in knowledge) get richer, and the poor stay relatively poor.

Our prior knowledge about the world often affects our ability to encode even the most basic kinds of information. For example, when you see someone walking away from you, that person does not appear to shrink, even though the image on your retinas is in fact getting smaller. You have learned from past experience that people do not shrink just because they move away from you, and so you make certain mental adjustments regarding people's sizes. What would happen if you had no such prior experience with perceiving people and other things at varying distances? The anthropologist Colin Turnbull (1961) observed exactly this situation while studying the Ba Mbuti pygmies, a tribe living in the thick jungle of the African Congo rain forest. With no open spaces in their environment, the Ba Mbuti never had the opportunity to see objects more than a few feet away from them. Turnbull described one particular incident in which a member of the tribe, a man named Kenge, traveled for the first time to an area of open grasslands. When Kenge spied a herd of buffalo grazing in the far distance, he asked, "What insects are those?" and dismissed as folly Turnbull's reply that they were actually buffalo that were very far away. A short time later, as the men approached the buffalo by car, Kenge grew increasingly frightened as he watched the buffalo "grow" in size, fearful that a magic trick was being played on him.

Numerous studies have illustrated the importance of previous knowledge for encoding and storing new information (Alexander, Kulikowich, & Schulze, 1994; Chiesi, Spilich, & Voss, 1979; Dole, Duffy, Roehler, & Pearson, 1991; Gauntt, 1991; Hall, 1989; Machiels-Bongaerts, Schmidt, & Boshuizen, 1991; Novak & Musonda, 1991; Rouet, Favart, Britt, & Perfetti, 1997; Schneider, 1993). For example, some of my colleagues and I once conducted a study of how well people from different disciplines learn and remember maps (Ormrod, Ormrod, Wagner, & McCallin, 1988). We asked faculty members and students in three disciplines—geography, sociology, and education—to study two maps and then

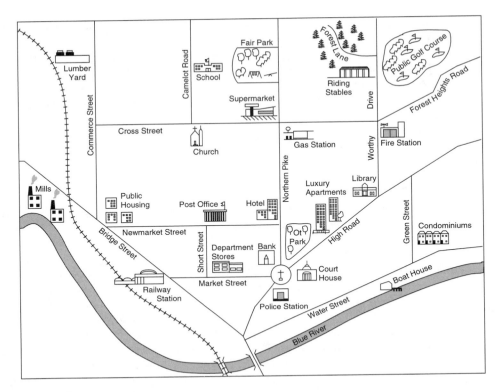

Figure 10–6

The logical city map from Ormrod et al. (1988).

Reprinted from "Reconceptualizing Map Learning" by J. E. Ormrod, R. K. Ormrod, E. D. Wagner, & R. C. McCallin, 1988, *American Journal of Psychology, 101,* p. 428. Reprinted with permission of the University of Illinois Press.

reproduce them from memory. The first of these maps, shown in Figure 10-6, depicts a city arranged in accordance with usual citylike patterns; that is, its arrangement is *logical.* Notice how the downtown business district is located at a point where it can be easily reached from different directions (this is typical), and the mills, lumberyard, and low-income housing are situated near the railroad tracks (also typical). The second map, shown in Figure 10-7, is on a larger scale and depicts several political regions (countries, perhaps). Several things about this map make no sense; that is, its arrangement is *illogical.* Notice how a river originates in the plains and runs *up* into the mountains, transportation networks do not interconnect, and towns are not located at transportation junctions. My colleagues and I predicted that geographers would remember more of the logical city map than either sociologists or educators because they could use their knowledge of typical urban patterns to learn the map meaningfully. We also predicted that the geographers would have no advantage over the other disciplines on the illogical "countries" map because geographic principles were largely inapplicable in making sense out of the map. Our predictions were confirmed: Geographers showed better recall

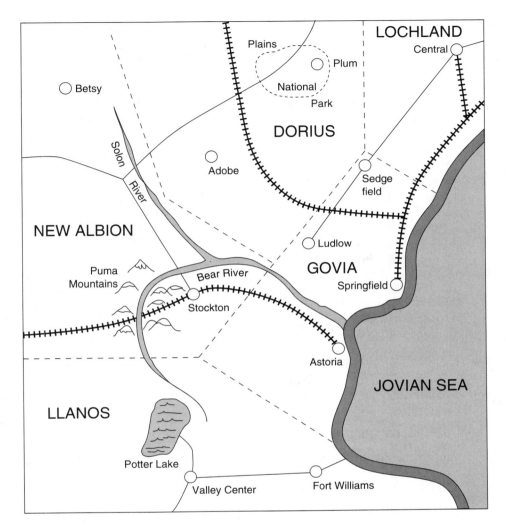

Figure 10–7

The illogical country map from Ormrod et al. (1988).

Reprinted from "Reconceptualizing Map Learning" by J. E. Ormrod, R. K. Ormrod, E. D. Wagner, & R. C. McCallin, 1988, *American Journal of Psychology, 101,* p. 429. Reprinted with permission of the University of Illinois Press.

than the other two groups for the logical city map but not for the illogical countries map. Because we had asked the participants to "think aloud" as they studied the maps, we were also able to examine the strategies they employed; as we expected, the geographers learned the maps more meaningfully than the other groups, and all three groups learned the city map more meaningfully than the countries map. Our nongeographers used primarily rote-learning strategies, mostly in the form of simple repetition.

Other studies have yielded similar results. For example, children who know a lot about spiders remember more from a reading passage about spiders than do children who initially know very little (Pearson, Hansen, & Gordon, 1979). People who know a lot about baseball or basketball can remember more new facts about those sports and more about what happened in a particular game than can people who are relatively uninformed about the two sports (Hall & Edmondson, 1992; Kuhara-Kojima & Hatano, 1991; Spilich, Vesonder, Chiesi, & Voss, 1979). Experts at the game of chess can remember the locations of chess pieces on a chessboard more accurately than chess novices, but only when the placement of pieces is logical within the framework of an actual game (Chase & Simon, 1973; deGroot, 1965). Second graders in Brazil who have experience as street vendors learn basic arithmetic more easily than students without street-vending experience (Saxe, 1988). Eighth graders who know a lot about American history engage in more elaborative processing when they read a history textbook (e.g., they are more likely to summarize the material, make inferences, and identify unanswered questions) than classmates who have less history knowledge (Hamman et al., 1995).

Although older children and adults usually learn most things more easily than younger children, we sometimes find the reverse to be true if younger children have more knowledge about the subject matter. For example, children who are expert chess players can better remember where chess pieces are on a chessboard than adults who are relative novices at chess (Chi, 1978). Similarly, 8-year-olds who know a lot about soccer remember more from a passage they read about soccer than 12-year-olds who know very little about the game (Schneider, Körkel, & Weinert, 1990).

Because everyone has somewhat different knowledge about the world, people are likely to elaborate on the same information in different ways and, as a result, to learn different things. For example, how would you interpret this newspaper headline (from Leinhardt, 1992)?

VIKINGS CREAM DOLPHINS

Your interpretation might depend on whether you are more attuned to American football or to possible early Scandinavian cuisine (Leinhardt, 1992). And consider the following passage from a study conducted by Anderson, Reynolds, Schallert, and Goetz (1977):

> Rocky slowly got up from the mat, planning his escape. He hesitated a moment and thought. Things were not going well. What bothered him most was being held, especially since the charge against him had been weak. He considered his present situation. The lock that held him was strong but he thought he could break it. He knew, however, that his timing would have to be perfect. Rocky was aware that it was because of his early roughness that he had been penalized so severely—much too severely from his point of view. The situation was becoming frustrating; the pressure had been grinding on him for too long. He was being ridden unmercifully. Rocky was getting angry now. He felt he was ready to make his move. He knew that his success or failure would depend on what he did in the next few seconds. (Anderson et al., 1977, p. 372)

Is this story about a wrestling match? Or is it about a prison escape? Read the passage again, and you should notice that it could be about either one. Anderson and his colleagues found that students' interpretations of the story depended on their background: Physical education majors more frequently viewed it as a wrestling match, whereas music education majors (most of whom had little or no knowledge of wrestling) were more likely to interpret it as a prison escape. Obviously, people elaborate on the same information in different ways, depending on their depth of knowledge about particular topics.

Prior Misconceptions

When people engage in elaboration, they use what they already know about a topic to expand on, and so presumably make better sense of, new information. But what happens when people use inaccurate "knowledge"—**misconceptions**—to elaborate? If people think that new information is clearly "wrong" within the context of what they currently believe about the world, they may sometimes ignore the information altogether. In other situations, they may change the information to be consistent with their "knowledge"; as a result, they learn something quite different from what was actually presented to them (Alexander & Judy, 1988; Bishop & Anderson, 1990; Dole et al., 1991; Lipson, 1982, 1983; Nussbaum, 1985; Roth & Anderson, 1988; Sneider & Pulos, 1983).

We saw one instance of such *mis*learning in Bartlett's (1932) study involving "The War of the Ghosts": Many students distorted the story to make it consistent with English culture. A study by Eaton, Anderson, and Smith (1984) provides another example. Fifth graders spent several weeks studying a unit on light in their science curriculum. A pretest had shown that many students had a particular misconception about light: They believed that people see things because the light shines on them and makes them brighter. During the unit, the correct explanation of human sight was presented: Light reflects off objects and travels to the eye, allowing people to see those objects. Yet despite reading and hearing this information, most students retained their misconceptions about vision in a test given at the end of the unit. Only 24 to 30% of them correctly indicated in their answers that light must travel not only from the light source to the object but also from the object to the eye.

Similar results have been reported by Champagne, Klopfer, and Gunstone (1982) for students studying physics. Many children have misconceptions about basic principles of physics that then interfere with their learning in a physics class. To illustrate, a misconception held by many students is that objects float on water because they are light rather than heavy, when in fact an object's *relative* weight, compared with water of equal volume, determines whether the object floats or sinks. Even when students correctly recite physics principles, they may continue to apply their earlier misconceptions when asked to explain real-world situations (Champagne et al., 1982). Hence, a student may accurately use the relative weight principle in describing how objects float on water yet have difficulty using that principle to explain why a heavy metal battleship doesn't immediately sink to the bottom of the ocean.

We see cases of distortion even at the college level (Bishop & Anderson, 1990; Holt-Reynolds, 1992). For example, students in teacher education programs may disregard a professor's definition of a concept, instead using their own (perhaps erroneous) understanding of what that concept means. And they are likely to ignore any recommendations for teaching practice that are inconsistent with their own beliefs about what "good teaching" is (Holt-Reynolds, 1992). Some of my own undergraduate teacher education students behave exactly as Holt-Reynolds has described. For example, they sometimes stick to their existing definitions of such words as *egocentrism, maturation,* and *elaboration,* even though I point out quite emphatically that a psychologist defines these words differently than a layperson does. And, despite the evidence I present regarding the effectiveness of meaningful learning, some of them stubbornly continue to believe that rote learning is a better approach.

Teachers often present information to students, thinking that it will correct any erroneous beliefs that students may have. Unfortunately, what often happens instead is that students stubbornly stick to their preconceived notions about the world and alter new information to fit those notions. Changing students' erroneous beliefs is therefore a difficult, although not impossible, task. We will identify some strategies for changing students' misconceptions in our discussion of conceptual change in Chapter 13.

Expectations

Read the sentence that follows:

> I pledge allegiance to the flag of the United Stetes of American, and to the Repulbic for which it stends, one nation, under God, indivsible, with liberty and justice for all.

You may have noticed one or two typographical errors in the passage. But did you catch them all? All together there were *five* mistakes, as shown in the following:

> I pledge allegiance to the flag of the United St*e*tes of Americ*a*n, and to the Repu*l*bic for which it st*e*nds, one nation, under God, indi*v*sible, with liberty and justice for all.

If you didn't notice all of the errors—and many people don't—then your expectation of what words *should* have been there influenced your interpretation of the sentence. If you have seen and heard the U.S. Pledge of Allegiance as many times as I have, you know that the phrase "I pledge allegiance" is usually followed by a certain sequence of words, and so you may have seen what you expected to see.

We often form expectations about the things we will see and hear—expectations based on our knowledge, and perhaps also on our misconceptions, about how the world typically operates. Such expectations can influence the ways in which we encode and store new information in long-term memory. In many cases we perceive and learn something more quickly when we have a good idea ahead of time about the information we are going to receive.[1] The process of reading is a case in point. Beginning readers pay close attention to the letters on the page as they read and, as a result, often read slowly and comprehend little. More mature readers tend not to look as carefully at the printed page. Instead, they rely on such things as context, sentence syntax, prior knowledge about a topic, and expectations about what the author is trying to communicate in order to draw hasty, although usually accurate, conclusions about what is on the page. It is precisely because mature readers jump to such conclusions that they read as quickly and efficiently as they do (Dole et al., 1991; Owens, 1996; Smith, 1988).

Yet such an efficient approach to reading has a potential drawback as well: Readers run the risk of jumping to the *wrong* conclusions and therefore misperceiving or misinterpreting what is on the page. They may have difficulty proofreading accurately, "seeing"

---

[1]In some contexts, this effect is known as *priming* (e.g., see Reisberg, 1997).

correctly spelled words that are actually misspelled. And they may have trouble learning how to spell the many new vocabulary words (e.g., *psychology, environment,* and *reinforcement*) that they encounter in their reading (Frith, 1978, 1980; Ormrod, 1985, 1986a, 1986b, 1986c). For example, people frequently misread my name—Jeanne Ormrod—as "Jeanne Orm*ond,*" an error that I find quite annoying. But let's face it: Ormrod is an unusual name, and Ormond is more common. One can almost not blame readers who see *Orm . . .* and just assume that the rest of the word is *. . . ond;* after all, using the first few letters of a word to identify that word is a common strategy in reading (Lima, 1993).

Earlier in the chapter I introduced the concept of *ambiguous stimulus*—a stimulus that can be interpreted in more than one way. Ambiguous stimuli are especially likely to be encoded in accordance with people's expectations (Eysenck & Keane, 1990). For instance, when I show the man-mouse picture (Figure 10-2) to students in my classes, I consistently find that the great majority of students who have been led to expect a mouse—by previously viewing a picture that is clearly a rodent—*do* in fact see a mouse or rat. Students who have similarly been led to expect a man see the bald-headed man. And notice how your expectations concerning how people typically behave influence your initial interpretation of the first statement in this verbal exchange (from Gleitman, 1985, p. 432):

"We're going to have my grandmother for Thanksgiving dinner."
"You are? Well, we're going to have turkey."

The behaviors that we see other people exhibit are often subject to numerous interpretations and so are prime examples of ambiguous stimuli. For example, if you see me smile at you (my behavior), you might draw any number of possible conclusions: I'm happy to see you, I'm *not* happy to see you but am being polite, I can't stand you but need a favor, I think that the outfit you're wearing is pretty ridiculous, and so on. People tend to interpret the behaviors of others in accordance with their own expectations (Juvonen, 1991; Nisbett & Bellows, 1977; Ritts, Patterson, & Tubbs, 1992; Snyder & Swann, 1978). People expect positive behaviors from a person they like or admire and so are likely to perceive that person's behaviors in a positive light—a phenomenon referred to as the **halo effect.** In much the same way, they expect inappropriate behaviors from a person they dislike, and their perceptions of that person's behaviors are biased accordingly— we could call this the **horns effect.** For example, imagine that Mr. Brighteyes, a fifth-grade teacher, has one student, Mary, who consistently performs well in classwork, and another, Susan, who more typically turns in sloppy and incomplete work. Let's say that both girls turn in an assignment of marginal quality. Mr. Brighteyes is likely to *over*rate Mary's performance and *under*rate Susan's.

Many factors affect people's expectations, and hence their interpretations, of another's behaviors. For example, people often expect higher-quality performance from people who are clean and well groomed than from people who are dirty and disheveled—hence the adage "Dress for success." Teachers expect well-behaved students to be more academically successful than poorly behaved students, and so their judgments of a specific student's academic performance is likely to be influenced by the way that student behaves in the classroom (Bennett, Gottesman, Rock, & Cerullo, 1993). Socioeconomic status also appears to make a difference; consider an experiment by Darley and Gross (1983) as an example. Undergraduate students were told that they were participating in a study on teacher evaluation methods and were asked to view a videotape of a fourth-grade girl named Hannah. Two versions of the videotape were designed to give two different impressions about Hannah's socioeconomic status; Hannah's clothing, the kind of playground on which she played, and information about her parents' occupations indirectly conveyed to some students that she was from a low socioeconomic background and to others that she was from a high socioeconomic background. All students then watched Hannah taking an oral achievement test (on which she performed at grade level) and were asked to rate Hannah on a number of characteristics. Students who had been led to believe that Hannah came from wealthy surroundings rated her ability well above grade level, whereas students believing she lived in an impoverished environment evaluated her as being below grade level. The two groups of students also rated Hannah differently in terms of her work habits, motivation, social skills, and general maturity.

Individuals' expectations and perceptions may even be influenced by other people's names. In an experiment by Harari and McDavid (1973), elementary school teachers were asked to grade essays written by 10-year-old children. Teachers who read an essay supposedly written by "Lisa" gave it a better grade than teachers who read the same essay but thought it was written by "Bertha." In the same way, "David" received better grades than "Hubert." Perhaps we should think of student essays as being ambiguous stimuli, because the criteria for perceiving (grading) them are often somewhat subjective. The grading of such ambiguous stimuli may be especially influenced by teachers' past experiences with—and therefore their expectations for—their students.

SOME FINAL REMARKS ABOUT LONG-TERM MEMORY STORAGE

Before we leave our discussion of long-term memory storage, we should note a few final points about storage processes:

- *Long-term memory storage is idiosyncratic.* Any two people store different information from the same situation. First of all, they attend to different aspects of the situation, so that different information is placed in their working memories. Second, they encode that information differently; for example, some people use visual imagery more than others (Clark & Paivio, 1991; Kosslyn, 1985; Riding & Calvey, 1981). And third, they bring their own unique background experiences to the situation so that the interpretations of what they observe are truly their own.

- *Storage of new information sometimes affects previously learned information as well.* Consistent with the process of elaboration, learners sometimes distort new material to fit their existing beliefs. Yet in other situations, a new piece of information may help learners recognize that something they stored earlier is inaccurate or that two previously learned pieces of information are related in a way they have not previously recognized.

- *The ways in which people store new information affect both the nature of the knowledge they possess and the ease with which they can retrieve that knowledge later on.* In the next two chapters, we will consider two other topics related to long-term memory: the nature of knowledge (Chapter 11) and retrieval (Chapter 12). As we address these topics, we will continually find that long-term memory storage processes are inextricably related both to what we know and how easily we can remember it.

SUMMARY

Many theorists believe that long-term memory storage processes are often constructive in nature. We typically store *less* than what we have sensed, because our working memories cannot hold all of the input that our sensory registers temporarily record. At the same time, we also store *more* than what we have sensed, using the often incomplete data we receive to construct a logical understanding of the events around us.

Long-term memory storage entails at least six processes. *Selection* is the process of determining what information we should process further and what information is irrelevant to our needs. *Rehearsal* is repeating something over and over again in a relatively meaningless (rote) fashion; its effectiveness in promoting long-term memory storage is questionable at best. *Meaningful learning* is connecting new material with similar ideas already stored in memory; in other words, it is a process of making sense out of that material. *Internal organization* is the integration of various pieces of new information into a cohesive, interrelated whole. *Elaboration* involves imposing one's own previously acquired knowledge and beliefs on new information. And *visual imagery* is encoding information in a mental "picture" that maintains its physical appearance to some extent.

Several factors affect how information is stored in long-term memory. For instance, it is often helpful to talk about, write about, or physically enact aspects of the things that are being learned. People can probably relate new material to their existing knowledge only when both things are in working memory at the same time. A greater degree of existing knowledge about a topic, provided that it is *accurate,* usually promotes long-term memory storage. Expectations about what will be seen or heard often yield more rapid and efficient learning. However, misconceptions and inaccurate predictions about the topic under consideration may often lead to distortions in what is learned and remembered.

CHAPTER 11

Long-Term Memory II: The Nature of Knowledge

Take a few minutes to answer the following questions:

1. What did you do yesterday?
2. In what kind of house or apartment did you live when you were 10 years old?
3. What is a *noun?*
4. How are rote learning and meaningful learning different?
5. Why do so many people raise cows?
6. In Great Britain's royal family, who is currently next in line after Queen Elizabeth to inherit the throne?
7. How do yu grow flowers from a package of flower seeds?
8. How do you order a chicken sandwich at a fast-food restaurant?

These questions asked you about eight very different topics, but I suspect that you could easily answer all of them. Even if you always lose at Trivial Pursuit and would never dream of becoming a contestant on the television game show *Jeopardy,* you nevertheless have a great deal of information stored in your long-term memory. Some of what you know relates to your own personal life experiences, but most of it is probably more general knowledge about the world. You've acquired some of your knowledge from teachers or textbooks, but you've probably picked up a vast amount on your own over the years. Furthermore, you don't just know things about your own past history and about the world around you; you also know how to *do* a great many things.

In this chapter, we continue our discussion of long-term memory, this time focusing on the nature of what is stored there—something we generally refer to as *knowledge.* As you will discover, theorists have gone in many different directions in describing the possible nature of human knowledge, and it will be virtually impossible for us to roll all of their ideas into one tight little package. For instance, several theorists have divided long-term memory into two distinctly different kinds of memory, but they don't all make the same kinds of distinctions. Theorists have different ideas, too, about how information is encoded in long-term memory and about how everything fits together into an overall organizational scheme.

In the pages that follow, we will examine some common views of the nature of knowledge in long-term memory. We will begin by exploring the diverse theories that psychologists have proposed regarding possible dichotomies, possible forms of encoding, and possible organizational schemes. We will then examine several of the particular forms that knowledge may take, with a focus on *concepts, schemas* and *scripts,* and *mental theories.* Finally, we will consider the overall quality of knowledge that people acquire and look at how expertise related to a particular field or discipline develops over the years.

POSSIBLE DICHOTOMIES IN LONG-TERM MEMORY

Up to this point, we have been talking about long-term memory as if it were a single, homogeneous entity. Many psychologists argue, however, that long-term memory may have two or more relatively distinct subcomponents. Following are three distinctions that theorists have made.

Episodic versus Semantic Memory

Tulving (1983) has made a distinction between **episodic memory**—one's memory of personal life experiences[1]—and **semantic memory**—one's general knowledge of the world independent of those experiences. Tulving points out that the two forms of memory are different in numerous ways. For instance, we *remember* events we have experienced (episodic) but *know* things about the world (semantic). We can often recall when a particular event happened to us (episodic) but usually can*not* recall when we acquired specific facts about the world (semantic). We are most likely to remember certain episodes in our lives when we are in the same context in which we first experienced those episodes, yet we can usually recall general information about the world regardless of the specific context in which we find ourselves. And our semantic memories typically stay with us longer than our episodic memories; for example, we are far more likely to recall how to order a chicken sandwich at a fast-food restaurant than to remember what we *did* order at a fast-food establishment a month ago last Tuesday.

Declarative versus Procedural Knowledge

Both episodic and semantic memory relate to the nature of "how things were or are"—something that many theorists refer to as **declarative knowledge.** But we also have something called **procedural knowledge:** We know "how to do things" (Anderson, 1983a; Hiebert & Lefevre, 1986; Phye, 1997a). For example, you probably know how to ride a bicycle, wrap a gift, and add the numbers 57 and 94. To perform such actions successfully, we must adapt our behaviors to changing conditions; for example, when riding a bicycle, we must be able to turn left or right when we find an object directly in our path, and we must be able to come to a complete stop when we reach our destination. Accordingly, as you will learn in our discussion of *productions* later in the chapter, our procedural knowledge must include information about how to respond under different circumstances.

Explicit versus Implicit Memory

How do you grow flowers from a package of flower seeds? You can probably describe the process fairly accurately, explaining that you need to plant the seeds in soil, make sure they have plenty of sunlight, water them regularly, and so on. But how do you keep your balance when you ride a bicycle? How do you move your legs when you skip? What things do you do to form a grammatically correct sentence when you speak? Such questions are more difficult to answer: Even though such activities are probably second nature to you, you really can't put your finger on exactly what you do when you perform them.

Some theorists distinguish between **explicit memory**—knowledge that we can easily recall and explain—and **implicit memory**—knowledge that we cannot consciously recall but that nevertheless influences our behavior (Ellis, 1994; Graf & Masson, 1993;

---

[1]Some theorists have developed the idea of episodic memory further, often using the term *autobiographic memory;* for example, see Conway and Rubin (1993) and Nelson (1993a, 1993b).

Reber, 1993; Schacter, 1993). Sometimes people have no conscious awareness that they have learned something, yet what they have learned clearly shows up in their behavior. This is the case, for example, for people who have suffered certain types of brain damage (Bachevalier, Malkova, & Beauregard, 1996; Cermak, 1993; Gabrieli et al., 1997; Kolers, 1975; Schacter, 1993). There is also evidence that we acquire some implicit knowledge when we learn either a first or second language: We can produce grammatically correct sentences even when we cannot explain how we do it (Ellis, 1994; Reber, 1993).

Not all theorists believe that long-term memory is necessarily comprised of such distinctly different subcomponents as those I have just described (e.g., see Conway & Rubin, 1993; Gabrieli, Fleischman, Keane, Reminger, & Morrell, 1995; Roediger, 1990; Schacter, 1993). Instead, it is quite possible that we have a wide variety of knowledge—episodic and semantic, declarative and procedural, explicit and implicit—all stored within a single long-term memory system. To some extent, the information we have in that long-term memory may also be encoded in several different ways, as we shall see now.

HOW INFORMATION IS ENCODED IN LONG-TERM MEMORY

Take a minute and think about a rose. What things come to mind? Perhaps words such as *flower, red, beautiful, long-stemmed,* or *expensive* pop into your head. Perhaps you can picture what a rose looks like or imagine its smell. Perhaps you can even feel a thorn prick your finger as you imagine yourself reaching out to clip a rose from its bush.

Information is probably encoded in long-term memory in a number of different ways. For one thing, it may be encoded *symbolically,* represented in memory by words, mathematical expressions, or other symbolic systems (e.g., "Roses are red, violets are blue"). Sometimes environmental input is stored as an *image* that retains some of its physical characteristics; for example, a rose has a certain look and a particular smell. Input may also be represented as one or more *propositions,* such that its underlying abstract meaning is stored; for example, the fact that "a rose is a flower" may be stored as an abstract idea. Still another way in which information can be stored in long-term memory is *productions*—the procedures involved in performing a particular task; for example, one learns the procedure necessary for clipping a rose from a rose bush. These four ways of encoding information—symbols, imagery, propositions, and productions—appear frequently in theories of long-term memory, and so we will examine each of them in more detail.

Encoding in Terms of Symbols: Words, Numbers, Etc.

A **symbol** is something that represents an object or event, often without bearing much direct resemblance to that object or event. As human beings, we probably represent much of our experience as symbols—as words, numbers, pictures, graphs, maps, models, and so forth (DeLoache, 1995; Flavell, Miller, & Miller, 1993).

As an example, there is no question that some information is stored in terms of actual words—in other words, as **verbal codes** (Bower, 1972; Clark & Paivio, 1991; Paivio, 1971,

1986).[2] First of all, people store verbal labels for most of the objects and events in their lives; for instance, this thing you are reading is called a *book*. Secondly, people sometimes learn information in a verbatim fashion; Hamlet's soliloquy ("To be or not to be . . .") and the Preamble to the U.S. Constitution are examples of things that people typically learn word for word (Rubin, 1977). On still other occasions people use language to help them associate things in memory. For example, the French word for "dog" is *chien;* I remember this word by thinking "dog chain." Many of the principles that emerged from verbal learning research (e.g., the serial learning curve) probably apply primarily to information stored in a verbal code.

Encoding in Terms of Appearance: Imagery

Can you imagine your mother's face? The melody of a favorite song? The smell of a rose? If so, then you are probably using mental imagery. Many psychologists believe that individuals store images in several modalities, including visual, auditory, and olfactory (smelling).[3] However, research and theory have emphasized visual imagery, so that is what we will focus on here.

Introspective reports have frequently been cited as support for the existence of visual imagery: People often say that they "see pictures" in their minds. However, given an inherent weakness of introspection—the fact that people cannot always describe their own cognitive processes accurately (Nisbett & Wilson, 1977; Zuriff, 1985)—psychologists have devised other research methods for demonstrating the existence of visual imagery. An example can be found in an ingenious experiment by Shepard and Metzler (1971) involving pictures of three-dimensional block configurations similar to those shown in Figure 11-1. In this experiment, adults compared pairs of these pictures and determined whether they represented the same three-dimensional configuration. For example, *a* and *b* in Figure 11-1 constitute a "match": if *b* were rotated 90 degrees clockwise, it would be identical to *a*. However, *a* and *c* are not a match: if *c* were rotated 90 degrees counterclockwise, it would become apparent that its top branch points in a different direction from that of *a*.

Shepard and Metzler measured people's reaction time to each pair of figures, assuming that more extensive cognitive processing would be reflected in longer reaction times. Results were quite dramatic: Reaction times were almost totally a function of how much a figure would have to be rotated for it to be lined up with another figure. In other words, the participants were responding as if they were mentally "rotating" mental images, with more rotation resulting in a longer reaction time. Similar results were obtained when people compared rotated letters (Cooper & Shepard, 1973).

Although at least one theorist has argued against the existence of visual imagery (Pylyshyn, 1973, 1979, 1981, 1984), most psychologists believe that it is a distinct form of

---

[2]If you have read Chapter 7, then you should recall that social learning theorists also talk about verbal codes as a way of remembering the things that one observes.

[3]For more on auditory imagery, see Intons-Peterson (1992), Intons-Peterson, Russell, and Dressel (1992), and Reisberg (1992).

Figure 11–1
Figures similar to those used by
Shepard and Metzler (1971).

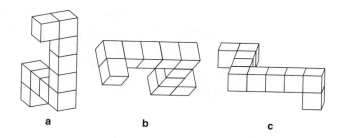

information storage (e.g., see Bower, 1972; Clark & Paivio, 1991; Farah, Hammond, Levine, & Calvanio, 1988; Kosslyn, 1980, 1983, 1994; Paivio, 1971, 1986). The exact nature of visual imagery is still an open question, but one thing is clear: A visual image is probably *not* a mental snapshot. Visual images tend to be imprecise representations of external objects, with many details omitted or altered (Chambers & Reisberg, 1985; Reed, 1974). Furthermore, individuals can construct mental images of things they have never seen; for example, you can probably visualize a rhinoceros with a pumpkin stuck on its horn even though you have never seen a rhino in that predicament. Some theorists are now beginning to think of imagery as being an *abstract analog* of visual input (Anderson, 1990; Glass, Holyoak, & Santa, 1979).

Encoding in Terms of Meanings: Propositions

People are more likely to remember the meaning of what they see or hear than precise, word-for-word detail. For example, think about the section you just read on imagery. What do you remember about it? You probably do not remember the specific words you read, but you should be able to recall the general ideas of the section. (If you cannot, go back and read the section again!)

Many learning theorists (e.g., Anderson, 1976, 1983a, 1990, 1995; Ellis & Hunt, 1983; E. Gagné, 1985; Kintsch & van Dijk, 1978; van Dijk & Kintsch, 1983; Weaver & Kintsch, 1991) believe that meanings are stored as **propositions**—that is, as small units of knowledge concerning relationships among objects or events. More specifically, to paraphrase John Anderson's (1990) definition, a proposition is the smallest unit of knowledge that (1) can stand as a separate statement or assertion and (2) can be judged as being either true or false. To illustrate, consider the following sentence:

Mary's uncle, whom she adores, owns a red Ferrari.

We can break up this complex sentence into four smaller assertions, each containing part of its meaning:

1.   Mary has an uncle.
2.   Mary adores the uncle.
3.   The uncle owns a Ferrari.
4.   The Ferrari is red.

Each assertion is either true or false; if any one of them is false, then the entire sentence is false. The four assertions are rough verbal analogs of the abstract propositions that may be stored in memory when the sentence itself is encountered.

Any proposition has two components. First, it includes one or more **arguments**—objects or events that are the topics of the proposition. Second, it involves a single **relation**—a description of an argument or a relationship among two or more arguments. For example, the assertion "Mary has an uncle" contains two arguments ("Mary" and "uncle") and one relation ("has"). Arguments are usually reflected by nouns and pronouns in a sentence, whereas relations are more typically reflected by verbs, adjectives, and adverbs.

Propositions provide a theoretical model of how meanings may be stored. It is becoming increasingly clear that a great deal of the information individuals receive is stored primarily in terms of underlying meanings. For example, participants in research studies can often remember information verbatim if asked to do so immediately after that information has been presented. When recall is delayed, their ability to remember the exact input declines rapidly, yet they continue to remember its *meaning* fairly accurately (Anderson, 1990; Brainerd & Reyna, 1992; Crowder & Wagner, 1992; Kintsch, 1977; Reder, 1982; Reyna, 1995).

Nonverbal visual information also appears to be stored at least partly in terms of meanings (Mandler & Johnson, 1976; Mandler & Parker, 1976; Mandler & Ritchey, 1977). An experiment by Mandler and Johnson (1976) illustrates this point well. In the experiment, college students looked at line drawings that included a number of different objects; for instance, one picture was a classroom scene that included a teacher, student, desk, bookshelf, flag, clock, globe, and large map. The students were then shown another set of pictures and asked whether each of the pictures was identical to a previous picture or had been changed in some way. Students were far more likely to notice changes in the pictures that reflected a change in the general meaning (e.g., the teacher was talking about a child's drawing instead of a world map) than in those that reflected a nonmeaningful change (e.g., the teacher's skirt and hairstyle were different).

Encoding in Terms of Actions: Productions

As we noted earlier, some of our knowledge is *procedural;* that is, we know how to perform various actions and activities. Some theorists have suggested that procedural knowledge is encoded in the form of **productions** (Anderson, 1976, 1983a, 1987, 1990, 1995; E. Gagné, 1985). Productions can best be described as a set of IF-THEN rules. For example, productions for riding a bicycle would include rules such as these:

1. IF I want to speed up, THEN I pedal at a faster rate.
2. IF I want to slow down, THEN I pedal at a slower rate.
3. IF my route turns to the right, THEN I turn the handlebars in a clockwise direction.
4. IF my route turns to the left, THEN I turn the handlebars in a counterclockwise direction.
5. IF an object is directly in front of me, THEN I must turn either right or left.
6. IF I want to stop, THEN I squeeze the brakes on the handlebars.

Similarly, productions for adding two two-digit numbers would include these rules:

1. IF the digits in the "ones" column equal nine or less, THEN I write their sum in the "ones" column of the answer space.
2. IF the digits in the "ones" column equal 10 or more, THEN I write the digit that appears in the "ones" column of that total in the "ones" column of the answer space and carry the "1" to the "tens" column of the problem.
3. IF the digits in the "tens" column equal nine or less, THEN I write their sum in the "tens" column of the answer space.
4. IF the digits in the "tens" column equal 10 or more, THEN I write the digit that appears in the "ones" column of that total in the "tens" column of the answer space and write the "1" in the "hundreds" column of the answer space.

As you can see, the "IF" part of a production specifies the condition under which a particular behavior will occur, and the "THEN" part specifies what that behavior will be. Productions, then, provide a means through which individuals can be responsive to different conditions in their environments.

In some cases, our knowledge about how to do something may begin as declarative knowledge (Anderson, 1983a, 1987). When we use declarative knowledge to guide our behavior, our performance is slow and laborious, the activity consumes a great deal of mental effort, and we must often talk ourselves through our actions (this idea should remind you of Vygotsky's *self-talk*). As we continue to perform the activity, however, our declarative knowledge gradually evolves into procedural knowledge, giving us productions that enable us to adapt more easily to changing circumstances. These productions become fine-tuned over time and eventually allow us to perform an activity quickly, efficiently, and effortlessly (Anderson, 1983a, 1987).

We may store information using any one of the four methods of encoding I have just described—symbols, images, propositions, and productions. Furthermore, we may sometimes encode the same information simultaneously in two or more different ways. In support of this idea, college students in an experiment by Pezdek (1977) confused information they had seen in pictures with information they had read in sentences. For example, some students first saw a picture of a car parked by a tree, then read the sentence, "The car by the tree had ski racks on it." These students tended to recognize a picture of a car with ski racks as being one they had seen before, even though the original picture had not included a rack; hence, they were probably storing the same information in both visual and verbal form. Similarly, in the study by Carmichael, Hogan, and Walters (1932) that I described in the preceding chapter (the study in which people looked at figures given one of two labels; see Figure 10–5 as a reminder), people probably stored the stimulus figures both as images (e.g., two balls connected by a line) and as words (e.g., *eyeglasses* or *dumbbells*). In fact, the more ways in which information is stored, the more likely it is that the information will be retrieved when it is needed at a later time (Clark & Paivio, 1991; Kulhavy, Lee, & Caterino, 1985; Paivio, 1975).

When the same information is coded in several ways, those different codes are apparently associated together in long-term memory (Heil, Rösler, & Hennighausen, 1994;

Reisberg, 1997; Sporer, 1991). It also appears that different but related pieces of information are frequently stored in connection with one another. We shall now look more closely at such interconnections—in other words, at the general organization of long-term memory.

THE ORGANIZATION OF LONG-TERM MEMORY

Contemporary theories of long-term memory are **associationistic:** They propose that pieces of information stored in long-term memory are associated, or connected, with one another. To show you what I mean, get a piece of paper and try this exercise. In just a minute, you will read a common, everyday word. As soon as you read it, write down the first word that comes into your head. Then write down the first word of which *that* word reminds you. Continue writing down the first word that each successive word brings to mind until you have a list of 10 words.

Ready? Here is the word to get your mind rolling:

beach

Once you have completed your list of 10 words, examine it carefully. It should give you an idea of what ideas are associated with what other ideas in your long-term memory.

Here is the list that I constructed using the same procedure and my own long-term memory:

> sand
>
> castle
>
> king
>
> queen
>
> Elizabeth
>
> England
>
> London
>
> theater
>
> *Hair*
>
> nude

Some of my associations might be similar to yours. For example, beach-sand and king-queen are common associates. Others might be unique to me. For instance, the last five items on my list reflect my trip to London many years ago when I attended a different play every night. The most memorable of the plays I saw was the musical *Hair,* in which several actors briefly appeared nude (quite shocking in 1969!).

Psychologists believe that virtually all pieces of information stored in long-term memory are directly or indirectly related to one another. Different individuals relate and organize their long-term memories somewhat idiosyncratically because their past

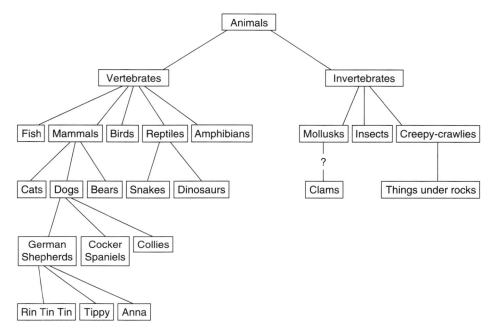

Figure 11–2
The author's hierarchical knowledge of the animal kingdom.

experiences have been different. Nevertheless, the organizational schemes that people use may share some common features. At least three models of long-term memory organization have been proposed: the hierarchy, the propositional network, and parallel distributed processing.

Long-Term Memory as a Hierarchy

An early view of long-term memory organization was that information was stored in a hierarchical arrangement, with more general, superordinate information at the top of the hierarchy and more specific, subordinate information below it (Ausubel, 1963, 1968; Ausubel & Robinson, 1969; Collins & Quillian, 1969, 1972). An example of such a hierarchy is my own knowledge of the animal kingdom, part of which is depicted in Figure 11-2. Notice how the most general category—animals—is at the top of the hierarchy. Next are two major categories of animals—vertebrates and invertebrates—followed by more and more subordinate categories, until finally specific instances of a category (Rin Tin Tin, Tippy, and Anna are all German Shepherds) are reached. As you can see, part of my hierarchy would resemble that of a biologist (my classes of vertebrates, for instance), but other parts are uniquely my own.

In a classic study, Collins and Quillian (1969) demonstrated how long-term memory might be organized hierarchically. Adults were given a number of statements (e.g., "A canary can sing") and asked to indicate whether they were true or false; individuals' reaction times to verify or reject the statements were recorded. Following are some examples of true statements and approximate reaction times to them:

Statements about Category Membership	Reaction Times (msec)
A canary is a canary.	1000
A canary is a bird.	1160
A canary is an animal.	1240

Statements about Characteristics	Reaction Times (msec)
A canary can sing.	1300
A canary can fly.	1380
A canary has skin.	1470

Notice how the reaction times increased for the three sentences regarding category membership: Participants most quickly verified that a canary is a canary and least quickly verified that a canary is an animal. Now notice the different reaction times for the three statements concerning a canary's characteristics: Participants found the statement about singing easiest and that about having skin most difficult. Collins and Quillian argued that the two sets of sentences are actually parallel, because most people associate singing directly with canaries, whereas they associate flying with birds and having skin with animals.

Collins and Quillian suggested that an individual's knowledge about categories and category characteristics is arranged in a hierarchical fashion similar to that depicted in Figure 11–3. To verify the statements, subjects had to locate the two components of the statement (e.g., "canary" and "skin") within their long-term memories and determine whether they were associated, either directly or indirectly. The farther apart the two components were in the hierarchy, the longer it would take to verify a statement (hence, the longer the reaction times).

Strictly hierarchical models of long-term memory have been the object of considerable criticism (Bourne, Dominowski, Loftus, & Healy, 1986; Loftus & Loftus, 1976; Wingfield & Byrnes, 1981). First of all, information is not always hierarchical in nature. Second, predictions consistent with hierarchically arranged information are not always confirmed. For example, just as people more quickly verify that a canary is a bird than they verify that a

Figure 11–3
A simplified version of the Collins and Quillian (1969) knowledge hierarchy.

Based on "Retrieval Time from Semantic Memory" by A. M. Collins & M. R. Quillian, 1969, *Journal of Verbal Learning and Verbal Behavior, 8,* pp. 240-247.

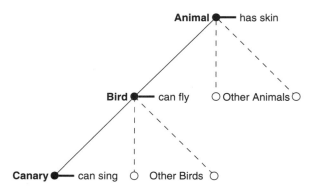

canary is an animal, we should expect that people would agree with the statement "A collie is a mammal" faster than the statement "A collie is an animal," because *collie* is closer to *mammal* than it is to *animal* in a logical hierarchy of animals. Yet the opposite holds true: People more quickly agree that a collie is an animal than that it is a mammal (Rips, Shoben, & Smith, 1973).

At this point, it appears that some information in long-term memory may be arranged hierarchically but that most information is probably organized less systematically. An alternative view of long-term memory, the propositional network, may provide a more useful and flexible theoretical model.

Long-Term Memory as a Propositional Network

A **network** model portrays memory as consisting of many pieces of information interconnected through a variety of associations. To illustrate, let's return again to my own previous list of successive associations resulting from the word *beach:* sand, castle, king, queen, Elizabeth, England, London, theater, *Hair,* nude. Such a list might have been generated from a long-term memory network such as the one in Figure 11–4. Different individuals should have networks with somewhat different associations and so should generate different lists. Some individuals, depending on their past experiences at the beach, might even associate *beach* and *nude* directly with each other!

Currently, the most popular model of long-term memory organization is the **propositional network** (Anderson, 1976, 1983a, 1983b, 1990; Anderson & Bower, 1973; E. Gagné, 1985; Lindsay & Norman, 1977; Norman & Rumelhart, 1975). A propositional network is

Figure 11–4

A hypothetical network of information in long-term memory.

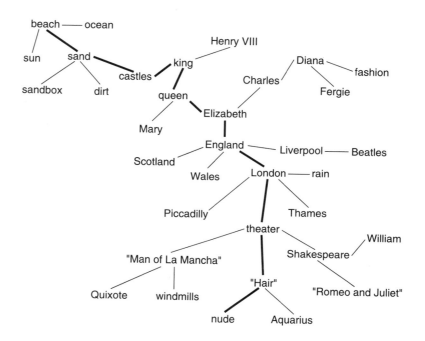

Figure 11–5
Diagrams of separate
propositions.

1. Mary has an uncle.

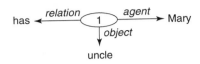

2. Mary adores the uncle.

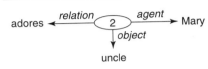

3. The uncle owns a Ferrari.

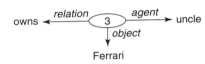

4. The Ferrari is red.

one in which propositions and their interrelationships are stored in a networklike fashion. As an illustration, let's return to a sentence we considered earlier in the chapter:

Mary's uncle, whom she adores, owns a red Ferrari

and to the four assertions it contains:

1. Mary has an uncle.
2. Mary adores the uncle.
3. The uncle owns a Ferrari.
4. The Ferrari is red.

The four assertions can be diagrammed as propositions, as shown in Figure 11–5. These diagrams, using Anderson's (1990) symbols, each show a proposition (symbolized by an oval) that encompasses one relation and one or more arguments.

As you should notice, the four diagrams in Figure 11–5 share several objects, or arguments; in particular, *Mary, uncle,* and *Ferrari* each appear in two or more propositions. Such commonalities allow the propositions to be linked in a network; an example is shown in Figure 11-6. A propositional network model of long-term memory is obviously more flexible than a hierarchical model. A hierarchy includes only superordinate-subordinate relationships; a network, on the other hand, can easily include a wide variety of relationships (e.g., possession, location, and opposition).

Network models are often conceptualized as including not only propositions (meanings) but other memory codes (such as imagery and productions) as well (E. Gagné, 1985; Glass et al., 1979; Paivio, 1971, 1986). For example, you might have a visual image of a Ferrari

Figure 11–6
A propositional
network.

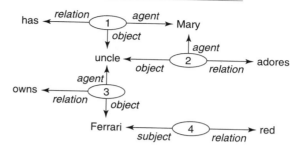

Mary's uncle, whom she adores, owns a red Ferrari.

stored in association with the information about Mary's uncle and his red sports car. Perhaps not too far away in the same network are productions related to how you drive a car.

In the preceding chapter, I described the process of *meaningful learning*—storing new information by relating it to knowledge already in long-term memory. Both hierarchical and propositional network models of memory give us an idea of how such meaningful learning might occur. For example, using a hierarchical model of long-term memory organization, Ausubel described the process as being one of **subsumption,** whereby people place new information under an appropriate superordinate category in their knowledge hierarchy (Ausubel, 1963, 1968; Ausubel, Novak, & Hanesian, 1978; Ausubel & Robinson, 1969). To illustrate, students are more likely to learn meaningful information about an animal called a "skink" if they are told that it is "a kind of lizard that looks like a snake" than if they are told that it is "brightly colored" or "a shy, seldom-seen creature." In the former case, they can store the concept *skink* under the more general concept *lizard;* in the latter two situations, they aren't really sure just *where* to put it.

Using a propositional network model of long-term memory, we can characterize meaningful learning as a process of storing new propositions with related propositions in the network. For example, let's assume that you have already stored some propositions concerning Mary's uncle and his red Ferrari in a form similar to what I depicted in Figure 11–6. You then read the following sentence:

The uncle is named Charles.

You might connect this proposition to your existing propositions about the uncle and perhaps to propositions concerning another Charles that you know, as illustrated in Figure 11–7.

Parallel Distributed Processing

Up until now, we have been speaking as if various items of information are each stored in a single "location" in long-term memory. However, some theorists believe that any given piece of information may actually be stored in *numerous* places, called **nodes,** throughout long-term memory. The nodes associated with each item are interconnected, so that when one is activated, the others become activated as well. At the same time, any single node may be associated with several pieces of information. Such a view of long-term memory is often called **parallel distributed processing (PDP):** Pieces of information

Figure 11–7
Meaningful learning
in a propositional
network.

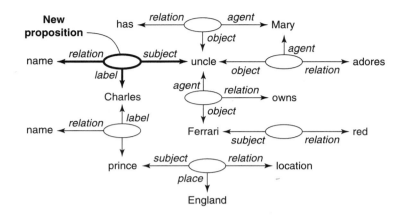

are stored in a "distributed" fashion throughout long-term memory, with numerous nodes being processed simultaneously in a parallel fashion (Ackley, Hinton, & Sejnowski, 1985; Ballard, 1986; Hinton & Anderson, 1981; Hinton, McClelland, & Rumelhart, 1986; McClelland & Rumelhart, 1986; Rumelhart & McClelland, 1986). Parallel distributed processing is also known as **connectionism,** but it should not be confused with Edward Thorndike's connectionism described in Chapter 2.

The parallel distributed processing model is still in the early stages of development, and it is not without its critics (Fodor & Pylyshyn, 1988; Holyoak, 1987; Lachter & Bever, 1988; Pinker & Prince, 1988; Sternberg, 1996). Nevertheless, the model provides a useful reminder that a single piece of information may in fact be stored in long-term memory in a multiple, "distributed" fashion, and that different pieces of information may overlap through the nodes they have in common.

Regardless of how long-term memory is organized, it clearly *is* organized. To some extent, people organize all of the information they store in their long-term memories. To an even greater extent, they organize their knowledge regarding very specific objects, events, and topics. At this point, let's turn to several specific examples of how people might organize their experiences, as we look at *concepts, schemas, scripts,* and *mental theories.*

CONCEPTS

One night in late May many years ago, my son Jeff and I had a discussion about the seasons. It went something like this:

Jeff: When are spring and summer coming?
Mom: Spring is already here. Haven't you noticed how warm it is, and how
            the leaves are back on the trees, and how the birds are singing again?

Jeff: Oh. Then when is summer coming?

Mom: Well, you only have one more week of school, and then a couple of
               weeks after that, summer will be here.

Jeff: Summer is when we go swimming, right?

Mom: [I pause and think about how to answer] Right.

As a 4-year-old, Jeff had not yet precisely defined the concepts of *spring* and *summer.*
When I was a child, summer was a season of heat, humidity, and no school. As an adult, I
now define it more formally as the three-month period between the summer solstice and
the autumn equinox. To Jeff, however, summer was simply the time when he could swim.

Generally speaking, you might think of a **concept** as a class of objects or events that
share one or more similarities (Flavell et al., 1993; Klausmeier, 1990; Schwartz & Reisberg,
1991). Some concepts are defined by readily observable characteristics and so are fairly
easy to learn. For example, the word *milk* refers to a white liquid with a particular taste.
Similarly, the word *red* refers to a certain range of light wavelengths (although people disagree about exactly where "red" ends and "orange" begins). Other concepts are defined by
less salient attributes, so are more slowly learned and more easily misconstrued. For
instance, the four seasons of the year are "officially" designated by the occurrences of sol-
stices and equinoxes that most people are unaware of, so many people erroneously define
them in terms of different weather conditions. Still other concepts may be even harder to
grasp, because they are based on abstract, relativistic, and sometimes elusive criteria. For
example, psychologists have wrestled with the concept of *intelligence* for many years and
still cannot agree on what the term means.

Theorists find it useful to distinguish between two general kinds of concepts
(Cohen, 1983; R. Gagné, 1985; Newby & Stepich, 1987; Wasserman, DeVolder, & Coppage, 1992). **Concrete concepts** are easily identified by their physical appearance; *cow,
red,* and *round* are examples. From a behaviorist perspective, concrete concepts may
develop, at least in part, as a result of stimulus generalization: Once an organism has
learned to respond in a certain way to one stimulus, it tends to respond in the same way
to similar stimuli. In contrast, **abstract concepts** are difficult to conceptualize in terms
of specific, observable characteristics; examples include *intelligence, charisma,* and
work. Abstract concepts are probably best described in terms of a formal definition (R.
Gagné, 1985). Consider the concept *cousin* as an example. There is no way to learn
what a cousin is simply by looking at examples of cousins and noncousins; all will have
one head, two arms, two legs, and so on. Instead, a person probably learns a rule (definition) for identifying cousins: A *cousin* is an offspring of a parent's sibling. Because stimulus generalization is unlikely to occur when objects or events don't *look* similar, abstract
concepts are most likely to develop as a result of specific training or instruction (Hull,
1943; Wasserman et al., 1992).

In many cases, people first learn a concept in a concrete form, then later acquire a
more abstract definition of it (R. Gagné, 1985). When I was a child, *summer* was a concrete concept for me: Heat, humidity, and no school were easily observable characteristics.
I later acquired an abstract concept of summer as I learned how the seasons are determined by the tilt of the earth in relation to the sun. In a similar way, children first learn
about a *circle* as a concrete concept (i.e., a "roundish" thing); later, perhaps in a high

One cannot learn abstract (defined) concepts such as *cousin* through physical examination alone.

Cousin Fred   Cousin Malcolm   Joe (no relation)   Tim (no relation)

school geometry class, they may develop an abstract concept of a circle (i.e., all points on a plane equidistant from another single point).

Most concepts are identified by a label—a word that symbolizes the concept and represents it in both thought and communication. For example, you have probably formed a concept that encompasses the many items you have seen with the following characteristics:

- Shorter and wider than most adult humans
- Covered with a short, bristly substance
- Appended at one end by an object similar in appearance to a paintbrush
- Appended at the other end by a lumpy thing with four pointy objects sticking upward (two soft and floppy, two hard and curved around)
- Held up from the ground by four spindly sticks, two at each end
- Usually observed in pastures or barns
- Almost always eating grass

You have no doubt attached a particular label to these similar-looking objects: *cow.*

We haven't truly acquired a concept until we can correctly identify all positive and negative instances of it. A **positive instance** is a particular example of a concept. To illustrate, you and I are positive instances of the concept *person,* and this thing you are reading is a positive instance of the concept *book.* A **negative instance** is a nonexample of the concept. You and I are negative instances of the concept *cow,* and this book is a negative instance of the concept *pencil.*

People often have "sort-of" understandings of concepts, in that they cannot always accurately separate positive instances from negative instances. A child who vehemently denies that a Chihuahua is a dog has not completely learned the concept of *dog,* and neither has the child who calls the neighbor's cow "doggie." Denying that a Chihuahua is a dog—**undergeneralization**—reflects an inability to recognize all positive instances. Identifying a cow as a dog—**overgeneralization**—reflects an inability to reject all negative instances. The various theories of concept learning that we now consider can help us to understand how such "sort-of" knowledge might exist.

Theories of Concept Learning

Several terms will be useful to us as we examine the various theories of concept learning that psychologists have proposed. In particular, I need to explain what I mean when I talk about different kinds of *features* and *rules*.

Features (some theorists instead use the term **attributes**) are the characteristics of a concept's positive instances. For instance, my dog Anna has numerous features worthy of note, including these:

- Hairy
- At one time physiologically equipped to give birth to live young
- Likely to bark loudly at any negative instance of an Ormrod
- Wearing a chain collar
- Presently located on my office floor

Some features are important for identifying positive instances of a concept, whereas others are not. **Defining features** are characteristics that must be present in all positive instances. For example, to be a dog, Anna must have hair and, as a female member of the species, must have (or once have had) the capability of giving birth to live young. **Correlational features** are frequently found in positive instances but are not essential for concept membership. For example, most dogs bark and many dogs wear collars, but neither of these features is a characteristic of *all* dogs. **Irrelevant features** are characteristics that are unrelated to membership in the concept. Anna's location on my office floor is totally irrelevant to her dogness.

Let's pause here for a brief exercise. Figure 11–8 presents eight positive instances and eight negative instances of the concept *gudge*. Can you identify one or more defining features of a gudge?

As you may have surmised, the two defining features of a gudge are that it be gray and square. A large black dot is a correlational feature: Black dots are found on six of the eight gudges but on only one nongudge. White dots and topside "whiskers" are irrelevant features, because they are found equally often on gudges and nongudges.

From some theoretical perspectives, concept learning is a process of learning what features are important for identifying positive instances of that concept. In essence, one must learn that certain features are an essential component of the concept and that other features are frequently present but unessential. Learning to differentiate between a concept's defining and correlational features takes time and experience, often many years' worth (Keil, 1989; Mervis, 1987). For example, consider this question that Saltz (1971) posed to children:

> A father goes to work. On the way home from work in the evening he stops at a bar to have a drink. His friends there are drunkards and he becomes a drunkard too. Is he still a father? (Saltz, 1971, p. 28)

Saltz found that, even at the age of eight, most children denied that a drunkard could still be a father. Apparently, many young children believe that "goodness" defines fatherhood rather than correlating with it, a belief that they are likely to discard only when they encounter enough "bad" positive instances of a father.

Figure 11–8
Positive and negative
instances of a *gudge.*

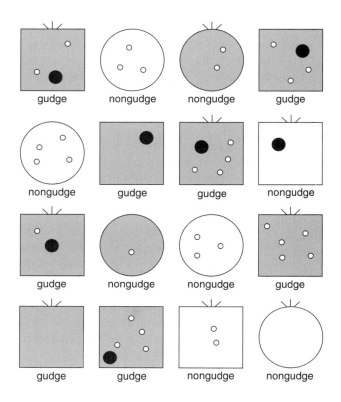

Some concepts have a single defining feature; others are likely to have two or more features that may or may not all need to be present at the same time. For instance, the concept *red* has one defining feature: a particular range of wavelengths. In contrast, the concept *gudge* has two that must both be present: square and gray. An *out* in baseball is an example of a concept for which no single defining feature is always present; for example, it can be three strikes while a player is at bat, the tagging of a player who is running from base to base, or a fly ball caught before it touches the ground.

Concept **rules** specify how defining features are combined to define the concepts. Theorists (Bourne, 1967; Bruner, Goodnow, & Austin, 1956; Dodd & White, 1980; Klein, 1987; Saltz, 1971) have identified a number of different concept rules. Four rules are most commonly described:

1. *Simple.* Only one particular feature must be present; for example, *red* is a specific range of wavelengths.
2. *Conjunctive.* Two or more features must all be present; for example, a *circle* must be two-dimensional and must have all points equidistant from a center point.
3. *Disjunctive.* Two or more defining features are not all present at the same time; for example, an *out* in baseball occurs in any one of several different situations.
4. *Relational.* The relationship between two or more features determines the concept; for example, the concept *between* requires three objects, two located on opposite sides of a third.

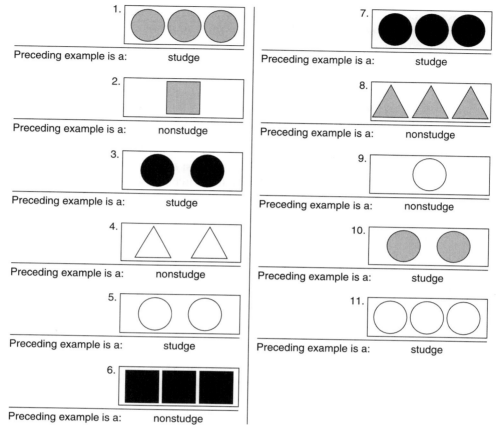

Figure 11–9
Positive and negative instances of a *studge.*

With these "concepts about concepts" in mind, let's look more closely at several theories that psychologists have offered regarding how people acquire concepts. In the following pages, we will consider four views of concept learning: hypothesis testing, prototypes, exemplars, and feature lists.[4]

Hypothesis Testing

Take a few minutes to learn the concept *studge* using Figure 11–9. Your first step is to get two three- by five-inch cards or similar-sized pieces of paper. Use one card to cover up the right-hand side of the figure. Now take the second card and cover the left-hand side, exposing only the top section above the first horizontal line. In this top section, you will

[4]For early behaviorist and neobehaviorist views of concept learning, refer to earlier editions of this book (first and second editions published in 1990 and 1995, respectively) or to my original sources (R. Gagné, 1985; Hull, 1920; Kendler & Kendler, 1959, 1961, 1962).

see a rectangle with three gray circles inside; take a wild guess and decide whether the rectangle is a studge. Once you have made your guess, move the left-hand card down to the next horizontal line, revealing the correct answer. In this section you will also see a second rectangle, one with a gray square inside; decide whether you think it is a studge. Keep moving the card down the page, one section at a time, on each occasion getting your feedback and then deciding whether the next rectangle is a studge. Continue the process with the rectangles in the right-hand side of the figure.

At this point, you have, I hope, learned that the concept *studge* is "two or three circles." Shape and number are defining features for the concept; color is irrelevant to studgeness. In learning about studges, perhaps you found yourself forming different hypotheses about what is and is not a studge. For instance, the first example was a studge. You may have used that positive instance to generate one or more hypotheses, such as the following:

- A studge is anything gray.
- A studge is round.
- A studge is three of something.
- A studge is three gray circles.

The second example in Figure 11–9 was a nonstudge, so, had you held the hypothesis that a studge is gray, you would have eliminated that particular hypothesis at that point. A hypothesis such as "three of something," however, would have been confirmed with the second example but disconfirmed with the third. Eventually you may have ended up with the correct hypothesis: A studge is two or three circles.

Bruner, Goodnow, and Austin (1956) have proposed that concept learning is a process of forming various hypotheses about the features and rules that define a concept and then using positive and negative instances to confirm or reject those hypotheses.[5] To demonstrate their theory, they used stimuli similar to my positive and negative instances of studges to study concept learning in adults. They gave participants in their experiment one positive instance of the concept and then asked them to try to select other positive instances from among an array of stimuli varying on four dimensions (shape, color, number of objects, and number of borders around the objects). By noting the selections that were made, Bruner and his colleagues observed several different approaches that the participants used in formulating and testing their hypotheses. Some people appeared to test one hypothesis at a time, choosing stimuli that varied on only one feature from a previous positive instance. If they received feedback that confirmed their hypothesis, they continued to test it; if they received contradictory feedback, they would form a different hypothesis and begin to test that one. Other people appeared to hold several hypotheses in mind at the same time and eliminate them simultaneously with their selection of different stimuli. This latter strategy would, of course, be faster, but it would also place greater demands on memory, hence leading to more errors. This tendency to test several hypotheses simultaneously has also been observed by Levine (1966).

Although some hypothesis testing may very well occur when people learn concepts, it is probably not the only process involved in concept learning. Experiments in which

---

[5]A similar perspective is seen in Pinker's (1984, 1987) theory of *semantic bootstrapping* in language learning.

hypothesis testing has been observed, such as those of Bruner et al. (1956) and Levine (1966), have been criticized as being artificial and not resembling real-world concept learning conditions (Glass et al., 1979; Rosch, 1973a). People rarely encounter a situation in which they can pick possible examples of a concept in any systematic fashion; more typically, they find a positive instance here, a negative instance there, and so on, in a somewhat haphazard fashion over a period of time. Furthermore, in several experiments (Brooks, 1978; Reber & Allen, 1978; Reber, Kassin, Lewis, & Cantor, 1980), people who were instructed to identify the rules underlying certain classification schemes (i.e., to form hypotheses) actually performed more poorly than people who were not so instructed. In these cases, the more successful learners were the less analytic ones: They simply remembered early positive instances and compared new examples with them. A different theory of concept learning—one involving the formation of prototypes—better explains such findings.

Prototypes

Eleanor Rosch (1973a, 1973b, 1977a; Rosch, Mervis, Gray, Johnson, & Boyes-Braem, 1976) and other theorists (Eysenck & Keane, 1990; Kemler Nelson, 1990; Smith, 1988; Wittgenstein, 1958) have argued that many real-world concepts are difficult to delineate in terms of defining features and precise rules. Objects can lack important features yet still be identified as positive instances of a particular concept. For example, a salient feature of human beings is that they have two legs, but you can still recognize a person with no legs at all as being a human. Similarly, although birds typically fly, most people correctly identify nonflying penguins and ostriches as birds. It appears that people often use correlational features rather than defining features to identify positive instances of a concept.

Furthermore, concepts often have fuzzy boundaries, so that in certain borderline cases correct identification of positive and negative instances is difficult (Labov, 1973; Oden, 1987; Rosch, 1973a, 1978; Zazdeh, Fu, Tanak, & Shimura, 1975). For example, is a stroke a *disease?* In a study by McCloskey and Glucksberg (1978), some people believed that it was and others did not. Is turquoise a shade of *blue* or a shade of *green?* My husband insists that turquoise is green, but I know better: it's blue.

Rosch (1973a, 1973b, 1977a, 1977b, 1978; Rosch, Mervis, Gray, Johnson, & Boyes-Braem, 1976) and others (Attneave, 1957; Tennyson & Cocchiarella, 1986; Walton & Bower, 1993) have proposed that people form concepts by developing a **prototype,** or representative example, of a typical member of that category. To illustrate, form an image in your mind of a *bird*. What probably comes to mind is a small creature, perhaps about the shape and size of a robin or sparrow. It is unlikely that you would instead imagine a penguin or an ostrich because these animals, although they are birds, are not as typically birdlike in appearance as robins and sparrows. Similarly, imagine a *vehicle*. Your image probably resembles a car or a truck rather than a canoe or hot-air balloon, because cars and trucks are more commonly observed instances of vehicles. Now imagine *red*. You probably picture a color similar to that red crayon you had when you were five rather than pink or maroon.

A prototype is likely to incorporate features of the most typical, commonly observed positive instances of the concept. For instance, your prototype of a human being probably has two arms and two legs, stands upright, and is slightly less than two meters tall. Your prototype of a table is likely to be a rectangular flat surface held up by four legs, one of them at each of the four corners. You identify new objects as positive instances of a particular concept when you compare them with the concept prototype and find them to be sufficiently similar. A positive identification does not require that all features be present, however; you can still recognize a legless man as a human being, and you can still recognize a three-legged object as a table.

At least two sources of evidence support the idea that concepts may be represented in memory in the form of prototypes. First of all, people easily identify positive instances of a concept that closely resemble the prototype but have difficulty identifying positive instances that are less similar (Glass, Holyoak, & O'Dell, 1974; Posner & Keele, 1968, 1970; Rips et al., 1973; Rosch, 1973b, 1978; Rosch & Mervis, 1975; Rosch, Simpson, & Miller, 1976; Wilkins, 1971). In one experiment by Rosch (1973b), elementary school and undergraduate students identified as birds those creatures that looked particularly birdlike (e.g., robins and sparrows) more quickly than they identified creatures less similar to the prototype (e.g., chickens and ducks).

A second source of evidence for prototypes is the fact that people usually recognize positive instances they have never encountered before when those instances closely resemble the prototype. In fact, people recognize them more easily than positive instances they *have* encountered that do *not* closely match the prototype (Franks & Bransford, 1971; Posner, Goldsmith, & Welton, 1967; Posner & Keele, 1968). For example, in an experiment by Franks and Bransford (1971), college students viewed a series of geometric patterns that involved one or more variations from a particular "base" pattern; the base pattern itself was not presented. The students were then shown another series of patterns (including the base pattern) and asked to identify which ones they had previously seen; they had actually seen *none* of these patterns earlier. Students were especially likely to "recognize" patterns that closely resembled the base pattern; they were most confident that they had seen the base pattern itself. Presumably, the base pattern represented the single best example of the various stimuli that the students had originally seen and thus most closely approximated the pattern prototype that they had formed.

Rosch, Mervis, and their colleagues (1976) have suggested that conceptual prototypes may be organized in a three-level hierarchy—a hierarchical organizational scheme similar to that described earlier in the chapter. **Basic-level concepts** are the ones we use most frequently—for instance, the ones we use when we name objects (this is a *chair,* this is a *hat,* this is a *car,* and so on). **Superordinate concepts** are more general categories that encompass a number of basic-level concepts (e.g., chairs and tables are both *furniture,* hats and shoes are two kinds of *clothing,* and cars and trucks are *vehicles*). **Subordinate concepts** are more specific subdivisions of basic-level concepts (e.g., *rocking chairs* and *lawn chairs* are types of chairs, *berets* and *bowlers* are types of hats, and *Volkswagen Beetles* and *Dodge Caravans* are types of cars). You can think of the three levels as reflecting varying degrees of abstraction: The superordinate concepts are most abstract, and the subordinate concepts are most concrete.

Exemplars

We probably cannot explain all human concept learning strictly in terms of the development of prototypes. For one thing, how we categorize an object depends on the context in which we find it. For instance, if a cuplike object contains flowers, we might identify it as a *vase* rather than a *cup;* if it contains mashed potatoes, we might instead identify it as a *bowl* (Labov, 1973; Schwartz & Reisberg, 1991). Furthermore, not all concepts lend themselves readily to a single prototypical representation (Eysenck & Keane, 1990; Hampton, 1981). For instance, I have a difficult time identifying a typical example of *music:* Classical, rock, jazz, and country-western are all quite different from one another.

In some cases, our knowledge of a concept may be based more on a variety of examples—that is, on **exemplars**—than on a single prototype (Reisberg, 1997; Ross & Spalding, 1994). Exemplars can give us an idea of the variability we are likely to see in any category of objects or events. As an illustration, consider the concept *fruit.* Many different things are likely to come to mind here: Apples, bananas, raspberries, mangos, and kiwifruit are all possibilities. If you encounter a new instance of fruit—a blackberry, let's say—you could compare it with the variety of exemplars you have already stored and find one (a raspberry, perhaps) that is relatively similar.

It is possible that prototypes or exemplars are used to identify positive instances in clear-cut situations, whereas formal definitions are used in other, more ambiguous ones (Andre, 1986; Glass & Holyoak, 1975; Glass et al., 1979). To illustrate, abstract concepts such as *rule, belief,* and *instinct* are difficult to conceptualize in terms of a typical example. In some cases, it may also be true that children rely on prototypes or exemplars in the early years and then acquire a formal definition later on. For example, as a preschooler, my son Jeff adamantly denied that the concept *animal* includes people, fish, and insects. The belief that these groups are nonanimals is a common phenomenon among young children, who often restrict their conception of animals to four-legged mammals (Kyle & Shymansky, 1989; Saltz, 1971). I suspect that Jeff's animal prototype might have resembled the family dog or perhaps the cows he often saw in the surrounding countryside. When he began studying the animal kingdom in school, he learned a biology-based definition of an animal that incorporates some of its major features: a form of life that derives its food from other organisms, responds immediately to its environment, and can move its body. At that point Jeff acknowledged that people, fish, and creepy-crawlies are legitimate animals. (If he takes college biology at a later date, however, he may learn that biologists do not really agree on a definition of *animal* and that true defining features of the concept are difficult to identify.)

Feature Lists

Feature list theory (Bourne, 1982; Bourne et al., 1986; Neumann, 1974, 1977; Rips et al., 1973; Smith, Shoben, & Rips, 1974; Ward, Vela, & Haas, 1990) is in some ways similar to prototype theory but focuses more on a concept's defining and correlational features. From this perspective, learning a concept involves developing a **feature list** that includes the following:

* Relevant features, both defining and correlational, of the concept
* The probability that each of these features is likely to be present in any specific instance—that is, the frequency with which each feature occurs
* The relationships among the features—that is, the rules for their combination

Recognizing an object as a positive instance of a concept, then, is a matter of determining whether the object possesses enough relevant features. Prototypes are recognized more quickly than other positive instances only because they encompass most or all of the concept's relevant features.

A prediction from feature list theory is that negative instances will be erroneously identified as positive instances if a sufficient number of relevant features is present. Bourne (1982) confirmed this prediction in an experiment involving an *exclusive disjunctive* concept. Earlier in the chapter, I described a disjunctive concept as being one with two or more defining features that do not all need to be present at once (the example I gave you was an *out* in baseball). An exclusive disjunctive concept is a subform of this kind of concept: An item possessing any of the defining features is a positive instance, but an item possessing all of them is not. (For example, a *pludge* is anything that is red or square, but things that are both red and square are nonpludges.) In an experiment involving undergraduate students, Bourne presented numerous positive and negative instances of an exclusive disjunctive concept that had two relevant features; an item that had one, but not both, of the features was a positive instance. Despite their training, when the students were later asked to identify examples of the concept, they were more likely to "recognize" those stimuli possessing both relevant features than those possessing only one of the two features.

Feature list theory is probably not the perfect explanation of concept learning, either. As we noted earlier, we cannot always identify the specific features on which concepts are based. But we probably *do* learn the relevant features of a concept to the extent that we can identify such features.

I suspect that each of the theories of concept learning we have just examined has an element of truth. As human beings, perhaps we represent any single concept in long-term memory as a prototype, a number of exemplars, *and* a set of defining and/or correlational features (e.g., Armstrong, Gleitman, & Gleitman, 1983). Perhaps we also form and test hypotheses about the nature of particular concepts. We do not necessarily need to choose just one theory of concept learning as being the "right" one, to the exclusion of the other three.

In our discussion of concepts, two factors have emerged as essential components of the concept learning process. First, people must learn the characteristics that determine concept membership (and discover which of those characteristics, if any, are truly definitive). Second, they must develop a realization of the degree of acceptable variation from best examples of the concept. For example, an ostrich is a bird even though it is much larger than the prototypical bird; however, a certain other creature that is the same size and also walks on two legs—a human being—falls outside of the bird category. In other words, to learn a concept completely one must eventually learn the boundaries of that concept.

Concepts are not the only mechanisms we use to help us make sense of the world around us. We may also form *schemas* and *scripts,* as we shall see now.

SCHEMAS AND SCRIPTS

As you should recall from Chapter 8, Jean Piaget used the concept *scheme* to refer to a mental unit representing a class of similar actions or thoughts. More recently, psychologists have been using a similar term but in a somewhat different sense. In contemporary cognitive theory, the term **schema** usually refers to an organized body of knowledge about a specific topic (Anderson & Pearson, 1984; Bartlett, 1932; Dansereau, 1995; Derry, 1996; Rumelhart & Ortony, 1977). For example, you probably have a schema for what a faculty member's office is typically like: It is usually a small room that contains a desk, one or more chairs, bookshelves with books, and other items useful in performing academic duties.

Schemas often influence how we perceive and remember new situations. For example, your schema of a faculty office might color your later memory of what a particular office was actually like. In a study by Brewer and Treyens (1981), 30 students were brought, one at a time, to a room they believed to be the experimenter's university office. After waiting in the office for less than a minute, they were taken to another room and asked to write down everything they could remember about the room. Most students correctly remembered things that one would expect to find in an office (e.g., a desk, a chair, and shelves). Relatively few of them remembered items not likely to be part of an office schema (e.g., a skull, a clown-shaped light switch, and a tennis racket). And 9 of the 30 "remembered" books that hadn't actually been there at all!

People often form schemas about events as well as objects; such event schemas are sometimes called **scripts** (Bower et al., 1979; Dansereau, 1995; Schank, 1975; Schank & Abelson, 1977). For example, what things usually happen when people go to a doctor's office? In a study by Bower et al. (1979), most people agreed that this series of activities is typical of a visit to the doctor:

They check in with the receptionist.

They sit down.

They read a magazine.

The nurse performs tests.

The doctor examines them.

They leave the office.

An individual's mental script of an event will influence what information is "learned" from a given instance of that event. For example, in another study by Bower et al. (1979), college students read this passage:

John was feeling bad today so he decided to go see the family doctor. He checked in with the doctor's receptionist, and then looked through several medical magazines that were on the table by his chair. Finally the nurse came and asked him to take off his clothes. The doctor was very nice to him. He eventually prescribed some pills for John. Then John left the doctor's office and headed home. (Bower et al., 1979, p. 190)

The students in the experiment "remembered" reading about many activities that were likely to be part of a visit to the doctor (e.g., arriving at the doctor's office) but that they had in fact *not* read.

Other research provides further support for the idea that schemas and scripts influence how learners process, store, and remember new information. To illustrate, many people (especially those with stereotypical schemas about how males and females behave) more accurately remember pictures and films that portray men and women behaving in a stereotypical manner (Cordua, McGraw, & Drabman, 1979; Martin & Halverson, 1981; Signorella & Liben, 1984). People also have an easier time remembering events similar to those in their own culture, presumably because such events are consistent with recognizable scripts (Lipson, 1983; Reynolds, Taylor, Steffensen, Shirey, & Anderson, 1982; Steffensen, Joag-Dev, & Anderson, 1979). And consider this story about two boys playing hooky:

> The two boys ran until they came to the driveway. "See, I told you today was good for skipping school," said Mark. "Mom is never home on Thursday," he added. Tall hedges hid the house from the road so the pair strolled across the finely landscaped yard. "I never knew your place was so big," said Pete. "Yeah, but it's nicer now than it used to be since Dad had the new stone siding put on and added the fireplace."
>
> There were front and back doors and a side door which led to the garage which was empty except for three parked 10-speed bikes. They went in the side door, Mark explaining that it was always open in case his younger sisters got home earlier than their mother.
>
> Pete wanted to see the house so Mark started with the living room. It, like the rest of the downstairs, was newly painted. Mark turned on the stereo, the noise of which worried Pete. "Don't worry, the nearest house is a quarter of a mile away," Mark shouted. Pete felt more comfortable observing that no houses could be seen in any direction beyond the huge yard.
>
> The dining room, with all the china, silver, and cut glass, was no place to play so the boys moved into the kitchen where they made sandwiches. Mark said they wouldn't go to the basement because it had been damp and musty ever since the new plumbing had been installed. (Pichert & Anderson, 1977, p. 310)

You will probably remember different details from the story, depending on whether you read it from the perspective of a potential home buyer or a potential burglar (Anderson & Pichert, 1978). Different schemas and scripts come into play for buying versus burgling a home.

As we noted in Chapter 9, the human memory system typically encounters more information than it can possibly handle. Schemas and scripts provide a means for reducing this information overload: They help people focus their attention on information that is likely to be important and to ignore what is probably unimportant (Goetz, Schallert, Reynolds, & Radin, 1983; Martin & Halverson, 1981; Wilson & Anderson, 1986). For example, when going to see the doctor, it is more important that you check in with the receptionist than that you attend to the style of clothing worn by other people in the waiting room. Schemas also enable people to make sense out of an incomplete set of information (R. Anderson, 1984; Dansereau, 1995; Martin & Halverson, 1981; Rumelhart & Ortony, 1977; Wilson & Anderson, 1986). As a result, individuals may "remember" information that they never specifically encountered but that they have filled in using their existing schemas and scripts regarding how objects and events typically are (Bower et al., 1979; Farrar & Goodman, 1992; Flavell et al., 1993; Kardash, Royer, & Greene, 1988). For example, if you hear someone describe an experience at the doctor's office, you can assume that the person entered the examination room, even if that statement is not explicitly stated. In the passage I presented earlier about John visiting the doctor's office, it is highly unlikely that the nurse asked John to take off his clothes in the waiting room, although that is in fact what the passage implies!

Schema theory has intuitive appeal as a way of helping us understand how we organize our past experiences and use what we've learned to predict and interpret future experiences. It has been criticized for being somewhat vague, however; for example, theorists have not been very specific regarding what schemas and scripts actually *are* (e.g., Dansereau, 1995). Furthermore, although we can reasonably assume that people form and modify schemas and scripts based on the specific objects and events they encounter in their lives (Flavell et al., 1993; Pressley, with McCormick, 1995; Rumelhart, 1980), the cognitive processes that occur during this learning are not at all clear.

Schemas and scripts usually relate to relatively specific objects and events. Another concept—that of *mental theories*—may help us understand how we organize our world on a much grander scale.

MENTAL THEORIES

Numerous psychologists have speculated that people form general **mental theories—** coherent belief systems that encompass cause-effect relationships—about many aspects of the world around them, including the physical world, the biological world, and mental phenomena (diSessa, 1996; Flavell et al., 1993; Glynn, Yeany, & Britton, 1991; Hatano & Inagaki, 1996; Keil & Silberstein, 1996; Magnusson, Boyle, & Templin, 1994; Wellman & Gelman, 1992). Such theories often begin to emerge in early childhood, long before formal "scientific" theories are encountered in school.

As an illustration, take a minute to read the two scenarios in Figure 11–10 and answer the questions that each one poses.

1. Doctors took a coffeepot that looked like this:

They sawed off the handle, sealed the top, took off the top knob, and sawed off and sealed the spout. They also sawed off the base and attached a flat piece of metal. They attached a little stick, cut a window in it, and filled the metal container with bird food. When they were done, it looked like this:

After the operation, was this a coffeepot or a bird feeder?

2. Doctors took this raccoon:

and shaved away some of its fur. They dyed what was left all black. Then they bleached a single stripe all white down the center of its back. Then, with surgery, they put in its body a sac of super-smelly odor, just like a skunk has. When they were all done, the animal looked like this:

After the operation, was this a skunk or a raccoon?

Figure 11–10
What the doctors did.
Both scenarios adapted from Keil, 1989, p. 184.

Chances are, you concluded that the coffeepot had been transformed into a bird feeder but that the raccoon was still a raccoon despite its radical surgery; even fourth graders come to these conclusions (Keil, 1986, 1989). Now how is it possible that the coffeepot could be made into something entirely different, whereas the raccoon could not?

The concepts that people form are influenced in part by the theories they have about how the world operates (Keil, 1986, 1989, 1994; Medin, 1989; Neisser, 1987; Reisberg, 1997). For example, even young children seem to make a basic distinction between man-made objects (e.g., coffeepots and bird feeders) and biological entities (e.g., raccoons and skunks) (Hatano & Inagaki, 1996; Massey & Gelman, 1988). Furthermore, children seem to conceptualize the two categories in fundamentally different ways: Man-made objects are defined largely by the *functions* they serve (e.g., keeping coffee warm or feeding birds), whereas biological entities are defined primarily by their origins (e.g., the parents who brought them into being or their DNA). Thus, when a coffeepot begins to hold birdseed rather than coffee, it becomes a bird feeder by virtue of the fact that its function has changed. But when a raccoon is surgically altered to look like a skunk, it still has raccoon parents and raccoon DNA, and so cannot possibly *be* a skunk (Keil, 1987, 1989). Thinking along similar lines, even preschoolers will tell you that you cannot change a yellow finch into a bluebird by giving it a coat of blue paint or dressing it in a "bluebird" costume (Keil, 1989).

Our mental theories about the world seem to guide us as we identify potential defining features of the concepts we are learning (Keil, 1987, 1989; McCauley, 1987; Mervis, 1987). For example, if you were trying to learn what a *horse* is, the fact that you know it's an animal would lead you to conclude that its location (in a stable, a pasture, a shopping mall, or wherever) is an irrelevant feature (Keil, 1989). On the other hand, if you were trying to learn what the *equator* is, knowing it's something on a map of the world should lead you to suspect that location is of the utmost importance.

The early mental theories that people form are not necessarily consistent with the theories that experts in a particular field have developed (diSessa, 1996; Duit, 1991; Halldén, 1994; Magnusson et al., 1994). For example, many people, especially before they take a course in physics, think that in order to keep an object moving through space one must continually apply force to the object; this notion is inconsistent with physicists' principle of *inertia* (diSessa, 1996). And many Japanese children develop the belief that plants and inanimate objects have "minds" similar to those of humans; although this idea isn't consistent with contemporary psychology, it *is* consistent with certain aspects of Japanese culture (Hatano & Inagaki, 1996). We'll identify additional misconceptions in our discussion of *conceptual change* in Chapter 13.

DEVELOPMENT OF EXPERTISE

Obviously, people acquire an increasing amount of information in their long-term memories over time. Many people eventually acquire a great deal of information about a particular topic or subject matter, to the point where we can say they are *experts* in their field. It appears, however, that experts don't just know more than their peers; their knowledge is also *qualitatively* different from that of others. In particular, their knowledge tends to be tightly organized, with many interrelationships among the things that they know and with many abstract generalizations unifying more concrete details (Alexander & Judy, 1988; Bédard & Chi, 1992; Proctor & Dutta, 1995; Zeitz, 1994). Such qualities enable experts to retrieve the things they need more easily, to find parallels between seemingly diverse situations, and to solve problems more effectively (Chi, Glaser, & Rees, 1982; De Corte et al., 1996; Rabinowitz & Glaser, 1985; Voss, Greene, Post, & Penner, 1983).

Patricia Alexander (in press) has described three somewhat distinct stages in the development of knowledge related to a particular subject matter. At the first stage, which she calls *acclimation,* learners familiarize themselves with a new content domain, much as someone might do by taking an introductory course in biology, economics, or art history. At this point, they pick up a lot of facts that they tend to store in relative isolation from one another. As a result of such "fragmented" learning, they are likely to hold on to many misconceptions that they may have acquired before they started studying the subject systematically.

At the second stage, which Alexander calls *competence,* learners acquire considerably more information about the subject matter, and they also acquire some general principles that help tie the information together. Because learners at the competence stage make numerous interconnections among the things they learn, they are likely to correct many of the specific misconceptions they have previously developed. (Those misconceptions that remain, however, are likely to pervade much of their thinking about the subject.) At the competence stage, learners' entire approach to the subject matter begins to resemble that of experts; for example, they may start to "think like a historian" or engage in some of their own scientific research. Competence is something that people acquire only after studying a particular subject in depth, perhaps through an undergraduate major, a master's degree, or several years of professional experience.

At the final stage—*expertise*—we can say that learners have truly mastered their field. They know a great deal about the subject matter, and they have pulled much of their knowledge together into a tightly integrated whole. At this point, they are helping to lead the way in terms of conducting research, proposing new ways of looking at things, solving problems, and, in general, making new knowledge. Expertise comes only after many years of studying and experience in a particular field; as a result, few learners ever reach this stage (also see Proctor & Dutta, 1995).

Alexander points out that the development of expertise depends not only on the acquisition of knowledge but also on effective learning strategies and a strong interest in the subject matter. We will identify many effective learning strategies in Chapter 14, and we will examine the specific benefits of interest in Chapter 18.

GENERALIZATIONS ABOUT THE NATURE OF KNOWLEDGE

In this chapter we have considered several aspects of the knowledge that we store in long-term memory, including the various kinds of knowledge that we are likely to acquire, the variety of ways in which we might encode it, the possible organizational structures that our long-term memories may have overall, and the particular mechanisms that we might use (e.g., concepts and schemas) to organize specific kinds of experiences. At this point, let's make some final generalizations about the nature of knowledge:

• *We often store information in long-term memory in more than one way.* Earlier in the chapter I mentioned a finding by Rips et al. (1973) that people can verify that "A collie is an animal" more quickly than they can verify that "A collie is a mammal." It is probably a more economical use of long-term memory "space" to remember that a collie is a mammal and that a mammal is an animal; people can then easily infer that a collie must be an animal. Yet it appears from these researchers' results that people store the fact that a collie is an animal as well—a fact that is redundant with other knowledge in long-term memory. Such redundancy may simply be a matter of convenience: If we have plenty of "room" in long-term memory, why not store the same information in the variety of ways in which we might need it later on?

• *Most of our knowledge is a summary of our experiences rather than information about specific events.* Early in the chapter, I made the distinction between episodic and semantic memory. Most of our knowledge is probably semantic in nature: Over the years, we have combined the specific experiences we have had into a general knowledge of the world that is somewhat independent of those experiences (e.g., Rosenfield, 1988).

Concepts are a prime example of how we summarize the objects and events that we encounter. As summaries of the things we have learned, concepts have several advantages:

1. *They reduce the world's complexity* (Bruner, 1957; Bruner et al., 1956; Sokal, 1977). Classifying similar objects and events makes life simpler and easier to understand. For example, when you drive along a country road, it is easier to think to yourself "There are some cows" than to think "There is a brown object, covered with bristly stuff, appended by a paintbrush and a lumpy thing, and held up by four sticks. Ah, yes, and I also see a black-and-white spotted object, covered with bristly stuff, appended by a paintbrush and a lumpy thing, and held up by four sticks. And over there is a brown-and-white spotted object. . . ."

2. *They facilitate generalization to new situations* (Bruner, 1957; Bruner et al., 1956; Johnson-Laird & Wason, 1977; Rosser, 1994). When we learn a concept, we associate certain characteristics with it. Then, when we encounter a new instance of the concept, we can draw on our knowledge of associated characteristics to form assumptions and inferences about the new instance. For example, if you see a herd of cattle as you drive through the countryside, you can assume that you are passing through either dairy or beef country, depending on whether you see large udders hanging down between two of the spindly sticks. If you purchase a potted flower, you know that you must water it regularly because of something you have learned about the concept *flower:* It needs water to live. Thanks to concepts, we don't have to learn from scratch in each new situation.

3. *They allow abstraction of the environment* (Bruner, 1966). An object covered with bristly stuff, appended by a paintbrush and a lumpy thing, and held up by four sticks is a very concrete thing. The concept *cow,* however, can be more abstract: It incorporates such characteristics as "female," "supplier of milk," and, to the dairy farmer, "economic asset." Concepts and their labels allow individuals to think about their experiences without necessarily having to consider all of their concrete, perceptual aspects.

4. *They enhance the power of thought* (Bruner, 1966). When you are thinking about an object covered with bristly stuff, appended by a paintbrush and a lumpy thing, held up by four sticks, and so on, you can think of little else; to express this point in terms of contemporary memory theory, your working memory capacity is exhausted. On the other hand, when you simply think *cow,* you can also think about *horse, dog, goat,* and *pig* at the same time.

5. *They make it easier for us to make connections among the things we know* (Bruner, 1957; Bruner et al., 1956). Once we have condensed and abstracted information into concepts, we can more easily make associations among those concepts in long-term memory. For instance, we can relate the concept *cow* to the concepts *bull* and *calf* in a familial sort of way and to *mammal, animal,* and *living thing* in a hierarchical fashion.

We must remember, however, that our summaries of the world will sometimes cause us to make mistakes. For example, when we identify a new stimulus as being a positive instance of a particular concept, we are likely to react to that stimulus as we would to any other instance of the concept. In the process, we may lose sight of the unique qualities of that particular stimulus. Furthermore, if we have identified a stimulus incorrectly, our response to it may be inappropriate. I remember as a young child trying to make a car using square pieces of wood for wheels. Calling those pieces of wood *wheels* was an inaccurate identification, and, as you can imagine, my car didn't move very far. Finally, in some situations we may *over*classify our experiences. For example, when we form **stereotypes** of certain groups of people (perhaps people of specific genders, races, or cultural backgrounds), we are likely to draw many incorrect inferences about how particular members of that group are likely to behave (Murray & Jackson, 1982/1983; Nelson & Miller, 1995).

• *In most situations, integrated knowledge is more useful than fragmented knowledge.* When we integrate the things we know, we are more likely to draw inferences that go beyond the specific things we have learned. Furthermore, as we will discover in the next chapter, organized information is easier to remember—in other words, to retrieve—than unorganized information.

Many theorists are now stressing the importance of teaching an integrated body of knowledge—knowledge that includes general principles, cause-effect relationships, and so on—rather than simply teaching isolated facts (Gregg & Leinhardt, 1994b; Linn, Songer, & Eylon, 1996; White & Rumsey, 1994). In the case of mathematics, for example, teachers should help students make associations between general concepts and principles of mathematics on the one hand and specific procedures for solving mathematical problems on the other hand (Hiebert & Lefevre, 1986). When students learn specific mathematical procedures (e.g., how to do long division or how to add two fractions by finding a common denominator) in association with the overall "logic" of mathematics, they are more likely to apply problem-solving procedures appropriately and to recognize occasions when they have obtained illogical and therefore incorrect problem solutions.

• *The in-depth study of a few topics is often more beneficial than the superficial study of many topics.* Historically, many people have seen the role of schools as being one of promoting **cultural literacy**—that is, of helping children learn the many facts that a seemingly "educated" person should know. For example, we are often chagrined when we hear how many children don't know the capital of France, can't list the nine planets of the solar system, or have no idea who wrote *Romeo and Juliet.*

Certainly schooling should, in part, be about helping children acquire a basic knowledge of the world and culture in which they live. Yet if schools focus exclusively on imparting isolated facts, an integrated body of knowledge about the world is unlikely to develop. Many theorists now suggest that teachers focus more on teaching a few topics in depth than on covering many topics at a superficial level (Brophy & Alleman, 1992; Onosko & Newmann, 1994; Sizer, 1992; Wiggins, 1989). They advocate the idea that "less is more": When students study *less* material so that they can study it more thoroughly, they learn it *more* completely and with greater understanding.

SUMMARY

Some theorists have proposed that long-term memory has two or more distinct subcomponents; for instance, they have made distinctions between episodic and semantic memory, between declarative and procedural knowledge, and between explicit and implicit memory. Information may be encoded in long-term memory in a number of different forms, including symbols (e.g., verbal codes), imagery (e.g., visual images), meanings (e.g., propositions), and actions (e.g., productions). These various forms of encoding are clearly interconnected in long-term memory; theorists have proposed at least three models (hierarchical model, network model, and parallel distributed processing) regarding the nature of such interconnections.

Concepts are classes of objects or events that share one or more common properties. Some concepts are concrete, in that they are easily identified by their physical appearance, whereas others are more abstract and difficult to pin down in terms of observable characteristics. Learning a concept often involves learning the features that determine which objects and events are members of that concept (i.e., positive instances) and which are nonmembers (i.e., negative instances). Drawing from several theories of concept learning, we can speculate that learning a concept may involve testing hypotheses about the nature of a particular concept, forming a prototype of a typical positive instance, storing exemplars that represent the variability of positive instances, and developing a feature list for the concept.

A *schema* is an organized body of knowledge about a specific topic; when a schema relates to a particular kind of event (e.g., a visit to the doctor's office), it is sometimes called a *script.* Schemas and scripts often influence how we process, store, and remember new situations; for example, they allow us to fill in any missing information with our own knowledge about how the world typically operates.

Some of the knowledge stored in long-term memory takes the form of a *mental theory,* a coherent belief system that encompasses cause-effect relationships. Mental theories influence concept learning by giving people some idea about the features that are likely to be important; not all mental theories are accurate ones, however.

The development of expertise in a particular subject area involves acquiring an increasing amount of knowledge, making numerous interconnections within that knowledge base, and eventually integrating what has been learned into an integrated whole. People typically become experts in their field only after many years of intensive study and practice.

Most of our knowledge probably represents a summary of our life experiences. For example, concepts summarize what we have learned about particular objects or events; as such, they reduce the complexity of the environment and facilitate generalization to new situations. In most situations, integrated knowledge about a topic is more useful than knowledge of separate facts.

CHAPTER 12

Long-Term Memory III: Retrieval, Forgetting, and Classroom Practice

H ere are definitions of words in the English language. Can you identify the specific words to which they refer?

- The fluid part of blood
- A picture form of writing used in ancient Egypt
- A game whose object is to snap small plastic disks into a container
- A zigzag trim used to decorate clothing
- A small, hard-shelled, ocean-dwelling animal that attaches itself to rocks and ships

You probably identified some of these words almost without thinking. But there is a good chance that you could not retrieve all five instantaneously. For one or more of them, you may have found yourself looking around in your long-term memory, perhaps for a lengthy period of time, in "places" where a word might be located. (In case you could not retrieve all five words, they are *plasma, hieroglyphics, tiddlywinks, rickrack,* and *barnacle.*)

Retrieving information from long-term memory is sometimes easy and automatic, at other times slow and strenuous, and at still other times virtually impossible. We tend to remember frequently used information without conscious effort. For instance, we can quickly retrieve the locations of our homes and the names of our close friends. It is more difficult to retrieve information that we seldom use, however. For example, we often have trouble remembering words that we rarely encounter in our everyday lives (words such as *hieroglyphics* and *barnacle*); in some cases, we may feel that such words are on the "tip of our tongues," yet we still cannot recall them (Brown, 1991; Brown & McNeill, 1966). Similarly, we may experience difficulty in identifying people whom we have not seen recently or frequently (Yarmey, 1973).

In this chapter we will look at how memory theorists believe long-term memory retrieval works and at how retrieval is related to storage. We will examine the concept of *retrieval cue,* a type of hint that helps us locate desired information in long-term memory. We will learn that retrieval, like storage, sometimes involves a process of construction; we will also learn that review and practice can facilitate retrieval over the long run. Later in the chapter, we will explore several explanations of why we are sometimes unable to retrieve the things we think we have learned—in other words, why we forget. Finally, we will apply principles of long-term memory storage and retrieval to classroom practice.

HOW RETRIEVAL WORKS

How easily we retrieve something from long-term memory depends on how well we stored it in the first place. Unlike working memory, which is functionally quite small, long-term memory is so large that an exhaustive exploration of it all is probably impossible. A search of long-term memory must therefore be selective and explore only certain "sections" (Hopkins & Atkinson, 1968). If the sought-after information is not stored in one of those sections, we will not retrieve it.

Our success in retrieving information from long-term memory depends to some extent on whether we initially stored the information in a well-organized fashion. To understand the role that organization plays in retrieval, let's first look at an analogous situation—your great-grandmother's attic. (I am going back three generations, because young families typically have homes without much attic space, and many grandparents seem to live in condominiums these days.) Granny probably kept many things in her attic, including furniture, books, old clothes, seldom-used cooking utensils, and holiday decorations. Granny may have been a very organized woman, one who stored all of the books in one place, all of the clothes in another, and all of the holiday decorations somewhere else. On the other hand, she may have been more haphazard, throwing things up there any old place, so that some cooking utensils were with books, others were with clothes, and still others were stuffed in an old dresser or on the top shelf of a dilapidated armoire. How Granny stored items in her attic undoubtedly affected her ability to find them later on. If she stored things systematically (e.g., books with books and cooking utensils with cooking utensils), she would have been able to find them easily when she needed them. But if she stored them in a helter-skelter fashion, she may have had to purchase new canning jars every summer because she couldn't locate her jars from any of the previous 13 years.

So it is with long-term memory. Retrieval is more effective when related pieces of information are stored in close association with one another, because we then have a good idea about where to find a certain piece of information. To illustrate, try answering this quick quiz item testing your memory of an earlier chapter:

What is a discriminative stimulus?

You may be able to answer the question quickly and easily, or you may have to search your long-term memory for a while. Your ability to retrieve the answer depends partly on how well you have organized the information you acquired from previous chapters. The word *stimulus* should, of course, lead you to look among the information you have stored about behaviorist learning theories. The word *discriminative* might suggest to you that you look more specifically in your information about discrimination. If your knowledge about discrimination is stored with what you know about stimulus control (and it should be, because the two concepts are related), then you should find the answer to the question. A discriminative stimulus sets the occasion in which a response is reinforced.

Lindsay and Norman (1977) have characterized long-term memory retrieval as being similar to looking for something in a large, dark room with just a small flashlight. Imagine that the electricity goes off in Granny's house on a dark, moonless night. Because Granny can no longer use either her electric can opener or her electric lights, she takes a flashlight up to the attic to find the manual can opener she put there last October. She switches on her flashlight and begins her search. Unfortunately, the flashlight cannot illuminate the whole attic at once. Instead, she must aim the light first at one spot, then at another, until eventually she finds the can opener. The necessity to search the attic one spot at a time will not be a problem if Granny knows the exact location of the can opener (e.g., in a drawer with other small cooking utensils), but she may search all night without success if she has no idea where she might have put the thing. In much the same way, retrieval from long-term memory may be a process of looking in various small "locations" in memory, just one location at a time. Information that has been stored in a logical place (i.e., associated with similar ideas) will probably be found quickly. Information that has been stored haphazardly, in a rote-learning fashion, will turn up only after a great deal of searching, or possibly not at all.

An experiment by Bower and Holyoak (1973) illustrates the dependence of retrieval on earlier storage. In this study, college students listened to a set of tape-recorded sounds and identified something that each sound might be (e.g., a sound might be chirping crickets or soldiers clumping down stairs). Two weeks later, they listened to a second set of sounds, including some sounds they had heard previously and some new sounds as well. Once again they were asked to identify what each sound might be and to indicate whether they had heard that exact sound during the first session. When students labeled a sound in the same way in the second session as they had in the first session, they were likely to recognize it as being one they had heard before. When they labeled it in a different way in the two sessions (e.g., once as a bouncing ball and once as a heartbeat), they were less likely to recognize it as being a familiar one. Other students, who had labels

An organized long-term memory makes things easier to retrieve.

provided for them by the experimenter, showed similar results. By using a label they had used before, the students apparently were more likely to search the part of long-term memory where the previous sound was stored.

You may recall the activation model of memory that I described in Chapter 9. According to this model, all information stored in memory is in either an active or inactive state. Information in an active state is what we might think of as being in working memory, whereas inactive information is in long-term memory. The activation model lends itself particularly well to an understanding of how long-term memory retrieval might work. From this perspective, our starting point in long-term memory might be an idea that something in the environment triggers. Retrieval is then a process of **spreading activation,** with the activation flowing through connections within the network of stored information (Anderson, 1990; Collins & Loftus, 1975; E. Gagné, 1985). Only a small part of the network can be activated at once, thus accounting for the limited-capacity, "flashlight" quality of retrieval. If the activation eventually spreads to that part of the network in which the information is located—something that is more likely to happen if similar ideas are closely associated in that network—we will retrieve the desired information.

We should note here that retrieval is typically easier when we are relaxed rather than anxious about retrieving information. To illustrate, think about what happens when you are looking for your car keys and are desperate to find them *immediately* because you are already late for an appointment. As you begin to panic, your search strategies become less and less efficient. You look in the same places over and over again; you don't think creatively about the wide variety of places in which the keys might be lurking. So, too, does anxiety adversely affect retrieval: We don't search long-term memory in an "open-minded" manner, reducing our chances of finding the desired information.

Retrieval is obviously easier when we know more or less where to look in our long-term memories—that is, when we know which part of long-term memory to activate. Therefore, hints about where to find a certain piece of information are helpful. It is to these hints—these **retrieval cues**—that we turn now.

RETRIEVAL CUES

In Chapter 10 you read a story called "The War of the Ghosts." Can you fill in the blank in this sentence from the story?

The warriors went on up the river to a town on the other side of _____.

See if you can remember the name of the town before you continue reading.

Any luck? If not, then perhaps you will recognize the town from among these four choices: (1) Bisantri, (2) Dormro, (3) Muckaruck, or (4) Kalama. Is it any easier to fill in the blank now? It should be. I hope you have now identified Kalama as the correct answer. In this question, I gave you a type of retrieval cue known as an **identity cue** (Bourne et al., 1986), because it was identical to the information you were trying to retrieve. Recognition tasks, such as multiple-choice tests, are often easier than recall tasks (e.g., Semb, Ellis, & Araujo, 1993), presumably because of the identity cues that recognition tasks provide.

Now try this exercise. Read the following list of 24 words *one time only.* I will ask you to recall them as soon as you have finished.

tulip	pencil	spoon	bed	baker	ruby
hat	mountain	doctor	paper	daisy	shirt
chair	fork	diamond	canyon	knife	table
hill	soldier	rose	pen	shoe	emerald

Now that you have read all 24 words, cover the page and write as many of them as you can remember. *Do not peek back at the list just yet.*

If you cannot remember all 24, see if these words and phrases help you:

clothing	professions
eating utensils	writing supplies
gemstones	furniture
flowers	land forms

These category names should help you remember more of the words, because all of the 24 words fall into one of those categories. Such **associate cues** are related to the words you were searching for; as such, they should direct your search toward relevant parts of your long-term memory.

Still a third kind of retrieval cue is an organizational structure, or **frame,** that guides the retrieval process systematically through long-term memory (e.g., Calfee, 1981). For example, in Chapter 10 I described an experiment by Bower and his colleagues (1969) in which presenting words in an organized format (e.g., the "minerals" hierarchy shown in Figure 10–4), rather than in a random order, facilitated learning. An overall organizational structure provides numerous cues that should facilitate retrieval (e.g., "Hmmm, now that I have remembered the rare and common metals, I need to remember the alloys").

Consider this sentence that science education students often tell me they use to remember the biological classification system:

King Philip comes over for good spaghetti.

The students use the first letter of each word in the sentence to help them remember these terms in their correct order: *kingdom, phylum, class, order, family, genus,* and *species.* Each word in the sentence provides a retrieval cue—it limits the search of long-term memory to words that begin with a particular letter.

Retrieval cues definitely aid recall of information (e.g., Tulving & Thomson, 1973).[1] They are likely to be most effective when we have frequently associated them with the specific information we are trying to remember (Tulving, 1968, 1975; Tulving & Thomson, 1971; Underwood, 1983). For example, when retrieving the list of 24 words I gave you earlier, once you remembered *table,* you should have had little trouble remembering *chair* as well (or vice versa), because the two words often occur together in conversation.

When we acquire a new piece of information, we sometimes store it in association with the environmental context in which we received it—a phenomenon known as **encoding specificity** (Tulving, 1983). Thus, being in the same environmental context later on can serve as an effective retrieval cue (Godden & Baddeley, 1975; Smith, Glenberg, & Bjork, 1978). In an unusual demonstration of this principle, Godden and Baddeley (1975) had scuba divers learn 36 unrelated words in either of two environments: on shore or 20 feet below the water's surface. They were then asked to remember the words in either the same or a different environment. On a free recall task, the divers were able to recall more words when they were in the same environment in which they had learned the words than when they were in the other environment. Yet even when the environment itself is not the specific one in which we originally learned something, exposure to some of the characteristics of that environment—perhaps the same smells or the same background music—can help us remember (Balch, Bowman, & Mohler, 1992; Cann & Ross, 1989; Schab, 1990).

Although retrieval cues usually facilitate our recall of information, they can hinder it when they direct our search to a part of long-term memory *other* than that which holds the information. For example, in a study by Brown (1968), an experimental group of college students was given a list of 25 U.S. states to read, while a control group had no such list. Both groups were then asked to recall as many of the 50 states as they could. Compared with the control group, the experimental group remembered more of the states

[1]Retrieval cues may even affect the extent to which organisms exhibit classically conditioned responses; see Bouton (1994) for an explanation.

they had previously read but *fewer* of the states they had *not* read. Thus, retrieval cues are helpful only to the extent that they direct us to that part of long-term memory containing the desired information.

CONSTRUCTION IN RETRIEVAL

Read the following passage *one time only:*

Carol Harris' Need for Professional Help

Carol Harris was a problem child from birth. She was wild, stubborn, and violent. By the time Carol turned eight, she was still unmanageable. Her parents were very concerned about her mental health. There was no good institution for her problem in her state. Her parents finally decided to take some action. They hired a private teacher for Carol. (Sulin & Dooling, 1974)

Now cover the passage and answer this question: Did you read the statement "She was deaf, dumb, and blind" anywhere in the passage?

My guess is that you correctly answered "no" to my question. But do you think you might have been fooled if you had read the same passage with the name Helen Keller substituted for Carol Harris? Sulin and Dooling (1974) compared what happened when people read a Carol Harris version of the story versus when they read a Helen Keller version: Immediately after reading the passage, 20% of the "Helen Keller" group stated that the passage had included a statement about the woman being "deaf, dumb, and blind," yet no one in the "Carol Harris" group made that mistake. One week later, the number asserting they had read such a statement rose to 50% for the "Helen Keller" group but only to 5% for the "Carol Harris" group. In a follow-up study using the same passage, Dooling and Christiaansen (1977) found that people who read about Carol Harris, but who were told at recall a week later that the passage was really about Helen Keller, were also likely to "remember" the statement about her being "deaf, dumb, and blind." At retrieval time, the participants in the two studies were apparently using their prior knowledge about Helen Keller as well as their actual memory of what they had read. The longer the time interval between storage and retrieval, the greater the impact their prior knowledge had.

Such results indicate that long-term memory retrieval, like long-term memory storage, may involve constructive processes. Individuals often retrieve only a portion of the information that has previously been presented to them; on such occasions, they may fill in holes in what they remember based on what is logical or consistent with their existing knowledge about the world (J. Anderson, 1983a; R. Anderson, 1984; Halpern, 1985; Heit, 1993; Kolodner, 1985; Loftus, 1991; Neisser, 1981; Rumelhart & Ortony, 1977; Spiro, 1980a, 1980b; Wilson & Anderson, 1986).

Construction can occur in retrieval of nonverbal as well as verbal material. For example, in Chapter 10 I described research by Carmichael, Hogan, and Walters (1932), in which people's reproductions of line drawings reflected the labels (e.g., eyeglasses or dumbbells) assigned to them. The participants probably remembered only parts of those drawings and filled in the rest based on what they knew about the objects that the labels identified. Another example of constructive retrieval of nonverbal material can be found in the recall of a crime one has witnessed. Eyewitness testimony is sometimes an inaccurate representation of what actually happened (Buckhout, 1974; Lindsay, 1993; Loftus, 1991, 1992; Wells & Loftus, 1984). People's descriptions of the crime may vary considerably, depending on prior knowledge about the individuals involved, expectations about what typically happens in such a situation, and additional information presented at a later time.

As an illustration of constructive processes in eyewitness retrieval, consider an experiment by Loftus and Palmer (1974). Five different groups of adults watched a film depicting a car accident, and then people in each group were asked one of five questions about how fast the car was going. The participants' estimates of the speed varied significantly, depending on how the question was worded (italics highlight the variations in wording):

Question Asked	Estimated Speed (mph)
About how fast were the cars going when they *contacted* each other?	31.8
About how fast were the cars going when they *hit* each other?	34.0
About how fast were the cars going when they *bumped* into each other?	38.1
About how fast were the cars going when they *collided* into each other?	39.3
About how fast were the cars going when they *smashed* into each other?	40.8

As you can see, the participants' reconstructions of the accident were influenced to some extent by the severity of the crash implied by the questions that were asked.

The Loftus and Palmer study illustrates the **misinformation effect:** We see distortions in people's memory for an event when they subsequently receive inaccurate information about that event (Lindsay, 1993; Loftus, 1991, 1992; Thelen, 1989; Titcomb & Reyna, 1995; Toglia, 1996; Zaragoza & Mitchell, 1996). Apparently, people integrate the misinformation with their original knowledge of the event and may use the two in combination to reconstruct what "must" have happened.

Even especially vivid memories can be partly reconstructed and therefore have the potential to be inaccurate. As an example, think about where you were and what you were doing when, on January 28, 1986, you first heard about the *Challenger* space shuttle disaster. (To refresh your memory, the *Challenger* plummeted into the ocean soon after liftoff, and seven astronauts, including teacher Christa McAuliffe, perished.) Neisser and Harsch (1992) asked college students to describe the circumstances in which they heard the news both the morning after the incident and then again two and a half years later. Even after more than two years, many students were quite confident about their recollections; despite their confidence, however, some of them were way off base. For example, one student gave this account the morning after hearing about the disaster:

> I was in my religion class and some people walked in and started talking about [it]. I didn't know any details except that it had exploded and the schoolteacher's students had all been watching which I thought was so sad. Then after class I went to my room and watched the TV program talking about it and I got all the details from that. (Neisser & Harsch, 1992, p. 9)

The same student had this recollection two and a half years later:

> When I first heard about the explosion I was sitting in my freshman dorm room with my roommate and we were watching TV. It came on a news flash and we were both totally shocked. I was really upset and I went upstairs to talk to a friend of mine and then I called my parents. (Neisser & Harsch, 1992, p. 9)

Our memories of hearing about significant and somewhat emotion-laden events are often quite vivid, detailed ones with a seemingly "snapshot" quality to them; hence, psychologists call them **flashbulb memories** (Brewer, 1992; Brown & Kulik, 1977). Yet we shouldn't let such vividness lead us astray; although many flashbulb memories are quite accurate, many others are not (Brewer, 1992; Rubin, 1992).

In their study of people's recollections of the *Challenger* disaster, Neisser and Harsch (1992) interviewed many students a third time, three years after the disaster itself and so six months after the second recall. On this third occasion, most students essentially repeated their stories from six months earlier. When those who inaccurately remembered the occasion were given hints as to the truth about where they had been and what they had been doing, they stuck with their prior misrecollections; furthermore, they were quite surprised when they were shown their original, morning-after descriptions. It appeared that these students were remembering not what had actually happened but what they had previously *said* had happened.

As the Neisser and Harsch study illustrates, describing an event that has happened to us often affects our later recall of that event, and such **storytelling** can definitely be constructive in nature (Bohannon & Symons, 1992; Rubin, 1992; Schank & Abelson, 1995). The author Marion Winik has described the process this way:

> Sometimes I think childhood memories are fabricated like pearls around a grain of sand. You know how it works: take one old photograph and the quick current of memory it sparks; add what you heard happened, what could have happened, what probably happened; then tell the story over and over until you get the details down. It doesn't take a degree in psychology to reverse-engineer your childhood based on the adult it produced.
>
> Even if I've made it all up, it doesn't matter. I'm stuck with the past I believe in, even if it's wrong. (Marion Winik, *Telling*, Vintage Books, 1994, p. 40)

The importance of storytelling in our later memories of events may be one reason why we remember few if any events from the first few years of our lives; as infants and toddlers, we simply never talked about the things that were happening to us (Nelson, 1993a).

Although constructive processes may be responsible for many errors in what we remember, construction usually facilitates long-term memory retrieval. When our memory of an event is incomplete, we can fill in details based on what makes sense (Halpern, 1985; Kintsch, Mandel, & Kozminsky, 1977; Kolodner, 1985; Reder, 1982). For example, a student may not immediately remember which general surrendered at Appomattox at the end of the American Civil War; however, the student might reasonably assume that, because the South lost the war and General Robert E. Lee commanded the Southern troops, it was probably General Lee who surrendered at Appomattox. Similarly, a student trying to remember how to spell the word *ascertain* may surmise that, because the word is related in meaning to the word *certain,* it should be spelled similarly.

In some cases, retrieval is almost entirely constructive, in that an individual is asked to provide information that has never actually been stored. For example, consider this arithmetic problem:

$$1/2 \times 0 = ?$$

You may never have been given the answer to this specific problem, yet you no doubt learned long ago that anything times zero equals zero. Hence you are able to construct the correct answer:

$$1/2 \times 0 = 0$$

Constructive retrieval enables individuals to produce information beyond what they have specifically stored. At the same time, we must realize that such construction takes time (Anderson, 1985). In a study by Stazyk, Ashcraft, and Hamann (1982), students easily retrieved multiplication facts they had practiced many times over so that they quickly answered such problems as 2×3 and 4×6. On the other hand, they were slower to answer "zero" problems such as 2×0 and 0×6. Many students probably store a general rule for such problems (i.e., that anything times zero equals zero) rather than specific answers to each problem, and they must therefore construct their answer from the rule each time such a problem is presented. When fast reaction times are essential (e.g., when numerous basic math facts are needed to solve complex problems), it is probably to a student's advantage to learn the specific information required rather than a more general rule from which the information can be derived.

VALUE OF REPETITION AND REVIEW

In Chapters 9 and 10 we noted that rehearsal—repeating information over and over within the course of a few seconds or minutes—maintains the information in working memory indefinitely but is probably a relatively ineffective way to promote long-term memory storage. In contrast to such short-lived rehearsal, repeating stored information at periodic intervals over the course of a few weeks, months, or years—for example, by occasionally reviewing or practicing it—clearly promotes retrieval over the long run. This principle seems to hold true for people of all ages, even young infants (Anderson & Schooler, 1991; Bahrick, et al., 1993; Belfiore, Skinner, & Ferkis, 1995; Dempster, 1991; Linton, 1986; Rovee-Collier, 1993; West & Stanovich, 1991). In fact, as we noted in our discussion of verbal learning research in Chapter 8, spreading a certain amount of study time over a series of sessions (*distributed* practice) is more effective than having the same amount of study time in a single session (*massed* practice).

By reviewing and practicing what we have learned over a period of time, we probably accomplish several things. First, we engage in additional processing—processing that may allow us to elaborate on learned information in new ways and so understand it more thoroughly (Dempster, 1991; McDaniel & Masson, 1985). Second, by reviewing the same information repeatedly, especially in different contexts, we are likely to develop new and better retrieval cues: The more frequently we use something we have learned, the more associations we will make with it and the stronger those associations will be (Anderson, 1990, 1995; Calfee, 1981). Continued practice seems to have a third benefit as well: It promotes automaticity in processing and retrieval, as we shall see now.

Development of Automaticity

Schneider and Shiffrin (1977; Shiffrin & Schneider, 1977) have distinguished between two types of information processing: controlled and automatic. **Controlled processing** requires much of an individual's attention and is likely to use most (possibly all) of the individual's working memory capacity. In other words, controlled processing requires conscious thought and effort. An example is the cognitive processing necessary for learning to drive a car. I still remember the summer evening in 1964 that my father tried to teach me to drive a standard shift in our 1951 Ford convertible. Trying to steer the car in the right direction while simultaneously monitoring the speed and negotiating the stick shift and clutch pedal consumed all of my attention and working memory capacity. In fact, my working memory must have been overflowing, because I kept forgetting to step on the clutch, thus jerking the car forward and almost catapulting my father into outer space. (Dad enrolled me in a drivers' education class the following morning.)

In contrast, **automatic processing,** more frequently known as **automaticity,** occurs with little or no conscious attention or effort and requires little working memory capacity; it is, in a sense, "thoughtless." For example, 30 years after that jerky start in our 1951 Ford, I can drive with few mistakes and little thought. I do not have to remind myself to step on the clutch every time I want to shift gears, nor do I need to remind myself to remove my foot from the brake when I want to increase speed. Except under difficult conditions such as heavy traffic or inclement weather, I can make the hour's drive to Denver while drinking coffee, talking to a friend, harmonizing with the "oldies" playing on the radio, or shouting at the kids to keep their hands to themselves. Even though I still drive with a standard transmission, driving has become an automatic activity for me.

Controlled processes become increasingly automatic through repetition and practice (Anderson, 1983a, 1987; Cheng, 1985; Fisk, 1986; Norman, 1976; Piontkowski & Calfee, 1979; Schneider & Shiffrin, 1977; Shiffrin & Schneider, 1977). As I continued to drive that 1951 Ford, I not only became more proficient, I was also able to devote less and less mental effort to the task of driving. With several months of persistent practice, I was cruising Main Street with my friends, tapping my fingers to early Beatles' music on the radio, munching McDonald's french fries (12 cents a bag in those days), and perusing the sidewalk for male classmates of particular interest.

As you should recall from Chapter 9, people can usually attend to only one demanding task—one task that requires conscious, controlled processing—at a time. On the other hand, people can probably attend to several tasks simultaneously when each of them involves only automatic processing. How many mental activities they can conduct at the same time, then, depends on how automatically they can perform each activity. Remember, working memory has a limited capacity; people can perform only as many activities simultaneously as that capacity will allow.

Many academic tasks, such as reading, writing, and mathematics, require performing a number of "subtasks" at more or less the same time. For successful performance of these tasks, some of the subtasks should probably be automatic (Lesgold, 1983; Mayer & Wittrock, 1996; Perfetti, 1983; Resnick, 1989; Resnick & Johnson, 1988). Consider the case of reading as an example. Comprehending what one reads is often a difficult task involving controlled, conscious effort. If students are going to understand what they read, more basic reading processes, such as letter and word identification, must occur automatically. In fact, research is clear on this point: The more effort a student must devote to identifying the words on the page, the lower the student's comprehension of a passage is likely to be (Greene & Royer, 1994; LaBerge & Samuels, 1974; Perfetti & Hogaboam, 1975; Perfetti & Lesgold, 1979).

Writing, too, is a multifaceted process that can easily exceed the limits of working memory unless some processes are automatic (Berninger, Fuller, & Whitaker, 1996; Flower & Hayes, 1981; McCutchen, 1996). Good writers devote most of their attention to the communicative aspect of writing—that is, to expressing their thoughts in a clear, logical, and organized fashion (Birnbaum, 1982; Pianko, 1979). Apparently, these individuals have already learned the mechanics of writing (e.g., spelling, grammar, and punctuation) thoroughly enough to apply them automatically. In contrast, poor writers devote a considerable amount of attention to writing mechanics and so can give little thought to communicating their ideas clearly (Birnbaum, 1982; Pianko, 1979). Becoming a good writer, then, is at least partly a matter of automatizing basic skills. People can devote themselves to the task of clear self-expression only if they are not bogged down in concerns about subject-verb agreement or the correct spelling of *psychology.*

Similarly, some aspects of mathematics—in particular, the basic math facts—need to become second nature (Gagné, 1983). For example, in my course on educational assessment, students must be able to solve problems such as the following before they can learn to interpret intelligence test (IQ) scores:

$$\frac{70 - 100}{15} = ?$$

To solve such a problem easily, my students must have certain arithmetic facts at their fingertips; in this case, they must be able to subtract 100 from 70 quickly and must automatically recognize that -30 divided by 15 equals -2. I have frequently observed that when my students must consciously and effortfully calculate a simple arithmetic problem, they lose sight of the overall task they are trying to accomplish.

In the preceding chapter I emphasized the importance of meaningful learning: When students understand the information they store in long-term memory, they can more easily retrieve it. At the same time, in the case of many basic skills, understanding is not enough, because these skills must be retrieved quickly and automatically. Such skills must be repeated and practiced often enough that they become second nature, so that students can perform them essentially without thinking. In a sense, practice makes perfect, at least in terms of retrieval.

Naturally, we often retrieve things that we haven't learned to a level of automaticity. But what about those occasions when we *can't* retrieve something we've learned, no matter how hard we try? Let's turn our attention now to explanations of why attempts at retrieval sometimes prove fruitless—in other words, to explanations of forgetting.

THEORIES OF FORGETTING

Over time, people remember less and less about the events they have experienced and the information they have acquired (e.g., Wixted & Ebbesen, 1991). But forgetting is not necessarily a bad thing. Many of the things we learn on any particular occasion have little use to us later (especially *much* later), and we rarely need to remember things *exactly* as we originally experienced them (Anderson & Schooler, 1991; Reisberg, 1997).

As you should recall from Chapter 10, most information loss from the sensory register and working memory is believed to be due to processes of decay and interference. Information is probably "forgotten" from long-term memory in a number of different ways. Let's look at seven possibilities: decay, obliterative subsumption, interference, failure to retrieve, repression, construction error, and failure to store.

Decay

Theorists disagree about the permanence of information stored in long-term memory (Loftus & Loftus, 1980). Some theorists believe that information, once stored in long-term memory, remains there permanently; they attribute information "loss" to such factors as interference or an inability to retrieve. Others, however, believe that information can fade, or **decay,** from long-term memory, particularly when that information is not used.

Some evidence indicates that information may indeed remain in long-term memory for a long time (Bahrick, 1984; Semb & Ellis, 1994). For example, in a study by Bahrick (1984), individuals remembered a considerable amount of the Spanish they had learned in high school or college as many as 50 years before, even if they had not spoken Spanish since that time. Other evidence is found in experiments in which people *re*learn information they have previously learned but can no longer recall or recognize: These individuals learn the information more quickly than people who have not previously learned the same material (Nelson, 1971, 1978).

The observations of neurosurgeon Wilder Penfield (1958, 1959; Penfield & Roberts, 1959) are widely cited as evidence for the permanence of long-term memory. Penfield sometimes operated on locally anesthetized but otherwise conscious patients. In doing so, he discovered that stimulating portions of the brain with a weak electric current could promote vivid sensations in his patients. Patients would describe hearing a song, delivering a baby, or going to a circus as if the experience were actually happening to them at that very moment. They acted almost as if they were reliving previous events in their lives.

Unfortunately, no conclusive evidence confirms the permanence of long-term memory: Research findings do not (and quite possibly *can*not) demonstrate that *all* information stored in long-term memory remains there for the life of the individual (Eysenck & Keane, 1990). Penfield's work has drawn additional criticism, because Penfield never determined whether the events his patients "remembered" had actually occurred. Ultimately, determining whether items in long-term memory are subject to decay over time may be an impossible task.

Obliterative Subsumption

A variation of the decay theory is Ausubel's notion of **obliterative subsumption** (Ausubel, 1963, 1968; Ausubel, Novak, & Hanesian, 1978; Ausubel & Robinson, 1969). According to Ausubel, meaningful learning is a process of subsuming new pieces of information into long-term memory under more general, superordinate pieces of information. Over time, these specific pieces of information may be absorbed by their superordinates; in other words, they are *obliteratively subsumed.* For example, a teacher may present a general concept and then illustrate that concept with a number of examples; the student probably subsumes the examples under the concept. Over time, however, some of the examples may lose their distinctiveness from the concept itself and eventually blend in with the subsuming concept. At that point, the concept continues to be remembered, but the examples are forgotten.

As evidence for his theory, Ausubel has pointed out that general ideas are more likely to be remembered than specific details. Furthermore, details that are distinctive in some way are remembered whereas less distinctive ones are forgotten or become a general blur (Eysenck, 1979; Reisberg, 1997). To illustrate, when I think back to my early lessons in U.S. history, I remember the general idea behind the American Revolution: The colonists were fighting for independence from British rule. I also remember certain distinctive details: For example, the Battle of Bunker Hill is commemorated by a monument I visited frequently as a child, and the Boston Tea Party was a unique and colorful illustration of American dissatisfaction with British taxation policies. However, I have forgotten the details of many other events, because, to my young mind, they consisted of nondistinctive people and places.

The notion of obliterative subsumption is certainly consistent with what we commonly observe to be true regarding the kinds of information we remember and the kinds of information we forget. However, as is true regarding decay theory, little evidence to date either supports or refutes its validity as a major, distinct factor in forgetting.

Interference

In Chapter 8 I described the phenomena of proactive and retroactive inhibition: In both situations, learning one set of verbal material interferes with the ability to recall another set. Verbal learning theorists (McGeoch, 1942; Melton & Irwin, 1940; Postman & Underwood, 1973; Underwood, 1948) proposed that such **interference** is a major cause of forgetting verbal information. In support of this idea, recall of word lists can be as high as 85% when sources of interference are removed from a serial learning task (Underwood, 1957).

Imagine that you need to learn a list of 20 words. You are then asked to learn another list of 20 more words. Now try to remember the first list. Learning the second list has probably made it more difficult to recall the first list; to some extent, you have forgotten which words are in which list. The interference theory of forgetting might best be described as a theory of confusion: An individual has learned numerous responses and gets them mixed up. Using more conventional behaviorist terminology, verbal learning theorists called this phenomenon **response competition** (e.g., Melton & Irwin, 1940).

An experiment by John Anderson (1974) helps us place interference within a contemporary cognitive framework. College students learned a long list of single-proposition sentences, each of which involved a person and a place; following are some examples:

A hippie is in the park.

A hippie is in the church.

A policeman is in the park.

A sailor is in the park.

The people and places appeared in varying numbers of sentences; some items (e.g., the policeman) appeared in only one sentence, whereas others (e.g., the park) appeared several times. The students studied the sentences until they knew them very well—more specifically, until they could respond to a long list of questions (e.g., "Who is in the park?" or "Where are the hippies?") with 100% accuracy. At that point, they were given a new set of sentences and asked to indicate whether these sentences had been among the previous set. The more frequently the person and the place had appeared in the previous set of sentences, the longer it took the students to determine whether the person and place had appeared *together* in that first set. Anderson (1974, 1976, 1983a, 1990) has explained these results as being a function of the numerous associations the students developed to the frequently appearing people and places. For example, the more frequently that certain places had been associated with *hippie* in the original set of sentences, the longer students would take to search among their associations with *hippie* to determine whether a new sentence about a hippie had been among the previous set. Thus, multiple associations with a concept can slow down retrieval time for information connected with that concept, a phenomenon that Anderson calls the **fan effect.**

Interference is probably more relevant in the forgetting of rote-learned information than in meaningfully learned information (Good & Brophy, 1986). In other words, response competition and confusion are more likely to be a problem when associations between pieces of information are arbitrary rather than logical.

Failure to Retrieve

You can probably think of occasions when you couldn't remember something at one time yet recalled it later on. Clearly, then, the information was still in your long-term memory; you just couldn't retrieve it the first time around.

Failure to retrieve is most likely to occur when people neglect to search that part of long-term memory storing the desired information. Given appropriate retrieval cues, they may eventually find what they are looking for (Tulving, 1975; Tulving & Psotka, 1971; Underwood, 1983).

Repression

Earlier in the chapter we discovered that emotionally laden news sometimes results in a flashbulb memory—a particularly vivid recollection of where we were and what we were doing when we heard the news. But in some situations we may have an experience that is so painful or emotionally distressing that we tend not to remember it at all. This phenomenon, known as **repression,** was first described by Sigmund Freud (1915/1957, 1922); more recently, several theorists have explained it within a contemporary cognitivist framework (Erdelyi, 1985; Erdelyi & Goldberg, 1979; Jones, 1993; Wegman, 1985). To describe repression in contemporary memory terminology, painful information begins to produce anxiety whenever the relevant part of long-term memory is approached. Because anxiety itself is unpleasant, the memory search will tend to steer clear of the anxiety-arousing part of long-term memory. Thus, the painful memory, as well as any other information stored in close association with it, will remain forgotten.

Repression is reportedly quite common in clinical settings (Erdelyi, 1985; Erdelyi & Goldberg, 1979; Pezdek & Banks, 1996). Over a series of therapy sessions, a client gradually recalls bits and pieces of a traumatic incident; eventually, the client may remember the entire event. Recalling the incident often relieves the symptoms for which the client has sought the therapist's assistance (Erdelyi & Goldberg, 1979). Unfortunately, however, many presumably repressed "memories" are never checked for accuracy; thus, they may or may not be based on something that actually occurred (Holmes, 1990; Loftus, 1993).

A few laboratory research studies support the existence of repression (Davis, 1987; Davis & Schwartz, 1987; Eriksen & Kuethe, 1956; Zeller, 1950), but overall the evidence is more spotty than that found in therapeutic settings. Repression is apparently difficult to create in the laboratory, leading at least one theorist to question its existence (Holmes, 1974, 1990). It may be, however, that events sufficiently traumatic to bring about repression cannot easily or ethically be created in a laboratory setting; it may also be that many adults simply do not repress painful information as a matter of course (Erdelyi, 1985; Jones, 1993). Until these various possibilities are investigated, theorists will undoubtedly have difficulty reaching consensus about the extent to which repression plays a role in human forgetting.

Construction Error

We have already seen how construction can lead to errors in recall. Construction may occur either at storage (i.e., learner-invented information is stored) or at retrieval (i.e., the learner "remembers" information that was never presented). Construction at retrieval time is particularly likely to occur when there are holes in the information retrieved—holes possibly due to decay, interference, or unsuccessful retrieval. So, as you might expect, erroneous reconstruction of an event or a body of learned information is increasingly likely to occur as time goes on (Anderson & Pichert, 1978; Dooling & Christiaansen, 1977; Spiro, 1977).

Failure to Store

A final explanation of "forgetting" is the fact that some information may never have been learned in the first place (Bourne et al., 1986; Ellis & Hunt, 1983). Perhaps we didn't pay attention to the information, so it never entered working memory. Or perhaps we didn't process it sufficiently to get it into long-term memory. Simple exposure to information does not guarantee long-term memory storage.

Perhaps all of the explanations I have just presented are partially responsible for the universal human problem of forgetting. Forgetting is often evident in classroom settings, where students sometimes seem to "lose" information almost as quickly as they acquire it. In the final section of the chapter, we use what we have learned about long-term memory to identify some strategies for maximizing students' long-term retention of important academic material.

FACILITATING STORAGE AND RETRIEVAL IN THE CLASSROOM

As a way of summing up our discussion of long-term memory in this and the preceding two chapters, let's reiterate some general principles of memory and consider how they might be useful in helping students learn and remember classroom subject matter more effectively over the long run:

• *Meaningful learning is more effective than rote learning.* As we have seen, meaningful learning—associating new information with things that have already been learned—promotes more effective storage and more successful retrieval than rote learning. Associative networks provide "routes" from one piece of information to another. The more routes to a particular piece of information, the more likely it is that the information will be discovered when it is needed.

Unfortunately, some educators seem to forget this basic principle. All too often, classroom instruction and assessment methods emphasize the learning of classroom material at a verbatim level, with little or no regard for its underlying meaning (Dansereau, 1978; Doyle, 1983, 1986b; Fennema, Carpenter, & Peterson, 1989; Schoenfeld, 1985b). Many school textbooks are equally guilty, presenting lists of facts with few interrelationships between them and without regard for what students are likely to know beforehand (Alleman & Brophy, 1992; Beck and McKeown, 1988; Calfee & Chambliss, 1988; Chambliss, Calfee, & Wong, 1990; McKeown & Beck, 1990). For example, Beck and McKeown (1988) examined a number of elementary school social studies textbooks and found them often lacking a meaningful presentation of concepts and events. Beck and McKeown illustrated their point by describing how four widely used history texts describe the events leading to the American Revolution. In these books, events are frequently described as isolated incidents (thus promoting a disorganized, rote learning of them) rather than as having any significant cause-effect relationships with one another or with the revolution in general. Beck and McKeown argued that history texts should instead help students make sense of history; for example, the French and Indian War, the Boston Tea Party, and the Intolerable Acts all contributed to the American colonists' eventual rebellion against Britain and should be learned within that context.

Perhaps as a result of instruction, assignments, and evaluation methods that downplay the importance of learning classroom subject matter in a meaningful fashion, students often engage in relatively ineffective rote-learning processes—processes that are, over the long run, unlikely to facilitate students' retrieval and use of the things they learn (Novak & Musonda, 1991; Perkins & Simmons, 1988; Prawat, 1989).

Let me list just a few of the countless possible ways in which teachers can promote meaningful learning. Among other things, teachers can show students how a new fact or procedure is similar to something students have previously learned. They can provide a series of reading assignments on a particular topic, such that each one builds on those that have preceded it (Beck, 1985; Wilson & Anderson, 1986). They can incorporate students' own backgrounds, both personal and cultural, into the topics being discussed in class (Garcia, 1992). They can use new material within the context of everyday activities and problems—for example, by using mapping skills to map the school or neighborhood or by studying metric units as part of a cooking class (Brophy & Alleman, 1991; Reesink, 1984). And teachers should of course be sure that classroom tests and assignments emphasize the *meaning* of material rather than its word-for-word repetition.

• *Meaningful learning can occur only when the learner has relevant prior knowledge to which to relate new material.* Students have considerable difficulty learning and remembering material that does not overlap with their existing knowledge. When students are observed processing material in a rote fashion (e.g., rehearsing it), they probably either lack the appropriate background knowledge for learning that material effectively or are unaware of the relevant knowledge that they *do* have. For example, history textbooks frequently refer to American distress over Britain's "taxation without representation" policy, without always providing an adequate explanation of why this policy was so upsetting to the colonists (Beck & McKeown, 1988; McKeown & Beck, 1990). Many adults can easily relate the idea of taxation without representation to their own frustrations with high taxes. Most fifth graders, however, have little if any experience upon which to draw in understanding the colonists' situation.

Whenever introducing a new topic, teachers must consider what related knowledge students already possess about the topic and begin instruction at that point. As an example, early mathematics instruction might build on the informal counting procedures children have developed on their own (Fennema et al., 1989). Or, when students seem to have almost no knowledge at all about a particular topic, teachers might create classroom experiences to which they can relate new concepts. For example, a teacher might introduce the concept of *taxation without representation* by conducting an activity in which students are told to give valued objects to fellow students (only temporarily) without regard for their own wishes in the matter.

• *The internal organization of a body of information facilitates its storage and retrieval.* When material is presented in an organized fashion—for example, when hierarchical structures, cause-effect relationships, and so on are clearly laid out—students are more likely to store it in a similar organizational network. And when information in long-term memory is organized, it can be more easily retrieved.

Some of my own students have found the following analogy useful in helping them understand the importance of organization for retrieval:

Imagine 10,000 buttons scattered on a hardwood floor. Randomly choose two buttons and connect them with a thread. Now put this pair down and randomly choose two more buttons, pick them up, and connect them with a thread. As you continue to do this, at first you will almost certainly pick up buttons that you have not picked up before. After a while, however, you are more likely to pick at random a pair of buttons and find that you have already chosen one of the pair. So when you tie a thread between the two newly chosen buttons, you will find three buttons tied together. In short, as you continue to choose random pairs of buttons to connect with a thread, after a while the buttons start becoming interconnected into larger clusters. (Kauffman, 1995, p. 56)

After a while, you will form a single giant cluster of buttons. At this point, you can pick up almost any button in the pile and have most of the others follow. Now think of the buttons as being individual pieces of information related to a particular topic and think of the threads as being your associations among those pieces. Eventually, you make enough associations that when you retrieve one idea about the topic, you can also retrieve, either directly or indirectly, most of the other things you know about that topic.[2]

When students *don't* know the appropriate interconnections to make among the ideas they are studying, they sometimes try to pull what they learn together in a constructive, perhaps creative—but often inaccurate—manner. Turning to U.S. history once again, here is what one fourth grader (a girl from Michigan) had to say about why the Americas were once called the New World:

> Because they used to live in England, the British, and they didn't know about. . . they wanted to get to China 'cause China had some things they wanted. They had some cups or whatever—no, they had furs. They had fur and stuff like that and they wanted to have a shorter way to get to China so they took it and they landed in Michigan, but it wasn't called Michigan. I think it was the British that landed in Michigan and they were there first and so they tried to claim that land, but it didn't work out for some reason so they took some furs and brought them back to Britain and they sold them, but they mostly wanted it for the furs. So then the English landed there and they claimed the land and they wanted to make it a state, and so they got it signed by the government or whoever, the big boss, then they were just starting to make it a state so the British just went up to the Upper Peninsula and they thought they could stay there for a little while. Then they had to fight a war, then the farmers, they were just volunteers, so the farmers went right back and tried to get their family put together back again. (VanSledright & Brophy, 1992, p. 849)

This student made some creative connections indeed; for instance, she made a connection between China and cups (after all, many cups *are* made of china). At the same time, she didn't make at least one essential connection that would help her understand early American history—the fact that the "British" and the "English" were the *same* group of people.

   • *In most situations, elaboration facilitates storage and retrieval.* Students are more likely to remember classroom material over the long run if they expand on that material based on the things they already know. As examples, they might draw an inference that has not been explicitly stated, form a visual image of what a story character might look like, or think about how they might apply a scientific principle at home.

Many classroom activities can potentially promote student elaboration of classroom subject matter. For example, asking students to talk about academic subject matter, perhaps within the context of a class discussion or cooperative learning activity, almost forces them to do *something* (mentally) with that material (Brown & Campione, 1986; Hiebert & Raphael, 1996; Prawat, 1989; Reiter, 1994; Yager, Johnson, & Johnson, 1985). Asking students to write about what they are learning—perhaps in a research paper or on an

---

[2]I am indebted to one of my former students, Jason Cole, for originally making the analogy between Kauffman's scenario and the organization of memory.

essay question—enables them to pull their thoughts together and perhaps to identify and resolve gaps and inconsistencies in their understanding (Prawat, 1989). And when students tutor their classmates on subject matter they presumably know quite well, they learn it at an even higher level of understanding (Brown & Palincsar, 1987; Inglis & Biemiller, 1997; Semb, Ellis, & Araujo, 1993).

• *Occasionally, elaboration leads to the learning of misinformation.* When students have misconceptions about a topic, they may inappropriately elaborate on new information related to that topic. Teachers must continually monitor students' understanding of classroom material—perhaps by asking questions, assigning regular homework, or giving occasional quizzes—and then take steps to correct any misinterpretations that students' responses reveal. As we noted in Chapter 11, some misconceptions are likely to be "stubborn" ones that are not easily corrected; we will identify strategies for changing such misconceptions in our discussion of *conceptual change* in Chapter 13.

• *Information that must be retrieved within a particular context should be stored within that context.* People are most likely to retrieve information relevant to a situation when they have stored it in close association with other aspects of that situation. If they have stored it elsewhere, they are much less likely to stumble on it at times when it will be useful. Thus, information should be stored with retrieval in mind.

In light of this principle, teachers should give students numerous opportunities to relate classroom material to the various situations that are later likely to require its retrieval. For example, a student is more likely to retrieve mathematical ideas relevant to accounting, surveying, or engineering if the mathematics teacher incorporates problems involving accounting, surveying, and engineering into instruction. Similarly, a student studying for a psychology test stressing application becomes better prepared by using study time to consider numerous situations in which psychological principles can be applied. Furthermore, students should have opportunities to use the things they learn in real-world contexts; we will consider such *authentic activities* in Chapter 16.

• *Periodic review and practice promote easier retrieval.* As we have seen, rehearsal of information within a short period of time (e.g., less than a minute) is a relatively ineffective way to store information in long-term memory. But occasional repetition of learned information over a longer period of time (e.g., over the course of a few days, weeks, or months) *does* facilitate retrieval of that information. Teachers, then, might find it helpful to have students review and practice important material throughout the school year, perhaps by integrating that material into the context of new lessons. Repetition is particularly important for facts and skills that students need every day—for example, for basic number factors, words frequently encountered in reading, and rules of punctuation. (Computer software can sometimes make such drill and practice more palatable; for example, see Lesgold [1983], Perfetti [1983], and Resnick and Johnson [1988].) Basic information and skills should certainly be learned as meaningfully as possible, but they should also be practiced until students can retrieve them quickly and automatically.

• *Students' memories will probably never be totally reliable records of information.* Long-term memory storage and retrieval are both constructive processes and therefore will always be fallible. Students' memories can undoubtedly be improved, but they will probably never be perfect.

In addition to the specific strategies I have just listed, contemporary memory theory yields many more general educational applications. We will consider several of them in the next chapter.

SUMMARY

Retrieval from long-term memory appears to be a process of searching, in one "location" at a time, until the desired information is found. Retrieval is easier when information has previously been stored in a meaningful, organized fashion and when retrieval cues are present. Retrieval is often a partially constructive process: Some pieces of information may be retrieved and others filled in so that an event is remembered completely, albeit sometimes inaccurately.

Although repetition of information within a period of a few seconds or minutes (rehearsal) is not an effective way of storing information in the first place, occasional repetition of information that has *already been stored* makes that information easier to remember over the long run. Knowledge and skills needed on a regular basis should in many cases be practiced over and over until they are learned to a level of automaticity—that is, until they can be retrieved quickly and effortlessly.

Numerous explanations have been offered for why people "forget" things they have presumably learned. Possibilities include decay, obliterative subsumption, interference, failure to retrieve, repression, reconstruction error, and failure to store information in the first place.

Principles of long-term memory storage and retrieval have many applications to educational practice. For example, teachers should help students to learn classroom material meaningfully and in an organized fashion. They should also encourage students to elaborate on the material, yet be on the lookout for possible inaccurate or inappropriate elaborations. And teachers should provide opportunities for students to store information in association with contexts in which the information is most likely to be useful later on.

CHAPTER 13

Applications of Cognitivism I: Promoting Effective Memory Processes

A s cognitive psychologists develop a better understanding of how people process and learn information, they are also identifying instructional practices that can help people learn more effectively. In this chapter, we will examine several instructional techniques that can help students store and retrieve information in productive ways. We will first consider how teachers can design and deliver classroom lectures and other forms of expository instruction in a manner that helps students process information in a meaningful and organized fashion. We will also identify strategies for teaching concepts—strategies that make use of the theories of concept learning that we examined in Chapter 11. Then, as we look at mnemonics, we will discover several techniques for helping students store information that, at least on the surface, is relatively "meaningless" and therefore difficult to learn and remember. We will see how teachers can encourage their students to elaborate on classroom material by asking certain kinds of questions and giving students time to formulate their responses. Later in the chapter, we will identify strategies for promoting conceptual change—for presenting new information in such a way that students are likely to discard or modify their existing misconceptions about the world. We will look at how classroom assessment practices, although usually designed to measure students' learning, also *influence* students' learning. And finally, we will consider the effects that a teacher's expectations for students' achievement have on the behaviors that the teacher exhibits toward students and ultimately on the levels at which students *do* achieve.

The instructional techniques described in this chapter all influence how students learn *as individuals;* what one student does has little effect on the learning and behaviors of other students. Yet other instructional techniques promote effective cognitive processing through sustained interaction between two or more people; classroom discussions and cooperative learning activities are two obvious examples. Interactive approaches to instruction may be especially useful in promoting effective study strategies and successful problem solving; accordingly, I will describe such approaches in Chapter 16, after we've had a chance to pursue some of the more complex aspects of cognition.

EXPOSITORY INSTRUCTION

Much of your education has undoubtedly taken the form of **expository instruction:** You were *exposed* to information that was in essentially the same form that you were expected to learn it. Lectures, explanations, textbooks, and educational films are all examples of expository instruction; in each case, all of the information you need to know is laid out before you.

Over the years, some psychologists and educators have criticized expository instruction—and especially the lecture method—as being a relatively ineffective pedagogical technique. For example, B. F. Skinner proposed that learning can occur only when an individual makes an active response; because the typical classroom lecture does not allow much active responding, it is unlikely to promote learning. Jerome Bruner (1961a, 1961b) has been similarly critical of lectures, proposing that students can better understand ideas when they have hands-on experiences with those ideas. Bruner has argued that a discovery approach to teaching—one in which students discover various properties of the environment through manipulation of concrete objects—should be more effective than a traditional lecture.

Nevertheless, the lecture method has some strong advocates, including many cognitive theorists (e.g., Ausubel, 1963; Ausubel et al., 1978; Ausubel & Robinson, 1969; Pressley, with McCormick, 1995; Weinert & Helmke, 1995). These theorists believe that students listening to a lecture are not necessarily the passive nonresponders whom Skinner portrayed. Instead, students, although perhaps not overtly active, are nevertheless *cognitively* active: They busily attend to and meaningfully interpret the information they hear. Furthermore, although some students (those whom Piaget would describe as being concrete operational) may require the concrete experiences that discovery learning provides, other students (those whom Piaget would describe as formal operational) are quite capable of understanding concepts presented at an abstract, verbal level. For the latter group of students, a concise, organized lecture may be the most rapid and efficient means of presenting classroom subject matter.

David Ausubel has pointed out, however, that expository instruction is not always as effective as it might be (Ausubel et al., 1978). For example, when it is delivered without regard for how students will learn material meaningfully, it may yield disappointing results in student achievement. Ausubel describes four particularly "inept" practices in expository teaching:

1. Premature use of pure verbal techniques with cognitively immature pupils [e.g., preoperational or concrete operational students].
2. Arbitrary presentation of unrelated facts without any organizing or explanatory principles.
3. Failure to integrate new learning tasks with previously presented materials.
4. The use of evaluation procedures that merely measure ability to recognize discrete facts or to reproduce ideas in the same words or in the identical context as originally encountered. (Ausubel et al., 1978, p. 119)

As you might guess, such practices are more likely to encourage rote learning than meaningful learning; thus, anything learned is unlikely to be retained over the long run.

Ausubel and his colleagues (1978) have suggested that, for meaningful learning to occur during expository instruction, three conditions must exist:

1. *Students must have previous knowledge to which they can relate new material.* As we discovered in Chapter 10, students who have a large body of information already stored in long-term memory have more ideas to which they can connect their new experiences and so can more easily learn new information at a meaningful level. Those who lack such relevant knowledge are likely to resort to inefficient rote learning.
2. *Students must be aware of the relationship between the new material and their existing knowledge.* Students are likely to make connections between the new and the old only when they know that such connections are possible. To use the terminology of contemporary memory theory, students must have both things in working memory at the same time.
3. *Students must have a meaningful learning set.* Students must approach new information with the attitude that they can understand and make sense

of it—something that Ausubel calls a **meaningful learning set.** Students are more likely to have this attitude when teachers emphasize understanding rather than verbatim recitation (Ausubel et al., 1978); for example, they are more apt to learn material meaningfully when they know they will be expected to explain it in their own words than when they will have to reproduce textbook definitions. A meaningful learning set is also more likely to occur when students are confident that they *can* understand new material. Students who have learned through past experience that a certain subject is confusing are more likely to resort to a rote-learning approach (Ausubel, 1963, 1968; Ausubel & Robinson, 1969).

A growing body of research confirms the belief that expository instruction, when delivered properly, is an effective pedagogical technique. Let's look at several mechanisms that are likely to promote student learning during expository instruction.

Advance Organizers

In Chapter 10 I distinguished between *internal organization*—how various ideas within a body of new information are interrelated—and *external organization*—how that information is related to what students already know. One means of facilitating both forms of organization is the use of **advance organizers** (Ausubel et al., 1978). An advance organizer is a general introduction to new material that is typically designed to accomplish either or both of two purposes. An **expository organizer** provides a rough overview or outline of the material, describing the general topics (superordinate concepts) that will be presented and their relationship to one another; thus, it provides the beginnings of an internal organizational scheme. (The outlines and introductory paragraphs appearing at the beginning of each chapter in this book are examples of expository organizers.) A **comparative organizer** shows how the new material relates to students' previous experiences, to information they have previously learned in school, or possibly to their own purposes for studying the material; it also points out the similarities between the new information and the old. In this way, the organizer facilitates external organization. An additional advantage of a comparative organizer, as Ausubel has pointed out, is that it establishes a meaningful learning set: Students anticipate being able to understand the new material at a meaningful level and thus are more likely to approach the learning task with meaningful learning in mind.

Research consistently demonstrates the effectiveness of advance organizers in facilitating student learning, especially when material is not clearly organized and students have trouble organizing it on their own (Ausubel et al., 1978; Corkill, 1992; Mayer, 1979a, 1979b). Advance organizers also appear to promote more meaningful learning and consequently to facilitate the application of learned information to new situations (Mayer, 1987).

Although Ausubel originally conceptualized them as abstract introductions, advance organizers are usually more effective when they are fairly concrete (Corkill, 1992; Corkill, Glover, & Bruning, 1988; Mayer & Bromage, 1980; Zook, 1991). A variety of formats of advance organizers—overviews, outlines, analogies, examples, and thought-provoking questions—all appear to be effective (Alexander, Frankiewicz, & Williams, 1979; Corkill,

1992; Frase, 1975; Glynn & Di Vesta, 1977; Mayer, 1984; Zook, 1991). What follows is an example of how a teacher might introduce a lesson on radar by means of an analogy—a comparative advance organizer:

> Radar means the detection and location of remote objects by reflection of radio waves. The phenomenon of acoustic echoes is familiar. Sound waves reflected from a building or cliff are received back at the observer after a lapse of a short interval. The effect is similar to you shouting in a canyon and, seconds later, hearing a nearly exact replication of your voice. Radar uses exactly the same principle except that the waves involved are radio waves, not sound waves. These travel very much faster than sound waves, 186,000 miles per second, and can cover much longer distances. Thus, radar involves simply measuring the time between transmission of the waves and their subsequent return or echo, and then converting that to a distance measure. (Mayer, 1984, p. 30)

In some situations, an advance organizer might even take a graphic rather than strictly verbal form. For example, when introducing a unit on minerals, a hierarchical diagram similar to the one in Figure 10–4 might provide a helpful visual overview—an expository advance organizer.

Ongoing Connections to Prior Knowledge

Instruction is clearly more effective when it begins with what students know and proceeds from there (e.g., Bobango, 1988; Wilson & Anderson, 1986). Too often, teachers assume that students know more than they really do and begin instruction at a point beyond what students can comprehend. Before any instructional unit, students' existing levels of knowledge should be ascertained through either formal assessment (perhaps a pretest) or informal questioning.

Even when students have existing knowledge to which they can relate new material, they frequently do not recognize the connections they might make (Paris & Lindauer, 1976; Spires, Donley, & Penrose, 1990; Stodolsky et al., 1991). Hence, theorists recommend that expository instruction include some means of **prior knowledge activation**—some means of encouraging students to retrieve relevant knowledge to working memory. For example, teachers and students might discuss a topic in class before they begin a reading assignment about that topic (Hansen & Pearson, 1983; Wilson & Anderson, 1986). And when content learned earlier in the year (or perhaps in previous years) is important for understanding something new, teachers might provide a quick review of that content—a "refresher," if you will.

Teachers should continue to make connections between the new and the old throughout an expository lesson. Such techniques as familiar examples, in-class activities, and small-group discussions about particular aspects of the instructional material may help students understand information within the context of their own experiences.

When students have little knowledge that is directly relevant to new subject matter, analogies to familiar concepts and situations once again provide a viable alternative; Figure 13–1 lists some examples. Analogies help students learn information more meaningfully and retrieve it more easily, particularly when the topic is a new one for students or when the material is relatively abstract (Anderson & Schustack, 1979; Donnelly & McDaniel, 1993; Hayes & Henk, 1986; Newby & Stepich, 1987; Royer & Cable,

- If we think of the earth's history as a *24-hour day,* then humans have been in existence only for the last minute of that day (Hartmann, Miller, & Lee, 1984).

- The growth of a glacier is like *pancake batter being poured into a frying pan.* As more and more substance is added to the middle, the edges spread farther and farther out (courtesy of R. K. Ormrod).

- The Ural Mountains in Russia are like *the Appalachian Mountains in the United States.* They are old, worn-down mountains that served as temporary barriers of migration (Andrews, 1987).

- The human circulatory system is similar to a *parcel delivery system.* "Red blood cells work like trucks, carrying needed materials from a central distribution point for delivery throughout the body. Arteries and veins are like roads, acting as access routes through which the various points of delivery are reached. The heart is like the warehouse or the central point in which vehicles are loaded and dispatched, and to which empty vehicles are returned to be reloaded" (Stepich & Newby, 1988, p. 136).

- Peristalsis, a process that moves food through the digestive system, is "like *squeezing ketchup out of a single-serving packet.* You squeeze the packet near one corner and run your fingers along the length of the packet toward an opening at the other corner. When you do this, you push the ketchup through the packet, in one direction, ahead of your fingers, until it comes out of the opening" (Newby, Ertmer, & Stepich, 1994, p. 4, emphasis added).

- Any horizontal surface, such as a table, exerts force on an object that rests upon it. You might think of the table as a *spring* that is compressed when something is put on top of it. The spring pushes up against the object (Brown, 1992).

- The process of heat flow is similar to *falling dominos.* In both cases, one thing affects the thing next to it, which in turn affects the thing next to *it,* and so on (Royer & Cable, 1976).

- Electricity going through a wire is like *people going through a tunnel.* Everything that enters at one end comes out at the other (Gentner & Gentner, 1983).

- Tying a bowline knot is like *a rabbit guarding the territory around its home.* You hold the rope vertically and make a loop near the middle. The loop is the rabbit hole, the upper end of the rope is the tree, and the lower end is the rabbit. The rabbit goes up and out of the hole, around the tree, and back down the hole again (Hayes & Henk, 1986).

- A dual-store model of memory is like *the information selection and storage system you use at home.* Some things (e.g., junk mail) are discarded as soon as they arrive, others (e.g., bills) are dealt with only briefly, and still others (e.g., driver's license) are used regularly and saved for a long period of time (see Chapter 9).

- Retrieval from long-term memory is like *looking for something in a large, dark room with just a small flashlight.* You can look at only one small spot at a time, and it is virtually impossible to look everywhere (Lindsay & Norman, 1977).

Figure 13–1

Examples of analogies that promote connections between new ideas and things students already know.

1976; Simons, 1984; Stepich & Newby, 1988; Zook, 1991). At the same time, teachers must be careful to point out ways in which the two things being compared are *different;* otherwise, students may take an analogy too far and draw some incorrect conclusions (Duit, 1990; Glynn, 1991; Zook & Di Vesta, 1991).

Coherent Organization

Expository instruction tends to be more effective when it presents new information in the basic organizational format in which students should store it in memory (Dansereau, 1995; Tennyson & Cocchiarella, 1986; Tennyson, Tennyson, & Rothen, 1980; Wade, 1992). For example, teachers facilitate students' learning when they present ideas in a logical sequence, identify any hierarchical relationships that exist among concepts, and make cause-effect relationships clear. Showing how material should be organized may be particularly important for low-ability students; apparently, high-ability students are better able to organize poorly sequenced information for themselves (Buckland, 1968; Krajcik, 1991; Mayer, 1989a).

One strategy for showing how the concepts and ideas of a lesson interrelate is a **concept map,** or **knowledge map**—a diagram of the concepts or main ideas of a unit (often identified by circles) and the interrelationships among them (often designated by lines and by words or phrases that link two concepts or ideas together). As an illustration, Figure 13–2 presents a concept map that a teacher might use to organize some of the key concepts in a lesson on ancient Egyptian art. Such organizational maps can frequently help students learn, organize, and remember the things that they hear in a lecture or read in a textbook (Hall, 1994; Hall & O'Donnell, 1994; Krajcik, 1991; Linn et al., 1996).

Signals

When expository instruction provides a great deal of information, students may have trouble deciding which things are important and which things are not (Alexander & Jetton, 1996; Dole et al., 1991; Garner, Alexander, Gillingham, Kulikowich, & Brown, 1991; Reynolds & Shirey, 1988). For example, students may focus their attention on interesting, relatively trivial details at the expense of less interesting but more important ideas (Alexander & Jetton, 1996; Garner et al., 1991; Ward, 1991). Or they may look at the equations they see in a scientific proof while disregarding any verbal explanation of those equations (Dee-Lucas & Larkin, 1991).

A variety of **signals** as to what information is most important can facilitate students' learning from expository instruction (Armbruster, 1984; Lorch, Lorch, & Inman, 1993; Reynolds & Shirey, 1988). For example, writing key points on the chalkboard is a means of emphasizing those points. Underlining important phrases and sentences in a textbook passage makes them more prominent (Hartley, Bartlett, & Branthwaite, 1980; McAndrew, 1983). Specific objectives for a lesson let students know what is expected of them (McAshan, 1979). Questions interspersed throughout a lecture or textbook passage draw students' attention to particular ideas (Anderson & Biddle, 1975; Andre, 1979; McDaniel & Einstein, 1989). Even just telling students what is important probably facilitates learning (Reynolds & Shirey, 1988).

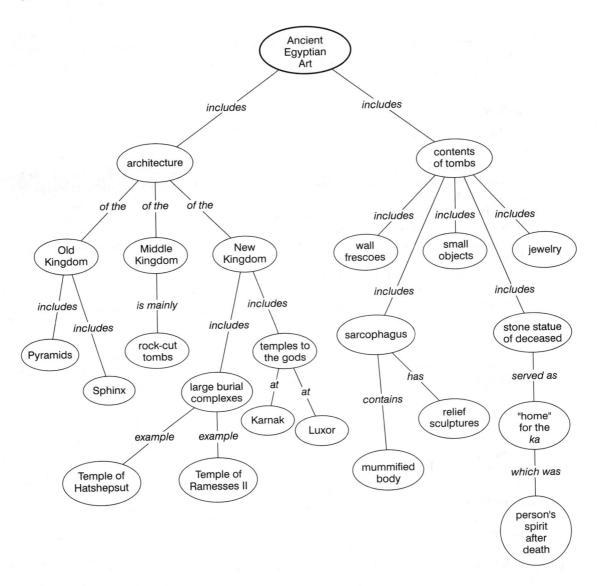

Figure 13–2
A possible concept map for a lesson on ancient Egyptian art.

Visual Aids

As we discovered in Chapter 10, visual imagery can be a highly effective way of encoding information. It may be particularly valuable when used in conjunction with other storage processes such as meaningful learning or elaboration. Thus, presenting information in visual form—through physical objects, pictures, maps, diagrams, live models, and so on—is often a helpful supplement to verbal material (Clark & Paivio, 1991; Denis, 1984; Levin, Anglin, & Carney, 1987; Levin & Mayer, 1993; Mayer, Steinhoff, Bower, & Mars, 1994; Prawat, 1989; Small et al., 1993; Waddill et al., 1988; Winn, 1991).

In most situations, visual aids should be simple and concise, including major ideas without overwhelming students with detail (Mayer, 1989b). In addition to promoting visual imagery, many visual aids can also show students how major ideas relate to and affect one another; thus they provide one more way of helping students organize the information they receive (Levin & Mayer, 1993; Mayer, 1989a; Winn, 1991). It is important, however, that pictures and other visual aids be relevant to the material students are studying; for example, irrelevant visual material in a reader or textbook, although possibly increasing the book's attractiveness, is unlikely to facilitate learning and can sometimes distract the learner's attention away from the more important part of the book—the text (Levin et al., 1987; Samuels, 1967, 1970).

Summaries

As we noted earlier in our discussion of advance organizers, students tend to learn more effectively when they receive advance notice of the things they will be learning. Students also tend to benefit from summaries presented at the end of a verbal lecture or written passage: They learn more effectively when they hear or read a synopsis of the information they have just studied (Hartley & Trueman, 1982; Lorch et al., 1993).

Summaries probably serve multiple functions for students. Among other things, they may help students to (1) review material, (2) determine which of the many ideas they have studied are most important, and (3) pull key ideas into a more cohesive organizational structure.

As we have seen, teachers can do many things to help students process material during expository instruction. When teachers use strategies that encourage students to engage in meaningful learning and to organize the ideas they are studying, such expository techniques as lectures and textbooks can be highly effective and efficient methods of presenting classroom subject matter to a large number of students.

Expository instruction often includes many new concepts for students to learn. Let's look at some specific strategies that teachers can use to teach such concepts.

TEACHING CONCEPTS

In Chapter 11 we examined several theories regarding how people learn concepts and what their resulting knowledge about a concept might include. More specifically, we characterized concept learning as possibly involving the following processes: testing *hypotheses* about the features important for concept membership, forming a *prototype* of what a typical positive instance of a concept might be like, remembering several *exemplars* that reflect the extent to which positive instances might differ from one another, and developing *feature lists* that include the defining and correlational features of a concept.

At this point, let's consider some of the factors that appear to affect how easily and quickly people learn new concepts. With these in mind, we can then identify strategies for teaching concepts more effectively.

Factors Influencing Concept Learning

Numerous factors influence the ease and rapidity of concept learning: the salience, redundancy, and number of features; the complexity of rules; the frequency and nature of positive and negative instances; and the extent to which these instances are presented in a simultaneous or sequential fashion.

Salience of Defining Features

The more salient, or obvious, a concept's defining features, the easier the concept is to learn. For example, my son Jeff easily learned the correct meanings of *milk, hot,* and *television,* presumably because the features that define these concepts are readily observable. However, he struggled with such words as *spring, summer, work,* and *university*—concepts whose defining features are not so obvious.

Because young children typically pay more attention to obvious features, their early concepts are likely to be based (sometimes erroneously) on such features. For example, in a study by DeVries (1969), children ranging in age from three to six played for a short time with a good-natured cat named Maynard. Then, as they looked on, the experimenter placed a ferocious-looking dog mask on Maynard and asked them, "What is this animal now?" Many of the three-year-olds asserted that Maynard was now a dog and refused to pet him. The six-year-olds, on the other hand, could overlook the dog mask, recognizing that it did not change Maynard's "catness." As children grow older, they begin to attend less to perceptually salient features and focus more on abstract qualities (Anglin, 1977; Ausubel et al., 1978; Keil, 1989).

Redundancy of Defining and Correlational Features

As defining and correlational features become increasingly redundant with one another, positive instances of a concept become easier to identify (Good & Brophy, 1986). For example, the concept *bird* is relatively easy to learn, because many characteristics—feathers, wings, beak, small size, and scrawny legs and feet—are either defining or correlational features. On the other hand, the concept *weed* is more difficult because it has only two defining features, and one of them is fairly abstract: It is a plant, and it is in the wrong place at the wrong time.

Number of Irrelevant Features

The more irrelevant features are present in positive instances of a concept, the more difficult the concept is to learn (Good & Brophy, 1986). For instance, the concept *animal* is difficult for many children, because most of the salient features of positive instances—body covering, nature and number of limbs, facial features, shape, and size—are somewhat irrelevant. So, too, might a true understanding of the concept *art* be a tough one to acquire. Things that stand out about a particular work of art are characteristics such as shape, color, medium (e.g., paint or clay), and subject matter (e.g., people or objects), yet these characteristics are only tangentially related to what art *is*.

Complexity of Rules

The rules that specify how defining features are combined influence the ease with which concepts are learned (Bourne, 1967; Haygood & Bourne, 1965; Neisser & Weene, 1962). Simple rules are typically the easiest to learn, conjunctive and disjunctive rules are moderately difficult, and relational rules are most difficult.[1] Young children often have trouble understanding such common relational concepts as *under, over, more,* and *less;* for example, children as old as seven years often do not fully understand what the concept *less* means (Owens, 1996; Palermo, 1973).

Positive Instances versus Negative Instances

Generally speaking, the presentation of positive instances leads to faster concept learning than the presentation of negative instances, although exceptions to this rule have been observed (Ausubel et al., 1978; Barringer & Gholson, 1979). In other words, it is generally more helpful to see what a concept is than what it is not.

Yet for truly accurate concept learning, both positive and negative instances are desirable. Positive instances should illustrate the full range of the concept, so that it will not be undergeneralized. For example, to learn an accurate concept of *dog,* the learner should see Chihuahuas and Great Danes as well as cocker spaniels and Irish setters. Negative instances can illustrate near misses, so that the concept will not be overgeneralized (Winston, 1973). For example, the learner must be informed that such creatures as cats, goats, and cows are nondogs to learn just where to draw the line on "dogness."

Sequential versus Simultaneous Presentation of Instances

In their everyday lives, people typically learn concepts through **sequential presentation:** They encounter a series of positive and negative instances one at a time over a period of weeks, months, or years and receive feedback about what is and is not an example of the concept. A faster way to learn concepts is **simultaneous presentation,** in which people can see a number of positive and negative instances all at once (Bourne, Ekstrand, & Dominowski, 1971). One likely reason for the difference in effectiveness of the two presentation methods is that in sequential presentation, the learner must store in memory what is learned from each instance, and that information can be forgotten from one instance to the next. In simultaneous presentation, on the other hand, the information to be gleaned from positive and negative instances is available all at once, so demands on memory are not as great.

---

[1] A refresher regarding these four kinds of rules may be in order here. To reiterate the definitions presented in Chapter 11: (1) *Simple concept:* one defining feature must always be present; (2) *conjunctive concept:* two or more features must all be present; (3) *disjunctive concept:* two or more defining features are not all present at the same time; and (4) *relational concept:* a relationship between two or more features determines the concept. You may want to refer back to Chapter 11 for specific examples of each of these rules.

Concepts are best learned through a simultaneous presentation of both positive and negative instances.

Each of these is a dog.

None of these is a dog.

Teaching Concepts Effectively

Theories and research related to concept learning yield a number of implications for educational practice. What follow are several points to keep in mind when teaching concepts in the classroom:

• *A definition of a concept facilitates concept learning* (R. Gagné, 1985; Merrill & Tennyson, 1977; Owen, Blount, & Moscow, 1978; Tennyson & Cocchiarella, 1986). A good definition includes defining features plus any rules related to them (e.g., "all defining features must be present"). Furthermore, it describes the concept in terms of other concepts with which students are already familiar (R. Gagné, 1985).

• *Numerous and varied positive instances help to illustrate a concept* (Clark, 1971; R. Gagné, 1985; Merrill & Tennyson, 1977, 1978; Owen et al., 1978; Tennyson & Cocchiarella, 1986). Through encountering many instances of concepts, people can form prototypes of those concepts. In fact, in some situations providing a "best example" is more helpful than offering a definition. To illustrate, Park (1984) used two instructional methods to teach basic psychology concepts (e.g., positive and negative reinforcement) to high school students. For some students, instruction focused on the defining features of the concepts; for others, it focused on illustrative examples of the concepts. Students for whom defining features were emphasized were better able to classify new examples during instruction. However, students who had been given examples of the concepts remembered more of what they had learned after instruction was completed. Ideally, of course, definitions and examples should be presented hand in hand, and in fact this combination of methods leads to more effective concept learning than either method alone (Dunn, 1983; Tennyson, Youngers, & Suebsonthi, 1983).

Concepts are better learned with many examples than with only one or two (Kinnick, 1990; Tennyson & Park, 1980; Tennyson & Tennyson, 1975). First examples should be simple and straightforward, with as few irrelevant features as possible (Clark, 1971; Merrill & Tennyson, 1977, 1978). Line drawings of concepts are often helpful because they can emphasize defining features and deemphasize or omit irrelevant features. Later examples should be more difficult, with more irrelevant features present (Clark, 1971; Kinnick, 1990; Merrill & Tennyson, 1977). Ultimately, examples should illustrate the full range of the concept so that students do not undergeneralize (Merrill & Tennyson, 1978; Tennyson & Cocchiarella, 1986); for example, the concept *mammal* should be illustrated by whales and platypuses as well as by cats and dogs.

- *Negative instances are useful in demonstrating what a concept is **not*** (Clark, 1971; Freiburgs & Tulving, 1961; R. Gagné, 1985; Merrill & Tennyson, 1977; Owen et al., 1978; Tennyson & Cocchiarella, 1986; Winston, 1973). Although negative instances were viewed as relatively unimportant by early theorists (Hovland & Weiss, 1953; Smoke, 1932), their importance has more recently been recognized. Negative instances, particularly when they are near misses to the concept, are helpful in defining the concept's limits and in preventing overgeneralization (Merrill & Tennyson, 1977; Winston, 1973). For example, in learning about mammals, students can be shown such similar-looking non-mammals as frogs and lizards.

- *Positive and negative instances are more effective when presented simultaneously* (Ellis & Hunt, 1983; R. Gagné, 1985). Research consistently indicates that people learn concepts more easily when they see examples and nonexamples simultaneously rather than sequentially (Bourne et al., 1971).

- *Students' understanding of a concept should be assessed by asking them to classify new examples* (Kinnick, 1990; Merrill & Tennyson, 1977; Owen et al., 1978; Tennyson & Cocchiarella, 1986). Do students truly understand what a concept is, or have they simply memorized a definition in a rote, meaning*less* fashion? To find out, teachers can ask students to select positive instances of the concept from among numerous possibilities—a strategy that Thiagarajan (1989) calls an *eg hunt* (a tongue-in-cheek variation of "e.g."). Students who have not mastered a concept will be unable to identify all positive and negative instances accurately, particularly in borderline cases. For example, as a preschooler, my son Jeff showed his limited understanding of the concept *animal* by denying that people, fish, and insects are positive instances. As another example, consider a study by Patricia Wilson (1988). Sixth and eighth graders were asked to define the concept *rectangle:* Many of them defined a rectangle in such a way that squares were (appropriately) included. Yet, when shown a variety of shapes and asked to identify the rectangles, the great majority of students who had correctly defined the concept of rectangle nevertheless did *not* identify any squares as being positive instances.

- *Students should be asked to generate their own examples and applications of a concept* (Ellis & Hunt, 1983; Watts & Anderson, 1971). Such a practice helps students test and refine their own understanding of the concept. The benefits of self-generated examples and applications are illustrated in an experiment in which high school students received instruction in basic psychological concepts (Watts & Anderson, 1971). Students who were asked to apply those concepts to new situations remembered more of the material than students who were asked merely to recall certain facts.

As we noted in Chapter 11, concepts enable students to interrelate and organize many of their observations and experiences. Furthermore, concept learning often involves meaningful learning to some degree, because students may be categorizing objects and events with which they are somewhat familiar. But what do teachers do in situations when important information is difficult to teach meaningfully and organize logically? In such situations, mnemonic devices provide an effective approach.

MNEMONICS

Looking back on your own educational experiences, you can no doubt recall many situations in which you had difficulty learning important information. Perhaps the troublesome material consisted of long lists of items, unfamiliar vocabulary words in a foreign language, or particular rules of grammar, spelling, or mathematics. **Mnemonics**—memory "tricks"—are devices that facilitate the learning and recall of many such forms of difficult material. In this section, we look at four different types of mnemonics—verbal mediation, visual imagery, superimposed meaningful structures, and external retrieval cues—and then examine some of the reasons that mnemonics are so effective.

Verbal Mediation

Imagine that you are trying to learn that the German word *Handschub* means *glove.* Playing off how the word sounds phonetically, you might remember this word by thinking of a glove as a "shoe for the hand." Such a mnemonic is an example of the use of **verbal mediation,** in which two words or ideas are associated by a word or phrase (the verbal mediator) that connects them. Following are some examples of verbal mediators for other German vocabulary words:

German Word	English Meaning	Mediator
der Hund	dog	hound
das Schwein	pig	swine
die Gans	goose	gander
der Stier	bull	steer

Notice that in every case, the verbal mediator bridges the gap between the German word and its English equivalent. By storing the mediator, you can make a connection between the two words.

Verbal mediators clearly facilitate learning (e.g., Bugelski, 1962), and their use is not necessarily restricted to the learning of foreign vocabulary words. For example, following is a mnemonic sometimes seen in spelling instruction:

The principal is my pal.

Retrieving this sentence will enable a student to remember that the correct spelling for a school administrator is "princi*pal*" rather than "princi*ple*." As another example, my daughter remembers the chemical symbol for gold—Au—by thinking "*Ay, you* stole my *gold* watch!"

Visual Imagery

As we discovered in Chapter 10, a visual image is a powerful storage mechanism that can be formed quickly and retained for a relatively long period of time (Shepard, 1967; Standing, 1973; Standing et al., 1970). Accordingly, visual imagery forms the basis for a number of effective mnemonic devices. Here we focus on three of them: the method of loci, the pegword method, and the keyword method.

Method of Loci

In the days of the Greek and Roman Empires, orators used a particular technique to help them remember the major ideas they wished to include in their hours-long harangues at the local forum (lecture notes were apparently not acceptable in those days). These orators would think about a familiar route that they walked frequently—the route from home to the forum, for example—and about the significant landmarks along the way—perhaps a bridge, a large tree, and a brothel, in that order. Then, when planning a speech, they would translate each key point into some sort of concrete, observable object and form a visual image of each successive key point located at each landmark along the familiar route. For example, let's say that an orator's first three points in his speech were the frequent traffic jams near the forum, the importance of a mass transit system in downtown Rome, and the consequent necessity for a tax increase. He might store images such as: (1) numerous horses and pedestrians entangled in a traffic jam on the bridge (first landmark), (2) a gigantic, 30-person chariot perched among the branches of the large tree (second landmark), and (3) several toga-clad prostitutes pitching coins at a tax collector from the upstairs window of the brothel (third landmark). Later, when pontificating at the forum, the orator would take a mental walk along his familiar route; as he passed each landmark, he would readily retrieve the image of that landmark and the object symbolizing the next major point of his speech. In this manner, he could easily remember all of the main ideas of the oration and their correct order.

This **method of loci** (*loci* is the Latin word for *places*) is clearly an effective mnemonic technique (Christen & Bjork, 1976; Groninger, 1971; Snowman, 1986) and lends itself readily to the storage and retention of lists of items. For example, in a study by Groninger (1971), some participants learned a list of 25 words using the method of loci while others learned the words simply by grouping them. People using the method of loci learned the words faster and remembered more of them on a free recall task five weeks later. Both groups performed equally well, however, when asked to recognize the words; thus, it appears that the benefit of the method of loci may lie in the imagery-based retrieval cues it provides.

Pegword Method

The **pegword method** is another technique for effectively learning a list of items and their relative positions (Bower, 1972; Bugelski et al., 1968; Higbee, 1976; Mastropieri & Scruggs, 1989, 1992). This method consists of using a well-known or easily learned list of items that then serves as a series of "pegs" on which another list is hung through visual imagery.

To illustrate, the following poem is sometimes used as a pegboard:

> *One is a bun.*
> *Two is a shoe.*
> *Three is a tree.*
> *Four is a door.*
> *Five is a hive.*
> *Six is sticks.*
> *Seven is heaven.*
> *Eight is a gate.*
> *Nine is a line; and*
> *Ten is a hen.*
> (Miller, Galanter, & Pribram, 1960, p. 135)

This poem should be an easy one to remember because its lines are composed of the numbers 1 through 10 in conjunction with rhyming nouns. Now suppose you need to remember a list of items in a certain order. You take the first item on the list and form a visual image of it interacting with the noun that rhymes with *one* (in this case, *bun*), then take the second list item and imagine it interacting with the noun that rhymes with *two* *(shoe)*, and so on. Images can be formed quickly and typically need not be practiced to be remembered.

Consider this food chain as an example of a list to be learned using the "One is a bun" poem:

> *Algae* in a lake are eaten by
> *Water fleas,* which are eaten by
> *Minnows,* which are eaten by
> *Larger fish,* which are eaten by
> *Eagles.*

Using the pegword method, you form an image of algae and a bun together—perhaps a hamburger bun covered with green algae. Similarly, you visualize water fleas in conjunction with a shoe—perhaps you see a shoe filled with water and several water fleas doing the backstroke across the surface. For the last three items of the food chain, you might form images of a tree with minnows hanging down like fruit, a door with a large fish stuffed through the keyhole, and an eagle wearing a beehive for a hat. Remembering the food chain, then, is simply a matter of thinking "One is a bun," conjuring up the image of the bun with algae, then thinking "Two is a shoe," retrieving the shoe image, and so on.

Keyword Method

I have already described the use of verbal mediation in learning foreign language words. But as you may have noticed, the German words I chose for my illustrations of verbal mediation closely resembled English words. More often, however, words in a foreign language are not so obviously related to their English meanings. In such situations, the **keyword method** provides an effective alternative. This technique, which is actually a combination of verbal mediation and visual imagery, involves two steps: (1) identifying an

Using a keyword to remember
that a horse is a *Pferd.*

English word or phrase (the keyword) that sounds similar to the foreign word and then
(2) forming a visual image of the English sound-alike word with the English meaning. For
example, consider how we might remember these German words:

German Word	English Meaning	Keyword(s)	Visual Image
das Pferd	horse	Ford	A *horse* driving a *Ford*
das Kaninchen	rabbit	can on chin	A *rabbit* with a *can on* its *chin*
der Waschbär	raccoon	wash, bar	A *raccoon wash*ing with a *bar* of soap
das Stachelschwein	porcupine	stash, swine	A *porcupine stash*ing nuts under a pig (*swine*)

The keyword method has been shown to be an effective instructional device in teaching both English and foreign language vocabulary words; it is also useful in teaching such
paired associates as states and their capitals or cities and their products (Atkinson, 1975;
Levin, 1981; Levin, McCormick, Miller, Berry, & Pressley, 1982; Mastropieri & Scruggs, 1989;
Pressley, Levin, & Delaney, 1982; Pressley, Levin, & McCormick, 1980; Raugh & Atkinson,
1975). Furthermore, older students (such as eighth graders) often spontaneously apply
this mnemonic to new learning tasks once they have been trained in its use (Jones & Hall,
1982; Mastropieri & Scruggs, 1989). Although only concrete objects can actually be visualized, the technique can be used with more abstract words as well, provided that they can
be adequately represented by a concrete object. For example, consider the Spanish word
for *love, el amor:* this word might be learned by picturing a heart (symbolizing *love*)
wearing a suit of armor (the keyword).

When presenting mnemonics based on visual imagery, teachers must keep three things
in mind. First, many young children cannot generate effective images on their own and so
probably need to have pictures provided for them (Mayer, 1987). Second, for imagery to be
an effective means of remembering a connection between two items (e.g., between a

bridge and mass transit or between love and *amor*), the two items must be incorporated into the same image in an *interacting* fashion (Bower, 1972; Dempster & Rohwer, 1974). Thus, while an image of a heart wearing armor is an effective way of remembering the Spanish word for *love,* an image of a heart standing beside a suit of armor probably is not. Third, as I indicated in Chapter 10, imagery does not preserve details very effectively (Anderson, 1990); therefore, it may not help one remember such specific information as the exact shape of a heart or the number of dents on a suit of armor.

Superimposed Meaningful Structure

One of my most vivid memories from my years as an undergraduate psychology major is being required to learn the 12 cranial nerves: olfactory, optic, oculomotor, trochlear, trigeminal, abducens, facial, auditory, glossopharyngeal, vagus, spinal accessory, and hypoglossal. It is not the nerves themselves that I remember but rather how painfully difficult it was to learn them all in their correct order. I had little luck drilling the list into my thick skull (I was using the tried-and-not-so-true method of rote memorization) until a friend passed along this mnemonic:

> *On old Olympus' towering top, a Finn and German viewed some hops.*

Notice that the first letters of the words in the sentence correspond with the first letters of the 12 cranial nerves: Just like in the list of nerves, the first three words in the sentence begin with *O,* the next two begin with *T,* and so on. And the sentence, though a bit strange, is fairly easy to remember because of the structure provided by its rhythm and rhyme.

"On old Olympus" is an example of a mnemonic I call a **superimposed meaningful structure.**[2] The technique is simple: The learner imposes a familiar structure on the body of information to be learned. That structure can be a sentence, story, poem, acronym, or anything else already meaningful to the learner. Figure 13–3 lists some examples.

Superimposed meaningful structures clearly facilitate memory for lists of items (Bower & Clark, 1969; Bulgren, Schumaker, & Deshler, 1994). As an example, let's look at an experiment by Bower and Clark (1969). Two groups of college students learned 12 lists of 10 nouns: Group 1 learned each list through repetition, while group 2 composed narrative stories that included all 10 words of each list. Following is an example of such a group 2 story (the nouns to be remembered are in capital letters):

> A LUMBERJACK DARTed out of a forest, SKATEd around a HEDGE past a COLONY of DUCKS. He tripped on some FURNITURE, tearing his STOCKING while hastening toward the PILLOW where his MISTRESS lay. (Bower & Clark, 1969, p. 182)

After the students had learned each of the 12 lists perfectly, they were then asked to recall all 120 words (the first word of each list was given as a retrieval cue). Students in group 1 (repetition) recalled only 13% of the words; in contrast, students in group 2 (stories) recalled 93%!

---

[2]I have also seen the terms *semantic elaboration* and *acrostic* used in reference to this technique.

The Mnemonic	What It Represents
ROY G. BIV	The spectrum: red, orange, yellow, green, blue, indigo, violet
HOMES	The five Great Lakes: Huron, Ontario, Michigan, Erie, Superior
Every good boy does fine.	The lines on the treble clef: E G B D F
Campbell's ordinary soup does make Peter pale.	The geologic time periods: Cambrian, Ordovician, Silurian, Devonian, Mississippian, Pennsylvanian, Permian
When the "mites" go up, the "tites" go down.	The distinction between stalagmites and stalactites
A "boot"	The shape of Italy
A "bearskin rug"	The shape of France
George Ellen's old grandmother rode a pig home yesterday.	The correct spelling of geography
I before E, except after C.	The correct spelling of words such as receive
Thirty days has September . . .	The number of days in each month

Figure 13–3
Examples of superimposed meaningful structures.

External Retrieval Cues

One of my own memory problems is remembering to remember. I forget to turn off my car lights after driving to work on a foggy morning. I occasionally forget important meetings. Sometimes I forget to bring crucial handouts or transparencies to class. Yes, yes, I know what you're thinking: I'm suffering from the absentminded professor syndrome.

It's not that I lose information from my long-term memory. When I go to the parking lot at the end of the day and find that my car has a dead battery, I readily remember the fact that I turned on my car lights that morning. When I'm reminded of the important meeting I've just missed or get to the point in a class session where I need the handout I've forgotten to bring, I think, "Of course!" My problem is that I *forget to retrieve* important information at the appropriate time. Given the number of my students who sometimes forget homework assignments (or even that they have class!), I know my problem is not unique to me.

When you need to remember to retrieve, an **external retrieval cue**—a physical object outside of (external to) your memory system—can be helpful. The classic example is the proverbial string around the finger: the string is tied in a spot impossible to overlook and serves as a reminder that something needs to be remembered. Finger strings are terribly unfashionable, but other external retrieval cues can be equally effective. Appointment books, to-do lists, and little self-reminder sticky notes increase the likelihood that students remember important assignments and engagements and also help students learn to be responsible for their own retrieval.

Why Mnemonics Work

It should be clear by now that mnemonics can be extremely helpful learning aids. As you may have noticed, their effectiveness lies in their conformity with a few critical principles of storage and retrieval. First, they often impose a structure or organization on the material to be learned. Second, they help the learner relate the new material to information already stored in long-term memory (e.g., to the number system or a familiar poetic meter). And third, they provide retrieval cues that help learners find the information at a later time.

Yet people rarely use mnemonics (Morris, 1977), perhaps because they are unaware of their existence or their benefits. Teachers can obviously help students learn difficult information if they identify or develop mnemonics for that information. Furthermore, they can help students become more independent learners by showing them how to develop effective mnemonics on their own.

The preceding discussions of expository instruction, concept learning, and mnemonics have, I hope, given you some useful ideas for promoting meaningful learning and internal organization. But how do teachers encourage students to *elaborate* on information as well? Teacher questioning is one possible strategy.

TEACHER QUESTIONS

In our discussion of instructional objectives in Chapter 5, we made a distinction between lower-level skills and higher-level skills. This was essentially a distinction between simply *knowing* something versus *doing* something (mentally) with that knowledge—for example, applying, analyzing, synthesizing, or evaluating it. We can make a similar distinction between **lower-level questions** and **higher-level questions:** The former ask students to retrieve something pretty much as they have stored it in memory, whereas the latter ask students to elaborate on that retrieved information.

Teacher questioning is a widely used teaching technique (e.g., Mehan, 1979), probably because it has several benefits. We noted one such benefit in Chapter 9: Questions help to focus students' attention on classroom activities. Questions also provide a feedback mechanism through which teachers and students alike can discover how much students have learned from a current lesson or can remember from previous lessons (Airasian, 1994; Connolly & Eisenberg, 1990; Fox & LeCount, 1991). When questions focus students' attention on previously studied material, they encourage review of that material—review that should promote greater recall later on (Wixson, 1984). And higher-level questions have the additional advantage of encouraging students to go beyond the information itself

(Feldhusen & Treffinger, 1980; Meece, 1994; Torrance & Myers, 1970). As examples, consider these questions from a lesson on the telegraph:

> Was the need for a rapid communications system [in North America] greater during the first part of the nineteenth century than it had been during the latter part of the eighteenth century? Why do you think so? (Torrance & Myers, 1970, p. 214)

To answer these questions, students must recall what they know about the eighteenth and nineteenth centuries (including the increasing movement of settlers to distant western territories) and pull that knowledge together in a way they have perhaps never done before.

All too often, however, teachers and instructional materials pose lower-level, fact-based questions, with few if any higher-level questions to facilitate student elaboration (Armbruster & Ostertag, 1993; Freiberg, 1987; Raudenbush, Rowan, & Cheong, 1993; Tobin, 1987). Such a state of affairs is unfortunate. Fact-based questions are certainly quite useful for helping students acquire and review basic knowledge and skills (Armbruster & Ostertag, 1993). Yet research indicates quite clearly that teachers and instructional materials (e.g., textbooks) promote greater student achievement when they ask higher-level questions in addition to lower-level ones—for example, when they call for inferences, applications, justifications, and solutions to problems as well as asking for knowledge (Armbruster & Ostertag, 1993; Brophy, 1992b; Frederiksen, 1984b; Liu, 1990; Redfield & Rousseau, 1981).

We should remind ourselves that elaboration takes *time*. It is unreasonable to expect students to formulate insightful, creative responses to higher-level questions in a split second. What happens when teachers give students the time they need to process and reprocess information? Let's find out.

WAIT TIME

When teachers ask students a question, they typically wait one second or less for a response; if students don't respond in that short time interval, teachers tend to speak again—perhaps by asking different students the same question, rephrasing the question, or even answering the question themselves (Rowe, 1974, 1987). Teachers are equally reluctant to let much time elapse after students answer questions or make comments in class; once again, they typically allow one second or less of silence before responding to a statement or asking another question (Rowe, 1987).

The amount of time teachers allow to pass after their own and students' questions and comments is known as **wait time.** In many instances, one second is probably *not* sufficient time for students to think about (process) the questions teachers ask and the comments students make in class. After all, they must retrieve the things they know and, in the case of higher-level questions, must construct a response they have not previously stored.

Research indicates that students benefit tremendously simply from being given a little time to think. For example, when teachers increase their wait time by allowing at least three seconds to elapse (instead of just one)[3] after both their own questions and students' remarks, we see changes in student behavior such as the following (Mohatt & Erickson, 1981; Rowe, 1974, 1987; Tharp, 1989; Tobin, 1987):

Increased student participation:
- Students talk more and are more likely to answer questions correctly.
- More students participate in class; previously quiet students (including many minority students) become more active contributors.
- Students are more likely to contribute spontaneously to a class discussion—for example, by asking questions and presenting their own perspectives.
- Students are more likely to talk *to one another* (as well as to their teacher) within the context of a classroom discussion.

Better quality of student responses:
- Students' responses are longer and more sophisticated.
- Students are more likely to support their responses with evidence or logic.
- Students are more likely to give a variety of responses to the same question.
- Students are more likely to speculate when they don't know an answer.

Better classroom performance:
- Students are less likely to feel confused by course content; they are more likely to feel confident that they can master the material.
- Students' motivation to learn class material increases.
- Students show higher achievement, especially for complex material.
- Discipline problems decrease (as one fifth-grade boy put it, "It's the first time in all my years in school that anybody cared what I really thought—not just what I am supposed to say" [Rowe, 1987, p. 40]).

We also see changes in teacher behavior when we increase wait time to at least three seconds. More specifically, we see such changes as the following (Rowe, 1974, 1987; Tobin, 1987):

Different kinds of questions:
- Teachers ask fewer "simple" questions (e.g., questions requiring the recall of facts).
- Teachers ask more complex questions (e.g., questions requiring students to elaborate or develop alternative explanations).

Increased flexibility in teaching:
- Teachers modify the direction of discussion to accommodate students' comments and questions.
- Teachers allow their classes to pursue a topic in greater depth than they originally anticipated.

Changes in expectations:
- Teachers' expectations for many students, especially previously low-achieving students, begin to improve.

---

[3]Note, however, that waiting *too* long may be detrimental in that students' attention begins to drift elsewhere, so that important information is no longer in working memory (Duell, 1994).

Increasing wait time during class discussions and question-answer sessions benefits student learning in two ways (Tobin, 1987). First, it allows students more time to process information. Second, it appears to change the very nature of teacher-student discussions; for example, teachers are more likely to ask challenging, thought-provoking questions. In fact, the nature of the questions that teachers ask is probably as important as—and perhaps even more important than—the amount of wait time per se (Giaconia, 1988).

Wait time may be equally important during expository instruction for the same reason—students need time to process (to encode and elaborate on) the things they see and hear (Rowe, 1987). For example, when giving a lecture, teachers might lecture for 8 or 10 minutes and then give students a 2-minute interval in which to compare notes and clarify subject matter with one another (Rowe, 1987). And when reading, students may want to provide wait time for *themselves,* pausing occasionally to draw inferences, generate examples, consider applications, and so on from the new ideas they encounter. Within this context, the whole notion of speed-reading becomes counterintuitive, and, in fact, speed-reading is probably effective only when readers already know much of the information they are reading (Carver, 1971, 1990; Crowder & Wagner, 1992).

When the objective is recall of facts—when students need to retrieve information very quickly, to "know it cold"—then wait time during a question-answer session should be short. There is a definite advantage to rapid-fire drill and practice for skills that teachers want students to learn to a level of automaticity (Tobin, 1987). But when objectives include more complex processing of ideas and issues, longer wait time provides both teachers and students the time they need to think things through.

CONCEPTUAL CHANGE

What is *rain?* Here is one seven-year-old's explanation:

> Clouds think it's too hot, and one day they start sweating. I guess they start sweating and then the sweat falls on us. (Stepans, 1991, p. 95)

And what shape is the earth that the rain falls upon? Some fifth graders might tell you that it is "round, like a thick pancake" (Vosniadou, 1994).

As we have seen, cognitive theorists believe that students rarely come to school as "blank slates"; instead, they bring prior knowledge into the classroom with them and use that knowledge to help them understand new material. Unfortunately, as we discovered in Chapter 10, some of this "knowledge" may include misconceptions that interfere with effective learning.

School-age children are likely to have numerous misconceptions about the world; Figure 13–4 lists some typical ones. Yet adults do not always have their facts straight, either. For example, my husband, who teaches geography at the college level, tells me that some of his students believe that rivers always run from north to south (after all, water can only run "downhill") and that the Great Lakes contain salt water. I find misconceptions in my own college classes as well, such as the belief that negative reinforcement involves the presentation of an aversive stimulus (see Chapter 4 for the correct explanation) and the belief that rote learning is more effective than meaningful learning (Lennon, Ormrod, Burger, & Warren, 1990).

In Biology

- A living thing is something that moves and/or grows. The sun, wind, clouds, and fire are living things (Kyle & Shymansky, 1989).

- Plants "eat" soil, fertilizer, and water, just as people eat more humanly food (Roth & Anderson, 1988). (From the perspective of biology, plants produce their own food through the process of photosynthesis.)

- Vision involves something moving outward from the eye toward the object being seen (Winer & Cottrell, 1996). (In reality, the opposite is true: light rays bounce off the object to the eye.)

In Astronomy

- The earth is bigger than the sun and stars (Vosniadou, 1991).

- The sun revolves around the earth. It "rises" in the morning and "sets" in the evening, at which point it "goes" to the other side of the earth (Vosniadou, 1991; Vosniadou & Brewer, 1987).

- The earth is shaped like a round, flat disk (Nussbaum, 1985; Sneider & Pulos, 1983; Vosniadou, 1994; Vosniadou & Brewer, 1987).

- Space has an absolute "up" and "down"; people standing at the South Pole will fall off the earth (Sneider & Pulos, 1983).

In Physics

- Any moving object has a force acting upon it. For example, a ball thrown in the air continues to be pushed upward by the force of the throw until it begins its descent (Carey, 1986; diSessa, 1996; Kyle & Shymansky, 1989). (In reality, force is needed only to change the direction or speed of an object—an idea known as *inertia*.)

- Gravity is the "glue" that holds people to the earth. There is no gravity without air (Kyle & Shymansky, 1989).

- When an electric current lights up a lightbulb, it is "used up" (consumed) by the lightbulb and disappears (Kyle & Shymansky, 1989). (In reality, the current flows back to the power source from which it originated.)

In Geography

- The lines separating countries or states are marked on the earth (Gardner, Torff, & Hatch, 1996).

- Islands float on top of the ocean (Gardner et al. 1996).

Figure 13–4
Examples of common student misconceptions.

Erroneous notions about the world probably have a variety of sources. Sometimes people's misconceptions result from how things *appear* to be (Byrnes, 1996; diSessa, 1996; Duit, 1991); for example, from our perspective living here on the earth's surface, the sun looks as if it moves around the earth rather than vice versa. Sometimes misconceptions are encouraged by common expressions in language; for instance, we often talk about the sun "rising" and "setting" (Duit, 1991; Mintzes, Trowbridge, Arnaudin, & Wandersee, 1991; Roth & Anderson, 1988; Stepans, 1991). Sometimes people infer incorrect cause-effect relationships between two events simply because those events often occur at the same time (Byrnes, 1996; Keil, 1991). Perhaps even fairy tales and television cartoon shows play a role in promoting misconceptions (Glynn et al., 1991); as an example, after cartoon "bad guys" run off the edge of a cliff, they usually remain suspended in air until they realize that there's nothing solid holding them up. And unfortunately it is sometimes the case that we acquire erroneous ideas because we have seen or heard such ideas from others; in some instances, teachers or textbooks even give us such misinformation (Begg, Anas, & Farinacci, 1992; Duit, 1991).

Research in classrooms indicates that students of all ages often hold quite stubbornly to their misconceptions, even after considerable instruction that explicitly contradicts those misconceptions (Anderson, Sheldon, & Dubay, 1990; Borko & Putnam, 1996; Carey, 1986; Chambliss, 1994; Champagne et al., 1982; Chinn & Brewer, 1993; Eaton et al., 1984; Holt-Reynolds, 1992; Roth, 1990; Shuell, 1996; Winer & Cottrell, 1996). Why are people's misconceptions often so resistant to change? Theorists have offered several possible explanations:

- As we noted in Chapter 10, people's existing misconceptions may often color their understanding of the new information they receive. Thanks to the processes of meaningful learning and elaboration—processes that usually facilitate learning—learners are more likely to interpret new information in ways that are consistent with what they already "know" about the world, to the point where they continue to believe what they have always believed.
- People tend not only to interpret new information in terms of what they already "know" but also to look for information that confirms their existing beliefs and to ignore any *dis*confirming evidence (Duit, 1991; Gunstone & White, 1981; Kuhn, Amsel, & O'Loughlin, 1988).
- People's existing beliefs are often consistent with their everyday experiences; in contrast, more accurate explanations (perhaps commonly accepted scientific principles or theories) may be fairly abstract and difficult to relate to everyday reality (Alexander, in press; Driver, Asoko, Leach, Mortimer, & Scott, 1994; Linn et al., 1996; Mintzes et al., 1991). For example, although the law of inertia tells us that force is needed to *start* an object in motion but not to *keep* it in motion, we know from experience that if we want to move a heavy object across the floor, we have to continue to push it (Driver et al., 1994).[4]
- Some erroneous beliefs are integrated into a cohesive whole, with many interrelationships existing among various ideas; in such a situation, changing misconceptions involves changing an entire organized body of knowledge rather than a single belief (Chambliss, 1994; Derry, 1996; Duit, 1991). For example, the

---

[4]Some theorists have proposed that such reality-based beliefs about the world, although scientifically incomplete or inaccurate, may be quite useful for interpreting everyday experiences; accordingly, the beliefs have some degree of "validity" and should be viewed as such (e.g., see Linn & Muilenburg, 1996; Linn et al., 1996).

belief that the sun revolves around the earth may be part of a more general "earth-centered" view of things, perhaps one that includes the moon, stars, and various other heavenly bodies revolving around the earth as well. In reality, of course, the moon revolves around the earth, the earth revolves around the sun, and the other stars are not directly involved with the earth one way or the other. Yet the earth-centered view is much easier to understand and accept (on the surface, at least), and everything fits so nicely together.

- In many situations, people learn new information without letting go of their prior beliefs, so that two inconsistent ideas are kept in memory simultaneously (Chambliss, 1994; Keil & Silberstein, 1996; Mintzes et al., 1991; Winer & Cottrell, 1996). Sometimes this happens because people learn the new information at a rote level, without relating it to the things they already know and believe (Chambliss, 1994; Strike & Posner, 1992). In other cases, it may occur because existing misconceptions take the form of *implicit knowledge*—knowledge that cannot consciously be accessed (Keil & Silberstein, 1996). In either situation, people do not realize that the new things they have learned contradict what they already believe.

When students have erroneous beliefs about the world, teachers face a twofold challenge. They must not only help their students learn new things but also help them *un*learn their existing misconceptions; in other words, teachers must promote **conceptual change**.[5] Although research on conceptual change is still in its infancy, theorists have offered several suggestions that should be helpful for teachers.

- *Before instruction begins, teachers should determine what misconceptions about a topic exist.* Teachers can more easily address students' misconceptions when they know what those misconceptions *are* (Kyle & Shymansky, 1989; Roth & Anderson, 1988; Stepans, 1991; Vosniadou & Brewer, 1987). Thus, a lesson might begin with informal questioning or a formal pretest to probe students' current view of the subject at hand. Teachers may need to ask a series of questions to get a clear understanding of what their students really believe; the following conversation illustrates the kinds of questions that may be in order:

Adult:	What is rain?
Child:	It's water that falls out of a cloud when the clouds evaporate.
Adult:	What do you mean, "clouds evaporate"?
Child:	That means water goes up in the air and then it makes clouds and then, when it gets too heavy up there, then the water comes and they call it rain.
Adult:	Does the water stay in the sky?
Child:	Yes, and then it comes down when it rains. It gets too heavy.
Adult:	Why does it get too heavy?
Child:	'Cause there's too much water up there.
Adult:	Why does it rain?
Child:	'Cause the water gets too heavy and then it comes down.

[5]Some theorists instead use such terms as *restructuring* or *reconstruction*.

Adult: Why doesn't the whole thing come down?

Child: Well, 'cause it comes down at little times like a salt shaker when you turn it upside down. It doesn't all come down at once 'cause there's little holes and it just comes out.

Adult: What are the little holes in the sky?

Child: Umm, holes in the clouds, letting the water out. (Adapted from Stepans, 1991, p. 94)

This conception of a cloud as a "salt shaker" of sorts is hardly consistent with the scientifically accepted view of how and why rain comes about. As teachers gain more experience teaching a particular topic over the years, they can begin to anticipate what students' prior beliefs and misbeliefs about that topic are likely to be (Hollon, Roth, & Anderson, 1991).

• *Students should learn correct information at a meaningful rather than rote level.* Students will only notice inconsistencies between new information and their previously acquired beliefs when they try to make connections between the new and the old. To use levels-of-processing terminology for a moment, students are most likely to modify their misconceptions in the light of new data if they process those data in depth—in other words, if they become actively engaged in learning and truly try to understand the information being presented to them (Brown, 1992; Chinn & Brewer, 1993; Howe, Tolmie, Greer, & Mackenzie, 1995; Lee & Anderson, 1993; Pintrich, Marx, & Boyle, 1993; Slusher & Anderson, 1996).

Instruction is most likely to encourage meaningful learning, and therefore to promote conceptual change, when it focuses on a few key ideas rather than covering many topics superficially (diSessa, 1996; Kyle & Shymansky, 1989; Roth & Anderson, 1988). To repeat a phrase I introduced in Chapter 11, "less is more."

• *Students are most likely to revise their current way of thinking when they believe revision is in order.* Thus, students should be shown how new information contradicts things they currently believe and why their existing conceptions are inadequate. With this point in mind, teachers might consider strategies such as the following to promote conceptual change:

- Asking questions that challenge students' current beliefs
- Presenting phenomena that students cannot adequately explain within their existing perspectives
- Engaging students in discussions of the pros and cons of various explanations
- Pointing out, explicitly, the differences between students' beliefs and "reality"
- Showing how the correct explanation of an event or phenomenon is more plausible (i.e., makes more sense) than anything students themselves can offer (Anderson, 1977; Brophy, 1992b; Chinn & Brewer, 1993; Gunstone, 1994; Guzzetti, Snyder, Glass, & Gamas, 1993; McKeown & Beck, 1990; Posner, Strike, Hewson, & Gertzog, 1982; Prawat, 1989; Roth, 1990; Roth & Anderson, 1988; Vosniadou & Brewer, 1987).

• *Students must **want** to learn the correct explanation.* Students are most likely to engage in deep processing and meaningful learning when they are motivated to do so (Hatano & Inagaki, 1993; Lee & Anderson, 1993; Pintrich et al., 1993). At a minimum, they must be interested in the subject matter, set their sights on mastering it, and have sufficient self-efficacy to believe that they *can* master it (Pintrich et al., 1993). In Chapters 17 and 18 we will identify specific strategies that teachers can use to promote such student motivation.

• *Throughout a lesson, students' understanding should be monitored for the existence of particularly tenacious misconceptions.* Because of students' natural tendency to reinterpret new information in light of what they already "know," some misconceptions may persist in spite of a teacher's best efforts. These misconceptions are sometimes blatantly incorrect; at other times, they may be "sort of but not quite" correct. To illustrate the latter situation, let's consider an example offered by Roth and Anderson (1988), once again dealing with the topic of vision. Students sometimes define *transparent* as "something you can see through." Although such a definition is consistent with how we speak about transparency on a day-to-day basis, it may nevertheless reflect the erroneous belief that sight originates with the eye and goes outward to and through the transparent object. *Transparent* is more accurately defined as "something light passes through."

Throughout a lesson, a prudent teacher continues to check students' beliefs about the topic at hand, looking for subtle signs that students' understanding is not quite accurate and giving corrective feedback when necessary. As an example, consider the following classroom discussion described by Roth and Anderson (1988, pp. 129–130):

Ms. Ramsey:	(Puts up transparency) Why can't the girl see around the wall?
Annie:	The girl can't see around the wall because the wall is opaque.
Ms. Ramsey:	What do you mean when you say the wall is opaque?
Annie:	*You can't see through it. It is solid.*
Brian:	(calling out) The rays are what can't go through the wall.
Ms. Ramsey:	I like that answer better. Why is it better?
Brian:	The rays of light bounce off the car and go to the wall. They can't go through the wall.
Ms. Ramsey:	Where are the light rays coming from originally?
Students:	The sun.
Annie:	*The girl can't see the car because she is not far enough out.*
Ms. Ramsey:	So you think her position is what is keeping her from seeing it. (She flips down the overlay with the answer.) Who was better?
Students:	Brian.
Ms. Ramsey:	(to Annie) Would she be able to see if she moved out beyond the wall?
Annie:	Yes.
Ms. Ramsey:	Why?
Annie:	*The wall is blocking her view.*
Ms. Ramsey:	Is it blocking her view? What is it blocking?
Student:	Light rays.
Ms. Ramsey:	Light rays that are doing what?
Annie:	If the girl moves out beyond the wall, then the light rays that bounce off the car are not being blocked.

Notice how Ms. Ramsey is not satisfied with Annie's original answer that the wall is opaque. With further questioning, it becomes clear that Annie's understanding of opaqueness is off target: She talks about the girl being unable to "see through" the wall rather than light's inability to pass through the wall. With Ms. Ramsey's continuing insistence on precise language, Annie eventually begins to bring light rays into her explanation (Roth & Anderson, 1988).

Assessment of students' comprehension is important *after* a lesson as well. Teachers are more likely to detect misconceptions when they ask students to *use* and *apply* the things they have learned (as Ms. Ramsey does in the conversation just described) rather than just spit back facts, definitions, and formulas memorized at a rote level (Roth, 1990; Roth & Anderson, 1988). Regular assessment in the classroom can have the additional benefit of *promoting* learning, as we shall see now.

CLASSROOM ASSESSMENT PRACTICES AND LEARNING

Teachers usually use tests, assignments, and other forms of classroom assessment to determine what their students have learned in a lesson or unit. Research tells us, however, that classroom assessment practices also *influence* what and how effectively students learn classroom subject matter. In this section of the chapter, we will examine the possible effects of paper-pencil tests. We will also discover why some theorists advocate the use of real-world (i.e., *authentic*) tasks rather than traditional paper-pencil tests to assess student learning.

Paper-Pencil Tests

As a college professor, I typically give my students a test every three to five weeks (undergraduate students get them more frequently than graduate students do). I use my tests as a means not only of assessing what my students have learned but also of helping them to learn and remember course material more effectively. Corny as it may sound, I think of my classroom tests as learning experiences in and of themselves.

Classroom tests can, *when designed appropriately*, potentially enhance students' long-term memory storage and retrieval in at least four ways:

1. *By encouraging review before the test.* As we discovered in Chapter 12, students have a better chance of remembering things over the long run when they review those things periodically. Studying for tests is one way of reviewing classroom material. Most students study class material more and learn it better when they are told they will be tested on it than when they are simply told to learn it (Frederiksen, 1984b; Halpin & Halpin, 1982). We should note, however, that students typically spend more time studying the information they think will be on a test than the things they think a test will not cover (Corbett & Wilson, 1988; Frederiksen, 1984b; Frederiksen & Collins, 1989).

2. *By promoting effective storage processes.* Students tend to study differently, depending on the kind of test they expect to take (Frederiksen, 1984b; Frederiksen & Collins, 1989; Lundeberg & Fox, 1991). For example, students are likely to focus on memorizing isolated facts at a rote level if they believe the test will require verbatim recall. They are more likely to try to make sense of what they are studying—that is, to engage in meaningful learning—when they know they will have to put things in their own words. And they are more likely to elaborate on

class material if such elaboration will be required at test time—for example, if their test questions will ask them to apply, analyze, or synthesize the material.

3. *By requiring review during the test itself.* Taking a test is, in and of itself, an occasion for retrieving and reviewing learned information. Generally speaking, the very process of taking a test on classroom material helps students learn that material better (Dempster, 1991; Foos & Fisher, 1988; Frederiksen, 1984b; Nungester & Duchastel, 1982). But once again, the nature of the test probably makes a difference here: A test that requires students to go beyond the material itself (e.g., to draw inferences) is likely to be more effective than one that asks only for recall of facts presented in class (Foos & Fisher, 1988). And test questions that require a broad search of long-term memory (as essay questions are likely to do) promote more comprehensive review than do relatively specific, recognition-type items (as true-false questions are likely to be) (Frederiksen & Ward, 1978; Murnane & Raizen, 1988).

4. *By providing feedback.* Tests provide a concrete mechanism for letting students know what things they have learned correctly and what things they have learned either *in*correctly or not at all. For example, when students get constructive comments on their essay tests—comments that point out the strengths and weaknesses of each response, indicate where answers are ambiguous or imprecise, suggest how an essay might be more complete or better organized, and so on—their understanding of class material and their writing skills are both likely to improve (e.g., Baron, 1987).

It is relatively easy to write test items that measure simple knowledge of facts. As a result, these fact-based questions turn up most frequently on both standardized and teacher-made achievement tests (Alleman & Brophy, 1997; Lohman, 1993; Nickerson, 1989; Poole, 1994; Silver & Kenney, 1995). But if a teacher wants students to do *more* than memorize facts, that teacher must construct a test that encourages students to process information in certain ways—perhaps to rephrase ideas in their own words, generate their own examples of concepts, relate principles and procedures to real-world situations, use course material to solve problems, or examine ideas with a critical eye.

Alternative Forms of Assessment

Concerned about the tendency of most paper-pencil tests to measure lower-level skills, many theorists propose that other forms of classroom assessment be used more frequently (Lester, Lambdin, & Preston, 1997; Magnusson et al., 1994; Mehrens, 1992; Paris & Ayres, 1994). More specifically, they advocate the use of *performance assessment* and *authentic assessment.* Although these terms are often used interchangeably, I make a distinction between the two. In **performance assessment,** students show what they have learned in a nonwritten fashion; for example, they might give an oral presentation about a topic they have studied, use a computer spreadsheet to analyze and summarize data, or identify acids and bases in a chemistry lab. In **authentic assessment,** students demonstrate their knowledge and skills in real-life (i.e., authentic) tasks; for example, they might write a letter to the editor of the newspaper, use addition and subtraction to balance a checkbook, or apply principles of both biology and economics to evaluate national wildlife preservation policies. The two terms overlap, of course; we are likely to find many instances of classroom assessment that are both performance based and authentic in nature.

Such forms of assessment are sometimes used to assess *extended performance*—that is, to determine what students are capable of doing over a period of time (Alleman & Brophy, 1997; De Corte et al., 1996; Greeno et al., 1996; Lester et al., 1997). Some assignments might last several weeks; for example, teachers might ask their students to plan a field trip—a task that would involve identifying a variety of possible outings, considering the logistics of each one, making detailed plans for a particular trip, going on the trip, and then evaluating the results (Bell, Burkhardt, & Swan, 1992). In addition, **portfolios**— systematic collections of students' work over the course of several months or years— can be used to show students' diversity of accomplishments and continuing development of skills (Silver & Kenney, 1995; Spandel, 1997).

Some evidence indicates that performance assessments and authentic assessments promote students' learning, in part because they influence the ways that teachers *teach*. Teachers tend to devote more class time to activities involving higher-level skills (e.g., application, synthesis, and problem solving) when they anticipate using assessment techniques that focus on such skills (Fuchs & Fuchs, 1997; Lester et al., 1997). Furthermore, students may benefit from complex activities in ways that are not possible during one-time assessments of discrete skills. For example, in a study by Gregg and Leinhardt (1994a), seventh graders in geography classes studied map skills (interpreting scale, latitude and longitude, and various map symbols) through one of two approaches. Some students ("map readers") studied existing maps of Canada and completed a series of activities that required them to apply their skills to an understanding of the maps. Other students ("map makers") had to construct a large map of Canada that reflected what they had learned about scale, latitude and longitude, and map symbols. The map makers acquired a better understanding of map interpretation skills than did the map readers; the map-making activity was especially beneficial for students who had previously had little or no prior knowledge about map interpretation.

We should note, however, that alternative forms of assessment are not without cost. For example, the map makers in the Gregg and Leinhardt (1994a) study often felt overwhelmed and frustrated by the enormity of their task. Furthermore, such assessment activities may in some cases take a considerable amount of time (Messick, 1994). The jury is still out on the question of whether such a time investment is worth the increased gains in achievement that these assessments may yield.

TEACHER EXPECTATIONS

One potential problem in any form of classroom assessment is the tendency for teachers to see what they expect to see in students' performance. As we discovered in our discussion of long-term memory storage in Chapter 10, expectations often affect how we encode and store new information. We further discovered that expectations are especially influential when stimuli are ambiguous and that other people's *behaviors* are prime examples of such ambiguity.

Students' behaviors can often be ambiguous enough that they suggest a variety of interpretations. For example, imagine that a student, Mary, fails to finish a classroom assignment on time. Her teacher, Mr. Jones, might conclude that Mary (a) didn't try very hard, (b) wasn't capable of doing the task, or (c) used her time poorly. Which conclusion Mr. Jones draws will depend to some extent on his prior beliefs about Mary—whether he thinks that she (a) is lazy and unmotivated, (b) has low ability, or (c) is both motivated and capable of doing the work.

Teachers' expectations for students definitely influence the ways that they evaluate those students (Good, 1987; Harari & McDavid, 1973; Ritts et al., 1992; Rosenthal, 1994). Furthermore, their expectations influence how they behave toward their students, thus indirectly affecting students' achievement and classroom performance (Copeland, 1993; Good, 1987). For example, teachers who hold high expectations for students' performance are likely to teach more material and more difficult material, insist on high student performance, give students more opportunities to respond to questions, rephrase questions when students are having trouble answering them, and provide specific feedback about the strengths and weaknesses of various responses (Brophy & Good, 1970; Cooper, 1979; Harris & Rosenthal, 1985; Rosenthal, 1994). In contrast, teachers who hold low expectations for their students are likely to

- Give them less time and attention and have less friendly interactions with them.
- Teach them less material and present *easier* material.
- Give them assistance when they don't really need it.
- Focus more on drill and practice of basic skills than on promoting higher-level thinking.
- Give them fewer opportunities to respond in class.
- Allow less wait time after asking them questions.
- Give them less feedback about how they are doing.
- Give them inaccurate feedback (e.g., by reinforcing incorrect responses).
- Accept lower levels of performance.
- Overlook good performance when it occurs.
  (Babad, 1993; Brophy & Good, 1970; Cooper, 1979; Good, 1987; Good & Brophy, 1994; Graham, 1991; Graham & Barker, 1990; Rosenthal, 1994; Schunk, 1989b)

When teachers behave in such ways, they may create a **self-fulfilling prophecy:** Their students may actually achieve at the low levels that their teachers expect of them (Harris & Rosenthal, 1985; Rosenthal & Jacobson, 1968; Shaffer, 1988).

We must keep in mind that not all teachers let their expectations govern their treatment of students (Good & Brophy, 1994; Snow et al., 1996). Furthermore, some accommodations are appropriate when students are clearly achieving at low levels; for example, it makes sense to be sure that students have mastered basic skills before focusing too much on higher-level thinking. Teachers' assessments of their students' capabilities, if realistic, can guide them in their daily decisions about how best to help every student achieve at the highest level possible (Goldenberg, 1992).

SUMMARY

Cognitive views of learning and memory have been translated into a variety of educational applications. Expository instruction (presenting information in the form that students are to learn it) promotes effective learning *if* it facilitates effective storage processes—for example, if it promotes meaningful rather than rote learning, emphasizes the structure and interrelationships within the material, and focuses student attention on important ideas.

Numerous factors affect the ease with which concepts are learned, including the salience and redundancy of defining and correlational features, the number of irrelevant features, the complexity of the rules determining the combination of features, and the frequency and timing with which positive and negative instances are presented. Teachers can help students learn new concepts by providing definitions, numerous and varied positive instances to illustrate the concept, and several negative instances to show what the concept is *not;* they can also ask students to generate their own examples of a concept.

Mnemonics are memory "tricks" that help learners store and retrieve relatively "meaningless" material more effectively. Examples of such mnemonics are verbal mediation, visual imagery, superimposed meaningful structures, and external retrieval cues.

Teacher questions asked in a rapid-fire fashion are useful for developing automaticity of basic facts and skills. But in other situations, higher-level questions—those that ask students to infer, apply, justify, problem solve, and so on—facilitate more effective long-term memory storage and retrieval. Students are more likely to respond appropriately to teacher questions, and to achieve at higher levels in general, when teachers allow sufficient wait time for students to process the information they receive and the questions they are asked.

When students have erroneous beliefs about a particular topic, they may impose those beliefs as they elaborate on new information; thus, they are likely to misinterpret the new information, learning something other than what their teacher actually presented. Several strategies may be useful in promoting conceptual change; for instance, teachers should encourage meaningful learning of a few key ideas rather than learning a great deal of material at a rote level, and they should show students how new explanations are better than the misconceptions students currently possess.

Classroom assessment techniques influence students' learning processes; for instance, some kinds of test items may encourage students to engage in rote learning, whereas others may encourage them to learn meaningfully and to elaborate. Because many paper-pencil tests seem to focus too much on lower-level skills, some theorists advocate alternative forms of assessment (e.g., performance assessment or authentic assessment) as a means of promoting more effective classroom learning.

Realistic assessments of students' current abilities can guide teachers as they make decisions about how to help each student learn most effectively. Erroneous expectations for students' performance can influence teacher behaviors in ways that are detrimental to students' learning, however—in some cases leading to a self-fulfilling prophecy.

CHAPTER 14

Metacognition and Study Strategies

When I look back on my days as a high school student, I think about how I used to learn, or at least *tried* to learn, and I shudder. Although I was a reasonably good student, my ideas about how I could best study for my classes were incredibly naive. For example, I remember sitting on my bed "reading" my history textbook at night: My eyes dutifully went down each page, focusing briefly on every line, but my mind was a thousand miles away. After completing the reading assignment, I couldn't remember a thing I had read, yet I had the crazy notion that my supposed "knowledge" of history would miraculously come to mind at test time (it didn't). I remember, too, studying vocabulary words for my class in Mandarin Chinese: I truly believed that simply repeating those words over and over again would get them through my thick skull. In retrospect, the only subject I learned well was mathematics, because the various mathematical concepts and principles I studied seemed logical based on what I already knew.

How, as a metacognitively naive high school student, the author read her history textbook.

When I went to college, I continued to bumble along, spending too much time in mindless "reading" and taking notes in class that I can now make very little sense of (I have to wonder how much they helped me even then). It was only after a great deal of studying experience and considerable trial and error that I began to realize how important it was that I pay attention to course material with my mind as well as my eyes and that I try to understand the things I was studying.

As you have been reading this book, I hope you have been learning a great deal about how *you* learn and remember; perhaps you have also been modifying your approach to your own learning tasks. For example, you may now be trying to pay closer attention to what you read in textbooks and what you hear in class. You may also be focusing more on understanding, organizing, and elaborating on your course material. In any case, I hope you are not reading this book the way I used to read my history text.

People's knowledge of their own learning and cognitive processes and their consequent regulation of those processes to enhance learning and memory are collectively known as **metacognition.** The more metacognitively sophisticated students are, the higher their school learning and achievement are likely to be (P. Peterson, 1988; Wittrock, 1994). Unfortunately, many students of all ages (even many adults) appear to know little about effective ways to learn and remember (Dryden & Jefferson, 1994; Mayer, 1996b; Pintrich & De Groot, 1990; Schofield & Kirby, 1994; Thomas, 1993).

You might think of metacognition as the "manager" or "coach" of a person's learning (Schoenfeld, 1985b): It guides information processing and monitors the effectiveness of various strategies being applied to a particular learning task. But just as the coach of a basketball team might be either quite knowledgeable about playing basketball or instead harbor some very counterproductive misconceptions about how best to play the game, so, too, can a learner's metacognitive knowledge be either a help or a hindrance in the learning process.

In this chapter, we will look at the many things that people's metacognitive knowledge and skills may include. We will revisit social learning theorists' notion of self-regulation, this time applying it to an understanding of how learners regulate their learning and cognitive processes in the pursuit of specific learning tasks. We will examine several learning and study strategies that appear to promote effective learning and retention of classroom material and consider how students' *epistemological beliefs*—their beliefs about the nature of knowledge and learning—influence the ways that they study and learn. We will discover that students' learning strategies develop and improve with age but that students don't always use effective strategies even when they may be capable of doing so. Finally, we will identify a number of teaching practices that can help students become metacognitively more sophisticated, and thus better able to learn and achieve in the classroom, over the long run.

METACOGNITIVE KNOWLEDGE AND SKILLS

Metacognition includes knowledge and skills such as the following:

- *Being aware of what one's own learning and memory capabilities are and of what learning tasks can realistically be accomplished* (e.g., recognizing that it is probably not possible to learn everything in a 200-page reading assignment in a single evening)
- *Knowing which learning strategies are effective and which are not* (e.g., realizing that meaningful learning is more effective than rote learning for long-term retention)
- *Planning an approach to a learning task that is likely to be successful* (e.g., finding a quiet place to study where there will be few distractions)
- *Using effective learning strategies* (e.g., taking detailed notes when lecture material is likely to be difficult to remember otherwise)
- *Monitoring one's present knowledge state* (e.g., knowing when information has been successfully learned and when it has not)
- *Knowing effective strategies for retrieval of previously stored information* (e.g., thinking about the context in which a certain piece of information was probably learned)

As you can see, metacognition involves some fairly complex (and often abstract) ideas and processes. Many of these ideas and processes are not specifically taught in the classroom. As a result, it is not surprising that students typically develop metacognitive knowledge and skills slowly and only after many challenging learning experiences, nor is it surprising that some students develop few if any effective study strategies at all.

As an example of metacognition, let's consider what happens when students study their school textbooks. Their reading in this situation is not just a process of identifying the words on the page, nor is it just making sense of the sentences and paragraphs within which those words appear. The students are also trying to store the information they read in long-term memory so that they can retrieve it later on. In other words, they are *reading for learning*.

What specifically do students do when they read for learning? Good readers—those who learn effectively from the things they read—do many of the following:

- Clarify their purpose for reading something
- Read differently depending on whether they want to ascertain the general gist of a passage, learn the passage's content thoroughly and in great detail, or merely read for pleasure
- Determine what is most important to learn and remember and focus their attention and efforts on that material
- Try to make sense of and elaborate on (e.g., draw inferences from and identify logical relationships within) what they read
- Bring their prior knowledge into play in understanding and elaborating on what they read
- Make predictions about what they are likely to read next in a passage
- Ask themselves questions that they try to answer as they read
- Periodically check themselves to make sure they understand and remember what they have read
- Attempt to clarify any ambiguous points they encounter
- Persist in their efforts to understand when they have initial difficulty comprehending what they are reading
- Envision possible examples and applications of the ideas presented

How the author *should* have read her history textbook.

A critical turning point of World War II was the Japanese attack on Pearl Harbor on December 7, 1941. . . why would the attack on Pearl Harbor have been so important for the outcome of the war? . . . probably because it forced the United States to enter the war, greatly increasing the number of ships, guns, and troops available to the Allies.

- Read for possible conceptual change—in other words, read with the understanding that the ideas they encounter may be inconsistent with things they now believe
- Critically evaluate what they read
- Summarize what they have read
  (Baker, 1989; Brown & Palincsar, 1987; Brown, Palincsar, & Armbruster, 1984; Chan, Burtis, & Bereiter, 1997; Dole et al., 1991; Myers & Duffy, 1990; Palincsar & Brown, 1989; Roth & Anderson, 1988; Schraw & Bruning, 1995; van der Broek, 1990)

In contrast, poor readers—those who have trouble learning and remembering the things they read—use few of the strategies I've just listed. For example, they have little focus and sense of purpose as they read a passage (Brown & Palincsar, 1987). They have difficulty drawing inferences from the ideas they encounter (Oakhill, 1993). They rarely ask themselves questions about the material, predict what's coming next, clarify ambiguous statements, or summarize what they have read (Palincsar & Brown, 1984). They overlook inconsistencies among ideas within the text, as well as inconsistencies between those ideas and their prior beliefs about the world (Brown & Palincsar, 1987; Roth & Anderson, 1988). And, in general, poor readers seem to have little metacognitive awareness of the things they should do mentally as they read (Baker, 1989). As examples, consider three high school students' descriptions of how they studied:

- . . . I stare real hard at the page, blink my eyes and then open them—and cross my fingers that it will be right here (points at head).
- It's easy. If [the teacher] says study, I read it twice. If she says read, it's just once through.
- I just read the first line in each paragraph—it's usually all there. (Brown & Palincsar, 1987, p. 83)

As you might guess, these students were *not* learning very effectively from the things they were reading (Brown & Palincsar, 1987).

The process of metacognition is consistent with social learning theorists' notion of *self-regulation:* It provides the mechanism through which people begin to regulate one aspect of their lives—their own learning. Let's look more closely at what self-regulated learning might involve.

SELF-REGULATED LEARNING

In our discussion of self-regulation in Chapter 7, we discovered that as children grow older, most of them begin to set standards and goals for their own performance. They then choose behaviors that they think will help them meet such standards and goals, and they evaluate the effects of their actions.

Social learning theorists and cognitivists alike have begun to portray effective learning in a similar manner—as a process of setting goals, choosing learning strategies that are likely to help one achieve those goals, and then evaluating the results of one's efforts (Paris & Cunningham, 1996; Schunk & Zimmerman, 1994; Winne, 1995a; Zimmerman,

1989; Zimmerman & Bandura, 1994). More specifically, **self-regulated learning** includes these elements:

- *Self-motivation:* Having the desire to accomplish a learning task effectively. Such motivation must come from within the individual rather than from such outside influences as external reinforcers. Learners are likely to be self-motivated only if they have high self-efficacy regarding their ability to accomplish the learning task successfully (Schunk, 1995; Zimmerman, 1995; Zimmerman & Risemberg, 1997).
- *Goal setting:* Identifying a desired end result for the learning activity. Self-regulated learners know what they want to accomplish when they read or study; for instance, they may want to learn specific facts, get an overall understanding of the ideas being presented, or simply acquire sufficient knowledge to do well on a classroom exam (Mayer, 1996b; Nolen, 1996; Winne, 1995a; Wolters, 1997; Zimmerman & Bandura, 1994).
- *Planning:* Determining how best to use the time available for the learning task. Self-regulated learners plan ahead with regard to a learning task and use their time effectively to accomplish their goals (Zimmerman & Risemberg, 1997).
- *Attention control:* Maximizing attention on the learning task. Self-regulated learners try to focus their attention on the subject matter at hand and to clear their minds of potentially distracting thoughts and emotions (Harnishfeger, 1995; Kuhl, 1985; Menec & Schonwetter, 1994; Winne, 1995a).
- *Application of learning strategies:* Selecting and using appropriate ways of processing the material to be learned. Self-regulated learners choose different learning strategies depending on the specific goal they wish to accomplish; for example, they read a magazine article differently, depending on whether they are reading it for entertainment or studying for an exam (Linderholm, Gustafson, van den Broek, & Lorch, 1997; Winne, 1995a).
- *Self-monitoring:* Checking periodically to see whether progress is being made toward the goal. Self-regulated learners continually monitor their progress during a learning activity, and they change their learning strategies or modify their goals if necessary (Butler & Winne, 1995; Carver & Scheier, 1990; Winne, 1995a; Zimmerman & Risemberg, 1997).
- *Self-evaluation:* Assessing the final outcome of one's efforts. Self-regulated learners determine whether what they have learned is sufficient for the goals they have set for themselves (Butler & Winne, 1995; Schraw & Moshman, 1995; Zimmerman & Risemberg, 1997).

When students are self-regulated learners, they set higher academic goals for themselves, learn more effectively, and achieve at higher levels in the classroom (Butler & Winne, 1995; Winne, 1995a; Zimmerman & Bandura, 1994; Zimmerman & Risemberg, 1997). Unfortunately, few students acquire a high level of self-regulation, perhaps in part because traditional instructional practices do little to promote it (Paris & Ayres, 1994; Zimmerman & Bandura, 1994).

Later in the chapter, we will consider several strategies that teachers can use to facilitate the development of self-regulation in students at a variety of age levels. Before we can do so, however, we must find out more about what metacognitive processes entail. At this point, let's consider what research has to say about effective learning and study strategies.

EFFECTIVE LEARNING AND STUDY STRATEGIES

People do a lot of things "in their heads" when they want to learn and remember new material, but some of their strategies are clearly more effective than others. In the next few pages, we will consider research findings regarding several effective learning and study strategies. The first three on our list—meaningful learning, elaboration, and organization—are long-term memory storage processes that we initially encountered in Chapter 10. The other four—note taking, identifying important information, comprehension monitoring, and summarizing—are additional strategies that researchers have consistently found to be valuable techniques in academic learning tasks.

Meaningful Learning and Elaboration

In Chapter 10 I described *meaningful learning* as a process of relating new material to knowledge already stored in long-term memory and *elaboration* as a process of using prior knowledge to interpret and expand on that new material. Both processes involve making connections between new information and the things we already know, and both processes clearly facilitate our learning as we study (Dole et al., 1991; Pressley, 1982; Waters, 1982; Weinstein, 1978; Wittrock & Alesandrini, 1990).

A study by Van Rossum and Schenk (1984) illustrates this point well. College students studied and took notes on a historical passage, then took a test on the contents of the passage and answered questions about how they had studied. Approximately half of the students described rote-learning approaches to studying; they interpreted the objective of the assignment as one of memorizing facts (as one student described it, "learning everything by heart"). The other half described meaningful learning approaches to the study process: They attempted to understand, interpret, abstract meaning, and apply what they read. One student's self-report illustrates this meaningful learning approach:

> First I read the text roughly through and try to form a picture of the content. The second time I read more accurately and try through the structure of the text to make the small connections in and between the paragraphs. The third or fourth time I try to repeat to myself, without looking at the text, the main lines of the argument, emphasizing reasonings. This is my usual way to study texts. (Van Rossum & Schenk, 1984, p. 77)

There were no differences between the two groups of students in their performance on multiple-choice questions that tested their knowledge of the passage. However, students who used meaningful learning strategies performed better on multiple-choice questions that required drawing inferences and produced better integrated and qualitatively superior responses on an essay test over the same material.

Students appear to interpret information differently depending on whether they are trying to remember facts or generate applications. In a study conducted by one of my doctoral students, Rose McCallin (McCallin, Ormrod, & Cochran, 1997), undergraduate education majors enrolled in two educational psychology classes completed a questionnaire that assessed their approach to learning the course material. Some students described themselves as wanting to learn specific teaching techniques; in other words, they wanted to be told exactly what they should do in the classroom. Other students described themselves as preferring to understand psychological principles of human learning and behavior so that they could develop their *own* classroom procedures. Following the course's unit on educational testing and measurement, McCallin gave the students a list of basic concepts in educational testing and asked them to draw a diagram (concept map) that showed how the concepts were related to one another. Students with a tell-me-what-to-do attitude tended to depict relationships among concepts that were simplistically factual or procedural (e.g., "*Raw scores* are used to compute a *mean*"). In contrast, students with a let-me-apply-it-myself attitude described conceptual interrelationships that reflected more sophisticated processing, including hierarchical structures, cause-effect relationships, and deductive reasoning (e.g., "*Reliability* affects the *standard error of measurement*"). Although McCallin did not study how well the students remembered course material after the semester was over, we could reasonably predict that the latter kind of students—those who develop a well-integrated and elaborated understanding of the topic in question so that they can apply it themselves—should be able to retrieve and reconstruct the course material more effectively. And, for reasons that you will discover in our discussion of transfer and problem solving in the next chapter, such students should also be able to apply principles of educational psychology more readily to new situations and problems.

Organization

In Chapter 10 we found evidence for the importance of *internal organization*—finding connections and interrelationships within a body of new information—for long-term memory storage. Making oneself aware of the inherent organizational structure of new material facilitates learning; so, too, does imposing an organizational structure on material when that structure does not initially exist (Gauntt, 1991; Kail, 1990; Wade, 1992).

Nevertheless, students often fail to develop appropriate organizational structures for information presented in lectures and written materials. Rather than recognizing and taking advantage of the interrelationships inherent in a body of information, students frequently "organize" various ideas simply as a list of unrelated facts (Meyer, Brandt, & Bluth, 1980). Furthermore, students are less likely to organize information as material becomes more difficult for them (Kletzien, 1988).

Students can use several techniques to help them organize classroom material effectively. One frequently used approach is to create an outline of the major topics and ideas. When students learn how to outline the things they hear in lectures and read in textbooks, their classroom learning often improves (McDaniel & Einstein, 1989; Wade, 1992). Curiously, however, good students are *less* likely to outline the things they read than their more "average" classmates (Baker, 1989). It may be that better students organize material easily enough in their heads that paper-pencil outlines aren't necessary.

A second approach is to create a graphic representation of the information to be learned—perhaps a map, flowchart, pie chart, or matrix (Dansereau, 1995; Jones, Pierce, & Hunter, 1988/1989; Scevak, Moore, & Kirby, 1993; Van Patten, Chao, & Reigeluth, 1986). For example, high school students can remember historical events more effectively when they put information about important events on a map depicting where each event took place (Scevak et al., 1993). As another example, consider how students might better remember the sequence in which various historical events took place. While I am writing this third edition of the book, my son Alex (now a high school senior) and I are both taking an undergraduate art history course at my university. The first unit of the course covered a 40,000-year span, including prehistoric art (e.g., cave paintings), Mesopotamian art (e.g., the Gates of Ishtar), and ancient Egyptian art (e.g., the pyramids at Giza). As we studied for our first test, Alex and I had a hard time keeping the time periods of all of the cultures and artistic styles straight. We finally developed a time line, depicted in Figure 14-1, which helped us remember what was happening when and kept us from going into severe "numbers shock." Graphics such as Alex's and my time line probably facilitate learning not only by organizing information but also by providing a way to encode the information visually as well as verbally (Jones et al., 1988/1989).

Still another technique for organizing information is concept mapping (Krajcik, 1991; Mintzes, Wandersee, & Novak, 1997; Novak & Gowin, 1984). In the preceding chapter, I described concept maps as a way that teachers can depict the overall organizational structure of a lesson or unit (refer back to Figure 13-2 as an example). Yet students can also develop their *own* concept maps for a lesson; for example, Figure 14-2 shows concept maps constructed by two fifth-grade students after they watched a slide-show lecture on Australia. Notice how very different the knowledge of the two children appears to be, even though both children received the same information.

Concept maps, constructed either by a teacher or by students themselves, often facilitate students' classroom performance (Alvermann, 1981; Hawk, 1986; Holley & Dansereau, 1984). Students benefit in numerous ways from constructing their own concept maps for classroom material (Mintzes et al., 1997; Novak & Gowin, 1984). By focusing on how concepts relate to one another, students organize material better. They are also more likely to notice how new concepts are related to things they already know; thus, they are more likely to learn the material meaningfully. And, like such graphic techniques as maps and time lines, concept maps can help students encode information in long-term memory visually as well as verbally. Concept maps are especially helpful to low-achieving students, perhaps because they provide a means of helping these students process information in ways that high-achieving students do more regularly (Dansereau, 1995; Lambiotte, Dansereau, Cross, & Reynolds, 1989; Mintzes et al., 1997; Stensvold & Wilson, 1990).

Student-constructed concept maps can provide information to teachers as well as to students; in particular, such maps may indicate possible misconceptions and "holes" in students' understanding (Novak & Gowin, 1984; Novak & Musonda, 1991). If you look carefully at the concept map on the left side of Figure 14-2, you should detect several misconceptions that the student has about Australia. For example, Adelaide is *not* part of Melbourne, it is a different city altogether! If geographic knowledge about Australia is an instructional objective, then this student clearly needs further instruction to correct such misinformation.

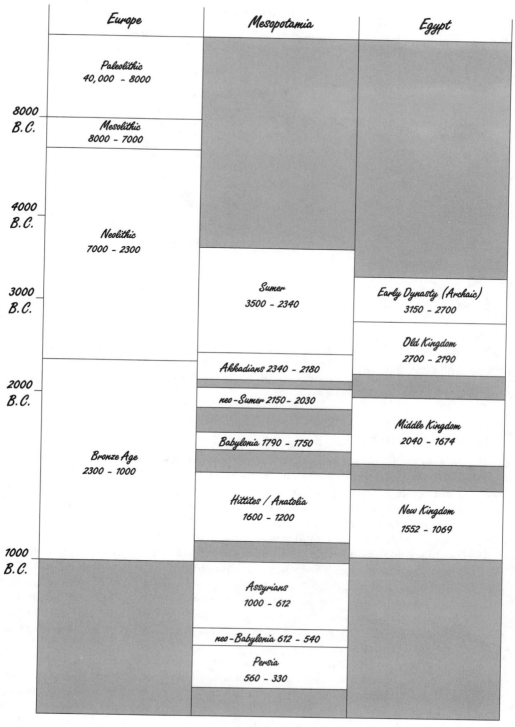

Figure 14–1

The Ormrod time line for prehistoric, Mesopotamian, and ancient Egyptian art.

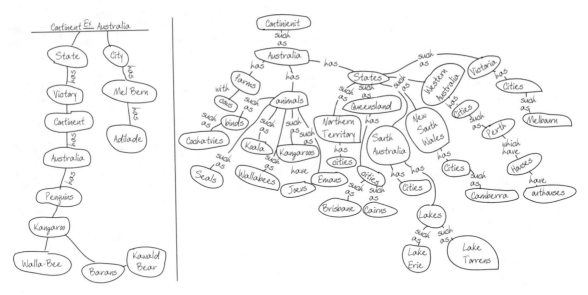

Figure 14–2
Concept maps constructed by two fifth-grade students after watching a slide lecture on Australia.
From *Learning How to Learn* (pp. 100–101) by J. D. Novak & D. B. Gowin, 1984, Cambridge, England: Cambridge University Press. Copyright 1984 by Cambridge University Press. Reprinted by permission.

Note Taking

In general, taking notes on the information presented in lectures and textbooks is positively correlated with student learning (Benton, Kiewra, Whitfill, & Dennison, 1993; Cohn, Hult, & Engle, 1990; Hale, 1983; Kiewra, 1989; Shrager & Mayer, 1989). Note taking probably serves two functions for students (Di Vesta & Gray, 1972; Kiewra, 1989). For one thing, it facilitates *encoding* of material: By writing information down and looking at it on paper, students are likely to encode it both verbally and visually. As evidence for the encoding function of note taking, students remember more when they take notes even if they have no opportunity to review those notes (Howe, 1970; Weinstein & Mayer, 1986). Secondly, notes serve as a form of concrete *external storage* for information presented in class: Given the notorious fallibility of long-term memory (see Chapter 12), pen and paper often provide a dependable alternative (Benton et al., 1993). Once lecture content is recorded on paper, it can be reviewed at regular intervals later on.

In my own classes, I have often observed how very different the notes of different students can be, even though all of the students have sat through the same lectures. Some students write extensively; others write very little. Some students try to capture all of the main ideas of a lecture, whereas others only copy the specific words I write on the board—mostly terms and their definitions. Some students include details and examples in their notes; others do not.

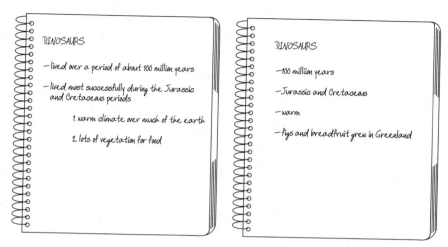

The effectiveness of note taking depends on the type of notes taken.

Not surprisingly, the effectiveness of note taking depends on the type of notes taken. Notes are more useful to students when they are relatively complete representations of the presented material (Benton et al., 1993; Cohn et al., 1990; Kiewra, 1989). They are more likely to promote learning when they represent an encoding of the information that is consistent with the objectives of the instructional unit; hence, those objectives should be clear to students (Barnett, Di Vesta, & Rogozinski, 1981; Snowman, 1986). Notes are also more likely to be effective when they summarize main ideas and include details that support those main ideas (Brown, Campione, & Day, 1981; Doctorow, Wittrock, & Marks, 1978; Kiewra, 1985; Taylor, 1982). And notes that go beyond the material—those that include students' own elaborations of it—may be especially beneficial (Barnett et al., 1981; Kiewra, 1989; King, 1992).

Another effective technique is reorganizing and elaborating on notes that have previously been taken during a lecture or reading assignment (DuBois et al., 1988; Kiewra, 1985; Kiewra et al., 1988; Shimmerlick & Nolan, 1976). Particularly in a lecture situation, students have no control over how fast information is presented and may not have time to process everything meaningfully. In such a case, students may need to focus merely on writing information during class and then organizing and encoding it appropriately afterward.

Unfortunately, many students (especially those at the junior high and high school levels) have difficulty understanding their own notes when they use them to review class material at a later time (Yokoi, 1997). Teachers can do some very simple things to improve the quality and completeness of the notes that their students take. Writing important ideas on the chalkboard may be helpful: Students are far more likely to write down things that their teacher also writes. Emphasizing important ideas (e.g., by repeating them) also increases the likelihood that students will record those ideas on paper. Furthermore, providing some kind of general organizational framework—a skeletal outline, a compare-and-contrast matrix, or the like—facilitates students' ability to organize information in the ways that the teacher envisions (Benton et al., 1993; Kiewra, 1989; Pressley, Yokoi, Van Meter, Van Etten, & Freebern, 1997; Van Meter, Yokoi, & Pressley, 1994; Yokoi, 1997).

Identifying Important Information

Students frequently encounter more information than they can possibly store in their long-term memories within a reasonable period of time. As a result, they must determine which things are most important for them to learn and study—for instance, they must separate main ideas from trivial details (Dole et al., 1991; Reynolds & Shirey, 1988). The task is often a challenging one, in part because the relative "importance" of different ideas is ultimately determined by the teacher, who may have a different perspective on the material than students do (Alexander & Jetton, 1996; Schellings, Van Hout-Wolters, & Vermunt, 1996).

The various *signals* present in a lecture or textbook (e.g., specified objectives of a lesson, underlined or italicized words, and ideas written on the chalkboard) can help students discriminate between important and unimportant information (see Chapter 13's discussion of expository instruction). In some instances, however, students may overlook or misinterpret such signals; in other instances, existing signals may be few and far between. In the absence of suitable signals, students often have trouble identifying the main points of a lecture or reading assignment; this is particularly true when they have little background knowledge about the subject matter they are studying (Byrnes, 1996; Dole et al., 1991; Garner et al., 1991). Many students use relatively inadequate methods of selecting information—for example, focusing on first sentences of paragraphs or on distinctive pieces of information (such as definitions and formulas)—and often miss critical ideas as a result (Mayer, 1984; Pallock & Surber, 1997). Even college students are fallible in this respect, because they are often distracted from central information by relatively unimportant but interesting (and perhaps more concrete) details (Garner et al., 1991; Garner, Brown, Sanders, & Menke, 1992; Sadoski et al., 1993; see Scholes & Kardash, 1996, for an exception).

Once students become proficient at identifying important information, underlining or highlighting the information, at least in purchased textbooks and students' lecture notes, is likely to be beneficial. I encourage my own students to underline or highlight the important points that their textbooks present; doing so is less time-consuming than taking notes on a book's content and keeps specific information within its larger context. But underlining and highlighting are probably only effective when used sparingly to emphasize main ideas and essential details (Snowman, 1986). Highlighting an entire page, as if with a paint roller, can hardly be of much value.

Comprehension Monitoring

Good students—those who learn most effectively—periodically check themselves to be sure they are actually absorbing what they are hearing in class or reading in a textbook. They also take steps to remediate any comprehension difficulties they have—for example, by asking questions or rereading a passage. In other words, good students engage in **comprehension monitoring** (Baker, 1989; Dansereau, 1978; Dole et al., 1991; Haller, Child, & Walberg, 1988; Pressley, Borkowski, & Schneider, 1987).

Unfortunately, many students of all ages *don't* monitor their comprehension as they sit in class or read a textbook (Baker & Brown, 1984; Flavell, 1979; Hacker, 1995; Markman, 1979; Mayer, 1992; Otero & Kintsch, 1992). As a result, they are often ignorant about what they know and what they don't know, and they may think they understand something they actually *mis*understand; such phenomena are sometimes referred to as the **illusion of knowing,** or **secondary ignorance** (Baker, 1989; Butler & Winne, 1995; Horgan, 1990; Brown, 1978; Voss & Schauble, 1992). As one simple example, students often think they know how to spell words that they actually do not (Adams & Adams, 1960; Johnson, Langford, & Quorn, 1981; Ormrod & Wagner, 1987).

When students think they know classroom material, they are likely to stop studying it. Thus, students who have only the *illusion* of knowing it will stop studying prematurely (Horgan, 1990; Voss & Schauble, 1992). And they are likely to be quite puzzled when, as a result, they perform poorly on an exam or assignment (Horgan, 1990). For example, students sometimes appear at my office, confused about why they did so poorly on an exam when they "knew" the information so well. When I ask these students specific questions about the material, I usually find that they don't really have a good grasp of it at all!

One strategy for facilitating students' comprehension monitoring is to have them formulate questions before a lesson or reading assignment that they then answer as they go along (Bragstad & Stumpf, 1982; Robinson, 1961; Rosenshine, Meister, & Chapman, 1996; Thomas & Robinson, 1972). For example, before reading a textbook, a student might turn each heading and subheading into a question to be answered and then read sections of text with the intention of finding answers to those questions (Robinson, 1961). Such **self-questioning** is probably even more effective when students do it *throughout* a lesson or reading assignment (Brozo, Stahl, & Gordon, 1985; Dole et al., 1991; Haller et al., 1988;

Students are not always accurate judges of what they know and what they do not.

Wong, 1985). For example, undergraduate students who ask themselves questions as they take notes during a class lecture take better notes, understand the material better, and remember it longer (King, 1992; Spires, 1990).

By asking themselves questions periodically, students are more likely to know when they know something and when they do not. After reviewing research on the effectiveness of self-questioning, however, Snowman (1986) concluded that positive effects are limited to the acquisition of facts, without any noticeable impact on more sophisticated behaviors such as application or evaluation of those facts. This may be because most students ask themselves primarily fact-based questions (e.g., "When did Columbus reach the New World?") rather than higher-level questions (e.g., "Why did Columbus risk his life to find a new route to India?"), perhaps because they have learned to expect mostly fact-based questions on their classroom examinations (Jackson, 1996; Ormrod, Jackson, & Salih, 1996). To promote meaningful learning, elaboration, and, in general, higher-level processing of information, teachers might encourage students to continually ask themselves questions such as the following:

- Explain why (how) . . . .
- What is the main idea of . . . ?
- How would you use . . . to . . . ?
- What is a new example of . . . ?
- What do you think would happen if . . . ?
- What is the difference between . . . and . . . ?
- How are . . . and . . . similar?
- What conclusions can you draw about . . . ?
- How does . . . affect . . . ?
- What are the strengths and weaknesses of . . . ?
- What is the best . . . and why?
- How is . . . related to . . . that we studied earlier? (King, 1992, p. 309)

Ideally, students should assess their understanding of class material at some later time as well. People are often inaccurate and overly optimistic judges of how much they will remember about something they have just read (Nelson & Dunlosky, 1991; Pressley, Borkowski, & Schneider, 1987; Weaver & Kelemen, 1997). In a simple illustration of this principle (Nelson & Dunlosky, 1991), undergraduate students studied a series of 60 paired associates (e.g., *ocean–tree*) for eight seconds apiece. Students were asked how confident they were that in 10 minutes' time they would be able to remember the second word in each pair when cued with the first; this question was sometimes asked immediately after a word pair had been presented (the immediate condition) and sometimes asked after several minutes had elapsed (the delayed condition). After studying all 60 pairs, students were tested for their actual ability to recall the second word in every pair. Their estimates of how much they would remember were far more accurate for word pairs in the delayed condition than for pairs in the immediate condition; for the latter word pairs, students believed they would remember many more than they actually did. The problem with judging one's knowledge of something immediately after studying it, Nelson and Dunlosky reasoned, is that the information is still in working memory and therefore can be easily retrieved. Ideally, students need to judge the likelihood that they can retrieve information from long-term memory as well—something they can do only when they monitor their comprehension after several minutes, hours, or days have elapsed.

Summarizing

Students are often encouraged to summarize the material they read and hear—for example, by condensing and integrating it, deriving abstract representations of it, or identifying suitable headings to label it. Doing so seems to facilitate learning and retention of that material (Dole et al., 1991; Jonassen, Hartley, & Trueman, 1986; King, 1992; Rinehart, Stahl, & Erickson, 1986; Wittrock & Alesandrini, 1990).

Unfortunately, many students have difficulty adequately summarizing the things they read and hear (Anderson & Hidi, 1988/1989; Brown & Palincsar, 1987; Byrnes, 1996; Jonassen et al., 1986). If we think about it, we realize that developing a good summary is not an easy task at all: Students must discriminate between important and unimportant information, identify main ideas that may or may not be explicitly stated, and organize critical elements into a cohesive whole (Anderson & Hidi, 1988/1989; Greene & Ackerman, 1995; Spivey, 1997). In classroom situations, students must also have some sense of how they are going to be evaluated and tailor their summaries to the evaluation criteria (Snowman, 1986).

Theorists have offered several suggestions for helping students create better summaries of classroom subject matter:

- Have students first practice developing summaries for short, easy, and well-organized passages (perhaps those only a few paragraphs in length), then gradually introduce longer and more difficult texts for them to summarize.
- Each time students develop a summary, ask them to
    - Identify or invent a topic sentence for each paragraph or section.
    - Identify superordinate concepts or ideas that subsume several more specific points.
    - Find supporting information for each main idea.
    - Delete trivial and redundant information.
- Have students compare and discuss their summaries, considering what ideas they thought were important and why.
  (Anderson & Hidi, 1988/1989; Brown & Day, 1983; Rinehart et al., 1986; Rosenshine & Meister, 1992)

Such strategies do seem to help students develop better summaries and, ultimately, to learn and remember classroom material more effectively (Bean & Steenwyk, 1984; Pressley, with McCormick, 1995; Rinehart et al., 1986).

In the last few pages, we have identified a number of effective learning and study strategies. Some of these strategies, such as outlining, taking notes, and writing summaries, are **overt strategies;** in other words, they are behaviors that we can actually see. Others—such as elaborating, identifying important information, and monitoring comprehension—are **covert strategies;** they are internal mental processes that we often can*not* see. Ultimately, it is probably the ways in which students process the information they receive—the covert strategies—that determine how effectively they learn and remember that information (Kardash & Amlund, 1991).

What kinds of learning and study strategies are we likely to see in students of different ages? Let's look at trends in the development of metacognitive knowledge and skills.

DEVELOPMENT OF METACOGNITIVE KNOWLEDGE AND SKILLS

Preschoolers know that *thinking* is different from such activities as *seeing, talking,* and *knowing* (Flavell, 1993). And they have a few simple strategies—for example, looking, pointing, and touching—for learning the things they want to remember (Kail, 1990). But more sophisticated metacognitive knowledge and skills emerge after children enter school (perhaps as a result of school learning experiences) and continue to improve throughout the school years (Duell, 1986; Flavell, 1979, 1985; Kail, 1990; Siegler, 1991). Following are several developmental trends in metacognition in school-age children:

- *Children become increasingly realistic about their memory capabilities and limitations* (Cavanaugh & Perlmutter, 1982; Duell, 1986; Flavell et al., 1993; Markman, 1979). Young children typically overestimate how much they can remember of the things they are about to learn. For example, in a study by Flavell, Friedrichs, and Hoyt (1970), four age groups of children (ranging from nursery school to fourth grade) were shown strips of paper picturing from 1 to 10 objects and asked to predict how many objects they thought they could remember at a time (a working memory task). The children were then tested to determine how many objects they actually could remember. All four groups of children tended to overestimate their working memory capacities, but the estimates of the older children were more realistic. For example, kindergarten children predicted that they could remember an average of 8.0 objects but in fact remembered only 3.6. The fourth graders, on the other hand, estimated that they could remember 6.1 objects and actually recalled 5.5 (a much closer guess).

- *Children develop an increasing ability to use effective learning and memory strategies.* Young children have little metacognitive awareness of effective strategies; older children are more likely to have a variety of strategies, to apply them broadly and flexibly, and to know when to use each one (Brown, Bransford, Ferrera, & Campione, 1983; Flavell et al., 1993; Kail, 1990; Lovett & Flavell, 1990; Siegler, 1991). Consider these research findings as illustrations:
  - When asked to study and remember 36 common objects (e.g., a bell, a flag, and a wagon) over a series of learning trials, and when given the opportunity to review half of the items after each trial, third graders choose to study those items they have failed to remember on the previous trial. In contrast, first graders choose their study items randomly, without consideration of past memory failures (Masur, McIntyre, & Flavell, 1973).
  - When young children use rehearsal to learn a list of items, they typically repeat each item a few times by itself. When they reach 9 or 10 years of age, they begin to use *cumulative rehearsal,* reciting the entire list at once and

continuing to add any new items (Gathercole & Hitch, 1993). Furthermore, children in the early elementary grades are not terribly discriminating about the things they rehearse; older children are more likely to emphasize important material in the process (Kail, 1990).

- The use of elaboration continues to increase throughout the school years (Flavell et al., 1993; Kail, 1990; Pressley, 1982; Siegler, 1991). For example, 10th graders are more likely than 8th graders to use elaboration when trying to remember paired associates (e.g., *doctor–machine,* and *acorn–bathtub*) (Waters, 1982). Sixth graders often draw inferences from the things they read, whereas first graders rarely do (Chan, Burtis, Scardamalia, & Bereiter, 1992).

Even when young children can verbally describe which learning and memory strategies are effective and which are not, when left to their own devices they often use relatively ineffective strategies (Strage et al., 1988).

- *Children engage in more comprehension monitoring as they get older; hence, they become increasingly able to determine when they actually know something.* Children's ability to monitor their comprehension appears to improve throughout the elementary and secondary school years (e.g., Hacker, 1995). For example, in the previously described study by Flavell et al. (1970), children of different ages were also asked to study a series of pictures until they were certain they could recall all of them in the correct order. Older children (second and fourth graders) were relatively accurate in ascertaining their own knowledge levels and were able to recall most of the pictures after their self-terminated study periods. On the other hand, younger children (those in nursery school and kindergarten) terminated their study sessions before they were able to recall the pictures accurately.

- *Some learning processes may be used unconsciously and automatically at first but become more conscious and deliberate with development.* It is not unusual to see students organizing or elaborating on the things they are learning without being consciously aware that they are doing so (Bjorklund, 1987; Flavell et al., 1993; Howe & O'Sullivan, 1990). For example, children may automatically group things into categories as a way of learning them more effectively; only later do they intentionally *try* to categorize the things they need to learn (Bjorklund, 1987). At what point do such processes become *strategies*? Theorists disagree on this point, some believing that any use of an effective learning process is a strategy and others arguing that it is strategic only when used intentionally (Flavell et al., 1993; Lange, 1978).

The specific learning strategies that students use depend, to some extent, on their beliefs about the nature of the knowledge they are trying to acquire, as well as about the nature of learning itself. Such *epistemological beliefs* are our next topic.

EPISTEMOLOGICAL BELIEFS

Earlier in the chapter I described how, as a high school student, I believed that I was "reading" my history textbook even when I was thinking about something else and that I could effectively "study" my Chinese vocabulary words by repeating them aloud to myself a few times. It is clear that I had a very naive notion of what learning involves: I thought that it was a relatively mindless process that would magically happen regardless of how much effort I invested.

I also had some pretty shaky beliefs about what "knowledge" is. I thought that the academic disciplines I was studying—history, science, and literature—were pretty much set in stone, with definite "right" and "wrong" ways of looking at things. Experts didn't know everything just yet (e.g., they still had not figured out how to cure the common cold), but that knowledge was "out there" somewhere and they would find it eventually. In the meantime, it was my job as a student to acquire as many facts as I could; I wasn't quite sure what I would do with them all, but I knew, deep down in my soul, that they would somehow make me a better person.

As people who learn new things every day, we all have ideas about what "knowledge" and "learning" are—ideas that are collectively known as **epistemological beliefs.** In many cases, such beliefs are pulled together into cohesive, although not necessarily accurate, "folk theories" about human learning and cognition (Hofer & Pintrich, 1997b; Lampert, Rittenhouse, & Crumbaugh, 1996); as such, they are examples of the *mental theories* I described in Chapter 11. Included in such theories are beliefs about

- *The certainty of knowledge:* Whether knowledge is a fixed, unchanging, absolute "truth" *or* a tentative, dynamic entity that will continue to evolve over time.[1]

- *The simplicity and structure of knowledge:* Whether knowledge is a collection of discrete and isolated facts *or* a set of complex and interrelated ideas.

- *The source of knowledge:* Whether knowledge comes from outside of the learner (i.e., from a teacher or an "authority" of some kind) *or* is derived and constructed by learners themselves.

- *The speed of learning:* Whether knowledge is acquired quickly if at all (in which case people either know something or they don't, in an all-or-none fashion) *or* is acquired gradually over a period of time (in which case people can partially know something).

- *The nature of learning ability:* Whether people's ability to learn is fixed at birth (i.e., inherited) *or* can improve over time with practice and use of better strategies.
(Hammer, 1994; Hofer & Pintrich, 1997b; Linn et al., 1996; Schommer, 1994a)

Keep in mind that epistemological beliefs are not necessarily as "either-or" as I have just described them. People's beliefs about each of these aspects of knowledge and learning are likely to vary somewhat, depending on the situation (Schommer, 1994a). For example, even though you and I may believe that scientific views of the world will probably continue to evolve over time (thus believing that knowledge is not certain), we know that other things are fairly black and white. Two plus two is four, the capital of France is Paris, and William Shakespeare wrote *Romeo and Juliet;* these facts are unlikely to change any time in the foreseeable future.

---

[1]The belief that there is an ultimate "truth" that experts will eventually find is sometimes referred to as *logical positivism.*

In addition to holding general beliefs about knowledge and learning, people may also hold beliefs about specific content domains. Following are some examples:

- Many students believe that knowledge in some disciplines is more certain than knowledge in others—for example, they may believe that knowledge in the sciences is less likely to change than knowledge in psychology (Hofer & Pintrich, 1997a; Schommer, 1994b).
- Many students think that learning physics means memorizing formulas and procedures (Hammer, 1994).
- Many students think that when they work on mathematics problems they will either solve the problems in a couple of minutes or else not solve them at all. Many also think that when an answer to a math problem isn't a whole number, it is probably wrong (Schoenfeld, 1988).

Researchers have found that people's epistemological beliefs often change over time. For example, young children typically believe in the certainty of knowledge; they think that there is an absolute truth about any topic out there somewhere (Astington & Pelletier, 1996). As they reach the high school and college years, some (although by no means all) of them begin to realize that knowledge is a subjective entity and that different perspectives on a topic may be equally valid (Perry, 1968; Schommer, 1994b, 1997). Other changes may also occur at the high school level; for example, students in 12th grade are more likely than 9th graders to believe that knowledge consists of complex interrelationships (rather than discrete facts), that learning happens slowly (rather than quickly), and that learning ability can improve with practice (rather than being fixed at birth) (Schommer, 1997). Cultural differences in epistemological beliefs may exist as well; for example, college students in Ireland are more likely to view learning as a complex and constructive process that results in somewhat tentative understandings of a topic, whereas their counterparts in the United States are more likely to view learning as a process of attending carefully to presented information and memorizing it as a set of isolated facts (McDevitt, Sheehan, Cooney, Smith, & Walker, 1994).

Students' epistemological beliefs clearly influence how they study and learn. Following are some of the specific effects that different beliefs are likely to have:

- *Beliefs regarding the certainty of knowledge:* When students believe that knowledge related to a topic is a fixed, certain entity, they are likely to jump to quick and potentially inaccurate conclusions based on the information they receive. In contrast, when students view knowledge as something that continues to evolve and doesn't necessarily include definitive right and wrong answers, they are more apt to enjoy cognitively challenging tasks, engage in meaningful learning, read course material critically, and recognize that some issues are controversial and not easily resolved (Kardash & Howell, 1996; Kardash & Scholes, 1996; Schommer, 1994a).

- *Beliefs regarding the simplicity and structure of knowledge:* Students who believe that knowledge is a collection of discrete facts are more likely to use rote-learning processes when they study and more likely to hold on to their misconceptions about a topic. They also tend to believe that they "know" the material they are studying if they can recall basic facts and definitions. In contrast, students who believe that knowledge is a complex set of interrelated ideas are more likely to engage in meaningful learning, organization, and elaboration when they study and more likely to evaluate the success of their learning efforts in terms of how well they understand and can apply what they have learned (Hammer, 1994; Hofer & Pintrich, 1997b; Purdie, Hattie, & Douglas, 1996; Schommer, 1994a, 1994b).

• *Beliefs regarding the source of knowledge:* Students who believe that knowledge originates outside of the learner and is passed along directly by authority figures are likely to be fairly passive learners, perhaps listening quietly to an explanation without asking questions when they don't understand. In contrast, students who believe that knowledge is something that one constructs for oneself are likely to be cognitively engaged in learning activities, make interconnections among ideas, read and listen critically, work to make sense of seemingly contradictory pieces of information, undergo conceptual change when it is warranted, and occasionally get emotionally involved with the things they are studying (Chan et al., 1997; Hogan, 1997; McDevitt, Spivey, Sheehan, Lennon, & Story, 1990; Schommer, 1994b; Schraw & Bruning, 1995).

• *Beliefs regarding the speed of learning:* When students believe that learning happens quickly in an all-or-none fashion, they are apt to believe that they have learned something before they really have, perhaps after just a single reading of their textbook; they are also apt to give up quickly in the face of failure and to express discouragement or dislike regarding the topic they are studying. In contrast, when students believe that learning is a gradual process that often takes time and effort, they are likely to use a wide variety of learning strategies as they study and to persist until they have made sense of the ideas presented (Butler & Winne, 1995; Kardash & Howell, 1996; Schommer, 1990, 1994a, 1994b).

• *Beliefs regarding the nature of learning ability:* As you might guess, students' beliefs about the nature of learning ability are correlated with their persistence in learning. If they think that learning ability is a fixed commodity, they will quickly give up on challenging tasks. In contrast, if they think that their ability to learn something is under their control, they will try, try again until they have mastered the subject matter (Schommer, 1994a, 1994b).

Not surprisingly, students with more sophisticated epistemological beliefs—for example, those who believe that knowledge is complex and uncertain and that learning is often a slow, gradual process—achieve at higher levels in the classroom (Schommer, 1994a). Furthermore, more advanced levels of academic achievement may bring about more advanced views about knowledge and learning (Schommer, 1994b; Strike & Posner, 1992). The more that students can get beyond the "basics" and explore the far reaches of the disciplines—whether those disciplines be science, mathematics, history, literature, or whatever—the more they will discover that learning involves acquiring an integrated and cohesive set of ideas, that even the experts don't know everything about a topic, and that truly complete and accurate "knowledge" of how the world operates may ultimately be an unattainable goal.

It is important to note here that students are not the only ones who can have relatively naive beliefs about the nature of knowledge and learning; some *teachers* appear to have such beliefs as well. Some teachers seem to believe that knowledge about a particular subject matter is a fixed and well-defined entity, that students need to "absorb" this knowledge in isolated bits and pieces, and that learning is a process of mindless memorization and rehearsal (Anderson, 1997; Berliner, 1997; Hofer & Pintrich, 1997b; Schommer, 1994b). Such beliefs are likely to influence the ways that teachers teach and assess their students; for example, teachers holding these beliefs will be more likely to focus on lower-level skills in their instructional objectives, classroom activities, assignments, and tests (Grossman, 1990; Hofer & Pintrich, 1997b).

WHY STUDENTS DON'T ALWAYS USE EFFECTIVE STRATEGIES

As we have seen, many students continue to use relatively ineffective learning and study strategies throughout their academic careers. Given what you have learned about metacognition up to this point, can you speculate about some reasons why this might be so? In the next few pages, I will suggest several possible reasons why effective learning strategies emerge relatively slowly. You will, I hope, find some of your own hypotheses in my list.

• *Students are uninformed or misinformed about effective strategies.* Many students, even those at the high school and undergraduate levels, are metacognitively naive about how they can best learn (Alexander & Judy, 1988; Flavell & Wellman, 1977; Knight, 1988; Ormrod & Jenkins, 1988; Palmer & Goetz, 1988). For example, some students believe that all they need to do to learn information better is to exert more effort—that is, to *try harder*—with little regard for how they should mentally process that information (O'Sullivan & Joy, 1990; Pressley, Borkowski, & Schneider, 1987). When I present a unit on cognitive psychology to my junior-level educational psychology class, my description of such basic strategies as organizing information and relating it to familiar concepts and experiences appears to be a major revelation to about half of my students; sadly, too many of these students have viewed learning as being best approached through rote memorization throughout their many years in school.[2] Furthermore, many students believe (incorrectly) that trying to learn information meaningfully—that is, trying to understand and make sense of the things they study—interferes with their ability to do well on classroom tests that emphasize rote memorization and knowledge of isolated facts (Crooks, 1988).

• *Students have epistemological beliefs that lead them to underestimate or misrepresent a learning task.* Students are unlikely to use effective strategies if they believe that the learning task before them is an easy one or that their success in learning is unrelated to the effort they put forth (Butler & Winne, 1995; Winne, 1995a). And as we have already seen, they will certainly not engage in such processes as meaningful learning, organization, and elaboration if they think that "knowledge" is nothing more than collecting a number of unrelated facts.

• *Students have little relevant prior knowledge on which they can draw.* Students who use ineffective learning and study strategies tend to know less about the subject mat-

---

[2]A belief in the value of rote memorization is probably more prevalent in some cultures than in others; for example, see Ho (1994) and Purdie and Hattie (1996).

ter they are studying, and less about the world in general, than students who use effective strategies (Alexander & Judy, 1988; Carpenter & Just, 1986; Chi, 1981; Hasselhorn & Körkel, 1986; Pressley, Borkowski, & Schneider, 1987; Schneider, 1993; Woloshyn, Pressley, & Schneider, 1992). For example, students may know too little about a topic to determine what is important and what is not (Alexander & Jetton, 1996; Carpenter & Just, 1986; McDaniel & Einstein, 1989). They may have few concepts or experiences to which they can relate new material in a meaningful fashion; thus, they have greater difficulty comprehending the things they read (Dole et al., 1991; Gauntt, 1991; Hall, 1989; Schneider, 1993; Voss, 1987; Wilson & Anderson, 1986; Woloshyn et al., 1992). And they are likely to have fewer organizational frameworks and schemas that they can impose on what might otherwise appear to be an unrelated set of ideas (Carpenter & Just, 1986).

- *Assigned learning tasks do not lend themselves to sophisticated strategies.* In some situations, teachers may assign tasks for which effective strategies are either counterproductive or impossible. For example, when teachers assign simple tasks that involve lower-level skills (e.g., when they insist that facts and definitions be learned verbatim), students are unlikely to engage in such processes as meaningful learning and elaboration (Turner, 1995; Van Meter et al., 1994). When teachers expect a great deal of material to be mastered for each test, students may have to devote the limited time that they have to getting a general "impression" of everything rather than to developing an in-depth understanding and integration of the subject matter (Thomas, 1993). When teachers tell students exactly what questions will be asked on a particular classroom test or assignment, students are likely to focus only on material related to those questions, without regard for the larger context in which the material appears (Thomas, 1993).

- *Students have goals that are inconsistent with effective learning.* Students are not always interested in learning for understanding; instead, they may be more interested in remembering information just long enough to get a passing grade, or they may want to complete an assigned task in as little time and with as little effort as possible. Effective learning strategies may be largely irrelevant to such motives (Mayer, 1996b; Nolen, 1996).

- *Students think that sophisticated learning strategies require too much effort to make them worthwhile.* If students believe that certain strategies involve too much time and effort, they are unlikely to use them, no matter how effective those strategies might be (Guttentag, 1984; Palmer & Goetz, 1988; Pressley et al., 1990). In many cases, students seem to be unaware of how much a few simple strategies can help them learn and remember classroom material (Pressley, Levin, & Ghatala, 1984; Zimmerman, 1994).

- *Students have low self-efficacy about their ability to learn in an academic setting.* Some students, especially those with a history of failure in the classroom, develop the belief that they are incapable of learning regardless of what they do. Such students may believe (erroneously) that *no* strategy is likely to make any appreciable difference in their school achievement (Palmer & Goetz, 1988; Pressley, Borkowski, & Schneider, 1987).

Teachers often assume that students will use the same relatively sophisticated study strategies that they themselves use—an assumption that is clearly unwarranted in many cases. But can metacognitive knowledge and skills be taught? Most psychologists believe that they can, and furthermore that they *should,* be taught. Let's look at some approaches to teaching metacognitive knowledge and skills.

PROMOTING EFFECTIVE LEARNING AND STUDY STRATEGIES

As students move through the grade levels—from elementary school to middle or junior high school, then to high school, and perhaps eventually on to college—their learning tasks become increasingly more complex and challenging (e.g., Eccles & Midgley, 1989; J. Wilson, 1988). For example, students must remember more information, do more with it (in terms of application, problem solving, critical analysis, and so on), and understand it at a more abstract level. Thus, there is a greater need for sophisticated learning and study strategies as the years go by (Baker, 1989).

Unfortunately, when teaching complex subject matter, teachers rarely teach effective strategies for learning that material (Pressley et al., 1990; J. Wilson, 1988). Yet when left to their own devices, students typically acquire effective strategies slowly if at all, and some students develop counterproductive misconceptions about how best to learn (e.g., Alexander & Judy, 1988; Kail, 1990).

Many theorists suggest that schools should provide explicit instruction in how to study and learn. This instruction may be especially valuable for at-risk students—those with a history of academic difficulties and a high probability of dropping out of school prematurely (Alderman, 1990; Brown & Palincsar, 1987; Weinstein, Hagen, & Meyer, 1991). In this final section of the chapter, we examine research regarding the effectiveness of study skills training; we also consider some specific classroom strategies for promoting and enhancing students' metacognitive capabilities.

Effectiveness of Study Skills Training Programs

Initially, most programs designed to enhance metacognitive knowledge and skills were at the college level (J. Wilson, 1988). But in recent years we have also seen these programs at the high school, junior high, and even upper elementary levels. The collective results of these programs indicate that students *can* be taught more effective learning and study strategies, with consequent improvements in their classroom performance and academic achievement; such training appears to be especially beneficial for low-ability students (Baker, 1989; DuBois et al., 1995; Haller et al., 1988; Hansen & Pearson, 1983; Hattie, Biggs, & Purdie, 1996; Holley & Dansereau, 1984; Kulik, Kulik, & Shwalb, 1983; Mastropieri & Scruggs, 1989; Palincsar & Brown, 1984, 1989; Paris, 1988; Pressley, 1982; Pressley, Borkowski, & Schneider, 1987; Shrager & Mayer, 1989; Thompson & Carr, 1995; Wade, 1983; Weinstein, Goetz, & Alexander, 1988; Weinstein et al., 1991; J. Wilson, 1988).

Effective programs tend to be multifaceted, teaching a wide variety of learning and study strategies. For example, successful reading-for-learning instruction is likely to teach students to (a) determine their purpose in reading a particular passage and modify their reading behavior accordingly, (b) retrieve background information and experiences relevant to the topic, (c) identify and attend to main ideas, (d) draw inferences from the things they read, and (e) monitor their reading comprehension as they go along. And general learning and study strategies programs typically include instruction about meaningful learning, organizational strategies, elaboration, mnemonics, note taking, and summarizing. Aside from such commonalities, training programs often differ markedly from one another; I invite you to explore some of the possibilities by consulting the references listed in the preceding paragraph.

Guidelines for Promoting Effective Strategies

Theorists and researchers have identified a number of practices that appear to promote the development of more sophisticated metacognitive knowledge and skills. Following are some guidelines to keep in mind:

• *Students learn strategies more effectively when those strategies are taught within the context of specific subject domains and actual academic learning tasks* (Brown & Palincsar, 1987; Hattie et al., 1996; Pressley, El-Dinary, Marks, Brown, & Stein, 1992; Pressley, Harris, & Marks, 1992). As students encounter specific academic content, they should simultaneously learn ways to study that content. For example, when presenting new information in class, a teacher might (a) suggest how students can organize their notes, (b) describe mnemonics for things that are difficult to remember, and (c) ask various students to summarize the ideas presented. When assigning textbook pages to be read over the weekend, a teacher might (a) suggest that students consider what they know about a topic *before* they begin reading about it, (b) ask students to use headings and subheadings to make predictions about upcoming content, and (c) provide questions for students to ask themselves as they read.

• *Students can use sophisticated learning strategies only when they have a knowledge base to which they can relate new material* (Brown et al., 1981; Weinstein & Mayer, 1986). The knowledge and skills that students bring to the classroom affect their ability to learn new information meaningfully, identify main ideas, and engage in such elaborative activities as drawing inferences and clarifying ambiguities. Teachers must be careful not to present difficult material until students have mastered the prerequisite knowledge and skills essential for a genuine understanding of that material.

• *Students should learn a wide variety of strategies, as well as the situations in which each one is appropriate* (Mayer & Wittrock, 1996; Nist, Simpson, Olejnik, & Mealey, 1991; Paris, 1988; Pressley, El-Dinary, et al., 1992; Pressley, Harris, & Marks, 1992). Different strategies are useful in different situations; for example, meaningful learning may be more effective for learning general principles within a discipline, whereas mnemonics may be more effective for learning hard-to-remember pairs and lists. Organizing ideas in a hierarchical fashion may be appropriate for one unit (e.g., see Figure 10–4); organizing them in a two-by-two matrix may be appropriate for another (e.g., see Figure 4–2).

• *Effective strategies should be practiced with a variety of tasks and on an ongoing basis* (Brown & Palincsar, 1987; Collins, Brown, & Newman, 1989; Pressley, El-Dinary, et al., 1992; Pressley, Harris, & Marks, 1992). When students learn a strategy only within the context of one particular task, they are unlikely to use that strategy in other contexts (Pressley et al., 1990). But when they learn to apply the same strategy to many different tasks over a long period of time, they are likely to recognize the strategy's value and to generalize its use to new situations. Effective strategy instruction is clearly not a one-shot deal.

• *Strategy instruction should include covert as well as overt strategies* (Kardash & Amlund, 1991). Certainly students stand to benefit from guidance about how to take notes from a lecture, underline the material they read in their textbooks, and write summaries of the material they study. But the sophisticated cognitive processes that underlie these behaviors—learning meaningfully, organizing, elaborating, comprehension monitoring, and so on—are ultimately the most important strategies for students to acquire.

• *Teachers can model effective strategies by thinking out loud about new material* (Brown & Palincsar, 1987; Pressley, El-Dinary, et al., 1992; Pressley, Harris, & Marks, 1992). When teachers think aloud about the content their classes are studying (e.g., "I remember that *Au* is the symbol for gold by remembering, '*Ay, you* stole my gold watch!'" or "Hmm . . . it seems to me that Napoleon's military tactics were quite similar to those of the ancient Assyrians"), they give their students specific, concrete examples of how to process information effectively.

• *Teachers should scaffold students' initial attempts at using new strategies, gradually phasing out the scaffolding as students become more proficient.* In Chapter 8 I introduced you to the concept of *scaffolding,* whereby a competent individual (e.g., a teacher) guides and supports a student's early attempts at a difficult task; as the student becomes more skilled at performing the task independently, such support is gradually removed. Many of the metacognitive activities we have considered in this chapter (e.g., note taking, comprehension monitoring, and summarizing) are challenging tasks indeed, and some teacher scaffolding to facilitate them is clearly in order (Brophy, 1992b; Dole et al., 1991; McCaslin & Good, 1996; Paris, 1988; Pontecorvo, 1993; Pressley, Harris, & Marks, 1992; Rogoff, 1990; Spires, Donley, & Penrose, 1990).

Earlier in the chapter we saw several illustrations of how teachers can scaffold students' learning and study strategies. For instance, teachers can provide a general organizational framework that students can follow while taking notes. They can provide examples of questions that students can use to monitor their comprehension as they read (e.g., "Explain how . . ." or "What is a new example of. . . ?"). They can provide guidance on how to develop a good summary (e.g., "Identify or invent a topic sentence" or "Find supporting information for each main idea"). Such scaffolding is most likely to be helpful when students are studying subject matter they find difficult to comprehend yet *can* comprehend if they apply appropriate metacognitive strategies (Pressley, El-Dinary, et al., 1992). As students become more proficient in the use of these strategies, instruction can gradually proceed through increasingly more challenging material (Rosenshine & Meister, 1992).

• *Students can often learn effective strategies by working cooperatively with their classmates.* A rapidly growing body of research indicates that group learning activities, especially when structured in particular ways, can promote more sophisticated cognitive processing. One approach is to teach students to ask one another higher-level questions about the material they are studying (questions along the line of "Why is it that such-and-such is true?") and then to develop answers for those questions. This technique, often called **elaborative interrogation,** appears to promote both better recall for facts and increased integration of ideas, perhaps in part by encouraging students to draw on their prior knowledge to understand new information (Kahl & Woloshyn, 1994; King, 1994; Martin & Pressley, 1991; Woloshyn et al., 1992; Wood, Willoughby, Reilley, Elliott, & DuCharme, 1994).

In Chapter 16 we will consider a variety of group learning activities that can help students learn. One approach that we will examine in that chapter—*reciprocal teaching*—shows particular promise as a way to help students develop effective metacognitive skills.

• *Students must understand why the skills they are taught are helpful.* Research indicates that strategy instruction is more successful when students not only learn effective strategies but also learn *how* and *why* these strategies are effective (Hattie et al., 1996;

Paris, 1988; Paris, Newman, & McVey, 1982; Pressley, Borkowski, & Schneider, 1987; Pressley, Harris, & Marks, 1992). In my own classes, I sometimes do little "experiments," presenting information that is difficult to learn and remember, then giving some students a mnemonic for learning the information while giving other students no guidance at all. We find out how much students in each group can recall by writing students' "test" scores on the board, and then we compare the two sets of numbers. The performance of the two groups is usually so dramatically different that my students readily acknowledge the usefulness of the mnemonic I've described to them.

Earlier in the chapter I mentioned that students often believe that effective strategies are too much trouble and so not worth the effort to use them. In many cases, they may not realize just how *in*effective their current strategies are. For example, in several studies, Pressley and his colleagues trained students at a variety of ages (ranging from 10 years to adulthood) to use the keyword method[3] to learn lists of vocabulary words (Pressley, Levin, & Ghatala, 1984, 1988; Pressley, Ross, Levin, & Ghatala, 1984). Although the students mastered the technique, many of them chose *not* to use it for a similar learning task later on. Students who were explicitly asked to consider just how much the keyword method had helped them learn the earlier words were far more likely to use it again in the new learning task. In a similar manner, teachers may sometimes need to show their students in a very concrete fashion (perhaps by using an ungraded quiz) just how little they are actually learning and remembering using their current, ineffective strategies and how much more they can learn using a different approach.

• *Students should have epistemological beliefs that are consistent with effective strategies.* As we have seen, students' epistemological beliefs influence the learning strategies that they use, and study strategies training, in and of itself, will not necessarily change those beliefs (Schraw & Moshman, 1995). In some cases, students' beliefs about the nature of knowledge and learning may be in the form of *implicit knowledge*—in other words, students are not consciously aware that they believe the things that they do—and so may be especially resistant to change (Schraw & Moshman, 1995).

One possible way to change students' epistemological beliefs is to talk specifically about the nature of knowledge and learning—for example, to describe learning as an active, ongoing process of finding interconnections among ideas and eventually constructing one's own understanding of the world (Schommer, 1994b). But probably an even more effective approach is to provide classroom experiences that lead students to discover that knowledge must necessarily be a dynamic, rather than static, entity and to realize that successful learning sometimes occurs only through effort and persistence. For example, teachers can give their students complex problems that have no clear-cut right or wrong answers (Schommer, 1994b). They can ask students to compare several possibly equally valid explanations of a particular phenomenon or event (Linn et al., 1996). And they can show students, perhaps by presenting puzzling phenomena, that their own current understandings, and perhaps even those of experts in the field, do not yet adequately explain all of human experience (Chan et al., 1997; Vosniadou, 1991).

• *Students must develop mechanisms for monitoring and evaluating their own learning.* As we noted earlier, self-regulated learners monitor their progress throughout a

---

[3]You can find a description of this technique in Chapter 13.

learning task and then evaluate their ultimate success in mastering the material they have been studying. In addition to teaching students self-questioning (a technique that facilitates comprehension monitoring), theorists have offered several recommendations for promoting self-monitoring and self-evaluation in students:

- Have students set specific behavioral objectives for each study session, and then describe their achievements relative to those objectives (Morgan, 1985; Stiggins, 1994).
- Provide specific criteria that students can use to judge their performance (Paris & Ayres, 1994; Stiggins, 1994; Winne, 1995b).
- On some occasions, delay teacher feedback so that students first have the opportunity to evaluate their own performance (Butler & Winne, 1995; Schroth, 1992).
- Encourage students to evaluate their performance realistically, and then reinforce them (e.g., with praise or extra-credit points) when their evaluations match the teacher's (McCaslin & Good, 1996; Schraw, Potenza, & Nebelsick-Gullet, 1993; Zuckerman, 1994).

By engaging regularly in self-monitoring and self-evaluation of classroom assignments, students should eventually develop appropriate standards for their performance and apply those standards regularly to the things they accomplish—true hallmarks of a self-regulated learner.

- *Students must believe that, with sufficient effort and appropriate strategies, they can learn and understand challenging material.* Strategy instruction must give students a sense of self-efficacy about their ability to learn classroom material (McCombs, 1988; Palmer & Goetz, 1988; Paris, 1988; Shapley, 1994). And it must show them that their success in learning *is,* in fact, related to the specific strategies they use (Butler & Winne, 1995; Pressley, Borkowski, & Schneider, 1987; Pressley, El-Dinary, et al., 1992).

Once students believe that they *can* learn academic subject matter successfully, they are more likely to *want* to learn it. Self-efficacy is a key ingredient in students' motivation to achieve in the classroom, for reasons that we will discover in Chapter 18.

By teaching students the metacognitive knowledge and skills they need to learn challenging classroom material, teachers not only help students learn that specific material more successfully but also help them become more effective learners over the long run. And it is the long run for which teachers must ultimately prepare their students.

SUMMARY

People's knowledge of effective learning and cognitive processes and their use of such processes to enhance learning are collectively known as metacognition. Students' metacognitive knowledge and skills are significantly related to their classroom performance and academic achievement. Successful students are *self-regulated learners:* They are intrinsically motivated to learn, set goals for their own performance, plan how best to use their learning time, keep their attention focused on the learning task before them, use effective learning strategies, monitor their progress, and evaluate the final outcome of their efforts.

Effective learning and study strategies include meaningful learning, elaboration, organizing, note taking, identifying important information, comprehension monitoring, and summarizing. Most important are the internal mental processes (covert strategies) that students use; any observable study behaviors (overt strategies) are likely to be effective only when the covert strategies that underlie them are productive ones. Children show increasing metacognitive sophistication as they grow older and gain more experience with academic learning tasks; nevertheless, many students at the high school and college levels are surprisingly uninformed about how best to learn.

People's *epistemological beliefs* are the things they believe about the nature of knowledge (whether it is static or continually evolving, whether it involves isolated facts or a body of interrelated ideas, and whether it comes from an outside authority or develops within) and the nature of learning (whether it occurs in an all-or-none fashion or slowly over a period of time, and whether it is determined more by inherited ability or more by effort and strategies). Students' epistemological beliefs influence the approaches they take to learning tasks and the criteria they use to decide when they have learned something successfully.

There are numerous possible reasons why students don't use effective strategies to learn classroom subject matter. For example, students may be uninformed about effective strategies or have overly simplistic beliefs about what "knowing" something means. They may have insufficient prior knowledge about a topic to enable meaningful learning and elaboration, or assigned classroom tasks may not lend themselves to such strategies. Students may be uninterested in mastering classroom subject matter or else believe that they *cannot* master it regardless of what they do.

Research indicates that training in effective learning and study strategies can significantly enhance students' classroom achievement. Theorists and researchers have offered a number of suggestions for promoting more sophisticated metacognitive knowledge and skills. For example, instruction regarding effective learning strategies is more successful when presented within the context of specific academic content rather than separate from academic subject areas. Such instruction is also more successful when students have numerous opportunities to practice specific strategies and when teachers and classmates scaffold early efforts. Students must develop epistemological beliefs consistent with effective learning strategies, and they must acquire mechanisms for monitoring and evaluating their learning efforts. Ultimately, students must discover that, with sufficient effort and appropriate strategies, they *can* learn and understand challenging classroom material.

Transfer and Problem Solving

Most semesters, I teach an undergraduate course in educational psychology for students who are preparing to become elementary or secondary teachers. In various class sessions, I introduce such topics as cognitive development, contemporary memory theory, operant conditioning, motivation, classroom management, and educational assessment. Many of my students seem to learn the material well: They carry on informed discussions in class and demonstrate comprehension and application on assignments and examinations. But I always wonder about what happens to these students when they finish my course. Does the information they have learned in educational psychology make a difference in the way they eventually teach their own students? Do they really apply the things I have taught them? Do principles and theories of educational psychology help them solve classroom problems?

When something you learn in one situation affects how you learn or perform in another situation, **transfer** has occurred. Sometimes you transfer knowledge and skills you have previously learned to solve a problem; hence, **problem solving** is a form of transfer.

Ideally, transfer and problem solving should be two of our educational system's top priorities. Schools at all levels, from preschools to doctoral programs, teach knowledge and skills with the assumption that students will somehow apply what they have learned to the "real world." Yet the things people learn in school do not always seem to transfer to new situations and new problems. Many adults cannot use basic addition and subtraction procedures to balance their checkbooks. Many teachers reinforce inappropriate behaviors in their classrooms, ignoring the basic operant conditioning principles they learned in their undergraduate education classes. People of all ages may know "right" from "wrong" without relating that knowledge to their own behavior.

In this chapter we will examine concepts, principles, theories, and research related to both transfer and problem solving. We will also consider a variety of factors that either facilitate or interfere with the successful application of acquired knowledge and skills to new situations and problems. At the end of the chapter, we will look at implications for educational practice.

TRANSFER

Transfer is a part of everyday life: People continually encounter new situations and draw on their previously acquired knowledge and skills to deal with them. In fact, transfer is an essential component of human functioning. Without it, people would have to learn from scratch about how to behave in every new circumstance and would spend most of their time in trial-and-error learning.

If you think back to our discussions of classical and operant conditioning in Chapters 3 and 4, you might realize that we have already talked about transfer to some extent. In those chapters we considered the phenomenon of *generalization:* After an organism learns a response to one stimulus, it often makes the same response to similar stimuli. Generalization is clearly an instance of transfer, because learning in one stimulus situation influences behavior in a slightly different situation. But here we will hardly be limiting ourselves to the behaviorist perspective; as you will discover, most contemporary explanations of transfer are decidedly cognitivist in nature.

In this first section of the chapter we will explore various aspects of transfer. After considering the different types of transfer that we might see, we will examine several theoretical perspectives of how transfer occurs, looking at both early theories and more contemporary views. We will also look at factors influencing the likelihood that transfer will take place.

Types of Transfer

The concept of transfer refers to several different, although related, phenomena. Theorists have made several distinctions among types of transfer, including positive versus negative transfer, vertical versus lateral transfer, and specific versus general transfer.

Positive versus Negative Transfer

When learning in one situation facilitates learning or performance in another situation, we say that **positive transfer** has occurred. Learning basic mathematics procedures should facilitate a person's ability to balance a checkbook. Learning principles of reinforcement should improve a teacher's ability to modify student behavior. Knowing the difference between right and wrong should have a positive impact on moral and ethical behavior.

In a sense, the processes of meaningful learning and elaboration are instances of positive transfer, because previously learned information is used in understanding and remembering new ideas (Ausubel et al., 1978; Brooks & Dansereau, 1987; Voss, 1987). "Old" information can help meaningful and elaborative learning in a variety of ways; for instance, it can serve as a conceptual framework to which new material is attached, help the learner fill in the holes when new ideas are ambiguous or incomplete, or provide an analogy that helps make those ideas better understood (e.g., Brooks & Dansereau, 1987).

On the other hand, when something learned in one situation hinders a person's ability to learn or perform in a second situation, then **negative transfer** has occurred. For example, when I play tennis after having played racquetball the day before, I find myself missing the ball a lot: I keep positioning myself too close to the ball because I am accustomed to a short racquetball racquet rather than to the much longer tennis racket. People accustomed to driving a standard transmission who then find themselves behind the wheel of a car with an automatic transmission often step on a clutch that isn't there. People who learn a second language typically apply patterns of speech production characteristic of their native tongue, thus giving them a foreign accent; they may also misapply spelling patterns from their native language (Fashola, Drum, Mayer, & Kang, 1996; Schmidt & Young, 1987). Students accustomed to memorizing facts in other college courses often don't perform well on my own application-oriented examinations.

An example of a situation in which negative transfer frequently rears its ugly head is in work with decimals: Students often erroneously apply mathematical rules they have learned for whole numbers. For example, when asked to compare two decimals such as these:

$$2.34 \text{ versus } 2.8$$

students sometimes apply the rule that "more digits mean a larger number," thus concluding that 2.34 is the larger of the two decimal numbers (Behr & Harel, 1988). Another rule inappropriately transferred to decimals is this whole-number rule: "When a number is divided, the result is a smaller number." Even college students show negative transfer of this rule; for instance, many assert that the answer to the following problem

$$5 \div 0.65$$

is a number smaller than 5 (Tirosh & Graeber, 1990). The answer is actually 7.69, a *larger* number.

As you can see, the occurrence of transfer may or may not be beneficial. At the end of the chapter we will look at ways to maximize positive transfer while minimizing negative transfer.

Vertical versus Lateral Transfer

In some subject areas topics build on one another in a hierarchical fashion, so that an individual must almost certainly know one topic before moving to the next. For example, a student should probably master principles of addition before moving on to multiplication, because multiplication is an extension of addition. Similarly, a medical student must have expertise in human anatomy before studying surgical techniques: It's difficult to perform an appendectomy when you can't find the appendix. **Vertical transfer** refers to such situations—an individual acquires new knowledge or skills by building on more basic information and procedures.

In other situations knowledge of one topic may affect learning a second topic even though the first is not a prerequisite to the second. Knowledge of French is not essential for learning Spanish, yet knowing French should facilitate one's learning of Spanish because many words are similar in the two languages. When knowledge of the first topic is not essential to learning the second one but is helpful in learning it just the same, we say that **lateral transfer** has occurred.

Specific versus General Transfer

In **specific transfer** the original learning task and the transfer task overlap in content. For example, having knowledge about the anatomy of a human should help a veterinary student learn the anatomy of a dog, because the two species have many parallel anatomical features. A student who knows Spanish should easily learn Portuguese, because the two languages have similar vocabulary and syntax.

In **general transfer,** the original task and the transfer task are different in content. For example, if knowledge of Latin helps a student learn physics, or if the study habits a student develops in a physics course facilitate the learning of sociology, then general transfer is occurring.

Research clearly shows that specific transfer is more common than general transfer (Gray & Orasanu, 1987; Perkins & Salomon, 1989). In fact, the question of whether general transfer can occur at all has been the subject of much debate over the years. We turn now to both early and contemporary theories of transfer, which vary considerably in their perspectives of what things transfer and when.

Theories of Transfer

How does transfer occur? Let's look first at an early view of transfer—one that predates twentieth-century learning theories—and then see what both behaviorists and cognitivists have had to say about how and when transfer takes place.

A Historical Perspective: Formal Discipline

In days of yore, serious scholars often studied rigorous and difficult topics—for instance, Latin, Greek, and formal logic—that are not as frequently studied today. Although these subject areas may have had no specific applicability to one's day-to-day functioning, scholars believed that learning such subjects would nevertheless improve their learning and performance in many other aspects of their lives. As recently as the middle of the twentieth century, students were given frequent practice in memorizing things (poems, for example), apparently as a method of improving their general learning capabilities. Such practices reflect the notion of **formal discipline:** Just as you exercise muscles to develop strength, you exercise your mind to learn more quickly and deal with new situations more effectively.

The theory of formal discipline, a predominant view in educational circles in the nineteenth century and early decades of the twentieth century, emphasized the importance and likelihood of general transfer, the idea being that learning in one situation improves learning and performance in another situation regardless of how different the two situations might be. As human learning began to be studied empirically, however, this notion of "mind as muscle" was soon discarded. For example, William James (1890) memorized a new poem each day over the course of several weeks, assuming that he would begin to learn poems more quickly with practice. Yet he found that his poem learning did not improve; if anything, he learned his later poems more *slowly* than his early ones. More recently, researchers have found that learning computer programming—a skill requiring precise, detailed thinking about a logical sequence of events—does *not* facilitate people's logical thinking in areas unrelated to computer use (Mayer & Wittrock, 1996; Perkins & Salomon, 1989). The consensus of contemporary learning theorists is that general transfer, in the extreme sense portrayed by the formal discipline perspective, probably does not occur.

An Early Behaviorist Theory: Thorndike's Identical Elements

Edward Thorndike (1903, 1924; Thorndike & Woodworth, 1901) proposed a theory of transfer that emphasized specific transfer: Transfer occurs only to the extent that the original and transfer tasks have *identical elements*. In an early study supporting Thorndike's theory (Thorndike & Woodworth, 1901), people received extensive training in estimating the areas of rectangles. This training improved their subsequent ability to estimate the areas of rectangles and other two-dimensional forms (e.g., triangles and circles) as well. However, training had less of an impact on the judgment of nonrectangular shapes, presumably because nonrectangles had elements both similar and dissimilar to the elements of rectangles. In a later study, Thorndike (1924) examined the interrelationships of high school students' academic achievement in various curricular areas. Achievement in one subject area appeared to facilitate students' achievement in another only when the two subjects were similar. For example, arithmetic achievement was related to performance in a bookkeeping course, but Latin proficiency was not. Thorndike concluded that the value of studying specific topics was due not to the benefits of mental exercise but to "the special information, habits, interests, attitudes, and ideals which they demonstrably produce" (Thorndike, 1924, p. 98).

A Later Behaviorist Perspective: Similarity of Stimuli and Responses

Since Thorndike's work, behaviorist views of transfer have focused on how transfer is affected by stimulus and response characteristics in both the original and transfer situations. As an illustration, consider these four lists of paired associates:

List 1	List 2	List 3	List 4
lamp – shoe	lamp – sock	rain – shoe	lamp – goat
boat – fork	boat – spoon	bear – fork	boat – shop
wall – lawn	wall – yard	sofa – lawn	wall – rice
corn – road	corn – lane	book – road	corn – fish

Imagine that you first learn list 1 and then are asked to learn list 2. Will your knowledge of the pairs in list 1 help you learn the pairs in list 2? Based on the results of verbal learning studies (Hall, 1966, 1971), the answer is yes: The stimulus words are identical in the two situations and the responses are similar, so positive transfer from one list to the other is likely to occur.

Now, however, imagine that you have to learn list 1 and then list 3. Will prior learning of list 1 help with list 3? The answer again is yes (Hall, 1966, 1971). Even though the stimulus words are very different, the responses in list 3 are identical to those of list 1—hence they have already been learned—and merely need to be attached to the new stimuli.

On the other hand, let's now suppose that, after learning list 1, you need to learn list 4. Here is a case in which very different responses from those of list 1 must be learned to the very same stimuli. Learning list 1 is likely to make learning list 4 more difficult because you will sometimes remember the list 1 response instead of the list 4 response (Hall, 1966, 1971), and negative transfer will result.

In general, principles of transfer that have emerged from behaviorist literature (Osgood, 1949; Thyne, 1963) include the following:

1. When stimuli and responses are similar in the two situations, maximal positive transfer will occur.
2. When stimuli are different and responses are similar, some positive transfer will occur.
3. When stimuli are similar and responses are different, negative transfer will occur.

As an example of this last point, I remember one year as a high school student when my class schedule included second-period Latin and third-period French. The word for "and" *(et)* is spelled the same in both languages but pronounced very differently ("et" in Latin and "ay" in French), hence meeting the conditions for negative transfer (similar stimuli, different responses). On several occasions I blurted out an "et" in my French class—a response that inevitably evoked a disgusted scowl from my French teacher.

As learning theorists have moved away from behaviorist perspectives to more cognitive explanations of how human beings learn, they have spoken less and less of specific stimulus-response connections. Nevertheless, we see hints of behaviorist notions even in today's conceptions of transfer. For example, similarity between something already learned and the demands of a new situation clearly *is* an important factor affecting the extent to which transfer occurs. And John Anderson (1987) has proposed that transfer occurs to the extent that procedures (productions) used in one situation apply to a second situation—a cognitive variation on Thorndike's theory of identical elements.

An Information Processing Perspective: Importance of Retrieval

From a cognitive perspective, we can probably best understand transfer as involving a process of retrieval: People are apt to transfer previously learned information and skills to a new situation only when they retrieve the information and skills at the appropriate time (Brooks & Dansereau, 1987; Cormier, 1987; Gick & Holyoak, 1987; Prawat, 1989). To make a connection between their current situation and any prior knowledge that might be relevant to the situation, they must have both things in working memory at the same time. Given the low probability that any particular piece of information will be retrieved, as well as the limited capacity of working memory, many potentially relevant pieces of information may very well *not* be transferred in situations in which they would be helpful.

The presence or absence of retrieval cues in the transfer situation determines what relevant knowledge, if any, is retrieved to working memory. A new event is more likely to call to mind previously learned information when aspects of the event are closely associated with the relevant information in long-term memory. This will happen, for instance, if the learner anticipated the situation when storing the new information, so that the situation and information relevant to it were stored in a connected fashion.

A Contextual Perspective: Situated Learning

In recent years, some cognitivists have proposed that most learning is context specific—that it is "situated" in the environment in which it takes place.[1] Such **situated learning** is unlikely to result in transfer to new contexts, especially when they are very different from the ones in which learning originally occurred (Brown, Collins, & Duguid, 1989; Greeno et al., 1996; Greeno, Moore, & Smith, 1993; Lave & Wenger, 1991; Light & Butterworth, 1993; Singley & Anderson, 1989).

Research indicates that some skills are indeed context bound (Butterworth, 1993; Hirschfeld & Gelman, 1994; Snow, 1994). For example, children who sell candy, gum, and other items on the street may readily use basic mathematical procedures when they calculate prices for various quantities of items or when they determine the amount of change they should give a particular customer yet not transfer such procedures to classroom mathematics lessons (Carraher, Carraher, & Schliemann, 1985; Schliemann & Carraher, 1993). Carpenters may learn such mathematical concepts as *parallel* and *perpendicular* within the context of carpentry yet not realize that their knowledge is applicable in other situations requiring the same concepts (Millroy, 1991). Furthermore, as we discovered in our discussion of Piaget's theory in Chapter 8, children can often apply logical thinking skills (e.g., proportional reasoning or separation and control of variables) to situations with which they have had previous experience yet *not* be able to use them in less familiar contexts.

Even in a school context, skills don't necessarily transfer from one classroom to another (Bassok & Holyoak, 1990, 1993). A study by Saljo and Wyndham (1992) provides an illustration. High school students were asked to figure out how much postage they should put on an envelope that weighed a particular amount, and they were given a table of postage rates that would enable them to determine the correct amount. When students were given the task in a social studies class, most of them used the postage table to find the answer. But when students were given the task in a math class, most of them tried to *calculate* the postage in some manner, sometimes figuring it to several decimal places. Curiously, the students in the social studies class were more likely to solve the problem correctly; as a former social studies teacher myself, I suspect that the students' work with topics in social studies gave them lots of experience finding information in tables and charts. On the other hand, many of the students in the math class apparently never considered pulling the correct postage directly from the table. Instead, they tried to apply some of the complex mathematical operations that served them so well in their daily assignments—operations that were often counterproductive in this situation.

It is important to note here that not all cognitivists believe that learning is as situated as some of their colleagues claim (e.g., see Anderson, Reder, & Simon, 1996, 1997; Perkins,

---

[1]This idea is similar to Tulving's notion of *encoding specificity,* which I described in Chapter 12.

1992). They point out that people often *do* use the things they have learned in school in real-world situations; for example, most individuals in our society engage in reading and simple mathematics—two skills they have probably learned at school—in nonschool contexts almost every day (Anderson et al., 1996). An additional criticism recently leveled at situated learning theory is that, in its present form at least, it is too vague to allow us to predict exactly when transfer will and will not take place (Anderson et al., 1997; Renkl, Mandl, & Gruber, 1996). Despite such concerns, situated learning theory has numerous supporters, many of whom argue that classroom learning activities should be as similar to real-world tasks as possible; we will consider such *authentic activities* in Chapter 16.

Current Views on General Transfer: Learning to Learn

We have already seen two extreme perspectives regarding general transfer. Advocates of formal discipline argued that learning rigorous and demanding subject matter facilitates later learning tasks because it strengthens and "disciplines" the mind. Thorndike, on the other hand, argued that one task will transfer to another only to the extent that the two tasks have identical elements. Current views concerning general transfer are somewhere in between: General transfer is not as common as specific transfer, but learning occurring at one time *can* facilitate learning at another time if, in the process, the individual *learns how to learn.*

In several early studies of learning to learn, Harry Harlow (1949, 1950, 1959) found that monkeys and young children became progressively faster at discrimination-learning tasks. More recently, a number of studies have examined the transfer value of metacognitive knowledge and skills; as we noted in Chapter 15, effective study methods and habits often do generalize from one subject matter to another (see also Brooks & Dansereau, 1987; Brown, 1978; Pressley, Snyder, & Cariglia-Bull, 1987).

As long as two tasks have something in common, the possibility of transfer from one task to the other exists (Gray & Orasanu, 1987). But commonalities among tasks do not guarantee transfer. In fact, regardless of theoretical orientation, most theorists agree that transfer does not occur nearly as often as it could or should. Much school learning seems to yield "inert" knowledge that students never use outside of the classroom (Mayer, 1996b; Perkins & Salomon, 1989; Renkl et al., 1996; Whitehead, 1929).

When is transfer most likely to take place? Let's look at some of the factors that seem to make a difference.

Factors Affecting Transfer

A number of factors influence the probability that information or skills learned in one situation will transfer to another situation. Let's look at several principles that can help us predict when transfer is most likely to occur:

• *Meaningful learning promotes better transfer than rote learning.* We have previously seen that meaningfully learned information is more easily stored and retrieved than information learned at a rote level. Now we see an additional advantage of meaningful learning: It promotes positive transfer (Ausubel et al., 1978; Brooks & Dansereau,

1987; Mayer & Wittrock, 1996; Prawat, 1989). For example, in a study by Brownell and Moser (1949, cited in Mayer, 1977), third-grade students were taught the idea of borrowing in subtraction in a presumably meaningful manner: Two-digit numbers were represented by individual sticks and groups of 10 sticks bundled together, with borrowing represented by the untying of one group of 10. These students solved a variety of subtraction problems more successfully than students taught the same information simply through verbally presented rules. Along a similar vein, in an experiment by Mayer and Greeno (1972), two groups of college students received one of two methods of instruction on a formula related to basic probability theory. Group 1 received instruction that focused on the formula itself, whereas group 2 received instruction that emphasized the relationship of the formula to students' general knowledge. Group 1 students were better able to apply the formula to problems similar to those they had studied during instruction, but group 2 students were better able to use the formula in ways that had not specifically been covered in instruction—that is, they could transfer the formula to a wider variety of situations. Apparently, group 2 students had made more connections between the new material and existing information in their long-term memories, and those connections enabled them to transfer probability theory in ways that group 1 students could not.

• *The more thoroughly something is learned, the more likely it is to be transferred to a new situation.* Research is clear on this point: the probability of transfer increases when students know something *well* (Brophy, 1992b; Cormier & Hagman, 1987; Gick & Holyoak, 1987; Voss, 1987).

Acquiring knowledge and skills thoroughly takes time. In fact, some conditions that make initial learning slower and more difficult may actually be beneficial for both retention and transfer over the long run. For example, increasing the variability of the tasks learners are asked to practice during instruction—having them perform several different tasks or several variations on the same task within a single instructional unit—lowers their performance initially but enhances their ability to transfer what they have learned to new situations later on (Schmidt & Bjork, 1992). Furthermore, although a certain amount of feedback is essential for learning to take place, occasional rather than continual feedback about one's performance appears to promote performance over the long run, even though it may result in slower improvement initially (Schmidt & Bjork, 1992). It may be that learners need practice not only in performing certain tasks but also in retrieving relevant knowledge in a multitask context and in providing their *own* feedback about their performance (Schmidt & Bjork, 1992).

Clearly, then, there is a trade-off between transfer and expediency. Teachers who teach a few things in depth are more likely to promote transfer than those who teach many things quickly—the "less is more" principle once again. Students should demonstrate thorough mastery of material if they will be expected to apply that material in future situations.

• *The more similar two situations are, the more likely it is that what is learned in one situation will be applied to the other situation.* Behaviorists have argued that similarity of either stimuli or responses is necessary for transfer to occur. Cognitivists have proposed instead that because transfer depends on retrieval of relevant information at the appropriate time, the *perceived* similarity rather than actual similarity of the two situations is important (Bassok, 1990; Bassok & Holyoak, 1993; Blake & Clark, 1990; Di Vesta & Peverly, 1984; Gick & Holyoak, 1987; Voss, 1987). Either way, one thing is clear: Similarity between two situations makes a difference in transfer.

• *Principles are more easily transferred than knowledge.* General principles and rules are more applicable than specific facts and information (Cheng, Holyoak, Nisbett, & Oliver, 1986; Fong, Krantz, & Nisbett, 1986; Gick & Holyoak, 1983, 1987; Judd, 1932; Perkins & Salomon, 1987; Perry, 1991). For example, if you have read Chapter 4's discussion of operant conditioning, then you probably remember the general principle of reinforcement: a reinforcer is a stimulus that increases the later frequency of a response it follows. This principle is easily transferable to a wide variety of situations, whereas specific facts that I mentioned in the same chapter (e.g., who did what research study and when) are not. Similarly, when students are trying to understand such current events as revolutions and international wars, general principles from history—for example, the principle that two groups of people will engage in battle when other attempts at reaching a mutually satisfying state of affairs have failed—are probably more applicable than precise knowledge of World War II battles. And when students study geography, general map interpretation skills—for example, determining why various features are located where they are—are probably more useful than the names and locations of specific rivers, mountain ranges, and state capitals (Bochenhauer, 1990). General and perhaps somewhat abstract principles are especially helpful when a new situation does not, on the surface, appear to be similar to one's previous experiences but when it shares underlying structural or conceptual similarities with those experiences (Anderson et al., 1996; Perkins, 1995; Perkins & Salomon, 1989).[2]

• *Numerous and varied examples and opportunities for practice increase the extent to which information and skills will be applied in new situations.* As situated learning theorists have suggested, knowledge is often stored in association with the context in which it has been encountered. People who store a particular skill or piece of information in connection with one situation are likely to retrieve that knowledge—and perhaps to use it—when they encounter the same situation once again; they are *less* likely to retrieve it when they are in a somewhat different situation (Di Vesta & Peverly, 1984; Stein, 1989; Sternberg & Frensch, 1993). For example, many elementary students don't recognize that the things they learn in science are useful in solving real-world problems (Rakow, 1984). And, in general, students don't see the connections between the things they learn in school and the situations they encounter in the outside world (Alexander & Judy, 1988; diSessa, 1982; Gick & Holyoak, 1987; Mayer & Wittrock, 1996; Perkins & Simmons, 1988; Schoenfeld, 1985a; Sternberg & Frensch, 1993).

[2]A distinction between high-road transfer and low-road transfer is relevant here. In *high-road transfer,* people must make a conscious and deliberate connection between a new situation and their previous experiences; such a connection is often made on the basis of an underlying, abstract similarity. In contrast, *low-road transfer* occurs when a new situation is superficially quite similar to prior experiences, such that relevant knowledge and skills are readily retrieved (Perkins & Salomon, 1989).

People are most likely to transfer something they have learned when they have encountered it in a wide variety of examples and practice situations (Anderson et al., 1996; Cheng et al., 1986; Cormier, 1987; Cox, 1997; Fong et al., 1986; Gick & Holyoak, 1987; Kotovsky & Fallside, 1989; Perkins, 1995; Perkins & Salomon, 1987; Schmidt & Bjork, 1992; Schmidt & Young, 1987; see Bassok & Holyoak, 1993, for an exception). Learners instructed in this fashion store the material they are studying in association with multiple contexts and are therefore more likely to retrieve the information when they again find themselves in one of those contexts. As an illustration, when students are learning basic arithmetic principles, they might be asked to apply those principles in determining best buys at a grocery store, dividing items equitably among friends, running a lemonade stand, and so on. Arithmetic will then be associated in long-term memory with all of these situations, and when the need arises to determine which of two grocery products yields the most for the money, relevant arithmetic procedures should be readily retrieved.

• *The probability of transfer decreases as the time interval between the original task and the transfer task increases.* Most research on transfer has focused on very short delays between the original task and the transfer task (Gick & Holyoak, 1987). Yet transfer decreases as the time interval between the original and transfer situations increases (Gick & Holyoak, 1987). Here is another principle that is probably due to retrieval: Information that has been learned recently is more likely, and more able, to be retrieved than information acquired further back in time.

How and when do people transfer information they have learned to find solutions to problems? It is to this topic—problem solving—that we turn next.

PROBLEM SOLVING

Can you solve these three problems?

1. What number is obtained when 3354 is divided by 43?
2. How can a 49-year-old educational psychologist be helped to control her junk food habit?
3. How can two groups of people of differing political persuasions and a mutual lack of trust be convinced to reduce their military defense spending and instead work toward cooperation and peaceful coexistence?

The world presents us with many different kinds of problems. Some, such as problem 1, are straightforward: all of the information necessary for a solution is presented, and the solution is definitely right or wrong. Others, such as problem 2, may necessitate seeking out additional information (e.g., does the educational psychologist keep physically active, or does she sit around the house all day reading mystery novels and watching television game shows?), and there may be two or more solutions to the problem (e.g., self-reinforcement for altered eating habits, or six months on a deserted island). Still others, such as problem 3, may be so complicated that, even after considerable research and creative thought, no easy solution emerges (as I write this, events in the Mideast and Eastern Europe come to mind). Different kinds of problems require different procedures and different solutions; this multifaceted nature of problem solving has made the theoretical study of problem solving a very challenging endeavor indeed.

In the following pages we will explore a number of topics related to the complex activity of human problem solving. We will first define some basic concepts that appear in problem-solving literature and then examine both behaviorist and cognitive theories of problem solving. Because cognitive theories predominate at the present time, we will also look in depth at several memory factors and cognitive strategies that are often involved when people solve problems successfully.

Basic Concepts in Problem Solving

Several basic concepts will be helpful to us as we explore the nature of problem solving: problem components, algorithms, heuristics, and well-defined problems versus ill-defined problems.

Components of a Problem

Any problem has at least three components (Glass et al., 1979; Wickelgren, 1974):

- **Givens**—pieces of information that are provided when the problem is presented
- **Goal**—the desired end state; what a problem solution will hopefully accomplish
- **Operations**—actions that can be performed to approach or reach the goal

Operations are frequently described in terms of *productions,* the "if-then" conditional actions described in Chapter 11 (e.g., see Anderson, 1983a, 1987). When one or more operations can be applied to reach the goal state, the problem is successfully solved.

Algorithms and Heuristics

Some problems can be approached using a set of specified operations that always lead to a correct solution. For example, the problem of dividing 3354 by 43 can be solved using either of two procedures: (1) applying prescribed methods of long division or (2) pushing the appropriate series of buttons on a calculator. Either approach leads to the correct answer—78. Similarly, a cherry pie recipe, if followed to the letter in terms of ingredients, measurements, and oven temperatures, provides a series of steps that guarantees a delicious dessert. Such specific, step-by-step procedures for solving problems are called **algorithms.**

Unfortunately, not all problems can be solved with algorithms. No specific algorithms exist for eliminating a junk food addiction or establishing world peace. In such situations, people use other approaches to problem solving—approaches that may or may not work. These approaches, known collectively as **heuristics,** include general problem-solving strategies, rules of thumb, and "best guesses" based on past experience with similar problems. For example, in helping an educational psychologist reduce her junk food intake, one heuristic is to think of as many different solutions as possible (a technique known as **brainstorming**), in hopes that one of them will be acceptable. The problem of disarmament of two warring factions can perhaps be solved by analogy: If two coworkers can resolve their differences when they sit down and talk about them, maybe the same strategy will be effective with political groups (hence the frequent summit conferences among world leaders).

Heuristics are also used when algorithms are impractical or time consuming. For example, I once coordinated a chili supper for the parent-teacher association (PTA) of the local elementary school and needed numerous volunteers to assist me. The PTA board suggested an algorithm for me to use: Contact the more than 200 individuals who had indicated on a questionnaire several months earlier that they would help at PTA functions. Being pressed for time, I instead chose a heuristic: I contacted people I knew personally, aware that I could shame many of them into helping out. Similarly, although an algorithm exists for determining the best move in a game of checkers, people tend not to use it because of its impracticality. This algorithm, as Samuel (1963) has described it, is as follows: Consider every possible move, then consider every possible next move that the opponent could make in response to each of those moves, then consider every follow-up move that could be made in response to each of *those* moves, and so on until the winner is projected for every conceivable series of moves. Such an algorithm would take either a sophisticated computer programmer or several lifetimes of total dedication to a single game of checkers.

Well-Defined versus Ill-Defined Problems

Problems vary greatly in terms of how well they are structured or defined. Many theorists have found it helpful to distinguish between well-defined and ill-defined problems (Eysenck & Keane, 1990; Frederiksen, 1984a; Reitman, 1964, 1965; Simon, 1973, 1978), a distinction that actually reflects a continuum of problem structure rather than a rigid dichotomy (Frederiksen, 1984a). At one extreme is the **well-defined problem,** one for which goals and givens are clearly stated, all of the necessary information for solving the problem is presented, and an algorithm exists that will lead to a correct solution. At the other extreme is the **ill-defined problem,** one in which the desired goal is ambiguous, some information necessary for problem solution is lacking, and no relevant algorithm for problem solution exists. Well-defined problems often have only one right solution, whereas ill-defined problems often have several possible solutions that vary in terms of their relative "rightness" or acceptability. The problem of dividing 3354 by 43 is well defined, while that of military disarmament is ill defined (e.g., the goal of "cooperation and peaceful coexistence" is ambiguous). As you might guess, ill-defined problems are typically more difficult to solve and require more complex problem-solving strategies than well-defined problems.

Unfortunately, researchers have focused more on well-defined problems (often somewhat artificial ones) than on the ill-defined problems that life so often presents (Eysenck & Keane, 1990; Ohlsson, 1983; Rosenshine et al., 1996). You will undoubtedly notice this bias as we proceed with our discussion of problem solving. Nevertheless, most of the theories and principles I present presumably apply to both kinds of problems. And, in fact, later in the chapter we will find that one strategy for solving ill-defined problems is to define them more specifically and concretely—in other words, to make them well defined.

Theories of Problem Solving

Since Edward Thorndike's early work with the cat in the puzzle box, several theories of problem solving have emerged from both the behaviorist and cognitive perspectives. We will first look at two behaviorist views: trial-and-error and response hierarchy. We will then examine three more cognitive approaches: Gestalt psychology, stages of problem solving, and information processing theory.

Trial-and-Error Learning

In Chapter 2 you read about Thorndike's (1898) classic work with a cat in a puzzle box. The cat needed to solve a problem: how to get out of a confining situation. It explored the box, manipulating its various parts, and eventually triggered the mechanism that opened the door. Once again the cat was put back into the box, and once again it tried different behaviors until it triggered the release mechanism. In each succeeding trial, escape from the box took less time than in the previous trial. The cat's approach to the problem situation appeared to be one of trial and error, with the correct solution being followed by a positive consequence (escape from the box).

A trial-and-error approach is often observed in the problem-solving behavior of children. For example, consider the way many young children assemble jigsaw puzzles: They try to fit different pieces into the same spot, often without considering each piece's shape and appearance, until eventually they find a piece that fits. Such an approach to problem solving is a workable one if there are only a limited number of possibilities that one can try; otherwise, it can be extremely time consuming, with no guarantee of finding a successful solution (Chi & Glaser, 1985).

Response Hierarchy

Another concept you encountered in Chapter 2 was Clark Hull's notion of a habit-family hierarchy, now more generally known as a **response hierarchy:** An organism learns several different responses to the same stimulus, each of which is associated with that stimulus but with a different degree of habit strength. When a stimulus is presented, an organism will, if possible, make the response for which the habit strength is the strongest. If that response fails or is prevented from occurring, the organism will make the second response, and so on down the hierarchy (Hull, 1934, 1937, 1938).

A response hierarchy can be graphically depicted like this:

In this case, three responses have been learned to the same stimulus, with stronger stimulus-response associations being indicated by thicker arrows. The organism first emits the response with the strongest association to the stimulus (R_1). If that response fails to achieve its goal, the response with the second strongest association (R_2) is emitted, then the third strongest response (R_3), and so on until eventually the goal is attained.

A number of behaviorists (e.g., Davis, 1966; Mayzner & Tresselt, 1958, 1966; Skinner, 1966a) have applied the notion of response hierarchy to a problem-solving situation. Stimuli in the problem situation may evoke several different responses, and those responses will be produced, one at a time and in order of their strength, until either the problem is solved or the organism exhausts its repertoire of responses. To illustrate, as my daughter Tina was growing up, she was often confronted with the same problem: getting permission from her parents to do something we didn't necessarily want her to do. Given this problem, she typically tried three different responses, usually in the same order. First she would smile sweetly and describe how much she wanted to engage in the forbidden activity (such a response, apparently, was associated most strongly with this particular problem situation). If that tactic was unproductive, she would speak indignantly about how her parents never let her do anything. As a last resort, she would run off to her room, slamming her door and shouting that her parents hated her. Unfortunately, Tina never did learn that some problems, such as engaging in forbidden activities, would be solved over her parents' dead bodies.

In their emphasis on trial-and-error learning and habit strength, behaviorists have obviously focused on the role that stimulus-response connections play in problem solving. Although such an approach can often be used to explain problem-solving behavior, contemporary theorists have largely abandoned it to focus more on the mental processes involved in problem solving. Consistent with this trend, we, too, will abandon behaviorism at this point and embrace a more cognitively oriented perspective for the rest of our discussion.

Gestalt Psychology

In Chapter 8 I described Wolfgang Köhler's (1925) observations of chimpanzee behavior in problem-solving situations. Köhler observed little trial-and-error behavior of the form that Thorndike had described. Rather, it appeared to him that the chimpanzees carefully examined the components of a problem situation (sizing things up, so to speak) and mentally combined and recombined those components until they eventually found a winning combination. At this point of **insight,** the chimps would immediately move into action, performing the required responses in a deliberate manner until the problem was solved. From such observations, Köhler (1925, 1929) concluded that problem solving was a process of mentally **restructuring** a problem situation until insight into the problem's solution was reached.

Stages of Problem Solving

Another early cognitive approach to problem solving was to identify the mental stages through which problem solving proceeded. For example, Wallas (1926) identified four steps in problem solving:

1. *Preparation:* Defining the problem and gathering information relevant to its solution

2. *Incubation:* Thinking about the problem at a subconscious level while engaging in other activities
3. *Inspiration:* Having a sudden insight into the solution of the problem
4. *Verification:* Checking to be certain that the solution is correct

Similarly, Polya (1957) listed these four steps:

1. *Understanding the problem:* Identifying the problem's knowns (givens) and unknowns and, if appropriate, using suitable notation, such as mathematical symbols, to represent the problem
2. *Devising a plan:* Determining appropriate actions to take to solve the problem
3. *Carrying out the plan:* Executing the actions that have been determined to solve the problem and checking their effectiveness
4. *Looking backward:* Evaluating the overall effectiveness of the approach to the problem, with the intention of learning something about how similar problems may be solved on future occasions

Unfortunately, Wallas and Polya derived their conceptualizations of problem solving more from introspection and informal observation than from controlled experimentation, and they were somewhat vague about how each of their four steps could be accomplished (Lester, 1985; Mayer, 1992; Schoenfeld, 1992). For example, Wallas's notion of incubation revealed little about how to behave to facilitate the occurrence of inspiration. Similarly, Polya recommended devising a plan, with little consideration of just how one would go about doing that. For such reasons, early stage theories of problem solving were of limited usefulness in helping psychologists determine what specific cognitive processes are involved in solving problems successfully.

Information Processing Theory

Most contemporary theories focus less on the steps people follow in solving problems and more on the specific mental processes they use to reach problem solutions (e.g., Andre, 1986; Siegler, 1991). These information processing theories emphasize the role of such factors as working memory capacity, meaningful learning, organization of long-term memory, retrieval of relevant information, and specific cognitive strategies. The bulk of current research in problem solving reflects inquiry into the nature of these cognitive processes; in the following pages, we will look at them in detail.

Cognitive Factors in Problem Solving

The ability to solve problems successfully depends on a number of factors related to the human information processing system. Here we will focus on five such factors: working memory capacity, encoding and storage in long-term memory, long-term memory retrieval, the specific knowledge base related to the problem, and metacognition. As we go along, we will identify several differences between problem-solving experts and novices within a particular content domain, discovering reasons why some individuals solve problems quickly, easily, and effectively while others solve them either with great difficulty or not at all.

Working Memory Capacity

As you should recall, working memory is the component of memory in which the active, conscious processing of information occurs. Yet this component has a limited capacity: It can hold and process only a small amount of information at a time. If the information and processes necessary to solve a problem exceed working memory capacity, the problem cannot be solved (Anderson, 1987; Johnstone & El-Banna, 1986; Pulos, 1980; Salthouse, 1991; Tourniaire & Pulos, 1985). For example, you may remember from Chapter 9 how difficult it can be to solve long-division problems in your head.

The working memory limitation can be overcome in problem-solving situations in a couple of ways. First of all, some of the information necessary to solve the problem can be stored externally (e.g., by writing it down on paper) or perhaps even processed externally (e.g., by using a calculator). Second, as I suggested in Chapter 12, some skills involved in problem solving should be learned well enough that they become automatic, thus requiring only minimal working memory capacity.

Encoding and Storage of the Problem

Consider this classic children's riddle:

> *As I was going to St. Ives,*
> *I met a man with seven wives.*
> *Every wife had seven sacks.*
> *Every sack had seven cats.*
> *Every cat had seven kits.*
> *Kits, cats, sacks, wives.*
> *How many were going to St. Ives?*

Many people take this logical approach to the problem: 1 traveler plus 1 man plus 7 wives plus 7^2 sacks (49) plus 7^3 cats (343) plus 7^4 kits (2401) equal a total of 2802 going to St. Ives. People who solve the problem in this manner have encoded the problem incorrectly. In particular, they have overlooked the first line of the riddle: "As *I* was going to St. Ives." The problem statement doesn't tell us where the polygamist was taking his harem and menagerie—perhaps to St. Ives, perhaps not.

Here is a passage containing some information you will need to solve a mathematical problem. Read the information; then, after you have finished, turn the page to read the problem:

I went to the store and made the following purchases:

- A roasting chicken for $4
- A dozen eggs for $1 per dozen
- Three avocados for 50¢ each
- Two cans of tomato sauce for 25¢ each
- Five apples for 20¢ each

Now for the problem:

How many items did I buy?

Did you find that you stored the wrong information? You may have been expecting the problem "How much did I spend?" If so, then you probably determined the total amount spent in each line of the problem and added the amounts together for a grand total. Using this approach, however, you would not have stored the information actually necessary for solving the problem: the number of items mentioned in each line.

One critical factor in problem solving is *what* specific information is stored in memory (Chi, Glaser, & Farr, 1988; Glaser, 1987; Sternberg, 1985; Sternberg & Davidson, 1982, 1983). A difficulty you may have had with the grocery shopping problem is that some irrelevant information was presented (i.e., the prices of items), and you may have stored that information instead of more essential data. Irrelevant information can be distracting, thus interfering with successful problem solving. For example, when I give examinations to my own students, I often present more information than is necessary to answer questions, and some students have difficulty sorting through it all. Similarly, I have noticed that my daughter Tina has trouble with mathematics problems that include superfluous information. My students and my daughter behave almost as if they have learned that they need to use *all* of the information they are given. This attitude may be the result of their own prior school experiences: Most problems presented in the classroom (especially mathematics problems) present only the information needed to solve the problem—no more, no less.

A second critical factor related to long-term storage is *how* a problem is encoded in memory (Mayer, 1982, 1986, 1992; Ormrod, 1979; Prawat, 1989; Resnick, 1989; Reusser, 1990; Schwartz, 1971; Sternberg & Davidson, 1982, 1983). For example, consider these two ways of presenting the same situation:

- There are 5 birds and 3 worms. How many more birds are there than worms?
- There are 5 birds and 3 worms. How many birds won't get a worm? (Hudson, 1983)

First graders often struggle with the first problem, yet they solve the second problem quite easily (Hudson, 1983). The first problem requires students to store *relational* information—the fact that there are more of one thing than another—and such information seems to be difficult to encode, even for adults. For instance, Mayer (1982) examined undergraduate students' ability to recall problems such as this one:

A truck leaves Los Angeles en route to San Francisco at 1 PM. A second truck leaves San Francisco at 2 PM en route to Los Angeles going along the same route. Assume the two cities are 465 miles apart and that the trucks meet at 6 PM. If the second truck travels at 15 mph faster than the first truck, how fast does each truck go? (Mayer, 1982, p. 202)

The students in Mayer's study had considerable difficulty remembering relational information (e.g., one truck traveling *15 mph faster* than another): They made three times as many errors in recalling relational aspects of problems as they did in recalling basic assertions (e.g., two cities being 465 miles apart).

Wertheimer (1945) has provided another example of the importance of encoding in problem solving: calculating the area of a parallelogram. As you probably know, the area of a rectangle is determined by multiplying its height by its width. But how is the area of a parallelogram determined? Problem solution is easier once you realize that the extra "triangle" at one end of the parallelogram is identical to the missing triangle at the other end, as illustrated in Figure 15-1.

How people encode a problem—and therefore how they solve it—is partly a function of how they classify the problem to begin with (Hinsley, Hayes, & Simon, 1977; Resnick, 1989; Sternberg & Davidson, 1982, 1983). For example, consider this situation:

> The students in Alice's ninth-grade social studies class have been working in pairs on an assigned project; their teacher has said that he will give a prize for the best project that a pair completes. Alice is now complaining to her younger sister Louisa that her partner, Meg, no longer wants to work with her; Meg thinks Alice is too bossy. Louisa suggests that the best course of action is simply for Alice and Meg to buckle down and finish the project so that they can win the prize. Alice, however, is thinking that she should instead talk with Meg and promise that she will be less bossy. (Adapted from Berg & Calderone, 1994)

Figure 15–1
Finding the area of a parallelogram.

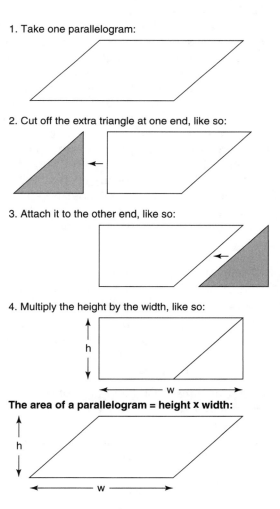

1. Take one parallelogram:

2. Cut off the extra triangle at one end, like so:

3. Attach it to the other end, like so:

4. Multiply the height by the width, like so:

h

w

The area of a parallelogram = height x width:

h

w

Louisa and Alice are classifying the problem in different ways here, and so they arrive at different solutions. In Louisa's eyes, the problem is one of completing the project. Alice sees the problem quite differently—as one of resolving an interpersonal conflict (Berg & Calderone, 1994).

As another example of problem classification, consider this problem:

> Ana went shopping. She spent $3.50 and then counted her money when she got home. She had $2.35 left. How much did Ana have when she started out? (Resnick, 1989, p. 165)

If you recognize this as an addition problem, you will probably get the correct answer of $5.85. However, if the word *left* in the problem leads you to classify the problem as one requiring subtraction (because many subtraction problems ask questions such as "How many are *left?*"), you may very well get an incorrect answer such as $1.15 (Resnick, 1989).

Expert and novice problem solvers within a particular content domain seem to classify problems differently (Alexander & Judy, 1988; Anderson, 1990; Anzai, 1991; Blake & Clark, 1990; Chi, Feltovich, & Glaser, 1981; Chi et al., 1988; De Corte et al., 1996; Di Vesta & Peverly, 1984; Larkin, 1980, 1983; Novick, 1988; Schoenfeld & Herrmann, 1982; Silver, 1981). Experts generally classify a problem on the basis of abstract concepts, principles, patterns, and schemas that can be applied to its solution. Novices, on the other hand, tend to focus on specific, concrete aspects of a problem and to retrieve information related only to those aspects. As an illustration, Schoenfeld and Herrmann (1982) compared the ways that mathematics professors and students classified a variety of mathematical problems. Professors classified them on the basis of abstract principles related to problem solution; for example, those solved by analogy were grouped together, as were those solved by contradiction, and so on. In contrast, students classified the problems on the basis of more superficial characteristics, such as whether they contained polynomial expressions or whether they included figures from plane geometry. After a course in mathematics, the students were asked to repeat the classification task; at this point, they began to classify the problems as their professors did.

Experts may also spend more time defining ill-defined problems before attempting to solve them (Mitchell, 1989; Swanson, O'Connor, & Cooney, 1990; Voss, Greene, Post, & Penner, 1983; Voss, Tyler, & Yengo, 1983; Voss, Wolfe, Lawrence, & Engle, 1991). Consider this problem as an example:

> Imagine that the year is 1983 and that you are the Minister of Agriculture in the Soviet Union. Crop productivity has been low for the past several years, and people are beginning to go hungry. What would you do to increase crop production? (Adapted from Voss, Greene, et al., 1983; Voss, Tyler, & Yengo, 1983)

Take a few minutes to jot down some of your ideas.

How much time did you spend defining the problem? Chances are, you didn't spend much time at all; you probably went right to work thinking about possible problem solutions. If you were a political scientist specializing in the Soviet Union, however, you might have spent considerable time identifying various aspects of the problem—perhaps considering Soviet political policies, the amount of available land for farming, and so on—before thinking about how you might solve it (Mitchell, 1989; Voss, Greene, et al., 1983; Voss, Tyler, & Yengo, 1983).

Mental Sets in Encoding   Individuals are often predisposed to approach and encode problems in particular ways, a phenomenon known as **mental set** (Gestalt psychologists called it *Einstellung*). Following is a problem for which people are often the victims of a mental set:

> How can you throw a tennis ball so that it goes a short distance, comes to a complete stop, then reverses its direction? You may not bounce the ball against a surface, nor may you attach any other object (such as a string) to it. (Adapted from Gardner, 1978)

I once gave this problem to a masters-level learning class, and only a handful of my 35 students were able to solve it. Most of them worked on the assumption that the ball had to be thrown horizontally (some may even have encoded the problem as a visual image of a pitcher). Once you break this mental set, the answer is quite simple: You throw the ball *up*.

As another example of mental set, consider this "candle" problem adapted from a similar one used by Duncker (1945):

> You are in a room with a bulletin board firmly affixed to the wall. Your task is to stand a candle upright beside the bulletin board about 4 feet above the floor. You do not want the candle touching the bulletin board, because the candle's flame must not singe the bulletin board. Instead, you need to place the candle about a centimeter away. How can you accomplish the task, given the following materials:
>
> - A small candle (birthday cake size)
> - A match
> - A box of thumbtacks
> - A 12-inch wooden ruler
> - A metal knitting needle

Develop a solution for the problem before you continue reading.

When I bring these materials to my graduate classes, students typically identify three different solutions. One solution is to stab the knitting needle through the candle and into the bulletin board; this action inevitably splits the candle and gouges the bulletin board. A second solution is to form a horizontal surface with the ruler, propping it against the bulletin board with thumbtacks, and then place the candle on top; however, the precariously placed ruler usually falls to the floor once the candle is placed on it. Only a third solution works: Take the thumbtacks out of the box, use the tacks to attach the box to the bulletin board, then affix the candle to the top side of the box (with either melted wax or a tack). The solution is obvious once you think about it, but many people have difficulty with the problem because they encode the box as a container and fail to consider its other possible functions.

The tendency to think of objects as having only one function, thereby overlooking other possible uses, is a form of mental set known as **functional fixedness** (Birch & Rabinowitz, 1951; Duncker, 1945; Maier & Janzen, 1968). The degree to which individuals experience functional fixedness depends, in part, on situational conditions. For instance, people more easily solve the candle problem if the tacks are presented *outside* of the box, presumably because they are less likely to think of the box only as a container for the tacks (Duncker, 1945). The problem is also easier to solve if the box itself is labeled "box" (Glucksberg & Weisberg, 1966), possibly because the label draws attention to the box as something that can be used in solving the problem.

Mental set and functional fixedness are partly the result of past experience: If a particular approach to a problem has worked in the past, an individual is likely to continue using that same approach even in situations in which it is inappropriate or unnecessarily cumbersome. Luchins's (1942; Luchins & Luchins, 1950) experiments with water jar problems illustrate just how strongly one's past experiences can influence problem solving. Imagine, if you will, that you have three jars of three different sizes:

Jar A holds 20 ounces of water.

Jar B holds 59 ounces of water.

Jar C holds 4 ounces of water.

You need exactly 31 ounces of water. Assuming that you have an unlimited amount of water, how can you get the exact amount of water using only the three jars you have? Try to find a solution before you read further.

The solution to the water jar problem is as follows:

1. Fill jar B. This gives you 59 ounces of water.
2. Pour water from jar B into jar A until A is full. This leaves 39 ounces in jar B.
3. Pour water from jar B into jar C until C is full. This leaves 35 ounces in jar B.
4. Pour the water out of jar C.
5. Once again pour water from jar B into C. At this point you have 31 ounces in jar B, the exact amount you need.

Mathematically speaking, the solution to the problem is

$$B - A - 2C$$

Luchins (1942) gave participants in his study a series of such problems, with the answer always being the same: $B - A - 2C$. He then presented these three problems:

Jar A holds	Jar B holds	Jar C holds	Obtain this amount
23	49	3	20
15	39	3	18
28	76	3	25

Almost everyone solved the first two problems using the same formula as before: $B - A - 2C$. They had difficulty solving the third problem because the standard formula did not apply. But notice that all three can be solved quite easily: The solution for the first and third problems is $A - C$, and that for the second problem is $A + C$. The participants in Luchins's study (who were professors and graduate students!) were victims of a problem-solving mental set established through prior experience.

In most situations, one's predisposition to approach similar problems in similar ways facilitates successful problem solving (Maier, 1945). A mental set influences the way in which a problem is encoded in memory, however, and this encoding in turn influences the parts of long-term memory that are searched for information potentially relevant to the problem. If a problem's encoding steers an individual in the wrong "direction" in long-term memory, then it hinders problem-solving performance (Alexander & Judy, 1988; Glass et al., 1979; Mayer, 1992; Stein, 1989). Let's now consider retrieval from long-term memory as yet another cognitive factor affecting problem-solving success.

Retrieval from Long-Term Memory

To use previously learned information to solve a problem, people must retrieve that information at the time they are thinking about the problem. Thus, the factors that facilitate long-term memory retrieval—for example, meaningful learning and organized storage—facilitate problem-solving success as well (Ausubel et al., 1978).

When they search long-term memory for information relevant to a problem, people begin by looking in logical "places." They tend to retrieve familiar ideas first, identifying original or unusual problem solutions later or not at all (Bourne et al., 1986). They also tend to retrieve information closely associated with aspects of the problem situation; for example, people more easily solve the candle problem when they have previously learned a paired-associate list that includes the pair *candle–box* (Weisberg, DiCamillo, & Phillips, 1979). Hints that provide important retrieval cues can be helpful, at least if individuals perceive their relevance (Bassok & Holyoak, 1993; Bourne et al., 1986; Gick & Holyoak, 1987). For example, the solution of anagrams such as this one:

Unscramble these letters to form a real word: NEEPLATH

is easier when you know that the solution belongs to a particular category such as *animals* (Safren, 1962). (The solution, by the way, is *elephant*.)

As I mentioned in Chapter 12, anxiety interferes with retrieval by restricting the part of long-term memory that is searched. Anxious individuals are therefore likely to have difficulty solving problems whose solutions are not readily apparent. For example, Glucksberg (1962) asked four groups of people to solve the candle problem I presented earlier. For two groups, the tacks were out of the box (the easy version of the problem), and for the other two groups, the tacks were in the box (the difficult version). Two groups were given no reason to be anxious about solving the problem; their success or failure in finding a solution had no consequences. The other two groups had an incentive to make them more eager and anxious about finding a solution: The fastest 25% of the problem solvers would receive $5, and the fastest individual of all would receive $25 (a tidy sum back in 1962). Following are the mean reaction times (in minutes) for the four groups of problem solvers; larger numbers indicate greater difficulty in solving the problem:

	Easy Version	Difficult Version
Low Anxiety	4.99	7.41
High Anxiety	3.67	11.08

When the box was empty, its use as a platform for the candle was obvious, and anxiety facilitated problem solving. But when the box was already being used as a container, anxiety made the problem even more difficult to solve than it already was!

The effects of anxiety on problem solving seem to be reduced or eliminated when individuals know where to search in long-term memory. Although high-anxiety individuals typically perform more poorly than low-anxiety individuals on problem-solving tasks, performance of the two groups is similar when memory aids that promote appropriate retrieval are provided (Gross & Mastenbrook, 1980; Leherissey, O'Neil, & Hansen, 1971).

If information relevant to a problem is to be retrieved from long-term memory, it must obviously be *in* long-term memory to begin with. So another factor affecting problem-solving success is an individual's knowledge base in a particular content domain, as we shall see now.

Knowledge Base

Successful (expert) problem solvers have a more complete and better organized knowledge base for the problems they solve (Alexander & Judy, 1988; Anzai, 1991; Bédard & Chi, 1992; Chi et al., 1982; Hiebert & Lefevre, 1986; Lawson & Chinnappan, 1994; Mayer, 1992; Smith, 1991). For example, using the concept mapping technique described in Chapters 13 and 14, Cochran (1988) examined the achievement (much of which involved problem solving) of high school physics students studying a unit on electricity. The higher achievers were students who had better organized information about concepts related to electricity in long-term memory; not only did they know better which concepts should be associated with which, but they also knew the particular relationships that different concepts had with one another. Low achievers were often uncertain about just how the different aspects of electricity fit together and were more often wrong about how the concepts interrelated. By having more information relative to a specific content domain, as well as more interconnections among various bits of information, expert problem solvers can more quickly and easily retrieve the things they need to solve a problem; they can also make inferences about the problem that may facilitate its solution (J. Anderson, 1993; Bédard & Chi, 1992; Chi et al., 1982; Hiebert & Lefevre, 1986; Mayer, 1992; Stein, 1989).

Successful problem solvers also appear to have more knowledge of specific strategies they can use to solve problems within their area of expertise. For example, once they have categorized a problem as falling into a particular category or being consistent with a certain schema, they readily apply certain procedures to solve that problem (Chi & Glaser, 1985; Gick, 1986; Mayer, 1986, 1992; Prawat, 1989; Reed, 1993). And they have often learned some of the more basic problem-solving procedures to a level of automaticity (Chi et al., 1988; Glaser, 1987). Novice problem solvers, lacking the rich knowledge base of experts, are more likely to engage in ineffective problem-solving strategies—for example, resorting to trial and error, persevering with unproductive procedures, making unwarranted assumptions, and applying procedures and equations in a rote, meaningless fashion (Perkins & Simmons, 1988).

Metacognition

Metacognition plays a key role in problem solving. In particular, successful problem solvers must

- Believe that they are capable of solving the problem successfully.
- Know which problem-solving strategies to use.
- Plan a course of action.

- Understand that some problems may take considerable time and effort to accomplish.
- Monitor progress toward the problem solution.
  (Cardelle-Elawar, 1992; De Corte et al., 1996; Delclos & Harrington, 1991; Geary, 1994; Kilpatrick, 1985; Lesgold & Lajoie, 1991; Lester, 1985; Pfeiffer, Feinberg, & Gelber, 1987; Schoenfeld, 1983, 1985a, 1988, 1992; Silver, 1982)

As an illustration, consider this train of thought regarding a particular problem:

> I'm sloppy at doing [algorithm]; I'd better go slow. This is complicated. I should go through the steps carefully. This method isn't working. I'll try something else. I need to vocalize what I'm doing to help me keep on track. I need to write these steps out. (Lester, 1985, p. 63)

This individual, while obviously not an expert at solving the problem in question, is bringing several beneficial metacognitive skills to bear on the problem—for example, acknowledging the need to go slowly and carefully, recognizing when a strategy is unproductive, and identifying specific behaviors that may facilitate problem-solving success.

Unfortunately, students sometimes have epistemological beliefs that interfere with effective problem solving. In the case of mathematics, for example, many students believe that successful problem solving is largely a matter of luck, that a problem can have only one right answer, that there is only one way to solve any particular problem, and that a problem is either solvable within a few minutes' time or else not solvable at all (De Corte et al., 1996; Geary, 1994; Schoenfeld, 1992).

We have spoken of the need to have appropriate strategies for solving particular problems and to regulate (metacognitively) the effectiveness of those strategies in achieving a problem solution. But what specific strategies do people use? We turn to this topic now.

Problem-Solving Strategies

Some types of problems—long division problems, for example—have specific algorithms associated with them that always yield a correct solution. Such algorithms are typically domain specific: They are useful with particular problems in a particular content area but are, for the most part, inapplicable to problems in other areas.

What do people do when they haven't learned an algorithm for solving a problem, or perhaps when no algorithm for a problem exists? In such cases, they typically resort to more general heuristic strategies (Gick, 1986; Perkins & Salomon, 1989; Prawat, 1989). Among such strategies are combining algorithms, hill climbing, means-ends analysis, working backward, drawing analogies, and "shortcut" heuristics.

Combining Algorithms
Sometimes, when a single algorithm is insufficient to solve a problem, several algorithms in combination may lead to a correct solution (R. Gagné, 1985). Mathematics problems (e.g., algebraic equations and geometric proofs) are frequently solved through a combination of algorithms.

Combining algorithms is not necessarily as easy as it sounds (e.g., Mayer & Wittrock, 1996). In some cases, individuals may have to learn, through either formal classroom instruction or informal experiences, the process of combining algorithms. A study by Scandura (1974) illustrates this point. Elementary school children were taught trading rules such as the following:

$$n \text{ caramels} = n + 1 \text{ toy soldiers}$$
$$n \text{ toy soldiers} = n + 2 \text{ pencils}$$

They were then asked to make trades that involved combining two of these rules (e.g., trading caramels for pencils). Children who were unable to combine rules successfully were identified, and half of them were given specific instruction on how to combine the rules. Subsequently, all of these instructed children effectively combined the trading rules (one of them first required additional instruction), while none of the children in an untrained control group were able to do so.

Hill Climbing

Hill climbing (Andre, 1986; Chi & Glaser, 1985; Mayer, 1983b; Wickelgren, 1974) is a problem-solving strategy in which individuals make any move that brings them closer to the problem goal. For example, consider this problem:

> You have a pile of 24 coins. Twenty-three of these coins have the same weight, and one is heavier. Your task is to determine which coin is heavier and to do so in the minimum number of weighings. You are given a beam balance (scale), which will compare the weight of any two sets of coins out of the total set of 24 coins. (Wickelgren, 1974, p. 34)

Stop to figure out a solution before you continue.

You undoubtedly used hill climbing to solve the problem, weighing different groups of coins against one another and gradually eliminating some of them, until eventually only the single heavier coin remained. How many weighings did you use? In fact, as Wickelgren (1974) has pointed out, the heavy coin can be identified with only *three* weighings, like so:

1. Divide the 24 coins into three groups of 8 coins each. Whichever of the three groups is heavier than the other two must contain the heavy coin. Weigh one group against a second; if one group tips the scale, it must contain the heavy coin. If the two groups balance each other, the third group must contain the heavy coin.
2. Divide the eight-coin group containing the heavy coin into three smaller groups, with two groups of three coins and one group of two coins. Weigh the two three-coin groups against each other. As before, the scale will tell you if one group is heavier (in which case it contains the heavy coin). If the two groups balance each other, the group of two coins must contain the heavy coin.
3. Using the same reasoning as in the previous two steps, the heavy coin can be identified from the group of two or three coins with only one additional weighing.

Hill climbing often leads to correct problem solution. It is ineffective, however, in situations in which the problem solution requires one or more temporary steps *backward*. To illustrate, consider this problem:

> A zookeeper must transport three lions and three giraffes across a river. She has a small barge that can hold only her and two other animals, so she will have to make several trips and leave some of her animals unattended some of the time. However, whenever she leaves a group of animals, the giraffes must outnumber the lions; otherwise, the lions will gang up on one of the giraffes and kill it. How can the zookeeper transport all six animals safely across the river?

Try to solve the zookeeper's problem before you read further.

The zookeeper can transport her animals across the river in this manner:

1. She takes two lions to the other side, leaving three giraffes and one lion behind. (The giraffes will be safe because they outnumber the lion.)
2. She comes back alone.
3. She takes one giraffe to the other side, leaving two giraffes and one lion behind.
4. She *brings back* the two lions, leaving one giraffe alone on the other side.
5. She takes the two giraffes to the other side, leaving the three lions behind.
6. She comes back alone, leaving the three giraffes behind.
7. She takes two lions to the other side, leaving one lion behind.
8. She comes back alone, leaving three giraffes and two lions behind.
9. She takes the last lion across the river.

Problem solution, then, requires a step backward: the zookeeper must bring two of the lions back to the first side of the river (step 4). A person using a hill-climbing strategy would not consider such a step and would be unable to solve the problem.

Means-Ends Analysis

Means-ends analysis (J. Anderson, 1990, 1993; Newell & Simon, 1972; Resnick & Glaser, 1976; Restle & Davis, 1962) is a process whereby an individual breaks a problem into two or more subgoals and then works successively on each of those subgoals. To illustrate, consider this situation:

> I have just had a brick barbecue built in my backyard. I have had it built with metric dimensions: The grill is 1 meter wide and 1.5 meters long. Rich and Marcy Jones look over from their yard next door and say, "Oooo, nice barbecue . . . almost as big as ours."
> "Mine is bigger," I reply.
> "Can't be," they say. "Our grill is 3.5 feet by 5 feet."

The question: Have I kept up with the Jones family by buying a bigger barbecue grill? I can solve this problem by breaking it into four subgoals and solving each one in turn:

1. Convert the dimensions of the Joneses' grill into metric units. One foot equals approximately 0.30 meters; multiplying the "feet" dimensions by 0.30 yields dimensions of 1.05 by 1.5 meters.
2. Compute the area of the Joneses' grill. Multiplying 1.05 by 1.5 equals 1.575 square meters.

3. Compute the area of my grill. Multiplying 1 by 1.5 equals 1.5 square meters.
4. Compare the areas of the two grills. Rich and Marcy's grill is still larger than mine. I have not kept up with the Joneses.

Means-ends analysis appears to be a relatively common method of solving problems (Greeno, 1973; Newell & Simon, 1972) and is most likely to be used when the goal is clearly specified (Sweller & Levine, 1982). However, a potential disadvantage of this approach is that, by attending to only one subgoal at a time, a person may lose sight of the problem as a whole (Sweller & Levine, 1982).

Working Backward

Consider this game, similar to one described by Wickelgren (1974):

> There are 21 pennies on a table. Two players, Mary and Susan, take turns removing pennies from the table; in any given turn, a player must take one, two, or three pennies. The player who removes the last penny from the table wins the game and keeps all 21 pennies. Mary begins by taking two pennies. What strategy can Susan use to be sure that she wins the game?

See if you can solve the problem before you read further.

The problem is solved by beginning at the *end* of the game, at the point where Susan removes the last penny, and then going backward to the first move. In what situation will Mary be in the position of enabling Susan to win? Remember, each player can remove one, two, or three pennies on a turn. Let's look at the solution as a series of steps:

1. Mary must be forced into a situation in which she has to leave one, two, or three pennies on the table. Susan can then take them all, and victory is hers.
2. If, on the preceding turn, Susan leaves four pennies, then Mary's options are such that she must leave one to three pennies on her turn.
3. For Susan to leave four pennies, Mary must, on the previous turn, leave five, six, or seven pennies.
4. For Mary to leave five to seven pennies, Susan must leave eight pennies for Mary to choose from.

Continuing the steps in this manner, we see a pattern: Susan must always leave a number divisible by four. Therefore, when Mary removes 2 pennies, leaving 19 on the table, Susan should take 3 pennies.

The method I used to help Susan figure out how to win the game every time illustrates the process of **working backward** (Chi & Glaser, 1985; Newell, Shaw, & Simon, 1958; Wickelgren, 1974). This strategy is to begin at the problem goal and then work backward, one step at a time, toward the initial problem state. In each step backward, the individual identifies one or more conditions that would produce the present condition. In a sense, working backward is the opposite approach to that of means-ends analysis.

Working backward is frequently used in solving algebra and geometry proofs. Students are given an initial situation—a formula or a geometric configuration with certain characteristics—and then are asked to prove, through a series of mathematically logical steps, how another formula or another characteristic (the goal) must also be true. Sometimes it is easier to move logically from the goal backward to the initial state; mathematically speaking, this approach is just as valid.

Drawing Analogies

See if you can solve the following problem originally used by Duncker (1945) and adapted by Gick and Holyoak (1980):

> Suppose you are a doctor faced with a patient who has a malignant tumor in his stomach. It is impossible to operate on the patient, but unless the tumor is destroyed the patient will die. There is a kind of ray that can be used to destroy the tumor. If the rays reach the tumor all at once at a sufficiently high intensity, the tumor will be destroyed. Unfortunately, at this intensity the healthy tissue that the rays pass through on the way to the tumor will also be destroyed. At lower intensities the rays are harmless to healthy tissue, but they will not affect the tumor either. What type of procedure might be used to destroy the tumor with the rays, and at the same time avoid destroying the healthy tissue? (Gick & Holyoak, 1980, pp. 307–308)

If you are having difficulty with the problem, then consider this situation:

> A general wishes to capture a fortress located in the center of a country. There are many roads radiating outward from the fortress. All have been mined so that, while small groups of men can pass over the roads safely, any large force will detonate the mines. A full-scale direct attack is therefore impossible. The general's solution is to divide his army into small groups, send each group to the head of a different road, and have the groups converge simultaneously on the fortress. (Gick & Holyoak, 1980, p. 309)

Now go back to the tumor problem. Perhaps the general's strategy in capturing the fortress has given you an idea about how to destroy the tumor. It can be destroyed by shooting a number of low-intensity rays from different directions, such that they all converge on the tumor simultaneously. Gick and Holyoak found that people are much more likely to solve the tumor problem when they have first read the solution to the fortress problem, because the two problems can be solved in analogous ways.

Drawing an analogy between a problem situation and another situation sometimes provides insights into how a problem can be solved (Clement, 1987; Holyoak, 1985; John-Steiner, 1997; Mayer & Wittrock, 1996; Novick, 1988; Schultz & Lochhead, 1991). For example, a student might solve a mathematics problem by finding a similar, "worked out" problem—one that has already been solved correctly using a particular procedure (Mayer & Wittrock, 1996; Reimann & Schult, 1996; Zhu & Simon, 1987). As another example, consider a problem that the Greek scientist Archimedes confronted sometime around 250 B.C.:

> King Hiero had ordered a crown of pure gold from the local goldsmith. He suspected that the goldsmith had cheated him by replacing some of the gold with silver, a cheaper metal. The only way to determine the goldsmith's honesty was to compare the crown's weight against its volume. Any metal has a particular volume for any given weight, and that ratio is different for each metal. The crown could be weighed easily enough. But how could its volume be measured?

Archimedes was pondering the problem one day as he stepped into his bathtub. He watched the bath water rise and, through analogy, immediately identified a solution to the king's problem: The crown's volume could be determined by placing it in a container of water and measuring the amount of water that was displaced.

Using analogies to solve problems has its difficulties, however. For one thing, people may make an incorrect analogy and solve a problem incorrectly as a result (Novick,

Analogies are
sometimes helpful in
solving problems.

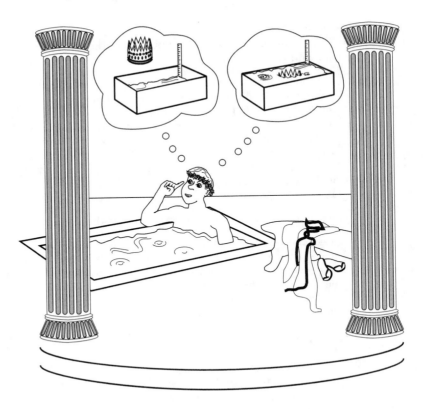

1988). Even when they identify a truly analogous situation, they may draw inappropriate parallels (Mayer & Wittrock, 1996). But the major drawback to using analogies as a problem-solving strategy is that individuals seldom retrieve analogous situations when they face a particular problem situation. The fact is, people rarely use analogies in solving problems unless a problem and its analogue are similar in terms of superficial features (Bassok, 1996; Gick & Holyoak, 1980; Hayes & Simon, 1974; Mayer & Wittrock, 1996; Reed, Ernst, & Banerji, 1974). When people *do* use analogies, it is often because they serendipitously encounter both the problem and the analogous situation at the same time. In other words, it may often be a matter of luck—of just happening to think of the right thing at the right time.

Shortcut Heuristics: Representativeness and Availability

Some problem-solving strategies can be executed quickly and simply. Two commonly described examples are representativeness and availability (Kahneman & Tversky, 1972, 1973; Klein, 1987; Mayer, 1992; Tversky & Kahneman, 1973, 1974). Unfortunately, such shortcuts sometimes lead to inaccurate problem solutions.

Representativeness involves jumping to conclusions about a solution based on obvious characteristics of the problem. Let me illustrate by adapting a problem used by Kahneman and Tversky (1973). Imagine that I have a stack of 100 personality profiles of

30 engineers and 70 lawyers, all of whom are successful in their careers. I pull this description randomly from the pile:

> Jack is a 45-year-old man. He is married and has four children. He is generally conservative, careful, and ambitious. He shows no interest in political and social issues and spends most of his free time on his many hobbies, which include home carpentry, sailing, and mathematical puzzles. (Kahneman & Tversky, 1973, p. 241)

Now for the problem: What is the probability that this man is one of the 30 engineers?

The probability that the man is an engineer is 30%, because the stack of 100 personality profiles contained 30 profiles of engineers. Yet many people in Kahneman and Tversky's study gave a higher figure; they jumped to a conclusion based on obvious characteristics about Jack that many people associate stereotypically with engineers (e.g., conservatism and enjoyment of mathematical puzzles).

A second shortcut heuristic, **availability,** is a strategy wherein a problem is solved based only on information that comes immediately to mind (i.e., is retrieved from long-term memory) when the problem is encountered. Typically, the problem will be solved using recently acquired information rather than information acquired in the distant past, because recent experiences are more likely to be retrieved than those from long ago. For example, imagine that you are trying to decide whether to go to California or Florida for a sunny March vacation at the beach. You learned many years ago that Florida has more rainfall than California. In February, just as you are about to make your choice, you hear on the news that California has just been drenched in a heavy rainstorm. You may easily book a flight to Florida, retrieving the available information about the California rainstorm rather than the overall frequency of rainfall in the two states.

At this point, we have examined a variety of different problem-solving strategies. Because many problems have no right or wrong solutions, no single "best" strategy may exist for solving them. Obviously, different strategies are appropriate in different situations. But sometimes people use strategies at the wrong times, often because they have learned such strategies at a rote, meaningless level. Let's look at what happens when individuals use problem-solving strategies either meaninglessly or meaningfully.

Meaningless versus Meaningful Problem Solving

See if you can solve this problem before you read further:

> The number of quarters a man has is seven times the number of dimes he has. The value of the dimes exceeds the value of the quarters by two dollars and fifty cents. How many has he of each coin? (Paige & Simon, 1966, p. 79)

If you found an answer to the problem—any answer at all—then you overlooked an important point: Quarters are worth more than dimes. If there are more quarters than dimes, the value of the dimes cannot possibly be greater than the value of the quarters. The fact is, the problem makes no sense, and so it cannot be solved.

When people learn algorithms at a rote level, without understanding their underlying logic, they may sometimes apply those algorithms "unthinkingly" and inappropriately (De Corte et al., 1996; Perkins & Simmons, 1988; Prawat, 1989; Resnick, 1989; Resnick &

Glaser, 1976; Schoenfeld, 1982, 1985a; Silver, Shapiro, & Deutsch, 1991). As a result, they may obtain illogical or physically impossible results. Consider the following instances of meaningless mathematical problem solving as examples:

- A student is asked to figure out how many chickens and how many pigs a farmer has if the farmer has 21 animals with 60 legs in all. The student adds 21 and 60, reasoning that, because the problem says "how many in all," addition is the logical operation (Lester, 1985).
- A student uses subtraction whenever a word problem contains the word *left*—even when a problem actually requiring addition includes the phrase "John left the room to get more apples" (Schoenfeld, 1982).
- Middle school students are asked to calculate how many 40-person buses are needed to transport 540 people to a baseball game. The majority give an answer that includes a fraction, without acknowledging that in the case of buses, only whole numbers are possible (Silver et al., 1991).

All too often, when schools teach problem solving, they focus on teaching algorithms for well-defined problems while omitting explanations of why the algorithms work (Cooney, 1991; Davis, 1986; Hiebert & Lefevre, 1986; Perkins & Salomon, 1989; Perkins & Simmons, 1988; Porter, 1989; Resnick, 1989). For example, perhaps you can remember learning how to solve a long-division problem, but you probably don't remember learning *why* you multiply the divisor by each digit in your answer and write the product in a particular location below the dividend. Or perhaps you were taught a "key word" method for solving word problems: Words such as *altogether* indicate addition, and words such as *left* mean subtraction. This approach is a meaningless one indeed and, as we noted in both the "Ana" and "John" examples presented earlier, often leads to an erroneous solution.

How can teachers help students engage in more meaningful problem solving? And, in general, how can they help students become more expert at problem solving and other forms of transfer? We turn now to the topic of facilitating transfer and problem solving in educational settings.

FACILITATING TRANSFER AND PROBLEM SOLVING IN THE CLASSROOM

As we noted earlier in the chapter, students often fail to see the relevance of what they have learned in school to new school tasks or to out-of-school problems. Thus, a major objective of our educational system—positive transfer—is probably not being achieved. At the same time, students sometimes erroneously apply what they have learned to situations in which it is not appropriate—a case of negative transfer.

Learning theorists are only beginning to understand the complex processes of transfer and problem solving. Nevertheless, theories and research in both areas provide numerous suggestions for educational practice:

- *Students need to learn information meaningfully and thoroughly.* Theorists agree that a solid knowledge base is a prerequisite for successful transfer and problem solving (Frederiksen, 1984a; Greeno, 1973; Hiebert & Lefevre, 1986; Mayer, 1975; Norman,

1980; Reif & Heller, 1982; Simon, 1980; Simon & Hayes, 1976). In the process of acquiring this knowledge base, students should develop a multitude of interconnections and relationships among the concepts and ideas they learn; they should also discover the potential relevance of such concepts and ideas for the various situations they may encounter later on (Bereiter, 1995; Brophy & Alleman, 1991; Perkins, 1995; Perkins & Salomon, 1987; Prawat, 1989; Sternberg & Frensch, 1993).

Unfortunately, many school curricula include long lists of topics that must be taught, the result being that no single topic is taught very thoroughly (e.g., see Porter, 1989). Breadth of coverage occurs at the expense of depth of coverage—and at the expense of successful transfer and problem solving as well.

• *Students should also learn problem-solving strategies at a meaningful level.* All too often, students learn problem-solving algorithms as procedures separate from anything they have previously learned about the world. For example, they may learn mathematics— its symbols, principles, and algorithms—in total isolation from the concrete physical world they deal with on a daily basis (Carpenter, 1985; Davis, 1987; Hiebert & Wearne, 1993; Resnick, 1989). When students learn an algorithm at a rote, meaningless level, they are likely to use it mechanically, thoughtlessly, and often incorrectly, and they are *un*likely to recognize many of the situations in which it might legitimately be applied (Greeno, 1991; Hiebert & Wearne, 1993; Kilpatrick, 1985; Perkins & Simmons, 1988).

Rather than simply learning algorithms at a rote level, students should understand *why* they do the things they do in order to solve problems; in other words, they should connect abstract, symbol-based procedures to things they already know and to concrete reality (Carpenter, 1985; Geary, 1994; Greeno, 1991; Heller & Hungate, 1985; Hiebert & Lefevre, 1986; Prawat, 1989; Resnick, 1983, 1989). As one simple example, a teacher might demonstrate the rationale behind "borrowing" in subtraction by using toothpicks, some of which have been bundled into groups of 10 or 100, then untying and borrowing from the bundles when necessary. By demonstrating the logic behind problem-solving procedures, a teacher increases the likelihood that students will apply those procedures at appropriate times and obtain plausible results.

• *Students must have a mental set for transfer.* We noted earlier that mental sets in problem solving—predispositions to solve problems in particular ways—sometimes interfere with successful problem solving. Yet a *general* mental set to transfer school learning—a predisposition to use and apply the things learned in the classroom—is clearly beneficial (Stein, 1989; Sternberg & Frensch, 1993). To promote such a mental set, teachers can point out how academic content can be applied to a variety of situations both in and out of school (Brophy, 1992b; Cox, 1997; Fennema et al., 1989; Perkins & Salomon, 1989; Prawat, 1989; Resnick, 1989; Sternberg & Frensch, 1993; Voss, 1987). And they can encourage their students to be constantly thinking "How might I use this information?" as they listen, read, and study (Perkins, 1992; Perkins & Salomon, 1987; Stein, 1989; Sternberg & Frensch, 1993).

• *Some prerequisite skills should be practiced until they are learned to the point of automaticity* (Anderson, 1983a, 1987; Frederiksen, 1984a; Gagné, 1982; Geary, 1994; Heller & Hungate, 1985; Mayer, 1985; Perkins & Salomon, 1987; Resnick, 1989). Remember that problem solving occurs in working memory—a component of the memory system that has a limited capacity for holding and processing information at any single moment.

To the extent that students can process the simple and familiar aspects of a problem automatically, thereby using only a minimal amount of working memory capacity, they can devote more working memory "space" to the problem's difficult and novel aspects.

• *Numerous and varied examples and opportunities for practicing transfer and problem solving should be provided* (Chase & Chi, 1980; Cormier, 1987; Frederiksen, 1984a; Gagné & Driscoll, 1988; Geary, 1994; Kilpatrick, 1985; Perkins & Salomon, 1987). Experience with many practice examples promotes associations in long-term memory between newly learned information and a variety of relevant situations; hence, the new information is more likely to be retrieved when it is needed later on. For example, in an experiment by Pepper (1981), students studied computer programming techniques from one of three instructional booklets. Two booklets were taken from actual programming textbooks. The third was a modified text in which simple examples were inserted to illustrate all major points and most minor ones; it was therefore longer and wordier than either of the other booklets. Despite its length, the example-filled booklet was liked most by students and led to the highest performance on an examination (83% for the example-filled booklet versus 58 to 67% for the other two booklets).

Occasionally, teachers should present problems in a somewhat mixed-up order (rather than having students solve a set of problems that all require the same procedure), so that students have practice in classifying problems before solving them (Geary, 1994; Mayer, 1985). It may also be beneficial to present real-life problems in addition to the more traditional word problems (De Corte et al., 1996; Lave, 1988, 1993). For instance, a teacher might have students predict how much helium they would need to put in a balloon to make it float or calculate the volume of a cylindrical punch bowl to determine whether it is large enough to hold a certain amount of punch for a class party.

• *Students should have experience identifying problems for themselves.* Teachers usually provide the problems they want their students to solve. But beyond the classroom—for example, at home and in the world of employment—people must often identify and define for themselves the problems that stand in their way. Some theorists suggest that students may benefit from getting a head start on such problem finding (Brown & Walter, 1990; Hiebert et al., 1996; Perkins & Simmons, 1988; Porter, 1989; Resnick, Bill, Lesgold, & Leer, 1991). For example, in a mathematics lesson, students might be given data describing the quantities and prices of items in a grocery store and asked to generate a number of questions that could be answered by those data. Or, in a history lesson, students might be given a scenario of an American Civil War battle in progress, instructed to identify the problems facing either the North or the South, and asked to propose possible solutions to those problems.

• *To minimize negative transfer, differences between two ideas should be emphasized.* Insects and spiders are similar stimuli—they are both small arthropods with exoskeletons and a generally creepy-crawly nature—and so students may inappropriately transfer what they know about one group of creepy-crawlies to the other. For similar stimuli, negative transfer can be reduced if differences rather than similarities are emphasized (Sternberg & Frensch, 1993). For instance, insects and spiders are different in a number of ways (e.g., six legs versus eight legs, three body parts versus two, and antennae versus no antennae); if emphasized, those differences could reduce negative transfer from one group to the other. Additionally, if negative transfer between two ideas is anticipated, it can be reduced by teaching each in a different environment (Bilodeau & Schlosberg, 1951; Greenspoon & Ranyard, 1957)—for example, by teaching students about insects while sitting in the classroom and teaching them about spiders while on a field trip to the natural history museum.

• *Problem-solving skills are sometimes better learned through a discovery approach.* Although expository instruction is in many cases the most efficient means of transmitting information to students in an organized fashion, instructional approaches that emphasize guided discovery learning may facilitate better transfer of problem-solving skills to new situations (Gagné & Brown, 1961; Hiebert et al., 1996; Mayer, 1974, 1987; McDaniel & Schlager, 1990; Roughead & Scandura, 1968; Shymansky, Hedges, & Woodworth, 1990). Discovery is probably most appropriate when problems are ill structured and students have a solid knowledge base (Doyle, 1983; Frederiksen, 1984a). However, for well-structured problems that can be solved by a specific algorithm (e.g., long-division problems), and for students relatively unsophisticated about a particular topic, direct instruction of the algorithm may be preferable (Frederiksen, 1984a; R. Gagné, 1985).

• *Teaching general learning and problem-solving skills may be helpful.* As I indicated in Chapter 14, training in study skills can be effective and appears to improve classroom learning and achievement. At the same time, remember that not everything will apply to everything else: Latin will help a student learn physics only to the extent that, while studying Latin, the student develops better learning strategies that are also applicable to the study of physics.

Many theorists believe that teaching general problem-solving strategies can enhance students' ability to solve problems successfully (Cardelle-Elawar, 1992; E. Gagné, 1985; Glaser, 1979; Mayer, 1987; Resnick, 1976; Schoenfeld, 1979, 1992; Simon, 1980). A study by Herrnstein, Nickerson, de Sánchez, and Swets (1986) provides some optimism about the effectiveness of training problem-solving skills: Seventh-grade Venezuelan students who took a year-long course in reasoning, problem-solving, and decision-making skills showed greater improvement in both the specific skills taught and general intellectual ability than did students in an untrained control group. Yet we should note here that, just as study strategies may be better learned when taught within the context of specific academic content areas (see Chapter 15), so, too, may general problem-solving strategies be more effectively learned when connected with content domains to which they are applicable (Mayer, 1992; Resnick, 1987; Schoenfeld & Herrmann, 1982).

Several problem-solving strategies may be transferable to a wide variety of problem situations. One helpful strategy is talking aloud about the problem; this approach may facilitate students' ability to guide and monitor their own progress (in a metacognitive sense) toward a problem solution (Gagné & Smith, 1962; Heller & Hungate, 1985; Stinessen, 1975; Vygotsky, 1962). A second is using paper and pencil to diagram a problem or list its components; this tactic may help students encode a problem more concretely and see the interrelationships among various elements more clearly (Anzai, 1991; Fuson & Willis, 1989; Lindvall, Tamburino, & Robinson, 1982; Mayer, 1992; Prawat, 1989; Schultz & Lochhead, 1991; Wickelgren, 1974). Still a third strategy is brainstorming—thinking of as many hypothetical problem solutions as possible without initially evaluating any of them (e.g., Osborn, 1963). The absence of evaluation when brainstorming ideas can potentially facilitate a broader search of long-term memory for unusual and creative possibilities.

After generating a long and seemingly exhaustive list of problem solutions, an individual can critically examine the various solutions to identify workable and unworkable ones.

Some theorists (e.g., Anderson, 1990; Ellis & Hunt, 1983; Wallas, 1926) have suggested that the incubation of a problem—letting it remain unsolved in memory for a period of time—can be a helpful strategy, although there are mixed reviews on its effectiveness (Anderson, 1990; Bourne et al., 1986; Dominowski & Jenrick, 1972). The benefits of an incubation period are more likely to be evident for difficult problems than for easy ones. For one thing, some of the factors that interfere with problem solving, such as fatigue and anxiety, may diminish during the incubation period (Ellis & Hunt, 1983). In addition, the individual may find more appropriate mental sets or more relevant information in long-term memory after leaving the problem alone for a while (Anderson, 1990; Ellis & Hunt, 1983).

• *Students should learn strategies for defining ill-defined problems.* As Frederiksen (1984a) has pointed out, most problems presented in classroom situations are well defined. Students are asked to identify the protagonist and antagonist in a story, use a dictionary to find two different pronunciations of the word *wind,* or calculate how many candy bars six boys can each have if there are 18 bars altogether. In contrast, most real-world problems are ill defined. People need to find viable means of home financing, decide what life insurance policy to purchase (if any), and maintain friendly and productive relationships with obnoxious work associates.

Ill-defined problems often require an individual to search outside sources to find relevant and potentially helpful information (Simon, 1978). Students should therefore be well versed in techniques for finding information through such resources as libraries, computer databases, and government agencies. Students should also learn techniques for more precisely defining ill-defined problems; for example, one helpful technique is to break a larger problem into a number of subproblems and to define and impose constraints on each of those subproblems (Chi & Glaser, 1985; Reitman, 1965; Simon, 1973). Finally, to the extent that students possess a solid knowledge base, they will be better able to define the problems they encounter (Bédard & Chi, 1992; Frederiksen, 1984a).

• *Students' early attempts to solve difficult problems should be scaffolded.* In Chapter 8 we encountered the concept of *scaffolding*—providing a structure that supports students in their efforts on difficult tasks. Then, in Chapter 14, we noted the importance of scaffolding students' early attempts to use sophisticated metacognitive strategies. Some theorists suggest that scaffolding may facilitate problem-solving performance as well (Heller & Hungate, 1985; Wood et al., 1976). Teachers can do several things to help students in their initial attempts at challenging problems: They can simplify early problems, model problem solutions, show students that they are making progress toward problem solutions, point out errors along the way, and in general keep students' frustration at a reasonable level. They can also give students questions to ask themselves as they proceed through a problem—perhaps questions such as the following:

> What (exactly) are you doing? Can you describe it precisely? Why are you doing it? How does it fit into your solution? (Schoenfeld, 1992, p. 356)

As students become more adept at solving problems on their own, such scaffolding can be gradually phased out.

• *The development of effective problem-solving strategies can often be facilitated through cooperative group problem solving.* The notion of *cooperative learning*—of students working together in small groups to help one another learn—is gaining popularity among today's educators. Several theorists have suggested that a cooperative learning environment may be ideal for promoting successful problem solving (Kilpatrick, 1985; Mayer, 1985; Noddings, 1985; Palincsar & Brown, 1989; Qin, Johnson, & Johnson, 1995; Schoenfeld, 1985b). By discussing concepts and principles relevant to the problem solution, students may identify more interrelationships among the things they know and clarify the things about which they are confused (Kilpatrick, 1985; Noddings, 1985). By thinking aloud about how to solve a problem, they may gain a better understanding of what they are mentally doing (Schoenfeld, 1985b; Whimbey & Lochhead, 1986). And, by observing the more effective strategies that their classmates sometimes use, they may begin to adopt those strategies themselves, leaving their inefficient strategies behind (Mayer, 1985; Noddings, 1985; Schoenfeld, 1985b). As an illustration of my last point, consider this incident in a cooperative problem-solving setting:

> [A] youngster suggested that the group should "add, subtract, and multiply these two numbers" and then see which answer "looked" best. Other members of the group were shocked and said, "Donna! We can't do that. We have to figure it out." Donna tried that strategy only once more and then it disappeared from her public repertoire. (Noddings, 1985, pp. 350–351)

• *Classroom evaluation practices should include measures of transfer and problem solving.* As we noted in Chapter 13, traditional classroom tests too often emphasize the learning of specific facts. Certainly basic knowledge and skills are important; among other things, they form the foundation for more sophisticated academic behaviors. But when teachers' instructional objectives also include transfer and problem solving, classroom assessment tasks should ask students to demonstrate the ability to apply classroom subject matter to a variety of situations (Foos & Fisher, 1988; Massialas & Zevin, 1983; Sternberg & Frensch, 1993). This practice can help successful transfer and problem solving become common phenomena rather than rare occurrences.

Teaching for effective transfer and problem solving takes time. Too often, schools seem to rush through a curriculum at the expense of providing sufficient practice at any single point along the way. Educators should probably slow down and give children time to use and apply the information and skills they learn. Students are likely to accomplish more over the long run.

SUMMARY

Transfer is the process of applying information and skills learned in one situation to one's learning or performance in another situation. Several theories of transfer have been proposed; current cognitive perspectives stress the importance of retrieval in the transfer situation and the possibility that knowledge and skills are "situated" to some extent in the context in which they were learned. Most contemporary theorists agree that transfer from one situation to another can occur only to the extent that the two situations are similar in some way. Among the factors that facilitate transfer are meaningful learning, thoroughness of learning, acquisition of general principles, and number and variety of examples and opportunities for practice.

Problem solving is a form of transfer, in that previously learned information is applied to resolve a problem situation. Both behaviorist and cognitive theories of problem solving have been proposed, with cognitive theories predominating today; such cognitive factors as working memory capacity, encoding, retrieval, one's knowledge base, and metacognition influence problem-solving success. Many problems can be solved through specific algorithms—procedures that guarantee correct solutions. Others may be solved through more general heuristics—shortcuts without guaranteed outcomes; examples of such heuristics include means-ends analysis, working backward, hill climbing, and drawing analogies. People often apply problem-solving procedures more effectively and appropriately when they understand the logic behind those procedures.

Theory and research yield numerous suggestions for promoting transfer and problem solving in classroom settings. For example, a school's prescribed curriculum should make it possible for teachers to teach a few things thoroughly and meaningfully rather than many things superficially and at a rote level (the "less is more" idea). Students should have a mental set for transfer; that is, they should approach school subject matter with the idea that they may be able to use it on future occasions. And such techniques as discovery learning, scaffolding, and cooperative learning may facilitate the development of effective problem-solving skills.

CHAPTER 16

Applications of Cognitivism II: Learning through Interactions with Others

O n several occasions in earlier chapters, we have noted the value of involving other people in the learning process. For instance, in our exploration of social learning theory in Chapter 7, we discovered that observing and imitating what other people do—*modeling*—provides an efficient way for learners to acquire new behaviors. In our discussion of Piaget's theory of cognitive development in Chapter 8, we found that social interactions (whether they be amicable conversations or not-so-amicable conflicts) are essential for helping young, egocentric children understand that their perspectives of the world are not necessarily shared by those around them. In the same chapter, we encountered Vygotsky's concept of the *zone of proximal development* and contemporary theorists' *contextual views* of learning, both of which remind us that people can often accomplish more difficult tasks when they have the assistance of other individuals. We found, too, that people often work together to make sense of and develop new knowledge about their world—a perspective known as *social constructivism*. Later, in our discussions of metacognition and problem solving in Chapters 14 and 15, we found that people can often acquire more effective learning strategies and solve problems more successfully when they work cooperatively with their peers.

In this chapter we will look at several teaching strategies that use social interaction as the primary mechanism for helping students learn. The first three strategies—*class discussions, reciprocal teaching,* and *cooperative learning*—involve students at the same general level of achievement working together as a group. Two others—*peer tutoring* and *apprenticeships*—involve students working intensively with someone who has greater proficiency with regard to a particular topic or skill. Later in the chapter we will examine *authentic activities,* in which students work on complex, real-world tasks, often in close collaboration with one another. Finally, we will consider the concept of a *community of learners*—a classroom in which teacher and students help one another learn in a systematic and sustained fashion.

CLASS DISCUSSIONS

Social constructivists propose that people often work together to construct meaningful interpretations of their world. Class discussions in which students feel that they can speak freely, asking questions and presenting their ideas and opinions in either a whole-class or small-group context, obviously provide an important mechanism for promoting such socially constructed understandings (Bruning, Schraw, & Ronning, 1995; De Corte et al., 1996; Fosnot, 1996; Greeno et al., 1996; Hatano & Inagaki, 1991; Hiebert & Fisher, 1992; Marshall, 1992; Webb & Palincsar, 1996; White & Rumsey, 1994).

Classroom discussions are likely to facilitate learning in several ways. When students explain their thinking to their peers, they must organize their thoughts and pull separate ideas into a logical, cohesive whole that makes sense to others and is likely to persuade them (Fosnot, 1996; Good et al., 1992; Hatano & Inagaki, 1993; Lampert et al., 1996; Stevens & Slavin, 1995). Furthermore, when students cannot adequately explain or defend their own perspective and so are questioned or challenged by their classmates, they may recognize that their own knowledge of a topic is inadequate and so try to enhance their knowledge (Damon, 1984; Hatano & Inagaki, 1993; Webb & Palincsar, 1996). In some situations, two or more conflicting perspectives may be presented during the course of a discussion, encouraging listeners either to adopt a perspective they have not previously considered or to integrate various viewpoints into a more multifaceted comprehension of the subject matter (Damon, 1984; Hatano & Inagaki, 1991, 1993; Lampert, 1990; Reiter, 1994; Sosniak & Stodolsky, 1994; Webb & Palincsar, 1996). And a group of students can sometimes co-construct a better understanding of a topic than students can construct when they work on their own (Webb & Palincsar, 1996).

Class discussions lend themselves readily to a variety of academic disciplines. For example, students may discuss various interpretations of classic works of literature, addressing questions that have no easy or "right" answers; when they do so, they are more likely to relate what they are reading to their personal lives and so to understand it better (Eeds & Wells, 1989; Hiebert & Raphael, 1996; McGee, 1992). In history classes, students may study and discuss various documents related to a single historical event and so begin to recognize that history is not necessarily as cut-and-dried as traditional history textbooks portray it (Leinhardt, 1994). In science classes, discussions of various and conflicting theoretical explanations of observed phenomena may help students come to grips with the idea that science is not "fact" as much as it is a dynamic and continually evolving understanding of the world (Bereiter, 1994). And in mathematics, class discussions that focus on alternative approaches to solving the same problem can promote a more meaningful understanding of mathematical principles and lead to better transfer of those principles to new situations and problems (Cobb et al., 1991; Hiebert & Wearne, 1992, 1996; Lampert, 1990).

Guidelines for Promoting Effective Discussions

Although students typically do most of the talking in classroom discussions, teachers nevertheless play a critical role. Theorists have offered several guidelines for how teachers can promote effective classroom discussions:

• *Class discussions should focus on topics that lend themselves to multiple perspectives, explanations, or approaches* (L. Anderson, 1993; Hiebert & Raphael, 1996; Lampert, 1990; Onosko, 1996). Controversial topics appear to have several benefits: Students are more likely to express their views to their classmates, seek out new information that resolves seemingly contradictory data, reevaluate their own positions on the issues under discussion, and develop a meaningful and well-integrated understanding of the subject matter (Cohen, 1994; Johnson & Johnson, 1985a; Smith, Johnson, & Johnson, 1981).

• *Students should have sufficient prior knowledge about the topic under discussion to discuss it intelligently.* Such knowledge may come from either previous class sessions or students' personal experiences (Bruning et al., 1995). In many cases, it is likely to come from studying a particular topic in depth (Onosko, 1996).

• *The classroom atmosphere should be conducive to open debate and the constructive evaluation of ideas.* Students are more likely to share their ideas and opinions if their teachers are supportive of multiple viewpoints and if disagreeing with classmates is socially acceptable (Cobb & Yackel, 1996; Eeds & Wells, 1989; Lampert et al., 1996; Onosko, 1996). To promote such an atmosphere in the classroom, teachers might

- Communicate the message that understanding a topic at the end of the discussion is more important than having the "correct" answer at the beginning of the discussion (Hatano & Inagaki, 1993).
- Communicate the beliefs that asking questions reflects curiosity, that differing perspectives on a controversial topic are both inevitable and healthy, and that changing one's opinion on a topic can be a sign of thoughtful reflection about the topic under discussion (Onosko, 1996).
- Encourage students to try to understand one another's reasoning and explanations (Cobb & Yackel, 1996).
- Encourage students to be open in their agreement or disagreement with their classmates—in other words, to "agree to disagree" (Cobb & Yackel, 1996; Lampert et al., 1996).

- Depersonalize challenges to a student's line of reasoning by framing questions in a third-person voice—for example, by asking, "What if someone were to respond to your claim by saying . . . ?" (Onosko, 1996).
- Occasionally ask students to defend a position that is in direct opposition to what they actually believe (Onosko, 1996; Reiter, 1994).
- Require students to develop compromise solutions that take into account opposing perspectives (Onosko, 1996).

• *Small-group discussions encourage a greater number of students to participate.* Students are more likely to speak openly when their audience is a handful of classmates rather than the class as a whole; the difference is especially noticeable for females (Théberge, 1994). On some occasions, teachers may want to have students discuss an issue in small groups first, thereby allowing students to voice and gain support for their ideas in a relatively private context, and then bring students together for a whole-class discussion (Onosko, 1996).

• *Class discussions are sometimes more effective when they are structured in some way.* Providing a structure for a class discussion—perhaps setting a particular goal toward which students should work—increases the likelihood that a teacher's instructional objectives will be accomplished (e.g., Calfee, Dunlap, & Wat, 1994). For example, before conducting an experiment, a science teacher might ask students to make predictions about what will happen in the experiment and to explain and defend why they think their predictions are correct; later, after students have observed the outcome of the experiment, the teacher might ask them to explain what happened and why (Hatano & Inagaki, 1991). Another strategy, useful when the topic under discussion is an especially controversial one, might be to follow a sequence such as this one:

1. The class is divided into groups of four students apiece. Each group of four subdivides into two pairs.
2. Within a group, each pair of students studies a particular position on the issue and presents its position to the other two students.
3. The group of four has an open discussion of the issue, giving each student an opportunity to argue persuasively for his or her own position.
4. Each pair presents the perspective of the *opposing* side as sincerely and persuasively as possible.
5. The group strives for consensus on a position that incorporates all of the evidence presented (Deutsch, 1993).

• *Students may have more productive discussions when they are given guidance about how to behave.* Teachers must take steps to ensure that students' reactions to one another's ideas are not disparaging or mean spirited (Onosko, 1996). For example, they might provide rules such as the following for acceptable behavior during small-group or whole-class discussions:

- Encourage everyone to participate and listen to everyone's ideas.
- Restate what someone else has said if you don't understand.
- Be critical of ideas rather than people.
- Try to pull ideas from both sides together in a way that makes sense.

- Focus not on winning but on resolving the issue in the best possible way.
- Change your mind if the arguments and evidence presented indicate that you should do so. (Adapted from Deutsch, 1993)
- *Some type of closure should be provided at the end of the discussion.* Although students may sometimes come to consensus about a topic at the end of a class discussion, such agreement is not always possible. Nevertheless, a class discussion should have some form of closure that helps students tie various ideas together. For instance, when I conduct discussions about controversial topics in my own classes, I spend about five minutes at the end of class identifying and summarizing the key issues that students have raised during the class period. Another strategy is to have students explain how a particular discussion has helped them understand the topic in question more fully (Onosko, 1996).

As you have seen, class discussions can help students think about and process classroom subject matter more completely. Yet such discussions can have an additional advantage as well: They can promote more effective learning strategies during reading and listening activities (Brown & Reeve, 1987; Cross & Paris, 1988; Palincsar & Brown, 1989; Paris & Winograd, 1990). One particular form of discussion—*reciprocal teaching*—is especially effective in this regard.

RECIPROCAL TEACHING

Annemarie Palincsar and Ann Brown (1984) have identified four key strategies that good readers typically use:

- *Summarizing:* They identify the gist and main ideas of what they read.
- *Questioning:* They ask themselves questions to make sure they understand what they are reading, thereby monitoring their comprehension as they proceed through reading material.
- *Clarifying:* They take steps to clarify confusing or ambiguous parts of the text, perhaps by rereading or imposing their own knowledge on those things.
- *Predicting:* They anticipate what they are likely to read next based on cues in the text (e.g., headings) and ideas that have already been presented.

Palincsar and Brown noted that poor readers—students who learn little from textbooks and other things they read—rarely summarize, question, clarify, or predict. For example, many students cannot adequately summarize a typical *fifth*-grade textbook until high school or even junior college (Brown & Palincsar, 1987; Palincsar & Brown, 1984).

Yet summarizing, questioning, clarifying, and predicting are activities that typically occur internally rather than externally; they are cognitive processes rather than observable behaviors. Palincsar and Brown reasoned that students might acquire these strategies more easily if they first practiced them out loud and in cooperation with their classmates. In **reciprocal teaching** (Brown & Palincsar, 1987; Palincsar, 1986; Palincsar & Brown, 1984, 1989), a classroom teacher and several students meet in a group to read a section of text, stopping to discuss that text as they proceed. Initially, the teacher leads the discussion, asking questions about the text to promote summarizing, questioning, clarifying, and predicting. But gradually, he or she turns the role of "teacher" over to different students, who then take charge of the discussion and ask one another the same kinds of questions their teacher has modeled. Eventually, students can read and discuss a text almost independently of the teacher, working together to construct its meaning and checking one another for comprehension and possible misunderstandings.

Reciprocal teaching sessions often begin with students making predictions about what they will read based on the title of a passage and their prior knowledge of a topic. Then, as they proceed through the text, they periodically stop to check their comprehension (e.g., by asking one another fact-based and inferential questions), clarify any potentially ambiguous statements or unfamiliar vocabulary, summarize what they have read, and predict what may be coming next. After finishing the passage, the "teacher" summarizes it, with other students possibly adding to and elaborating on that summary.

As an illustration, let's look at a reciprocal teaching session for a group of six first graders reading a passage about snowshoe rabbits. In this particular case, the classroom teacher reads the text in small segments (at higher grade levels, the students themselves take turns reading). After each segment, the teacher pauses while students discuss and process that segment. As you read the dialogue, look for examples of summarizing, questioning, clarifying, and predicting (there is at least one instance of each):

The children were reading about the snowshoe rabbit and it was the sixteenth day of dialogue. The teacher had just read a segment of text describing the season in which baby rabbits are born and the ways in which the mother rabbit cares for her babies. A student named Kam is the dialogue leader.

Kam:	When was the babies born?
Teacher:	That's a good question to ask. Call on someone to answer that question.
Kam:	Robby? Milly?
Milly:	Summer.
Teacher:	What would happen if the babies were born in the winter? Let's think.

Several children make a number of responses including: "The baby would be very cold." "They would need food." "They don't have no fur when they are just born."

Kam:	I have another question. How does she get the babies safe?
Kris:	She hides them.
Kam:	That's right but something else....
Teacher:	There is something very unusual about how she hides them that surprised me. I didn't know this.
Travis:	They are all in a different place.
Teacher:	Why do you think she does this?
Milly:	Probably because I heard another story and when they're babies they usually eat each other or fight with each other.
Teacher:	That could be! And what about when that lynx comes?

Several children comment that that would be the end of all the babies.

Travis:	If I was the mother, I would hide mine, I would keep them all together.

Kris:	If the babies are hidden and the mom wants to go and look at them how can she remember where they are?
Teacher:	Good question. Because she does have to find them again. Why? What does she bring them?
Milly:	She needs to bring food. She probably leaves a twig or something.
Teacher:	Do you think she puts out a twig like we mark a trail?

Several children disagree and suggest that she uses her sense of smell. One child, recalling that the snowshoe rabbit is not all white in the winter, suggests that the mother might be able to tell her babies apart by their coloring.

Teacher:	So we agree that the mother rabbit uses her senses to find her babies after she hides them. Kam, can you summarize for us now?
Kam:	The babies are born in the summer....
Teacher:	The mother ...
Kam:	The mother hides the babies in different places.
Teacher:	And she visits them....
Kam:	To bring them food.
Travis:	She keeps them safe.
Teacher:	Any predictions?
Milly:	What she teaches her babies ... like how to hop.
Kris:	They know how to hop already.
Teacher:	Well, let's read and see.

(Dialogue courtesy of A. Palincsar.)

Reciprocal teaching provides a mechanism through which both the teacher and students can model effective reading and learning strategies. Furthermore, the structured nature of a reciprocal teaching session scaffolds students' efforts to make sense of the things they read and hear. For example, if you look back at the previous dialogue for a moment, you may notice how the teacher models elaborative questions and connections to prior knowledge ("What would happen if the babies were born in the winter?"; "Do you think she puts out a twig like we mark a trail?") and provides general guidance and occasional hints about how students should process the passage about snowshoe rabbits ("Kam, can you summarize for us now?"; "And she visits them . . ."). Also notice in the dialogue how students support one another in their efforts to process what they are reading; consider this exchange as an example:

Kam:	I have another question. How does she get the babies safe?
Kris:	She hides them.
Kam:	That's right but something else....

Effectiveness of Reciprocal Teaching

Studies of reciprocal teaching have yielded significant and often dramatic improvements in students' reading and listening comprehension (Brown & Palincsar, 1987; Campione, Shapiro, & Brown, 1995; Palincsar, 1986; Palincsar & Brown, 1984, 1989; Rosenshine & Meister, 1994). Furthermore, students continue to show the benefits of this approach for at least six months after instruction (Brown & Palincsar, 1987). For example, in an early study of reciprocal teaching (Palincsar & Brown, 1984), six seventh-grade students with a history of reading difficulty participated in 20 reciprocal teaching sessions, each lasting about 30 minutes. Despite the relatively short intervention, the students showed changes such as the following:

- They became increasingly able to process reading material in an effective manner—for example, by summarizing and questioning—and to do so independently of their classroom teacher.
- They demonstrated increasingly better comprehension of the passages they were reading. Average scores on daily comprehension tests increased from 30% before instruction to 70 to 80% (a level similar to that for average readers) after instruction.
- Three months after the reciprocal teaching intervention, their scores on a standardized reading comprehension test reflected an improvement in reading comprehension typically observed after 15 months of traditional schooling—more than a year's worth!
- They generalized their new reading strategies to other classes; for instance, they showed improved performance in their science and social studies classes, sometimes even surpassing the level of their classmates (Brown & Palincsar, 1987; Palincsar & Brown, 1984).

A reciprocal teaching approach to reading instruction has been used successfully with a wide variety of students, ranging from third graders to learning-disabled college students. Furthermore, it can be used to foster more effective listening comprehension beginning in first grade (the earlier dialogue is an example). And it can be employed with an entire classroom of students almost as easily as in a small group. Although teachers are often very skeptical of such a radically different approach to teaching and learning, their enthusiasm grows once they have tried it themselves (Brown & Palincsar, 1987; Palincsar & Brown, 1989).

COOPERATIVE LEARNING

In **cooperative learning** (e.g., Johnson & Johnson, 1991; Slavin, 1983a, 1990a), students work in small groups to achieve a common goal. Cooperative learning groups vary in duration, depending on the task to be accomplished. On some occasions, groups are formed on a short-term basis to accomplish specific tasks—perhaps to study new material, solve a problem, or complete an assigned project. On other occasions, groups are formed to work toward long-term classroom goals. For instance, **base groups** are cooperative groups that last the entire semester or school year; they provide a means through which students can clarify assignments for one another, help one another with class notes, and provide one another with a general sense of support and belonging in the classroom (Johnson & Johnson, 1991).

We find justification for cooperative learning in a number of theoretical perspectives. From a behaviorist point of view, rewards for group success are consistent with the operant conditioning notion of a group contingency. From the standpoint of social learning theory, students are likely to have higher self-efficacy for performing a task when they know that they will have the help of other group members; furthermore, students can model effective learning and problem-solving strategies for one another (Brown & Palincsar, 1989; Good et al., 1992).

Cognitive theories of development and learning provide further justification for a cooperative learning approach. First of all, we see the same benefits that emerge from class discussions: greater comprehension and integration of the subject matter, recognition of inadequacies or misconceptions in understanding, and increased perspective taking. Furthermore, when students help one another learn, they create scaffolding for one another's efforts, and they may co-construct more sophisticated ideas and strategies than any single group member might be able to construct alone (Good et al., 1992; Hatano & Inagaki, 1991; O'Donnell & O'Kelly, 1994; Webb & Palincsar, 1996).

Common Features of Cooperative Learning

Cooperative learning is not simply a process of putting students in groups and setting them loose to work on an assignment together. Oftentimes students will be more accustomed to learning on an individual basis, or perhaps even to competing with classmates, than they are to engaging in cooperative endeavors with other students. For a cooperative learning approach to be successful, teachers must structure classroom activities in such a way that cooperation is not only helpful for academic success but in fact even necessary for it (e.g., Johnson & Johnson, 1991). Following are several features that enhance the effectiveness of cooperative groups:

• *Students work in small, teacher-assigned groups.* Groups are typically comprised of two to six members; groups of three to four students are especially effective (Hatano & Inagaki, 1991; Lou et al., 1996). In most cases, the teacher forms the groups, choosing combinations of students that are likely to be most productive (Johnson & Johnson, 1991). Many advocates of cooperative learning suggest that each group be relatively heterogeneous in makeup—that each group include high achievers and low achievers, boys and girls, and children of various ethnic backgrounds (Johnson & Johnson, 1991; Shachar & Sharan, 1994; Slavin, 1983a; Stevens & Slavin, 1995).

• *Groups have one or more common goals toward which to work.* At the beginning of a cooperative group activity, the teacher should specify clearly and concretely what each group should accomplish (Johnson & Johnson, 1991).

• *Students are given clear guidelines about how to behave.* Without instruction about appropriate group behaviors, students may act in a decidedly uncooperative manner; for example, they may try to dominate discussions, ridicule one another's ideas, or exert pressure to complete the task in a particular way (Blumenfeld, Marx, Soloway, & Krajcik, 1996; Webb & Palincsar, 1996). Instruction on group skills such as the following seems to increase cooperative and productive group behaviors:

- Listening to others politely and attentively
- Giving encouragement to others
- Making sure everyone has an equal chance to participate
- Refraining from insulting or yelling at others

- Offering assistance to others
- Asking clear, precise questions when one doesn't understand
(Cohen, 1994; Deutsch, 1993; Johnson & Johnson, 1991; Lou et al., 1996;
O'Donnell & O'Kelly, 1994; Webb & Farivar, 1994; Webb & Palincsar, 1996)

• *Group members are dependent on one another for their success.* Group tasks should be structured so that each student's success depends on the help and participation of other group members; furthermore, each student must believe it is to his or her advantage that other group members do well (Deutsch, 1993; Johnson & Johnson, 1991; Lou et al., 1996; Schofield, 1995; Slavin, 1983a). For instance, tasks that involve creative problem solving and have more than one right answer are more likely to encourage students to work cooperatively with one another (Blumenfeld et al., 1996). In some situations, each student might have a unique and essential function within the group, perhaps serving as group leader, critic, bookkeeper, summarizer, or the like (Brown & Palincsar, 1989; Johnson & Johnson, 1991). In other situations, the **jigsaw** technique is useful: New information is divided equally among all group members, and each student must teach his or her portion to the other group members (Aronson, 1997).

• *A structure is provided to encourage productive learning behaviors.* When students are novices at cooperative learning, it is often helpful to give them a set of steps (a "script" to follow) that guides their interaction (Cohen, 1994; Dansereau, 1988; Fantuzzo, King, & Heller, 1992; Meloth & Deering, 1994; Palincsar, Anderson, & David, 1993; Webb & Palincsar, 1996). In one approach, known as **scripted cooperation,** students work together in pairs to read and study expository text (Dansereau, 1988). One member of the pair might act as "recaller," summarizing the contents of a textbook passage. The other student acts as "listener," correcting any errors and recalling additional important information. For the next passage, the two students switch roles. Such an approach can help students improve such learning strategies as elaboration, summarizing, and comprehension monitoring (Dansereau, 1988).

• *The teacher serves primarily as a resource and monitor.* During cooperative learning activities, the teacher monitors each group to be sure that interactions are productive and socially appropriate (Johnson & Johnson, 1991). The teacher may also provide assistance in situations in which group members are unable to provide information or insights critical for accomplishing the group's goal. Too much intervention may be counterproductive, however: Students tend to talk less with one another when their teacher joins the group (Cohen, 1994).

• *Students are individually accountable for their achievement.* Each student demonstrates individual mastery or accomplishment of the group's goal—for example, by taking a quiz or answering questions in class. This strategy minimizes the likelihood that some students will do most or all of the work while others get a free ride (Johnson & Johnson, 1991; Karau & Williams, 1995; Slavin, 1983b, 1990a; Webb & Palincsar, 1996).

• *Students are rewarded for group success.* In addition to being accountable for their own learning and achievement, group members are rewarded for the success of the group as a whole (Lou et al., 1996; Slavin, 1983b, 1990a). Such group rewards often promote higher achievement overall, perhaps because students have a vested interest in helping one another learn and so make a concerted effort to help fellow group members understand the material being studied (Slavin, 1983b; Stevens & Slavin, 1995).

- *At the completion of an activity, each group evaluates its effectiveness.* Once a cooperative group has accomplished its goal, it looks analytically and critically (often with the assistance of the teacher) at the ways in which it has functioned effectively and the ways in which it needs to improve (Cohen, 1994; Deutsch, 1993; Johnson & Johnson, 1991).

How Heterogeneous Should Cooperative Groups Be?

As I mentioned earlier, cooperative groups are usually heterogeneous with respect to students' achievement levels, with high and low achievers being asked to work together. In recent years, however, some theorists have begun to question this practice (Cohen, 1994; Cohen & Lotan, 1995; Good et al., 1992; McCaslin & Good, 1996; O'Donnell & O'Kelly, 1994; Peterson, 1993; Webb & Palincsar, 1996). One potential problem with heterogeneous grouping is that ability differences among students become more obvious. High-ability students are apt to dominate discussions and may discourage low-ability students from fully participating. Low-ability students may be reluctant to ask for help in understanding the material being studied, or they may simply sit back and let other group members do most or all of the work. And if a group fails to achieve its goal, the high performers in the group may resent and blame those who contributed little or nothing to the group's efforts.

Findings regarding the achievement gains of students in heterogeneous ability groupings have been somewhat mixed. Some studies indicate that heterogeneous groups benefit both high-ability students, who can sharpen their understanding of class material by explaining it to their classmates, and low-ability students, who benefit from hearing such explanations (Cohen, 1994; Fuchs et al., 1996; Lou et al., 1996; Stevens & Slavin, 1995; Webb & Palincsar, 1996). Yet other studies indicate that high-ability students do not always gain from working with their low-ability peers; in fact, these students occasionally even lose ground (Lou et al., 1996; Tudge, 1990). And middle-ability students may sometimes do better when grouped with *either* high-ability students (who can help them learn) or low-ability students (whom they can help learn) rather than being placed in the middle of a wide range of student abilities (Lou et al., 1996; McCaslin & Good, 1996; Webb & Palincsar, 1996).

Two strategies that I mentioned earlier—assigning different roles to different group members and providing scripts for interaction—are possible ways of equalizing the participation of students who have varying abilities. A third approach is to assign projects that require such a wide range of talents and skills that every group member is likely to have something truly unique and useful to contribute to the group's overall success (Cohen, 1994; Cohen & Lotan, 1995; Schofield, 1995).

Effectiveness of Cooperative Learning Activities

Numerous research studies indicate that cooperative learning activities, when designed and structured appropriately, are effective in many ways. For one thing, students of all ability levels show higher academic achievement; females, members of minority groups, and students at risk for academic failure are especially likely to show increased achievement (Lampe & Rooze, 1994; Lou et al., 1996; Pigott et al., 1986; Qin et al., 1995; Shachar &

Sharan, 1994; Slavin, 1983a, 1990a; Stevens & Slavin, 1995). Cooperative learning activities may also promote higher-level thinking skills: Students essentially "think aloud," modeling various learning and problem-solving strategies for one another and developing greater metacognitive awareness as a result (Brown & Palincsar, 1989; Good et al., 1992; Paris & Winograd, 1990).

The benefits of cooperative learning activities are not limited to gains in learning and achievement. Students have higher self-efficacy about their chances of being successful, express more intrinsic motivation to learn school subject matter, and participate more actively in classroom activities. They better understand the perspectives of others and more frequently engage in prosocial behavior—making decisions about how to divide a task fairly and equitably, resolving interpersonal conflicts, and encouraging and supporting one another's learning. Furthermore, they are more likely to believe that they are liked and accepted by their classmates, and increased numbers of friendships across racial and ethnic groups and between students with and without disabilities are likely to form (Deutsch, 1993; Good et al., 1992; Johnson & Johnson, 1985b, 1987; Lou et al., 1996; Marsh & Craven, 1997; Slavin, 1983a, 1990a; Stevens & Slavin, 1995; Webb & Palincsar, 1996).

Some potential disadvantages of cooperative learning should also be noted, however. Students may sometimes be more interested in achieving a group reward with the least possible effort and so will focus more on getting the "right" answer than on ensuring that all group members understand the subject matter being studied (Good et al., 1992; Hatano & Inagaki, 1991; Linn et al., 1996). The students who do most of the work and most of the talking may learn more than other group members (Blumenfeld, 1992; Gayford, 1992; Webb, 1989). Students may occasionally agree to use an incorrect strategy or method that a particular group member has suggested, or they may share misconceptions about the topic they are studying (Good et al., 1992; Stacey, 1992). And in some cases, students may simply not have the skills to help one another learn (O'Donnell & O'Kelly, 1994). Clearly, then, teachers must keep a close eye on the discussions that cooperative groups have and the products that they produce, providing additional structure and guidance when necessary to promote maximal learning and achievement.

One of the reasons that cooperative learning is so often effective is that students are likely to tutor one another in the subject matter they are studying. Such peer tutoring is our next topic of discussion.

PEER TUTORING

Teachers cannot always devote as much time as they would like to one-on-one instruction with their students. In such situations, **peer tutoring,** whereby students who have mastered a topic teach those who have not, can provide an effective alternative for teaching fundamental knowledge and skills (Brown & Palincsar, 1987; Durkin, 1995; Greenwood, Carta, & Hall, 1988; Pigott et al., 1986).

In some cases, peer tutoring leads to greater academic gains than more traditional forms of instruction (Greenwood et al., 1988). One possible reason for its effectiveness is that it provides a context in which struggling students may be more comfortable asking questions when they don't understand something. For example, in one study (Graesser & Person, 1994), students asked 240 times as many questions during peer tutoring as they did during whole-class instruction!

Peer tutoring typically benefits the tutors as well as those being tutored (Durkin, 1995; Fuchs, Fuchs, Mathes, & Simmons, 1997; Greenwood et al., 1988; Inglis & Biemiller, 1997; Semb et al., 1993; Webb & Palincsar, 1996). When students study material with the expectation that they will be teaching it to someone else, they are more intrinsically motivated to learn it, find it more interesting, process it in a more meaningful fashion, and remember it longer (Benware & Deci, 1984; Semb et al., 1993). Peer tutoring has nonacademic benefits as well: cooperation and other social skills improve, classroom behavior problems diminish, and friendships develop between students of different ethnic groups and between students with and without disabilities (Greenwood et al., 1988).

Guidelines for Facilitating Effective Tutoring

Peer tutoring, like other interactive approaches to instruction, is most effective when teachers follow certain guidelines in its use. Following are several suggestions for using peer tutoring effectively:

• *Teachers should be sure that their tutors have mastered the material they are teaching and use sound instructional techniques.* Good tutors have a meaningful understanding of the subject matter they are teaching and provide explanations that focus on such understanding; poor tutors are more likely to describe procedures without explaining why the procedures are useful (Fuchs et al., 1996). Good tutors also use teaching strategies that are likely to promote learning: They ask questions, give hints, scaffold responses when necessary, provide feedback, and so on (Lepper, Aspinwall, Mumme, & Chabey, 1990).

• Students don't always have the knowledge and skills that will enable them to become effective tutors, especially at the elementary school level (Greenwood et al., 1988; Kermani & Moallem, 1997; Wood, Wood, Ainsworth, & O'Malley, 1995). It is essential, then, that tutoring sessions be limited to subject matter that the student tutors know well. Training in effective tutoring skills is also helpful; for example, student tutors might be shown how to establish a good relationship with the students they are tutoring, how to break a task into simple steps, how and when to give feedback, and so on (Inglis & Biemiller, 1997; Kermani & Moallem, 1997).

• *Structured interactions can enhance the effectiveness of peer tutoring.* Studies by Lynn and Douglas Fuchs and their colleagues (D. Fuchs et al., 1997; L. Fuchs et al., 1996) indicate that providing a structure for tutoring sessions can help elementary students effectively tutor their classmates in reading comprehension skills. In one study (D. Fuchs et al., 1997), 20 second- through sixth-grade classrooms participated in a project called Peer-Assisted Learning Strategies (PALS). In each classroom, students were ranked with regard to their reading performance, and the ranked list was divided in two. The first-ranked student in the top half of the list was paired with the first-ranked student in the bottom half of the list, the second student in the top half was paired with the second student in the bottom half, and so on down the line; through this procedure, students who were paired together had moderate but not extreme differences in their reading levels. Each pair read reading material at the level of the weaker reader and engaged in these activities:

- *Partner reading with retell:* The stronger reader read aloud for five minutes, and then the weaker reader read the same passage of text. Reading something that had previously been read presumably enabled the weaker reader to read the material easily. After the double reading, the weaker reader described the material that the pair had just read.
- *Paragraph summary:* The students both read a passage one paragraph at a time. Then, with help from the stronger reader, the weaker reader tried to identify the subject and main idea of the paragraph.
- *Prediction relay:* Both students read a page of text, and then, with help from the stronger reader, the weaker reader would summarize the text and also make a prediction about what the next page would say. The students would read the following page, and then the weaker reader would confirm or disconfirm the prediction, summarize the new page, make a new prediction, and so on.

Such a procedure enabled students in the PALS program to make significantly greater progress in reading than students who had more traditional reading instruction, even though the amount of class time devoted to reading instruction was similar for both groups. The researchers speculated that the superior performance of the PALS students was probably due to the fact that they had more frequent opportunities to make verbal responses to the things they were reading, received more frequent feedback about their performance, and, in general, were more frequently encouraged to use effective reading strategies.

- *Teachers must be careful that their use of higher-ability students to tutor lower-ability students is not excessive or exploitive.* As we have seen, tutors often gain just as much from tutoring sessions as the students they are tutoring. When students teach something to a classmate, they must pull their knowledge together sufficiently to explain it in a way that someone else can understand; in the process, they review, organize, and elaborate on the things they have learned. Nevertheless, teachers must not assume that high-achieving students will always learn from a tutoring session; teachers should therefore monitor the effects of a peer tutoring program to make sure that all of their students are reaping its benefits.

- *Teachers can use peer tutoring to help students with special educational needs.* Peer tutoring has been used effectively to help students with learning disabilities, physical disabilities, and other special educational needs (Cushing & Kennedy, 1997; D. Fuchs et al., 1997). For example, in one study (Cushing & Kennedy, 1997), low-achieving students were assigned as regular tutors for classmates who had moderate or severe intellectual or physical disabilities. The student tutors clearly benefited from their tutoring assignments: They became more attentive in class, completed classroom tasks more frequently, and participated in class more regularly. I suspect that the opportunity to tutor classmates less capable than themselves may have enhanced their own self-efficacy for learning classroom subject matter, which in turn would encourage them to engage in the kinds of behaviors that would ensure academic success.

- *Tutoring does not necessarily need to be limited to same-age pairs.* In many instances, students at one grade level can effectively tutor students at a lower grade level; for example, fourth or fifth graders can tutor students in kindergarten or first grade (Brown & Campione, 1994; Inglis & Biemiller, 1997; Kermani & Moallem, 1997). Such a practice is consistent with Vygotsky's belief that older and more competent individuals are invaluable in promoting the cognitive development of younger children. Another approach to instruction—the *apprenticeship*—is also consistent with this idea, as we shall see now.

APPRENTICESHIPS

In an **apprenticeship,** a learner works intensively with an expert to accomplish complex tasks; in doing so, the learner performs activities that he or she could never do independently. The expert provides considerable structure and guidance throughout the process, gradually removing scaffolding and giving the learner more responsibility as competence increases (Rogoff, 1990, 1991). Many cultures use apprenticeships as a way of gradually introducing children to the practices of the adult community—practices that might include such skills as weaving, tailoring, or midwifery (Lave, 1991; Lave & Wenger, 1991; Rogoff, 1990). We also see apprenticeships frequently in music instruction— for instance, in teaching a student how to play a musical instrument (Elliott, 1995; Gardner et al., 1996).

Through an apprenticeship, an expert often learns not only how to perform a task but also how to *think about* a task; such a situation is sometimes called a **cognitive apprenticeship** (Brown et al., 1989; Collins et al., 1989; John-Steiner, 1997; Rogoff, 1990, 1991). An example is the relationship between a university professor and a graduate student (Roth & Bowen, 1995). For instance, as I am writing this third edition of *Human Learning,* I am also teaching a doctoral seminar called Cognition and Instruction. I have assigned my students a gigantic collection of outside readings (at last count, the assigned articles and book chapters stacked up to a pile about two feet high), but as a class we have spent two or three hours over the course of the semester talking about how to read such a large amount of material productively. I have shared such strategies as skimming, reading with particular goals in mind, and relating one theorist's perspectives to another's, and I have given my students a list of focus questions that they should try to answer as they read. The students in my class must also complete a major research project by the end of the semester; I meet with each of them periodically to help them narrow their topic, identify fruitful directions to pursue, organize their thoughts, and consider possible conclusions.

Although apprenticeships can differ widely from one context to another, they typically have some or all of the following features (Collins et al., 1989):

- *Modeling:* The teacher carries out the task, thinking aloud about the process at the same time, while the student observes and listens.
- *Coaching:* As the student performs the task, the teacher gives frequent suggestions, hints, and feedback.

- *Scaffolding:* The teacher provides various forms of support for the student, perhaps by simplifying the task, breaking it down into smaller and more manageable components, or providing less complicated equipment.
- *Increasing complexity and diversity of tasks:* As the student gains greater proficiency, the teacher presents more complex, challenging, and varied tasks to complete.
- *Articulation:* The student explains what he or she is doing and why, allowing the teacher to examine the student's knowledge, reasoning, and problem-solving strategies.
- *Reflection:* The teacher asks the student to compare his or her performance with that of experts, or perhaps with an ideal model of how the task should be done.
- *Exploration:* The teacher encourages the student to frame questions and problems on his or her own and in doing so to expand and refine acquired skills.

Apprenticeships are clearly a labor-intensive approach to instruction; as such, their use in the classroom is not always practical or logistically feasible (De Corte et al., 1996). At the same time, teachers can certainly use elements of an apprenticeship model to help their students develop more complex skills. For example, Scardamalia and Bereiter (1985) have used prompts such as the following to help students think about writing tasks in the same ways that expert writers do:

- "My purpose ..."
- "My main point ..."
- "An example of this ..."
- "The reason I think so ..."
- "To liven this up I'll ..."
- "I'm not being very clear about what I just said so ..."
- "I'm getting off the topic so ..."
- "This isn't very convincing because ..."
- "I can tie this together by ..."

Such prompts provide the same sort of scaffolding that an expert writer might provide, and they help students develop more sophisticated writing strategies (Scardamalia & Bereiter, 1985).

Apprenticeships frequently take place in natural settings—for example, in a studio, workshop, or place of employment—and involve real-life tasks. Many theorists believe that such *authentic activities* are an essential part of effective instruction. In the next section we will look more closely at what such activities entail.

AUTHENTIC ACTIVITIES

Authentic activities are tasks that are identical or similar to those that students will eventually encounter in the outside world (De Corte et al., 1996; Greeno et al., 1996; Hiebert & Fisher, 1992; Lave, 1993; Newmann & Wehlage, 1993). Given what we have learned about learning, we can speculate that such activities are likely to have several benefits. For one thing, when students work in a naturalistic environment, using the physical and social resources (e.g., tools and colleagues) that such an environment offers, students should be able to accomplish more than they might accomplish in relatively artificial and unscaffolded classroom tasks (Greeno et al., 1996). Second, complex authentic tasks can help students make meaningful connections among the various ideas and skills they have learned in the classroom. Finally, because authentic activities resemble real-world tasks and problems, they should help students transfer the things they learn at school to out-of-school contexts (Collins et al., 1989).

Authentic activities can be developed for virtually any area of the school curriculum. For example, teachers might have students

Give an oral presentation.
Write an editorial.
Write a letter to a business
  or government agency.
Participate in a debate.
Find information in the library.
Conduct an experiment.
Graph data.
Construct a chart, model, or map.
Design an electrical circuit.
Create a museum display.
Create and distribute a class
  newsletter.

Converse in a foreign language.
Play in an athletic event.
Conduct field work to study and
  document local flora and fauna.
Complete an art project.
Perform in a concert.
Design a model city.
Make a videotape.
Perform a workplace routine.
Plan a family budget.
Write a computer program.
Develop a home page for the
  Internet.

It may occasionally be possible to assign authentic activities as homework; for example, teachers might ask students to write an editorial, design an electrical circuit, or plan a family budget while working at home in the evening. But many authentic activities may require considerable classroom dialogue, with students asking questions of one another, sharing their ideas, offering explanations of their thinking, and synthesizing their efforts into an integrated whole (Newmann & Wehlage, 1993; Paris & Turner, 1994). For example, creating a school newspaper, designing a model city, debating controversial social or political issues, and conversing in a foreign language may be activities that students can perform only as a group. Furthermore, because authentic activities are typically more complex and more ill defined than traditional classroom tasks, they may require considerable teacher scaffolding (Brophy, 1992a). For obvious reasons, then, many authentic activities can be accomplished more effectively in class than at home, or perhaps through a combination of group work during class and independent work after school hours.

Effectiveness of Authentic Activities

Researchers have only begun to study the effects of authentic activities on students' learning and achievement, but preliminary results are encouraging (Cognition and Technology Group at Vanderbilt, 1993; Gregg & Leinhardt, 1994a; Hiebert & Fisher, 1992). For example, students' writing skills may show greater improvement in both quality and quantity when they practice writing via stories, essays, and letters to real people rather than via short, artificial writing exercises (Hiebert & Fisher, 1992). Likewise, students gain a more complete understanding of how to use and interpret maps effectively when they construct their own maps than when they engage in workbook exercises involving map interpretation (Gregg & Leinhardt, 1994a).

Theorists have suggested that an authentic activity is most likely to be effective when it has characteristics such as the following:

- It requires a fair amount of background knowledge about a particular topic; in other words, students must know the subject matter thoroughly and have learned it in a meaningful fashion.
- It promotes higher-level thinking skills; for example, it may involve synthesizing information, forming and testing hypotheses, solving problems, and drawing conclusions.
- It requires students to seek out information in a variety of contexts and perhaps from a variety of academic disciplines.
- It conveys high expectations for students' performance yet also encourages students to take risks and experiment with new strategies.
- Its final outcome is complex and somewhat unpredictable; there is not necessarily a single "right" response or answer.
  (Newmann & Wehlage, 1993; Paris & Turner, 1994)

We should note, however, that it is not necessarily desirable to fill the entire school day with complex, authentic tasks. For one thing, students can often master basic skills more effectively when they practice them in relative isolation from other activities; for example, when learning to play the violin, they need to master their fingering before they join an orchestra, and when learning to play soccer, they need to practice dribbling and passing before they play in a game (Anderson et al., 1996). Second, some authentic tasks may be too expensive and time-consuming to warrant their use on a regular basis in the classroom (Griffin & Griffin, 1994). It is probably most important that classroom tasks encourage students to engage in such cognitive processes as meaningful learning, organization, and elaboration—processes that promote long-term retention and transfer of classroom subject matter—than that tasks always be authentic in nature (Anderson et al., 1996).

By encouraging students to work and learn together through authentic activities, as well as through such other group-based strategies as class discussions, reciprocal teaching, cooperative learning, and peer tutoring, teachers can ultimately create a *community of learners* in their classrooms. We turn to this concept now.

COMMUNITY OF LEARNERS

Throughout the chapter we have been talking about ways in which students can work cooperatively together to help one another learn. A cooperative classroom has several benefits: It encourages students to clarify and organize their own thoughts sufficiently to express them to someone else, it gives them an opportunity to observe the learning and problem-solving strategies that their classmates use, and it increases their sense of self-efficacy about performing classroom tasks successfully.

An effective teacher typically creates a *sense of community* in the classroom—a sense that teacher and students have shared goals, respect and support one another's efforts, and believe that everyone makes an important contribution to classroom learning (Emmer, Evertson, Clements, & Worsham, 1994; Hom & Battistich, 1995; Kim, Solomon, & Roberts, 1995; Lickona, 1991). Some theorists suggest that one way to create this sense of community is to transform the classroom into a **community of learners** in which teacher and students actively and cooperatively work to help one another learn (A. L. Brown et al., 1993; Brown & Campione, 1990, 1994; Campione et al., 1995; Prawat, 1992; Rogoff, 1994). A classroom that operates as a community of learners is likely to have certain characteristics:

- All students are active participants in classroom activities.
- Discussion and collaboration among two or more students are common occurrences and play a key role in learning.
- Diversity in students' interests and rates of progress are expected and respected.
- Students and teacher coordinate their efforts at helping one another learn; no one has exclusive responsibility for teaching others.
- Everyone is a potential resource for the others; different individuals are likely to serve as resources on different occasions, depending on the topics and tasks at hand.
- The teacher provides some guidance and direction for classroom activities, but students may also contribute to such guidance and direction.
- Constructive questioning and critique of one another's work is commonplace.
- The process of learning is emphasized as much as, and sometimes more than, the finished product.
(Brown & Campione, 1994; Campione et al., 1995; Rogoff, 1994; Rogoff, Matusov, & White, 1996)

Brown and Campione (1994) have described one simple example of how a community of learners might be structured. In this situation, students were divided into five groups to study five different subtopics falling within a general theme; for instance, subtopics for the theme *changing populations* were *extinct, endangered, artificial, assisted,* and *urbanized.* Each group conducted research and prepared teaching materials related to its subtopic. The class then reassembled into five new groups that included at least one representative from each of the previous groups; within these groups, the students taught one another the things they had learned. (Here we see an example of the *jigsaw* technique that I described in the section on cooperative learning.)

Researchers have not yet systematically compared the academic achievement of communities of learners with the achievement of more traditional classes. Case studies indicate that classes structured as communities of learners have some positive effects, however. For one thing, these classes appear to promote higher-level thinking processes for extended periods of time (Brown & Campione, 1994). They are also highly motivating for students; for instance, students often insist on going to school even when they are ill, and they are disappointed when summer vacation begins (Rogoff, 1994). Communities of learners may be especially useful as a way of encouraging students with diverse backgrounds, cultural perspectives, and specialized talents to make unique and valued contributions to the classroom learning environment (e.g., Garcia, 1994).

At the same time, communities of learners have a couple of potential weaknesses (Brown & Campione, 1994). For one thing, what students learn will inevitably be limited to the knowledge that they themselves acquire and share with one another. Second, students may occasionally pass on their own misconceptions to their classmates. Obviously, then, teachers who structure their classrooms as communities of learners must carefully monitor student interactions to make sure that instructional objectives are being achieved and that students ultimately acquire accurate understandings of the subject matter they are studying.

ADVANTAGES OF INTERACTIVE APPROACHES

At this point, it might be useful to reiterate some of the advantages of interactive instructional strategies in general:

- They provide a means through which two or more students work cooperatively together to make sense of their world; in doing so, students may arrive at more complete understandings than any single student could develop working alone. (Here we see the influence of both social constructivist and contextual views of learning.)
- They encourage students to elaborate on the material they are studying—for example, to analyze, compare, synthesize, evaluate, and apply it.
- They enable individuals with greater proficiency to model more sophisticated behaviors and cognitive processes for individuals with less proficiency.
- When they involve discussion or debate of controversial subject matter, they may promote more sophisticated epistemological beliefs, including the beliefs that acquiring "knowledge" involves developing an integrated set of ideas about a topic and that such knowledge is likely to evolve gradually over a lengthy period of time.
- They are often highly motivating for students.

The last advantage in my list—motivation—is certainly not limited to interactive models of instruction. In the final two chapters of the book, we will look at the nature of motivation more closely; we will also consider many teaching strategies that can keep students regularly engaged in, and perhaps even excited about, studying classroom subject matter.

SUMMARY

Three interactive approaches to instruction—class discussions, reciprocal teaching, and cooperative learning—involve students at the same general level of achievement working together as a group to study classroom subject matter. In *class discussions,* students must clarify and organize their ideas and opinions sufficiently to express them to others, and they may acquire a more accurate and complete understanding of a topic after hearing what their classmates have to say. Class discussions are often more effective when they address complex or controversial issues about which students have some prior knowledge and when they are structured in such a way that all students actively participate.

Reciprocal teaching is an approach to instruction whereby students learn to ask one another certain kinds of questions about textual material they are reading or (in the case of students in the early elementary grades) their teacher is reading to them. In the process, students develop such metacognitive strategies as clarifying, making predictions about, and summarizing the material they are studying.

In *cooperative learning,* students work in small groups to accomplish specific goals. Successful cooperative learning groups have several key features: (1) students must have clear guidelines for appropriate behavior, (2) successful learning depends on students' working cooperatively and supporting one another's efforts, (3) students are individually accountable for what they have learned, and (4) students are rewarded for the overall success of their group.

In two additional interactive approaches to instruction—peer tutoring and apprenticeships—a more capable student works one-on-one with a less capable student to promote learning. *Peer tutoring* involves two students at either the same grade level or different grade levels. Tutors and tutees typically both benefit from tutoring sessions; this is especially true when tutors have a good command of the subject matter and use sound instructional techniques or when tutoring sessions are structured to promote effective instruction.

In an *apprenticeship,* a learner works intensively with an expert to accomplish a complex task that the learner could never do on his or her own. In some situations (cognitive apprenticeships), the expert shares not only ways to perform the task but also ways of thinking about the task. The expert guides the learner's behavior by using such strategies as modeling, coaching, and scaffolding. As the learner develops greater proficiency, more complex, challenging, and varied tasks are introduced.

Authentic activities are tasks similar to those that students may eventually encounter in the outside world. They are typically complex in nature, and they may involve two or more students working together, often over an extended period of time. From a theoretical standpoint, authentic activities are likely to promote meaningful learning and transfer of classroom subject matter.

A *community of learners* is a classroom in which teacher and students actively and cooperatively work to help one another learn; it often incorporates other interactive approaches such as class discussions and cooperative learning. Although the teacher provides some guidance and direction for classroom activities, students assume much of the responsibility for facilitating one another's learning.

Motivation and Affect

Over the years, I have learned how to do a great many things. For example, I have learned how to teach and write about psychology. I have learned how to find my favorite junk food in the supermarket and my favorite television game show in *TV Guide*. I have learned how to control my tongue and temper in a university committee meeting. I have learned how to mow the lawn, file a tax return, cook lima beans, clean the garage, and pick up after slovenly children.

Yet you don't see me doing all of these things on a regular basis. I engage in some activities (e.g., writing about psychology, eating junk food, and watching television game shows) because I like doing them. I engage in others (e.g., behaving myself at committee meetings, filing tax returns, and mowing the lawn) not because I enjoy them but because they bring me things I *do* enjoy, such as productive relationships with my university colleagues, IRS refunds, or a well-kept backyard. But there are some things that I never do because they aren't fun and they reap me few if any rewards. For example, you won't find me cooking lima beans (yuck), cleaning the garage (who cares if it's clean?), or picking up children's messy bedrooms (a never-ending battle).

Once we have learned how to do something, the extent to which we continue to do it is a function of **motivation**—an internal state that arouses us to action, pushes us in particular directions, and keeps us engaged in certain activities. Learning and motivation are equally essential for performance: The former enables us to acquire new knowledge and skills, and the latter provides the impetus for demonstrating the things we have learned.

People are almost always motivated in one way or another. For example, Lee and Anderson (1991) found that students in a sixth-grade classroom had a variety of motives. Some students clearly wanted to learn the subject matter being presented in class. Others were more interested in getting good grades, outperforming their classmates, pleasing their teacher and parents, or simply completing assignments as quickly and painlessly as possible.

We have touched on human motivation in previous chapters—for example, within the context of reinforcement in Chapter 4 and in our discussion of modeling in Chapter 7. In this chapter we begin to look at the topic in greater depth. We will identify the specific ways in which motivation influences behavior, cognition, and learning. We will make a distinction between extrinsic and intrinsic motivation, finding that each influences learning and performance somewhat differently. We will examine several theoretical perspectives of motivation, including drive and incentive theories, Abraham Maslow's hierarchy of needs, self-worth theory, individual differences in motives, and the contemporary cognitive viewpoint. We will consider the role of *affect* (emotional state) in learning and behavior, with particular attention to anxiety. Finally, we will identify several things teachers can do to motivate their students in appropriate and productive directions. In the following chapter, we will return to the cognitive perspective once again as we see how motivation and cognition are very much intertwined.

GENERAL EFFECTS OF MOTIVATION

In general, more motivated people achieve at higher levels (Walberg & Uguroglu, 1980). Motivation appears to affect learning and performance in at least four ways:

• *It increases an individual's energy and activity level* (Maehr, 1984; Pintrich et al., 1993; Vernon, 1969). It influences the extent to which an individual is likely to engage in a certain activity intensively and vigorously or half-heartedly and lackadaisically.

• *It directs an individual toward certain goals* (Csikszentmihalyi & Nakamura, 1989; Dweck & Elliott, 1983; Eccles & Wigfield, 1985; Maehr, 1984; Pintrich et al., 1993). Motivation affects the choices people make and the consequences they find reinforcing.

We should note here that when people exert effort toward some goals, they often must direct it away from others. For example, as a freshman at a small high school, my son Jeff wanted to enroll in both French I and Musical Theater, but the two classes were offered at the same time, so he could enroll in only one of them. In a similar way, a student may sometimes have to choose between pleasing a parent who values academic success versus pleasing a friend who thinks schoolwork is for nerds (Dodge, Asher, & Parkhurst, 1989).

• *It promotes initiation of certain activities and persistence in those activities* (Eccles & Wigfield, 1985; Maehr, 1984; Pintrich et al., 1993; Stipek, 1993). Motivation increases the likelihood that people will begin something on their own initiative, persist in the face of difficulty, and resume a task after a temporary interruption.

Educators have long recognized that **time on task** is an important factor affecting school learning and achievement (e.g., Davis & Thomas, 1989). The more time students spend engaged in a particular learning activity, the more academically successful they will be. Although time on task is partly determined by how teachers plan and schedule the classroom curriculum—that is, by how much time they devote to different topics—it is also determined to some extent by students' motivation to study and persist with those topics, both in and out of school.

• *It affects the learning strategies and cognitive processes an individual employs* (e.g., Dweck & Elliott, 1983; Eccles & Wigfield, 1985). Motivation increases the likelihood that people will pay attention to something, study and practice it, and try to learn it in a meaningful fashion. It also increases the likelihood that they will seek help when they encounter difficulty.

Here we should note that time on task is, in and of itself, insufficient for successful learning. Certain cognitive processes—paying attention, learning meaningfully, elaborating, monitoring comprehension, identifying inconsistencies between new information and prior knowledge, and so on—must occur as people engage in a particular learning activity. In other words, learners must be *thinking about* what they are seeing, hearing, and doing (Carroll, 1989; Lee, 1991; Lee & Anderson, 1993; Pintrich et al., 1993; Tobin, 1986; Wittrock, 1986). Such **cognitive engagement** is one of the benefits of a high level of motivation.

Not all forms of motivation have exactly the same effect on human learning and performance. In fact, extrinsic motivation and intrinsic motivation yield somewhat different results, as we shall see now.

EXTRINSIC VERSUS INTRINSIC MOTIVATION

At the beginning of the chapter, I mentioned that I engage in some activities because they bring about desirable consequences (i.e., they are extrinsically reinforced), whereas I engage in others simply because they are intrinsically enjoyable. Just as operant conditioning theorists distinguish between extrinsic and intrinsic reinforcement, motivation theorists distinguish between extrinsic and intrinsic motivation.

Extrinsic motivation exists when the source of motivation lies outside of the individual and the task being performed. For example, I file an income tax return every year partly because I usually get a refund when I do so and partly because I will be fined if I *don't* file. I go to university committee meetings because university service is part of my job description and I am quite dependent on my monthly paycheck. I give my house a thorough cleaning when preparing to host a party, because I would hate for my friends to discover I'm a slob. In contrast, **intrinsic motivation** exists when the source of motivation lies within the individual and task: The individual finds the task enjoyable or worthwhile in and of itself. For example, I frequently read books and articles about human learning because they continue to shed new light on a topic that is, to me, utterly fascinating. I watch television game shows because I enjoy playing along as a home viewer. I eat junk food because it tastes good.

Extrinsic motivation can certainly promote successful learning and productive behavior, as evidenced by the effectiveness of behavior modification programs (see Chapter 5). Extrinsic reinforcement for engaging in a particular activity increases an individual's time on task, and performance is likely to improve as a result (Emmer & Evertson, 1981). Extrinsic motivation in the classroom has its drawbacks, however: Extrinsically motivated students are likely to exert only the minimal behavioral and cognitive effort they need to execute a task successfully (occasionally this may mean copying someone else's work), and they may stop an activity as soon as reinforcement disappears (Flink, Boggiano, Main, Barrett, & Katz, 1992; Lee, 1991).

Intrinsic motivation has numerous advantages over extrinsic motivation. For any particular task, intrinsically motivated learners are more likely to

- Pursue the task on their own initiative, without having to be prodded or cajoled.
- Be cognitively engaged in the task (e.g., by keeping attention focused on it).
- Undertake more challenging aspects of the task.
- Learn information in a meaningful rather than rote fashion.
- Undergo conceptual change when such change is warranted.
- Show creativity in performance.
- Persist in the face of failure.
- Experience pleasure, sometimes even exhilaration, in what they are doing.
- Regularly evaluate their own progress, often using their own criteria.
- Seek out additional opportunities to pursue the task.
- Achieve at high levels.
  (Brophy, 1986; Csikszentmihalyi, 1990, 1996; Csikszentmihalyi & Nakamura, 1989; Flink et al., 1992; Gottfried, 1990; Harter, 1981a; Hennessey, 1995; Hennessey & Amabile, 1987; Lee, 1991; Lee & Anderson, 1991; Maehr, 1984; Pintrich et al., 1993; Russ, 1993; Spaulding, 1992; Stipek, 1993)

Csikszentmihalyi (1990, 1996; Csikszentmihalyi & Nakamura, 1989) has used the term **flow** to describe an intense form of intrinsic motivation, characterizing it as a state of complete absorption, focus, and concentration in a challenging activity, to the point that the individual loses track of time and completely ignores other tasks.

Obviously, intrinsic motivation is the optimal state of affairs in the classroom. Unfortunately, although many children first enter school with a high degree of intrinsic motivation to learn classroom subject matter, they gradually lose this motivation as they move through the grade levels (Csikszentmihalyi & Nakamura, 1989; Eccles & Midgley, 1989; Harter, 1992). At the end of the chapter, we will identify several ways in which teachers can help students become more intrinsically motivated to learn classroom material. And in Chapter 18 we will discover the cognitive factors likely to influence students' intrinsic motivation to achieve academic success.

In the pages that follow, we will explore varying perspectives of both extrinsic and intrinsic motivation that psychologists have proposed over the years. In particular, we will consider drives and incentives, Maslow's hierarchy of needs, self-worth theory, individual differences in motivation, and the contemporary cognitive viewpoint.

DRIVES AND INCENTIVES

Drive theory (Freud, 1949; Hull, 1943, 1951, 1952; Woodworth, 1918) is based on the notion that people and other animals (*organisms*) try to maintain physiological homeostasis; in other words, they try to keep their bodies at an optimal state of functioning. A **drive** is an internal state of need within an organism: Something necessary for optimal functioning (e.g., food, water, warmth, or rest) is missing. When a drive exists, the organism behaves in ways that reduce the need and bring the body back into balance. For example, a hungry person eats, a thirsty person drinks, a cold person seeks out a source of heat, and a tired person goes to bed. If a response that reduces the need is not immediately possible, the organism shows a general increase in activity—activity that may eventually lead to an encounter with a need-reducing stimulus.

From the perspective of drive theory, a reinforcer is effective to the extent that it reduces a need state, thereby simultaneously reducing drive. For example, a drink of water is reinforcing only if an organism is thirsty, and a source of heat is reinforcing only if an organism is cold. Behaviors that reduce a need state—behaviors that are reinforced—are likely to be repeated when the same need emerges at some later point in time.

Probably the most widely cited version of drive theory is that of Clark Hull (1943, 1951, 1952), a perspective I described briefly in Chapter 2. In 1943 Hull proposed that drive was due to physiological needs such as hunger and thirst. All of these needs contributed to the general drive state of the organism; drive was not specific to a particular need. Hull further proposed that the strength and intensity of a behavior is a function of both *habit strength* (i.e., the degree to which associations between a particular stimulus and response have been learned) and drive:

$$\text{Strength of behavior} = \text{Habit} \times \text{Drive}$$

In such a multiplicative relationship, both habit (prior learning) and drive must be present; if either is zero, the strength of the behavior—the likelihood that it will occur—is also zero.

Hull based his notion of *habit times drive* on experiments conducted by two of his students (Perin, 1942; Williams, 1938). In these experiments, rats were placed in Skinner boxes and trained to press a bar for a food reinforcer. Different groups of rats received varying amounts of training, with a greater number of reinforced responses presumably leading to greater habit strength. Later, after going without food for either 3 hours (low drive) or 22 hours (high drive), the rats were once again placed in Skinner boxes, and their frequency of bar pressing was recorded under nonreinforcement (extinction) conditions. The hungrier rats pressed the bar many more times than the less hungry rats; similarly, rats who had received more training pressed the bar more often than those who had undergone little training. Rats with little drive (three hours of food deprivation) and low habit strength (five training trials) pressed the bar, on the average, only once.

In 1951 Hull revised his thinking in two significant ways. First of all, he observed that some behaviors serve no apparent biological purpose. He therefore proposed that some drives are **acquired drives**: They develop when previously neutral stimuli are associating with drive-reducing stimuli such as food. (To repeat the example I presented in Chapter 2, an individual might become "driven" by a need for approval if approval has previously been associated with candy.) Reinforcement therefore became strictly a function of drive reduction rather than being due to the reduction of specific physiological needs.

At the same time, Hull also took into account research by Crespi (1942) and others indicating that reinforcers may affect performance rather than learning. (We encountered Crespi's experiment in our discussion of reinforcement in Chapter 4. To refresh your memory, rats running down a runway for food began to run faster when the amount of reinforcement was increased; they began to run more slowly when the amount of reinforcement was decreased.) Accordingly, Hull introduced the concept of *incentive* into his theory, acknowledging that behaviors are influenced by the characteristics of a goal object—for example, by the amount of food at the end of a runway. Incentive became a third essential ingredient for a behavior to occur, as follows:

$$\text{Strength of behavior} = \text{Habit} \times \text{Drive} \times \text{Incentive}$$

The absence of any of the three factors—habit strength, drive, or incentive—meant that the behavior was not emitted.

Other theorists expanded on Hull's notion that the characteristics of goal objects (incentives) are motivating forces in behavior (Mowrer, 1960; Overmier & Lawry, 1979; Spence, 1956). From their perspective, **incentive motivation** serves as a mediator (M) between stimuli and responses, affecting which stimuli are responded to and which are not. Symbolically, we could describe the relationship this way:

$$S \rightarrow M_{\text{incentive}} \rightarrow R$$

For example, I find a bag of Cheetos quite enticing after several hours of food-free book writing (thus leading to a reach-in-and-grab-a-handful response); however, the same bag provokes no response whatsoever right after a Thanksgiving dinner, when I have stuffed myself with turkey, mashed potatoes, and pumpkin pie.

Incentives undoubtedly play a role in human motivation. Just as Crespi's rats ran faster when they knew that mass quantities of food lay waiting at the end of the runway, so, too, do we humans apparently work harder when incentives are more attractive (Klinger, 1975, 1977). When our progress toward particular goals is temporarily stymied, we often intensify our efforts (Klinger, 1975). And when our progress is permanently blocked, we are likely to respond with regression (i.e., immature behavior) or aggression (Barker, Dembo, & Lewin, 1941; Dollard, Doob, Miller, Mowrer, & Sears, 1939; Hinton, 1968; Johnson, 1972).

Although incentives remain in vogue as a probable source of motivation, theorists have largely left drive reduction theory by the wayside (Bolles, 1975; Graham & Weiner, 1996). For one thing, learning sometimes occurs in the absence of any apparent drive reduction (Sheffield & Roby, 1950; Sheffield, Roby, & Campbell, 1954; Sheffield, Wulff, & Backer, 1951). For example, male rats will make responses that allow them to mount receptive female rats, even though they are pulled away from the females before they can consummate their affectionate relationship and reduce their sexual drive (Sheffield et al., 1951). And a great deal of human behavior seems to be aimed at accomplishing long-term goals rather than satisfying short-term needs (Pintrich & Schunk, 1996). Furthermore, organisms sometimes behave in ways that actually *increase* their drive states (Olds & Milner, 1954; Rachlin, 1991; Sheffield, 1966a, 1966b). For example, when rats have electrodes implanted in particular areas of their brains (called "pleasure centers"), they eagerly press a bar to obtain electrical stimulation of those areas, and they continue in their bar-pressing until they're completely exhausted (Olds & Milner, 1954). In much the same way, we humans voluntarily increase our drive states by going to scary movies, reading suspense novels, and riding roller coasters; some of us are even **sensation seekers** who put ourselves in risky or dangerous situations on a regular basis for the physiological thrills that such situations yield (e.g., Snow et al., 1996).

As a result of such observations, drive theory plays little part in contemporary views of motivation. Physiological needs figure prominently in Maslow's theory of motivation, however, as we shall see now.

MASLOW'S HIERARCHY OF NEEDS

Another early perspective of motivation was that of Abraham Maslow (1959, 1973a, 1973b, 1987). Maslow's theory is a critical aspect of **humanism,** a movement in psychology that gained prominence in the 1960s and 1970s. Humanism has its roots in counseling psychology and focuses its attention on how individuals acquire emotions, attitudes, values, and interpersonal skills. Humanist perspectives tend to be grounded more in philosophy than in research, but they provide useful insights into human motivation nevertheless.

In an attempt to pull together his informal observations of human behavior, Maslow proposed that people have five different sets of needs:

1. **Physiological needs:** People are motivated to satisfy needs related to their immediate physical survival—needs for food, water, oxygen, warmth, exercise, rest, sex, and so on. For example, if you've been sitting still in class for a long time, you may find yourself getting restless and fidgety, and if you're hungry, you may think more about your growling stomach than about a professor's lecture. Maslow's physiological needs are essentially the same as those of Hull's early drive theory.

2. **Safety needs:** People have a need to feel safe and secure in their environment. Although they may enjoy an occasional surprise, generally speaking they prefer structure and order in their lives. For example, most students like to know what things are expected of them and prefer classroom routines that are somewhat predictable.

3. **Love and belongingness needs:** People seek affectionate relationships with others and like to feel that they "belong" and are accepted as part of a group. For example, a fourth grader may place great importance on having a best friend. And

many adolescents take great pains to fit in with the cool crowd—for example, by wearing a certain hairstyle or buying clothes with a certain brand name placed conspicuously upon them.

4. **Esteem needs:** People need to feel good about themselves (**need for self-esteem**) and to believe that others also feel positively about them (**need for esteem from others**). To develop positive self-esteem, individuals strive for achievement and mastery of their environment. To attain the esteem and respect of others, they behave in ways that gain them recognition, appreciation, and prestige. For example, a second grader can partially satisfy the need for self-esteem by reading a book "all by myself" or by achieving a special merit badge in Cub Scouts or Campfire Girls. A high school student may try to satisfy the need for esteem from others by running for student council treasurer or becoming a star athlete. When their esteem needs are satisfied, people are self-confident and have a sense of self-worth; when these needs go unmet, people feel weak and inferior.

5. **Need for self-actualization:** People have a need to **self-actualize**—to develop and become all they are capable of becoming (also see Rogers, 1951, 1961). Individuals striving toward self-actualization seek out new activities as a way of expanding their horizons and want to learn simply for the sake of learning. For example, people seeking self-actualization might be driven by their own curiosity to learn everything they can about a particular topic, or they might pursue an active interest in ballet both as a means of developing muscle tone and as an outlet for creative self-expression.

Maslow proposed that the five sets of needs form a hierarchy, as illustrated in Figure 17-1. When two or more of these needs are unmet, people tend to satisfy them in a particular sequence. They begin with the lowest needs in the hierarchy, satisfying physiological needs first, safety needs next, and so on. They attempt to fulfill higher needs only when lower needs have been at least partially met.

Figure 17–1
Maslow's hierarchy of needs.

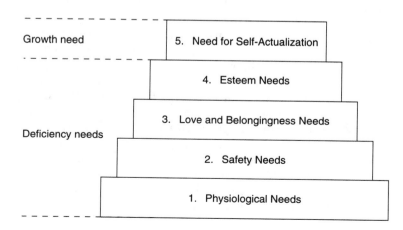

Growth need

5. Need for Self-Actualization

4. Esteem Needs

3. Love and Belongingness Needs

Deficiency needs

2. Safety Needs

1. Physiological Needs

To illustrate Maslow's hierarchy, a boy with a need for exercise (a physiological need) may become excessively restless in class even though he is scolded by his teacher for his hyperactivity (thereby *not* satisfying his need for esteem from others). A girl with an unfulfilled need for love and belonging may choose not to enroll in intermediate algebra—a class that would satisfy her desire to learn more math—if the peers whose friendships she most values tell her the class is only for nerds and various other uncool individuals. I once knew a boy living in a Philadelphia ghetto who had a strong interest in learning yet often stayed home from school to avoid the violent gangs that hung out on the local street corner. This boy's need for safety took precedence over any higher needs that he might have had.

According to Maslow, the first four needs on the hierarchy—physiological, safety, love and belonging, and esteem needs—result from things that a person *lacks*; hence, Maslow called them **deficiency needs.** Deficiency needs can be met only by external sources—by people and events in one's environment. Furthermore, once these needs are fulfilled, there is no reason to satisfy them further. Self-actualization, on the other hand, is a **growth need:** Rather than addressing a deficiency in a person's life, it serves to enhance the person's growth and development and thus is rarely satisfied completely. Self-actualizing activities tend to be intrinsically motivated: People engage in them because doing so gives them pleasure and satisfies their desire to know and grow.

Needs that are satisfied most of the time have little effect on behavior. For example, many people in our society routinely satisfy their physiological and safety needs. The needs for love and esteem are more likely to go unfulfilled; hence, people may direct much of their effort toward gaining the acceptance and respect of others and toward developing their own sense of competence and self-worth. But people are likely to strive for self-actualization—a need that is almost never completely satisfied—only when all four deficiency needs are at least partially met.

According to Maslow, self-actualized individuals have a number of noteworthy characteristics. For example, they are independent, spontaneous, creative, and sympathetic to the plights of others. They perceive themselves, other people, and the world in general in an objective, realistic light, and they are quite comfortable with who they are. They typically have a mission in life—an important problem that they are concerned about solving. Maslow suggested that few people—probably less than 1% of the population—become fully self-actualized, and then only in the later years of life.

Despite its intuitive appeal, Maslow's hierarchy has been criticized on several counts. For one thing, little hard evidence exists to substantiate the hierarchical nature of human motivation. Maslow derived his theory from his informal, subjective observations of presumably "self-actualized" personal friends and from published descriptions of such historical figures as Thomas Jefferson and Abraham Lincoln; it would be almost impossible for other investigators to confirm that these individuals had the characteristics Maslow identified. Furthermore, self-actualization is so rare that the hierarchy may not provide an accurate description of people in general (Petri, 1991).

At the same time, aspects of Maslow's theory clearly have some merit. It makes intuitive sense, for instance, that people will worry about their physiological well-being and personal safety before they aim to address more social needs. And Maslow's notion of *esteem needs* is evident in contemporary self-worth theory—a perspective to which we turn now.

SELF-WORTH THEORY

Maslow has hardly been the only one to suggest that people have a need for esteem. In 1959 Robert White proposed that people (and other animals as well) have an intrinsic need to feel *competent*—to believe that they can deal effectively with their environment or, as social learning theorists would put it, to have a sense of self-efficacy. To achieve a sense of competence, young children spend a great deal of time engaged in exploring and attempting to master the world. As an illustration, let's look once again at an example I presented in Chapter 8, in which Jean Piaget's son Laurent tried to reach a piece of bread that was beyond his reach:

> Laurent is seated before a table and I place a bread crust in front of him, out of reach. Also, to the right of the child I place a stick about 25 cm. long. At first Laurent tries to grasp the bread without paying attention to the instrument, and then he gives up. I then put the stick between him and the bread. . . . Laurent again looks at the bread, without moving, looks very briefly at the stick, then suddenly grasps it and directs it toward the bread. But he grasped it toward the middle and not at one of its ends so that it is too short to attain the objective. Laurent then puts it down and resumes stretching out his hand toward the bread. Then, without spending much time on this movement, he takes up the stick again, this time at one of its ends . . . and draws the bread to him. (Piaget, 1952, p. 335)

According to White, the need for competence has biological significance: It pushes people to develop ways of dealing more effectively with environmental conditions and thus increases their chances of survival.

More recently, Martin Covington (1992) has proposed that *protecting* one's sense of competence—something he refers to as **self-worth**—is one of people's highest priorities. Obviously, achieving success on a regular basis is one way of maintaining, perhaps even enhancing, this self-worth. But consistent success isn't always possible, especially when people face challenging tasks. In such instances, people may protect their sense of self-worth by making excuses that seemingly justify their poor performance, or they may refuse to engage in the tasks at all (Covington, 1992). They may also do things that actually *undermine* their chances of success—a phenomenon known as **self-handicapping.** Self-handicapping takes a variety of forms, including:

- *Setting unattainably high goals:* Working toward goals that even the most able individuals couldn't achieve
- *Procrastinating:* Putting a task off until success is virtually impossible
- *Reducing effort:* Putting forth an obviously insufficient amount of effort to succeed
- *Using alcohol or drugs:* Taking substances that will inevitably reduce performance (Covington, 1992; Ford, 1996; Jones & Berglas, 1978; Riggs, 1992)

It might seem paradoxical that people who want to be successful would engage in such behaviors. But if people believe they are unlikely to succeed at a particular task, they increase their chances of *justifying* their lack of success (and therefore they maintain self-worth) by acknowledging that, under the circumstances, success wasn't very likely to begin with (Covington, 1992; Jones & Berglas, 1978; Riggs, 1992). Curiously, people are more likely to perform at their best, and less likely to display self-handicapping behaviors, when their chances of success are slim; in such situations, failure does not indicate low ability and so does not threaten their sense of self-worth (Covington, 1992).

Ideally, students should probably have a reasonably accurate sense of what they can and cannot accomplish. Students who underestimate their abilities will set unnecessarily low goals for themselves and give up easily in the face of temporary failure. Those who overestimate their abilities (perhaps because they have been lavished with praise by parents or teachers, or perhaps because school assignments have been consistently easy and nonchallenging) may set themselves up for failure by forming unrealistically high expectations for themselves or by not exerting a sufficient amount of effort to succeed (Paris & Cunningham, 1996; Phillips & Zimmerman, 1990; Pintrich & Schunk, 1996; Stevenson, Chen, & Uttal, 1990).

INDIVIDUAL DIFFERENCES IN MOTIVATION

Up to this point, we have been talking about forms of motivation that might characterize all of us at one time or another. Some theorists have proposed, however, that people differ with respect to the kinds of motivation they display. Much of their research has focused on three motives in particular: the need for affiliation, the need for approval, and the need for achievement.

Need for Affiliation

The **need for affiliation** is the degree to which a person wants and needs friendly relationships with others (Boyatzis, 1973; Connell & Wellborn, 1991; Ford & Nichols, 1991; Hill, 1987; McClelland, 1984). For example, as high school students, my oldest two children couldn't stand the thought of being home "alone" (i.e., with their parents and siblings) on a Friday or Saturday night and so always found something to do with their friends. When they *were* home on a weeknight, they spent long hours talking to friends on the telephone, to the point where their schoolwork sometimes didn't get done. In contrast, my youngest child, Jeff, has always been able to work or play alone quite happily for hours at a time.

People with a high need for affiliation have a number of characteristics in common. For example, they tend to become nervous when other individuals observe their performance (Boyatzis, 1973). They spend considerable time communicating with others, and their attitudes and opinions are easily influenced by those around them (Boyatzis, 1973). They are more interested in interpersonal relationships than in task accomplishment; hence, when choosing a work partner, they are apt to select an incompetent friend over a competent person they don't particularly care for (Boyatzis, 1973; French, 1956; Vernon, 1969). Children with a high need for affiliation tend to have lower grade point averages than their equal-ability peers (Ringness, 1967), and they earn better classroom grades when they have warm, nurturing teachers (McKeachie, 1961; McKeachie, Lin, Milholland, & Isaacson, 1966).

Many children and adolescents appear to have high affiliation needs. A high priority during the school day is socializing with friends, and they may spend only the minimum energy and effort necessary to finish their classwork (Doyle, 1986a). Unfortunately, they may find that it is impossible to please everyone simultaneously; for example, maintaining friendships with classmates who place little value on academics may occur at the expense of not pleasing parents and teachers who look for high classroom performance.

Need for Approval

In addition to having a high need for affiliation, some people have a strong desire to "look good" to others; in other words, they have a high **need for approval** (Boyatzis, 1973; Crowne & Marlowe, 1964; Urdan & Maehr, 1995). For example, one student may continually seek teacher recognition for even the smallest accomplishments in the classroom. Another may do everything possible to appear cool in front of peers.

Many elementary school students have a strong desire to attain the approval of their teacher; at the secondary level, students are more likely to seek the approval of their classmates (Juvonen & Weiner, 1993; Urdan & Maehr, 1995). Students with a high need for approval are often those with low self-esteem (Crowne & Marlowe, 1964). They may go out of their way to behave in ways they think will please others, often compromising any standards that they themselves may have regarding appropriate behavior (Crowne & Marlowe, 1964). But such efforts are often counterproductive: Perhaps because they are trying *too* hard to be liked, students with a high need for approval tend to be relatively unpopular with their peers (Boyatzis, 1973; Crowne & Marlowe, 1964).

Need for Achievement

The **need for achievement,** sometimes called **achievement motivation,** is the need for excellence for its own sake, without regard for any external rewards that one's accomplishments might bring (Atkinson, 1957, 1964; Atkinson & Feather, 1966; McClelland, Atkinson, Clark, & Lowell, 1953; Vernon, 1969; Veroff, McClelland, & Ruhland, 1975). For example, a person with a high need for achievement might work diligently to maintain a 4.0 grade point average, practice long hours to become a professional basketball player, or play Monopoly with a vengeance.

People with a high need for achievement are realistic about the tasks they can accomplish, and they persist at tasks that are challenging yet achievable (Vernon, 1969; Veroff et al., 1975). They rarely rest on their laurels; instead, they set increasingly higher standards for excellence as their current standards are met (Veroff et al., 1975). And they are willing and able to delay gratification: They put off small, immediate rewards for the larger rewards that their long-term efforts are likely to bring (French, 1955; Vernon, 1969; Veroff et al., 1975).

An early and widely cited theory of achievement motivation is that of John Atkinson and his associates (Atkinson, 1957, 1964; Atkinson & Birch, 1978; Atkinson & Feather, 1966; Atkinson & Raynor, 1978). These theorists proposed that the tendency to strive for achievement is a function of two related needs: the **motive for success,** or M_s (the desire to do well and accomplish goals), and the **motive to avoid failure,** or M_{af} (anxiety about failing to accomplish goals and the resulting inhibition of activities that are likely to result in failure). For many people, one of these needs is stronger than the other, and achievement behavior depends on which need predominates.

Individuals with a stronger motive for success tend to seek and tackle moderately difficult tasks—those that are challenging yet can feasibly be accomplished. Because these individuals have a relatively low motive to avoid failure, they don't worry about the mistakes they may make or the stumbling blocks they may encounter. Furthermore, they recognize that success on difficult tasks is more noteworthy than success on easy tasks.

In contrast, individuals with a stronger motive to avoid failure typically forego such risks in favor of a sure thing. They steer clear of the moderately difficult tasks that their high M_s counterparts select. Instead, they often choose tasks they can almost certainly accomplish. Even though their success on such tasks may be meaningless, they are nevertheless able to avoid the failure they fear. Curiously, though, high M_{af} individuals sometimes choose extremely difficult tasks—those at which they cannot possibly succeed. When they fail at such tasks, they have a built-in explanation—after all, the task was impossible—and so the failure is easily rationalized. (This tendency to choose very difficult tasks should remind you of the self-handicapping phenomenon I described earlier.)

Atkinson and Litwin (1960) demonstrated the hypothesized effects of M_s and M_{af} in a concrete fashion. Their experiment involved a ring toss game—throwing rings to land around an upright peg. Male undergraduate students, some of whom had been identified as having a higher M_s and others as having a higher M_{af}, were told that they could stand wherever they wished, within a 15-foot range, as they attempted to throw 10 rings, 1 at a time, around the peg. The great majority of the high M_s students opted to stand about 8 to 12 feet away from the peg (thus taking on a moderate challenge). Of the high M_{af} students, only half stood in the 8- to 12-foot range; the other half stood either within 7 feet of the peg (thus making the task an easy one) or at least 13 feet away from it (thus making it extremely difficult). Isaacson (1964) found the same pattern in the course selections of college students: Those with a higher M_s tended to choose classes of moderate difficulty, whereas those with a higher M_{af} chose either very easy or very difficult classes.

Researchers have noted that the need for achievement does not necessarily remain constant throughout a person's lifetime. For example, it may decrease as children progress through the school grades and may be especially low when they make the often anxiety-arousing transition from elementary school to junior high school (Eccles & Midgley, 1989; Harter, 1981b). And children's very conception of what achievement *is* changes as they develop: As they progress through the elementary school years, they increasingly define success as doing better than their peers rather than as achieving a particular goal per se (Feld, Ruhland, & Gold, 1979; Ruble, 1980).

In its earliest conceptualization, the need for achievement was thought to be a general characteristic that people exhibit consistently in a variety of tasks across many domains. More recently, however, theorists have proposed that this need may instead be somewhat specific to particular tasks and occasions (Dweck & Elliott, 1983; Eccles & Wigfield, 1985; Jackson, Ahmed, & Heapy, 1976; Paris & Turner, 1994; Ruble, 1980; Stipek, 1996; Weinstein, 1969; Wigfield, 1997). As one simple example, research indicates that most males and females have greater achievement motivation in arenas that are stereotypically appropriate for their gender (Berk, 1989; Lueptow, 1984; Shaffer, 1988; Stein, 1971; Tobin & Fox, 1980). Theorists are also beginning to explain people's need for achievement in terms of specific cognitive factors that influence the choices they make and the tasks they pursue. In the next section we will look briefly at what the contemporary cognitive perspective of motivation encompasses.

THE CONTEMPORARY COGNITIVE PERSPECTIVE OF MOTIVATION

Within the past four decades, theorists have radically changed their approach to the study of human motivation (Dweck, 1986; Graham & Weiner, 1996). Talk of physiological needs and drives has largely gone by the wayside. Concrete, external reinforcers play less of a role in conceptions of human learning (e.g., consider the declining popularity of the operant conditioning perspective in recent years). And interest in global needs that may vary from one individual to another—needs for achievement, affiliation, and the like—is diminishing.

Most contemporary theorists describe human motivation as being a function of human cognition (e.g., see Dweck, 1986; Dweck & Elliott, 1983; Graham & Weiner, 1996; Voss & Schauble, 1992). For example, people set specific *goals* toward which they strive. They form *expectations* regarding the likelihood of success in different activities. They construct *interpretations* (in Chapter 18 we will use the term *attributions*) of why certain consequences come their way, and they make *predictions* about the future consequences of their behavior. As we noted at the beginning of the chapter, motivation affects cognition as well—for example, by increasing attention and cognitive engagement and by promoting effective learning strategies. Ultimately, motivation and cognition are probably inextricably intertwined (e.g., Nenniger, 1992).

Some contemporary cognitive theorists also propose that motivation, rather than being a relatively permanent characteristic that people bring with them to various situations, is largely a function of the particular context in which people find themselves; this phenomenon is sometimes called **situated motivation** (Graham & Weiner, 1996; Greeno et al., 1996; Paris & Turner, 1994; Rueda & Moll, 1994). In school classrooms, many factors are likely to influence students' motivation; for instance, the kinds of instructional materials that a teacher uses (whether they are interesting, challenging, relevant to students' needs, and so on), the extent to which students find themselves having to compete with one another, and the ways in which students are evaluated are all likely to play a role (Boykin, 1994; Paris & Turner, 1994; Stipek, 1996).

Cognitive theorists have offered a number of ideas regarding the cognitions involved in motivation and the specific circumstances under which various "motivating" cognitions are most likely to occur; we will explore many of these ideas in Chapter 18. In the meantime, let's turn to a concept that has implications for our understanding of both motivation and cognition—the concept of *affect*.

THE ROLE OF AFFECT

When we talk about motivation, it is difficult not to talk about **affect**—the feelings and emotions that an individual brings to bear on a task—at the same time. For example, earlier in the chapter we noted that intrinsically motivated individuals typically find pleasure in what they are doing. Yet too much motivation—perhaps wanting something too much—may lead to an intense sense of anxiety. Pleasure, anxiety, excitement, pride, depression, anger, guilt—all of these are forms of affect.

Affect is clearly a factor in learning and cognition. For example, while learning how to perform a task, we simultaneously learn whether or not we like doing it (Zajonc, 1980). Problem solving is easier when we enjoy what we are doing, and successful attempts at learning and problem solving often bring on feelings of excitement, pleasure, and pride (Bloom & Broder, 1950; Carver & Scheier, 1990; Cobb, Yackel, & Wood, 1989; McLeod & Adams, 1989; Smith, 1991; Snow et al., 1996; Thompson & Thompson, 1989). Our failed attempts at a task are likely to make us feel frustrated or anxious, especially if the task is an easy one, and we are apt to develop a dislike for that task (Carver & Scheier, 1990; Eccles & Wigfield, 1985; Stodolsky et al., 1991).

As we are thinking about, learning, or remembering something, our very thoughts and memories may have emotional overtones—a phenomenon called **hot cognition** (e.g., Hoffman, 1991; Lazarus, 1991). Affect clearly influences both storage and retrieval processes. When we are in a good mood (for instance, when we feel happy or excited rather than sad or depressed), we are more likely to pay attention to information, to relate it to things we already know, and to remember it (Bower, 1994; Hertel, 1994; Hettena & Ballif, 1981; Isen, Daubman, & Gorgoglione, 1987; Oatley & Nundy, 1996; Snow et al., 1996). A good mood is also likely to help us retrieve things we have previously stored in long-term memory (Oatley & Nundy, 1996). And we can retrieve information from long-term memory more successfully when our mood at the time of retrieval is the same as our mood when we initially stored the information—an effect known as **mood-dependent memory** (Bower, 1994; Eich, 1995; Gilligan & Bower, 1984; Macauley, Ryan, & Eich, 1993).

The nature of the material we are trying to learn or remember can also induce hot cognition. For example, when information is emotionally charged, we are more likely to pay attention to it, continue to think about it over a period of time, and repeatedly elaborate on it (Bower, 1994; Edwards & Bryan, 1997; Heuer & Reisberg, 1992). Furthermore, although we may repress extremely painful memories (see Chapter 12), in general we can more easily retrieve information with high emotional content than we can recall relatively nonemotional information (Baddeley, 1982; Bower, 1994; Heuer & Reisberg, 1992; Kleinsmith & Kaplan, 1963; Reisberg, 1997; Russ, 1993; Winograd & Neisser, 1992).

As an example of the last principle, let's consider an experiment by Heuer and Reisberg (1990). Undergraduate students looked at a series of slides that depicted one of two stories. Both stories involved a boy and his mother visiting the boy's father at his workplace. For some students (the emotional-content group), the father was a surgeon operating on an accident victim; among other things, these students saw slides of surgery in progress (with a person's internal organs in full view) and the badly scarred legs of a child. For other students (the neutral-content group), the father was an auto mechanic repairing a broken-down car; these students saw the internal workings of the car, including a piece that was clearly broken. Two weeks later, all of the students were given an unexpected quiz about the things they had observed. Students who had seen the emotion-laden sequence remembered both the general gist of the story and many of the tiny details depicted in the slides far more accurately than did students who had

People often remember more when information packs an emotional wallop.

The Serial Killer, the Relentless Nymphomaniac, and Me

seen the neutral sequence. In fact, although they did not expect to be tested on what they had seen, people in the emotional-content group remembered more than people who had watched the neutral sequence and specifically been told to remember its plot and details.

Probably the most widely studied form of affect, at least within the context of human learning, is anxiety. For example, in Chapter 3 we discovered that anxiety may be acquired through classical conditioning, becoming a conditioned response to previously neutral stimuli. In Chapter 6 we noted that fear or anxiety may play a prominent role in avoidance learning. In Chapters 12 and 15 we found that anxiety often interferes with both long-term memory retrieval and problem-solving performance. Anxiety has numerous other effects as well; some are beneficial whereas others are not. Let's look more closely at how anxiety influences learning and performance.

Anxiety

Anxiety is a feeling of uneasiness and apprehension about a situation, typically one with an uncertain outcome. Fear and anxiety are related concepts, but with a distinct difference: Fear is a response to a specific threat, whereas anxiety is vague and relatively unfocused. For example, people are *afraid* of certain things, but they don't always know exactly what they're *anxious* about (e.g., Lazarus, 1991). Anxiety probably has two components: worry and emotionality (Liebert & Morris, 1967; Tryon, 1980). **Worry** is the cognitive aspect of anxiety, which includes troubling thoughts and beliefs about one's ability to deal with a situation. **Emotionality** is the affective aspect of anxiety, which includes such physiological responses as muscular tension (e.g., stomach "butterflies"), increased heartbeat, and perspiration and such behavioral responses as restlessness and pacing.

Psychologists have found it useful to distinguish between two types of anxiety: state versus trait. **State anxiety** is a temporary condition elicited by a particular stimulus. For example, you might experience state anxiety when working on an especially challenging

Figure 17–2
The inverted U curve, depicting a curvilinear relationship between arousal and performance.

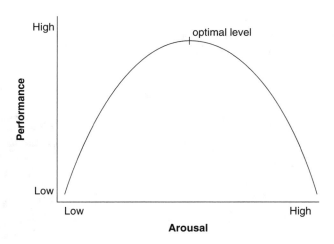

mathematics problem or when thinking about an upcoming exam in a notoriously difficult class. **Trait anxiety** is a relatively stable state of affairs, such that an individual is chronically anxious in certain situations. For example, you might have general mathematics anxiety or test anxiety, becoming anxious whenever you encounter numbers or think about exams.

Effects of Anxiety

Early studies focused on the effects of anxiety on learning and performance. More recently, with the advent of cognitivism, studies have investigated the effects anxiety is likely to have on cognitive processes. Let's consider the evidence in each of these areas.

Effects on learning and performance.   Psychologists use the term **arousal** to refer to the level of internal energy an organism is currently experiencing. Organisms experiencing low levels of arousal are relaxed, perhaps even asleep. Organisms experiencing high levels of arousal are highly energized, perhaps to the point of being excessively anxious.

Early researchers found that arousal affects learning and performance in a curvilinear ("inverted U") fashion (Broadhurst, 1959; Fiske & Maddi, 1961; Hebb, 1955; Yerkes & Dodson, 1908). More specifically, a small degree of arousal (e.g., a low level of anxiety) facilitates learning and performance. A high degree of arousal (e.g., high anxiety) may facilitate learning and performance when the task is easy but is likely to interfere when the task is more difficult. For any task, there is probably some **optimal level of arousal** (reflected by the top point of the inverted U) at which learning and performance are maximized (see Figure 17–2).

A classic experiment with mice by Yerkes and Dodson (1908) provides a concrete illustration of how arousal level and task difficulty interact. Each mouse was placed in a chamber from which it could escape by either of two doors. The wall opposite the doors was slowly moved to make the chamber smaller and smaller, until the mouse was

Figure 17–3

Arousal level interacts with task difficulty, resulting in different optimal levels for different tasks.

From data reported in "The relation of strength of stimulus to rapidity of habit-formation" by R. M. Yerkes & J. D. Dodson, 1908, *Journal of Comparative Neurology and Psychology*, *18*, pp. 459–482.

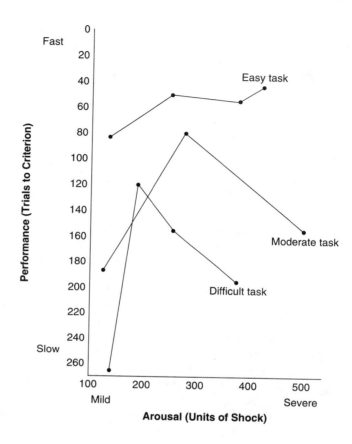

eventually forced to escape through one door or the other. One door led to a safe, comfortable "nest box"; the other led to electric shock. The experimenters provided a clue to help the mouse determine which door was which: The doorway leading to the nest box was consistently brighter than the doorway leading to shock.

For different groups of mice, the experimenters varied arousal level by the amount of shock they administered—mild, intense, or somewhere in between—when the "wrong" door was entered. They varied task difficulty by the relative similarity or difference between the two doorways: some mice had to choose between white and black (an easy task), others between light and dark gray (a moderately difficult task), and still others between similar shades of gray (a very difficult, although not impossible, task).

The experimenters established a criterion of 30 correct door choices in a row as an indication that a mouse had successfully learned the brightness discrimination. Figure 17–3 shows the average number of learning trials for mice in each condition; because the y-axis reflects quality of performance (speed of learning), groups needing fewer trials to criterion appear higher in the figure than groups with more trials. Notice how the mice with an easy choice performed best under high arousal (intense shock) conditions. Those with a moderately difficult task performed better with moderate arousal (moderate shock). Those with an extremely difficult discrimination performed best when shock and arousal were relatively low.

This principle—that easy tasks are best accomplished with a relatively high level of arousal but more difficult tasks are better accomplished with a low or moderate level—is often known as the **Yerkes-Dodson law.** The principle holds true not only for mice but for human beings as well. A high level of anxiety enhances our performance on easy and automatic tasks, such as running a mile or reciting the alphabet; here we have a case of **facilitating anxiety.** But the same high level interferes with our performance on a difficult task, such as writing a psychology textbook or speaking before a large audience; in this situation, we have **debilitating anxiety.**

We find the Yerkes-Dodson law at work in the classroom as well. For example, students who experience a small amount of muscular tension during mathematical problem solving are more successful problem solvers than students who experience no tension at all (Bloom & Broder, 1950). Highly anxious students sometimes perform better than low-anxiety students on tasks requiring verbatim recall of simple information; however, they perform comparatively poorly on tasks requiring flexible, creative thought (Kirkland, 1971). Low levels of anxiety throughout the course of instruction may facilitate students' learning; a high degree of anxiety at the tail end of the same course (e.g., at final exam time) is likely to be counterproductive (Kirkland, 1971). And the same degree of anxiety about a test may enhance the performance of high-ability students, for whom the test is easy, while lowering the performance of low-ability students, for whom the test is more difficult (Spielberger, 1966).

A useful distinction in this context is the difference between threat and challenge (Combs, Richards, & Richards, 1976). A **threat** is a situation in which individuals believe they have little chance of success—they see failure as an almost inevitable outcome. In contrast, a **challenge** is a situation in which individuals believe they can probably succeed if they try hard enough. Students are likely to have debilitating anxiety when they perceive a situation to be threatening. They respond to challenges more favorably; for example, they are likely to be highly motivated to do their best, and they express considerable excitement and satisfaction when they succeed (Cobb et al., 1989; Natriello & Dornbusch, 1984; Thompson & Thompson, 1989).

For most students, school tasks are more often challenging than easy. Accordingly, we should expect students with lower levels of anxiety to perform more effectively in the classroom, which is in fact the case: Students with relatively low trait anxiety achieve greater academic success (e.g., higher grade point averages) than their peers of equal ability who have high trait anxiety (Gaudry & Spielberger, 1971; Stipek, 1993; Tobias, 1980).

Effects on cognition.   Imagine yourself sitting in class taking a test. Here are some possible thoughts running through your mind as you do so:

- Oh, yes, my professor introduced this concept last week. It refers to . . .
- Here is a situation we didn't specifically talk about in class. Let me see if I can relate it to something we *did* talk about. . . .
- The best way to solve this problem might be to . . .

- These questions are getting harder and harder. . . .
- Oh, no, I only have 10 minutes left. I can't possibly finish. . . .
- What if I fail this test? It's required for my program. . . .

The first three thoughts are clearly relevant to the task at hand and should help you do your best on the test. In contrast, the last three are irrelevant to your task: You are spending your time worrying rather than thinking about how to answer the test questions. As you should recall from our discussion of attention and working memory in Chapter 9, we can attend to and process only a small amount of information at any one time. The more time and attention we devote to worrying about the test we are taking, the less capacity we have for dealing with and responding to the test itself.

Anxiety interferes with an individual's attention to a task (Covington, 1992; Easterbrook, 1959; Eysenck, 1992; Green, 1980; Tobias, 1980; Wine, 1980). And because "worrying" thoughts take up a certain amount of working memory capacity, anxiety also interferes with effective cognitive processing (Eccles & Wigfield, 1985; Eysenck, 1992; Mueller, 1980; Naveh-Benjamin, 1991; Tobias, 1985). Such effects are particularly likely when a learning or memory task is a difficult one, and when it involves considerable retrieval of information from long-term memory (Tobias, 1980).

In general, anxiety's debilitative effect is a distractive one: when performing a difficult task, highly anxious people are more likely to think irrelevant thoughts, be diverted by irrelevant stimuli, and exhibit irrelevant responses (Dusek, 1980; Eccles & Wigfield, 1985; Eysenck & Keane, 1990; Wine, 1980).

Common Sources of Anxiety

People become anxious about a variety of things. For example, they may be anxious about physically hurting themselves (King & Ollendick, 1989). They may be concerned about their personal appearance (King & Ollendick, 1989). They may worry about how they perform in comparison with their peers and about what their peers might think of them as a result (King & Ollendick, 1989; Vernon, 1969). They are likely to feel insecure when entering a new, unknown, and perhaps unsettling situation—for example, when, as budding adolescents, they make the transition from elementary school to junior high school (Eccles & Midgley, 1989). Adolescence brings additional sources of anxiety as well, including the high expectations that many secondary school teachers have for students' performance, the increasingly challenging nature of class material, and general concerns about what the future will bring (Eccles & Midgley, 1989; Phelan, Yu, & Davidson, 1994; Snow et al., 1996). And, in general, people are likely to become anxious whenever their sense of self-worth is threatened—when they receive some form of feedback that portrays them in an unflattering light (Covington, 1992).

Two forms of trait anxiety—test anxiety and mathematics anxiety—have been the focus of considerable study. Let's look at what research tells us about each of these.

Test anxiety.   Most of us get a little bit anxious about tests, and, as we have already seen, a small amount of anxiety may actually help us do better on tests. But some students become extremely anxious in test-taking situations, and these students typically get lower test scores than their less anxious classmates (Covington, 1992; Hembree, 1988; Hill, 1984; Sarason, 1972). Such students appear to be concerned primarily about the *evaluative* aspect of tests: They are terribly concerned that someone else (such as their teacher) will make negative judgments about them (Harter, Whitesell, & Kowalski, 1992; Phillips, Pitcher, Worsham, & Miller, 1980; Wine, 1980).

Test anxiety is rare in the early grades but increases throughout the elementary school years (Kirkland, 1971; Sarason, 1972). Many secondary and upper elementary students have test anxiety that interferes with their test performance; we are especially likely to see such debilitative test anxiety in students from minority groups, students with special needs, and students with a history of academic failure (Kirkland, 1971; Phillips et al., 1980).

Mathematics anxiety.   Of all the subjects taught in schools, none seems to elicit as much anxiety for as many students as mathematics. Mathematics anxiety has both worry and emotionality components. First, math-anxious people firmly believe that they are incapable of succeeding at mathematical tasks. Second, they have negative emotional reactions to math: They fear and dislike it, often intensely so (Wigfield & Meece, 1988).

One possible reason why students become anxious about math is that, as we noted in our discussion of classical conditioning (Chapter 3), school curricula frequently introduce mathematical concepts and procedures before students are cognitively ready to handle them. For example, developmentalists have proposed that the abilities to understand proportions and to deal with abstract ideas don't usually emerge until early adolescence and then continue to develop for several years after that (Schliemann & Carraher, 1993; Tourniaire & Pulos, 1985; also see the discussion of Piaget's theory in Chapter 8). Yet we often expose students to such proportions as fractions and ratios, and to such abstract ideas as negative numbers and *pi* (π), in the upper elementary and early junior high school years. If students are asked to deal with mathematical tasks they can't understand, many of them will undoubtedly encounter frustration and failure. And when students associate frequent failure with math, we can expect them to develop a dislike for the subject and a belief that they are incapable of doing well in it.

As you might expect, students with high math anxiety do more poorly in mathematics classes than students with low math anxiety; furthermore, highly math-anxious students are less likely to enroll in additional mathematics classes of their own volition (Eccles & Jacobs, 1986; McCoy, 1990; Meece, Wigfield, & Eccles, 1990). Such differences between high-math-anxious and low-math-anxious students appear even when the two groups of students have done equally well in previous math classes. In fact, math anxiety may have a greater influence on students' future plans for taking (or not taking) mathematics than do their previous achievement level and degree of success in math (Eccles & Jacobs, 1986). Math anxiety, which is more common in girls than in boys even when achievement levels are the same, may be a key reason why so few girls pursue advanced study or careers in mathematics (Eccles & Jacobs, 1986; Fennema, 1980). And for students of both genders, math anxiety may inhibit the desire to pursue a career in science (Chipman, Krantz, & Silver, 1992).

To perform most effectively in the classroom, students should be motivated to do their best yet not be overly anxious about their performance. In the final section of this chapter, we will consider some general strategies for promoting students' motivation to achieve academic success and for keeping their anxiety at productive levels.

PROMOTING STUDENT MOTIVATION

The principles and theories we've examined in this chapter have numerous implications for classroom practice. Following are several principles that can guide teachers in their efforts to promote student motivation:

• *Students learn more effectively and demonstrate more productive classroom behaviors when they are intrinsically motivated to learn and achieve.* Historically, parents, teachers, and society in general have emphasized the extrinsic advantages of classroom success (Harter, 1992; Spaulding, 1992). For example, parents give their children money and privileges for good report cards. Schools award athletic letters for sports participation. Teachers and guidance counselors point out that students will gain admission to college, find more employment opportunities, and earn higher salaries if they obtain their high school diplomas. Yet as we have seen, *intrinsically* motivated students are more likely to exhibit initiative, independence, ambition, meaningful learning, and enjoyment regarding academic activities than is true for their extrinsically motivated counterparts, and they ultimately achieve at higher levels in the classroom.

Researchers have identified several strategies that appear to promote intrinsic motivation. Talking about intrinsic rather than extrinsic motives for pursuing classroom activities is one effective approach (Amabile & Hennessey, 1992; Graham & Weiner, 1996; Hennessey & Amabile, 1987). For example, a teacher might say, "It's always nice to get good grades, but it's more important that you understand what you are studying and enjoy what you are doing," or, "You must be very proud of yourself for passing the district writing test." Adult models who visibly pursue their own interests and express intrinsic enjoyment of something they are doing (e.g., saying "I feel wonderful" after giving something generously to someone else) promote observers' intrinsic motivation for the same activities (Bryan, 1971; Csikszentmihalyi, Rathunde, & Whalen, 1993). And relating classroom topics to students' own lives, experiences, needs, and feelings (e.g., in geography, identifying students with roots in the regions being studied, or, in history, having students imagine how they might have felt leaving home at the age of 12 to work as an apprentice during the Middle Ages) increases the likelihood that students will genuinely want to study those topics (Brophy, 1986; Wlodkowski & Ginsberg, 1995; Zahorik, 1994).

Intrinsic motivation is also more likely to emerge when certain cognitive factors are present—for example, when students believe they are capable of accomplishing tasks successfully and when they feel in control of their lives. As we study such cognitive factors in the following chapter, we will identify additional strategies for helping students genuinely *want* to learn and achieve.

It is important to note, however, that students' intrinsic motivation to learn classroom material will not develop overnight but instead will emerge slowly over a period of time, especially if students have previously become accustomed to receiving extrinsic reinforcement for their efforts. In such situations, teachers might want to increase their focus on the intrinsic rewards of learning while gradually weaning their students from an overdependence on external reinforcers (Covington, 1992; Lepper, 1981; Stipek, 1996).

• *Students are more likely to focus on their schoolwork when their nonacademic needs have been met.* As we examined drive theory, Maslow's hierarchy, self-worth theory, and individual differences, we identified a number of nonacademic needs that students may have. They are likely to have physiological needs on some occasions; for example, they may be hungry, thirsty, tired, or restless. They may feel uncertain or insecure about what will happen to them in class, in the schoolyard, or on the way home from school. Many students will have a strong desire to socialize with others (classmates and teachers alike), gaining the companionship, acceptance, approval, and respect of those around them. And students will want to maintain their own sense of self-worth—to believe that they are competent, capable individuals.

Teachers can do a number of simple things to ensure students' physiological needs are met. For example, they can help students from low-income families apply for free lunch programs. They can alternate quiet, in-seat tasks with opportunities for physical activity. They can refer students with apparently untreated illnesses to the school nurse. And they should certainly include bathroom breaks and trips to the drinking fountain in the daily schedule.

To meet students' need for safety and security in the classroom, and to keep their anxiety about academic tasks and activities at a reasonable, facilitative level, teachers must create an environment that is somewhat orderly and predictable (Brophy, 1987; Dowaliby & Schumer, 1973; Grimes & Allinsmith, 1970; Klein, 1975; Wlodkowski, 1978). For example, teachers might have regular procedures for handing out and sharing materials, meeting with cooperative learning groups, doing homework, and turning in assignments. They should clearly describe expectations for academic performance and classroom behavior. They should deal with misbehaviors in a fair and consistent fashion. And they should provide opportunities for students to voice any questions and concerns that may arise.

Students' needs for love, belonging, affiliation, and approval can be met in a variety of ways. Teacher-student relationships are, by their very nature, somewhat businesslike; after all, both teachers and students have a job to do. At the same time, teachers can express their interest and affection for students through the many little things they do throughout the day—for example, by acknowledging birthdays and other special occasions, taking students' ideas and opinions seriously, and offering a supportive and nonjudgmental ear when a particular student seems angry or depressed. And they can provide opportunities for students to interact frequently with their classmates—for example, through such group-oriented instructional techniques as discussions, cooperative learning, reciprocal teaching, and role-playing.

To help students gain the esteem of others and maintain their own sense of self-worth, teachers can acknowledge students' accomplishments both in and out of class. They can schedule activities in such a way that all students are able to demonstrate their particular strengths at some point during the school day or at special events after school (e.g., Jenlink, 1994). They can "brag" about their students' accomplishments in many subtle ways—for example, by posting students' art projects on the wall, describing noteworthy achievements at parent-teacher conferences, displaying students' best work at open houses, and sending occasional good-news reports home to parents. But most importantly, teachers must do everything they can to help students achieve classroom success.

• *Teachers can capitalize on the role that affect plays in learning.* There is no reason that academic subject matter needs to be dry and emotionless. On the contrary, students will probably remember more if they have feelings about the things they study. For example, a scientific discovery might be exciting. A look at social injustices might make students angry. A poem might convey peace and serenity. One simple way that teachers can promote positive affect is to model their own enthusiasm and excitement about classroom subject matter—perhaps by bringing in newspaper articles and other outside materials they have run across, presenting material in an animated or even impassioned fashion, and sharing the particular questions and issues about which they themselves are concerned (Brophy, 1986, 1987; Wlodkowski, 1978).

We must remember, too, that students should associate pleasure and other forms of positive affect with classroom activities. For example, although teachers don't necessarily want to give the impression that schoolwork is all fun and games, they can occasionally incorporate a few gamelike features into classroom tasks and activities (Brophy, 1986)—perhaps by using simple crossword puzzles to introduce new spelling words or by using a television game show format for a class history review. And, in general, teachers must make sure that most of students' experiences with any task or subject matter, and especially their *early* experiences, are positive and nonthreatening ones (Wlodkowski, 1978).

- *Assessments of students' performance should be portrayed as means of enhancing future achievement rather than as judgments of ability and worth.* Under the best of circumstances, tests and other forms of classroom assessment *can* serve as effective motivators for student learning. For example, most students study class material more and learn it better when they are told they will be tested on it than when they are simply told to learn it (Frederiksen, 1984b; Halpin & Halpin, 1982). Classroom assessments are especially effective as motivators when they challenge students to perform at their very best (Natriello & Dornbusch, 1984). However, we should note several situations in which an assessment will definitely *not* motivate students to do well or—even worse—may motivate them to do *poorly*:
  - When they believe they will be penalized for doing too well on the assessment—for example, when they think they will receive more challenging work (e.g., extra readings or more difficult assignments) if they attain a high score (Sax, 1989)
  - When they think they will lose the esteem of their peers for doing too well—for example, when they are afraid of becoming nerds or "school girls" (Sax, 1989)
  - When they think their teacher's high standards for performance on the assessment are impossible to attain (Natriello & Dornbusch, 1984)
  - When they consistently perform at lower levels than most of their classmates (Natriello, 1987)
  - When they believe an assessment is a poor reflection of what they know (Paris, Lawton, Turner, & Roth, 1991; Paris & Turner, 1994)

Thus, a classroom assessment tool is most likely to serve as a motivator for learning when students perceive it to be a valid measure of course objectives, when they believe that successful performance on the assessment is possible, and when they are confident that successful performance will be rewarded rather than punished.

But as we discovered in our discussion of test anxiety, many students are so concerned about performing well on classroom assessments that they become overly anxious about taking them. There are probably several reasons that high school and upper elementary students experience debilitative anxiety in assessment situations. Perhaps when teachers talk about an upcoming assessment they too often imply that it is an event to be feared or revered. Perhaps they too often stress the dire consequences of failing. Perhaps teachers and other school personnel make too many major decisions—about grades, scholarships, admission to special programs, and so on—based on the results of a single test score.

Researchers and theorists offer numerous suggestions for keeping students' anxiety about classroom assessments at a facilitative level. First of all, teachers should help students master class material and effective study strategies to the point where successful performance on an assessment is highly likely (Covington, 1992; Naveh-Benjamin, 1991). Second, teachers can base students' classroom grades on many sources of data (perhaps including scores on numerous small assessments) instead of on only one or two test scores (Gaudry & Bradshaw, 1971; Gaynor & Millham, 1976; Sax, 1989). Third, teachers can encourage students to do their best without creating unnecessary anxiety about the consequences of doing poorly (I. Sarason, 1980; S. Sarason, 1972; Sax, 1989; Sinclair, 1971). Fourth, a classroom assessment should be short enough that students can easily complete it within the allotted time; this strategy is especially beneficial for high-anxiety students (Brophy, 1986; Hill, 1984). And fifth, students should be given whatever support (scaffolding) is appropriate to help them perform successfully on a classroom assessment task. For example, students can be given pretests for practice and feedback, instructed on effective test-taking strategies, and allowed to use notes or other resources when there is no inherent value in committing certain information (e.g., formulas and trivial facts) to memory (Brophy, 1986; Kirkland, 1971; Leherissey et al., 1971; Sax, 1989; Sieber, Kameya, & Paulson, 1970; Stipek, 1993; Wine, 1980).

Above all, teachers and students alike must keep tests and other forms of classroom assessment in the proper context—as means of promoting learning and achievement, especially over the long run, rather than as means of making judgments about students' ability and worth. For example, evaluation procedures should provide frequent and informative feedback to students about what they have mastered and how they can improve (Brophy, 1986; Spaulding, 1992; Wine, 1980). Such procedures should also allow for the mistakes that are an inevitable part of the learning process. When students know they will have the chance to correct their errors, they are more likely to take on challenging, risky tasks (Brophy, 1986; Wlodkowski, 1978).

Students are more likely to exhibit high motivation to achieve, and therefore to gain the maximum benefits of classroom instruction, when they find the subject matter they are studying to be interesting, when they are more concerned about learning than about looking "good" for their teacher and classmates, when they know they are capable of achieving instructional objectives, and when they believe they have some control over the things that happen in the classroom. We will consider these points further when we examine cognitive factors in motivation in the next chapter.

SUMMARY

Motivation is an internal state that arouses us to action, pushes us in particular directions, and keeps us engaged in certain activities. Motivation determines the extent to which we exhibit the particular responses we have learned. It also affects the ways in which we process the information we receive. Intrinsic motivation is ultimately more beneficial than extrinsic motivation; for example, intrinsically motivated individuals do things on their own initiative, maintain their attention on tasks, and process information in a meaningful fashion.

Numerous theories of motivation have been proposed. Drive theorists postulate that human beings and other organisms behave in ways that reduce their physiological needs and thus maintain homeostasis. Incentive theorists propose that characteristics of goal objects mediate a stimulus-response relationship, affecting which stimuli are responded to and which are not. From the perspective of Maslow's hierarchy, people have five different sets of needs (ranging from physiological needs to self-actualization) that they strive to meet in a particular order. Self-worth theory tells us that people have a need to maintain the belief that they are competent, capable individuals and that they may paradoxically undermine their own success as a way of protecting this belief. Other theories focus on the individual differences that may exist in such motives as the need for affiliation, the need for approval, and the need for achievement. Most contemporary theories emphasize the cognitive aspects of motivation; these theories are described in Chapter 18.

Related to motivation is the concept of *affect*—the feelings and emotions that an individual brings to bear on a task. Affect influences learning; for example, we can typically store and retrieve information with highly emotional content more easily than we can recall relatively nonemotional information. Anxiety is the form of affect that has been most thoroughly studied by researchers. It facilitates performance on easy tasks, but high levels interfere with performance on difficult tasks, presumably by interfering with effective cognitive processing and otherwise distracting people from what they are doing.

Theorists and researchers offer numerous suggestions for promoting students' motivation to achieve and succeed in the classroom. For example, teachers should emphasize the intrinsically motivating aspects of school learning more than the external rewards. Assessment of students' performance should be portrayed as a means of enhancing future achievement rather than as a judgment of ability and worth. And students are more likely to focus on school tasks and activities when their nonacademic needs have been met.

CHAPTER 18

Cognitive Factors in Motivation

Many of the people I meet marvel at how anyone could have the fortitude and persistence to get a doctoral degree. And, to be honest, when I was growing up in the 1950s and 1960s, I expected only to become a housewife and mother, certainly not a college professor with "Ph.D." attached to my name. So how did I get here? It's really quite simple.

For one thing, I've always been concerned about children, and in particular about their education. While attending a small liberal arts college during the late 1960s—the era of the Vietnam War, the civil rights movement and sit-ins on the home front, and heightened soul-searching on many campuses across the country—I realized that I wanted my life to have an impact on society far beyond that of my own family and friends. By the end of my senior year, I had identified what I wanted to do when I grew up: I wanted to make education better for my children's generation than it had been for mine.

I began applying to graduate schools and ultimately chose Penn State's educational psychology program, partly because of the reputation of its faculty, partly because of the financial package it offered, and partly because of central Pennsylvania's incredible pastoral charm and serenity. I had been a psychology major as an undergraduate and knew that psychology was something I was "good at." I had also done well in the required statistics courses that led half of my fellow psychology majors to find a different major by their junior year. So I worked hard during my years at Penn State, knowing I would certainly be successful if I was conscientious about my studies. Besides, I found educational psychology to be absolutely fascinating; the many books and articles I read were hard to put down because they gave me innumerable insights into how human beings learn and many intriguing ideas about how to help people learn more effectively. My doctoral dissertation took longer than I had anticipated (a year and a half from start to finish), but with each passing month I came noticeably closer to completing it, and I *did* complete it in time to graduate in June of 1975.

So why did I initiate and persist in my efforts to earn a doctoral degree? Because, among other things, I valued a better world, had a goal for myself, and discovered an interest in human learning theory. Furthermore, I believed I was capable of graduate work in educational psychology. All of these things—values, goals, interests, and beliefs—are among the cognitive factors that kept me motivated throughout my doctoral program.

In the preceding chapter, we found that motivation affects cognition: Motivated individuals are more likely to pay attention to and process information in ways that promote effective learning and memory. But cognition affects motivation as well: The things we think and believe have a significant influence on the tasks we pursue and the activities in which we engage.

In this chapter we will explore the cognitive aspects of human motivation. We will talk first about the various goals that people set for themselves and the effects that different kinds of goals are likely to have on behavior. We will examine two factors that influence people's decisions to pursue particular goals: their values regarding what's important and their expectations for success. We will consider, too, the role that interest plays in human behavior, looking at personal characteristics and situational variables that determine whether a particular topic or task is interesting. Later in the chapter we will explore attribution theory—the perspective that people's behaviors after reinforcing and punishing consequences are a function of their beliefs about the causes of those consequences. We will identify two probable prerequisites for intrinsic motivation—competence and self-determination—and find out why extrinsic reinforcement for academic achievement may sometimes *not* be such a good idea. We will also learn that some behaviors that are initially motivated extrinsically may become *internalized* over time, to the point where an individual eventually engages in them freely and willingly. Finally, we will look at how challenging situations often promote motivation and at how competition often undermines it, and we will consider additional strategies for promoting student motivation in the classroom.

GOALS

As we discovered in our discussion of social learning theory in Chapter 7, setting goals is a critical part of self-regulated behavior. Social learning theorists propose that people's internal goals and standards for success motivate them to move in particular directions. Goal attainment results in considerable self-satisfaction; it also leads to greater self-efficacy and higher standards for future performance (Bandura, 1986, 1989). Furthermore, people are more likely to work toward goals, and thus are more likely to accomplish them, when they have set those goals for themselves rather than when others have imposed goals upon them (Schunk, 1985, 1996b). We must note, however, that goals are beneficial only to the extent that they are accomplishable; if they are unrealistically high, the consistent failure to achieve them may result in excessive stress or depression (Bandura, 1986).

In our discussion of metacognition in Chapter 13, we found that goal setting is also an important component of self-regulated learning. Self-regulated learners know what they want to accomplish when they read or study, they direct their thoughts and learning strategies accordingly, and they continually monitor their progress toward the goals they have set for themselves (Carver & Scheier, 1990; Schunk & Zimmerman, 1994; Zimmerman & Bandura, 1994; Zimmerman & Risemberg, 1997).

Goals figure prominently in motivation theory as well (Dweck & Elliott, 1983; Locke & Latham, 1994; Pintrich & Schunk, 1996). In our discussion of motivation's general effects in the preceding chapter, we noted that motivation revolves around the accomplishment of certain goals, with such goals influencing both the choices people make and the consequences they find reinforcing. People's goals also influence their cognitive processing; for instance, goals affect the extent to which learners become cognitively engaged in particular tasks and the cognitive strategies that they use to study and learn (Anderman & Maehr, 1994; Brickman, Miller, & Roedel, 1997; Nolen, 1996; Winne & Marx, 1989).

Researchers have identified a wide variety of goals that people may set for themselves, including the following:

- Gaining physical comfort and personal well-being
- Achieving and maintaining a sense of competence and self-worth
- Mastering information or skills
- Obtaining extrinsic rewards
- Doing well in school (e.g., getting good grades)
- Making a good impression on others
- Gaining the recognition or approval of superiors or peers
- Bringing honor to one's family or social group
- Developing productive interpersonal relationships
- Developing long-term, intimate relationships (e.g., getting married and having children)
- Helping others

- Doing better than others in competitive situations
- Becoming a productive member of society
- Achieving a desired career
- Gaining material wealth
- Gaining social or political power
- Finding novelty and adventure
    (Durkin, 1995; Lee & Anderson, 1991; McInerney, Roche, McInerney, & Marsh, 1997; Schutz, 1994; Urdan & Maehr, 1995; Wentzel, 1989; Wolters, 1997)

Most of us have and work for many of these goals; for example, I achieve some degree of physical comfort by popping Cheetos into my mouth, I strive to maintain my sense of self-worth by playing along at home as I watch television game shows, and I continually embarrass myself in front of family and friends as I practice and try to master parallel turns on the ski slopes of Colorado. But many of us have **core goals**—general goals of considerable priority for us at any given point in time—that seem to drive much of what we do (Schutz, 1994). For instance, at the age of 49, my number one goal is to be a productive member of society—to leave the world a better place than I found it—and many of my behaviors (e.g., raising socially responsible children, supporting my friends through difficult times, and writing books that can help teachers) are in one way or another directed toward that end.

Some theorists have proposed that many goals fall into one of two general categories, learning goals and performance goals. These two types of goals lead to somewhat different behaviors and cognitions, as we shall see now.

Learning Goals versus Performance Goals

As I mentioned in the preceding chapter, achievement motivation (also known as the need for achievement) was originally conceptualized as a general characteristic that people exhibit consistently across a variety of tasks and in many domains. But some contemporary theorists have proposed that achievement motivation takes one of several forms, depending on the specific goal an individual has in mind (Ames & Archer, 1988; Dweck & Elliott, 1983; Stipek, 1993). To illustrate, let's consider what three different girls might be thinking during the first day of a basketball unit in a physical education class:

Jane: This is my chance to show all the girls what a great basketball player I am. If I stay near the basket, Joan and June will keep passing to me, and I'll score a lot of points. I can really impress Coach and my friends.

Joan: Boy, I hope I don't screw this up. If I shoot at the basket and miss, I'll look like a real jerk. Maybe I should just stay outside the three-point line and keep passing to Jane and June.

June: I'd really like to become a better basketball player. I can't figure out why I don't get more of my shots into the basket. I'll ask Coach to give me feedback about how I can improve my game. Maybe some of my friends will have suggestions, too.

All three girls want to play basketball well but for different reasons. Jane is concerned mostly about her performance—that is, about looking good in front of her coach and classmates—and so she wants to maximize opportunities to demonstrate her skill on the court. Joan is also concerned about the impression she will make, but she just wants to make sure she *doesn't* look *bad*. Unlike Jane and Joan, June isn't even thinking about how her performance will appear to others. Instead, she is interested mainly in developing her skill—in mastering the game of basketball—and doesn't expect herself to be an expert on the first day. For June, making mistakes is an inevitable part of learning a new skill, not a source of embarrassment or humiliation.

June's approach to basketball illustrates a **learning goal**—a desire to achieve competence by either acquiring additional knowledge or mastering new skills. In contrast, Jane and Joan are each setting a **performance goal**—a desire to look good and receive favorable judgments from others or *not* to look bad and receive unfavorable judgments (Dweck & Elliott, 1983).[1]

Before they reach school age, children seem to focus primarily on learning goals. For instance, even infants seek out experiences that are likely to increase their competence and mastery of the environment, and they derive genuine pleasure from new accomplishments (Dweck & Elliott, 1983). But when children enter school at five or six years of age, two things happen that orient them more toward performance goals (Dweck & Elliott, 1983). First of all, they suddenly have many peers around them to whom they can compare their own behavior; as a result, they may begin to define success more in terms of doing better than their classmates than in terms of task mastery. Second, whereas they have previously dealt primarily with physical tasks (e.g., learning to walk, fasten buttons, and ride a tricycle), they are now being asked to deal with tasks of an intellectual and somewhat abstract nature (e.g., learning to read, write, and add). The value of these school tasks may not be readily apparent to them, and their efforts in accomplishing them might therefore seem unnecessarily laborious. Furthermore, they may have greater difficulty assessing their progress on such tasks, to the point where they must rely on others (e.g., their teachers) to make judgments about their competence.

When we compare individuals who set learning goals with those who set performance goals, we often find different behaviors, beliefs, attitudes, learning strategies, and affect. Table 18-1 describes some of the differences we are likely to see.

Let's look at learning and performance goals in the context of schools and classrooms. As Table 18-1 indicates, students with learning goals tend to engage in the very activities that will help them learn; for example, they pay attention in class, process information in ways that promote effective long-term memory storage, and approach class assignments with the intention of getting the maximum benefit from them. Furthermore, students with learning goals have a healthy perspective about learning, effort, and failure: They realize that learning is a process of trying hard and continuing to persevere even in the face of temporary setbacks. Consequently, it is usually these students who achieve at high levels and benefit the most from their classroom experiences (e.g., Schunk, 1996a). In contrast, students with performance goals—those concerned primarily about how they appear to others—may stay away from some of the very tasks that, because of their challenging nature, would do the most to promote mastery of new

---

[1]Nicholls (1984, 1992) has made a similar distinction but uses the terms *task involvement* and *ego involvement*.

Table 18–1

Characteristics of people with learning versus performance goals.

People with Learning Goals	People with Performance Goals
Believe that competence develops over time through practice and effort	Believe that competence is a stable characteristic (people either have talent or they don't) and think that competent people shouldn't have to try very hard
Choose tasks that maximize opportunities for learning	Choose tasks that maximize opportunities for demonstrating competence and avoid tasks that might make them look incompetent
React to easy tasks with feelings of boredom or disappointment	React to success on easy tasks with feelings of pride or relief
Are more likely to be intrinsically motivated to learn course material reinforcement	Are more likely to be extrinsically motivated—that is, motivated by expectations of external and punishment
Invest considerable effort in tasks	Invest the minimal effort needed to succeed
Use learning strategies that promote true comprehension of course material (e.g., meaningful learning, elaboration, and comprehension monitoring)	Use learning strategies that promote only rote learning of course material (e.g., repetition copying, and word-for-word memorization)
Seek feedback that accurately describes their ability and helps them improve	Seek feedback that flatters them
Evaluate their own performance in terms of the progress they make	Evaluate their own performance in terms of how they compare with others
View errors as a normal and useful part of the learning process and use their errors to help improve performance	View errors as a sign of failure and incompetence
Are satisfied with their performance if they try hard and make progress, even if their efforts result in failure	Are satisfied with their performance only if they succeed
Interpret failure as a sign that they need to exert more effort	Interpret failure as a sign of low ability and therefore predictive of continuing failure in the future
Persist in the face of failure	Give up easily when they fail and avoid tasks that have previously led to failure
View a teacher as a resource and guide to help them learn	View a teacher as a judge and as a rewarder or punisher
As students, are more likely to be enthusiastic about, and become actively involved in, school activities	As students, are more likely to distance themselves from the school environment

Sources: Ames & Archer, 1988; Anderman & Maehr, 1994; Brophy, 1986; Duda & Nicholls, 1992; Dweck, 1986; Dweck & Elliott, 1983; Garcia, 1992; Graham & Weiner, 1996; Hagen, 1994; Jaqacinski & Nicholls, 1984, 1987; Newman & Schwager, 1995; Nicholls, 1992; Nolen, 1988, 1996; Powell, 1990; Stipek, 1993

skills (Dweck, 1986). Furthermore, because these students may exert only the minimal effort necessary to achieve desired performance outcomes, they may learn only a fraction of what their teachers have to offer them (Brophy, 1986, 1987).

Some people seem to choose learning goals over performance goals fairly consistently. These people can be thought of as having a strong **motivation to learn**—a tendency to find learning activities meaningful and worthwhile and therefore to attempt to get the maximum benefit from them (Brophy, 1986, 1987; McCombs, 1988). The motivation to learn puts a new twist on the concept of achievement motivation: People want to engage in the cognitive processes that lead to successful learning as well as the behaviors that lead to achievement.

Coordinating Multiple Goals

Learning and performance goals are not necessarily mutually exclusive; on many occasions, people are likely to have *both* kinds of goals at the same time (Anderman & Maehr, 1994). For instance, students may have a strong desire to learn and understand classroom subject matter while at the same time wanting to achieve the good grades so important for gaining admission to college. Students may simultaneously have other goals as well; for example, most students have social goals as well as academic ones (Dodge, Asher, & Parkhurst, 1989; Urdan & Maehr, 1995; Wigfield et al., 1996).

Achieving multiple goals at the same time can be a challenging task indeed. People take a variety of approaches when they have several goals that they want to accomplish (Dodge et al., 1989; McCaslin & Good, 1996). They may find activities that allow them to achieve several goals simultaneously; for instance, they may satisfy both their academic goals and their social goals by participating in cooperative learning activities (Dodge et al., 1989; Phelan et al., 1994; Urdan & Maehr, 1995). They may pursue some goals while putting others on the "back burner." For example, as I pursue the goal of completing this book, I leave dirty dishes in the sink, thereby ignoring my lower-priority goal of having a clean house. People may also modify their idea of what it means to achieve a particular goal. For example, as I have become increasingly busy with my professional writing in recent years (thereby, I hope, satisfying my desire to make the world a better place), my definition of a clean house has deteriorated rapidly from being a spotless home that would make Martha Stewart green with envy to one in which my husband, children, and I can successfully find a pathway through the clutter on the family room floor.

In some situations, however, accomplishing one goal may be incompatible with accomplishing another; for example, achieving at a high level in the classroom may interfere with one's ability to maintain a friendship with a peer who doesn't value academic achievement (Berndt & Perry, 1990; McCaslin & Good, 1996; Phelan et al., 1994). On such occasions, an individual may seemingly have little choice but to abandon one goal in favor of another (McCaslin & Good, 1996).

Goals are only one of the factors influencing people's decisions to engage in some activities over others. At least two additional variables—expectancies and values—also influence the choices that people make.

EXPECTANCIES AND VALUES

Some theorists (e.g., Atkinson, 1964; Dweck & Elliott, 1983; Eccles [Parsons], 1983; Feather, 1982; Wigfield, 1994; Wigfield & Eccles, 1992) have proposed that motivation for performing a particular task is a function of two variables. First of all, people must believe they can succeed; in other words, they must have a high **expectancy** about their task performance (a notion similar to social learning theorists' concept of self-efficacy). Second, people must believe that there are direct or indirect benefits in performing a task; in other words, they must place **value** on the task itself or on the outcomes that are likely to result.

From this perspective, motivated behavior occurs only when both expectancy and value are present. For example, as a doctoral student in educational psychology, I found value in human learning theory and had a high expectancy that I could master it; thus, I was motivated to learn as much as I could about how human beings learn. I value good music, too, but have a low expectancy for becoming an accomplished musician (I have an uninspired singing voice and am all butterfingers on the piano), so I don't work very hard or very often at my music. I'm much better at cooking lima beans than I am at singing, but I never cook them because I place absolutely no value on cooking the abominable things. And there are some things that, for me, are associated with both low expectancy and low value; playing my sons' video games and walking barefoot on hot coals are two activities that spring to mind.

People's expectancies are probably the result of several factors. Prior successes and failures at a particular task of course make a difference; for example, people form increasingly lower expectations after experiencing a series of failures (Dweck, Goetz, & Strauss, 1980). Other factors affect expectancy level as well: the perceived difficulty of a task, one's general work habits, environmental resources, the quality of instruction, and the anticipated effort necessary to succeed are all likely to make a difference (Dweck & Elliott, 1983; Eccles [Parsons], 1983; Wigfield & Eccles, 1992; Zimmerman et al., 1992). From such factors, an individual comes to a conclusion—perhaps correct, perhaps not—about the likelihood of success.

Value is equally subjective in nature. Eccles and Wigfield (1985; Eccles [Parsons], 1983) have suggested several possible reasons why value might be high or low. Some activities are valued because they are associated with certain personal qualities; for example, a boy who wants to be smart and thinks that smart people do well in school will place a premium on academic success. Other activities have high value because they are seen as means to a desired goal; for example, much as she detests mathematics, my daughter Tina struggled through four years of high school math classes because so many colleges require that much math. Still other activities are valued simply because they bring pleasure and enjoyment; for example, junk food doesn't help me achieve any of my long-range goals (it may even interfere with my goal of losing 15 pounds this year), but it sure does taste good.

We can also anticipate the circumstances in which an activity will probably *not* be valued very much (Eccles & Wigfield, 1985; Eccles [Parsons], 1983, 1984). Some activities may require so much effort that they are simply not worth it. For example, I could undoubtedly improve my piano-playing skills with lessons and practice, but right now I have more important things to which I need to devote my time and energy. Other activities may be associated with too many bad feelings. For example, I can't imagine hang gliding or bungee jumping because I am deathly afraid of heights. And anything likely to threaten one's self-esteem is a "must" to avoid. For example, you may know individuals who rarely make the first move with people of the opposite sex for fear that they might be rejected.

While examining operant conditioning in Chapter 4, we discovered that people may sometimes not exhibit certain behaviors, despite potential reinforcement, because they have too much to lose or too little to gain by doing so. We can explain such a cost-benefit analysis quite easily within an expectancies/values framework (Eccles [Parsons], 1984; Eccles & Wigfield, 1985; Feather, 1982; Paris & Byrnes, 1989). We will see people engage in a particular activity when they believe that (a) they can perform the activity successfully with a reasonable amount of effort (high expectancy) and (b) the activity or its outcome is worthwhile (high value). We will probably *not* see them engage in that activity if they think they will have to exert an inordinate amount of effort to achieve success (if they achieve it at all), nor will we see them do so when they place little value on the activity and its consequence.

One common reason we value something is that we find it interesting. Let's find out what theorists have said about the role of interest in human motivation.

INTEREST

When we say that people have **interest** in a particular topic or activity, we mean that they find the topic or activity intriguing and enticing. Interest, then, is one form of intrinsic motivation. Positive affect accompanies interest; for example, people pursuing a task in which they are interested experience such feelings as pleasure, excitement, and liking (Hidi & Anderson, 1992).

Theorists distinguish between two general types of interest (Alexander & Jetton, 1996; Hidi & Anderson, 1992; Krapp, Hidi, & Renninger, 1992). Some interests reside within the individual; people tend to have personal preferences regarding the topics they pursue and the activities in which they engage. Because such **personal interests** are relatively stable over time, we see a consistent pattern in the choices that people make. For example, my husband has a strong interest in football and so can often be found in front of the television set on Saturdays, Sundays, and Monday nights from September to January. (Fortunately, these are not the times when my favorite television game shows are broadcast.) And each of my children has shown unique individual interests from an early age. When Tina was growing up, she spent many hours either talking to or talking about boys, and now, as a college student, she resides in a coeducational "fraternity" house with a ratio of three males to every female. For many years, Alex had a thing for critters; he was fascinated with ants as a toddler, and he had an intense interest in various kinds of reptiles (lizards, snakes, and dinosaurs) throughout the elementary and middle school years. Jeff has always been a Lego man, putting all of his allowance toward Lego sets and spending many long hours in the basement designing architectural wonders. A few months ago, Jeff finally put his Legos away, but, knowing that the family plans to move to a new community in a few months, he continues to draw various Lego-like house plans on graph paper for me.

In contrast to personal interest, **situational interest** is evoked by something in the environment—something that is perhaps new, unusual, or surprising. For example, as I was driving to Boulder one day a number of years ago, I saw what looked like a llama out of the corner of my eye. Well, I knew very well that Colorado's eastern plains are cattle and horse country, not llama country, so I slowed down to take a closer look, eventually confirming the unlikely llama hypothesis. For the time being, I was more interested in identifying the strange creature I saw than in getting to Boulder. In much the same way, you might have your interest temporarily piqued by a traffic accident at the side of the road, a strange-but-true tidbit in the newspaper, or a large, brightly wrapped gift with your name on it.

Effects of Interest

Although situational interest can temporarily capture one's attention, personal interest is the force that ultimately sustains involvement in an activity over the long run (Alexander et al., 1994). When people are interested in a particular activity, they are likely to set learning goals (rather than performance goals) related to that activity (Schiefele, 1992; Schiefele & Wild, 1994). For example, for a year or so, Alex's interest in lizards led him to subscribe to a herpetologists' magazine and to read every issue from cover to cover. Similarly, people interested in antique automobiles might tinker with an old Model T engine until they know that engine inside and out. And people interested in gymnastics might spend a good portion of their free time at the gym practicing, practicing, practicing.

In addition, interest promotes more effective information processing. People who are interested in a particular topic show greater cognitive engagement in that topic (Pintrich, et al., 1993; Schiefele & Wild, 1994; Wigfield, 1994). They are also more likely to process information in a meaningful and elaborative fashion—for example, by relating it to things they already know, drawing inferences, forming visual images, generating their own examples, and identifying potential applications (Hidi, 1990; Hidi & Anderson, 1992; Pintrich & Schrauben, 1992; Schiefele, 1991, 1992; Schiefele & Wild, 1994; Tobias, 1994). As an illustration, ninth graders in an experiment by Bernstein (1955) read two prose passages that, in terms of objective measures, were equally readable. "The Get-Away Boy" was an action-packed, suspenseful story with a teenage hero and colorful images. "The House on Smith Street," adapted from Nathaniel Hawthorne's *The House of the Seven Gables,* contained dull, descriptive passages and included no human action whatsoever. After reading both stories, students rated them for their interest level and took a test that measured meaningful learning and elaboration of each one (items assessed such elaborative processes as drawing inferences, recognizing literary devices, and determining the writer's purpose). Students' ratings of the two stories confirmed the experimenters' belief that "The Get-Away Boy" was considerably more interesting than "The House on Smith Street." Furthermore, the students' test results revealed significantly more meaningful learning and elaboration for "The Get-Away Boy."

As you might guess, then, students who are interested in the things they study are more likely to remember them over the long run and thus are able to build on them in future learning (Garner et al., 1991, 1992; Hidi, 1990; Renninger, 1992; Scholes & Kardash, 1996; Wigfield, 1994). As a result, interested students show higher academic achievement (Krapp et al., 1992; Schiefele, Krapp, & Winteler, 1992).

Factors Promoting Interest

Researchers have identified several sources of situational interest. Some topics—for example, death, destruction, danger, money, romance, and sex—appear to be inherently interesting for human beings (Schank, 1979). Things that are new, different, or unexpected often generate interest, as do things with a high activity level or intense emotions (Deci, 1992; Hidi, 1990; Hidi & Anderson, 1992; Schank, 1979; Wade, 1992). Works of fiction—novels, short stories, movies, and so on—are more engaging when they include themes and characters with which people can personally identify (Hidi, 1990; Hidi & Anderson, 1992; Schank, 1979; Wade, 1992). Nonfiction is more interesting when it is easy to understand and relationships among ideas are clear (Wade, 1992). And, for children at least, challenging tasks are often more interesting than easy ones (Danner & Lonky, 1981; Harter, 1978), a fortunate state of affairs if, as Lev Vygotsky proposed, challenges promote cognitive growth.

Interesting information sometimes appears within the context of larger, less interesting content. Consider this passage as an example:

> Some insects live alone, and some live in large families. Wasps that live alone are called solitary wasps. A Mud Dauber Wasp is a solitary wasp. Click Beetles live alone. When a click beetle is on its back, it flips itself into the air and lands right side up while it makes a clicking noise. Ants live in large families. There are many kinds of ants. Some ants live in trees. Black Ants live in the ground. (Garner, Gillingham, & White, 1989, p. 46)

If you are like me, you may have found the sentence about an upside-down beetle making a clicking noise as it rights itself to be the one interesting detail in an otherwise ho-hum passage. Yet notice that this sentence does *not* contribute to the paragraph's general theme—the social or nonsocial nature of various species of insects. Such "seductive details"—interesting but irrelevant tidbits—do not necessarily enhance learning and retention of the overall content in which they appear; in fact, they may in many cases steal readers' attention from more important, and perhaps more abstract, ideas (Garner et al., 1989, 1991, 1992). Seductive details are particularly likely to be distracting when readers have only limited background knowledge about a topic and therefore have little basis for determining what is and is not important (Alexander & Jetton, 1996; Garner et al., 1991).

The origins of personal interest have not been investigated to the extent that sources of situational interest have. Many personal interests probably come from people's prior experiences with various topics and activities; for example, objects or events that initially invoke situational interest may provide the seed from which personal interest will eventually grow (Alexander, in press). People may also find that acquiring more knowledge and skill in a particular area enhances their sense of self-efficacy, thereby providing intrinsic reinforcement. To some extent, interest and knowledge seem to perpetuate each other: Personal interest in a topic fuels a quest to learn more about the topic, and the increasing knowledge that one gains in turn promotes greater interest (Alexander, in press; Hidi & McLaren, 1990; Kintsch, 1980; Tobias, 1994).

People are more likely to be interested in pursuing an activity when they think their behaviors will lead to desired outcomes. But some individuals fail to recognize existing contingencies between the behaviors they exhibit and the consequences that result. To what sources do people attribute the events that occur in their lives? To what things do they give credit when they succeed? What things do they blame when they fail? We will find out as we explore attribution theory in the next section.

ATTRIBUTIONS

You have undoubtedly gotten As on some of the classroom exams you have taken. On those occasions, why do you think you did so well? Did you study hard? Were the exams easy? Did you luck out and guess right on questions you knew little about? Or is it simply that you are an incredibly intelligent human being?

And now let's consider those exams on which you haven't done so well. To what did you attribute your failures? Did you spend too little time studying, or did you perhaps study the wrong things? Were the exams too difficult? Were the questions poorly worded, so that you misinterpreted many that you should have answered correctly? Were you too tired or sick to think clearly? Or do you just not have what it takes?

People's various explanations for success and failure—their beliefs about what causes what—are **attributions**.[2] Many theorists contend that attributions play a major role in the choices people make and the behaviors they ultimately exhibit (Dweck, 1986; Graham, 1994; Weiner, 1979, 1980, 1984, 1986). From an attribution theory perspective, how people interpret the reinforcements and punishments they experience—for example, whether they think an event is the result of something that they themselves have done or instead the result of something that has been done *to* them—influences the long-term effects that reinforcement and punishment are likely to have.

Attribution theory has been a major focus of scientific investigation in recent years. In the pages that follow, we will look at the kinds of attributions we are likely to see and at their varying effects on behavior and cognition. We will identify reasons why different people form different attributions. We will discover that many individuals are consistent in their interpretations of events and consequences, with some exhibiting a mastery orientation and others demonstrating learned helplessness. And we will find that, given certain environmental conditions, people can acquire more productive attributions than they currently have.

Dimensions Underlying People's Attributions

People are apt to explain events in a variety of ways. For example, school children may attribute their successes and failures in the classroom to such things as effort, ability, luck, task difficulty, health, mood, physical appearance, or teachers' or peers' behaviors (Schunk, 1990). It is important to note that attributions are as much a function of people's *perceptions* as of reality; thus, they are often distorted in line with one's self-concept and existing

---

[2]Some theorists use the term *causal attributions*.

schemas about how the world operates (Dweck, 1978; Dweck & Elliott, 1983; Paris & Byrnes, 1989). For example, your poor performance on exams in years past may very well have been due to ineffective study strategies; like many students, you may have tried to learn class material in a rote, meaningless fashion (you obviously hadn't read this book yet!). But because you thought of yourself as a smart person and believed that you *had* studied adequately, you instead attributed your low score to the exam's exceptional difficulty or your teacher's capriciousness.

Bernard Weiner (1984, 1986) has proposed that attributions differ from one another in five ways—locus, temporal stability, cross-situational generality, controllability, and intentionality:

- *Locus ("place"): internal versus external.* We sometimes attribute the causes of events to *internal* things—that is, to factors within ourselves. Thinking that a good grade is due to your own hard work and believing that a poor grade is due to your lack of ability are examples of internal attributions. At other times, we attribute events to *external* things—to factors outside of ourselves. Concluding that you received a scholarship because you were lucky and interpreting a classmate's scowl as being due to her bad mood (rather than to anything you have done to deserve such a scowl) are examples of external attributions. Theorists sometimes refer to this "locus" dimension as **locus of control.**

- *Temporal stability: stable versus unstable.* Sometimes we believe that events are due to *stable* factors—to things that probably won't change much in the near future. For example, if you believe that you do well in school because of inherited ability or that you have trouble making friends because you're too fat, then you may be attributing events to stable, relatively unchangeable causes. But sometimes we instead believe that events are the result of *unstable* factors—to things that can change from one time to the next. Thinking that winning a tennis game was just a "fluke" and believing that you got a bad test grade because you were tired when you took the test are examples of attributions involving unstable factors.

- *Cross-situational generality: global versus specific.* We sometimes attribute events to *global* factors that influence many aspects of our lives. For example, you may believe that you did poorly on an exam because you are a complete ignoramus about anything academic. At other times, we attribute events to causes that are *specific* to a particular situation. For example, you may think you landed an especially lucrative job simply because you were in the right place at the right time.

- *Controllability: controllable versus uncontrollable.* On some occasions we attribute events to *controllable* factors—to things we can influence and change. For example, if you believe that a classmate invited you to coffee because you always smile and say nice things to her, and if you think you probably failed a test simply because you didn't study the right things, then you are attributing these events to controllable factors. On other occasions, we attribute events to *uncontrollable* factors—to things over which we have no control. For example, if you think that you were chosen for a title role in *Romeo and Juliet* because the director thinks you have the right face for the part, or that you played a lousy game of basketball because you had a mild case of the flu, then you are attributing these events to uncontrollable factors.[3]

- *Intentionality: intentional versus unintentional.* Our attributions may be due to either *intentional* or *unintentional* factors—to things we either did or didn't mean to do. Believing you failed an exam because you didn't study hard enough is an intentional factor: You consciously chose to do things other than study. On the other hand, using ineffective learning strategies is *un*intentional: You approached your class material in a rote, meaningless fashion only because you didn't know any better.

We can analyze virtually any attribution in terms of these five dimensions. For example, viewing success on a task as being due to inherited ability is an internal, stable, global, uncontrollable, and unintentional attribution. Believing failure on a task was a case of bad luck is an external, unstable, specific, uncontrollable, and unintentional attribution. Table 18-2 analyzes eight common attributions that students are likely to make along three of the five dimensions—locus, stability, and controllability.

As you look at Table 18-2, you might think to yourself that "ability can change with practice, so is unstable and controllable" or that "teachers' attitudes toward students often depend on how students behave in the classroom, so are really due to internal, unstable, and controllable factors." Perhaps you are right, but keep in mind that people's *beliefs* about the locus, stability, and controllability of their attributions, not the reality of the situation, are what affect their future behavior (Dweck & Leggett, 1988; Weiner, 1994).

Generally speaking, we tend to attribute our successes to internal causes (e.g., high ability or hard work) and our failures to external causes (e.g., bad luck or the inconsiderate behavior of others) (Igoe & Sullivan, 1991; Marsh, 1986, 1990; Weisz & Cameron, 1985; Whitley & Frieze, 1985). By patting ourselves on the back for the things we do well and putting the blame elsewhere for poor performance, we are able to maintain a positive self-concept (Katkovsky, Crandall, & Good, 1967; Paris & Byrnes, 1989) and so presumably maintain our sense of self-worth. When we attribute our failures inaccurately to factors outside of ourselves, however, we are unlikely to change our behavior in ways that will lead to greater success (Seligman, 1991). Let's look more closely at the various effects that attributions, accurate or otherwise, are likely to have on how we think, feel, and behave.

---

[3]Weisz and Cameron (1985) have suggested that a sense of control has two components. First, one must believe that there is a *contingency* between the behavior and the outcome—in other words, that a particular behavior can cause a certain event to occur. Second, one must have a sense of *competence* (i.e., self-efficacy) that one is actually capable of performing the necessary behavior. According to Weisz and Cameron, an individual is apt to feel that an event is uncontrollable if either one of these components is missing. For example, a student may know that good grades will result from making correct responses in class but may not believe that he or she has the ability to make those responses; in this situation there is a sense of contingency but no sense of competence (Weisz, 1986). As another example, a person from a minority group may have high self-efficacy for achieving a particular goal yet feel that the racial prejudice and discrimination of others will nevertheless make success impossible; in this case there is a sense of competence but no sense of contingency (Pintrich & Schunk, 1996; Sue & Chin, 1983).

Table 18–2
Analyzing various student attributions in terms of the three dimensions.

Success or Failure Attributed to	Locus	Stability	Controllability
Inherited "ability"	Internal	Stable	Uncontrollable
Personality	Internal	Stable	Uncontrollable
Effort	Internal	Unstable	Controllable
Health	Internal	Unstable	Uncontrollable
Energy level	Internal	Unstable	Uncontrollable
Task difficulty	External	Stable	Uncontrollable
Teacher's attitudes	External	Stable	Uncontrollable
Luck or chance	External	Unstable	Uncontrollable

Effects of Attributions

Attributions influence numerous aspects of behavior and cognition. Among other things, they affect an individual's (a) emotional reactions to success and failure, (b) expectations for future success or failure, (c) effort and persistence, (d) learning strategies, (e) future choices, (f) self-efficacy, and (g) responses to failure situations.

Emotional Reactions to Success and Failure

People are, of course, happy when they succeed. But do they also feel *proud* of their accomplishments? When they believe that their successes are due to the actions of another person or to some other outside force, they are apt to feel grateful rather than proud. Individuals feel pride and satisfaction about their successes only when they attribute those successes to internal causes—that is, to something that they themselves have done (Weiner, Russell, & Lerman, 1978, 1979).

Along a similar vein, people usually feel a certain amount of sadness after a failure. When they believe that failure is due to external causes—to events and people outside of themselves—they are apt to feel angry and resentful. When they instead believe that their failure is due to their own lack of ability or effort, they are apt to feel guilty or ashamed (Eccles & Wigfield, 1985; Weiner et al., 1978, 1979). People who attribute failure to internal causes, and especially to their lack of ability, often have lower self-esteem as a result (Covington, Spratt, & Omelich, 1980).

Expectations for Future Success or Failure

When people attribute their successes and failures to stable factors, they will expect their future performance to be similar to their current performance. In this situation success leads to an anticipation of future success, and failure breeds an expectation of more failure to come. In contrast, when people attribute their successes and failures to *un*stable factors—for example, to effort or luck—then their current success rate will have less influence on their expectation for future success (Dweck, 1978; Fennema, 1987; Schunk, 1990; Weiner, 1986). The most optimistic individuals—those who have the highest expectations for future success—are the ones who attribute their successes to stable factors (such as innate ability) and their failures to unstable yet controllable factors (such as lack of effort) (Eccles [Parsons], 1983; Fennema, 1987; Murray & Jackson, 1982/1983; Schunk, 1990; Weiner, 1984).

We should note here that as children grow older they change their beliefs about the stability of intelligence and ability. When they first enter school, they typically believe that ability is a function of effort and therefore is an unstable and controllable entity. However, as they progress through the elementary and middle school grades, they gradually begin to view ability as an inherited characteristic that they either do or do not possess—thus, as something that is stable and uncontrollable (Dweck, 1986; Nicholls, 1990; Paris & Byrnes, 1989; Ruble, 1980; Schunk, 1990). As you might predict, then, younger children who experience a temporary failure are far more optimistic about their chances for future success than are older children and adolescents (Dweck & Elliott, 1983; Eccles & Wigfield, 1985; Paris & Byrnes, 1989; Stipek & Gralinski, 1990).

We should also note a difference between males and females that appears consistently in research studies (Carr & Jessup, 1994; Deaux, 1984; Durkin, 1987; Dweck, 1978; Fennema, 1987; Huston, 1983; Stipek & Gralinski, 1990). Males are more likely to attribute their successes to ability and their failures to lack of effort, thus having the attitude that *I know I can do this because I have the ability.* Females show the reverse pattern: They attribute their successes to effort and their failures to lack of ability, believing that *I don't know if I can keep on doing it, because I'm not very good at this type of thing.* This gender difference is evident even when males' and females' previous levels of achievement are the same; we are especially likely to see it for stereotypically "male" activities such as mathematics and sports (Eccles & Jacobs, 1986; Eccles, Jacobs, Harold-Goldsmith, Jayaratne, & Yee, 1989; Stipek, 1984). As a result, males set higher expectations for themselves than females do, especially in traditionally masculine arenas.

Effort and Persistence

When people believe that their failures are due to their own lack of effort—that they *do* have the ability to succeed if they try hard enough—they are likely to exert more effort in future situations and to persist in the face of difficulty. When they instead attribute failure to a lack of innate ability (they couldn't do it even if they tried), they give up easily and sometimes cannot even perform tasks they have previously accomplished successfully (Brophy, 1986; Dweck, 1978; Eccles [Parsons], 1983; Feather, 1982; Rowe, 1983; Weiner, 1984). Students with a history of academic failure are especially likely to attribute their classroom difficulties to low ability, and they often stop trying as a result (Pressley, Borkowski, & Schneider, 1987).

Learning Strategies

People's attributions and resulting expectations for future performance clearly affect the cognitive strategies they apply to learning tasks. Students who expect to succeed in the classroom and believe that academic success is a result of their own doing are more likely to apply effective study strategies when trained in their use (Palmer & Goetz, 1988;

Pressley, Borkowski, & Schneider, 1987). These students are also more likely to seek their teacher's assistance when they don't understand course material and to attend extra help sessions when they need them (Ames, 1983; Ames & Lau, 1982). And students with high expectations for success are more likely to approach problem-solving tasks in a logical, systematic, and meaningful fashion (Tyler, 1958). In contrast, students who expect failure and believe that their academic performance is largely out of their hands often reject effective learning and problem-solving strategies in favor of rote-learning approaches.

Future Choices

As you might expect, individuals whose attributions lead them to expect success in a particular subject area are more likely to pursue that area—for example, by enrolling in more courses in the same discipline (Dweck, 1986; Eccles [Parsons], 1984; Stipek & Gralinski, 1990; Weiner, 1986). Individuals who believe their chances for future success in an activity are slim will avoid that activity whenever they can. And when people don't continue to pursue an activity, they can't possibly get better at it.

Self-Efficacy

In our culture young children, particularly those in kindergarten and first grade, tend to believe they have the ability to do well in school if they expend a reasonable amount of effort (Dweck & Elliott, 1983; Stipek & Gralinski, 1990). As children get older, many of them increasingly begin to attribute their successes and failures to inherited intelligence or natural talent—things they believe to be stable and beyond their control. If these students are usually successful at school activities, they come to believe that they have high ability; in other words, they develop a high sense of self-efficacy for academic tasks. But if, instead, students experience frequent failure in their schoolwork, and especially if they attribute this failure to low ability rather than to lack of effort or poor study strategies, they may develop low self-efficacy concerning their competence in academic subjects (Dweck, 1986; Dweck & Elliott, 1983; Eccles [Parsons], 1983; Hong, Chiu, & Dweck, 1995; Schunk, 1990).

This state of affairs is likely to lead to a self-fulfilling prophecy. As we discovered in Chapter 7, people with low self-efficacy choose less challenging tasks, give up more easily, and ultimately learn and achieve at lower levels than their more self-confident peers. As a result, they will experience few of the successes they need to feel more efficacious. Furthermore, children with low self-efficacy tend to attribute the successes they do achieve to external factors and the failures to internal factors, thereby giving themselves little credit for the things they do well and blaming themselves for the things they do poorly (Ickes & Layden, 1978).

Responses to Failure Situations

As we have seen, many people believe that ability is an uncontrollable, stable characteristic—a built-in, "natural" talent. Many also believe that there is an inverse relationship between ability and effort: Success with little effort reflects high ability, and success that comes only with a great deal of effort is a sign of low ability (Barker & Graham, 1987; Covington & Omelich, 1979; Dweck & Elliott, 1983; Eccles [Parsons], 1983; Graham, 1990). These beliefs are especially prevalent when people have performance goals rather than learning goals (see Table 18-1).

For such individuals, effort is probably a "double-edged sword" (Covington & Omelich, 1979; Covington et al., 1980; Eccles & Wigfield, 1985). Those who perceive themselves to have low ability are in a no-win situation. If they don't try hard, failure is inevitable. If they *do* try hard and fail anyway, they look "stupid," at least in their own eyes. Many of them therefore do not try very hard (one form of self-handicapping), perhaps as a way of saving face and hiding the low ability they believe they have (Covington, 1992; Covington & Beery, 1976; Covington et al., 1980; Dweck, 1986; Eccles & Wigfield, 1985; Jagacinski & Nicholls, 1990; Murray & Jackson, 1982/1983; Schunk, 1990). They may also decide that the activity isn't worth doing—in other words, they attach little value to it (Covington & Beery, 1976; Eccles & Wigfield, 1985).

Attribution theorists propose that people respond most favorably to failure situations when they attribute these failures to internal, unstable, and controllable variables such as effort and strategies (Clifford, 1984; Curtis & Graham, 1991; Pressley, Borkowski, & Schneider, 1987). But blaming lack of effort alone can backfire. Individuals who try hard and still fail are likely to reach the conclusion that they have low ability— that they simply don't have what it takes. Therefore, it is more beneficial to attribute failure to strategies as well—to believe that they could succeed if they did things *differently* (Curtis & Graham, 1991; Pressley, Borkowski, & Schneider, 1987). Such attributions often characterize good students, who know that they need not only to work hard but also to work strategically (Brophy, 1987; Pressley, Borkowski, & Schneider, 1987; Weinstein et al., 1991).

Why do different people attribute the same events to different causes? For example, why does one individual believe that a failure is merely a temporary setback due to an inappropriate strategy, while another attributes the same failure to low ability, and still another believes it to be the result of someone else's capricious and unpredictable actions? Let's look at variables affecting the development of different attributions.

Factors Influencing the Development of Attributions

Researchers have identified at least five variables that influence the development of different attributions for success and failure: past successes and failures, the degree to which successes and failures have been followed by reinforcement or punishment, situational cues, the expectations that others communicate, and the attributions that others assign to one's performance.[4]

Past Successes and Failures

As you might expect, the attributions that people develop result partly from their previous success and failure experiences (Klein, 1990; Paris & Byrnes, 1989; Pressley, Borkowski, & Schneider, 1987; Schunk, 1990; Stipek, 1993). Those who have tried and succeeded in the past are more likely to believe that success is due to internal factors, such as effort or high ability. Those who have tried and failed, or who have had an

---

[4]The specific attributions that people make may also be influenced by cultural variables (e.g., see Hidalgo, Siu, Bright, Swap, & Epstein, 1995; Lillard, 1997; Miller, 1986; Triandis, 1995).

inconsistent pattern of successes and failures, are likely to believe that success is due to something beyond their control—perhaps to an ability they don't possess or to such external factors as a tough break or poor instruction.

When we consider students in the classroom, metacognition plays a role here as well. In Chapter 14 we discovered that students often think they have learned something they actually have *not* learned; in other words, they have an *illusion of knowing*. When these students do poorly on an exam, they cannot attribute their performance to internal factors; after all, they studied hard and so "know" the material. Instead, they are likely to attribute it to such external factors as bad luck, exam difficulty, or teacher capriciousness (Horgan, 1990).

Reinforcement and Punishment

Generally speaking, children are more likely to attribute events to internal, controllable causes when adults reinforce their successes but don't punish their failures. Conversely, children are more likely to make external attributions when adults punish failures and ignore successes (Katkovsky et al., 1967). It appears that people are more likely to accept responsibility for their failures if others don't made a big deal of them.

Situational Cues

Characteristics specific to a particular situation may influence the attributions that people make. Features of the task being performed are one influential characteristic; for example, complex math problems (e.g., those that include more numbers) are perceived as being more difficult, and so failure to solve those problems can readily be attributed to task difficulty rather than to internal causes (Schunk, 1990). The performance of others provides another cue; for example, a failure is apt to be attributed to task difficulty if everyone else is failing, whereas it is more likely to be attributed to an internal source such as lack of ability if others are succeeding (Schunk, 1990; Weiner, 1984).

Others' Expectations

Other people communicate their beliefs about an individual's ability, and thus their expectations for the individual's performance, in a variety of subtle ways. For example, as we discovered in Chapter 13, teachers who hold high expectations for students' performance are likely to teach more material and more difficult material, insist on high student performance, give students more opportunities to respond to questions, rephrase questions when students are having trouble answering them, and provide specific feedback about the strengths and weaknesses of various responses. In contrast, teachers who hold low expectations for their students often present easy rather than challenging tasks, give students more assistance than necessary, accept low levels of performance, criticize incorrect answers to questions, and overlook good performance when it occurs. Minority students with a history of academic failure are especially likely to be the recipients of such low-ability signals (Graham, 1990).

To some extent, teachers' expectations are based on the performance students have previously demonstrated. Yet even when several students all have the same history of success and failure, teachers and other adults may hold different expectations for each of these students, and their expectations in turn lead to different student attributions and varying levels of performance (Brophy & Good, 1970; Eccles & Wigfield, 1985; Eccles [Parsons] et al., 1983; Harris & Rosenthal, 1985; Miller, Brickman, & Bolen, 1975; Murray & Jackson, 1982/1983; Palardy, 1969; Yee & Eccles, 1988). As an illustration, a study by Miller and his colleagues (1975) demonstrates the effect of teacher expectations on students' littering behavior. One group of fifth graders was repeatedly labeled neat and clean; for example, a poster of a Peanuts character on the wall proclaimed that "We are Andersen's litter-conscious class," and, after noticing a piece of litter on the floor, the teacher stated that "Our class is clean and would not do that." For a second group of students, persuasion was used in various forms to alter littering behavior; for example, a poster of a Peanuts character advocated, "Don't be a litterbug," and the teacher explained why garbage should always be thrown away (e.g., it draws flies and endangers health). To test the relative effects of the two treatments, the experimenters provided opportunities for the students to litter (by distributing candy wrapped in cellophane and, two weeks later, by handing out toy puzzles in disposable plastic containers); they also scattered several candy wrappers and plastic puzzle containers on the floor while the students were at recess. A short time later, the experimenters counted the number of candy wrappers and plastic containers that remained on the floor: Students who had consistently been labeled neat and clean left significantly fewer pieces of litter than those who had specifically been persuaded not to litter.

With the effects of teacher expectations in mind, we should note that teacher assistance, while often a valuable source of scaffolding on difficult tasks, may be counterproductive if students don't really need it. When students struggle temporarily with a task, the unsolicited help of their teacher may communicate the message that they have low ability and little control regarding their own successes and failures. In contrast, allowing students to struggle on their own for a reasonable period of time conveys the belief that students do have the ability to succeed on their own (Graham, 1990, 1997; Graham & Barker, 1990; Stipek, 1996; Weiner, 1984).

Others' Attributions

Just as we ourselves form attributions regarding the causes of our performance, those around us may form their own opinions regarding why we have succeeded or failed (Eccles & Wigfield, 1985; Graham, 1990; Seligman, 1991; Weiner, 1984). Research indicates that children's attributions for their own successes and failures are often similar to the attributions that parents and teachers assign to those successes and failures (Dweck, Davidson, Nelson, & Enna, 1978; Lueptow, 1984; Parsons, Adler, & Kaczala, 1982; Schunk, 1982; Yee & Eccles, 1988).

In some cases other people communicate their attributions verbally and explicitly. For example, consider the things a teacher might say about a student's success:

- You did it! You're so smart!
- That's wonderful. Your hard work has really paid off, hasn't it?
- You've done very well. It's clear that you really know how to study.
- Terrific! This is definitely your lucky day!

Consider, also, the statements a teacher might make about a student's failure:

- Hmmm, maybe this just isn't something you're good at. Perhaps we should try something different.
- Why don't you practice a little more and then try again?

- Let's see if we can come up with some study strategies that might work better for you.
- Maybe you're just having a bad day.

All of these are well-intended comments, presumably designed to make a student feel good, but notice the different attributions they imply. In some cases success or failure is attributed to controllable (and therefore changeable) student behaviors—that is, to hard work or lack of practice or to the use of effective or ineffective study strategies. But in other cases the student's success or failure is attributed to uncontrollable ability— that is, to being smart or not "good at" something. And in still other cases the student's success is attributed to external, uncontrollable causes—that is, to a lucky break or a bad day.

Other individuals may also communicate their attributions indirectly through the things that they say and do. For example, when teachers criticize and express anger about students' poor performance, they convey the message that students have sufficient ability to master the task and simply aren't trying hard enough. But when teachers express pity for the same performance, they communicate their belief that students' low ability is the reason for their failure (Graham, 1984, 1990, 1991, 1997; Pintrich & Schunk, 1996; Weiner, 1984). Frequent praise is often a message that students' successes are due to their efforts; however, by praising students for *easy* tasks, teachers may simultaneously convey the message that success wasn't expected—in other words, that students have low ability (Graham, 1990, 1991; Schunk, 1989b; Stipek, 1993, 1996).

As an illustration, Barker and Graham (1987) asked 4- to 12-year-old children to watch a videotape depicting two boys either solving single-digit math problems at the blackboard or throwing balls through a large hoop in the gymnasium; the two tasks appeared to be easy ones for the boys to accomplish. Some of the children saw a videotape in which both boys succeeded; the teacher praised one boy (e.g., "Great job!") but gave the other only neutral feedback (e.g., "Correct"). Other children saw a videotape in which the two boys failed at their task; one was criticized for this failure (e.g., "What's the matter with you? That's not the right answer!") and the others, again, given neutral feedback (e.g., "No, not quite"). The children were subsequently asked to rate the two boys for either intelligence (for the math problem videos) or throwing ability (for the ball-throwing videos) on a five-point scale. Younger children (4- and 5-year-olds) concluded that the boy praised for his success had higher ability than the other boy; in contrast, older children (11- and 12-year-olds) concluded that the praised boy had *lower* ability. At the same time, younger children deduced that the boy criticized for his failure had lower ability, while older children came to the opposite conclusion. Children who were 8 or 9 years old assigned similar ratings to both boys in both success and failure situations. Thus, we see a developmental change as children grow older: They become increasingly likely to interpret praise for an easy success as a sign of low ability and to interpret blame for failure on an easy task as an indication of high ability.

Operant conditioning theorists propose that praise is a form of reinforcement; hence, it should increase the behavior it follows. Here we see an opposing viewpoint: Praise may sometimes be counterproductive, at least for easy tasks. When it communicates low ability, students may be unwilling to exert much effort on later tasks. Praise for students' effort is likely to be effective only when students *have* exerted that effort.

For reasons we have just identified, different people may interpret the same events in very different ways. Over time, students gradually develop predictable patterns of attributions and expectations for their future performance. Some remain optimistic, confident that they can master new tasks and succeed in a variety of endeavors. But others, either unsure of their own chances for success or else convinced that they *can't* succeed, display a growing sense of futility. Theorists have characterized this difference among students as being a difference in *explanatory style*.

Explanatory Style: Mastery Orientation versus Learned Helplessness

When we discussed the effects of aversive stimuli in Chapter 6, we encountered the phenomenon of learned helplessness: When organisms repeatedly encounter aversive stimuli that they cannot avoid, escape, or terminate, they eventually give up and passively accept those stimuli. Although much of the early research on learned helplessness was conducted with animals, this concept has been incorporated into cognitive theorists' notion of explanatory style.

A person's **explanatory style** is the general way in which the individual interprets daily events and consequences.[5] Some people typically attribute their accomplishments to their own abilities and efforts; they have an I-can-do-it attitude known as a **mastery orientation.** Others attribute successes to outside and uncontrollable factors and believe that their failures reflect a lack of ability; they have an I-can't-do-it attitude known as **learned helplessness** (Dweck, 1986; Dweck & Licht, 1980; Dweck & Reppucci, 1973; Eccles & Wigfield, 1985; Mikulincer, 1994; Peterson, Maier, & Seligman, 1993; Wood et al., 1990). You should think of this distinction as a continuum of individual differences rather than a complete dichotomy. You might also look at it as a difference between *optimists* and *pessimists* (Peterson, 1990; Seligman, 1991).

To illustrate, consider these two boys, keeping in mind that both boys have the same ability level:

- Jerry is an enthusiastic, energetic learner. He enjoys working hard at school activities and takes obvious pleasure in doing well. He is always looking for a challenge and especially likes to solve the brainteaser problems that his teacher assigns as extra-credit work each day. He can't always solve the problems, but he takes failure in stride and is eager for more problems the following day.
- Jason is an anxious, fidgety student. He doesn't seem to have much confidence in his ability to accomplish school tasks successfully. In fact, he is always underestimating what he can do; even when he has succeeded, he doubts that he can do it again. He seems to prefer filling out drill-and-practice worksheets that

[5]Some theorists instead use the term *attributional style*.

help him practice skills he's already mastered rather than attempting new tasks and problems. As for those daily brainteasers, he sometimes takes a stab at them, but he gives up quickly if the answer isn't readily apparent.

Jerry exhibits a mastery orientation: He clearly has his life (and his attributions) under control, and he is optimistic about his future performance. In contrast, Jason displays learned helplessness: He believes that challenging tasks are out of his reach and beyond his control, and he expects failure rather than success.

Researchers have identified a number of ways in which people with a mastery orientation differ from those with learned helplessness. For example, in an academic context, those with a mastery orientation tend to perform better in the classroom than we would predict from their aptitude test scores and previous grade point averages (Seligman, 1991). In an athletic context, optimists bounce back from a lost game more readily, and overcome injuries more quickly, than do equally capable but more pessimistic athletes (Peterson, 1990).

Table 18-3 lists additional differences between a mastery orientation and learned helplessness. As you can see from this table, people with a mastery orientation behave in ways that lead to higher achievement over the long run: They set high goals, seek challenging situations, and persist in the face of failure. People feeling learned helplessness behave very differently: Because they underestimate their own ability, they set goals they can easily accomplish, avoid situations likely to maximize their learning and growth, and respond to failure in counterproductive ways.

In a nutshell, people with a mastery orientation attribute their successes to internal, global, and somewhat stable factors, and they believe that the reasons for their failures are temporary and often within their control. In contrast, those with learned helplessness attribute their successes to external and uncontrollable factors, and they interpret their failures as reflecting a relatively pervasive and permanent lack of ability (Seligman, 1991).

Young children rarely show signs of learned helplessness; we are more likely to see it in adolescents and adults (Paris & Cunningham, 1996; Peterson et al., 1993). As I indicated in Chapter 6, helplessness sometimes develops when people consistently find that they have little or no control over the things that happen to them. It may also develop when people observe *other* individuals having little control over their lives (Brown & Inouye, 1978; Peterson et al., 1993). In some cases, entire *groups* can begin to feel helpless when group members are asked to work together on tasks that, despite their best efforts, they cannot accomplish successfully (Simkin, Lederer, & Seligman, 1983). When people have a history of experiences in which they *have* had control of their successes and failures, however, they are less likely to succumb to learned helplessness in the face of temporarily uncontrollable events (Peterson et al., 1993).

Can people's attributions and explanatory styles be changed? Let's look at what research tells us about this question.

Changing Attributions

Several studies have shown that, for school-age children at least, attributions can be altered, with more persistence in the face of failure being the result (Andrews & Debus,

Table 18–3

Characteristics of a mastery orientation versus learned helplessness.

People with a Mastery Orientation	People with Learned Helplessness
• Have higher self-esteem and greater self-efficacy about their chances for success	• Have low self-esteem and poor self-efficacy
• Set high goals for themselves	• Set low, easily accomplished goals for themselves
• Prefer new and challenging tasks	• Prefer easy tasks and tasks they have already completed successfully
• Strive for success	• Try to avoid failure
• Believe that prior successes are an indication of high ability and future success	• Don't see prior successes as indicative of high ability and future success; *do* see prior failures as an indication of low ability and future failure
• Accurately estimate their number of prior successes	• Underestimate their prior successes; may even forget about them
• View failure as a challenge to be met	• Define themselves as "failures" when they fail
• Persist when facing difficulty; try to determine the source of difficulty; seek assistance if needed	• Become anxious and discouraged when facing difficulty; use ineffective strategies; may experience depression
• Increase effort and concentration after failure	• Decrease effort and concentration after failure; give up quickly
• Take pride in their accomplishments	• Don't take pride in their accomplishments because they don't believe they *caused* them; may take more responsibility for their failures than is warranted
• Perform and achieve at higher levels	• Perform and achieve at lower levels

Sources: Abramson, Seligman, & Teasdale, 1978; Diener & Dweck, 1978; Dweck, 1975, 1986; Dweck & Licht, 1980; Dweck & Reppucci, 1973; Meyer, Turner, & Spencer, 1994; Peterson, 1990; Peterson & Barrett, 1987; Peterson, Colvin, & Lin, 1992; Peterson et al., 1993; Seligman, 1991; Wood et al., 1990

1978; Chapin & Dyck, 1976; Dweck, 1975; Fowler & Peterson, 1981). In these **attribution retraining** studies, children are asked to engage in a particular task (e.g., reading difficult sentences, solving arithmetic problems, or constructing geometric puzzles), with occasional failures interspersed among more frequent successes. Within this context, one viable approach for changing attributions is for an adult to interpret each success in terms of the effort a child has exerted and each failure in terms of insufficient effort (Chapin &

Dyck, 1976; Dweck, 1975; Fowler & Peterson, 1981). Another effective approach is to reinforce children for attributing their *own* successes and failures to effort or a lack thereof (Andrews & Debus, 1978; Fowler & Peterson, 1981).

Early studies focused on effort attributions, but later studies indicated that effort attributions are not always the most beneficial attributions for children to acquire. For example, greater self-efficacy may result when an experimenter attributes a child's successes (but not failures) to ability rather than effort (e.g., "You're good at this") (Schunk, 1983a). And attributions to effective and ineffective learning strategies (for success and failure, respectively) are often more productive than effort attributions, particularly when such attribution retraining accompanies a study strategies training program (Pressley, Borkowski, & Schneider, 1987; Weinstein et al., 1991).

Yet we must remember that people's views of themselves and their abilities are not likely to change dramatically overnight. Efforts to change attributions probably need to be an ongoing endeavor rather than a one-shot deal (Meece, 1994; Paris, 1990). In classroom contexts, teachers can do a variety of things to promote internal, controllable attributions and an overall mastery orientation. For instance, they can portray knowledge and skills as things that, with hard work and occasional inevitable errors, will undoubtedly increase over time (Good & Brophy, 1994). They can describe and model how they themselves learn—for example, by recalling situations in which they have mastered something only after they've exerted considerable effort or tried several different strategies (Good & Brophy, 1994). They can give students numerous opportunities to improve assignments and overall class grades (Ames, 1992). And they should certainly evaluate students on the basis of mastery of class material rather than on how students compare with one another (Ames, 1992; Good & Brophy, 1994).

Ultimately, people are most likely to be optimistic about their futures when they have the confidence that they can succeed in their endeavors and believe that they can control their destinies. In the next few pages, we will look more closely at the role that such beliefs about *competence* and *self-determination* play in human motivation.

COMPETENCE AND SELF-DETERMINATION

As you should recall from the preceding chapter, intrinsic motivation has several advantages over extrinsic motivation. For instance, when people are intrinsically motivated, they are more likely to pursue a task on their own initiative, keep their attention focused on it, learn meaningfully, and persist in the face of failure. Edward Deci and Richard Ryan (1985, 1987, 1992; also see Boggiano & Pittman, 1992; Connell & Wellborn, 1991; McCombs, 1988; Spaulding, 1992) have proposed that intrinsic motivation is most likely to be present when two conditions exist. First of all, individuals must believe that they are capable of successfully executing the tasks before them; that is, they must have a sense of **competence.** Second, individuals must believe that they can, to some extent, choose and regulate the course of their lives; in other words, they must have a sense of **self-determination.** When both conditions are present, people experience greater pleasure and satisfaction in performing a task.

Let's look more closely at the concepts of competence and self-determination. As we do so, we'll identify a number of variables likely to promote intrinsic motivation.

Competence

We first encountered the concept of *competence* in the preceding chapter, when we considered White's (1959) proposal that people have an intrinsic need to believe that they can deal successfully with their environment. But we also encountered a similar idea much earlier, in our discussion of social learning theory in Chapter 7. At that time, we found that people are more inclined to engage in an activity when they believe they are or can become competent at the activity—in other words, when they have high *self-efficacy*. Within the context of contemporary motivation theory, we find an additional benefit of perceived competence or self-efficacy: It promotes interest and intrinsic motivation. Conversely, as you might guess, feelings of incompetence lead to decreased interest and motivation (Deci, 1992; Deci & Ryan, 1985, 1987; Harter, 1992; Harter et al., 1992; MacIver, Stipek, & Daniels, 1991).

As we discussed self-efficacy in Chapter 7, we identified three variables that help us believe we can succeed at a task. One such variable is an encouraging message—having someone else either directly or indirectly convince us that we can do it. A second is the successful performance of our peers; after all, if they can do it, so can we. But ultimately the most important variable affecting feelings of competence and self-efficacy is our own success, success, and more success.

Self-Determination

I should first point out that Deci and Ryan's concept of self-determination overlaps with, yet is also somewhat different from, attribution theory's notion of controllability (Deci & Ryan, 1987). Attribution to controllable factors relates to our belief that environmental events and circumstances are within our purview to influence and alter. In contrast, self-determination refers to our belief that we can autonomously choose our behaviors and, ultimately, our fate (also see deCharms, 1968, 1984). For example, when we think "I *want* to do this" or "I would *find it valuable* to do that," we have a high sense of self-determination. In contrast, when we think "I *have to*" or "I *should*," we are telling ourselves that someone or something else is making our choices for us.

When circumstances and events confirm our feelings of self-determination, we are likely to engage in tasks for long periods, to think meaningfully and creatively about those tasks, to experience pleasure in our activities, and to achieve at higher levels (Amabile & Hennessey, 1992; deCharms, 1972; Deci, 1992; Deci & Ryan, 1987; Wang & Stiles, 1976). Furthermore, we are likely to undertake the challenges that will maximize our long-term learning and development (Deci & Ryan, 1985).

In contrast, when environmental circumstances and events lead us to conclude that we have little involvement in determining the course of our lives, we may comply with external demands but are unlikely to have much intrinsic motivation (Deci & Ryan, 1987). As an example, I think back to 1989 when the Berlin Wall came down: East German workers reportedly showed little initiative or stick-to-itiveness on the job, quite possibly because they had for so long been told exactly what to do and what not to do under the

Communist regime. Furthermore, when our reasons for doing something lie outside of ourselves, we are likely to undertake the easy things we know we can do rather than challenges at which we might fail (Stipek, 1993).

Deci and Ryan (1987) have identified several variables that influence people's sense of self-determination one way or the other. Here we will look at five of them: choices, threats and deadlines, controlling statements, extrinsic rewards, and surveillance and evaluation.

Choices

People have a greater sense of self-determination, and are therefore more intrinsically motivated, when they are able to make choices, within reasonable limits, about the things that they do (Deci & Ryan, 1987, 1992; Morgan, 1984; Stipek, 1993). For example, in an early study by Lewin, Lippitt, and White (1939), 10-year-old boys participating in after-school recreational programs were in one of three experimental conditions. In the *autocratic* group, adults made all of the decisions about what the boys would do. In the *laissez-faire* group, the boys did as they pleased, with little if any adult input. In the *democratic* group, the adults and boys engaged in group decision making about daily activities. The boys were most productive in the democratic setting: They showed greater initiative and on-task behavior related to group projects, and they were less likely to be aggressive toward other group members. Other researchers have found similar results in classroom settings: When students have choices (again, within appropriate limits) about the activities in which they engage, they show greater interest and involvement in their classwork, and they display fewer off-task behaviors (Condry, 1977; Dunlap et al., 1994; Foster-Johnson, Ferro, & Dunlap, 1994; Morgan, 1984; Paris & Turner, 1994; Powell & Nelson, 1997; Stipek, 1993, 1996; Vaughn & Horner, 1997).

Threats and Deadlines

Threats (e.g., "Do this or else!") and deadlines (e.g., "This is due by January 15—no exceptions!") are typically experienced as controlling people's behaviors. As a result, they lessen self-determination and intrinsic motivation (Clifford, 1990; Deci & Ryan, 1987).

Controlling Statements

Some of the things that people say to us, even though they aren't threatening in nature, nevertheless convey the message that others control our fate and so may undermine our sense of self-determination (Amabile & Hennessey, 1992; Boggiano, Main, & Katz, 1988; Koestner, Ryan, Bernieri, & Holt, 1984). As an example, in an experiment by Koestner and colleagues (1984), first and second graders were asked to paint a picture of a house they would like to live in. The children were given the materials they needed—a paintbrush, a set of watercolor paints, two sheets of paper, and several paper towels—and then told some rules about how to proceed. For some children (the controlling-limits condition), restrictions described things that they could and couldn't do, as follows:

> Before you begin, I want to tell you some things that you will have to do. They are rules that we have about painting. You have to keep the paints clean. You can paint only on this small sheet of paper, so don't spill any paint on the big sheet. And you must wash out your brush and wipe it with a paper towel before you switch to a new color of paint, so that you don't get the colors all mixed up. In general, I want you to be a good boy (girl) and don't make a mess with the paints. (Koestner et al., 1984, p. 239)

For other children (the informational-limits condition), restrictions were presented only as information, like this:

> Before you begin, I want to tell you some things about the way painting is done here. I know that sometimes it's really fun to just slop the paint around, but here the materials and room need to be kept nice for the other children who will use them. The smaller sheet is for you to paint on, the larger sheet is a border to be kept clean. Also, the paints need to be kept clean, so the brush is to be washed and wiped in the paper towel before switching colors. I know that some kids don't like to be neat all the time, but now is a time for being neat. (Koestner et al., 1984, p. 239)

Each child was allowed 10 minutes of painting time. The experimenter then took the child's painting to another room, saying he would return in a few minutes. As he departed, he placed two more sheets of paper on the child's table, saying, "You can paint some more on this piece of paper if you like, or, if you want, you can play with the puzzles over on that table." In the experimenter's absence, the child was surreptitiously observed, and painting time was measured. Children in the informational-limits condition spent more time painting (so were apparently more intrinsically motivated to paint), and their paintings were judged to be more creative, than was true for their counterparts in the controlling-limits condition.

Extrinsic Rewards

In Chapter 5 one of the concerns I expressed about using extrinsic reinforcement is that it may undermine the intrinsic reinforcement that an activity provides. Extrinsic reinforcers are apparently most likely to have this adverse influence when people perceive the reinforcers as controlling or manipulating their behavior rather than as providing information about their progress.[6] Rewards are unlikely to be beneficial, at least over the long run, when people interpret them as bribes or as limits on their freedom (Deci & Ryan, 1985, 1987, 1992; Hennessey, 1995; Lepper & Hodell, 1989; Ryan, Mims, & Koestner, 1983; Spaulding, 1992). This finding may be due, in part, to the fact that providing rewards for particular behaviors communicates the message that a task is not worth doing for its own sake (Hennessey, 1995; Stipek, 1993).[7]

On the other hand, as we have noted on previous occasions, extrinsic reinforcement may be useful when desirable behaviors will apparently not occur any other way. People

---

[6]Theorists haven't specifically talked about the informational or controlling messages that punishment might communicate, but we can logically deduce that a similar pattern exists here as well. Certainly punishment can be presented in either of two ways—as a means of control or as a source of information about appropriate behavior. As we discovered in Chapter 6, punishment is more effective when it is accompanied by reasons (information) about why the punished behavior is unacceptable.

[7]You should be aware that one meta-analysis of 96 studies (Cameron & Pierce, 1994) indicated that, in general, extrinsic rewards do *not* decrease intrinsic motivation. This meta-analysis has been criticized, however, for failing to differentiate among various kinds of rewards—for instance, between rewards that were perceived as controlling versus informational—and for excluding studies in which strong undermining effects were found (Kohn, 1996; Lepper, Keavney, & Drake, 1996; Ryan & Deci, 1996; also see the rebuttal from Cameron & Pierce, 1996).

may initially find a new activity difficult or frustrating and therefore need external encouragement to continue. With continuing practice, however, their competence and skill are likely to improve, and they may eventually begin to find the activity intrinsically rewarding.

Surveillance and Evaluation

People who know they are going to be evaluated on their performance have a lower sense of self-determination and, as a result, are less intrinsically motivated; this is especially likely to be so when the task at hand is a difficult one (Clifford, 1990; Deci & Ryan, 1987, 1992; Harter et al., 1992; Hennessey, 1995; Stipek, 1996). In fact, the mere presence of a potential evaluator is likely to undermine intrinsic motivation (Clifford, 1990; Deci & Ryan, 1987). For example, even though I have a mediocre singing voice, I like to sing and will often do so when no one else is around to hear me (e.g., when I'm mowing the lawn or driving alone on business). But my intrinsic motivation to sing vanishes when anyone else is in earshot (fortunately for the "anyone else").

In Chapter 13 we discovered that classroom tests often promote long-term memory storage. Among other things, tests encourage students to review classroom material more regularly and process information more thoroughly. But here we see the downside of tests: They may undermine students' intrinsic motivation to learn (Benware & Deci, 1984; Grolnick & Ryan, 1987; Spaulding, 1992; Stipek, 1993). A study by Benware and Deci (1984) illustrates this point well. College students studied an article about brain functioning under either of two conditions: Some studied it with the expectation of being tested on it, while others studied it with the expectation that they would have to teach the material to someone else (a presumably nonevaluative situation). Compared with those in the first group, students in the second group enjoyed their learning experience more, found

Feelings of self-determination and intrinsic motivation are often greater when potential evaluators are absent from the scene.

the material more interesting, and learned it in a more meaningful (rather than rote) fashion. Grolnick and Ryan (1987) have found similar results with fifth graders.

Curiously, people can sometimes undermine their own sense of self-determination simply by *imagining* that others may be evaluating their performance (Deci & Ryan, 1992; Ryan, 1982). For example, in a study by Ryan (1982), undergraduate students worked on a series of hidden-figure puzzles—puzzles in which they had to find drawings of particular objects embedded within the context of more complex drawings. Some students were told that the task was an indication of "creative intelligence." Even though these students were not specifically told that their performance would be evaluated, they were less likely than students in a control group to continue doing the puzzles in a free-choice situation later on. The mere idea that the task was indicative of intelligence may have led these students to consider how an outside person might evaluate their performance, and accordingly to have less intrinsic motivation for engaging in the task (Deci & Ryan, 1992; Ryan, 1982).

We should keep in mind that no amount of self-determination is going to make us feel intrinsically motivated to do something if we don't also have a sense of competence. To show you what I mean, let's consider a study by Spaulding (1992, pp. 54–55). Seventh-grade students, including some who believed themselves to be competent writers and some who did not, were asked to write an essay concerning what they had learned in English class that year. Some students were asked to write it for their teacher, someone they believed would evaluate their work; hence, this group experienced low self-determination. Other students were asked to write the essay for the researcher so that she could tell future teachers what students study in English; without the threat of evaluation looming over them, these students presumably experienced relatively high self-determination. As the students wrote the essay, Spaulding measured their task engagement (and, indirectly, their intrinsic motivation) in several different ways. Students who believed themselves to be competent writers showed greater intrinsic motivation in the high self-determination condition—that is, when writing for the researcher. In contrast, students who believed they were poor writers were more engaged in the task when writing for the teacher; apparently self-determination in the absence of perceived competence did not promote intrinsic motivation.

Effects of Feedback

In Chapter 4 I talked about positive feedback as a form of reinforcement; from an operant conditioning perspective, then, the behavior it follows should increase in frequency. But motivation theorists tell us that the effects of feedback are not so simple. From their perspective, positive feedback is most likely to enhance performance when it affirms an individual's feelings of competence and self-determination; it is *un*likely to do so when it either diminishes one's sense of competence or communicates an attempt to control one's behavior (Deci & Ryan, 1992; Ryan et al., 1983; Stipek, 1996). For example, I respond to my children more favorably when they tell me

> Boy, Mom, these brownies you made are really good. *(a competence-enhancing statement)*

than when they say

> It's a good thing you finally baked something around here, Ma. All my friends' mothers do it all the time. *(a controlling statement)*

Compliments about things I do well are always welcome. But statements about what "good" parents are supposed to do make me feel as if I'm not really in charge in my own home. Furthermore, I have no intention of letting my children tell *me* how to behave.

Even *negative* feedback can be effective when it promotes competence and self-determination (Butler, 1987, 1988; Butler & Nisan, 1986; Corno & Rohrkemper, 1985; Stipek, 1996). If it provides information about how to improve in the future, thereby presuming an individual's ability to be successful eventually, it is likely to facilitate intrinsic motivation. If it instead conveys the message that an individual is incompetent or imposes a feeling of outside control, it is apt to undermine any intrinsic motivation to continue engaging in a task.

Intrinsic motivation is essential for the process of *self-regulated learning* that I described in Chapter 14. Self-regulated learners set goals for their learning efforts, choose cognitive strategies that are likely to help them achieve those goals, and then evaluate the results of their efforts. To engage in such self-regulated activities, learners must feel confident that they can be successful at a learning task and must also believe that they can control the direction in which they are going; in other words, they must have a sense of both competence and self-determination (Corno & Rohrkemper, 1985; McCombs, 1996; Paris & Turner, 1994; Schunk, 1995; Zimmerman, 1995; Zimmerman & Risemberg, 1997).

Yet there are times when, for a variety of reasons, people must do things that they wouldn't necessarily choose to do of their own accord. In many instances, we find people willingly doing such things even in the absence of any obvious extrinsic reinforcers. These behaviors may reflect *internalized motivation,* a concept we turn to now.

INTERNALIZED MOTIVATION

As I mentioned in Chapter 14, my son Alex and I are currently taking an undergraduate course in art history. We are both taking the course primarily to gain a greater understanding of the many works of art we've seen in museums over the years. Alex also has a second reason for taking the course: to earn credit toward his high school diploma. Alex must, of course, get a passing grade in the course. As for me, it matters little whether I get an A or F. Yet I diligently study for every test, often foregoing things I'd rather be doing, such as reading a mystery novel or watching a television game show. Why am I doing this? Although I enjoy attending class, studying the material before a test is definitely *not* an intrinsically motivating activity for me; although the textbook has lots of beautiful pictures, its prose is about as interesting and engaging as the telephone book. Yet there is no extrinsic motivation for me to study, either; the grade I get in the course will in no way affect my future physical, emotional, or financial well-being. The bottom line is that, over my many years as a student, I acquired a desire to achieve good grades, more or less for their own sake.

In our discussion so far, we have thought of intrinsic versus extrinsic motivation as an either-or state of affairs. In fact, there is a third possibility. The concept of **internalized motivation** refers to situations in which, over time, people gradually adopt behaviors that other individuals value, without regard for the external consequences that such behaviors may or may not bring (Deci & Ryan, 1995; Deci, Vallerand, Pelletier, & Ryan, 1991; Harter, 1992; Ryan & Connell, 1989; Ryan, Connell, & Grolnick, 1992).

Deci and Ryan (1995; Deci et al., 1991; Ryan et al.,1992) have described four stages through which internalized motivation may evolve:

1. *External regulation:* The individual is motivated to behave, or else *not* to behave, in certain ways based primarily on the external consequences that will follow behaviors; in other words, the individual is extrinsically motivated. For instance, students at this stage may do schoolwork primarily to avoid being punished for poor grades, and they are likely to need a lot of prodding to get their work done.

2. *Introjection:* The person behaves in particular ways to gain the approval of others; for example, a student may willingly complete an easy, boring assignment as a means of gaining the teacher's approval. At the introjection stage, we see some internal pressure to behave in particular ways; for instance, the individual may feel guilty if he or she violates certain standards or rules for behavior. However, the person does not fully understand the rationale behind such standards and rules. Instead, the primary motives tend to be feelings about self-worth and the desire to avoid a negative self-evaluation.

3. *Identification:* The individual now sees certain behaviors as being personally important or valuable. Students at this stage value learning and academic success for their own sake, perceive assigned classroom tasks as being essential for helping them learn, and so need little prodding to get their work done.

4. *Integration:* The individual has fully accepted the desirability of certain behaviors and has integrated them into an overall system of motives and values. For example, a student at this stage might have acquired a keen interest in science as a career goal; if so, we are likely to see that interest reflected in many things the student does on a regular basis.

Internalized motivation is an important aspect of self-regulated learning; it fosters a general work ethic in which the learner spontaneously engages in activities that, although not always fun or immediately gratifying, are essential for reaching one's long-term goals (Harter, 1992; McCombs, 1996; Ryan et al., 1992; Stipek, 1993). Ryan and his colleagues (1992) have suggested that three conditions promote the development of internalized motivation:

- *The learner operates within the context of a warm, responsive, and supportive environment:* The learner feels a sense of relatedness to, and regard for, important other people (i.e., *significant others*) within his or her environment.
- *The learner is given some autonomy:* The significant others who are controlling the learner's behavior (e.g., parents and teachers) exert no more control than necessary, as a way of maximizing the extent to which the learner maintains a sense of self-determination. And, over time, they gradually relinquish that control to the learner.
- *The learner operates within a certain degree of structure:* The environment provides information about expected behaviors and why they are important. Response-consequence contingencies are clearly spelled out.

Fostering the development of internalized motivation, then, involves a delicate balancing act between giving the learner sufficient opportunities for experiencing self-determination and providing a certain degree of guidance about how the learner should behave. In a sense, significant others "scaffold" desired behaviors at first, gradually reducing such scaffolding as the learner exhibits the behaviors more easily and frequently.

Obviously, many aspects of the environment promote various kinds of motivation in learners. At this point, let's turn to two kinds of events that motivation theorists often mention as affecting motivation in one way or another—challenge and competition.

EFFECTS OF CHALLENGE AND COMPETITION

In various places throughout the book I have alluded to the positive effects of challenging tasks. For example, as we discovered in Chapter 8, challenges promote cognitive development. From Piaget's perspective, accommodation occurs and new schemes emerge only when events cannot be readily assimilated into existing schemes. From Vygotsky's perspective, tasks within a child's zone of proximal development are optimal for long-term cognitive growth. Furthermore, as we learned in Chapter 14, students are most likely to develop maximally effective metacognitive strategies when the learning tasks they face are not easily accomplished using such simplistic strategies as repetition and rote memorization.

Competition and other forms of social comparison also play a role in learning. For example, when we examined the "good behavior game" in Chapter 5, we discovered that when two groups of students compete for privileges based on good behavior, students in both groups show marked improvements in classroom behavior. Furthermore, as we learned in Chapter 7, students develop high or low self-efficacy partially as a function of what they see their peers being able to do.

Challenge and competition have implications for human motivation as well as learning. Let's look at both of these within the context of the cognitive motivational factors we have explored in this chapter.

Challenge

As I defined it in the preceding chapter, a challenge is a situation in which individuals believe that, although they risk possible failure, they are likely to succeed if they exert sufficient effort. From a motivational standpoint, the advantages of challenges are threefold:

• *Challenges heighten interest and minimize boredom* (Brophy, 1987; Csikszentmihalyi & Nakamura, 1989; Deci & Ryan, 1992; Malone & Lepper, 1987; Spaulding, 1992; Stipek, 1996; Turner, 1995). We typically become bored with easy tasks, yet we are frustrated by tasks at which we always seem to fail. Challenges provide a happy medium: They have those unexpected little twists and turns that maintain our interest, but we know that, with persistence, we can achieve success.

• *It is difficult to attribute success on challenging tasks to external factors, such as task ease or luck* (Clifford, 1990; Eisenberger, 1992; Lan, Repman, Bradley, & Weller, 1994; C. Peterson, 1988, 1990). When we succeed at a very easy task—one on which we have exerted very little effort—we are likely to attribute our success to the fact that, hey, anybody can do it. When we succeed at an extremely difficult task—something we thought ourselves incapable of doing—we might attribute our success to good luck or somebody else's assistance. However, when we succeed on a challenging task—one that we know we can do if we try long and hard enough—we cannot dismiss it as being due to task ease, and we have little reason to attribute our performance to luck or assistance. Our best alternative is to attribute our hard-won success to our own efforts and clever strategies.

• *Success at challenging tasks promotes a greater sense of competence and self-efficacy* (Clifford, 1990; Deci & Ryan, 1992; Lan et al., 1994; Stipek, 1993). Take a minute to do this little exercise:

> Write the numbers 1 to 10 on a piece of paper. See if you can do it in less than 10 seconds.

Were you successful? If so, how good does your success make you feel? I just did the task in about four seconds' time, and I had little reason to feel particularly proud. After all, I'm 49 years old; if I can't write these numbers quickly and accurately by now, something must be terribly wrong.

Success on easy tasks, while virtually guaranteed, does little to enhance our sense of competence and self-efficacy. Sure, we can do it, but so can anyone else. On the other hand, challenges are not so easily accomplished: Perhaps we have failed to accomplish them in the past, or perhaps we know others who have failed. When we successfully meet a challenge, we must obviously be pretty competent folks. Success on a challenging task, then, gives us feelings of satisfaction that are not possible with an easier task. Furthermore, because it enhances our feelings of competency, success in a challenging situation also increases our intrinsic motivation (Clifford, 1990; Deci & Ryan, 1985; Stipek, 1996).

When are people most likely to take on new risks and challenges? Theorists suggest that conditions such as the following are optimal:

- There are few, if any, penalties for errors.
- The same rewards cannot be obtained by engaging in easier tasks, or rewards are greater for challenging tasks than they are for easy ones.
- Standards for success are realistic for each individual.
- Scaffolding is sufficient to make success possible.
- People attribute their success to their own ability, efforts, and strategies.
- People have a sense of competence and a sense of self-determination (Brophy & Alleman, 1992; Clifford, 1990; Corno & Rohrkemper, 1985; Deci & Ryan, 1985; Dweck & Elliott, 1983; Lan et al., 1994; Stipek, 1993).

A moment ago, I stated that success on challenging tasks promotes feelings of competence. But the last of the conditions I just listed indicates that the reverse is also true; that is, competence increases the challenges that people undertake. In other words, we have a happily "vicious" cycle here: Challenge promotes competence, and competence promotes challenge.

Competition

In a competitive situation, success doesn't depend on absolute mastery of a task; instead, it results from performing better than others. Competition is a pervasive element of our society. In the business world, the people who have the best ideas, make the most money, or work the longest hours are (usually) the ones who get ahead. We often see competition in recreation, too—for example, in the games we play and the athletic events we watch on television. And our democratic political system is based on competition in the most basic sense: Those who get more votes than anybody else are the ones who end up in office.

Competition is prevalent in our schools as well (Ames, 1984). We find school personnel comparing students in virtually every arena. For example, when teachers grade on the curve, their grades reflect how students stack up against one another, and only those at the top of the stack are identified as being successful. When students take college aptitude tests, their test scores reflect not what they know and can do but how their performance compares with that of their peers. Participation in sports is competitive, especially at the high school level: Even before students compete against other teams, they compete among themselves to make the team and achieve first-string status. And many of the concepts we use when we talk about students' abilities—intelligence, giftedness, special needs, and so on—are defined by psychologists only in a normative sense.

What conditions promote a competitive atmosphere? One likely condition is uncertainty regarding others' expectations for our performance: In the absence of definitive criteria about what "good" performance is, we compare ourselves with our peers as a general indication of how well we are doing (Ames, 1984). A second condition, certainly, is a competitive reward structure, one that reinforces us for outperforming everyone else.

Many people are motivated by competition *if* they believe they have a reasonable chance of winning (Brophy, 1986; Deci & Ryan, 1992; Krampen, 1987; Stipek, 1996). But competition has several negative side effects, both behavioral and cognitive, of which you should be aware:

• *Competition sometimes leads to undesirable or counterproductive behaviors* (Ames, 1984). In a competitive situation, people often behave in ways that interfere with their own learning and achievement or with the learning and achievement of others. For example, they may cheat if cheating puts them ahead of the pack. They may deny others access to the resources necessary for success. They may have little regard for equity and fairness. And because they are accustomed to working against one another, they may have a difficult time working cooperatively *with* one another.

• *Competition promotes performance goals rather than learning goals* (Ames, 1984; Hagen, 1994; Nicholls, 1984; Spaulding, 1992; Stipek, 1996). When the key to success is doing better than everyone else, people inevitably focus their attention on how good they appear to others rather than on how much they are learning. And they define success as being better than everyone else rather than as improving their abilities and skills over time.

• *For the losers, competition promotes a low sense of competence and poor self-efficacy* (Ames, 1984; Ames & Ames, 1981). When people define success as mastery of a task or improvement in an activity over time, success is likely to come frequently and so will enhance self-efficacy. But when people instead define success as coming out on top, most will inevitably be losers. In the face of such "failure," they may understandably begin to believe themselves to be incompetent.

• *Competition promotes attributions to ability rather than to effort* (Ames, 1984; Nicholls, 1984; Stipek, 1993). Many people lose in competitive situations even when they exert a great deal of effort. They quite logically reach the conclusion that effort is not enough—that some sort of natural ability is the critical ingredient for success. Their failures, then, are due to their lack of that elusive ability, and they become pessimistic about their future chances for success.

• *Competition ultimately leads to lower achievement for most students.* When students' classroom success is judged on the basis of how well they perform relative to one another rather than on how much improvement they make, most students earn lower grades, show less creativity, and develop more negative attitudes toward school (Amabile & Hennessey, 1992; Covington, 1992; Graham & Golen, 1991; Krampen, 1987). Competitive classroom environments may be especially disadvantageous to female students (Eccles, 1989; Inglehart, Brown, & Vida, 1994).

As you can see, competition is not productive in situations in which we want and expect *all* individuals to learn and achieve at the highest possible level. Thus, it is generally not a recommended strategy in school settings, where individual student achievement is the number one goal.

What other educational implications can we draw from what we have learned about cognitive factors in motivation? Let's take a look.

PROMOTING COGNITIONS THAT MOTIVATE

We have considered several cognitive factors that influence motivation, including goals, expectancies, values, interests, attributions, and perceptions of self-determination and competence. Teachers can often help students think about and interpret classroom events in productive ways—in ways that ultimately lead students to direct their efforts and behaviors toward effective learning and classroom achievement. Following are some guidelines that we can derive from cognitive views of motivation:

• *Teachers should encourage students to set goals for themselves.* When we talked about instructional objectives in Chapter 5, we were essentially talking about goals that teachers set for their students. But it is equally important that students set their *own* goals regarding what they want to accomplish at school. Their self-chosen goals will help them make appropriate choices and direct their efforts as they work in the classroom.

Although students should eventually be encouraged to develop long-term goals for themselves—perhaps going to college or becoming an environmental scientist—many students initially respond more favorably to short-term goals—perhaps learning a certain number of spelling words or solving a certain number of mathematics problems (Bandura & Schunk, 1981; Good & Brophy, 1994; Schunk & Rice, 1989).[8] By setting and working toward a series of short-term goals, students get regular feedback about the progress they are making and thereby develop a sense of self-efficacy that they can master school subject matter (Bandura, 1981; Schunk, 1991, 1996a).

---

[8]Some theorists use the terms *distal goals* and *proximal goals* when referring to long-term and short-term goals, respectively.

- *Teachers should encourage students to focus more on learning goals than on performance goals.* Performance goals—for example, completing classroom assignments, obtaining high scores on college admissions tests, and graduating from high school—are often important for students to attain. But learning goals are the ones most likely to promote effective learning and performance over the long run. Learning goals are especially motivating when they are specific ("I want to learn how to ride a bicycle"), challenging ("Writing a limerick looks difficult, but I'm sure I can do it"), and short term ("I'm going to learn to count to 100 in French by the end of the month") (Alderman, 1990; Brophy, 1987; Good & Brophy, 1994).

Through their own classroom behaviors, teachers can demonstrate that improving and mastering skills and subject matter are the objectives most important for students to accomplish. For example, teachers can present tasks that students find valuable in and of themselves (Ames, 1992; Dweck & Elliott, 1983; Pintrich et al., 1993). They can provide mechanisms and criteria through which students may easily record and assess academic progress (Good & Brophy, 1994; Spaulding, 1992). They can communicate that mistakes are a normal part of learning and therefore to be expected (Ames, 1992; Clifford, 1990; Dweck, 1975; Dweck & Elliott, 1983; Stipek, 1996). They can give specific feedback about how students can improve rather than simply assigning relatively uninformative grades (Brophy, 1986; Butler, 1987; Graham & Weiner, 1996; Spaulding, 1992). And they should *not* repeatedly remind students that classwork will be evaluated and graded (Stipek, 1993; Thomas & Oldfather, 1997).

- *Instruction should help students see value in learning school subject matter.* Teachers can do many things to enable students to find value in school activities. For example, they can identify the specific knowledge and skills that students will acquire from an instructional unit (Keller, 1987). They can show how things learned in the classroom will help fulfill students' present needs and long-term goals (Brophy, 1986, 1987; Keller, 1987; Parsons, Kaczala, & Meece, 1982). They can demonstrate how they themselves value academic activities—for example, by sharing their fascination with certain topics and describing how they use the things they've learned in school (Brophy, 1987; Brophy & Alleman, 1991). And they should refrain from asking students to engage in activities with little long-term benefit—memorizing trivial facts for no good reason, reading material that is clearly beyond students' comprehension level, and so on (Brophy, 1987).

- *Students should find classroom material interesting as well as informative.* Almost all students learn more when subject matter is interesting; students with little background knowledge in the topic are especially likely to benefit (Alexander, in press; Garner et al., 1991).

Certainly teachers should capitalize on students' personal interests whenever possible (Alexander et al., 1994; Brophy, 1986, 1987; Wlodkowski, 1978). But situational interest factors can also be incorporated into classroom subject matter and activities. For example, students typically enjoy opportunities to respond actively during a learning activity—perhaps by manipulating and experimenting with physical objects, creating new products, or discussing controversial issues with classmates (Brophy, 1987; Sadker & Sadker, 1985; Zahorik, 1994). They enjoy subject matter to which they can relate on a personal level—for instance, mathematics lessons that involve students' favorite foods, works of literature that feature characters with whom students can readily identify, or history textbooks that portray historical figures as real people with distinctly human qualities (Anand & Ross, 1987; Levstik, 1994). Students are often curious about things that are new and different and about events that are surprising and puzzling (Brophy, 1986, 1987; Lepper & Hodell, 1989; Sheveland, 1994; Spaulding, 1992; Stipek, 1993; Wlodkowski, 1978). They like to engage in fantasy and make-believe—for example, playing out the roles of key figures in historical events or imagining what it must be like to be weightless in space (Brophy, 1986, 1987; Lepper & Hodell, 1989). Keep in mind, however, that adding interesting but *non*important information may be counterproductive, distracting students' attention from more important material (Wade, 1992).

• *Teachers should attribute students' successes to both stable and unstable internal factors but attribute their failures only to unstable and controllable internal factors.* To be most optimistic about their future performance, students should attribute their successes partly to stable internal factors such as natural talent (thus, they will know that success wasn't a fluke) and partly to unstable but controllable factors such as effort and strategies (thus, they will continue to work hard). At the same time, they should attribute their failures primarily to factors they can control and change.

Teachers can help promote such attributions in their students through the causes they themselves attribute to student performance (Alderman, 1990; Brophy, 1987; Schunk, 1990; Spaulding, 1992; Stipek, 1993). Consider these teacher statements as examples:

• "You've done very well. Obviously you're good at this, and you've been trying very hard to get better."
• "Your project shows a lot of talent and a lot of hard work."
• "The more you practice, the better you will get."
• "Perhaps you need to study a little more next time. And let me give you some suggestions on how you might study a little differently, too."

Teachers should attribute student failures solely to a lack of effort only when students clearly haven't given classroom tasks their best shot. When students fail at a task at which they have expended a great deal of effort and are then told that they didn't try hard enough, they are likely to conclude that they simply don't have the ability to perform the task successfully (Alderman, 1990; Curtis & Graham, 1991; Schunk, 1990). In many cases, it may be more productive, and probably more accurate, to attribute failures to ineffective strategies and subsequently to help students acquire more effective ones (Clifford, 1984; Curtis & Graham, 1991; Pressley, Borkowski, & Schneider, 1987; Weinstein et al., 1991).

• *Students must feel competent about classroom activities and have high expectations for academic success.* Throughout the book, we have encountered strategies for promoting students' academic success. For example, we have found that students learn new material more effectively when they have sufficient knowledge and skills to which they can relate that material. We have found that expository instruction is more successful when it provides advance organizers, visual aids, mnemonics, and so on to help students process information in a meaningful, organized, and elaborative fashion. We have found that some learning and study strategies promote more effective learning and memory than others and that students can learn to use such strategies.

In addition to promoting success itself, several strategies may also enhance students' sense of competence and expectations for academic success. For one thing, teachers can communicate their own high expectations for student performance. They can help students develop a realistic perspective as to what success *is* (monthly improvement qualifies, consistent perfection does not). And they can cast students' errors in an appropriate light—as inevitable minor stumbling blocks on the road to success—and make sure that, despite such errors, students eventually do succeed with effort, persistence, and appropriate strategies.

• *Students should believe that they have some self-determination regarding classroom events.* For both pedagogical and logistical reasons, students often have little control over the things that happen in school. For example, societal needs and district curricula often dictate the objectives that students must achieve. The use of the same facilities and resources by many different students requires adhering to certain schedules. To keep students' attention focused on school tasks, teachers must maintain some semblance of order in the classroom. And as we have seen, a certain amount of structure regarding expectations for students' behavior is an important condition for promoting internalized motivation.

Yet some degree of self-determination is essential for both intrinsic motivation and the development of internalized motivation. Teachers can do numerous little things to give students a sense of self-determination about classroom activities. For example, they can establish general routines and procedures that students should typically follow, thus minimizing the need to give explicit instructions for each and every assignment (Spaulding, 1992). They can inform students well ahead of time about upcoming deadlines, so that students can budget their time accordingly (Spaulding, 1992). They can ask for regular feedback about how classroom activities might be improved (Keller, 1987). They can structure classroom tasks sufficiently to facilitate successful performance but not so much that students feel unnecessarily constrained (deCharms, 1984). They can provide opportunities for students to learn independently—through computer-assisted instruction, for example (Swan, Mitrani, Guerrero, Cheung, & Schoener, 1990). When the same objective can be accomplished in two or more different ways, they can give students a choice about how best to proceed (Hennessey & Amabile, 1987; Paris & Turner, 1994; Spaulding, 1992). When extrinsic reinforcers are used as a way of encouraging students to perform dull but necessary tasks, teachers can preserve students' sense of self-determination by giving them choices regarding the specific reinforcers they can earn by completing those tasks (Spaulding, 1992). And when evaluation is useful in promoting academic progress, teachers can provide mechanisms (e.g., checklists and feedback sheets) through which students can evaluate *themselves* (McCaslin & Good, 1996; Spaulding, 1992; Wlodkowski, 1978).

• *Feedback and other forms of extrinsic reinforcement should communicate information, rather than decreasing students' sense of control.* In an ideal world, all students would be intrinsically motivated to learn in the classroom and succeed at classroom activities. But in reality, external stimuli—feedback, praise, privileges, and so on—are sometimes necessary to keep students on task.

As we discovered earlier in the chapter, reinforcement may undermine students' intrinsic motivation, particularly if it conveys the idea that adults are trying to control their behavior. Yet feedback and other forms of reinforcement can be beneficial when they instead communicate information about students' current performance and offer suggestions for improvement (Bangert-Drowns et al., 1991; Clifford, 1990; Deci & Ryan, 1985, 1987; Harris & Rosenthal, 1985). Whenever possible, teachers should provide such information immediately, so that students can store it in working memory simultaneously with their recollection of what they have just done; in this way, the two are easily integrated (Anderson, 1987).

• *Teachers should encourage students to take on challenges and risks.* Success on difficult and challenging tasks promotes feelings of competence and self-efficacy in ways that easier tasks never can. Teachers should help students recognize that a hard-won success is far more significant than the "easy A." And they shouldn't penalize students for trying new approaches that don't pan out.

On the other hand, the school day shouldn't necessarily be one challenge after another. Such a state of affairs would be absolutely exhausting, and probably quite discouraging as well. Instead, teachers should probably strike a balance between easy tasks—those that will boost students' self-confidence over the short run—and the challenging tasks so critical for a long-term sense of competence and self-efficacy (Keller, 1987; Spaulding, 1992; Stipek, 1993, 1996).

• *Most classroom activities should be noncompetitive in nature.* In any public situation, including the classroom, people will invariably compare themselves with one another. Yet teachers can take steps to minimize the extent to which comparison and competition among students occur. For example, they can keep students' performance on classroom tasks private and confidential, minimizing the degree to which students are even aware of classmates' performance levels (Schunk, 1990; Spaulding, 1992). At any one time, they can have different students doing different tasks (Stipek, 1996). They can assess students' performance independently of how well classmates are doing and encourage students to assess their own performance in a similar manner (Spaulding, 1992; Wlodkowski, 1978). When little competitions among students (e.g., debates and team math games) do seem appropriate, teachers can make sure that all students or teams have a reasonable (perhaps equal) chance of winning (Brophy, 1986, 1987) and make no big deal about whomever the ultimate winners are.

We must recognize that school activities will not always be intrinsically enjoyable. But when students see the value of those activities, believe themselves capable of school success, and ultimately achieve that success, they are likely to be motivated and productive learners.

SUMMARY

Numerous cognitions influence the amount and type of motivation we see. As one example, people set goals toward which they direct their behaviors. Learning goals tend to promote more effective learning and performance than performance goals: People with learning goals seek challenging tasks and are persistent until they succeed at those tasks, with little concern for the errors they make along the way. People are also likely to pursue certain activities when they place value on those activities, find them interesting, and expect to succeed at them.

People's attributions for the things that happen to them—their interpretations regarding the causes of their successes and failures—are equally important variables affecting behavior. People are most likely to take pride in a success when they believe they themselves were responsible for that success. And they are most likely to modify their behavior after a failure when they see that failure as being due to internal factors they can control—factors such as effort and strategies.

Some theorists believe that intrinsic motivation is the result of two conditions. First, people must have a sense of competence—they must believe they are capable of successfully executing the tasks before them. Second, they must have a sense of self-determination—they must believe they can make choices and regulate the course of their lives. In some situations, extrinsic forms of motivation become increasingly internalized over time, such that people begin to value and adopt the behaviors that those around them value and encourage.

Such cognitive motivational factors have numerous implications for classroom practice. For example, challenging tasks are likely to enhance students' sense of competence and expectations for future success. Competitive situations are usually counterproductive, in that most students are the inevitable losers. Students are more intrinsically motivated when they have choices and an appropriate degree of control over their classroom activities. And, ultimately, students must experience academic success on a regular basis.

References

Abrams, R. A. (1994). The forces that move the eyes. *Current Directions in Psychological Science, 3,* 65-67.

Abramson, L. Y., Seligman, M. E. P., & Teasdale, J. (1978). Learned helplessness in humans: Critique and reformulation. *Journal of Abnormal Psychology, 87,* 49-74.

Ackley, D. H., Hinton, G. E., & Sejnowski, T. J. (1985). A learning algorithm for Boltzmann machines. *Cognitive Science, 9,* 147-169.

Adams, P. A., & Adams, J K. (1960). Confidence in the recognition and reproduction of words difficult to spell. *American Journal of Psychology, 73,* 544-552.

Airasian, P. W. (1994). *Classroom assessment* (2nd ed.). New York: McGraw-Hill.

Alberto, P. A., & Troutman, A. C. (1990). *Applied behavior analysis for teachers* (3rd ed.). Columbus, OH: Merrill.

Alderman, K. (1990). Motivation for at-risk students. *Educational Leadership, 48* (1), 27-30.

Alexander, L., Frankiewicz, R., & Williams, R. (1979). Facilitation of learning and retention of oral instruction using advance and post organizers. *Journal of Educational Psychology, 71,* 701-707.

Alexander, P. A. (in press). Mapping the multidimensional nature of domain learning: The interplay of cognitive, motivational, and strategic forces. In P. R. Pintrich & M. L. Maehr (Eds.), *Advances in motivation and achievement* (Vol. 10). Greenwich, CT: JAI Press.

Alexander, P. A., & Jetton, T. L. (1996). The role of importance and interest in the processing of text. *Educational Psychology Review, 8,* 89-121.

Alexander, P. A., & Judy, J. E. (1988). The interaction of domain-specific and strategic knowledge in academic performance. *Review of Educational Research, 58,* 375-404.

Alexander, P. A., Kulikowich, J. M., & Schulze, S. K. (1994). How subject-matter knowledge affects recall and interest. *American Educational Research Journal, 31,* 313-337.

Alford, G. S., & Rosenthal, T. L. (1973). Process and products of modeling in observational concept attainment. *Child Development, 44,* 714-720.

Alleman, J., & Brophy, J. (1992). Analysis of the activities in a social studies curriculum. In J. Brophy (Ed.), *Advances in research on teaching: Vol. 3. Planning and managing learning tasks and activities.* Greenwich, CT: JAI Press.

Alleman, J., & Brophy, J. (1997). Elementary social studies: Instruments, activities, and standards. In G. D. Phye (Ed.), *Handbook of classroom assessment: Learning, achievement, and adjustment.* San Diego: Academic Press.

Alvermann, D. E. (1981). The compensatory effect of graphic organizers on descriptive text. *Journal of Educational Research, 75,* 44-48.

Amabile, T. M., & Hennessey, B. A. (1992). The motivation for creativity in children. In A. K. Boggiano & T. S. Pittman (Eds.), *Achievement and motivation: A social-developmental perspective.* Cambridge, UK: Cambridge University Press.

Ames, C. (1984). Competitive, cooperative, and individualistic goal structures: A cognitive-motivational analysis. In R. Ames & C. Ames (Eds.), *Research on motivation in education: Vol. 1. Student motivation.* Orlando: Academic Press.

Ames, C. (1992). Classrooms: Goals, structures, and student motivation. *Journal of Educational Psychology, 84,* 261-271.

Ames, C., & Ames, R. (1981). Competitive versus individualistic goal structures: The salience of past performance information for causal attributions and affect. *Journal of Educational Psychology, 73,* 411-418.

Ames, C., & Archer, J. (1988). Achievement goals in the classroom: Students' learning strategies and motivation processes. *Journal of Educational Psychology, 80,* 260-267.

Ames, R. (1983). Help-seeking and achievement orientation: Perspectives from attribution theory. In A. Nadler, J. Fisher, & B. DePaulo (Eds.), *New directions in helping* (Vol. 2). New York: Academic Press.

Ames, R., & Lau, S. (1982). An attributional analysis of student help-seeking in academic settings. *Journal of Educational Psychology, 74,* 414-423.

Anand, P., & Ross, S. (1987). A computer-based strategy for personalizing verbal problems in teaching mathematics. *Educational Communication and Technology Journal, 35,* 151-162.

Anderman, E. M., & Maehr, M. L. (1994). Motivation and schooling in the middle grades. *Review of Educational Research, 64,* 287–309.

Anderson, C. W., Sheldon, T. H., & Dubay, J. (1990). The effects of instruction on college nonmajors' conceptions of respiration and photosynthesis. *Journal of Research in Science Teaching, 27,* 761–776.

Anderson, J. R. (1974). Retrieval of propositional information from long-term memory. *Cognitive Psychology, 6,* 451–474.

Anderson, J. R. (1976). *Language, memory, and thought.* Hillsdale, NJ: Erlbaum.

Anderson, J. R. (1983a). *The architecture of cognition.* Cambridge, MA: Harvard University Press.

Anderson, J. R. (1983b). A spreading activation theory of memory. *Journal of Verbal Learning and Verbal Behavior, 22,* 261–295.

Anderson, J. R. (1984). Spreading activation. In J. R. Anderson & S. M. Kosslyn (Eds.), *Tutorials in learning and memory.* San Francisco: W. H. Freeman.

Anderson, J. R. (1985). *Cognitive psychology and its implications* (2nd ed.). New York: W. H. Freeman.

Anderson, J. R. (1987). Skill acquisition: Compilation of weak-method problem solutions. *Psychological Review, 94,* 192–210.

Anderson, J. R. (1990). *Cognitive psychology and its implications* (3rd ed.). New York: W. H. Freeman.

Anderson, J. R. (1993). Problem solving and learning. *American Psychologist, 48,* 35–44.

Anderson, J R. (1995). *Learning and memory: An integrated approach.* New York: Wiley.

Anderson, J. R., & Bower, G. H. (1973). *Human associative memory.* Washington, DC: Winston.

Anderson, J. R., Reder, L. M., & Simon, H. A. (1996). Situated learning and education. *Educational Researcher, 25* (4), 5–11.

Anderson, J. R., Reder, L. M., & Simon, H. A. (1997). Situative versus cognitive perspectives: Form versus substance. *Educational Researcher, 26* (1), 18–21.

Anderson, J. R., & Schooler, L. J. (1991). Reflections of the environment in memory. *Psychological Science, 2,* 396–408.

Anderson, J. R., & Schustack, M. W. (1979). Effects of analogy to prior knowledge on memory for new information. *Journal of Verbal Learning and Verbal Behavior, 18,* 565–583.

Anderson, L. M. (1993). Auxiliary materials that accompany textbooks: Can they promote "higher-order" learning? In B. K. Britton, A. Woodward, & M. Binkley (Eds.), *Learning from textbooks: Theory and practice.* Hillsdale, NJ: Erlbaum.

Anderson, L. M. (1997, March). Taking students' entering knowledge and beliefs seriously when teaching about learning and teaching. In. H. Borko (Chair), *Educational psychology and teacher education: Perennial issues.* Symposium conducted at the annual meeting of the American Educational Research Association, Chicago.

Anderson, R. C. (1977). The notion of schemata and the educational enterprise. In R. C. Anderson, R. J. Spiro, & W. E. Montague (Eds.), *Schooling and the acquisition of knowledge.* Hillsdale, NJ: Erlbaum.

Anderson, R. C. (1984). Role of reader's schema in comprehension, learning, and memory. In R. C. Anderson, J. Osborn, & R. J. Tierney (Eds.), *Learning to read in American schools: Basal readers and content texts.* Hillsdale, NJ: Erlbaum.

Anderson, R. C., & Biddle, B. (1975). On asking people questions about what they are reading. In G. H. Bower (Ed.), *Psychology of learning and motivation* (Vol. 9). New York: Academic Press.

Anderson, R. C., & Pearson, P. D. (1984). A schema-theoretic view of basic processes in reading. In P. D. Pearson (Ed.), *Handbook of reading research.* New York: Longman.

Anderson, R. C., & Pichert, J. W. (1978). Recall of previously unrecallable information following a shift in perspective. *Journal of Verbal Learning and Verbal Behavior, 17,* 1–12.

Anderson, R. C., Reynolds, R. E., Schallert, D. L., & Goetz, E. T. (1977). Frameworks for comprehending discourse. *American Educational Research Journal, 14,* 367–381.

Anderson, V., & Hidi, S. (1988/1989). Teaching students to summarize. *Educational Leadership, 46* (4), 26–28.

Anderson-Inman, L., Walker, H. M., & Purcell, J. (1984). Promoting the transfer of skills across settings: Transenvironmental programming for handicapped students in the mainstream. In W. Heward, T. E. Heron, D. S. Hill, & J. Trap-Porter (Eds.), *Focus on behavior analysis in education.* Columbus, OH: Merrill.

Andre, T. (1979). Does answering higher-level questions while reading facilitate productive learning? *Review of Educational Research, 49,* 280–318.

Andre, T. (1986). Problem solving and education. In G. D. Phye & T. Andre (Eds.), *Cognitive classroom learning: Understanding, thinking, and problem solving.* Orlando: Academic Press.

Andrews, A. C. (1987). The analogy theme in geography. *Journal of Geography, 86,* 194–197.

Andrews, G. R., & Debus, R. L. (1978). Persistence and the causal perception of failure: Modifying cognitive attributions. *Journal of Educational Psychology, 70,* 154–166.

Anglin, J. M. (1977). *Word, object, and conceptual development.* New York: W. W. Norton.

Anker, A. L., & Crowley, T. J. (1982). Use of contingency contracts in specialty clinics for cocaine abuse. *National Institute on Drug Abuse: Research Monograph Series, 4,* 452–459.

Anzai, Y. (1991). Learning and use of representations for physics expertise. In K. A. Ericsson & J. Smith (Eds.), *Toward a general theory of expertise: Prospects and limits.* Cambridge, UK: Cambridge University Press.

Appel, J. B., & Peterson, N. J. (1965). Punishment: Effects of shock intensity on response suppression. *Psychological Reports, 16,* 721–730.

Arlin, M. (1984). Time, equality, and mastery learning. *Review of Educational Research, 54,* 65–86.

Armbruster, B. B. (1984). The problem of "inconsiderate text." In G. G. Duffy, L. R. Roehler, & J. Mason (Eds.), *Comprehension instruction: Perspectives and suggestions.* New York: Longman.

Armbruster, B. B., & Ostertag, J. (1993). Questions in elementary science and social studies textbooks. In B. K. Britton, A. Woodward, & M. Binkley (Eds.), *Learning from textbooks: Theory and practice.* Hillsdale, NJ: Erlbaum.

Armstrong, S. L., Gleitman, L. R., & Gleitman, H. G. (1983). What some concepts might not be. *Cognition, 13,* 263–308.

Aronfreed, J. (1968). Aversive control of socialization. In W. J. Arnold (Ed.), *Nebraska Symposium on Motivation.* Lincoln, NE: University of Nebraska Press.

Aronfreed, J., & Reber, A. (1965). Internalized behavioral suppression and the timing of social punishment. *Journal of Personality and Social Psychology, 1,* 3–16.

Aronson, E. (1997). *The jigsaw classroom: Building cooperation in the classroom* (2nd ed.). New York: Longman.

Assor, A., & Connell, J. P. (1992). The validity of students' self-reports as measures of performance affecting self-appraisals. In D. H. Schunk & J. L. Meece (Eds.), *Student perceptions in the classroom.* Hillsdale, NJ: Erlbaum.

Astington, J. W., & Pelletier, J. (1996). The language of mind: Its role in teaching and learning. In D. R. Olson & N. Torrance (Eds.), *The handbook of education and human development: New models of learning, teaching, and schooling.* Cambridge, MA: Blackwell Publishers.

Atkinson, J. W. (1957). Motivational determinants of risk-taking behavior. *Psychological Review, 64,* 359-372.

Atkinson, J. W. (1958). *Motives in fantasy, action, and sobriety.* Princeton, NJ: Van Nostrand.

Atkinson, J. W. (1964). *Introduction to motivation.* Princeton, NJ: Van Nostrand.

Atkinson, J. W., & Birch, D. (1978). *Introduction to motivation* (2nd ed.). New York: Van Nostrand.

Atkinson, J. W., & Feather, N. T. (Eds.). (1966). *A theory of achievement motivation.* New York: Wiley.

Atkinson, J. W., & Litwin, G. H. (1960). Achievement motive and test anxiety conceived as motive to approach success and motive to avoid failure. *Journal of Abnormal and Social Psychology, 60,* 52-63.

Atkinson, J. W., & Raynor, J. O. (1978). *Personality, motivation, and achievement.* Washington, DC: Hemisphere.

Atkinson, R. C. (1975). Mnemotechnics in second-language learning. *American Psychologist, 30,* 821-828.

Atkinson, R. C., & Shiffrin, R. M. (1968). Human memory: A proposed system and its control processes. In K. W. Spence & J. T. Spence (Eds.), *The psychology of learning and motivation: Advances in research and theory* (Vol. 2). New York: Academic Press.

Atkinson, R. C., & Shiffrin, R. M. (1971). The control of short-term memory. *Scientific American, 225* (2), 82-90.

Attneave, A. (1957). Transfer of experience with a class schema to identification learning of patterns and shapes. *Journal of Experimental Psychology, 54,* 81-88.

Ausubel, D. P. (1963). *The psychology of meaningful verbal learning.* New York: Grune & Stratton.

Ausubel, D. P. (1968). *Educational psychology: A cognitive view.* New York: Holt, Rinehart & Winston.

Ausubel, D. P., Novak, J. D., & Hanesian, H. (1978). *Educational psychology: A cognitive view* (2nd ed.). New York: Holt, Rinehart & Winston.

Ausubel, D. P., & Robinson, F. G. (1969). *School learning: An introduction to educational psychology.* New York: Holt, Rinehart & Winston.

Ayllon, T., Layman, D., & Kandel, H. J. (1975). A behavioral-educational alternative to drug control of hyperactive children. *Journal of Applied Behavior Analysis, 8,* 137-146.

Azrin, N. H. (1960). Effects of punishment intensity during variable-interval reinforcement. *Journal of the Experimental Analysis of Behavior, 3,* 123-142.

Azrin, N. H. (1967, May). Pain and aggression. *Psychology Today, 1,* 27-33.

Azrin, N. H., & Holz, W. C. (1966). Punishment. In W. K. Honig (Ed.), *Operant behavior: Areas of research and application.* New York: Appleton-Century-Crofts.

Babad, E. (1993). Teachers' differential behavior. *Educational Psychology Review, 5,* 347-376.

Bachevalier, J., Malkova, L., & Beauregard, M. (1996). Multiple memory systems: A neuropsychological and developmental perspective. In G. R. Lyon & N. A. Krasnegor (Eds.), *Attention, memory, and executive function.* Baltimore: Paul H. Brookes.

Baddeley, A. D. (1978). The trouble with levels: A reexamination of Craik and Lockhart's framework for memory research. *Psychological Review, 85,* 139-152.

Baddeley, A. D. (1982). *Your memory: A user's guide.* New York: Macmillan.

Baddeley, A. D. (1986). *Working memory.* Oxford, UK: Clarendon Press.

Baddeley, A. D., & Hitch, G. (1974). Working memory. In G. H. Bower (Ed.), *The psychology of learning and motivation* (Vol. 8). New York: Academic Press.

Baddeley, A. D., & Logie, R. (1992). Auditory imagery and working memory. In D. Reisberg (Ed.), *Auditory imagery.* Hillsdale, NJ: Erlbaum.

Bahrick, H. P. (1984). Semantic memory content in permastore: Fifty years of memory for Spanish learned in school. *Journal of Experimental Psychology: General, 113,* 1-29.

Bahrick, H. P., Bahrick, L. E., Bahrick, A. S., & Bahrick, P. E. (1993). Maintenance of foreign language vocabulary and the spacing effect. *Psychological Science, 4,* 316-321.

Baillargeon, R. (1987). Object permanence in 3.5- and 4.5-month-old infants. *Developmental Psychology, 23,* 655-664.

Baker, L. (1989). Metacognition, comprehension monitoring, and the adult reader. *Educational Psychology Review, 1,* 3-38.

Baker, L., & Brown, A. L. (1984). Metacognitive skills of reading. In D. Pearson (Ed.), *Handbook of reading research.* New York: Longman.

Baker, L., Scher, D., & Mackler, K. (1997). Home and family influences on motivations for reading. *Educational Psychologist, 32,* 69-82.

Balch, W., Bowman, K., & Mohler, L. (1992). Music-dependent memory in immediate and delayed word recall. *Memory and Cognition, 20,* 21-28.

Ballard, D. H. (1986). Cortical connections and parallel processing. *Behavioural and Brain Sciences, 9* (1), 67-120.

Bandura, A. (1965a). Behavioral modification through modeling practices. In L. Krasner & L. Ullman (Eds.), *Research in behavior modification.* New York: Holt, Rinehart & Winston.

Bandura, A. (1965b). Influence of models' reinforcement contingencies on the acquisition of imitative responses. *Journal of Personality and Social Psychology, 1,* 589-595.

Bandura, A. (1969). *Principles of behavior modification.* New York: Holt, Rinehart & Winston.

Bandura, A. (1973). *Aggression: A social learning analysis.* Englewood Cliffs, NJ: Prentice Hall.

Bandura, A. (1977a). Self-efficacy: Toward a unifying theory of behavioral change. *Psychological Review, 84,* 191-215.

Bandura, A. (1977b). *Social learning theory.* Englewood Cliffs, NJ: Prentice Hall.

Bandura, A. (1981). Self-referent thought: A developmental analysis of self-efficacy. In J. Flavell & L. Ross (Eds.), *Social cognitive development: Frontiers and possible futures.* Cambridge, UK: Cambridge University Press.

Bandura, A. (1982). Self-efficacy mechanism in human agency. *American Psychologist, 37,* 122-147.

Bandura, A. (1986). *Social foundations of thought and action: A social cognitive theory.* Englewood Cliffs, NJ: Prentice Hall.

Bandura, A. (1989). Human agency in social cognitive theory. *American Psychologist, 44,* 1175-1184.

Bandura, A., Grusec, E., & Menlove, F. L. (1967). Vicarious extinction of avoidance behavior. *Journal of Personality and Social Psychology, 516-23.*

Bandura, A., & Jeffery, R. W. (1973). Role of symbolic coding and rehearsal processes in observational learning. *Journal of Personality and Social Psychology, 26,* 122-130.

Bandura, A., Jeffery, R. W., & Bachicha, D. L. (1974). Analysis of memory codes and cumulative rehearsal in observational learning. *Journal of Research in Personality, 7,* 295-305.

Bandura, A., & Kupers, C. J. (1964). Transmission of patterns of self-reinforcement through modeling. *Journal of Abnormal and Social Psychology, 69,* 1-9.

Bandura, A., & McDonald, F. J. (1963). Influences of social reinforcement and the behavior of models in shaping children's moral judgments. *Journal of Abnormal and Social Psychology, 67,* 274-281.

Bandura, A., & Menlove, F. L. (1968). Factors determining vicarious extinction of avoidance behavior through symbolic modeling. *Journal of Personality and Social Psychology, 5,* 16-23.

Bandura, A., & Perloff, B. (1967). Relative efficacy of self-monitored and externally imposed reinforcement systems. *Journal of Personality and Social Psychology, 7,* 111-116.

Bandura, A., Ross, D., & Ross, S. A. (1961). Transmission of aggression through imitation of aggressive models. *Journal of Abnormal and Social Psychology, 63,* 575-582.

Bandura, A., Ross, D., & Ross, S. A. (1963). Imitation of film-mediated aggressive models. *Journal of Abnormal and Social Psychology, 66,* 3-11.

Bandura, A., & Schunk, D. (1981). Cultivating competence, self-efficacy, and intrinsic interest through proximal self-motivation. *Journal of Personality and Social Psychology, 41,* 586-598.

Bandura, A., & Walters, R. H. (1963). *Social learning and personality development.* New York: Holt, Rinehart & Winston.

Bandura, A., & Whalen, C. K. (1966). The influence of antecedent reinforcement and divergent modeling cues on patterns of self-reward. *Journal of Personality and Social Psychology, 3,* 373-382.

Bangert-Drowns, R. L., Kulik, C. C., Kulik, J. A., & Morgan, M. (1991). The instructional effect of feedback in test-like events. *Review of Educational Research, 61,* 213-238.

Barbetta, P. M. (1990). GOALS: A group-oriented adapted levels system for children with behavior disorders. *Academic Therapy, 25,* 645-656.

Barbetta, P. M., Heward, W. L., Bradley, D. M., & Miller, A. D. (1994). Effects of immediate and delayed error correction on the acquisition and maintenance of sight words by students with developmental disabilities. *Journal of Applied Behavior Analysis, 27,* 177-178.

Barker, G. P., & Graham, S. (1987). Developmental study of praise and blame as attributional cues. *Journal of Educational Psychology, 79,* 62-66.

Barker, R. H., Dembo, T., & Lewin, K. (1941). Frustration and regression: An experiment with young children. *University of Iowa Studies in Child Welfare, 18,* 1-314.

Barkley, R. A. (1996a). Critical issues in research on attention. In G. R. Lyon & N. A. Krasnegor (Eds.), *Attention, memory, and executive function.* Baltimore: Paul H. Brookes.

Barkley, R. A. (1996b). Linkages between attention and executive functions. In G. R. Lyon & N. A. Krasnegor (Eds.), *Attention, memory, and executive function.* Baltimore: Paul H. Brookes.

Barnett, J. E., Di Vesta, F. J., & Rogozinski, J. T. (1981). What is learned in note taking? *Journal of Educational Psychology, 73,* 181-192.

Baron, A., Kaufman, A., & Stauber, K. A. (1969). Effects of instructions and reinforcement feedback on human operant behavior maintained by fixed-interval reinforcement. *Journal of the Experimental Analysis of Behavior, 12,* 701-712.

Baron, J. B. (1987). Evaluating thinking skills in the classroom. In J. B. Baron & R. J. Sternberg (Eds.), *Teaching thinking skills: Theory and practice.* New York: W. H. Freeman.

Barringer, C., & Gholson, B. (1979). Effects of type and combination of feedback upon conceptual learning by children: Implications for research in academic learning. *Review of Educational Research, 49,* 459-478.

Barrish, H. H., Saunders, M., & Wolf, M. M. (1969). Good behavior game: Effects of individual contingencies for group consequences on disruptive behavior in a classroom. *Journal of Applied Behavior Analysis, 2,* 119-124.

Barth, R. (1979). Home-based reinforcement of school behavior: A review and analysis. *Review of Educational Research, 49,* 436-458.

Bartlett, F. C. (1932). *Remembering: A study in experimental and social psychology.* Cambridge, UK: Cambridge University Press.

Bassok, M. (1990). Transfer of domain-specific problem-solving procedures. *Journal of Experimental Psychology: Learning, Memory, and Cognition, 16,* 522-533.

Bassok, M. (1996). Using content to interpret structure: Effects on analogical transfer. *Current Directions in Psychological Science, 5,* 54-58.

Bassok, M., & Holyoak, K. (1990, April). *Transfer of solution procedures between quantitative domains.* Paper presented at the annual meeting of the American Educational Research Association, Boston.

Bassok, M., & Holyoak, K. J. (1993). Pragmatic knowledge and conceptual structure: Determinants of transfer between quantitative domains. In D. K. Detterman & R. J. Sternberg (Eds.), *Transfer on trial: Intelligence, cognition, and instruction.* Norwood, NJ: Ablex.

Bates, J. A. (1979). Extrinsic reward and intrinsic motivation: A review with implications for the classroom. *Review of Educational Research, 49,* 557-576.

Baumrind, D. (1983). Rejoinder to Lewis's reinterpretation of parental firm control effects: Are authoritative families really harmonious? *Psychological Bulletin, 94,* 132-142.

Bay-Hinitz, A. K., Peterson, R. F., & Quilitch, H. R. (1994). Cooperative games: A way to modify aggressive and cooperative behaviors in young children. *Journal of Applied Behavior Analysis, 27,* 435-446.

Bean, T. W., & Steenwyk, F. L. (1984). The effect of three forms of summarization instruction on sixth graders' summary writing and comprehension. *Journal of Reading Behavior, 16,* 297-306.

Bechterev, V. M. (1913). *The psychologie objective.* Paris: Alcan.

Beck, I. L. (1985). Comprehension instruction in the primary grades. In J. Osborn, P. Wilson, & R. C. Anderson (Eds.), *Reading education: Foundations for a literate America.* Lexington, MA: Lexington Books.

Beck, I. L., & McKeown, M. G. (1988). Toward meaningful accounts in history texts for young learners. *Educational Researcher, 47* (6), 31-39.

Becker, W. C. (1971). *Parents are teachers.* Champaign, IL: Research Press.

Becker, W. C., Madsen, C. H., Arnold, C. R., & Thomas, D. R. (1967). The contingent use of teacher attention and praise in reducing classroom behavior problems. *Journal of Special Education, 1,* 287-307.

Bédard, J., & Chi, M. T. H. (1992). Expertise. *Current Directions in Psychological Science, 1,* 135-139.

Begg, I., Anas, A., & Farinacci, S. (1992). Dissociation of processes in belief: Source recollection, statement familiarity, and the illusion of truth. *Journal of Experimental Psychology: General, 121,* 446-458.

Behr, M., & Harel, G. (1988, April). Cognitive conflict in procedure applications. In D. Tirosh (Chair), *The role of inconsistent ideas in learning mathematics.* Symposium conducted at the annual meeting of the American Educational Research Association, New Orleans.

Belfiore, P. J., Lee, D. L., Vargas, A. U., & Skinner, C. H. (1997). Effects of high-preference single-digit mathematics problem completion on multiple-digit mathematics problem performance. *Journal of Applied Behavior Analysis, 30,* 327-330.

Belfiore, P. J., Skinner, C. H., & Ferkis, M. A. (1995). Effects of response and trial repetition on sight-word training for students with learning disabilities. *Journal of Applied Behavior Analysis, 28,* 347-348.

Bell, A., Burkhardt, H., & Swan, M. (1992). Assessment of extended tasks. In R. Lesh & S. J. Lamon (Eds.), *Assessment of authentic performance in school mathematics.* Washington, DC: American Association for the Advancement of Science.

Bellezza, F. S. (1986). Mental cues and verbal reports in learning. In G. H. Bower (Ed.), *The psychology of learning and motivation: Advances in research and theory* (Vol. 20). Orlando: Academic Press.

Bell-Gredler, M. E. (1986). *Learning and instruction: Theory into practice.* New York: Macmillan.

Beneke, W. N., & Harris, M. B. (1972). Teaching self-control of study behavior. *Behaviour Research and Therapy, 10,* 35-41.

Bennett, R. E., Gottesman, R. L., Rock, D. A., & Cerullo, F. (1993). Influence of behavior perceptions and gender on teachers' judgments of students' academic skill. *Journal of Educational Psychology, 85,* 347-356.

Benton, S. L. (1997). Psychological foundations of elementary writing instruction. In G. D. Phye (Ed.), *Handbook of academic learning: Construction of knowledge.* San Diego: Academic Press.

Benton, S. L., Kiewra, K. A., Whitfill, J. M., & Dennison, R. (1993). Encoding and external-storage effects on writing processes. *Journal of Educational Psychology, 85,* 267-280.

Benware, C., & Deci, E. L. (1984). Quality of learning with an active versus passive motivational set. *American Educational Research Journal, 21,* 755-765.

Bereiter, C. (1994). Implications of postmodernism for science, or, science as progressive discourse. *Educational Psychologist, 29* (1), 3-12.

Bereiter, C. (1995). A dispositional view of transfer. In A. McKeough, J. Lupart, & A. Marini (Eds.), *Teaching for transfer: Fostering generalization in learning.* Mahwah, NJ: Erlbaum.

Berg, C. A., & Calderone, K. S. (1994). The role of problem interpretations in understanding the development of everyday problem solving. In R. J. Sternberg & R. K. Wagner (Eds.), *Mind in context: Interactionist perspectives on human intelligence.* Cambridge, UK: Cambridge University Press.

Berk, L. E. (1989). *Child development.* Boston: Allyn & Bacon.

Berk, L. E. (1994). Why children talk to themselves. *Scientific American, 271,* 78-83.

Berkowitz, L., & LePage, A. (1967). Weapons as aggression-eliciting stimuli. *Journal of Personality and Social Psychology, 7,* 202-207.

Berliner, D. C. (1989). The place of process-product research in developing the agenda for research on teacher thinking. *Educational Psychologist, 24,* 325-344.

Berliner, D. C. (1997, March). Discussant's comments. In H. Borko (Chair), *Educational psychology and teacher education: Perennial issues.* Symposium conducted at the annual meeting of the American Educational Research Association, Chicago.

Berlyne, D. E. (1960). *Conflict, arousal, and curiosity.* New York: McGraw-Hill.

Berndt, T., & Perry, T. (1990). Distinctive features and effects of early adolescent friendships. In R. Montemayor, G. Adams, & T. Gullotta (Eds.), *From childhood to adolescence: A transitional period?* Newbury Park, CA: Sage.

Berninger, V. W., Fuller, F., & Whitaker, D. (1996). A process model of writing development across the life span. *Educational Psychology Review, 8,* 193-218.

Bernstein, M. R. (1955). Relationship between interest and reading comprehension. *Journal of Educational Research, 49,* 283-288.

Bersh, P. J. (1951). The influence of two variables upon the establishment of a secondary reinforcer for operant responses. *Journal of Experimental Psychology, 41,* 62-73.

Bilodeau, I. M., & Schlosberg, H. (1951). Similarity in stimulating conditions as a variable in retroactive inhibition. *Journal of Experimental Psychology, 41,* 199-204.

Birch, H. G., & Rabinowitz, H. S. (1951). The negative effect of previous experience on productive thinking. *Journal of Experimental Psychology, 41,* 121-125.

Birnbaum, J. C. (1982). The reading and composing behaviors of selected fourth- and seventh-grade students. *Research in the Teaching of English, 16,* 241-260.

Bishop, B. A., & Anderson, C. W. (1990). Student conceptions of natural selection and its role in evolution. *Journal of Research in Science Teaching, 27,* 415-427.

Bjork, R. A. (1972). Theoretical implications of directed forgetting. In A. W. Melton & E. Martin (Eds.), *Coding processes in human memory.* Washington, DC: V. H. Winston.

Bjorklund, D. F. (1987). How age changes in knowledge base contribute to the development of children's memory: An interpretive review. *Developmental Review, 7,* 93-130.

Blake, S. B., & Clark, R. E. (1990, April). *The effects of metacognitive selection on far transfer in analogical problem solving tasks.* Paper presented at the annual meeting of the American Educational Research Association, Boston.

Blanchard, F. A., Lilly, T., & Vaughn, L. A. (1991). Reducing the expression of racial prejudice. *Psychological Science, 2,* 101-105.

Block, J. H. (1980). Promoting excellence through mastery learning. *Theory into Practice, 19* (1), 66-74.

Block, J. H., & Burns, R. B. (1976). Mastery learning. In L. Shulman (Ed.), *Review of research in education* (Vol. 4). Itasca, IL: Peacock.

Bloom, B. S. (1968). Mastery learning. In *Evaluation comment* (Vol. 1, No. 2). Los Angeles: University of California at Los Angeles, Center for the Study of Evaluation of Instructional Programs.

Bloom, B. S. (1974). An introduction to mastery learning theory. In J. H. Block (Ed.), *Schools, society, and mastery learning.* New York: Holt, Rinehart & Winston.

Bloom, B. S. (1976). *Human characteristics and school learning.* New York: McGraw-Hill.

Bloom, B. S. (1981). *All our children learning.* New York: McGraw-Hill.

Bloom, B. S. (1984). The search for methods of group instruction as effective as one-to-one tutoring. *Educational Leadership, 41* (8), 4-17.

Bloom, B. S., & Broder, L. J. (1950). *Problem-solving processes of college students.* Chicago: University of Chicago Press.

Bloom, B. S., Englehart, M. B., Furst, E. J., Hill, W. H., & Krathwohl, D. R. (1956). *Taxonomy of educational objectives. The classification of educational goals. Handbook I: Cognitive domain.* New York: Longmans Green.

Blumenfeld, P. C. (1992). The task and the teacher: Enhancing student thoughtfulness in science. In J. Brophy (Ed.), *Advances in research on teaching: Vol. 3. Planning and managing learning tasks and activities.* Greenwich, CT: JAI Press.

Blumenfeld, P. C., Marx, R. W., Soloway, E., & Krajcik, J. (1996). Learning with peers: From small group cooperation to collaborative communities. *Educational Researcher, 25* (8), 37-40.

Bobango, J. C. (1988, April). *The effect of phase-based instruction on high school geometry students' van Hiele levels and achievement.* Paper presented at the annual meeting of the American Educational Research Association, New Orleans.

Bobrow, S., & Bower, G. H. (1969). Comprehension and recall of sentences. *Journal of Experimental Psychology, 80,* 455-461.

Bochenhauer, M. H. (1990, April). *Connections: Geographic education and the National Geographic Society.* Paper presented at the annual meeting of the American Educational Research Association, Boston.

Boe, E. E., & Church, R. M. (1967). Permanent effects of punishment during extinction. *Journal of Comparative and Physiological Psychology, 63,* 486-492.

Boggiano, A. K., Main, D. S., & Katz, P. A. (1988). Children's preference for challenge: The role of perceived competence and control. *Journal of Personality and Social Psychology, 54,* 134-141.

Boggiano, A. K., & Pittman, T. S. (Eds.). (1992). *Achievement and motivation: A social-developmental perspective.* Cambridge, UK: Cambridge University Press.

Bohannon, J. N., III, & Symons, V. L. (1992). Flashbulb memories: Confidence, consistency, and quantity. In E. Winograd & U. Neisser (Eds.), *Affect and accuracy in recall: Studies of "flashbulb" memories.* Cambridge, UK: Cambridge University Press.

Bolles, R. C. (1975). *Theory of motivation* (2nd ed.). New York: Harper & Row.

Bolstad, O., & Johnson, S. (1972). Self-regulation in the modification of disruptive classroom behavior. *Journal of Applied Behavior Analysis, 5,* 443-454.

Borko, H., & Putnam, R. T. (1996). Learning to teach. In D. C. Berliner & R. C. Calfee (Eds.), *Handbook of educational psychology.* New York: Macmillan.

Born, D. G., & Davis, M. L. (1974). Amount and distribution of study in a personalized instruction course and in a lecture course. *Journal of Applied Behavior Analysis, 7,* 365-375.

Boschee, F., & Baron, M. A. (1993). *Outcome-based education: Developing programs through strategic planning.* Lancaster, PA: Technomic Publishing.

Bourbeau, P. E., Sowers, J., & Close, D. E. (1986). An experimental analysis of generalization of banking skills from classroom to bank settings in the community. *Education and Training of the Mentally Retarded, 21,* 98-107.

Bourne, L. E., Jr. (1967). Learning and utilization of conceptual rules. In B. Kleinmuntz (Ed.), *Concepts and the structure of memory.* New York: Wiley.

Bourne, L. E., Jr. (1982). Typicality effects in logically defined concepts. *Memory and Cognition, 10,* 3-9.

Bourne, L. E., Jr., Dominowski, R. L., Loftus, E. F., & Healy, A. F. (1986). *Cognitive processes* (2nd ed.). Englewood Cliffs, NJ: Prentice Hall.

Bourne, L. E., Jr., Ekstrand, D. R., & Dominowski, R. L. (1971). *The psychology of thinking.* Englewood Cliffs, NJ: Prentice Hall.

Bousfield, W. A. (1953). The occurrence of clustering in the recall of randomly arranged associates. Journal of General Psychology, *49,* 229-240.

Bouton, M. E. (1994). Context, ambiguity, and classical conditioning. *Current Directions in Psychological Science, 3,* 49-53.

Bower, G. H. (1972). Mental imagery and associative learning. In L. W. Gregg (Ed.), *Cognition in learning and memory.* New York: Wiley.

Bower, G. H. (1994). Some relations between emotions and memory. In P. Ekman & R. J. Davidson (Eds.), *The nature of emotion: Fundamental questions.* New York: Oxford University Press.

Bower, G. H., Black, J. B., & Turner, T. J. (1979). Scripts in memory for text. *Cognitive Psychology, 11,* 177-220.

Bower, G. H., & Clark, M.C. (1969). Narrative stories as mediators for serial learning. *Psychonomic Science, 14,* 181-182.

Bower, G. H., Clark, M. C., Lesgold, A. M., & Winzenz, D. (1969). Hierarchical retrieval schemes in recall of categorized word lists. *Journal of Verbal Learning and Verbal Behavior, 8,* 323-343.

Bower, G. H., & Hilgard, E. R. (1981). *Theories of learning* (5th ed.). Englewood Cliffs, NJ: Prentice Hall.

Bower, G. H., & Holyoak, K. J. (1973). Encoding and recognition memory for naturalistic sounds. *Journal of Experimental Psychology, 101,* 360-366.

Bower, G. H., Karlin, M. B., & Dueck, A. (1975). Comprehension and memory for pictures. *Memory and Cognition, 3,* 216-220.

Bower, G. H., McLean, J., & Meachem, J. (1966). Value of knowing when reinforcement is due. *Journal of Comparative and Physiological Psychology, 62,* 184-192.

Bower, G. H., & Springston, F. (1970). Pauses as recoding points in letter series. *Journal of Experimental Psychology, 83,* 421-430.

Boyatzis, R. E. (1973). Affiliation motivation. In D. C. McClelland & R. S. Steele (Eds.), *Human motivation: A book of readings.* Morristown, NJ: General Learning Press.

Boykin, A. W. (1994). Harvesting talent and culture: African-American children and educational reform. In R. J. Rossi (Ed.), *Schools and students at risk: Context and framework for positive change.* New York: Teachers College Press.

Bragstad, B. J., & Stumpf, S. M. (1982). *A guidebook for teaching study skills and motivation.* Boston: Allyn & Bacon.

Brainerd, C. J., & Reyna, V. F. (1992). Explaining "memory free" reasoning. *Psychological Science, 3,* 332-339.

Bramel, D., Taub, B., & Blum, B. (1968). An observer's reaction to the suffering of his enemy. *Journal of Personality and Social Psychology, 8,* 384-392.

Bransford, J. D., & Franks, J. J. (1971). The abstraction of linguistic ideas. *Cognitive Psychology, 2,* 331-350.

Bransford, J. D., & Johnson, M. K. (1972). Contextual prerequisites for understanding: Some investigations of comprehension and recall. *Journal of Verbal Learning and Verbal Behavior, 11,* 717-726.

Braukmann, C. J., Ramp, K. K., & Wolf, M. M. (1981). Behavioral treatment of juvenile delinquency. In S. W. Bijou & R. Ruiz (Eds.), *Behavior modification: Contributions to education.* Hillsdale, NJ: Erlbaum.

Bredo, E. (1997). The social construction of learning. In G. D. Phye (Ed.), *Handbook of academic learning: Construction of knowledge.* San Diego: Academic Press.

Breitmeyer, B. B., & Ganz, L. (1976). Implications of sustained and transient channels for theories of visual pattern masking, saccadic suppression, and information processing. *Psychological Review, 83,* 1-36.

Brewer, W. F. (1992). The theoretical and empirical status of the flashbulb memory hypothesis. In E. Winograd & U. Neisser (Eds.), *Affect and accuracy in recall: Studies of "flashbulb" memories.* Cambridge, UK: Cambridge University Press.

Brewer, W. F., & Treyens, J. C. (1981). Role of schemata in memory for places. *Cognitive Psychology, 13,* 207-230.

Brickman, S., Miller, R. B., & Roedel, T. D. (1997, March). *Goal valuing and future consequences as predictors of cognitive engagement.* Paper presented at the annual meeting of the American Educational Research Association, Chicago.

Briggs, L. J., & Reed, H. B. (1943). The curve of retention for substance material. *Journal of Experimental Psychology, 32,* 513-517.

Broadbent, D. E. (1958). *Perception and communication.* London: Pergamon Press.

Broadhurst, P. L. (1959). The interaction of task difficulty and motivation: The Yerkes-Dodson law revived. *Acta Psychologia, 16,* 321-338.

Bronfenbrenner, U. (1970). *Two worlds of childhood: U.S. and U.S.S.R.* New York: Russell Sage Foundation.

Brooke, R. R., & Ruthren, A. J. (1984). The effects of contingency contracting on student performance in a PSI class. *Teaching of Psychology, 11,* 87-89.

Brooks, L. R. (1978). Nonanalytic concept formation and memory for instances. In E. Rosch & B. B. Lloyd (Eds.), *Cognition and categorization.* Hillsdale, NJ: Erlbaum.

Brooks, L. W., & Dansereau, D. F. (1987). Transfer of information: An instructional perspective. In S. M. Cormier & J. D. Hagman (Eds.), *Transfer of learning: Contemporary research and applications.* San Diego: Academic Press.

Brophy, J. E. (1981). Teacher praise: A functional analysis. *Review of Educational Research, 51,* 5-32.

Brophy, J. E. (1986). *On motivating students.* Occasional Paper No. 101, Institute for Research on Teaching, Michigan State University, East Lansing, MI.

Brophy, J. E. (1987). Synthesis of research on strategies for motivating students to learn. *Educational Leadership, 45* (2), 40-48.

Brophy, J. E. (1992a). Conclusions: Comments on an emerging field. In J. Brophy (Ed.), *Advances in research on teaching: Vol. 3. Planning and managing learning tasks and activities.* Greenwich, CT: JAI Press.

Brophy, J. E. (1992b). Probing the subtleties of subject-matter teaching. *Educational Leadership, 49* (7), 4-8.

Brophy, J. E., & Alleman, J. (1991). Activities as instructional tools: A framework for analysis and evaluation. *Educational Researcher, 20* (4), 9-23.

Brophy, J., & Alleman, J. (1992). Planning and managing learning activities: Basic principles. In J. Brophy (Ed.), *Advances in research on teaching: Vol. 3. Planning and managing learning tasks and activities.* Greenwich, CT: JAI Press.

Brophy, J. E., & Good, T. L. (1970). Teachers' communication of differential expectations for children's classroom performance: Some behavioral data. *Journal of Educational Psychology, 61,* 365-374.

Brothers, K. J., Krantz, P. J., & McClannahan, L. E. (1994). Office paper recycling: A function of container proximity. *Journal of Applied Behavior Analysis, 27,* 153-160.

Brown, A. (1991). A review of the tip-of-the-tongue experience. *Psychological Bulletin, 109,* 204-223.

Brown, A. L. (1978). Knowing when, where, and how to remember: A problem of metacognition. In R. Glaser (Ed.), *Advances in instructional psychology.* Hillsdale, NJ: Erlbaum.

Brown, A. L., Ash, D., Rutherford, M., Nakagawa, K., Gordon, A., & Campione, J. C. (1993). Distributed expertise in the classroom. In G. Salomon (Ed.), *Distributed cognitions: Psychological and educational considerations.* Cambridge, UK: Cambridge University Press.

Brown, A. L., Bransford, J. D., Ferrera, R. A., & Campione, J. C. (1983). Learning, remembering, and understanding. In J. Flavell & E. Mankman (Eds.), *Carmichael's manual of children psychology* (Vol. 1). New York: Wiley.

Brown, A. L., & Campione, J. C. (1986). Psychological theory and the study of learning disabilities. *American Psychologist, 41,* 1059-1068.

Brown, A. L., & Campione, J. C. (1990). Communities of learning and thinking, or, a context by any other name. *Contributions to Human Development, 21,* 108-126.

Brown, A. L., & Campione, J. C. (1994). Guided discovery in a community of learners. In K. McGilly (Ed.), *Classroom lessons: Integrating cognitive theory and classroom practice.* Cambridge, MA: MIT Press/Bradford.

Brown, A. L., Campione, J., & Day, J. (1981). Learning to learn: On training students to learn from texts. *Educational Researcher, 10* (2), 14-21.

Brown, A. L., & Day, J. D. (1983). Macrorules for summarizing texts: The development of expertise. *Journal of Verbal Learning and Verbal Behavior, 22,* 1-14.

Brown, A. L., & Palincsar, A. S. (1987). Reciprocal teaching of comprehension strategies: A natural history of one program for enhancing learning. In J. Borkowski & J. D. Day (Eds.), *Cognition in special education: Comparative approaches to retardation, learning disabilities, and giftedness.* Norwood, NJ: Ablex.

Brown, A. L., & Palincsar, A. S. (1989). Guided, cooperative learning and individual knowledge acquisition. In L. B. Resnick (Ed.), *Knowing, learning, and instruction: Essays in honor of Robert Glaser.* Hillsdale, NJ: Erlbaum.

Brown, A. L., Palincsar, A. S., & Armbruster, B. B. (1984). Instructing comprehension fostering activities in interactive learning situations. In H. Mandl, N. Stein, & T. Trabasso (Eds.), *Learning and comprehension of text.* Hillsdale, NJ: Erlbaum.

Brown, A. L., & Reeve, R. A. (1987). Bandwidths of competence: The role of supportive contexts in learning and development. In L. S. Liben (Ed.), *Development and learning: Conflict or congruence?* Hillsdale, NJ: Erlbaum.

Brown, D. E. (1992). Using examples and analogies to remediate misconceptions in physics: Factors influencing conceptual change. *Journal of Research in Science Teaching, 29,* 17-34.

Brown, I., & Inouye, D. K. (1978). Learned helplessness through modeling: The role of perceived similarity in competence. *Journal of Personality and Social Psychology, 36,* 900-908.

479

Brown, J. (1968). Reciprocal facilitation and impairment of free recall. *Psychonomic Science, 10*, 41–42.

Brown, J. S., Collins, A., & Duguid, P. (1989). Situated cognition and the culture of learning. *Educational Researcher, 18* (1), 32–42.

Brown, R., & Herrnstein, R. J. (1975). *Psychology*. Boston: Little, Brown.

Brown, R., & Kulik, J. (1977). Flashbulb memories. *Cognition, 5*, 73–99.

Brown, R., & McNeill, D. (1966). The "tip of the tongue" phenomenon. *Journal of Verbal Learning and Verbal Behavior, 5*, 325–337.

Brown, S. I., & Walter, M. I. (1990). *The art of problem posing* (2nd ed.). Hillsdale, NJ: Erlbaum.

Brown, W. H., Bryson-Brockmann, W., & Fox, J. J. (1986). The usefulness of J. R. Kantor's setting event concept for research on children's social behavior. *Child and Family Behavior Therapy, 8* (2), 15–25.

Brown, W. H., Fox, J. J., & Brady, M. P. (1987). Effects of spatial density on 3- and 4-year-old children's socially directed behavior during freeplay: An investigation of a setting factor. *Education and Treatment of Children, 10*, 247–258.

Brozo, W. G., Stahl, N. A., & Gordon, B. (1985). Training effects of summarizing, item writing, and knowledge of information sources on reading test performance. In J. A. Niles & R. V. Lalik (Eds.), Issues in literacy. Rochester, NY: National Reading Conference.

Bruck, M., Cavanagh, P., & Ceci, S. (1991). Fortysomething: Recognizing faces at one's 25th reunion. *Memory and Cognition, 19*, 221–228.

Bruner, J. S. (1957). On going beyond the information given. In *Contemporary approaches to cognition*. Cambridge, MA: Harvard University Press.

Bruner, J. S. (1961a). The act of discovery. *Harvard Educational Review, 31*, 21–32.

Bruner, J. S. (1961b). *The process of education*. Cambridge, MA: Harvard University Press.

Bruner, J. S. (1966). *Toward a theory of instruction*. New York: W. W. Norton.

Bruner, J. S., Goodnow, J., & Austin, G. (1956). *A study of thinking*. New York: Wiley.

Bruning, R. H., Schraw, G. J., & Ronning, R. R. (1995). *Cognitive psychology and instruction* (2nd ed.). Englewood Cliffs, NJ: Prentice Hall/Merrill.

Bryan, J. H. (1971). Model affect and children's imitative altruism. *Child Development, 42*, 2061–2065.

Bryan, J. H. (1975). Children's cooperation and helping behaviors. In E. M. Hetherington (Ed.), *Review of child development research* (Vol. 5). Chicago: University of Chicago Press.

Buckhout, R. (1974). Eyewitness testimony. *Scientific American, 231* (6), 23–31.

Buckland, P. R. (1968). The ordering of frames in a linear program. *Programmed Learning and Educational Technology, 5*, 197–205.

Bufford, R. K. (1976). Evaluation of a reinforcement procedure for accelerating work rate in a self-paced course. *Journal of Applied Behavior Analysis, 9*, 208.

Bugelski, B. R. (1962). Presentation time, total time, and mediation in paired-associate learning. *Journal of Experimental Psychology, 63*, 409–412.

Bugelski, B. R., & Alampay, D. A. (1961). The role of frequency in developing perceptual sets. *Canadian Journal of Psychology, 15*, 205–211.

Bugelski, B. R., Kidd, E., & Segmen, J. (1968). Image as a mediator in one-trial paired-associate learning. *Journal of Experimental Psychology, 76*, 69–73.

Bulgren, J. A., Schumaker, J. B., & Deshler, D. D. (1994). The effects of a recall enhancement routine on the test performance of secondary students with and without learning disabilities. *Learning Disabilities Research and Practice, 9*, 2–11.

Burnett, R. E., & Kastman, L. M. (1997). Teaching composition: Current theories and practices. In G. D. Phye (Ed.), *Handbook of academic learning: Construction of knowledge*. San Diego: Academic Press.

Burron, A., & Claybaugh, A. (1992). *Basic concepts in reading instruction: A programmed approach*. Longmont, CO: Sopris.

Buschke, H. (1977). Two-dimensional recall: Immediate identification of clusters in episodic and semantic memory. *Journal of Verbal Learning and Verbal Behavior, 16*, 201–215.

Bushell, D., Wrobel, P. A., & Michaelis, M. L. (1968). Applying "group" contingencies to the classroom study behavior of preschool children. *Journal of Applied Behavior Analysis, 1*, 55–61.

Butler, D. L., & Winne, P. H. (1995). Feedback and self-regulated learning: A theoretical synthesis. *Review of Educational Research, 65*, 245–281.

Butler, R. (1987). Task-involving and ego-involving properties of evaluation: Effects of different feedback conditions on motivational perceptions, interest, and performance. *Journal of Educational Psychology, 79*, 474–482.

Butler, R. (1988). Enhancing and undermining intrinsic motivation: The effects of task-involving and ego-involving evaluation on interest and performance. *British Journal of Educational Psychology, 58*, 1–14.

Butler, R., & Nisan, M. (1986). Effects of no feedback, task-related comments, and grades on intrinsic motivation and performance. *Journal of Educational Psychology, 78*, 210–216.

Butterworth, G. (1993). Context and cognition in models of cognitive growth. In P. Light & G. Butterworth (Eds.), *Context and cognition: Ways of learning and knowing*. Hillsdale, NJ: Erlbaum.

Byrnes, J. P. (1996). *Cognitive development and learning in instructional contexts*. Boston: Allyn & Bacon.

Calfee, R. (1981). Cognitive psychology and educational practice. In D. C. Berliner (Ed.), *Review of Research in Education* (Vol. 9). Washington, DC: American Educational Research Association.

Calfee, R. C., & Chambliss, M. J. (1988, April). *The structure of social studies textbooks: Where is the design?* Paper presented at the annual meeting of the American Educational Research Association, New Orleans.

Calfee, R., Dunlap, K., & Wat, A. (1994). Authentic discussion of texts in middle grade schooling: An analytic-narrative approach. *Journal of Reading, 37*, 546–556.

Cameron, J., & Pierce, W. D. (1994). Reinforcement, reward, and intrinsic motivation: A meta-analysis. *Review of Educational Research, 64*, 363–423.

Cameron, J., & Pierce, W. D. (1996). The debate about rewards and intrinsic motivation: Protests and accusations do not alter the results. *Review of Educational Research, 66*, 39–51.

Campione, J. C., Shapiro, A. M., & Brown, A. L. (1995). Forms of transfer in a community of learners: Flexible learning and understanding. In A. McKeough, J. Lupart, & A. Marini (Eds.), *Teaching for transfer: Fostering generalization in learning*. Mahwah, NJ: Erlbaum.

Cann, A., & Ross, D. (1989). Olfactory stimuli as context cues in human memory. *American Journal of Psychology, 102*, 91–102.

Cardelle-Elawar, M. (1992). Effects of teaching metacognitive skills to students with low mathematics ability. *Teaching and Teacher Education, 8*, 109–121.

480

Carey, R. G., & Bucher, B. D. (1986). Positive practice overcorrection: Effects of reinforcing correct performance. *Behavior Modification, 10,* 73-92.

Carey, S. (1985). Are children fundamentally different kinds of thinkers and learners than adults? In S. F. Chipman, J. W. Segal, & R. Glaser (Eds.), *Learning and thinking skills: Vol. 2. Research and open questions.* Hillsdale, NJ: Erlbaum.

Carey, S. (1986). Cognitive science and science education. *American Psychologist, 41,* 1123-1130.

Carlson, B. E. (1984). The father's contribution to child care: Effects on children's perceptions of parental roles. *American Journal of Orthopsychiatry, 54,* 123-136.

Carmichael, L., Hogan, H. P., & Walters, A. A. (1932). An experimental study of the effect of language on the reproduction of visually perceived form. *Journal of Experimental Psychology, 15,* 73-86.

Carpenter, P. A., & Just, M. A. (1986). Cognitive processes in reading. In J. Orasanu (Ed.), *Reading comprehension: From research to practice.* Hillsdale, NJ: Erlbaum.

Carpenter, T. P. (1985). Learning to add and subtract: An exercise in problem solving. In E. A. Silver (Ed.), *Teaching and learning mathematical problem solving: Multiple research perspectives.* Hillsdale, NJ: Erlbaum.

Carr, M., & Jessup, D. (1994, April). *Gender differences in first grade mathematics strategy use: Social, metacognitive, and attributional influences.* Paper presented at the annual meeting of the American Educational Research Association, New Orleans.

Carraher, T. N., Carraher, D. W., & Schliemann, A. D. (1985). Mathematics in the streets and in the schools. *British Journal of Developmental Psychology, 3,* 21-29.

Carroll, J. B. (1963). A model of school learning. *Teachers College Record, 64,* 723-733.

Carroll, J. B. (1989). The Carroll model: A 25-year retrospective and prospective view. *Educational Researcher, 18* (1), 26-31.

Carver, C. S., & Scheier, M. F. (1990). Origins and functions of positive and negative affect: A control-process view. *Psychological Review, 97,* 19-35.

Carver, R. P. (1971). *Sense and nonsense in speed reading.* Silver Springs, MD: Revrac.

Carver, R. P. (1990). *Reading rate: A review of research and theory.* San Diego: Academic Press.

Case, R. (1985). *Intellectual development: Birth to adulthood.* Orlando: Academic Press.

Case, R. (1996). Changing views of knowledge and their impact on educational research and practice. In D. R. Olson & N. Torrance (Eds.), *The handbook of education and human development: New models of learning, teaching, and schooling.* Cambridge, MA: Blackwell Publishers.

Catania, A. C. (1985). The two psychologies of learning: Blind alleys and nonsense syllables. In S. Koch & D. E. Leary (Eds.), *A century of psychology as science.* New York: McGraw-Hill.

Catania, A. C., & Reynolds, G. S. (1968). A quantitative analysis of the responding maintained by interval schedules of reinforcement. *Journal of the Experimental Analysis of Behavior, 11,* 327-383.

Cavanaugh, J. C., & Perlmutter, M. (1982). Metamemory: A critical examination. *Child Development, 53,* 11-28.

Ceci, S. J., & Roazzi, A. (1994). The effects of context on cognition: Postcards from Brazil. In R. J. Sternberg & R. K. Wagner (Eds.), *Mind in context: Interactionist perspectives on human intelligence.* Cambridge, UK: Cambridge University Press.

Cermak, L. S. (1993). Automatic versus controlled processing and the implicit task performance of amnesic patients. In P. Graf & M. E. J. Masson (Eds.), *Implicit memory: New directions in cognition, development, and neuropsychology.* Hillsdale, NJ: Erlbaum.

Cermak, L. S., & Craik, F. I. M. (Eds.). (1979). *Levels of processing in human memory.* Hillsdale, NJ: Erlbaum.

Chambers, D., & Reisberg, D. (1985). Can mental images be ambiguous? *Journal of Experimental Psychology: Human Perception and Performance, 11,* 317-328.

Chambliss, M. J. (1994). Why do readers fail to change their beliefs after reading persuasive text? In R. Garner & P. A. Alexander (Eds.), *Beliefs about text and instruction with text.* Hillsdale, NJ: Erlbaum.

Chambliss, M. J., Calfee, R. C., & Wong, I. (1990, April). *Structure and content in science textbooks: Where is the design?* Paper presented at the annual meeting of the American Educational Research Association, Boston.

Champagne, A. B., Klopfer, L. E., & Gunstone, R. F. (1982). Cognitive research and the design of science instruction. *Educational Psychologist, 17,* 31-53.

Chan, C., Burtis, J., & Bereiter, C. (1997). Knowledge building as a mediator of conflict in conceptual change. *Cognition and Instruction, 15,* 1-40.

Chan, C. K. K., Burtis, P. J., Scardamalia, M., & Bereiter, C. (1992). Constructive activity in learning from text. *American Educational Research Journal, 29,* 97-118.

Chapin, M., & Dyck, D. G. (1976). Persistence in children's reading behavior as a function of N length and attribution retraining. *Journal of Abnormal Psychology, 85,* 511-515.

Chase, W. G., & Chi, M. T. H. (1980). Cognitive skill: Implications for spatial skill in large-scale environments. In J. Harvey (Ed.), Cognition, social behavior, and the environment. Potomac, MD: Erlbaum.

Chase, W. G., & Simon, H. A. (1973). Perception in chess. *Cognitive Psychology, 4,* 55-81.

Cheng, P. W. (1985). Restructuring versus automaticity: Alternative accounts of skill acquisition. *Psychological Review, 92,* 414-423.

Cheng, P. W., Holyoak, K. J., Nisbett, R. E., & Oliver, L. M. (1986). Pragmatic versus syntactic approaches to training deductive reasoning. *Cognitive Psychology, 18,* 293-328.

Cherry, E. C. (1953). Some experiments on the recognition of speech, with one and with two ears. *Journal of the Acoustical Society of America, 25,* 975-979.

Cheyne, J. A., & Walters, R. H. (1970). Punishment and prohibition: Some origins of self-control. In T. M. Newcomb (Ed.), *New directions in psychology.* New York: Holt, Rinehart & Winston.

Chi, M. T. H. (1978). Knowledge structures and memory development. In R. S. Siegler (Ed.), *Children's thinking: What develops?* Hillsdale, NJ: Erlbaum.

Chi, M. T. H. (1981). Knowledge development and memory performance. In M. P. Friedman, J. P. Das, & N. O'Connor (Eds.), *Intelligence and learning.* New York: Plenum Press.

Chi, M. T. H., Feltovich, P., & Glaser, R. (1981). Categorization and representation of physics problems by experts and novices. *Cognitive Science, 5,* 121-152.

Chi, M. T. H., & Glaser, R. (1985). Problem-solving ability. In R. J. Sternberg (Ed.), *Human abilities: An information-processing approach.* New York: W. H. Freeman.

Chi, M. T. H., Glaser, R., & Farr, M. J. (Eds.). (1988). *The nature of expertise*. Hillsdale, NJ: Erlbaum.

Chi, M. T. H., Glaser, R., & Rees, E. (1982). Expertise in problem solving. In R. J. Sternberg (Ed.), *Advances in the psychology of human intelligence*. Hillsdale, NJ: Erlbaum.

Chiesi, H. L., Spilich, G. J., & Voss, J. F. (1979). Acquisition of domain-related information in relation to high and low domain knowledge. *Journal of Verbal Learning and Verbal Behavior, 18,* 257-273.

Chinn, C. A., & Brewer, W. F. (1993). The role of anomalous data in knowledge acquisition: A theoretical framework and implications for science instruction. *Review of Educational Research, 63,* 1-49.

Chipman, S. F., Krantz, D. H., & Silver, R. (1992). Mathematics anxiety and science careers among able college women. *Psychological Science, 3,* 292-295.

Chomsky, N. (1957). *Syntactic structures*. The Hague: Mouton.

Christen, F., & Bjork, R. A. (1976). *On updating the loci in the method of loci*. Paper presented at the annual meeting of the Psychonomic Society, St. Louis.

Church, R. M. (1993). Human models of animal behavior. *Psychological Science, 4,* 170-173.

Clark, D. C. (1971). Teaching concepts in the classroom: A set of teaching prescriptions derived from experimental research. *Journal of Educational Psychology, 62,* 253-278.

Clark, J. M., & Paivio, A. (1991). Dual coding theory and education. *Educational Psychology Review, 3,* 149-210.

Clement, J. (1987). Overcoming students' misconceptions in physics: The role of anchoring intuitions and analogical validity. In *Proceedings of the Second International Seminar on Misconceptions and Educational Strategies in Science and Mathematics* (Vol. 3). Ithaca, NY: Cornell University.

Clifford, M. M. (1984). Thoughts on a theory of constructive failure. *Educational Psychologist, 19,* 108-120.

Clifford, M. M. (1990). Students need challenge, not easy success. *Educational Leadership, 48* (1), 22-26.

Coates, B., & Hartup, W. W. (1969). Age and verbalization in observational learning. *Developmental Psychology, 1,* 556-562.

Cobb, P., Wood, T., Yackel, E., Nicholls, J., Wheatley, G., Trigatti, B., & Perlwitz, M. (1991). Assessment of a problem centered second-grade mathematics project. *Journal for Research in Mathematics Education, 22,* 3-29.

Cobb, P., & Yackel, E. (1996). Constructivist, emergent, and sociocultural perspectives in the context of developmental research. *Educational Psychologist, 31,* 175-190.

Cobb, P., Yackel, E., & Wood, T. (1989). Young children's emotional acts while engaged in mathematical problem solving. In D. B. McLeod & V. M. Adams (Eds.), *Affect and mathematical problem solving: A new perspective*. New York: Springer-Verlag.

Cochran, K. F. (1988, April). *Cognitive structure representation in physics*. Paper presented at the annual meeting of the American Educational Research Association, New Orleans.

Cofer, C. (1971). Properties of verbal materials and verbal learning. In J. Kling & L. Riggs (Eds.), *Woodworth and Schlosberg's experimental psychology*. New York: Holt, Rinehart & Winston.

Cognition and Technology Group at Vanderbilt. (1993). Anchored instruction and situated cognition revisited. *Educational Technology, 33* (3), 52-70.

Cohen, E. G. (1994). Restructuring the classroom: Conditions for productive small groups. *Review of Educational Research, 64,* 1-35.

Cohen, E. G., & Lotan, R. A. (1995). Producing equal-status interaction in the heterogeneous classroom. *American Educational Research Journal, 32,* 99-120.

Cohen, G. (1983). *The psychology of cognition* (2nd ed.). London: Academic Press.

Cohen, R. L. (1989). Memory for action events: The power of enactment. *Educational Psychology Review, 1,* 57-80.

Cohn, S., Hult, R. E., & Engle, R. W. (1990, April). *Working memory, notetaking, and learning from a lecture*. Paper presented at the annual meeting of the American Educational Research Association, Boston.

Cole, N. S. (1990). Conceptions of educational achievement. *Educational Researcher, 19* (3), 2-7.

Collier, G., Hirsh, E., & Hamlin, P. H. (1972). The ecological determinants of reinforcement in the rat. *Physiology and Behavior, 9,* 705-716.

Collins, A., Brown, J. S., & Newman, S. E. (1989). Cognitive apprenticeship: Teaching the crafts of reading, writing, and mathematics. In L. B. Resnick (Ed.), *Knowing, learning, and instruction: Essays in honor of Robert Glaser*. Hillsdale, NJ: Erlbaum.

Collins, A. M., & Loftus, E. F. (1975). A spreading-activation theory of semantic processing. *Psychological Review, 82,* 407-428.

Collins, A. M., & Quillian, M. R. (1969). Retrieval time from semantic memory. *Journal of Verbal Learning and Verbal Behavior, 8,* 240-247.

Collins, A. M., & Quillian, M. R. (1972). How to make a language user. In E. Tulving & W. Donaldson (Eds.), *Organization of memory*. New York: Academic Press.

Collins, E., & Green, J. L. (1992). Learning in classroom settings: Making or breaking a culture. In H. H. Marshall (Ed.), *Redefining student learning: Roots of educational change*. Norwood, NJ: Ablex.

Collins, J. L. (1982, March). *Self-efficacy and ability in achievement behavior*. Paper presented at the annual meeting of the American Educational Research Association, New York.

Coltheart, M., Lea, C. D., & Thompson, K. (1974). In defense of iconic memory. *Quarterly Journal of Experimental Psychology, 26,* 633-641.

Colwill, R. M. (1993). An associative analysis of instrumental learning. *Current Directions in Psychological Science, 2,* 111-116.

Colwill, R. M., & Rescorla, R. A. (1986). Associative structures in instrumental learning. In G. H. Bower (Ed.), *The psychology of learning and motivation* (Vol. 20). Orlando: Academic Press.

Combs, A. W., Richards, A. C., & Richards, F. (1976). *Perceptual psychology: A humanistic approach to the study of persons*. New York: Harper & Row.

Condry, J. (1977). Enemies of exploration: Self-initiated versus other-initiated learning. *Journal of Personality and Social Psychology, 35,* 4459-4477.

Connell, J. P., & Wellborn, J. G. (1991). Competence, autonomy, and relatedness: A motivational analysis of self-system processes. In M. R. Gunnar & L. A. Sroufe (Eds.), *Self processes and development: The Minnesota Symposia on Child Psychology* (Vol. 23). Hillsdale, NJ: Erlbaum.

Connolly, F. W., & Eisenberg, T. E. (1990). The feedback classroom: Teaching's silent friend. *T.H.E. Journal, 17* (5), 75-77.

Conrad, R. (1962). An association between memory errors and errors due to acoustic masking of speech. *Nature, 193,* 1314-1315.

Conrad, R. (1964). Acoustic confusions in immediate memory. *British Journal of Psychology, 55,* 75-84.

Conrad, R. (1971). The chronology of the development of covert speech in children. *Developmental Psychology, 5,* 398-405.

Conrad, R. (1972). Short-term memory in the deaf: A test for speech coding. *British Journal of Psychology, 63,* 173-180.

Conrad, R., & Hull, A. J. (1964). Information, acoustic confusion, and memory span. *British Journal of Psychology, 55,* 429-432.

Conway, M. A., & Rubin, D. C. (1993). The structure of autobiographical memory. In A. F. Collins, S. E. Gathercole, M. A. Conway, & P. E. Morris (Eds.), *Theories of memory.* Hove, UK: Erlbaum.

Cooney, J. B. (1991). Reflections on the origin of mathematical intuition and some implications for instruction. *Learning and Individual Differences, 3,* 83-107.

Cooper, H. M. (1979). Pygmalion grows up: A model for teacher expectation communication and performance influence. *Review of Educational Research, 49,* 389-410.

Cooper, L. A., & Shepard, R. N. (1973). The time required to prepare for a rotated stimulus. *Memory and Cognition, 1,* 246-250.

Copeland, J. T. (1993). Motivational approaches to expectancy confirmation. *Current Directions in Psychological Science, 2,* 117-121.

Corbett, H. D., & Wilson, B. (1988). Raising the stakes in statewide mandatory minimum competency testing. *Politics of Education Association Yearbook,* 27-39.

Cordua, G. D., McGraw, K. O., & Drabman, R. S. (1979). Doctor or nurse: Children's perception of sex typed occupations. *Child Development, 50,* 590-593.

Corkill, A. J. (1992). Advance organizers: Facilitators of recall. *Educational Psychology Review, 4,* 33-67.

Corkill, A. J., Glover, J. A., & Bruning, R. H. (1988). Advance organizers: Concrete versus abstract. *Journal of Educational Research, 82,* 76-81.

Cormier, S. M. (1987). The structural processes underlying transfer of training. In S. M. Cormier & J. D. Hagman (Eds.), *Transfer of learning: Contemporary research and applications.* San Diego: Academic Press.

Cormier, S. M., & Hagman, J. D. (1987). Introduction. In S. M. Cormier & J. D.

Hagman (Eds.), *Transfer of learning: Contemporary research and applications.* San Diego: Academic Press.

Corno, L., & Rohrkemper, M. M. (1985). The intrinsic motivation to learn in classrooms. In C. Ames & R. Ames (Eds.), *Research on motivation in education: Vol. 2. The classroom milieu.* Orlando: Academic Press.

Corte, H. E., Wolf, M. M., & Locke, B. J. (1971). A comparison of procedures for eliminating self-injurious behavior of retarded adolescents. *Journal of Applied Behavior Analysis, 4,* 201-214.

Cothern, N. B., Konopak, B. C., & Willis, E. L. (1990). Using readers' imagery of literary characters to study text meaning construction. *Reading Research and Instruction, 30,* 15-29.

Covington, M. V. (1992). *Making the grade: A self-worth perspective on motivation and school reform.* Cambridge, UK: Cambridge University Press.

Covington, M. V., & Beery, R. M. (1976). *Self-worth and school learning.* New York: Holt, Rinehart & Winston.

Covington, M. V., & Omelich, C. (1979). Effort: The double-edged sword in school achievement. *Journal of Educational Psychology, 71,* 169-182.

Covington, M. V., Spratt, M., & Omelich, C. (1980). Is effort enough or does diligence count too? Student and teacher reactions to effort stability in failure. *Journal of Educational Psychology, 72,* 717-729.

Cowan, N. (1994). Mechanisms of verbal short-term memory. *Current Directions in Psychological Science, 3,* 185-189.

Cowan, N. (1995). *Attention and memory: An integrated framework.* New York: Oxford University Press.

Cowan, N., Wood, N. L., Nugent, L. D., & Treisman, M. (1997). There are two word-length effects in verbal short-term memory: Opposed effects of duration and complexity. *Psychological Science, 8,* 290-295.

Cox, B. D. (1997). The rediscovery of the active learner in adaptive contexts: A developmental-historical analysis of transfer of training. *Educational Psychologist, 32,* 41-55.

Craik, F. I. M., & Lockhart, R. S. (1972). Levels of processing: A framework for memory research. *Journal of Verbal Learning and Verbal Behavior, 11,* 671-684.

Craik, F. I. M., & Tulving, E. (1975). Depth of processing and the retention of

words in episodic memory. *Journal of Experimental Psychology: General, 104,* 268-294.

Craik, F. I. M., & Watkins, M. J. (1973). The role of rehearsal in short-term memory. *Journal of Verbal Learning and Verbal Behavior, 12,* 598-607.

Crespi, L. P. (1942). Quantitative variation of incentive and performance in the white rat. *American Journal of Psychology, 55,* 467-517.

Crooks, T. J. (1988). The impact of classroom evaluation practices on students. *Review of Educational Research, 58,* 438-481.

Crosbie, J., & Kelly, G. (1994). Effects of imposed postfeedback delays in programmed instruction. *Journal of Applied Behavior Analysis, 27,* 483-491.

Cross, D. R., & Paris, S. G. (1988). Developmental and instructional analyses of children's metacognitive and reading comprehension. *Journal of Educational Psychology, 80,* 131-142.

Crowder, N. A., & Martin, G. (1961). *Trigonometry.* Garden City, NY: Doubleday.

Crowder, R. G. (1993). Short-term memory: Where do we stand? *Memory and Cognition, 21,* 142-145.

Crowder, R. G., & Wagner, R. K. (1992). *The psychology of reading: An introduction* (2nd ed.). New York: Oxford University Press.

Crowley, T. J. (1984). Contingency contracting treatment of drug-abusing physicians, nurses, and dentists. *National Institute on Drug Abuse: Research Monograph Series, 46,* 68-83.

Crowne, D. P., & Marlowe, D. (1964). *The approval motive: Studies in evaluative dependence.* New York: Wiley.

Csikszentmihalyi, M. (1990). *Flow: The psychology of optimal experience.* New York: Harper & Row.

Csikszentmihalyi, M. (1996). *Creativity: Flow and the psychology of discovery and invention.* New York: HarperCollins.

Csikszentmihalyi, M., & Nakamura, J. (1989). The dynamics of intrinsic motivation: A study of adolescents. In C. Ames & R. Ames (Eds.), *Research on motivation in education: Vol. 3. Goals and cognitions.* Orlando: Academic Press.

Csikszentmihalyi, M., Rathunde, K., & Whalen, S. (1993). *Talented teenagers: A longitudinal study of their development.* New York: Cambridge University Press.

Curtis, K. A., & Graham, S. (1991, April). *Altering beliefs about the importance of strategy: An attributional intervention.* Paper presented at the annual meeting of the American Educational Research Association, Chicago.

Cushing, L. S., & Kennedy, C. H. (1997). Academic effects of providing peer support in general education classrooms on students without disabilities. *Journal of Applied Behavior Analysis, 30,* 139-151.

Cuvo, A. J. (1975). Developmental differences in rehearsal and free recall. *Journal of Experimental Child Psychology, 19,* 65-78.

Dallett, K. M. (1964). Implicit mediators in paired-associate learning. *Journal of Verbal Learning and Verbal Behavior, 3,* 209-214.

D'Amato, M. R. (1955). Secondary reinforcement and magnitude of primary reinforcement. *Journal of Comparative and Physiological Psychology, 48,* 378-380.

D'Amato, M. R. (1970). *Experimental psychology: Methodology, psychophysics, and learning.* New York: McGraw-Hill.

Damon, W. (1984). Peer education: The untapped potential. *Journal of Applied Developmental Psychology, 5,* 331-343.

Daneman, M. (1987). Reading and working memory. In J. R. Beech & A. M. Colley (Eds.), *Cognitive approaches to reading.* Chichester, UK: Wiley.

Daneman, M., & Carpenter, P. A. (1980). Individual differences in working memory and reading. *Journal of Verbal Learning and Verbal Behavior, 19,* 450-466.

Danner, F. W., & Lonky, E. (1981). A cognitive-developmental approach to the effects of rewards on intrinsic motivation. *Child Development, 52,* 1043-1052.

Dansereau, D. F. (1978). The development of a learning strategies curriculum. In H. F. O'Neil, Jr. (Ed.), *Learning strategies.* New York: Academic Press.

Dansereau, D. F. (1988). Cooperative learning strategies. In C. E. Weinstein, E. T. Goetz, & P. A. Alexander (Eds.), *Learning and study strategies: Issues in assessment, instruction, and evaluation.* San Diego: Academic Press.

Dansereau, D. F. (1995). Derived structural schemas and the transfer of knowledge. In A. McKeough, J. Lupart, & A. Marini (Eds.), *Teaching for transfer: Fostering generalization in learning.* Mahwah, NJ: Erlbaum.

Darley, J. M., & Gross, P. H. (1983). A hypothesis-confirming bias in labeling effects. *Journal of Personality and Social Psychology, 44,* 20-33.

Darwin, C. J., Turvey, M. T., & Crowder, R. G. (1972). An auditory analogue of the Sperling partial report procedure: Evidence for brief auditory storage. *Cognitive Psychology, 3,* 255-267.

Davis, G. A. (1966). Current status of research and theory in human problem solving. *Psychological Bulletin, 66,* 36-54.

Davis, G. A., & Thomas, M. A. (1989). *Effective schools and effective teachers.* Boston: Allyn & Bacon.

Davis, P. J. (1987). Repression and the inaccessibility of affective memories. *Journal of Personality and Social Psychology, 53,* 585-593.

Davis, P. J., & Schwartz, G. E. (1987). Repression and the inaccessibility of affective memories. *Journal of Personality and Social Psychology, 52,* 155-162.

Davis, R. B. (1986). Conceptual and procedural knowledge in mathematics: A summary analysis. In J. Hiebert (Ed.), *Conceptual and procedural knowledge: The case of mathematics.* Hillsdale, NJ: Erlbaum.

Deaux, K. (1984). From individual differences to social categories: Analysis of a decade's research on gender. *American Psychologist, 39,* 105-116.

deCharms, R. (1968). *Personal causation: The internal affective determinants of behavior.* New York: Academic Press.

deCharms, R. (1972). Personal causation training in the schools. *Journal of Applied Social Psychology, 2,* 95-113.

deCharms, R. (1984). Motivation enhancement in educational settings. In R. Ames & C. Ames (Eds.), *Research on motivation in education: Vol. 1. Student motivation.* Orlando: Academic Press.

Deci, E. L. (1971). Effects of externally mediated rewards on intrinsic motivation. *Journal of Personality and Social Psychology, 18,* 105-115.

Deci, E. L. (1992). The relation of interest to the motivation of behavior: A self-determination theory perspective. In K. A. Renninger, S. Hidi, & A. Krapp (Eds.), *The role of interest in learning and development.* Hillsdale, NJ: Erlbaum.

Deci, E. L., & Ryan, R. M. (1985). *Intrinsic motivation and self-determination in human behavior.* New York: Plenum Press.

Deci, E. L., & Ryan, R. M. (1987). The support of autonomy and the control of behavior. *Journal of Personality and Social Psychology, 53,* 1024-1037.

Deci, E. L., & Ryan, R. M. (1992). The initiation and regulation of intrinsically motivated learning and achievement. In A. K. Boggiano & T. S. Pittman (Eds.), *Achievement and motivation: A social-developmental perspective.* Cambridge, UK: Cambridge University Press.

Deci, E. L., & Ryan, R M. (1995). Human autonomy: The basis for true self-esteem. In M. H. Kernis (Ed.), *Efficacy, agency, and self-esteem.* New York: Plenum Press.

Deci, E. L., Vallerand, R. J., Pelletier, L. G., & Ryan, R. M. (1991). Motivation and education: The self-determination perspective. *Educational Psychologist, 26,* 325-346.

De Corte, E., Greer, B., & Verschaffel, L. (1996). Mathematics teaching and learning. In D. C. Berliner & R. C. Calfee (Eds.), *Handbook of educational psychology.* New York: Macmillan.

Dee-Lucas, D., & Larkin, J. H. (1991). Equations in scientific proofs: Effects on comprehension. *American Educational Research Journal, 28,* 661-682.

deGroot, A. D. (1965). *Thought and choice in chess.* The Hague: Mouton.

Delclos, V. R., & Harrington, C. (1991). Effects of strategy monitoring and proactive instruction on children's problem-solving performance. *Journal of Educational Psychology, 83,* 35-42.

DeLoache, J. S. (1995). Early understanding and use of symbols: The model model. *Current Directions in Psychological Science, 4,* 109-113.

Dempster, F. N. (1991). Synthesis of research on reviews and tests. *Educational Leadership, 48* (7), 71-76.

Dempster, F. N., & Rohwer, W. D. (1974). Component analysis of the elaborative encoding effect in paired-associate learning. *Journal of Experimental Psychology, 103,* 400-408.

Denis, M. (1984). Imagery and prose: A critical review of research on adults and children. *Text, 4,* 381-401.

Denny, M. R., & Weisman, R. G. (1964). Avoidance behavior as a function of the length of nonshock confinement. Journal of Comparative and Physiological Psychology, 58, 252-257.

Derry, S. J. (1996). Cognitive schema theory in the constructivist debate. *Educational Psychologist, 31,* 163-174.

Deutsch, M. (1993). Educating for a peaceful world. *American Psychologist, 48,* 510-517.

de Villiers, P. A. (1977). Choice in concurrent schedules and a quantitative formulation of the law of effect. In W. K. Honig & J. E. R. Staddon (Eds.),

Handbook of operant behavior. Englewood Cliffs, NJ: Prentice Hall.

DeVries, R. (1969). Constancy of generic identity in the years three to six. *Monographs of the Society for Research in Child Development, 34* (Whole No. 127).

Dewhurst, S. A., & Conway, M. A. (1994). Pictures, images, and recollective experience. *Journal of Experimental Psychology: Learning, Memory, and Cognition, 20,* 1088-1098.

Díaz, R. M., Neal, C. J., & Amaya-Williams, M. (1990). The social origins of self-regulation. In L. C. Moll (Ed.), *Vygotsky and education: Instructional implications and applications of sociohistorical psychology.* Cambridge, UK: Cambridge University Press.

Diener, C. I., & Dweck, C. S. (1978). An analysis of learned helplessness: Continuous changes in performance, strategy, and achievement cognitions following failure. *Journal of Personality and Social Psychology, 36,* 451-462.

Dinsmoor, J. A. (1954). Punishment: I. The avoidance hypothesis. *Psychological Review, 61,* 34-46.

Dinsmoor, J. A. (1955). Punishment: II. An interpretation of empirical findings. *Psychological Review, 62,* 96-105.

DiSciullo, M. (1984). In-school suspension: An alternative to unsupervised out-of-school. *Clearing House, 57,* 328-330.

diSessa, A. A. (1982). Unlearning Aristotelian physics: A study of knowledge-based learning. *Cognitive Science, 6,* 37-75.

diSessa, A. A. (1996). What do "just plain folk" know about physics? In D. R. Olson & N. Torrance (Eds.), *The handbook of education and human development: New models of learning, teaching, and schooling.* Cambridge, MA: Blackwell Publishers.

DiVesta, F. J. & Gray, S. G. (1972). Listening and notetaking. *Journal of Educational Psychology, 63,* 8-14.

DiVesta, F. J. & Ingersoll, G. M. (1969). Influence of pronouceability, articulation, and test mode on paired-associate learning by the study-recall procedure. *Journal of Experimental Psychology, 79,* 104-108

DiVesta, F. J. & Peverly, S. T. (1984). The effects of encoding variability, processing activity, and rule example sequences on the transfer of conceptual rules. *Journal of Educational Psychology, 76,* 108-119.

Doctorow, M., Wittrock, M. C., & Marks, C. (1978). Generative processes in reading comprehension. *Journal of Educational Psychology, 70,* 109-118.

Dodd, D. H., & White, R. M. (1980). *Cognition: Mental structures and processes.* Boston: Allyn & Bacon.

Dodge, K. A., Asher, S. R., & Parkhurst, J. T. (1989). Social life as a goal-coordination task. In C. Ames & R. Ames (Eds.), *Research on motivation in education: Vol. 3. Goals and cognitions.* San Diego: Academic Press.

Dole, J. A., Duffy, G. G., Roehler, L. R., & Pearson, P. D. (1991). Moving from the old to the new: Research on reading comprehension instruction. *Review of Educational Research, 61,* 239-264.

Dollard, J. C., Doob, L., Miller, N., Mowrer, O., & Sears, R. (1939). *Frustration and aggression.* New Haven, CT: Yale University Press.

Dominowski, R. L., & Jenrick, R. (1972). Effects of hints and interpolated activity on solution of an insight problem. *Psychonomic Science, 26,* 335-338.

Donaldson, M. (1978). *Children's minds.* New York: W. W. Norton.

Donnelly, C. M., & McDaniel, M. A. (1993). Use of analogy in learning scientific concepts. *Journal of Experimental Psychology: Learning, Memory, and Cognition, 19,* 975-987.

Dooling, D. J., & Christiaansen, R. E. (1977). Episodic and semantic aspects of memory for prose. *Journal of Experimental Psychology: Human Learning and Memory, 3,* 428-436.

Dowaliby, F. J., & Schumer, H. (1973). Teacher-centered versus student-centered mode of college classroom instruction as related to manifest anxiety. *Journal of Educational Psychology, 64,* 125-132.

Downs, R. M., & Stea, D. (1977). *Maps in minds.* New York: Harper & Row.

Doyle, W. (1983). Academic work. *Review of Educational Research, 53,* 159-199.

Doyle, W. (1986a). Classroom organization and management. In M. C. Wittrock (Ed.), *Handbook of research on teaching* (3rd ed.). New York: Macmillan.

Doyle, W. (1986b). Content representation in teachers' definitions of academic work. *Journal of Curriculum Studies, 18,* 365-379.

Doyle, W. (1990). Classroom management techniques. In O. C. Moles (Ed.), *Student discipline strategies: Research and practice.* Albany, NY: State University of New York Press.

Drabman, R. S. (1976). Behavior modification in the classroom. In W. E. Craighead & M. J. Mahoney (Eds.), *Behavior modification principles, issues, and applications.* Boston: Houghton Mifflin.

Dressel, P. L. (1977). The nature and role of objectives in instruction. *Educational Technology, 17* (5), 7-15.

Drevno, G. E., Kimball, J. W., Possi, M. K., Heward, W. L., Gardner, R., III, & Barbetta, P. M. (1994). Effects of active student responding during error correction on the acquisition, maintenance, and generalization of science vocabulary by elementary students: A systematic replication. *Journal of Applied Behavior Analysis, 27,* 179-180.

Driver, R. (1995). Constructivist approaches to science teaching. In L. P. Steffe & J. Gale (Eds.), *Constructivism in education.* Hillsdale, NJ: Erlbaum.

Driver, R., Asoko, H., Leach, J., Mortimer, E., & Scott, P. (1994). Constructing scientific knowledge in the classroom. *Educational Researcher, 23* (7), 5-12.

Dryden, M. A., & Jefferson, P. (1994, April). *Use of background knowledge and reading achievement among elementary school students.* Paper presented at the annual meeting of the American Educational Research Association, New Orleans.

DuBois, N. F. (1987, April). *Training students to become autonomous learners.* Paper presented at the annual meeting of the American Educational Research Association, Washington, DC.

DuBois, N. F., Kiewra, K. A., & Fraley, J. (1988, April). *Differential effects of a learning strategy course.* Paper presented at the annual meeting of the American Educational Research Association, New Orleans.

DuBois, N. F., Staley, R., Guzy, L., & DiNardo, P. (1995, April). *Durable effects of a study skills course on academic achievement.* Paper presented at the annual meeting of the American Educational Research Association, San Francisco.

Duda, J., & Nicholls, J. (1992). Dimensions of achievement motivation in schoolwork and sport. *Journal of Educational Psychology, 84,* 290-299.

Duell, O. K. (1986). Metacognitive skills. In G. D. Phye & T. Andre (Eds.), *Cognitive classroom learning: Understanding, thinking, and problem solving.* Orlando: Academic Press.

Duell, O. K. (1994). Extended wait time and university student achievement. *American Educational Research Journal, 31,* 397-414.

Duit, R. (1990, April). *On the role of analogies, similes, and metaphors in learning science.* Paper presented at the annual meeting of the American Educational Research Association, Boston.

Duit, R. (1991). Students' conceptual frameworks: Consequences for learning science. In S. M. Glynn, R. H. Yeany, & B. K. Britton (Eds.), *The psychology of learning science.* Hillsdale, NJ: Erlbaum.

DuNann, D. G., & Weber, S. J. (1976). Short- and long-term effects of contingency managed instruction on low, medium, and high GPA students. *Journal of Applied Behavior Analysis, 9,* 375-376.

Duncker, K. (1945). On problem solving. *Psychological Monographs, 58* (Whole No. 270).

Dunlap, G., dePerczel, M., Clarke, S., Wilson, D., Wright, S., White, R., & Gomez, A. (1994). Choice making to promote adaptive behavior for students with emotional and behavioral challenges. *Journal of Applied Behavior Analysis, 27,* 505-518.

Dunn, C. S. (1983). The influence of instructional methods on concept learning. *Science Education, 67,* 647-656.

Durkin, K. (1987). Social cognition and social context in the construction of sex differences. In M. A. Baker (Ed.), *Sex differences in human performance.* Chichester, UK: Wiley.

Durkin, K. (1995). *Developmental social psychology: From infancy to old age.* Cambridge, MA: Blackwell Publishers.

Durst, R. K., & Newell, G. E. (1989). The uses of function: James Britton's category system and research on writing. *Review of Educational Research, 59,* 375-394.

Dusek, J. B. (1980). The development of test anxiety in children. In I. G. Sarason (Ed.), *Test anxiety: Theory, research, and applications.* Hillsdale, NJ: Erlbaum.

Dweck, C. S. (1975). The role of expectations and attributions in the alleviation of learned helplessness. *Journal of Personality and Social Psychology, 31,* 674-685.

Dweck, C. S. (1978). Achievement. M. E. Lamb (Ed.), *Social and personality development.* New York: Holt, Rinehart & Winston.

Dweck, C. S. (1986). Motivational processes affecting learning. *American Psychologist, 41,* 1040-1048.

Dweck, C. S., Davidson, W., Nelson, S., & Enna, B. (1978). Sex differences in learned helplessness: II. The contingencies of evaluative feedback in the classroom; III. An experimental analysis. *Developmental Psychology, 14,* 268-276.

Dweck, C. S., & Elliott, E. S. (1983). Achievement motivation. In E. M. Hetherington (Ed.), *Handbook of child psychology: Vol. 4. Socialization, personality, and social development* (4th ed.). New York: Wiley.

Dweck, C. S., Goetz, T. E., & Strauss, N. L. (1980). Sex differences in learned helplessness: IV. An experimental and naturalistic study of failure generalization and its mediators. *Journal of Personality and Social Psychology, 38,* 441-452.

Dweck, C. S., & Leggett, E. L. (1988). A social-cognitive approach to motivation and personality. *Psychological Review, 95,* 256-273.

Dweck, C. S., & Licht, B. (1980). Learned helplessness and intellectual achievement. In J. Garber & M. E. P. Seligman (Eds.), *Human helplessness: Theory and applications.* New York: Academic Press.

Dweck, C. S., & Reppucci, N. D. (1973). Learned helplessness and reinforcement responsibility in children. *Journal of Personality and Social Psychology, 25,* 109-116.

Dyer, H. S. (1967). The discovery and development of educational goals. *Proceedings of the 1966 Invitational Conference on Testing Problems.* Princeton, NJ: Educational Testing Service.

Easterbrook, J. A. (1959). The effect of emotion on cue utilization and the organization of behavior. *Psychological Review, 66,* 183-201.

Eaton, J. F., Anderson, C. W., & Smith, E. L. (1984). Students' misconceptions interfere with science learning: Case studies of fifth-grade students. *Elementary School Journal, 84,* 365-379.

Ebbinghaus, H. (1913). *Memory: A contribution to experimental psychology* (H. A. Ruger & C. E. Bussenius, Trans.). New York: Teachers College. (Original work published 1885.)

Eccles, J. S. (1989). Bringing young women to math and science. In M. Crawford & M. Gentry (Eds.), *Gender and thought: Psychological perspectives.* New York: Springer-Verlag.

Eccles, J. S., & Jacobs, J. E. (1986). Social forces shape math attitudes and performance. *Signs: Journal of Women in Culture and Society, 11,* 367-380.

Eccles, J. S., Jacobs, J., Harold-Goldsmith, R., Jayaratne, T., & Yee, D. (1989, April). *The relations between parents' category-based and target-based beliefs: Gender roles and biological influences.* Paper presented at the annual meeting of the Society for Research in Child Development, Kansas City.

Eccles, J. S., & Midgley, C. (1989). Stage-environment fit: Developmentally appropriate classrooms for young adolescents. In C. Ames & R. Ames (Eds.), *Research on motivation in education: Vol. 3. Goals and cognition.* New York: Academic Press.

Eccles, J. S., & Wigfield, A. (1985). Teacher expectations and student motivation. In J. B. Dusek (Ed.), *Teacher expectancies.* Hillsdale, NJ: Erlbaum.

Eccles (Parsons), J. (1983). Expectancies, values, and academic behaviors. In J. T. Spence (Ed.), *Achievement and achievement motivation.* San Francisco: W. H. Freeman.

Eccles (Parsons), J. (1984). Sex differences in mathematics participation. In M. Steinkamp & M. Maehr (Eds.), *Women in science.* Greenwich, CT: JAI Press.

Eccles (Parsons), J. S., Adler, T. F., Futterman, R., Goff, S. B., Kaczala, C. M., Meece, J. L., & Midgley, C. (1983). Expectations, values, and academic behaviors. In J. T. Spence (Ed.), *Achievement and achievement motivation.* San Francisco: W. H. Freeman.

Edwards, K., & Bryan, T. S. (1997). Judgmental biases produced by instructions to disregard: The (paradoxical) case of emotional information. *Personality and Social Psychology Bulletin, 23,* 849-864.

Eeds, M., & Wells, D. (1989). Grand conversations: An explanation of meaning construction in literature study groups. *Research in the Teaching of English, 23,* 4-29.

Eich, R. (1995). Searching for mood dependent memory. *Psychological Science, 6,* 67-75.

Eisenberger, R. (1992). Learned industriousness. *Psychological Review, 99,* 248-267.

Elliott, D. J. (1995). *Music matters: A new philosophy of music education.* New York: Oxford University Press.

Elliott, R., & Vasta, R. (1970). The modeling of sharing: Effects associated with vicarious reinforcement, symbolization, age, and generalization. *Journal of Experimental Child Psychology, 10,* 8-15.

Elliott, S. N., & Busse, R. T. (1991). Social skills assessment and intervention with children and adolescents. *School Psychology International, 12,* 63-83.

Ellis, H. C., & Hunt, R. R. (1983). *Fundamentals of human memory and cognition* (3rd ed.). Dubuque, IA: Wm. C. Brown.

Ellis, N. C. (Ed.). (1994). *Implicit and explicit learning of languages.* London: Academic Press.

Emmer, E. T., & Evertson, C. M. (1981). Synthesis of research on classroom management. *Educational Leadership, 38,* 342-347.

Emmer, E. T., Evertson, C. M., Clements, B. S., & Worsham, M. E. (1994). *Classroom management for secondary teachers* (3rd ed.). Boston: Allyn & Bacon.

Emshoff, J. G., Redd, W. H., & Davidson, W. S. (1976). Generalization training and the transfer of treatment effects with delinquent adolescents. *Journal of Behavior Therapy and Experimental Psychiatry, 7,* 141-144.

English, H. B., Welborn, E. L., & Killian, C. D. (1934). Studies in substance memorization. *Journal of General Psychology, 11,* 233-260.

Epstein, H. (1978). Growth spurts during brain development: Implications for educational policy and practice. In J. Chall & A. Mirsky (Eds.), *Education and the brain: The 77th yearbook of the National Society for the Study of Education, Part II.* Chicago: University of Chicago Press.

Epstein, R. (1991). Skinner, creativity, and the problem of spontaneous behavior. *Psychological Science, 2,* 362-370.

Erdelyi, M. H. (1985). *Psychoanalysis: Freud's cognitive psychology.* New York: W. H. Freeman.

Erdelyi, M. H., & Goldberg, B. (1979). Let's not sweep repression under the rug: Toward a cognitive psychology of repression. In J. F. Kihlstrom & F. J. Evans (Eds.), *Functional disorders of memory.* Hillsdale, NJ: Erlbaum.

Eriksen, C. W., & Kuethe, J. L. (1956). Avoidance conditioning of verbal behavior without awareness: A paradigm of repression. *Journal of Abnormal and Social Psychology, 53,* 203-209.

Estes, W. K. (1969a). New perspectives on some old issues in association theory. In N. J. Mackintosh & W. K. Honig (Eds.), *Fundamental issues in associative learning.* Halifax, Canada: Dalhousie University Press.

Estes, W. K. (1969b). Outline of a theory of punishment. In B. A. Campbell & R. M. Church (Eds.), *Punishment and aversive behavior.* New York: Appleton-Century-Crofts.

Evans, G. W., & Oswalt, G. L. (1968). Acceleration of academic progress through the manipulation of peer influence. *Behaviour Research and Therapy, 6,* 189-195.

Eysenck, M. W. (1979). Depth, elaboration, and distinctiveness. In L. S. Cermak & F. I. M. Craik (Eds.), *Levels of processing in human memory.* Hillsdale, NJ: Erlbaum.

Eysenck, M. W. (1992). *Anxiety: The cognitive perspective.* Hove, UK: Erlbaum.

Eysenck, M. W., & Keane, M. T. (1990). *Cognitive psychology: A student's handbook.* Hove, UK: Erlbaum.

Fabes, R. A., Fultz, J., Eisenberg, N., May-Plumlee, T., & Christopher, F. S. (1989). Effect of rewards on children's prosocial motivation: A socialization study. *Developmental Psychology, 25,* 509-515.

Fagen, J. W., & Rovee, C. K. (1976). Effects of qualitative shifts in a visual reinforcer in the instrumental response of infants. *Journal of Experimental Child Psychology, 21,* 349-360.

Fantino, E. (1973). Aversive control. In J. A. Nevin & G. S. Reynolds (Eds.), *The study of behavior.* Glenview, IL: Scott, Foresman.

Fantuzzo, J. W., King, J., & Heller, L. R. (1992). Effects of reciprocal peer tutoring on mathematics and school adjustment: A component analysis. *Journal of Educational Psychology, 84,* 331-339.

Farah, M. J., Hammond, K. M., Levine, D. N., & Calvanio, R. (1988). Visual and spatial mental imagery: Dissociable systems of representation. *Cognitive Psychology, 20,* 439-462.

Farnham-Diggory, S. (1972). The development of equivalence systems. In S. Farnham-Diggory (Ed.), *Information processing in children.* New York: Academic Press.

Farrar, M. J., & Goodman, G. S. (1992). Developmental changes in event memory. *Child Development, 63,* 173-187.

Fashola, O. S., Drum, P. A., Mayer, R. E., & Kang, S. (1996). A cognitive theory of orthographic transitioning: Predictable errors in how Spanish-speaking children spell English words. *American Educational Research Journal, 33,* 825-843.

Faust, G. W., & Anderson, R. C. (1967). Effects of incidental material in a programmed Russian vocabulary lesson. *Journal of Educational Psychology, 58,* 3-10.

Feather, N. T. (1982). *Expectations and actions: Expectancy-value models in psychology.* Hillsdale, NJ: Erlbaum.

Feld, S., Ruhland, D., & Gold, M. (1979). Developmental changes in achievement motivation. *Merrill-Palmer Quarterly, 25,* 43-60.

Feldhusen, J. F. (1963). Taps for teaching machines. *Phi Delta Kappan, 44,* 265-267.

Feldhusen, J. F., & Treffinger, D. J. (1980). *Creative thinking and problem solving in gifted education.* Dubuque, IA: Kendall/Hunt.

Fennema, E. (1980). Sex-related differences in mathematics achievement: Where and why. In L. H. Fox, L. Brody, & D. Tobin (Eds.), *Women and the mathematical mystique.* Baltimore: Johns Hopkins University Press.

Fennema, E. (1987). Sex-related differences in education: Myths, realities, and interventions. In V. Richardson-Koehler (Ed.), *Educators' handbook: A research perspective.* New York: Longman.

Fennema, E., Carpenter, T. P., & Peterson, P. L. (1989). Learning mathematics with understanding: Cognitively guided instruction. In J. Brophy (Ed.), *Advances in research on teaching* (Vol. 1). Greenwich, CT: JAI Press.

Ferguson, E. L., & Hegarty, M. (1995). Learning with real machines or diagrams: Application of knowledge to real-world problems. *Cognition and Instruction, 13,* 129-160.

Ferster, C. B., & Skinner, B. F. (1957). *Schedules of reinforcement.* Englewood Cliffs, NJ: Prentice Hall.

Field, D. (1987). A review of preschool conservation training: An analysis of analyses. *Developmental Review, 7,* 210-251.

Fischer, S. M., Iwata, B. A., & Mazaleski, J. L. (1997). Noncontingent delivery of arbitrary reinforcers as treatment for self-injurious behavior. *Journal of Applied Behavior Analysis, 30,* 239-249.

Fisk, A. D. (1986). Frequency encoding is not inevitable and is not automatic: A reply to Hasher & Zacks. *American Psychologist, 41,* 215-216.

Fiske, D. W., & Maddi, S. R. (1961). *Functions of varied experience.* Homewood, IL: Dorsey.

Flaherty, C. F. (1985). *Animal learning and cognition.* New York: Alfred Knopf.

Flavell, J. H. (1963). *The developmental psychology of Jean Piaget.* New York: Van Nostrand Reinhold.

Flavell, J. H. (1979). Metacognition and cognitive monitoring: A new area of cognitive-developmental inquiry. *American Psychologist, 34,* 906-911.

Flavell, J. H. (1985). *Cognitive development* (2nd ed.). Englewood Cliffs, NJ: Prentice Hall.

Flavell, J. H. (1993). Young children's understanding of thinking and consciousness. *Current Directions in Psychological Science, 2,* 40-43.

Flavell, J. H. (1996). Piaget's legacy. *Psychological Science, 7,* 200-203.

Flavell, J. H., Friedrichs, A. G., & Hoyt, J. D. (1970). Developmental changes in memorization processes. *Cognitive Psychology, 1,* 324-340.

Flavell, J. H., Miller, P. H., & Miller, S. A. (1993). *Cognitive development* (3rd ed.). Upper Saddle River, NJ: Prentice Hall.

Flavell, J. H., & Wellman, H. M. (1977). Metamemory. In R. V. Kail, Jr., & J. W. Hagen (Eds.), *Perspectives on the development of memory and cognition.* Hillsdale, NJ: Erlbaum.

Flink, C., Boggiano, A. K., Main, D. S., Barrett, M., & Katz, P. A. (1992). Children's achievement-related behaviors: The role of extrinsic and intrinsic motivational orientations. In A. K. Boggiano & T. S. Pittman (Eds.), *Achievement and motivation: A social-developmental perspective.* Cambridge, UK: Cambridge University Press.

Flower, L. S., & Hayes, J. R. (1981). A cognitive process theory of writing. *College Composition and Communication, 32,* 365-387.

Fodor, J. A., & Pylyshyn, Z. W. (1988). Connectionism and cognitive architecture: A critical analysis. *Cognition, 28,* 3-71.

Fong, G. T., Krantz, D. H., & Nisbett, R. E. (1986). The effects of statistical training on thinking about everyday problems. *Cognitive Psychology, 18,* 253-292.

Foos, P. W., & Fisher, R. P. (1988). Using tests as learning opportunities. *Journal of Educational Psychology, 80,* 179-183.

Ford, D. Y. (1996). *Reversing underachievement among gifted black students.* New York: Teachers College Press.

Ford, M. E., & Nichols, C. W. (1991). Using goal assessments to identify motivational patterns and facilitate behavioral regulation and achievement. In M. Maehr & P. R. Pintrich (Eds.), *Advances in motivation and achievement: Vol. 7. Goals and self-regulatory processes.* Greenwich, CT: JAI Press.

Fosnot, C. T. (1996). Constructivism: A psychological theory of learning. In C. T. Fosnot (Ed.), *Constructivism: Theory, perspectives, and practice.* New York: Teachers College Press.

Foster-Johnson, L., Ferro, J., & Dunlap, G. (1994). Preferred curriculum activities and reduced problem behaviors in students with intellectual disabilities. *Journal of Applied Behavior Analysis, 27,* 493-504.

Fowler, J. W., & Peterson, P. L. (1981). Increasing reading persistence and altering attributional style of learned helpless children. *Journal of Educational Psychology, 73,* 251-260.

Fowler, S. A., & Baer, D. M. (1981). "Do I have to be good all day?" The timing of delayed reinforcement as a factor in generalization. *Journal of Applied Behavior Analysis, 14,* 13-24.

Fox, P. W., & LeCount, J. (1991, April). *When more is less: Faculty misestimation of student learning.* Paper presented at the annual meeting of the American Educational Research Association, Chicago.

Foxx, R. M., & Azrin, N. H. (1973). The elimination of autistic self-stimulatory behavior by overcorrection. *Journal of Applied Behavior Analysis, 6,* 1-14.

Foxx, R. M., & Bechtel, D. R. (1983). Overcorrection: A review and analysis. In S. Axelrod & J. Apsche (Eds.), *The effects of punishment on human behavior.* New York: Academic Press.

Foxx, R. M., & Shapiro, S. T. (1978). The timeout ribbon: A nonexclusionary timeout procedure. *Journal of Applied Behavior Analysis, 11,* 125-136.

Frankel, F., & Simmons, J. Q. (1985). Behavioral treatment approaches to pathological unsocialized physical aggression in young children. *Journal of Child Psychiatry, 26,* 525-551.

Franks, J. J., & Bransford, J. D. (1971). Abstraction of visual patterns. *Journal of Experimental Psychology, 90,* 65-74.

Frase, L. T. (1975). Prose processing. In G. H. Bower (Ed.), *The psychology of learning and motivation* (Vol. 9). New York: Academic Press.

Frederiksen, J. R., & Collins, A. (1989). A systems approach to educational testing. *Educational Researcher, 18*(9), 27-32.

Frederiksen, N. (1984a). Implications of cognitive theory for instruction in problem-solving. *Review of Educational Research, 54,* 363-407.

Frederiksen, N. (1984b). The real test bias: Influences of testing on teaching and learning. *American Psychologist, 39,* 193-202.

Frederiksen, N., & Ward, W. C. (1978). Measures for the study of creativity in scientific problem solving. *Applied Psychological Measurement, 2,* 1-24.

Freiberg, H. J. (1987). Teacher self-evaluation and principal supervision. *NASSP Bulletin, 71,* 85-92.

Freiburgs, V., & Tulving, E. (1961). The effect of practice on utilization of information from positive and negative instances in concept identification. *Canadian Journal of Psychology, 15,* 101-106.

French, E. G. (1955). Some characteristics of achievement motivation. *Journal of Experimental Psychology, 50,* 232-236.

French, E. G. (1956). Motivation as a variable in work partner selection. *Journal of Abnormal and Social Psychology, 53,* 96-99.

Freud, S. (1922). *Beyond the pleasure principle.* London: International Psychoanalytic Press.

Freud, S. (1949). Instincts and their vicissitudes. In *Collected papers of Sigmund Freud* (Vol. 4). (J. Riviere, Trans.). London: Hogarth. (Original work published 1915.)

Freud, S. (1957). Repression. In J. Strachey (Ed.), *The standard edition of the complete psychological works of Sigmund Freud* (Vol. 14). London: Hogarth Press. (Original work published 1915.)

Friedrich, L. K., & Stein, A. H. (1973). Aggressive and pro-social television programs and the natural behavior of preschool children. *Society for Research in Child Development Monographs, 38* (Whole No. 151).

Friman, P. C., & Poling, A. (1995). Making life easier with effort: Basic findings and applied research on response effort. *Journal of Applied Behavior Analysis, 28,* 583-590.

Frith, U. (1978). From print to meaning and from print to sound, or how to read without knowing how to spell. *Visible Language, 12,* 43-54.

Frith, U. (1980). Unexpected spelling problems. In U. Frith (Ed.), *Cognitive processes in spelling.* London: Academic Press.

Fuchs, D., Fuchs, L. S., Mathes, P. G., & Simmons, D. C. (1997). Peer-assisted learning strategies: Making classrooms more responsive to diversity. *American Educational Research Journal, 34,* 174-206.

Fuchs, L. S., & Fuchs, D. (1997, March). *Mathematics performance assessments in the classroom: Effects on teacher planning and student learning.* Paper presented at the annual meeting of the American Educational Research Association, Chicago.

Fuchs, L. S., Fuchs, D., Karns, K., Hamlett, C. L., Dutka, S., & Katzaroff, M. (1996). The relation between student ability and the quality and effectiveness of explanations. *American Educational Research Journal, 33,* 631-664.

Furedy, J. J., & Riley, D. M. (1987). Human Pavlovian autonomic conditioning and the cognitive paradigm. In G. Davey

(Ed.), *Cognitive processes and Pavlovian conditioning in humans.* Chichester, UK: Wiley.

Furst, E. J. (1981). Bloom's taxonomy of educational objectives for the cognitive domain: Philosophical and educational issues. *Review of Educational Research, 51,* 441-453.

Fuson, K. C., & Willis, G. B. (1989). Second graders' use of schematic drawings in solving addition and subtraction word problems. *Journal of Educational Psychology, 81,* 514-520.

Gabrieli, J. D. E., Fleischman, D. A., Keane, M. M., Reminger, S. L., & Morrell, F. (1995). Double dissociation between memory systems underlying explicit and implicit memory in the human brain. *Psychological Science, 6,* 76-82.

Gabrieli, J. D. E., Keane, M. M., Zarella, M. M., & Poldrack, R. A. (1997). Preservation of implicit memory for new associations in global amnesia. *Psychological Science, 8,* 326-329.

Gagné, E. D. (1985). *The cognitive psychology of school learning.* Boston: Little, Brown.

Gagné, R. M. (1982). Developments in learning psychology: Implications for instructional design; and effects of computer technology on instructional design and development. *Educational Technology, 22* (6), 11-15.

Gagné, R. M. (1983). Some issues in the psychology of mathematics instruction. *Journal of Research in Mathematics Education, 14* (1), 7-18.

Gagné, R. M. (1985). *The conditions of learning and theory of instruction* (4th ed.). New York: Holt, Rinehart & Winston.

Gagné, R. M., & Brown, L. T. (1961). Some factors in the programming of conceptual learning. *Journal of Experimental Psychology, 62,* 313-321.

Gagné, R. M., & Driscoll, M. P. (1988). *Essentials of learning for instruction* (2nd ed.). Englewood Cliffs, NJ: Prentice Hall.

Gagné, R. M., & Smith, E. C. (1962). A study of the effects of verbalization on problem solving. *Journal of Experimental Psychology, 63,* 12-18.

Gallimore, R., & Tharp, R. (1990). Teaching mind in society: Teaching, schooling, and literate discourse. In L. C. Moll (Ed.), *Vygotsky and education: Instructional implications and applications of sociohistorical psychology.* Cambridge, UK: Cambridge University Press.

Gambrell, L. B., & Bales, R. J. (1986). Mental imagery and the comprehension-monitoring performance of fourth- and fifth-grade poor readers. *Reading Research Quarterly, 21,* 454-464.

Garb, J. L., & Stunkard, A. J. (1974). Taste aversions in man. *American Journal of Psychiatry, 131,* 1204-1207.

Garcia, E. E. (1992). "Hispanic" children: Theoretical, empirical, and related policy issues. *Educational Psychology Review, 4,* 69-93.

Garcia, E. E. (1994). *Understanding and meeting the challenge of student cultural diversity.* Boston: Houghton Mifflin.

Garcia, J., & Koelling, R. A. (1966). The relation of cue to consequence in avoidance learning. *Psychonomic Science, 4,* 123-124.

Gardner, H., Torff, B., & Hatch, T. (1996). The age of innocence reconsidered: Preserving the best of the progressive traditions in psychology and education. In D. R. Olson & N. Torrance (Eds.), *The handbook of education and human development: New models of learning, teaching, and schooling.* Cambridge, MA: Blackwell Publishers.

Gardner, M. (1978). *Aha! Insight.* New York: Scientific American.

Garner, R., Alexander, P. A., Gillingham, M. G., Kulikowich, J. M., & Brown, R. (1991). Interest and learning from text. *American Educational Research Journal, 28,* 643-659.

Garner, R., Brown, R., Sanders, S., & Menke, D. J. (1992). "Seductive details" and learning from text. In K. A. Renninger, S. Hidi, & A. Krapp (Eds.), *The role of interest in learning and development.* Hillsdale, NJ: Erlbaum.

Garner, R., Gillingham, M. G., & White, C. S. (1989). Effects of "seductive details" on macroprocessing and microprocessing in adults and children. *Cognition and Instruction, 6,* 41-57.

Gasper, K. L. (1980). The student perspective. *Teaching Political Science, 7,* 470-471.

Gathercole, S. E., & Hitch, G. J. (1993). Developmental changes in short-term memory: A revised working memory perspective. In A. F. Collins, S. E. Gathercole, M. A. Conway, & P. E. Morris (Eds.), *Theories of memory.* Hove, UK: Erlbaum.

Gaudry, E., & Bradshaw, G. D. (1971). The differential effect of anxiety on performance in progressive and terminal school examinations. In E. Gaudry & C. D. Spielberger (Eds.), *Anxiety and educational achievement.* Sydney, Australia: Wiley.

Gaudry, E., & Spielberger, C. D. (Eds.). (1971). *Anxiety and educational achievement.* Sydney, Australia: Wiley.

Gauntt, H. L. (1991, April). *The roles of prior knowledge of text structure and prior knowledge of content in the comprehension and recall of expository text.* Paper presented at the annual meeting of the American Educational Research Association, Chicago.

Gayford, C. (1992). Patterns of group behavior in open-ended problem solving in science classes of 15-year-old students in England. *International Journal of Science Education, 14,* 41-49.

Gaynor, J., & Millham, J. (1976). Student performance and evaluation under variant teaching and testing methods in a large college course. *Journal of Educational Psychology, 68,* 312-317.

Geary, D. C. (1994). *Children's mathematical development: Research and practical applications.* Washington, DC: American Psychological Association.

Gentner, D., & Gentner, D. R. (1983). Flowing waters or teeming crowds: Mental models of electricity. In D. Gentner & A. L. Stevens (Eds.), *Mental models.* Hillsdale, NJ: Erlbaum.

Gerst, M. S. (1971). Symbolic coding processes in observational learning. *Journal of Personality and Social Psychology, 19,* 7-17.

Giaconia, R. M. (1988). Teacher questioning and wait-time (doctoral dissertation, Stanford University, 1988). *Dissertation Abstracts International, 49,* 462A.

Gibson, E., & Rader, N. (1979). Attention: The perceiver as performer. In G. A. Hale & M. Lewis (Eds.), *Attention and cognitive development.* New York: Plenum Press.

Gick, M. L. (1986). Problem-solving strategies. *Educational Psychologist, 21,* 99-120.

Gick, M. L., & Holyoak, K. J. (1980). Analogical problem solving. *Cognitive Psychology, 12,* 306-355.

Gick, M. L., & Holyoak, K. J. (1983). Schema induction and analogical transfer. *Cognitive Psychology, 15,* 1-38.

Gick, M. L., & Holyoak, K. J. (1987). The cognitive basis of knowledge transfer. In S. M. Cormier & J. D. Hagman (Eds.), *Transfer of learning: Contemporary research and applications.* San Diego: Academic Press.

Gilligan, S. G., & Bower, G. H. (1984). Cognitive consequences of emotional arousal. In C. Izard, J. Kagen, & R. Zajonc (Eds.), *Emotions, cognition, and behaviour.* New York: Cambridge University Press.

Girotto, V., & Light, P. (1993). The pragmatic bases of children's reasoning. In P. Light & G. Butterworth (Eds.), *Context and cognition: Ways of learning and knowing.* Hillsdale, NJ: Erlbaum.

Glanzer, M., & Cunitz, A. R. (1966). Two storage mechanisms in free recall. *Journal of Verbal Learning and Verbal Behavior, 5,* 351-360.

Glanzer, M., & Nolan, S. D. (1986). Memory mechanisms in text comprehension. In G. H. Bower (Ed.), *The psychology of learning and motivation: Advances in research and theory* (Vol. 20). Orlando: Academic Press.

Glaser, R. (1979). Trends and research questions in psychological research on learning and schooling. *Educational Researcher, 8,* 6-13.

Glaser, R. (1987). Thoughts on expertise. In C. Schooler & W. Schaie (Eds.), *Cognitive functioning and social structure over the life course.* Norwood, NJ: Ablex.

Glass, A. L., & Holyoak, K. J. (1975). Alternative conceptions of semantic memory. *Cognition, 3,* 313-339.

Glass, A. L., Holyoak, K. J., & O'Dell, C. (1974). Production frequency and the verification of quantified statements. *Journal of Verbal Learning and Verbal Behavior, 13,* 237-254.

Glass, A. L., Holyoak, K. J., & Santa, J. L. (1979). *Cognition.* Reading, MA: Addison-Wesley.

Gleitman, H. (1985). Some trends in the study of cognition. In S. Koch & D. E. Leary (Eds.), *A century of psychology as science.* New York: McGraw-Hill.

Glenberg, A. (1976). Monotonic and nonmonotonic lag effects in paired-associate and recognition memory paradigms. *Journal of Verbal Learning and Verbal Behavior, 15,* 1-16.

Glover, J., & Gary, A. L. (1976). Procedures to increase some aspects of creativity. *Journal of Applied Behavior Analysis, 9,* 79-84.

Glucksberg, S. (1962). The influence of strength of drive on functional fixedness and perceptual recognition. *Journal of Experimental Psychology, 63,* 36-41.

Glucksberg, S., & Weisberg, R. W. (1966). Verbal behavior and problem solving: Some effects of labeling in a functional fixedness problem. *Journal of Experimental Psychology, 71,* 659-664.

Glueck, S., & Glueck, E. (1950). *Unraveling juvenile delinquency.* Cambridge, MA: Harvard University Press.

Glynn, S. M. (1991). Explaining science concepts: A teaching-with-analogies model. In S. M. Glynn, R. H. Yeany, & B. K. Britton (Eds.), *The psychology of learning science.* Hillsdale, NJ: Erlbaum.

Glynn, S. M., & Di Vesta, F. J. (1977). Outline and hierarchical organization as aids for study and retrieval. *Journal of Educational Psychology, 69,* 89-95.

Glynn, S. M., Yeany, R. H., & Britton, B. K. (1991). A constructive view of learning science. In S. M. Glynn, R. H. Yeany, & B. K. Britton (Eds.), *The psychology of learning science.* Hillsdale, NJ: Erlbaum.

Godden, D. R., & Baddeley, A. D. (1975). Context-dependent memory in two natural environments: On land and underwater. *British Journal of Psychology, 66,* 325-332.

Goetz, E. T., Schallert, D. L., Reynolds, R. E., & Radin, D. I. (1983). Reading in perspective: What real cops and pretend burglars look for in a story. *Journal of Educational Psychology, 75,* 500-510.

Goldenberg, C. (1992). The limits of expectations: A case for case knowledge about teacher expectancy effects. *American Educational Research Journal, 29,* 517-544.

Good, T. L. (1987). Two decades of research on teacher expectations: Findings and future directions. Journal of Teacher Education, 38 (4), 32-47.

Good, T. L., & Brophy, J. E. (1986). *Educational psychology: A realistic approach.* New York: Longman.

Good, T. L., & Brophy, J. E. (1994). *Looking in classrooms* (6th ed.). New York: HarperCollins.

Good, T. L., McCaslin, M. M., & Reys, B. J. (1992). Investigating work groups to promote problem solving in mathematics. In J. Brophy (Ed.), *Advances in research on teaching: Vol. 3. Planning and managing learning tasks and activities.* Greenwich, CT: JAI Press.

Gorman, A. M. (1961). Recognition memory for nouns as a function of abstractness and frequency. *Journal of Experimental Psychology, 61,* 23-29.

Gottfried, A. E. (1990). Academic intrinsic motivation in young elementary school children. *Journal of Educational Psychology, 82,* 525-538.

Gottfried, A. E., Fleming, J. S., & Gottfried, A. W. (1994). Role of parental motivational practices in children's academic intrinsic motivation and achievement. *Journal of Educational Psychology, 86,* 104-113.

Grabe, M. (1986). Attentional processes in education. In G. D. Phye & T. Andre (Eds.), *Cognitive classroom learning: Understanding, thinking, and problem solving.* Orlando: Academic Press.

Graesser, A. C., & Bower, G. H. (Eds.). (1990). *Inferences and text comprehension. The psychology of learning and motivation: Advances in research and theory* (Vol. 25). Orlando: Academic Press.

Graesser, A. C., & Person, N. K.(1994). Question asking during tutoring. *American Educational Reasearch Journal, 31,* 104-137.

Graf, P., & Masson, M. E. J. (Eds.). (1993). *Implicit memory: New directions in cognition, development, and neuropsychology.* Hillsdale, NJ: Erlbaum.

Graham, S. (1984). Communicating sympathy and anger to black and white students: The cognitive (attributional) consequences of affective cues. *Journal of Personality and Social Psychology, 47,* 40-54.

Graham, S. (1990). Communicating low ability in the classroom: Bad things good teachers sometimes do. In S. Graham & V. S. Folkes (Eds.), *Attribution theory: Applications to achievement, mental health, and interpersonal conflict.* Hillsdale, NJ: Erlbaum.

Graham, S. (1991). A review of attribution theory in achievement contexts. *Educational Psychology Review, 3,* 5-39.

Graham, S. (1994). Classroom motivation from an attributional perspective. In H. F. O'Neil, Jr., & M. Drillings (Eds.), *Motivation: Theory and research.* Hillsdale, NJ: Erlbaum.

Graham, S. (1997). Using attribution theory to understand social and academic motivation in African American youth. *Educational Psychologist, 32,* 21-34.

Graham, S., & Barker, G. (1990). The downside of help: An attributional-developmental analysis of helping behavior as a low ability cue. *Journal of Educational Psychology, 82,* 7-14.

Graham, S., & Golen, S. (1991). Motivational influences on cognition: Task involvement, ego involvement, and depth of information processing. *Journal of Educational Psychology, 83,* 187-194.

Graham, S., & Weiner, B. (1996). Theories and principles of motivation. In D. C. Berliner & R. C. Calfee (Eds.), *Handbook of educational psychology.* New York: Macmillan.

Granger, R. H., Jr., & Schlimmer, J. C. (1986). The computation of contingency in classical conditioning. In G. H. Bower (Ed.), *The psychology of learning and motivation: Advances in research and theory* (Vol. 20). Orlando: Academic Press.

Grant, C. A., & Gomez, M. L. (1996). *Making schooling multicultural: Campus and classroom.* Englewood Cliffs, NJ: Merrill/Prentice Hall.

Gray, J. A., & Wedderburn, A. A. I. (1960). Grouping strategies with simultaneous stimuli. *Quarterly Journal of Experimental Psychology, 12,* 180-184.

Gray, W. D., & Orasanu, J. M. (1987). Transfer of cognitive skills. In S. M. Cormier & J. D. Hagman (Eds.), *Transfer of learning: Contemporary research and applications.* San Diego: Academic Press.

Green, L., Fry, A. F., & Myerson, J. (1994). Discounting of delayed rewards: A life-span comparison. *Psychological Science, 5,* 33-36.

Green, L., & Rachlin, H. (1977). Pigeon's preferences for stimulus information: Effects of amount of information. *Journal of the Experimental Analysis of Behavior, 27,* 255-263.

Green, R. G. (1980). Test anxiety and cue utilization. In I. G. Sarason (Ed.), *Test anxiety: Theory, research, and applications.* Hillsdale, NJ: Erlbaum.

Greene, B. A., & Royer, J. M. (1994). A developmental review of response time data that support a cognitive components model of reading. *Educational Psychology Review, 6,* 141-172.

Greene, R. L. (1986). Sources of recency effects in free recall. *Psychological Bulletin, 99,* 221-228.

Greene, S., & Ackerman, J. M. (1995). Expanding the constructivist metaphor: A rhetorical perspective on literacy research and practice. *Review of Educational Research, 65,* 383-420.

Greeno, J. G. (1973). The structure of memory and the process of solving problems. In R. L. Solso (Ed.), *Contemporary issues in cognitive psychology: The Loyola Symposium.* Washington, DC: Winston.

Greeno, J. G. (1991). A view of mathematical problem solving in school. In M. U. Smith (Ed.), *Toward a unified theory of problem solving: Views from the content domains.* Hillsdale, NJ: Erlbaum.

Greeno, J. G., Collins, A. M., & Resnick, L. B. (1996). Cognition and learning. In D. C. Berliner & R. C. Calfee (Eds.), *Handbook of educational psychology.* New York: Macmillan.

Greeno, J. G., Moore, J. L., & Smith, D. R. (1993). Transfer of situated learning. In D. K. Detterman & R. J. Sternberg (Eds.), *Transfer on trial: Intelligence, cognition, and instruction.* Norwood, NJ: Ablex.

Greenspoon, J., & Ranyard, R. (1957). Stimulus conditions and retroactive inhibition. *Journal of Experimental Psychology, 53,* 55-59.

Greenwood, C. R., Carta, J. J., & Hall, R. V. (1988). The use of peer tutoring strategies in classroom management and educational instruction. *School Psychology Review, 17,* 258-275.

Greer, R. D. (1983). Contingencies of the science and technology of teaching and pre-behavioristic research practices in education. *Educational Researcher, 12* (1), 3-9.

Gregg, M., & Leinhardt, G. (1994a, April). *Constructing geography.* Paper presented at the annual meeting of the American Educational Research Association, New Orleans.

Gregg, M., & Leinhardt, G. (1994b). Mapping out geography: An example of epistemology and education. *Review of Educational Research, 64,* 311-361.

Greiner, J. M., & Karoly, P. (1976). Effects of self-control training on study activity and academic performance: An analysis of self-monitoring, self-reward, and systematic planning components. *Journal of Counseling Psychology, 23,* 495-502.

Griffin, M. M., & Griffin, B. W. (1994, April). *Some can get there from here: Situated learning, cognitive style, and map skills.* Paper presented at the annual meeting of the American Educational Research Association, New Orleans.

Griffore, R. J. (1981). *Child development: An educational perspective.* Springfield, IL: Charles C. Thomas.

Grimes, J. W., & Allinsmith, W. (1961). Compulsivity, anxiety, and school achievement. *Merrill-Palmer Quarterly, 7,* 247-271.

Grimes, J. W., & Allinsmith, W. (1970). Compulsivity, anxiety, and school achievement. In P. H. Mussen, J. J. Conger, & J. Kagan (Eds.), *Readings in child development and personality.* New York: Harper & Row.

Grolnick, W. S., & Ryan, R. M. (1987). Autonomy in children's learning: An experimental and individual difference investigation. *Journal of Personality and Social Psychology, 52,* 890-898.

Groninger, L. D. (1971). Mnemonic imagery and forgetting. *Psychonomic Science, 23,* 161-163.

Gronlund, N. E. (1995). *How to write and use instructional objectives* (5th ed.). Upper Saddle River, NJ: Merrill/Prentice Hall.

Gross, T. F., & Mastenbrook, M. (1980). Examination of the effects of state anxiety on problem-solving efficiency under high and low memory conditions. *Journal of Educational Psychology, 72,* 605-609.

Grossman, P. L. (1990). *The making of a teacher: Teacher knowledge and teacher education.* New York: Teachers College Press.

Guevremont, D. C., Osnes, P. G., & Stokes, T. F. (1988). The functional role of preschoolers' verbalization in the generalization of self-instructional training. *Journal of Applied Behavior Analysis, 21,* 45-55.

Gunstone, R. F. (1994). The importance of specific science content in the enhancement of metacognition. In P. J. Fensham, R. F. Gunstone, & R. T. White (Eds.), *The content of science: A constructivist approach to its teaching and learning.* London: Falmer Press.

Gunstone, R. F., & White, R. T. (1981). Understanding of gravity. *Science Education, 65,* 291-299.

Guskey, T. R. (1985). *Implementing mastery learning.* Belmont, CA: Wadsworth.

Guskey, T. R. (1994, April). *Outcome-based education and mastery learning: Clarifying the differences.* Paper presented at the annual meeting of the American Educational Research Association, New Orleans.

Gustafsson, J., & Undheim, J. O. (1996). Individual differences in cognitive functions. In D. C. Berliner & R. C. Calfee (Eds.), *Handbook of educational psychology.* New York: Macmillan.

Guthrie, E. R. (1935). *The psychology of learning.* New York: Harper & Row.

Guthrie, E. R. (1942). Conditioning: A theory of learning in terms of stimulus, response, and association. In *The psychology of learning, 41st Yearbook of the National Society for the Study of Education, Part II.* Chicago: University of Chicago Press.

Guttentag, R. E. (1984). The mental effort requirement of cumulative rehearsal: A developmental study. *Journal of Experimental Child Psychology, 37,* 92-106.

Guzzetti, B. J., Snyder, T. E., Glass, G. V., & Gamas, W. S. (1993). Promoting conceptual change in science: A comparative meta-analysis of instructional interventions from reading education and science education. *Reading Research Quarterly, 28,* 117-159.

Haberlandt, K. (1997). *Cognitive psychology* (2nd ed.). Needham Heights, MA: Allyn & Bacon.

Hacker, D. J. (1995, April). *Comprehension monitoring of written discourse across early-to-middle adolescence.* Paper presented at the annual meeting of the American Educational Research Association, San Francisco.

Hagen, A. S. (1994, April). *Achievement motivation processes and the role of classroom context.* Paper presented at the annual meeting of the American Educational Research Association, New Orleans.

Hale, G. A. (1983). Students' predictions of prose forgetting and the effects of study strategies. *Journal of Educational Psychology, 75,* 708-715.

Hall, J. F. (1966). *The psychology of learning.* Philadelphia: J. B. Lippincott.

Hall, J. F. (1971). *Verbal learning and retention.* Philadelphia: J. B. Lippincott.

Hall, R. H. (1994, April). *Spatially directed post organization in learning from knowledge maps.* Paper presented at the annual meeting of the American Educational Research Association, New Orleans.

Hall, R. H., & O'Donnell, A. (1994, April). *Alternative materials for learning: Cognitive and affective outcomes of learning from knowledge maps.* Paper presented at the annual meeting of the American Educational Research Association, New Orleans.

Hall, R. V., Axelrod, S., Foundopoulos, M., Shellman, J., Campbell, R. A., & Cranston, S. S. (1971). The effective use of punishment to modify behavior in the classroom. *Educational Technology, 11* (4), 24-26. Reprinted in K. D. O'Leary & S. O'Leary (Eds.). (1972). *Classroom management: The successful use of behavior modification.* New York: Pergamon.

Hall, R. V., Cristler, C., Cranston, S. S., & Tucker, B. (1970). Teachers and parents as researchers using multiple baseline designs. *Journal of Applied Behavior Analysis, 3,* 247-255.

Hall, V. C., & Edmondson, B. (1992). Relative importance of aptitude and prior domain knowledge on immediate and delayed posttests. *Journal of Educational Psychology, 84,* 219-223.

Hall, W. S. (1989). Reading comprehension. *American Psychologist, 44,* 157-161.

Hallahan, D. P., Marshall, K. J., & Lloyd, J. W. (1981). Self-recording during group instruction: Effects of attention to task. *Learning Disabilities Quarterly, 4,* 407-413.

Halldén, O. (1994). On the paradox of understanding history in an educational setting. In G. Leinhardt, I. L. Beck, & C. Stainton (Eds.), *Teaching and learning in history.* Hillsdale, NJ: Erlbaum.

Haller, E. P., Child, D. A., & Walberg, H. J. (1988). Can comprehension be taught? A quantitative synthesis of "metacognitive" studies. *Educational Researcher, 17* (9), 5-8.

Halpern, D. F. (1985). The influence of sex-role stereotypes on prose recall. *Sex Roles, 12,* 363-375.

Halpin, G., & Halpin, G. (1982). Experimental investigations of the effects of study and testing on student learning, retention, and ratings of instruction. *Journal of Educational Psychology, 74,* 32-38.

Hamman, D., Shell, D. F., Droesch, D., Husman, J., Handwerk, M., Park, Y., & Oppenheim, N. (1995, April). *Middle school readers' on-line cognitive processes: Influence of subject-matter knowledge and interest during reading.* Paper presented at the annual meeting of the American Educational Research Association, San Francisco.

Hammer, D. (1994). Epistemological beliefs in introductory physics. *Cognition and Instruction, 12,* 151-183.

Hampton, J. A. (1981). An investigation of the nature of abstract concepts. *Memory and Cognition, 9,* 149-156.

Hansen, J., & Pearson, P. D. (1983). An instructional study: Improving the inferential comprehension of good and poor fourth-grade readers. *Journal of Educational Psychology, 75,* 821-829.

Harari, H., & McDavid, J. W. (1973). Name stereotypes and teachers' expectations. *Journal of Educational Psychology, 65,* 222-225.

Haring, N. G., & Liberty, K. A. (1990). Matching strategies with performance in facilitating generalization. *Focus on Exceptional Children, 22* (8), 1-16.

Haring, T. G., Roger, B., Lee, M., Breen, C., & Gaylord-Ross, R. (1986). Teaching social language to moderately handicapped students. *Journal of Applied Behavior Analysis, 19,* 159-171.

Harlow, H. F. (1949). The formation of learning sets. *Psychological Review, 56,* 51-65.

Harlow, H. F. (1950). Analysis of discrimination learning by monkeys. *Journal of Experimental Psychology, 40,* 26-39.

Harlow, H. F. (1959). Learning set and error factor theory. In S. Koch (Ed.), *Psychology: A study of science.* New York: McGraw-Hill.

Harlow, H. F., & Zimmerman, R. R. (1959). Affectional responses in the infant monkey. *Science, 130,* 421-432.

Harnishfeger, K. K. (1995). The development of cognitive inhibition: Theories, definitions, and research evidence. In F. N. Dempster & C. J. Brainerd (Eds.), *Interference and inhibition in cognition.* San Diego: Academic Press.

Harris, K. R. (1986). Self-monitoring of attentional behavior versus self-monitoring of productivity: Effects of on-task behavior and academic response rate among learning disabled children. *Journal of Applied Behavior Analysis, 19,* 417-423.

Harris, M. (1985). Visualization and spelling competence. *Journal of Developmental Education, 9* (2), 2-5; 31.

Harris, M. J., & Rosenthal, R. (1985). Mediation of interpersonal expectancy effects: 31 meta-analyses. *Psychological Bulletin, 97,* 363-386.

Harris, R. J. (1977). Comprehension of pragmatic implications in advertising. *Journal of Applied Psychology, 62,* 603-608.

Harris, V. W., & Sherman, J. A. (1973). Use and analysis of the "Good Behavior Game" to reduce disruptive classroom behavior. *Journal of Applied Behavior Analysis, 6,* 405-417.

Harrow, A. J. (1972). *A taxonomy of the psychomotor domain: A guide for developing behavioral objectives.* New York: David McKay.

Harter, S. (1978). Pleasure derived from optimal challenge and the effects of extrinsic rewards on children's difficulty level choices. *Child Development, 49,* 788-799.

Harter, S. (1981a). A model of mastery motivation in children: Individual differences and developmental change. In W. A. Collins (Ed.), *The Minnesota symposia on child psychology: Vol. 14. Aspects of the development of competence.* Hillsdale, NJ: Erlbaum.

Harter, S. (1981b). A new self-report scale of intrinsic versus extrinsic orientation in the classroom: Motivational and informational components. *Developmental Psychology, 17,* 300-312.

Harter, S. (1983). Developmental perspectives on the self-system. In E. M. Hetherington (Ed.), *Handbook of child psychology: Vol. 4. Socialization, personality, and social development.* New York: Wiley.

Harter, S. (1992). The relationship between perceived competence, affect, and motivational orientation within the classroom: Processes and patterns of change. In A. K. Boggiano & T. S. Pittman (Eds.), *Achievement and motivation: A social-developmental perspective.* Cambridge, UK: Cambridge University Press.

Harter, S., Whitesell, N. R., & Kowalski, P. (1992). Individual differences in the effects of educational transitions on young adolescents' perceptions of competence and motivational orientation. *American Educational Research Journal, 29,* 777-807.

Hartley, J., Bartlett, S., & Branthwaite, A. (1980). Underlining can make a difference—sometimes. *Journal of Educational Research, 73*, 218-224.

Hartley, J., & Trueman, M. (1982). The effects of summaries on the recall of information from prose: Five experimental studies. *Human Learning, 1*, 63-82.

Hartmann, W. K., Miller, R., & Lee, P. (1984). *Out of the cradle: Exploring the frontiers beyond earth.* New York: Workman.

Hasher, L., & Zacks, R. T. (1984). Automatic processing of fundamental information. *American Psychologist, 39*, 1372-1388.

Hasselhorn, M., & Körkel, J. (1986). Metacognitive versus traditional reading instructions: The mediating role of domain-specific knowledge on children's text-processing. *Human Learning, 5*, 75-90.

Hastings, W. M. (1977). In praise of regurgitation. *Intellect, 105*, 349-350.

Hatano, G., & Inagaki, K. (1991). Sharing cognition through collective comprehension activity. In L. B. Resnick, J. M. Levine, & S. D. Teasley (Eds.), *Perspectives on socially shared cognition.* Washington, DC: American Psychological Association.

Hatano, G., & Inagaki, K. (1993). Desituating cognition through the construction of conceptual knowledge. In P. Light & G. Butterworth (Eds.), *Context and cognition: Ways of learning and knowing.* Hillsdale, NJ: Erlbaum.

Hatano, G., & Inagaki, K. (1996). Cognitive and cultural factors in the acquisition of intuitive biology. In D. R. Olson & N. Torrance (Eds.), *The handbook of education and human development: New models of of learning, teaching, and schooling.* Cambridge, MA: Blackwell Publishers.

Hativa, N., & Shorer, D. (1989). Socioeconomic status, aptitude, and gender differences in CAI gains of arithmetic. *Journal of Educational Research, 83* (1), 11-21.

Hattie, J., Biggs, J., & Purdie, N. (1996). Effects of learning skills interventions on student learning: A meta-analysis. *Review of Educational Research, 66*, 99-136.

Hawk, P. P. (1986). Using graphic organizers to increase achievement in middle school life science. *Science Education, 70*, 81-87.

Hayes, D. A., & Henk, W. A. (1986). Understanding and remembering complex prose augmented by analogic and pictorial illustration. *Journal of Reading Behavior, 18*, 63-78.

Hayes, J. R., & Simon, H. A. (1974). Understanding written problem instructions. In L. W. Gregg (Ed.), *Knowledge and cognition.* Hillsdale, NJ: Erlbaum.

Hayes, K. J., & Hayes, C. (1952). Imitation in a home-raised chimpanzee. *Journal of Comparative and Physiological Psychology, 45*, 450-459.

Hayes, S. C., Rosenfarb, I., Wulfert, E., Munt, E. D., Korn, Z., & Zettle, R. D. (1985). Self-reinforcement effects: An artifact of social standard setting? *Journal of Applied Behavior Analysis, 18*, 201-214.

Hayes-Roth, B., & Thorndyke, P. W. (1979). Integration of knowledge from text. *Journal of Verbal Learning and Verbal Behavior, 18*, 91-108.

Haygood, R. C., & Bourne, L. E., Jr. (1965). Attribute- and rule-learning aspects of conceptual behavior. *Psychological Review, 72*, 175-195.

Hebb, D. O. (1955). Drives and the c. n. s. (conceptual nervous system). *Psychological Review, 62*, 243-254.

Heil, M., Rösler, F., & Hennighausen, E. (1994). Dynamics of activation in long-term memory: The retrieval of verbal, pictorial, spatial, and color information. *Journal of Experimental Psychology: Learning, Memory, and Cognition, 20*, 169-184.

Heindel, P., & Kose, G. (1990). The effects of motoric action and organization on children's memory. *Journal of Experimental Child Psychology, 50*, 416-428.

Heins, E. D., Lloyd, J. W., & Hallahan, D. P. (1986). Cued and noncued self-recording of attention to task. *Behavior Modification, 10*, 235-254.

Heit, E. (1993). Modeling the effects of expectations on recognition memory. *Psychological Science, 4*, 244-251.

Heller, J. I., & Hungate, H. N. (1985). Implications for mathematics instruction of research on scientific problem solving. In E. A. Silver (Ed.), *Teaching and learning mathematical problem solving: Multiple research perspectives.* Hillsdale, NJ: Erlbaum.

Helmke, A. (1988). The role of classroom context factors for the achievement-impairing effect of test anxiety. *Anxiety Research, 1*, 37-52.

Helmke, A. (1989). Affective student characteristics and cognitive development: Problems, pitfalls, perspectives. *International Journal of Educational Research, 13*, 915-932.

Hembree, R. (1988). Correlates, causes, effects, and treatment of test anxiety. *Review of Educational Research, 58*, 47-77.

Hemphill, L., & Snow, C. (1996). Language and literacy development: Discontinuities and differences. In D. R. Olson & N. Torrance (Eds.), *The handbook of education and human development: New models of learning, teaching, and schooling.* Cambridge, MA: Blackwell Publishers.

Henle, M. (1985). Rediscovering Gestalt psychology. In S. Koch & D. E. Leary (Eds.), *A century of psychology as science.* New York: McGraw-Hill.

Hennessey, B. A. (1995). Social, environmental, and developmental issues and creativity. *Educational Psychology Review, 7*, 163-183.

Hennessey, B. A., & Amabile, T. M. (1987). *Creativity and learning.* Washington, DC: National Education Association.

Herbert, J. J., & Harsh, C. M. (1944). Observational learning by cats. *Journal of Comparative Psychology, 37*, 81-95.

Hergenhahn, B. R., & Olson, M. H. (1997). *An introduction to theories of learning* (5th ed.). Upper Saddle River, NJ: Prentice Hall.

Herrnstein, R. J. (1969). Method and theory in the study of avoidance. *Psychological Review, 76*, 49-69.

Herrnstein, R. J. (1977). The evolution of behaviorism. *American Psychologist, 32*, 593-603.

Herrnstein, R. J. (1990). Behavior, reinforcement, and utility. *Psychological Science, 1*, 217-223.

Herrnstein, R. J., Nickerson, R. S., de Sánchez, M., & Swets, J. A. (1986). Teaching thinking skills. *American Psychologist, 41*, 1279-1289.

Hertel, P. T. (1994). Depression and memory: Are impairments remediable through attentional control? *Current Directions in Psychological Science, 3*, 190-193.

Hess, R. D., & McDevitt, T. M. (1984). Some cognitive consequences of maternal intervention techniques: A longitudinal study. *Child Development, 55*, 2017-2030.

Hess, R. D., & McDevitt, T. M. (1989). Family. In E. Barnouw (Ed.), *International encyclopedia of communications.* New York: Oxford University Press.

Hettena, C. M., & Ballif, B. L. (1981). Effects of mood on learning. *Journal of Educational Psychology, 73*, 505-508.

Heuer, F., & Reisberg, D. (1990). Vivid memories of emotional events: The accuracy of remembered minutiae. *Memory and Cognition, 18*, 496-506.

Heuer, F., & Reisberg, D. (1992). Emotion, arousal, and memory for detail. In S. Christianson (Ed.), *Handbook of emotion and memory*. Hillsdale, NJ: Erlbaum.

Heward, W. L. (1996). *Exceptional children: An introduction to special education* (5th ed.). Englewood Cliffs, NJ: Merrill/Prentice Hall.

Hidalgo, N. M., Siu, S., Bright, J. A., Swap, S. M., & Epstein, J. L. (1995). Research on families, schools, and communities: A multicultural perspective. In J. A. Banks & C. A. M. Banks (Eds.), *Handbook of research on multicultural education*. New York: Macmillan.

Hidi, S. (1990). Interest and its contribution as a mental resource for learning. *Review of Educational Research, 60,* 549-571.

Hidi, S., & Anderson, V. (1992). Situational interest and its impact on reading and expository writing. In K. A. Renninger, S. Hidi, & A. Krapp (Eds.), *The role of interest in learning and development*. Hillsdale, NJ: Erlbaum.

Hidi, S., & McLaren, J. (1990). The effect of topic and theme interestingness on the production of school expositions. In H. Mandl, E. De Corte, N. Bennett, & H. F. Friedrich (Eds.), *Learning and instruction in an international context*. Oxford, UK: Pergamon.

Hiebert, E. H., & Fisher, C. W. (1992). The tasks of school literacy: Trends and issues. In J. Brophy (Ed.), *Advances in research on teaching: Vol. 3. Planning and managing learning tasks and activities*. Greenwich, CT: JAI Press.

Hiebert, E. H., & Raphael, T. E. (1996). Psychological perspectives on literacy and extensions to educational practice. In D. C. Berliner & R. C. Calfee (Eds.), *Handbook of educational psychology*. New York: Macmillan.

Hiebert, J., Carpenter, T. P., Fennema, E., Fuson, K., Human, P., Murray, H., Olivier, A., & Wearne, D. (1996). Problem solving as a basis for reform in curriculum and instruction: The case of mathematics. *Educational Researcher, 25* (4), 12-21.

Hiebert, J., & Lefevre, P. (1986). Conceptual and procedural knowledge in mathematics: An introductory analysis. In J. Hiebert (Ed.), *Conceptual and procedural knowledge: The case of mathematics*. Hillsdale, NJ: Erlbaum.

Hiebert, J., & Wearne, D. (1992). Links between teaching and learning place value with understanding in first grade. *Journal for Research in Mathematics Education, 23,* 98-122.

Hiebert, J., & Wearne, D. (1993). Instructional tasks, classroom discourse, and students' learning in second-grade arithmetic. *American Educational Research Journal, 30,* 393-425.

Hiebert, J. & Wearne, D. (1996). Instruction, understanding, and skill in multidigit addition and substraction. *Cognition and Instruction, 14,* 251-283.

Higbee, K. L. (1976). Can young children use mnemonics? *Psychological Reports, 38,* 18.

Hill, C. A. (1987). Affiliation motivation: People who need people . . . but in different ways. *Journal of Personality and Social Psychology, 52,* 1008-1018.

Hill, K. T. (1984). Debilitating motivation and testing: A major educational problem, possible solutions, and policy applications. In R. Ames & C. Ames (Eds.), *Research on motivation in education: Vol. 1. Student motivation*. New York: Academic Press.

Hinsley, D., Hayes, J. R., & Simon, H. A. (1977). From words to equations. In P. Carpenter & M. Just (Eds.), *Cognitive processes in comprehension*. Hillsdale, NJ: Erlbaum.

Hinton, B. L. (1968). Environmental frustration and creative problem solving. *Journal of Applied Psychology, 52,* 211-217.

Hinton, G. E., & Anderson, J. A. (1981). *Parallel models of associative memory*. Hillsdale, NJ: Erlbaum.

Hinton, G. E., McClelland, J. L., & Rumelhart, D. E. (1986). Distributed representations. In D. E. Rumelhart, J. L. McClelland, & the PDP Research Group (Eds.), *Parallel distributed processing: Vol. 1. Foundations*. Cambridge, MA: M.I.T. Press.

Hiroto, D. S. (1974). Locus of control and learned helplessness. *Journal of Experimental Psychology, 102,* 187-193.

Hiroto, D. S., & Seligman, M. E. P. (1975). Generality of learned helplessness in man. *Journal of Personality and Social Psychology, 31,* 311-327.

Hirschfeld, L. A., & Gelman, S. A. (Eds.). (1994). *Mapping the mind: Domain specificity in cognition and culture*. Cambridge, UK: Cambridge University Press.

Hitch, G. J. (1984). Working memory. *Psychological Medicine, 14,* 265-271.

Ho, D. Y. F. (1994). Cognitive socialization in Confucian heritage cultures. In P. M. Greenfield & R. R. Cocking (Eds.), *Cross-cultural roots of minority child development*. Hillsdale, NJ: Erlbaum.

Hobbs, T. R., & Holt, M. M. (1976). The effects of token reinforcement on the behavior of delinquents in cottage settings. *Journal of Applied Behavior Analysis, 9,* 189-198.

Hockman, C. H., & Lipsitt, L. P. (1961). Delay-of-reward gradients in discrimination learning with children for two levels of difficulty. *Journal of Comparative and Physiological Psychology, 54,* 24-27.

Hofer, B. K., & Pintrich, P. R. (1997a, March). *Disciplinary ways of knowing: Epistemological beliefs in science and psychology*. Paper presented at the annual meeting of the American Educational Research Association, Chicago.

Hofer, B. K., & Pintrich, P. R. (1997b). The development of epistemological theories: Beliefs about knowledge and knowing and their relation to learning. *Review of Educational Research, 67,* 88-140.

Hoffman, M. L. (1984). Interaction of affect and cognition in empathy. In C. E. Izard, J. Kagan, & R. B. Zajonc (Eds.), *Emotions, cognition, and behavior*. Cambridge, UK: Cambridge University Press.

Hoffman, M. L. (1991). Empathy, social cognition, and moral action. In W. M. Kurtines & J. L. Gewirtz (Eds.), *Moral behavior and development: Vol. 1. Theory*. Hillsdale, NJ: Erlbaum.

Hogan, K. (1997, March). *Relating students' personal frameworks for science learning to their cognition in collaborative contexts*. Paper presented at the annual meeting of the American Educational Research Association, Chicago.

Hokanson, J. E., & Burgess, M. (1962). The effects of three types of aggression on vascular processes. *Journal of Abnormal and Social Psychology, 64,* 446-449.

Holley, C. D., & Dansereau, D. F. (1984). *Spatial learning strategies: Techniques, applications, and related issues*. Orlando: Academic Press.

Holliday, B. G. (1985). Towards a model of teacher-child transactional processes affecting black children's academic achievement. In M. B. Spencer, G. K. Brookins, & W. R. Allen (Eds.), *Beginnings: The social and affective development of black children*. Hillsdale, NJ: Erlbaum.

Hollis, K. L. (1997). Contemporary research on Pavlovian conditioning: A "new" functional analysis. *American Psychologist, 52,* 956-965.

Hollon, R. E., Roth, K. J., & Anderson, C. W. (1991). Science teachers' conceptions of teaching and learning. In

494

J. Brophy (Ed.), *Advances in research on teaching: Vol. 2. Teachers' knowledge of subject matter as it relates to their teaching practice*. Greenwich, CT: JAI Press.

Holmes, D. S. (1974). Investigation of repression: Differential recall of material experimentally or naturally associated with ego threat. *Psychological Bulletin, 81,* 632-653.

Holmes, D. S. (1990). The evidence for suppression: An examination of sixty years of research. In J. Singer (Ed.), *Repression and dissociation: Implications for personality theory, psychopathology, and health.* Chicago: University of Chicago Press.

Holt-Reynolds, D. (1992). Personal history-based beliefs as relevant prior knowledge in course work. *American Educational Research Journal, 29,* 325-349.

Holyoak, K. J. (1985). The pragmatics of analogical transfer. In G. H. Bower (Ed.), *The psychology of learning and motivation: Advances in research and theory* (Vol. 19). Orlando: Academic Press.

Holyoak, K. J. (1987). Review of parallel distributed processing. *Science, 236,* 992.

Holz, W. C., & Azrin, N. H. (1962). Recovery during punishment by intense noise. *Psychological Reports, 11,* 655-657.

Hom, A., & Battistich, V. (1995, April). *Students' sense of school community as a factor in reducing drug use and delinquency.* Paper presented at the annual meeting of the American Educational Research Association, San Francisco.

Homme, L. E., Csanyi, A. P., Gonzales, M. A., & Rechs, J. R. (1970). *How to use contingency contracting in the classroom.* Champaign, IL: Research Press.

Homme, L. E., deBaca, P. C., Devine, J. V., Steinhorst, R., & Rickert, E. J. (1963). Use of the Premack principle in controlling the behavior of nursery school children. *Journal of the Experimental Analysis of Behavior, 6,* 544.

Hong, Y., Chiu, C., & Dweck, C. S. (1995). Implicit theories of intelligence: Reconsidering the role of confidence in achievement motivation. In M. H. Kernis (Ed.), *Efficacy, agency, and self-esteem.* New York: Plenum Press.

Hopkins, R. H., & Atkinson, R. C. (1968). Priming and the retrieval of names from long-term memory. *Psychonomic Science, 11,* 219-220.

Horgan, D. (1990, April). *Students' predictions of test grades: Calibration and metacognition.* Paper presented at the annual meeting of the American Educational Research Association, Boston.

Hovland, C. I., & Weiss, W. (1953). Transmission of information concerning concepts through positive and negative instances. *Journal of Experimental Psychology, 43,* 175-182.

Howard, D. V. (1983). *Cognitive psychology: Memory, language, and thought.* New York: Macmillan.

Howe, C., Tolmie, A., Greer, K., & Mackenzie, M. (1995). Peer collaboration and conceptual growth in physics: Task influences on children's understanding of heating and cooling. *Cognition and Instruction, 13,* 483-503.

Howe, M. J. A. (1970). Using students' notes to examine the role of the individual learner in acquiring meaningful subject matter. *Journal of Educational Research, 64,* 61-63.

Howe, M. L., & O'Sullivan, J. T. (1990). The development of strategic memory: Coordinating knowledge, metamemory, and resources. In D. F. Bjorklund (Ed.), *Children's strategies: Contemporary views of cognitive development.* Hillsdale, NJ: Erlbaum.

Hudson, T. (1983). Correspondences and numerical differences between disjoint sets. *Child Development, 54,* 84-90.

Hudspeth, W. J. (1985). Developmental neuropsychology: Functional implications of quantitative EEG maturation [Abstract]. *Journal of Clinical and Experimental Neuropsychology, 7,* 606.

Huff, J. A. (1988). Personalized behavior modification: An in-school suspension program that teaches students how to change. *School Counselor, 35,* 210-214.

Hughes, J. N. (1988). *Cognitive behavior therapy with children in schools.* New York: Pergamon.

Hull, C. L. (1920). Quantitative aspects of the evolution of concepts: An experimental study. *Psychological Monographs, 28* (Whole No. 123).

Hull, C. L. (1934). The concept of the habit-family hierarchy and maze learning. *Psychological Review, 41,* 33-54.

Hull, C. L. (1937). Mind, mechanism, and adaptive behavior. *Psychological Review, 44,* 1-32.

Hull, C. L. (1938). The goal-gradient hypothesis applied to some "field-force" problems in the behavior of young children. *Psychological Review, 45,* 271-299.

Hull, C. L. (1943). *Principles of behavior: An introduction to behavior theory.* New York: Appleton-Century-Crofts.

Hull, C. L. (1951). *Essentials of behavior.* New Haven, CT: Yale University Press.

Hull, C. L. (1952). *A behavior system: An introduction to behavior theory concerning the individual organism.* New Haven, CT: Yale University Press.

Hulse, S. H. (1993). The present status of animal cognition: An introduction. *Psychological Science, 4,* 154-155.

Humphreys, L. G. (1939). Acquisition and extinction of verbal expectations in a situation analogous to conditioning. *Journal of Experimental Psychology, 25,* 294-301.

Hundert, J. (1976). The effectiveness of reinforcement, response cost, and mixed programs on classroom behaviors. *Journal of Applied Behavior Analysis, 9,* 107.

Hunter, M. (1982). *Mastery teaching.* El Segundo, CA: TIP Publications.

Huston, A. C. (1983). Sex-typing. In E. M. Hetherington (Ed.), *Handbook of child psychology: Vol. 4. Socialization, personality, and social development* (4th ed.). New York: Wiley.

Huston, A. C., Watkins, B. A., & Kunkel, D. (1989). Public policy and children's television. *American Psychologist, 44,* 424-433.

Hyde, T. S., & Jenkins, J. J. (1969). Differential effects of incidental tasks on the organization of recall of a list of highly associated words. *Journal of Experimental Psychology, 82,* 472-481.

Ickes, W. J., & Layden, M. A. (1978). Attributional styles. In J. Harvey, W. Ickes, & R. Kidd (Eds.), *New directions in attributional research* (Vol. 2). Hillsdale, NJ: Erlbaum.

Igoe, A. R., & Sullivan, H. (1991, April). *Gender and grade-level differences in student attributes related to school learning and motivation.* Paper presented at the annual meeting of the American Educational Research Association, Chicago.

Inglehart, M., Brown, D. R., & Vida, M. (1994). Competition, achievement, and gender: A stress theoretical analysis. In P. R. Pintrich, D. R. Brown, & C. E. Weinstein (Eds.), *Student motivation, cognition, and learning: Essays in honor of Wilbert J. McKeachie.* Hillsdale, NJ: Erlbaum.

Inglis, A., & Biemiller, A. (1997, March). *Fostering self-direction in mathematics: A cross-age tutoring program that enhances math problem solving.*

Paper presented at the annual meeting of the American Educational Research Association, Chicago.

Inhelder, B., & Piaget, J. (1958). *The growth of logical thinking from childhood to adolescence* (A. Parsons & S. Milgram, Trans.). New York: Basic Books.

Intons-Peterson, M. J. (1992). Components of auditory imagery. In D. Reisberg (Ed.), *Auditory imagery*. Hillsdale, NJ: Erlbaum.

Intons-Peterson, M. J., Russell, W., & Dressel, S. (1992). The role of pitch in auditory imagery. *Journal of Experimental Psychology: Human Perception and Performance, 18*, 233-240.

Irwin, D. E. (1996). Integrating information across saccadic eye movements. *Current Directions in Psychological Science, 5*, 94-100.

Isaacson, R. L. (1964). Relation between achievement, test anxiety, and curricular choices. *Journal of Abnormal and Social Psychology, 68*, 447-452.

Isen, A., Daubman, K. A., & Gorgoglione, J. M. (1987). The influence of positive affect on cognitive organization: Implications for education. In R. E. Snow & M. J. Farr (Eds.), *Aptitude, learning and instruction* (Vol. 3). Hillsdale, NJ: Erlbaum.

Iwata, B. A. (1987). Negative reinforcement in applied behavior analysis: An emerging technology. *Journal of Applied Behavior Analysis, 20*, 361-378.

Iwata, B. A., & Bailey, J. S. (1974). Reward versus cost token systems: An analysis of the effects on students and teacher. *Journal of Applied Behavior Analysis, 7*, 567-576.

Iwata, B. A., Pace, G. M., Cowdery, G. E., & Miltenberger, R. G. (1994). What makes extinction work: An analysis of procedural form and function. *Journal of Applied Behavior Analysis, 27*, 131-144.

Jackson, D. L. (1996). *Effects of training in self-generation on the quality of students' questions, class notes, and examination scores.* Unpublished doctoral dissertation, University of Northern Colorado, Greeley.

Jackson, D. N., Ahmed, S. A., & Heapy, N. A. (1976). Is achievement motivation a unitary construct? *Journal of Research in Personality, 10*, 1121.

Jacobsen, B., Lowery, B., & DuCette, J. (1986). Attributions of learning disabled children. *Journal of Educational Psychology, 78*, 59-64.

Jacoby, L. L., & Hayman, C. A. G. (1987). Specific visual transfer in word identification. *Journal of Experimental Psychology: Learning, Memory, and Cognition, 13*, 456-463.

Jagacinski, C. M., & Nicholls, J. (1984). Conceptions of ability and related affects in task involvement and ego involvement. *Journal of Educational Psychology, 76*, 909-919.

Jagacinski, C. M., & Nicholls, J. (1987). Competence and affect in task involvement and ego involvement: The impact of social comparison information. *Journal of Educational Psychology, 79*, 107-114.

Jagacinski, C. M., & Nicholls, J. G. (1990). Reducing effort to protect perceived ability: "They'd do it but I wouldn't." *Journal of Educational Psychology, 82*, 15-21.

James, W. (1890). *Principles of psychology*. New York: Holt.

Jenkins, J. J., & Russell, W. A. (1952). Associative clustering during recall. *Journal of Abnormal and Social Psychology, 47*, 818-821.

Jenlink, C. L. (1994, April). *Music: A lifeline for the self-esteem of at-risk students*. Paper presented at the annual meeting of the American Educational Research Association, New Orleans.

Johnson, D. W., & Johnson, R. T. (1985a). Classroom conflict: Controversy versus debate in learning groups. *American Educational Research Journal, 22*, 237-256.

Johnson, D. W., & Johnson, R. T. (1985b). Motivational processes in cooperative, competitive, and individualistic learning situations. In C. Ames & R. Ames (Eds.), *Research on motivation in education: Vol. 2. The classroom milieu*. Orlando: Academic Press.

Johnson, D. W., & Johnson, R. T. (1987). *Learning together and alone: Cooperative, competitive, and individualistic learning* (2nd ed.). Englewood Cliffs, NJ: Prentice Hall.

Johnson, D. W., & Johnson, R. T. (1991). *Learning together and alone: Cooperative, competitive, and individualistic learning* (3rd ed.). Upper Saddle River, NJ: Prentice Hall.

Johnson, M. K., Bransford, J. D., & Solomon, S. K. (1973). Memory for tacit implications of sentences. *Journal of Experimental Psychology, 98*, 203-205.

Johnson, R. N. (1972). *Aggression in man and animals*. Philadelphia: Saunders.

Johnson, T. D., Langford, K. G., & Quorn, K. C. (1981). Characteristics of an effective spelling program. *Language Arts, 58*, 581-588.

Johnson-Laird, P. N., & Wason, P. C. (1977). Introduction to conceptual thinking. In P. N. Johnson-Laird & P. C. Wason (Eds.), *Thinking: Readings in cognitive science*. Cambridge, UK: Cambridge University Press.

John-Steiner, V. (1997). *Notebooks of the mind: Explorations of thinking* (rev. ed.). New York: Oxford University Press.

Johnston, J. C., McCann, R. S., & Remington, R. W. (1995). Chronometric evidence for two types of attention. *Psychological Science, 6*, 365-369.

Johnstone, A. H., & El-Banna, H. (1986). Capacities, demands, and processes—a predictive model for science education. *Education in Chemistry, 23*, 80-84.

Jonassen, D. H., Hartley, J., & Trueman, M. (1986). The effects of learner-generated versus text-provided headings on immediate and delayed recall and comprehension: An exploratory study. *Human Learning, 5*, 139-150.

Jones, B. F., & Hall, J. W. (1982). School applications of the mnemonic keyword method as a study strategy by eighth graders. *Journal of Educational Psychology, 74*, 230-237.

Jones, B. F., Pierce, J., & Hunter, B. (1988/1989). Teaching students to construct graphic representations. *Educational Leadership, 46* (4), 20-25.

Jones, B. P. (1993). Repression: The evolution of a psychoanalytic concept from the 1890's to the 1990's. *Journal of the American Psychoanalytic Association, 41* (1), 63-93.

Jones, E. E., & Berglas, S. (1978). Control of attributions about the self through self-handicapping strategies: The appeal of alcohol and the role of underachievement. *Personality and Social Psychology Bulletin, 4*, 200-206.

Jones, H. E., & English, H. B. (1926). Notional vs. rote memory. *American Journal of Psychology. 37*, 602-603.

Jones, M. C. (1924). The elimination of children's fears. *Journal of Experimental Psychology, 7*, 382-390.

Judd, C. H. (1932). Autobiography. In C. Murchison (Ed.), *History of psychology in autobiography* (Vol. 2). Worcester, MA: Clark University. Press.

Juvonen, J. (1991, April). *The effect of attributions and interpersonal attitudes on social emotions and behavior*. Paper presented at the annual meeting of the American Educational Research Association, Chicago.

496

Juvonen, J., & Weiner, B. (1993). An attributional analysis of students' interactions: The social consequences of perceived responsibility. *Educational Psychology Review, 5,* 325-345.

Kahl, B., & Woloshyn, V. E. (1994). Using elaborative interrogation to facilitate acquisition of factual information in cooperative learning settings: One good strategy deserves another. *Applied Cognitive Psychology, 8,* 465-478.

Kahneman, D. (1973). *Attention and effort.* Englewood Cliffs, NJ: Prentice Hall.

Kahneman, D., & Tversky, A. (1972). Subjective probability: A judgment of representativeness. *Cognitive Psychology, 3,* 430-454.

Kahneman, D., & Tversky, A. (1973). On the psychology of prediction. *Psychological Review, 80,* 237-251.

Kail, R. (1990). *The development of memory in children* (3rd ed.). New York: W. H. Freeman.

Kamin, L. J. (1956). The effects of termination of the CS and avoidance of the US on avoidance learning. *Journal of Comparative and Physiological Psychology, 49,* 420-424.

Kamin, L. J., Brimer, C. J., & Black, A. H. (1963). Conditioned suppression as a monitor of fear of the CS in the course of avoidance training. *Journal of Comparative and Physiological Psychology, 56,* 497-501.

Kantor, J. R. (1959). *Interbehavioral psychology.* Granville, OH: Principia Press.

Karau, S. J., & Williams, K. D. (1995). Social loafing: Research findings, implications, and future directions. *Current Directions in Psychological Science, 4,* 134-140.

Kardash, C. A. M., & Amlund, J. T. (1991). Self-reported learning strategies and learning from expository text. *Contemporary Educational Psychology, 16,* 117-138.

Kardash, C. A. M., & Howell, K. L. (1996, April). *Effects of epistemological beliefs on strategies employed to comprehend dual-positional text.* Paper presented at the annual meeting of the American Educational Research Association, New York.

Kardash, C. A. M., Royer, J. M., & Greene, B. A. (1988). Effects of schemata on both encoding and retrieval of information from prose. *Journal of Educational Psychology, 80,* 324-329.

Kardash, C. A. M., & Scholes, R. J. (1996). Effects of pre-existing beliefs, epistemological beliefs, and need for cogni-

tion on interpretation of controversial issues. *Journal of Educational Psychology, 88,* 260-271.

Katkovsky, W., Crandall, V. C., & Good, S. (1967). Parental antecedents of children's beliefs in internal-external control of reinforcements in intellectual achievement situations. *Child Development, 38,* 765-776.

Katz, L. G. (1993). All about me: Are we developing our children's self-esteem or their narcissism? *American Educator, 17* (2), 18-23.

Kauffman, S. (1995). *At home in the universe: The search for laws of self-organization and complexity.* New York: Oxford University Press.

Kaufman, A., Baron, A., & Kopp, R. E. (1966). Some effects of instructions on human operant behavior. *Psychonomic Monograph Supplements, 1,* 243-250.

Kazdin, A. E. (1972). Response cost: The removal of conditional reinforcers for therapeutic change. *Behavior Therapy, 3,* 533-546.

Keele, S. W. (1973). *Attention and human performance.* Pacific Palisades, CA: Goodyear.

Keil, F. C. (1986). The acquisition of natural kind and artifact terms. In W. Demopolous & A. Marras (Eds.), *Language learning and concept acquisition.* Norwood, NJ: Ablex.

Keil, F. C. (1987). Conceptual development and category structure. In U. Neisser (Ed.), *Concepts and conceptual development: Ecological and intellectual factors in categorization.* Cambridge, UK: Cambridge University Press.

Keil, F. C. (1989). *Concepts, kinds, and cognitive development.* Cambridge, MA: M.I.T. Press.

Keil, F. C. (1991). Theories, concepts, and the acquisition of word meaning. In S. A. Gelman & J. P. Byrnes (Eds.), *Perspectives on language and thought: Interrelations in development.* Cambridge, UK: Cambridge University Press.

Keil, F. C. (1994). The birth and nurturance of concepts by domains: The origins of concepts of living things. In L. A. Hirschfeld & S. A. Gelman (Eds.), *Mapping the mind: Domain specificity in cognition and culture.* Cambridge, UK: Cambridge University Press.

Keil, F. C., & Silberstein, C. S. (1996). Schooling and the acquisition of theoretical knowledge. In D. R. Olson & N. Torrance (Eds.), *The handbook of education and human development:*

New models of learning, teaching, and schooling. Cambridge, MA: Blackwell Publishers.

Keller, F. S. (1968). Goodbye teacher. *Journal of Applied Behavior Analysis, 1,* 79-89.

Keller, F. S. (1974). An international venture in behavior modification. In F. S. Keller & E. Ribes-Inesta (Eds.), *Behavior modification: Applications to education.* New York: Academic Press.

Keller, J. M. (1987). Development and use of the ARCS model of instructional design. *Journal of Instructional Development, 10* (3), 2-10.

Kelley, M. L., & Carper, L. B. (1988). Home-based reinforcement procedures. In J. C. Witt, S. N. Elliott, & F. M. Gresham (Eds.), *Handbook of behavior therapy in education.* New York: Plenum Press.

Kemler Nelson, D. G. (1990). When experimental findings conflict with everyday observations: Reflections on children's category learning. *Child Development, 61,* 606-610.

Kendler, H. H. (1985). Behaviorism and psychology: An uneasy alliance. In S. Koch & D. E. Leary (Eds.), *A century of psychology as science.* New York: McGraw-Hill.

Kendler, H. H., & Kendler, T. S. (1961). Effect of verbalization on reversal shifts in children. *Science, 134,* 1619-1620.

Kendler, H. H., & Kendler, T. S. (1962). Vertical and horizontal processes in problem solving. *Psychological Review, 69,* 1-16.

Kendler, T. S., & Kendler, H. H. (1959). Reversal and nonreversal shifts in kindergarten children. *Journal of Experimental Psychology, 58,* 56-60.

Keppel, G., & Underwood, B. J. (1962). Proactive inhibition in short-term retention of single items. *Journal of Verbal Learning and Verbal Behavior, 1,* 153-161.

Kermani, H., & Moallem, M. (1997, March). *Cross-age tutoring: Exploring features and processes of peer-mediated learning.* Paper presented at the annual meeting of the American Educational Research Association, Chicago.

Kernaghan, K., & Woloshyn, V. E. (1994, April). *Explicit versus implicit multiple strategy instruction: Monitoring grade one students' spelling performances.* Paper presented at the annual meeting of the American Educational Research Association, New Orleans.

Kiewra, K. A. (1985). Investigating notetaking and review: A depth of processing alternative. *Educational Psychologist, 20,* 23-32.

Kiewra, K. A. (1989). A review of notetaking: The encoding-storage paradigm and beyond. *Educational Psychology Review, 1,* 147-172.

Kiewra, K. A., DuBois, N. F., Christian, D., McShane, A., Meyerhoffer, M., & Roskelly, D. (1988, April). *Theoretical and practical aspects of taking, reviewing, and borrowing conventional, skeletal, or matrix lecture notes.* Paper presented at the annual meeting of the American Educational Research Association, New Orleans.

Killeen, P. R. (1991). Behavior's time. In G. H. Bower (Ed.), *The psychology of learning and motivation: Advances in research and theory* (Vol. 27). San Diego: Academic Press.

Kilpatrick, J. (1985). A retrospective account of the past 25 years of research on teaching mathematical problem solving. In E. A. Silver (Ed.), *Teaching and learning mathematical problem solving: Multiple research perspectives.* Hillsdale, NJ: Erlbaum.

Kim, D., Solomon, D., & Roberts, W. (1995, April). *Classroom practices that enhance students' sense of community.* Paper presented at the annual meeting of the American Educational Research Association, San Francisco.

King, A. (1992). Comparison of self-questioning, summarizing, and notetaking-review as strategies for learning from lectures. *American Educational Research Journal, 29,* 303-323.

King, A. (1994). Guiding knowledge construction in the classroom: Effects of teaching children how to question and how to explain. *American Educational Research Journal, 31,* 338-368.

King, N. J., & Ollendick, T. H. (1989). Children's anxiety and phobic disorders in school settings: Classification, assessment, and intervention issues. *Review of Educational Research, 59,* 431-470.

Kinnick, V. (1990). The effect of concept teaching in preparing nursing students for clinical practice. *Journal of Nursing Education, 29,* 362-366.

Kintsch, W. (1977). Reading comprehension as a function of text structure. In A. S. Reber & D. L. Scarborough (Eds.), *Toward a psychology of reading.* New York: Wiley.

Kintsch, W. (1980). Learning from text, levels of comprehension, or: Why anyone would read a story anyway. *Poetics, 9,* 87-98.

Kintsch, W., Mandel, T. S., & Kozminsky, E. (1977). Summarizing scrambled stories. *Memory and Cognition, 5,* 547-552.

Kintsch, W., & van Dijk, T. A. (1978). Toward a model of text comprehension and production. *Psychological Review, 85,* 363-394.

Kirkland, M. C. (1971). The effect of tests on students and schools. *Review of Educational Research, 41,* 303-350.

Klatzky, R. L. (1975). *Human memory.* San Francisco: W. H. Freeman.

Klausmeier, H. J. (1990). Conceptualizing. In B. F. Jones & L. Idol (Eds.), *Dimensions of thinking and cognitive instruction.* Hillsdale, NJ: Erlbaum.

Klein, J. D. (1990, April). *The effect of interest, task performance, and reward contingencies on self-efficacy.* Paper presented at the annual meeting of the American Educational Research Association, Boston.

Klein, P. S. (1975). Effects of open vs. structured teacher-student interaction on creativity of children with different levels of anxiety. *Psychology in the Schools, 12,* 286-288.

Klein, S. B. (1987). *Learning: Principles and applications.* New York: McGraw-Hill.

Kleinsmith, L. J., & Kaplan, S. (1963). Paired associate learning as a function of arousal and interpolated interval. *Journal of Experimental Psychology, 65,* 190-193.

Kletzien, S. B. (1988, April). *Achieving and non-achieving high school readers' use of comprehension strategies for reading expository text.* Paper presented at the annual meeting of the American Educational Research Association, New Orleans.

Klinger, E. (1975). Consequences of commitment to and disengagement from incentives. *Psychological Review, 82,* 1-25.

Klinger, E. (1977). *Meaning and void: Inner experience and the incentives in people's lives.* Minneapolis: University of Minnesota Press.

Knight, S. L. (1988, April). *Examining the relationship between teacher behaviors and students' cognitive reading strategies.* Paper presented at the annual meeting of the American Educational Research Association, New Orleans.

Koestner, R., Ryan, R. M., Bernieri, F., & Holt, K. (1984). Setting limits on children's behavior: The differential effects of controlling vs. informational styles on intrinsic motivation and creativity. *Journal of Personality, 52,* 233-248.

Koffka, K. (1935). *Principles of Gestalt psychology.* New York: Harcourt, Brace.

Köhler, W. (1925). *The mentality of apes.* London: Routledge & Kegan Paul.

Köhler, W. (1929). *Gestalt psychology.* New York: Liveright.

Köhler, W. (1938). *The place of value in a world of facts.* New York: Liveright.

Köhler, W. (1940). *Dynamics in psychology.* New York: Liveright.

Köhler, W. (1947). *Gestalt psychology: An introduction to new concepts in modern psychology.* New York: Liveright.

Köhler, W. (1959). Gestalt psychology today. *American Psychologist, 14,* 727-734.

Köhler, W. (1969). *The task of Gestalt psychology.* Princeton, NJ: Princeton University Press.

Kohn, A. (1996). By all available means: Cameron and Pierce's defense of extrinsic motivators. *Review of Educational Research, 66,* 1-4.

Kolers, P. A. (1975). Specificity of operations in sentence recognition. *Cognitive Psychology, 1,* 283-306.

Kolodner, J. (1985). Memory for experience. In G. H. Bower (Ed.), *The psychology of learning and motivation: Advances in research and theory,* (Vol. 19). Orlando: Academic Press.

Konopak, B. C., Martin, S. H., & Martin, M. A. (1990). Using a writing strategy to enhance sixth-grade students' comprehension of content material. *Journal of Reading Behavior, 22,* 19-37.

Kosslyn, S. M. (1980). *Image and mind.* Cambridge, MA: Harvard University Press.

Kosslyn, S. M. (1983). *Ghosts in the mind's machine: Creating and using images in the brain.* New York: W. W. Norton.

Kosslyn, S. M. (1985). Mental imagery ability. In R. J. Sternberg (Ed.), *Human abilities: An information-processing approach.* New York: W. H. Freeman.

Kosslyn, S. M. (1994). *Image and brain: The resolution of the imagery debate.* Cambridge, MA: M.I.T. Press.

Kotovsky, K., & Fallside, D. (1989). Representation and transfer in problem solving. In D. Klahr & K. Kotovsky (Eds.), *Complex information processing: The impact of Herbert A. Simon.* Hillsdale, NJ: Erlbaum.

Krajcik, J. S. (1991). Developing students' understanding of chemical concepts. In S. M. Glynn, R. H. Yeany, & B. K. Britton (Eds.), *The psychology of learning science.* Hillsdale, NJ: Erlbaum.

Krampen, G. (1987). Differential effects of teacher comments. *Journal of Educational Psychology, 79,* 137-146.

Krapp, A., Hidi, S., & Renninger, K. A. (1992). Interest, learning, and development. In K. A. Renninger, S. Hidi, & A. Krapp (Eds.), *The role of interest in learning and development.* Hillsdale, NJ: Erlbaum.

Krathwohl, D. R. (1994). Reflections on the taxonomy: Its past, present, and future. In L. W. Anderson & L. A. Sosniak (Eds.), *Bloom's taxonomy: A forty-year perspective. Ninety-third yearbook of the National Society for the Study of Education, Part II.* Chicago: National Society for the Study of Education.

Krathwohl, D. R., Bloom, B. S., & Masia, B. B. (1964). *Taxonomy of educational objectives. Handbook II: Affective domain.* New York: David McKay.

Krueger, W. C. F. (1929). The effect of overlearning on retention. *Journal of Experimental Psychology, 12,* 71-78.

Krumboltz, J. D., & Krumboltz, H. B. (1972). *Changing children's behavior.* Englewood Cliffs, NJ: Prentice Hall.

Kuhara-Kojima, K., & Hatano, G. (1991). Contribution of content knowledge and learning ability to the learning of facts. *Journal of Educational Psychology, 83,* 253-263.

Kuhl, J. (1985). Volitional mediators of cognition-behavior consistency: Self-regulatory processes and actions versus state orientation. In J. Kuhl & J. Beckmann (Eds.), *Action control: From cognition to behavior.* Berlin: Springer-Verlag.

Kuhn, D., Amsel, E., & O'Loughlin, M. (1988). *The development of scientific thinking skills.* San Diego: Academic Press.

Kulhavy, R. W., Lee, J. B., & Caterino, L. C. (1985). Conjoint retention of maps and related discourse. *Contemporary Educational Psychology, 10,* 28-37.

Kulhavy, R. W., Peterson, S., & Schwartz, N. H. (1986). Working memory: The encoding process. In G. D. Phye & T. Andre (Eds.), *Cognitive classroom learning: Understanding, thinking, and problem solving.* Orlando: Academic Press.

Kulhavy, R. W., Schwartz, N. H., & Shaha, S. H. (1983). Spatial representation of maps. *American Journal of Psychology, 96,* 337-351.

Kulik, C. C., Kulik, J. A., & Bangert-Drowns, R. L. (1990). Effectiveness of mastery learning programs: A meta-analysis. *Review of Educational Research, 60,* 265-299.

Kulik, C. C., Kulik, J. A., & Shwalb, B. J. (1983). College programs for high-risk and disadvantaged students: A meta-analysis of findings. *Review of Educational Research, 53,* 397-414.

Kulik, J. A., & Kulik, C. C. (1988). Timing of feedback and verbal learning. *Review of Educational Research, 58,* 79-97.

Kulik, J. A., Kulik, C. C., & Cohen, P. A. (1979). A meta-analysis of outcome studies of Keller's Personalized System of Instruction. *American Psychologist, 34,* 307-318.

Kulik, J. A., Kulik, C. C., & Cohen, P. A. (1980). Effectiveness of computer-based college teaching: A meta-analysis of findings. *Review of Educational Research, 50,* 525-544.

Kyle, W. C., & Shymansky, J. A. (1989, April). Enhancing learning through conceptual change teaching. *NARST News, 31,* 7-8.

LaBerge, D., & Samuels, S. J. (1974). Toward a theory of automatic information processing in reading. *Cognitive Psychology, 6,* 293-323.

Labov, W. (1973). The boundaries of words and their meanings. In C.-J. N. Bailey & R. W. Shuy (Eds.), *New ways of analyzing variations in English.* Washington, DC: Georgetown University Press.

Lachter, J., & Bever, T. G. (1988). The relation between linguistic structure and associative theories of language learning—a critique of some connectionist learning models. *Cognition, 28,* 195-247.

Lambiotte, J. G., Dansereau, D. F., Cross, D. R., & Reynolds, S. B. (1989). Multirelational semantic maps. *Educational Psychology Review, 1,* 331-367.

Lampe, J. R., & Rooze, G. E. (1994, April). *Enhancing social studies achievement among Hispanic students using cooperative learning work groups.* Paper presented at the annual meeting of the American Educational Research Association, New Orleans.

Lampert, M. (1990). When the problem is not the question and the solution is not the answer: Mathematical knowing and teaching. *American Educational Research Journal, 17,* 29-63.

Lampert, M., Rittenhouse, P., & Crumbaugh, C. (1996). Agreeing to disagree: Developing sociable mathematical discourse. In D. R. Olson & N. Torrance (Eds.), *The handbook of education and human development: New mod-* els of learning, teaching, and schooling. Cambridge, MA: Blackwell Publishers.

Lan, W. Y., Repman, J., Bradley, L., & Weller, H. (1994, April). *Immediate and lasting effects of criterion and payoff on academic risk taking.* Paper presented at the annual meeting of the American Educational Research Association, New Orleans.

Landauer, T. K. (1962). Rate of implicit speech. *Perceptual and Motor Skills, 15,* 646.

Lange, G. (1978). Organization-related processes in children's recall. In P. A. Ornstein (Ed.), *Memory development in children.* Hillsdale, NJ: Erlbaum.

Lange, P. C. (1972). What's the score on programmed instruction? *Today's Education, 61,* 59.

Larkin, J. H. (1980). Teaching problem solving in physics: The psychological lab and the practical classroom. In D. T. Tuma & F. Reif (Eds.), *Problem solving and education: Issues in teaching and research.* Hillsdale, NJ: Erlbaum.

Larkin, J. H. (1983). The role of problem representation in physics. In D. Gentner & A. L. Stevens (Eds.), *Mental models.* Hillsdale, NJ: Erlbaum.

Lave, J. (1988). *Cognition in practice: Mind, mathematics, and culture in everyday life.* Cambridge, UK: Cambridge University Press.

Lave, J. (1991). Situating learning in communities of practice. In L. B. Resnick, J. M. Levine, & S. D. Teasley (Eds.), *Perspectives on socially shared cognition.* Washington, DC: American Psychological Association.

Lave, J. (1993). Word problems: A microcosm of theories of learning. In P. Light & G. Butterworth (Eds.), *Context and cognition: Ways of learning and knowing.* Hillsdale, NJ: Erlbaum.

Lave, J., & Wenger, E. (1991). *Situated learning: Legitimate peripheral participation.* Cambridge, UK: Cambridge University Press.

Lawson, M. J., & Chinnappan, M. (1994). Generative activity during geometry problem solving: Comparison of the performance of high-achieving and low-achieving high school students. *Cognition and Instruction, 12,* 61-93.

Lazarus, R. S. (1991). *Emotion and adaptation.* New York: Oxford University Press.

Lee, J. F., Jr., & Pruitt, K. W. (1984). *Providing for individual differences in student learning: A mastery learning approach.* Springfield, IL: Charles C. Thomas.

Lee, O. (1991, April). *Motivation to learn subject matter content: The case of science*. Paper presented at the annual meeting of the American Educational Research Association, Chicago.

Lee, O., & Anderson, C. W. (1991, April). *Student motivation in middle school science classrooms*. Paper presented at the annual meeting of the American Educational Research Association, Chicago.

Lee, O., & Anderson, C. W. (1993). Task engagement and conceptual change in middle school science classrooms. *American Educational Research Journal, 30,* 585-610.

Leff, R. (1969). Effects of punishment intensity and consistency on the internalization of behavioral suppression in children. *Developmental Psychology, 1,* 345-356.

Leherissey, B. L., O'Neil, H. F., Jr., & Hansen, D. N. (1971). Effects of memory support on state anxiety and performance in computer-assisted learning. *Journal of Educational Psychology, 62,* 413-420.

Leinhardt, G. (1992). What research on learning tells us about teaching. *Educational Leadership, 49* (7), 20-25.

Leinhardt, G. (1994). History: A time to be mindful. In G. Leinhardt, I. L. Beck, & C. Stainton (Eds.), *Teaching and learning in history*. Hillsdale, NJ: Erlbaum.

Lennon, R., Ormrod, J. E., Burger, S. F., & Warren, E. (1990, October). *Belief systems of teacher education majors and their possible influences on future classroom performance*. Paper presented at the annual meeting of the Northern Rocky Mountain Educational Research Association, Greeley, CO.

Lentz, F. E. (1988). Reductive procedures. In J. C. Witt, S. N. Elliott, & F. M. Gresham (Eds.), *Handbook of behavior therapy in education*. New York: Plenum Press.

Leon, J. A., & Pepe, H. J. (1983). Self-instructional training: Cognitive behavior modification for remediating arithmetic deficits. *Exceptional Children, 50,* 54-60.

Lepper, M. R. (1981). Intrinsic and extrinsic motivation in children: Detrimental effects of superfluous social controls. In W. A. Collins (Ed.), *Minnesota Symposia on Child Psychology* (Vol. 14). Hillsdale, NJ: Erlbaum.

Lepper, M. R., Aspinwall, L. G., Mumme, D. L., & Chabey, R. W. (1990). Self-perception and social-perception processes in tutoring: Subtle social control strategies of expert tutors. In

J. M. Olson & M. P. Zanna (Eds.), *Self-inference processes: The Ontario Symposium*. Hillsdale, NJ: Erlbaum.

Lepper, M. R., & Greene, D. (Eds.). (1978). *The hidden costs of reward*. Hillsdale, NJ: Erlbaum.

Lepper, M. R., Greene, D., & Nisbett, R. E. (1973). Understanding children's intrinsic interest with extrinsic rewards: A test of the "overjustification" hypothesis. *Journal of Personality and Social Psychology, 28,* 129-137.

Lepper, M. R., & Gurtner, J. (1989). Children and computers: Approaching the twenty-first century. *American Psychologist, 44,* 170-178.

Lepper, M. R., & Hodell, M. (1989). Intrinsic motivation in the classroom. In C. Ames & R. Ames (Eds.), *Research on motivation in education: Vol. 3. Goals and cognitions*. San Diego: Academic Press.

Lepper, M. R., Keavney, M., & Drake, M. (1996). Intrinsic motivation and extrinsic rewards: A commentary on Cameron and Pierce's meta-analysis. *Review of Educational Research, 66,* 5-32.

Lerman, D. C., & Iwata, B. A. (1995). Prevalence of the extinction burst and its attenuation during treatment. *Journal of Applied Behavior Analysis, 28,* 93-94.

Lesgold, A. M. (1983). A rationale for computer-based reading instruction. In A. C. Wilkinson (Ed.), *Classroom computers and cognitive science*. New York: Academic Press.

Lesgold, A. M., & Lajoie, S. (1991). Complex problem-solving in electronics. In R. J. Sternberg & P. A. Frensch (Eds.), *Complex problem solving: Principles and mechanisms*. Hillsdale, NJ: Erlbaum.

Lester, F. K., Jr. (1985). Methodological considerations in research on mathematical problem-solving instruction. In E. A. Silver (Ed.), *Teaching and learning mathematical problem solving: Multiple research perspectives*. Hillsdale, NJ: Erlbaum.

Lester, F. K., Jr., Lambdin, D. V., & Preston, R. V. (1997). A new vision of the nature and purposes of assessment in the mathematics classroom. In G. D. Phye (Ed.), *Handbook of classroom assessment: Learning, achievement, and adjustment*. San Diego: Academic Press.

Lett, B. T. (1973). Delayed reward learning: Disproof of the traditional theory. *Learning and Motivation, 4,* 237-246.

Lett, B. T. (1975). Long delay learning in the T-maze. *Learning and Motivation, 6,* 80-90.

Levin, J. R. (1981). The mnemonic '80s: Keywords in the classroom. *Educational Psychologist, 16,* 65-82.

Levin, J. R., Anglin, G. J., & Carney, R. N. (1987). On empirically validating functions of pictures in prose. In D. M. Willows & H. A. Houghton (Eds.), *The psychology of illustration: I. Basic research*. New York: Springer-Verlag.

Levin, J. R., & Mayer, R. E. (1993). Understanding illustrations in text. In B. K. Britton, A. Woodward, & M. Binkley (Eds.), *Learning from textbooks: Theory and practice*. Hillsdale, NJ: Erlbaum.

Levin, J. R., McCormick, C. B., Miller, G. E., Berry, J. K., & Pressley, M. (1982). Mnemonic versus nonmnemonic vocabulary learning strategies for children. *American Educational Research Journal, 19,* 121-136.

Levine, M. (1966). Hypothesis behavior by humans during discrimination learning. *Journal of Experimental Psychology, 71,* 331-338.

Levstik, L. S. (1994). Building a sense of history in a first-grade classroom. In J. Brophy (Ed.), *Advances in research on teaching: (Vol. 4). Case studies of teaching and learning in social studies*. Greenwich, CT: JAI Press.

Lewin, K., Lippitt, R., & White, R. (1939). Pattern of aggressive behavior in experimentally created "social climates." *Journal of Social Psychology, 10,* 271-299.

Lewis, D. J., & Maher, B. A. (1965). Neural consolidation and electroconvulsive shock. *Psychological Review, 72,* 225-239.

Lhyle, K. G., & Kulhavy, R. W. (1987). Feedback processing and error correction. *Journal of Educational Psychology, 79,* 320-322.

Lickona, T. (1991). Moral development in the elementary school classroom. In W. M. Kurtines & J. L. Gewirtz (Eds.), *Moral behavior and development: Vol. 3. Application*. Hillsdale, NJ: Erlbaum.

Liebert, R. M., & Morris, L. W. (1967). Cognitive and emotional components of test anxiety: A distinction and some initial data. *Psychological Reports, 20,* 975-978.

Light, P., & Butterworth, G. (Eds.). (1993). *Context and cognition: Ways of learning and knowing*. Hillsdale, NJ: Erlbaum.

Lillard, A. S. (1997). Other folks' theories of mind and behavior. *Psychological Science, 8,* 268-274.

Lima, S. D. (1993). Word-initial letter sequences and reading. *Current Directions in Psychological Science, 2,* 139–142.

Linderholm, T., Gustafson, M., van den Broek, P., & Lorch, R. F., Jr. (1997, March). *Effects of reading goals on inference generation.* Paper presented at the annual meeting of the American Educational Research Association, Chicago.

Lindsay, D. S. (1993). Eyewitness suggestibility. *Current Directions in Psychological Science, 2,* 86–89.

Lindsay, P. H., & Norman, D. A. (1977). *Human information processing.* New York: Academic Press.

Lindvall, C. M., Tamburino, J. L., & Robinson, L. (1982, March). *An exploratory investigation of the effect of teaching primary grade children to use specific problem-solving strategies in solving simple story problems.* Paper presented at the annual meeting of the American Educational Research Association, New York.

Linn, M. C., & Muilenburg, L. (1996). Creating lifelong science learners: What models form a firm foundation? *Educational Researcher, 25* (5), 18–24.

Linn, M. C., Songer, N. B., & Eylon, B. (1996). Shifts and convergences in science learning and instruction. In D. C. Berliner & R. C. Calfee (Eds.), *Handbook of educational psychology.* New York: Macmillan.

Linton, M. (1986). Ways of searching and the contents of memory. In D. C. Rubin (Ed.), *Autobiographical memory.* Cambridge, UK: Cambridge University Press.

Lipsitt, L. P., & Kaye, H. (1964). Conditioned sucking in the human newborn. *Psychonomic Science, 1,* 29–30.

Lipsitt, L. P., & Kaye, H. (1965). Change in neonatal response to optimizing and non-optimizing sucking stimulation. *Psychonomic Science, 2,* 221–222.

Lipson, M. Y. (1982). Learning new information from text: The role of prior knowledge and reading ability. *Journal of Reading Behavior, 14,* 243–261.

Lipson, M. Y. (1983). The influence of religious affiliation on children's memory for text information. *Reading Research Quarterly, 18,* 448–457.

Liu, L. G. (1990, April). *The use of causal questioning to promote narrative comprehension and memory.* Paper presented at the annual meeting of the American Educational Research Association, Boston.

Locke, E. A., & Latham, G. P. (1994). Goal setting theory. In H. F. O'Neil, Jr., &

M. Drillings (Eds.), *Motivation: Theory and research.* Hillsdale, NJ: Erlbaum.

Loftus, E. F. (1991). Made in memory: Distortions in recollection after misleading information. In G. H. Bower (Ed.), *The psychology of learning and motivation: Advances in research and theory* (Vol. 27). San Diego: Academic Press.

Loftus, E. F. (1992). When a lie becomes memory's truth: Memory distortion after exposure to misinformation. *Current Directions in Psychological Science, 1,* 121–123.

Loftus, E. F. (1993). The reality of repressed memories. *American Psychologist, 48,* 518–537.

Loftus, E. F., & Loftus, G. R. (1980). On the permanence of stored information in the human brain. *American Psychologist, 35,* 409–420.

Loftus, E. F., & Palmer, J. C. (1974). Reconstruction of automobile destruction: An example of the interaction between language and memory. *Journal of Verbal Learning and Verbal Behavior, 13,* 585–589.

Loftus, G. R., & Bell, S. M. (1975). Two types of information in picture memory. *Journal of Experimental Psychology: Human Learning and Perception, 104,* 103–113.

Loftus, G. R., & Loftus, E. F. (1976). *Human memory: The processing of information.* New York: Wiley.

Logue, A. W. (1979). Taste aversion and the generality of the laws of learning. *Psychological Bulletin, 86,* 276–296.

Lohman, D. (1993). Teaching and testing to develop fluid abilities. *Educational Researcher, 22,* 12–23.

Lorch, R. F., Jr., Lorch, E. P., & Inman, W. E. (1993). Effects of signaling topic structure on text recall. *Journal of Educational Psychology, 85,* 281–290.

Lou, Y., Abrami, P. C., Spence, J. C., Poulsen, C., Chambers, B., & d'Apollonia, S. (1996). Within-class grouping: A meta-analysis. *Review of Educational Research, 66,* 423–458.

Lovett, S. B., & Flavell, J. H. (1990). Understanding and remembering: Children's knowledge about the differential effects of strategy and task variables on comprehension and memorization. *Child Development, 61,* 1842–1858.

Lovitt, T. C., Guppy, T. E., & Blattner, J. E. (1969). The use of free-time contingency with fourth graders to increase spelling accuracy. *Behaviour Research and Therapy, 7,* 151–156.

Luchins, A. S. (1942). Mechanization in problem solving: The effect of Einstellung. *Psychological Monographs, 54* (Whole No. 248).

Luchins, A. S., & Luchins, E. H. (1950). New experimental attempts at preventing mechanization in problem solving. *Journal of General Psychology, 42,* 279–297.

Lueptow, L. B. (1984). *Adolescent sex roles and social change.* New York: Columbia University Press.

Lundeberg, M. A., & Fox, P. W. (1991). Do laboratory findings on test expectancy generalize to classroom outcomes? *Review of Educational Research, 61,* 94–106.

Macauley, D., Ryan, L., & Eich, E. (1993). Mood dependence in implicit and explicit memory. In P. Graf & M. E. J. Masson (Eds.), *Implicit memory: New directions in cognition, development, and neuropsychology.* Hillsdale, NJ: Erlbaum.

Mace, F. C., Belfiore, P. J., & Shea, M. C. (1989). Operant theory and research on self-regulation. In B. J. Zimmerman & D. H. Schunk (Eds.), *Self-regulated learning and academic achievement: Theory, research, and practice.* New York: Springer-Verlag.

Mace, F. C., Hock, M. L., Lalli, J. S., West, B. J., Belfiore, P., Pinter, E., & Brown, D. K. (1988). Behavioral momentum in the treatment of noncompliance. *Journal of Applied Behavior Analysis, 21,* 123–141.

Mace, F. C., & Kratochwill, T. R. (1988). Self-monitoring. In J. C. Witt, S. N. Elliott, & F. M. Gresham (Eds.), *Handbook of behavior therapy in education.* New York: Plenum Press.

Mace, F. C., Page, T. J., Ivancic, M. T., & O'Brien, S. (1986). Effectiveness of brief time-out with and without contingent delay: A comparative analysis. *Journal of Applied Behavior Analysis, 19,* 79–86.

Macfarlane, A. (1978). What a baby knows. *Human Nature, 1,* 74–81.

Machiels-Bongaerts, M., Schmidt, H. G., & Boshuizen, H. P. A. (1991, April). *The effects of prior knowledge activation on free recall and study time allocation.* Paper presented at the annual meeting of the American Educational Research Association, Chicago.

MacIver, D., Stipek, D. J., & Daniels, D. (1991). Explaining within-semester changes in student effort in junior high school and senior high school courses. *Journal of Educational Psychology, 83,* 201–211.

MacPherson, E. M., Candee, B. L., & Hohman, R. J. (1974). A comparison of three methods for eliminating disruptive lunchroom behavior. *Journal of Applied Behavior Analysis, 7,* 287–297.

Madsen, C. H., Becker, W. C., & Thomas, D. R. (1968). Rules, praise, and ignoring: Elements of elementary classroom control. *Journal of Applied Behavior Analysis, 1,* 139-150.

Maehr, M. L. (1984). Meaning and motivation: Toward a theory of personal investment. In R. Ames & C. Ames (Eds.), *Research on motivation in education: Vol. 1. Student motivation.* Orlando: Academic Press.

Mager, R. F. (1962). *Preparing instructional objectives.* Belmont, CA: Fearon.

Mager, R. F. (1972). *Goal analysis.* Belmont, CA: Fearon.

Mager, R. F. (1984). *Preparing instructional objectives* (2nd ed.). Belmont, CA: David S. Lake.

Magnusson, S. J., Boyle, R. A., & Templin, M. (1994, April). *Conceptual development: Re-examining knowledge construction in science.* Paper presented at the annual meeting of the American Educational Research Association, New Orleans.

Mahoney, M. J., & Thoresen, C. E. (1974). *Self-control: Power to the person.* Monterey, CA: Brooks-Cole.

Maier, N. R. F. (1945). Reasoning in humans III: The mechanisms of equivalent stimuli and of reasoning. *Journal of Experimental Psychology, 35,* 349-360.

Maier, N. R. F., & Janzen, J. C. (1968). Functional values as aids and distractors in problem solving. *Psychological Reports, 22,* 1021-1034.

Maier, S. F., & Seligman, M. E. P. (1976). Learned helplessness: Theory and evidence. *Journal of Experimental Psychology: General, 105,* 3-46.

Malone, T. W., & Lepper, M. R. (1987). Making learning fun: A taxonomy of intrinsic motivation for learning. In R. E. Snow & M. J. Farr (Eds.), *Aptitude, learning, and instruction: Vol. 3. Conative and affective process analyses.* Hillsdale, NJ: Erlbaum.

Mandler, G., & Pearlstone, Z. (1966). Free and constrained concept learning and subsequent recall. *Journal of Verbal Learning and Verbal Behavior, 5,* 126-131.

Mandler, J. M., & Johnson, N. S. (1976). Some of the thousand words a picture is worth. *Journal of Experimental Psychology: Human Learning and Memory, 2,* 529-540.

Mandler, J. M., & Parker, R. E. (1976). Memory for descriptive and spatial information in complex pictures. *Journal of Experimental Psychology: Human Learning and Memory, 2,* 38-48.

Mandler, J. M., & Ritchey, G. H. (1977). Long-term memory for pictures. *Journal of Experimental Psychology: Human Learning and Memory, 3,* 386-396.

Markman, E. (1979). Realizing that you don't understand: Elementary school children's awareness of inconsistencies. *Child Development, 50,* 643-655.

Marsh, H. W. (1986). Verbal and math self-concepts: An internal external frame of reference model. *American Educational Research Journal, 23,* 129-149.

Marsh, H. W. (1990). A multidimensional, hierarchical model of self-concept: Theoretical and empirical justification. *Educational Psychology Review, 2,* 77-172.

Marsh, H. W., & Craven, R. (1997). Academic self-concept: Beyond the dustbowl. In G. D. Phye (Ed.), *Handbook of classroom assessment: Learning, achievement, and adjustment.* San Diego: Academic Press.

Marshall, H. H. (Ed.). (1992). *Redefining student learning: Roots of educational change.* Norwood, NJ: Ablex.

Marshall, J. (1987). The effects of writing on students' understanding of literary texts. *Research in the Teaching of English, 21,* 30-63.

Martin, C. L., & Halverson, C. F. (1981). A schematic processing model of sex typing and stereotyping in children. *Child Development, 52,* 1119-1134.

Martin, I., & Levey, A. B. (1987). Learning what will happen next: Conditioning, evaluation, and cognitive processes. In G. Davey (Ed.), *Cognitive processes and Pavlovian conditioning in humans.* Chichester, UK: Wiley.

Martin, S. S., Brady, M. P., & Williams, R. E. (1991). Effects of toys on the social behavior of preschool children in integrated and nonintegrated groups: Investigation of a setting event. *Journal of Early Intervention, 15,* 153-161.

Martin, V. L., & Pressley, M. (1991). Elaborative-interrogation effects depend on the nature of the question. *Journal of Educational Psychology, 83,* 113-119.

Maslow, A. H. (1959). *New knowledge in human values.* New York: Harper & Row.

Maslow, A. H. (1973a). Self-actualizing people: A study of psychological health. In R. J. Lowry (Ed.), *Dominance, self-esteem, self-actualization: Germinal papers of A. H. Maslow.* Monterey, CA: Brooks-Cole.

Maslow, A. H. (1973b). Theory of human motivation. In R. J. Lowry (Ed.), *Dominance, self-esteem, self-actualization: Germinal papers of A. H. Maslow.* Monterey, CA: Brooks-Cole.

Maslow, A. H. (1987). *Motivation and personality* (3rd ed.). New York: Harper & Row.

Massey, C. M., & Gelman, R. (1988). Preschoolers' ability to decide whether a photographed unfamiliar object can move itself. *Developmental Psychology, 24,* 307-317.

Massialas, B. G., & Zevin, J. (1983). *Teaching creatively: Learning through discovery.* Malabar, FL: Robert E. Krieger.

Mastropieri, M. A., & Scruggs, T. E. (1989). Constructing more meaningful relationships: Mnemonic instruction for special populations. *Educational Psychology Review, 1,* 83-111.

Mastropieri, M. A., & Scruggs, T. E. (1992). Science for students with disabilities. *Review of Educational Research, 62,* 377-411.

Mastropieri, M. A., Scruggs, T. E., McLoone, B., & Levin, J. R. (1985). Facilitating learning disabled students' acquisition of science classifications. *Learning Disability Quarterly, 8,* 299-309.

Masur, E. F., McIntyre, C. W., & Flavell, J. H. (1973). Developmental changes in apportionment of study time among items in a multitrial free recall task. *Journal of Experimental Child Psychology, 15,* 237-246.

Mathews, J. R., Friman, P. C., Barone, V. J., Ross, L. V., & Christophersen, E. R. (1987). Decreasing dangerous infant behaviors through parent instruction. *Journal of Applied Behavior Analysis, 20,* 165-169.

Maurer, A. (1974). Corporal punishment. *American Psychologist, 29,* 614-626.

Mayer, G. R., & Butterworth, T. N. (1979). A preventive approach to school violence and vandalism: An experimental study. *Personnel Guidance Journal, 57,* 436-441.

Mayer, R. E. (1974). Acquisition processes and resilience under varying testing conditions for structurally different problem solving procedures. *Journal of Educational Psychology, 66,* 644-656.

Mayer, R. E. (1975). Information processing variables in learning to solve problems. *Review of Educational Research, 45,* 525-541.

Mayer, R. E. (1977). *Thinking and problem solving: An introduction to human recognition and learning.* Glenview, IL: Scott, Foresman.

Mayer, R. E. (1979a). Can advance organizers influence meaningful learning? *Review of Educational Research, 49,* 371-383.

Mayer, R. E. (1979b). Twenty years of research on advance organizers:

Assimilation theory is still the best predictor of results. *Instructional Science, 8,* 133-167.

Mayer, R. E. (1982). Memory for algebra story problems. *Journal of Educational Psychology, 74,* 199-216.

Mayer, R. E. (1983a). Can you repeat that? Qualitative effects of repetition and advance organizers on learning from science prose. *Journal of Educational Psychology, 75,* 40-49.

Mayer, R. E. (1983b). *Thinking, problem solving, and cognition.* New York: W. H. Freeman.

Mayer, R. E. (1984). Aids to text comprehension. *Educational Psychologist, 19,* 30-42.

Mayer, R. E. (1985). Implications of cognitive psychology for instruction in mathematical problem solving. In E. A. Silver (Ed.), *Teaching and learning mathematical problem solving: Multiple research perspectives.* Hillsdale, NJ: Erlbaum.

Mayer, R. E. (1986). Mathematics. In R. F. Dillon & R. J. Sternberg (Eds.), *Cognition and instruction.* San Diego: Academic Press.

Mayer, R. E. (1987). *Educational psychology: A cognitive approach.* Boston: Little, Brown.

Mayer, R. E. (1989a). Models for understanding. *Review of Educational Research, 59,* 43-64.

Mayer, R. E. (1989b). Teaching for thinking: Research on the teachability of thinking skills. In I. S. Cohen (Ed.), *The G. Stanley Hall Lecture Series* (Vol. 9). Washington, DC: American Psychological Association.

Mayer, R. E. (1992). *Thinking, problem solving, cognition* (2nd ed.). New York: W. H. Freeman.

Mayer, R. . (1996a). Learners as information processors: Legacies and limitations of educational psychology's second metaphor. *Educational Psychologist, 31,* 151-161.

Mayer, R. E. (1996b). Learning strategies for making sense out of expository text: The SOI model for guiding three cognitive processes in knowledge construction. *Educational Psychology Review, 8,* 357-371.

Mayer, R. E., & Bromage, B. (1980). Different recall protocols for technical texts due to advance organizers. *Journal of Educational Psychology, 72,* 209-225.

Mayer, R. E., & Greeno, J. G. (1972). Structural differences between learning outcomes produced by different instructional methods. *Journal of Educational Psychology, 63,* 165-173.

Mayer, R. E., Steinhoff, K., Bower, G., & Mars, R. (1994, April). *Using illustrations to foster understanding of science text.* Paper presented at the annual meeting of the American Educational Research Association, New Orleans.

Mayer, R. E., & Wittrock, M. C. (1996). Problem-solving transfer. In D. C. Berliner & R. C. Calfee (Eds.), *Handbook of educational psychology.* New York: Macmillan.

Mayzner, M. S., & Tresselt, M. E. (1958). Anagram solution times: A function of letter-order and word frequency. *Journal of Experimental Psychology, 56,* 350-376.

Mayzner, M. S., & Tresselt, M. E. (1966). Anagram solution times: A function of multiple-solution anagrams. *Journal of Experimental Psychology, 71,* 66-73.

Mazur, J. E. (1993). Predicting the strength of a conditioned reinforcer: Effects of delay and uncertainty. *Current Directions in Psychological Science, 2,* 70-74.

McAllister, W. R., & McAllister, D. E. (1965). Variables influencing the conditioning and the measurement of acquired fear. In W. F. Prokasy (Ed.), *Classical conditioning.* New York: Appleton-Century-Crofts.

McAndrew, D. A. (1983). Underlining and notetaking: Some suggestions from research. *Journal of Reading, 27,* 103-108.

McAshan, H. H. (1979). *Competency-based education and behavioral objectives.* Englewood Cliffs, NJ: Educational Technology.

McCallin, R. C., Ormrod, J. E., & Cochran, K. C. (1997, March). *Algorithmic and heuristic learning sets and their relationship to cognitive structure.* Paper presented at the annual meeting of the American Educational Research Association, Chicago.

McCaslin, M., & Good, T. L. (1996). The informal curriculum. In D. C. Berliner & R. C. Calfee (Eds.), *Handbook of educational psychology.* New York: Macmillan.

McCauley, R. N. (1987). The role of theories in a theory of concepts. In U. Neisser (Ed.), *Concepts and conceptual development: Ecological and intellectual factors in categorization.* Cambridge, UK: Cambridge University Press.

McClelland, D. C. (1984). *Motives, personality, and society: Selected papers.* New York: Praeger.

McClelland, D. C., Atkinson, J. W., Clark, R. A., & Lowell, E. L. (1953). *The achievement motive.* New York: Appleton-Century-Crofts.

McClelland, J. L., & Rumelhart, D. E. (1986). *Parallel distributed processing* (Vol. 2). Cambridge, MA: M.I.T. Press.

McCloskey, M. E., & Glucksberg, S. (1978). Natural categories: Well-defined or fuzzy sets? *Memory and Cognition, 6,* 462-472.

McCombs, B. L. (1988). Motivational skills training: Combining metacognitive, cognitive, and affective learning strategies. In C. E. Weinstein, E. T. Goetz, & P. A. Alexander (Eds.), *Learning and study strategies: Issues in assessment, instruction, and evaluation.* San Diego: Harcourt Brace Jovanovich.

McCombs, B. L. (1996). Alternative perspectives for motivation. In L. Baker, P. Afflerbach, & D. Reinking (Eds.), *Developing engaged readers in school and home communities.* Hillsdale, NJ: Erlbaum.

McCord, W., McCord, J., & Zola, I. K. (1959). *Origins of crime: A new evaluation of the Cambridge-Somerville Youth Study.* New York: Columbia University Press.

McCoy, L. P. (1990, April). *Correlates of mathematics anxiety.* Paper presented at the annual meeting of the American Educational Research Association, Boston.

McCrary, J. W., & Hunter, W. S. (1953). Serial position curves in verbal learning. *Science, 117,* 131-134.

McCutchen, D. (1996). A capacity theory of writing: Working memory in composition. *Educational Psychology Review, 8,* 299-325.

McDaniel, M. A., & Einstein, G. O. (1989). Material-appropriate processing: A contextualist approach to reading and studying strategies. *Educational Psychology Review, 1,* 113-145.

McDaniel, M. A., & Masson, M. E. J. (1985). Altering memory representations through retrieval. *Journal of Experimental Psychology: Learning, Memory, and Cognition, 11,* 371-385.

McDaniel, M. A., & Schlager, M. S. (1990). Discovery learning and transfer of problem-solving skills. *Cognition and Instruction, 7,* 129-159.

McDevitt, T. M., Sheehan, E. P., Cooney, J. B., Smith, H. V., & Walker, I. (1994). Conceptions of listening, learning processes, and epistemologies held by American, Irish, and Australian university students. *Learning and Individual Differences, 6,* 231-256.

McDevitt, T. M., Spivey, N., Sheehan, E. P., Lennon, R., & Story, R. (1990). Children's beliefs about listening: Is it enough to be still and quiet? *Child Development, 55,* 810-820.

McGee, L. M. (1992). An exploration of meaning construction in first graders' grand conversations. In C. K. Kinzer & D. J. Leu (Eds.), *Literacy research, theory, and practice: Views from many perspectives.* Chicago: National Reading Conference.

McGeoch, J. A. (1942). *The psychology of human learning.* New York: David McKay.

McHale, M. A., Brooks, Z., & Wolach, A. H. (1982). Incentive shifts with different massed and spaced trial cues. *Psychological Record, 32,* 85-92.

McInerney, D. M., Roche, L. A., McInerney, V., & Marsh, H. W. (1997). Cultural perspectives on school motivation: The relevance and application of goal theory. *American Educational Research Journal, 34,* 207-236.

McKeachie, W. J. (1961). Motivation, teaching methods, and college learning. In M. R. Jones (Ed.), *Nebraska symposium on motivation.* Lincoln, NE: University of Nebraska Press.

McKeachie, W. J., Lin, Y., Milholland, J., & Isaacson, R. (1966). Student affiliation motives, teacher warmth, and academic achievement. *Journal of Personality and Social Psychology, 4,* 457-461.

McKenzie, H. S., Clark, M., Wolf, M. M., Kothera, R., & Benson, C. (1968). Behavior modification of children with learning disabilities using grades as tokens and allowances as back up reinforcers. *Exceptional Children, 34,* 745-752.

McKeown, M. G., & Beck, I. L. (1990). The assessment and characterization of young learners' knowledge of a topic in history. *American Educational Research Journal, 27,* 688-726.

McLaughlin, T. F., & Malaby, J. (1972). Intrinsic reinforcers in a classroom token economy. *Journal of Applied Behavior Analysis, 5,* 263-270.

McLaughlin, T. F., & Williams, R. L. (1988). The token economy. In J. C. Witt, S. N. Elliott, & F. M. Gresham (Eds.), *Handbook of behavior therapy in education.* New York: Plenum Press.

McLeod, D. B., & Adams, V. M. (Eds.). (1989). *Affect and mathematical problem solving: A new perspective.* New York: Springer-Verlag.

McNamara, E. (1987). Behavioural approaches in the secondary school. In K. Wheldall (Ed.), *The behaviourist in the classroom.* London: Allen & Unwin.

Medin, D. L. (1989). Concepts and conceptual structure. *American Psychologist, 44,* 1469-1481.

Meece, J. L. (1994). The role of motivation in self-regulated learning. In D. H. Schunk & B. J. Zimmerman (Eds.), *Self-regulation of learning and performance: Issues and educational applications.* Hillsdale, NJ: Erlbaum.

Meece, J. L., Wigfield, A., & Eccles, J. S. (1990). Predictors of math anxiety and its influence on young adolescents' course enrollment intentions and performance in mathematics. *Journal of Educational Psychology, 82,* 60-70.

Meehl, P. E. (1950). On the circularity of the law of effect. *Psychological Bulletin, 47,* 52-75.

Mehan, H. (1979). *Social organization in the classroom.* Cambridge, MA: Harvard University Press.

Mehrens, W. A. (1992). Using performance assessment for accountability purposes. *Educational Measurement: Issues and Practices, 11* (1), 3-9.

Meichenbaum, D. (1977). *Cognitive-behavior modification: An integrative approach.* New York: Plenum Press.

Meichenbaum, D. (1985). Teaching thinking: A cognitive-behavioral perspective. In S. F. Chipman, J. W. Segal, & R. Glaser (Eds.), *Thinking and learning skills: Vol. 2. Research and open questions.* Hillsdale, NJ: Erlbaum.

Meloth, M. S., & Deering, P. D. (1994). Task talk and task awareness under different cooperative learning conditions. *American Educational Research Journal, 31,* 138-165.

Melton, A. W. (1963). Implications of short-term memory for a general theory of memory. *Journal of Verbal Learning and Verbal Behavior, 2,* 1-21.

Melton, A. W., & Irwin, J. M. (1940). The influence of degree of interpolated learning on retroactive inhibition and the overt transfer of specific responses. *American Journal of Psychology, 53,* 173-203.

Melton, R. F. (1978). Resolution of conflicting claims concerning the effect of behavioral objectives on student learning. *Review of Educational Research, 48,* 291-302.

Menec, V. H., & Schonwetter, D. J. (1994, April). *Action control, motivation, and academic achievement.* Paper presented at the annual meeting of the American Educational Research Association, New Orleans.

Merrill, M. D., & Tennyson, R. D. (1977). *Concept teaching: An instructional design guide.* Englewood Cliffs, NJ: Educational Technology.

Merrill, M. D., & Tennyson, R. D. (1978). Concept classification and classification errors as a function of relationships between examples and non-examples. *Improving Human Performance, 7,* 351-364.

Mervis, C. B. (1987). Child-basic object categories and early lexical development. In U. Neisser (Ed.), *Concepts and conceptual development: Ecological and intellectual factors in categorization.* Cambridge, UK: Cambridge University Press.

Messick, S. (1994). The interplay of evidence and consequences in the validation of performance assessments. *Educational Researcher, 23* (2), 13-23.

Metz, K. E. (1995). Reassessment of developmental constraints on children's science instruction. *Review of Educational Research, 65,* 93-127.

Meyer, B. J. F., Brandt, D. H., & Bluth, G. J. (1980). Use of top-level structure in text: Key for reading comprehension of ninth-grade students. *Reading Research Quarterly, 16,* 72-103.

Meyer, D. K., Turner, J. C., & Spencer, C. A. (1994, April). *Academic risk taking and motivation in an elementary mathematics classroom.* Paper presented at the annual meeting of the American Educational Research Association, New Orleans.

Michael, J. L. (1974). The essential components of effective instruction and why most college teaching is not. In F. S. Keller & E. Ribes-Inesta (Eds.), *Behavior modification: Applicaitons to education.* New York: Academic Press.

Mikulincer, M. (1994). *Human learned helplessness: A coping perspective.* New York: Plenum Press.

Miller, D. L., & Kelley, M. L. (1994). The use of goal setting and contingency contracting for improving children's homework performance. *Journal of Applied Behavior Analysis, 27,* 73-84.

Miller, G. A. (1956). The magical number seven, plus or minus two: Some limits on our capacity for processing information. *Psychological Review, 63,* 81-97.

Miller, G. A., Galanter, E., & Pribram, K. H. (1960). *Plans and the structure of behavior.* New York: Holt, Rinehart & Winston.

Miller, J. G. (1986). Early cross-cultural commonalities in social explanation. *Developmental Psychology, 22,* 514-520.

Miller, N. E. (1948). Studies of fear as an acquirable drive: I. Fear as motivation and fear-reduction as reinforcement in the learning of new responses. *Journal of Experimental Psychology, 38,* 89-101.

Miller, N. E., & Dollard, J. C. (1941). *Social learning and imitation.* New Haven, CT: Yale University Press.

Miller, R. L., Brickman, P., & Bolen, D. (1975). Attribution versus persuasion as a means for modifying behavior. *Journal of Personality and Social Psychology, 31,* 430-441.

Miller, R. R.., & Barnet, R. C. (1993). The role of time in elementary associations. *Current Directions in Psychological Science, 2,* 106-111.

Millroy, W. L. (1991). An ethnographic study of the mathematical ideas of a group of carpenters. *Learning and Individual Differences, 3,* 1-25.

Mintzes, J. J., Trowbridge, J. E., Arnaudin, M. W., & Wandersee, J. H. (1991). Children's biology: Studies on conceptual development in the life sciences. In S. M. Glynn, R. H. Yeany, & B. K. Britton (Eds.), *The psychology of* Erlbaum.

Mintzes, J. J., Wandersee, J. H., & Novak, J. D. (1997). Meaningful learning in science: The human constructivist perspective. In G. D. Phye (Ed.), *Handbook of academic learning: Construction of knowledge.* San Diego: Academic Press.

Mischel, W., & Grusec, J. E. (1966). Determinants of the rehearsal and transmission of neutral and aversive behaviors. *Journal of Personality and Social Psychology, 3,* 197-205.

Mitchell, J. B. (1989). Current theories on expert and novice thinking: A full faculty considers the implications for legal education. *Journal of Legal Education, 39,* 275-297.

Mohatt, G., & Erickson, F. (1981). Cultural differences in teaching styles in an Odawa school: A sociolinguistic approach. In H. T. Trueba, G. P. Guthrie, & K. H. Au (Eds.), *Culture and the bilingual classroom: Studies in classroom ethnography.* Rowley, MA: Newbury House.

Moles, O. C. (Ed.). (1990). *Student discipline strategies: Research and practice.* Albany, NY: State University of New York Press.

Moletzsky, B. (1974). Behavior recording as treatment: A brief note. *Behavior Therapy, 5,* 107-111.

Mooney, C. M. (1957). Age in the development of closure ability in children. *Canadian Journal of Psychology, 11,* 219-226.

Moray, N., Bates, A., & Barnett, R. (1965). Experiments on the four-eared man. *Journal of the Acoustical Society of America, 38,* 196-201.

Morgan, M. (1984). Reward-induced decrements and increments in intrinsic motivation. *Review of Educational Research, 54,* 5-30.

Morgan, M. (1985). Self-monitoring of attained subgoals in private study. *Journal of Educational Psychology, 77,* 623-630.

Morris, C. D., Bransford, J. D., & Franks, J. J. (1977). Levels of processing versus transfer appropriate processing. *Journal of Verbal Learning and Verbal Behavior, 16,* 519-533.

Morris, E. K. (1982). Some relationships between interbehavioral psychology and radical behaviorism. *Behaviorism, 10,* 187-216.

Morris, P. (1977). Practical strategies for human learning and remembering. In M. J. A. Howe (Ed.), *Adult learning: Psychological research and applications.* London: Wiley.

Morris, R. J. (1985). *Behavior modification with exceptional children: Principles and practices.* Glenview, IL: Scott, Foresman.

Morris, R. J., Kratochwill, T. R., & Aldridge, K. (1988). Fears and phobias. In J. C. Witt, S. N. Elliott, & F. M. Gresham (Eds.), *Handbook of behavior therapy in education.* New York: Plenum Press.

Mowrer, O. H. (1938). Preparatory set (expectancy): A determinant in motivation and learning. *Psychological Review, 45,* 62-91.

Mowrer, O. H. (1939). A stimulus-response analysis and its role as a reinforcing agent. *Psychological Review, 46,* 553-565.

Mowrer, O. H. (1956). Two-factor learning theory reconsidered, with special reference to secondary reinforcement and the concept of habit. *Psychological Review, 63,* 114-128.

Mowrer, O. H. (1960). *Learning theory and behavior.* New York: Wiley.

Mowrer, O. H., & Lamoreaux, R. R. (1942). Avoidance conditioning and signal duration: A study of secondary motivation and reward. *Psychological Monographs, 54* (Whole No. 247).

Mueller, J. H. (1980). Test anxiety and the encoding and retrieval of information. In I. G. Sarason (Ed.), *Test anxiety: Theory, research, and applications.* Hillsdale, NJ: Erlbaum.

Murnane, R. J., & Raizen, S. A. (Eds.). (1988). *Improving indicators of the quality of science and mathematics education in grades K-12.* Washington, DC: National Academy Press.

Murray, C. B., & Jackson, J. S. (1982/1983). The conditioned failure model of black educational underachievement. *Humboldt Journal of Social Relations, 10,* 276-300.

Murray, F. B. (1978). Teaching strategies and conservation training. In A. M. Lesgold, J. W. Pellegrino, S. D. Fokkema, & R. Glaser (Eds.), *Cognitive psychology and instruction.* New York: Plenum Press.

Myers, J. L., & Duffy, S. A. (1990). Causal inferences and text memory. In A. C. Graessner & G. H. Bower (Eds.), *Inferences and text comprehension. The psychology of learning and motivation: Advances in research and theory* (Vol. 25). Orlando: Academic Press.

Natriello, G. (1987). The impact of evaluation processes on students. *Educational Psychologist, 22,* 155-175.

Natriello, G., & Dornbusch, S. M. (1984). *Teacher evaluative standards and student effort.* New York: Longman.

Naveh-Benjamin, M. (1991). A comparison of training programs intended for different types of text-anxious students: Further support for an information-processing model. *Journal of Educational Psychology, 83,* 134-139.

Neisser, U. (1967). *Cognitive psychology.* New York: Appleton-Century-Crofts.

Neisser, U. (1981). John Dean's memory: A case study. *Cognition, 9,* 1-22.

Neisser, U. (Ed.). (1987). *Concepts and conceptual development: Ecological and intellectual factors in categorization.* Cambridge, UK: Cambridge University Press.

Neisser, U., & Harsch, N. (1992). Phantom flashbulbs: False recollections of hearing the news about *Challenger.* In E. Winograd & U. Neisser (Eds.), *Affect and accuracy in recall: Studies of "flashbulb" memories.* Cambridge, UK: Cambridge University Press.

Neisser, U., & Weene, P. (1962). Hierarchies in concept formation. *Journal of Experimental Psychology, 64,* 644-645.

Nelson, K. (1993a). Explaining the emergence of autobiographical memory in early childhood. In A. F. Collins, S. E. Gathercole, M. A. Conway, & P. E. Morris (Eds.), *Theories of memory.* Hove, UK: Erlbaum.

Nelson, K. (1993b). The psychological and social origins of autobiographical memory. *Psychological Science, 4,* 7-14.

Nelson, L. J., & Miller, D. T. (1995). The distinctiveness effect in social categorization: You are what makes you unusual. *Psychological Science, 6,* 246-249.

Nelson, T. O. (1971). Savings and forgetting from long-term memory. *Journal of Verbal Learning and Verbal Behavior, 10,* 568-576.

Nelson, T. O. (1977). Repetition and depth of processing. *Journal of Verbal Learning and Verbal Behavior, 16,* 151-171.

Nelson, T. O. (1978). Detecting small amounts of information in memory: Savings for nonrecognized items. *Journal of Experimental Psychology: Human Learning and Memory, 4,* 453-468.

Nelson, T. O., & Dunlosky, J. (1991). When people's judgments of learning (JOLs) are extremely accurate at predicting subsequent recall: The "delayed-JOL effect." *Psychological Science, 2,* 267-270.

Nelson, T. O., & Rothbart, R. (1972). Acoustic savings for items forgotten from long-term memory. *Journal of Experimental Psychology, 93,* 357-360.

Nenniger, P. (1992). Task motivation: An interaction between the cognitive and content-oriented dimensions in learning. In K. A. Renninger, S. Hidi, & A. Krapp (Eds.), *The role of interest in learning and development.* Hillsdale, NJ: Erlbaum.

Neumann, P. G. (1974). An attribute frequency model for the abstraction of prototypes. *Memory and Cognition, 2,* 241-248.

Neumann, P. G. (1977). Visual prototype formation with discontinuous representation of dimensions of variability. *Memory and Cognition, 5,* 187-197.

Nevin, J. A., Mandell, C., & Atak, J. R. (1983). The analysis of behavioral momentum. *Journal of the Experimental Analysis of Behavior, 39,* 49-59.

Newby, T. J., Ertmer, P. A., & Stepich, D. A. (1994, April). *Instructional analogies and the learning of concepts.* Paper presented at the annual meeting of the American Educational Research Association, New Orleans.

Newby, T. J., & Stepich, D. A. (1987). Learning abstract concepts: The use of analogies as a mediational strategy. *Journal of Instructional Development, 10* (2), 20-26.

Newell, A., Shaw, J. C., & Simon, H. A. (1958). Elements of a theory of human problem solving. *Psychological Review, 65,* 151-166.

Newell, A., & Simon, H. A. (1972). *Human problem solving.* Englewood Cliffs, NJ: Prentice Hall.

Newman, R. S., & Schwager, M. T. (1995). Students' help seeking during problem solving: Effects of grade, goal, and prior achievement. *American Educational Research Journal, 32,* 352-376.

Newmann, F. M., & Wehlage, G. G. (1993). Five standards of authentic instruction. *Educational Leadership, 50* (7), 8-12.

Nicholls, J. G. (1984). Conceptions of ability and achievement motivation. In R. Ames & C. Ames (Eds.), *Research on motivation in education: Vol. 1. Student motivation.* Orlando: Academic Press.

Nicholls, J. G. (1990). What is ability and why are we mindful of it? A developmental perspective. In R. J. Sternberg & J. Kolligian (Eds.), *Competence considered.* New Haven, CT: Yale University Press.

Nicholls, J. G. (1992). Students as educational theorists. In D. Schunk & J. L. Meece (Eds.), *Student perception in the classroom.* Hillsdale, NJ: Erlbaum.

Nickerson, R. S. (1989). New directions in educational assessment. *Educational Researcher, 18* (9), 3-7.

Nisbett, R. E., & Bellows, N. (1977). Verbal reports about causal influences on social judgments: Private access versus public theories. *Journal of Personality and Social Psychology, 35,* 613-624.

Nisbett, R. E., & Wilson, T. D. (1977). Telling more than we can know: Verbal reports on mental processes. *Psychological Review, 84,* 231-259.

Nist, S. L., Simpson, M. L., Olejnik, S., & Mealey, D. L. (1991). The relation between self-selected study processes and test performance. *American Educational Research Journal, 28,* 849-874.

Noddings, N. (1985). Small groups as a setting for research on mathematical problem solving. In E. A. Silver (Ed.), *Teaching and learning mathematical problem solving: Multiple research perspectives.* Hillsdale, NJ: Erlbaum.

Nolen, S. B. (1988). Reasons for studying: Motivational orientations and study strategies. *Cognition and Instruction, 5,* 269-287.

Nolen, S. B. (1996). Why study? How reasons for learning influence strategy selection. *Educational Psychology Review, 8,* 335-355.

Norman, D. A. (1969). *Memory and attention: An introduction to human information processing.* New York: Wiley.

Norman, D. A. (1976). *Memory and attention: An introduction to human information processing* (2nd ed.). New York: Wiley.

Norman, D. A. (1980). Cognitive engineering and education. In D. T. Tuma & F. Reif (Eds.), *Problem solving and education: Issues in teaching and research.* Hillsdale, NJ: Erlbaum.

Norman, D. A., & Bobrow, D. G. (1975). On data-limited and resource-limited processes. *Cognitive Psychology, 7,* 44-64.

Norman, D. A., & Rumelhart, D. E. (1975). *Explorations in cognition.* San Francisco: W. H. Freeman.

Northup, J., Broussard, C., Jones, K., George, T., Vollmer, T. R., & Herring, M. (1995). The differential effects of teachers and peer attention on the disruptive classroom behavior of three children with a diagnosis of attention deficit hyperactivity disorder. *Journal of Applied Behavior Analysis, 28,* 227-228.

Novak, J. D., & Gowin, D. B. (1984). *Learning how to learn.* Cambridge, UK: Cambridge University Press.

Novak, J. D., & Musonda, D. (1991). A twelve-year longitudinal study of science concept learning. *American Educational Research Journal, 28,* 117-153.

Novick, L. R. (1988). Analogical transfer, problem similarity, and expertise. *Journal of Experimental Psychology: Learning, Memory, and Cognition, 14,* 510-520.

Nungester, R. J., & Duchastel, P. C. (1982). Testing versus review: Effects on retention. *Journal of Educational Psychology, 74,* 18-22.

Nussbaum, J. (1985). The earth as a cosmic body. In R. Driver (Ed.), *Children's ideas of science.* Philadelphia: Open University Press.

Oakhill, J. (1993). Children's difficulties in reading comprehension. *Educational Psychology Review, 5,* 223-237.

Oatley, K., & Nundy, S. (1996). Rethinking the role of emotions in education. In D. R. Olson & N. Torrance (Eds.), *The handbook of education and human development: New models of learning, teaching, and schooling.* Cambridge, MA: Blackwell Publishers.

Oden, G. C. (1987). Concept, knowledge, and thought. *Annual Review of Psychology, 38,* 203-227.

O'Donnell, A. M., & O'Kelly, J. (1994). Learning from peers: Beyond the rhetoric of positive results. *Educational Psychology Review, 6,* 321-349.

Ohlsson, S. (1983). On natural and technical knowledge domains. *Scandinavian Journal of Psychology, 25,* 89–91.

Olds, J., & Milner, P. (1954). Positive reinforcement produced by electrical stimulation of septal area and other regions of rat brain. *Journal of Comparative and Physiological Psychology, 47,* 419–427.

O'Leary, K. D., & Becker, W. C. (1967). Behavior modification of an adjustment class: A token reinforcement program. *Exceptional Children, 33,* 637–642.

O'Leary, K. D., Kaufman, K. F., Kass, R. E., & Drabman, R. S. (1970). The effects of loud and soft reprimands on the behavior of disruptive students. *Exceptional Children, 37,* 145–155.

O'Leary, K. D., & O'Leary, S. G. (Eds.). (1972). *Classroom management: The successful use of behavior modification.* New York: Pergamon Press.

Onosko, J. J. (1996). Exploring issues with students despite the barriers. *Social Education, 60* (1), 22–27.

Onosko, J. J., & Newmann, F. M. (1994). Creating more thoughtful learning environments. In J. N. Mangieri & C. C. Block (Eds.), *Creating powerful thinking in teachers and students: Diverse perspectives.* Fort Worth, TX: Harcourt Brace.

Ormrod, J. E. (1979). Cognitive processes in the solution of three-term series problems. *American Journal of Psychology, 92,* 235–255.

Ormrod, J. E. (1985). Proofreading *The Cat in the Hat*: Evidence for different reading styles of good and poor spellers. *Psychological Reports, 57,* 863–867.

Ormrod, J. E. (1986a). Differences between good and poor spellers in reading style and short-term memory. *Visible Language, 20,* 437–447.

Ormrod, J. E. (1986b). Learning to spell: Three studies at the university level. *Research in the Teaching of English, 20,* 160–173.

Ormrod, J. E. (1986c). Learning to spell while reading: A follow-up study. *Perceptual and Motor Skills, 63,* 652–654.

Ormrod, J. E. (1995). *Educational psychology: Principles and applications.* Upper Saddle River, NJ: Merrill/Prentice Hall.

Ormrod, J. E., Jackson, D. L., & Salih, D. J. (1996, April). *The nature of students' metacognitive processes, as reflected in their self-generated questions and class notes.* Paper presented at the annual meeting of the American Educational Research Association, New York.

Ormrod, J. E., & Jenkins, L. (1988, April). *Study strategies for learning spelling: What works and what does not.* Paper presented at the annual meeting of the American Educational Research Association, New Orleans.

Ormrod, J. E., Ormrod, R. K., Wagner, E. D., & McCallin, R. C. (1988). Reconceptualizing map learning. *American Journal of Psychology, 101,* 425–433.

Ormrod, J. E., & Wagner, E. D. (1987, October). *Spelling conscience in undergraduate students: Ratings of spelling accuracy and dictionary use.* Paper presented at the annual meeting of the Northern Rocky Mountain Educational Research Association, Park City, UT.

Ornstein, R. E. (1972). *The psychology of consciousness.* San Francisco: W. H. Freeman.

Osborn, A. F. (1963). *Applied imagination* (3rd ed.). New York: Scribner.

Osborne, J. G. (1969). Free-time as a reinforcer in the management of classroom behavior. *Journal of Applied Behavior Analysis, 2,* 113–118.

Osgood, C. E. (1949). The similarity paradox in human learning: A resolution. *Psychological Review, 56,* 132–143.

O'Sullivan, J. T., & Joy, R. M. (1990, April). *Children's theories about reading difficulty: A developmental study.* Paper presented at the annual meeting of the American Educational Research Association, Boston.

Otero, J., & Kintsch, W. (1992). Failures to detect contradictions in a text: What readers believe versus what they read. *Psychological Science, 3,* 229–235.

Overmier, J. B., & Lawry, J. A. (1979). Pavlovian conditioning and the mediation of behavior. In G. H. Bower (Ed.), *The psychology of learning and motivation* (Vol. 13). New York: Academic Press.

Owen, S., Blount, H., & Moscow, H. (1978). *Educational psychology: An introduction.* Boston: Little, Brown.

Owens, J., Bower, G. H., & Black, J. B. (1979). The "soap opera" effect in story recall. *Memory and Cognition, 7,* 185–191.

Owens, R. E., Jr. (1996). *Language development* (4th ed.). Boston: Allyn & Bacon.

Packard, R. G. (1970). The control of "classroom attention": A group contingency for complex behavior. *Journal of Applied Behavior Analysis, 3,* 13–28.

Paige, J. M., & Simon, H. A. (1966). Cognitive processes in solving algebra word problems. In B. Kleinmuntz (Ed.), *Problem solving.* New York: Wiley.

Paivio, A. (1963). Learning of adjective-noun paired associates as a function of adjective-noun word order and noun abstractness. *Canadian Journal of Psychology, 17,* 370–379.

Paivio, A. (1971). *Imagery and verbal processes.* New York: Holt, Rinehart & Winston.

Paivio, A. (1975). Coding distinctions and repetition effects in memory. In G. H. Bower (Ed.), *The psychology of learning and motivation* (Vol. 9). New York: Academic Press.

Paivio, A. (1986). *Mental representations: A dual-coding approach.* New York: Oxford University Press.

Pajares, F. (1996). Self-efficacy beliefs in academic settings. *Review of Educational Research, 66,* 543–578.

Palardy, J. M. (1969). What teachers believe—what children achieve. *Elementary School Journal, 69,* 370–374.

Palermo, D. S. (1973). More about less: A study of language comprehension. *Journal of Verbal Learning and Verbal Behavior, 12,* 211–221.

Palincsar, A. S. (1986, April). *Interactive cognition to promote listening comprehension.* Paper presented at the annual meeting of the American Educational Research Association, San Francisco.

Palincsar, A. S., Anderson, C., & David, Y. M. (1993). Pursuing scientific literacy in the middle grades through collaborative problem solving. *Elementary School Journal, 93,* 643–658.

Palincsar, A. S., & Brown, A. L. (1984). Reciprocal teaching of comprehension-fostering and comprehension-monitoring activities. *Cognition and Instruction, 1,* 117–175.

Palincsar, A. S., & Brown, A. L. (1989). Classroom dialogues to promote self-regulated comprehension. In J. Brophy (Ed.), *Advances in research on teaching* (Vol. 1). Greenwich, CT: JAI Press.

Pallock, L., & Surber, J. R. (1997, March). *Effect of topic frequency and importance on recall of text.* Paper presented at the annual meeting of the American Educational Research Association, Chicago.

Palmer, D. J., & Goetz, E. T. (1988). Selection and use of study strategies: The role of the studier's beliefs about self and strategies. In C. E. Weinstein, E. T. Goetz, & P. A. Alexander (Eds.), *Learning and study strategies: Issues in assessment, instruction, and evaluation.* San Diego: Academic Press.

Paris, S. G. (1988). Models and metaphors of learning strategies. In C. E. Weinstein, E. T. Goetz, & P. A. Alexander (Eds.), *Learning and study strategies: Issues in assessment, instruction, and evaluation*. San Diego: Academic Press.

Paris, S. G. (1990, April). Discussant's comments. In B. McCombs (Chair), *Theoretical perspectives on socialization and children's development of self-regulated learning*. Symposium presented at the annual meeting of the American Educational Research Association, Boston.

Paris, S. G., & Ayres, L. R. (1994). *Becoming reflective students and teachers with portfolios and authentic assessment*. Washington, DC: American Psychological Association.

Paris, S. G., & Byrnes, J. P. (1989). The constructivist approach to self-regulation and learning in the classroom. In B. J. Zimmerman & D. H. Schunk (Eds.), *Self-regulated learning and academic achievement: Theory, research, and practice*. New York: Springer-Verlag.

Paris, S. G., & Cunningham, A. E. (1996). Children becoming students. In D. C. Berliner & R. C. Calfee (Eds.), *Handbook of educational psychology*. New York: Macmillan.

Paris, S. G., Lawton, T. A., Turner, J. C., & Roth, J. L. (1991). A developmental perspective on standardized achievement testing. *Educational Researcher, 20* (5), 12-20, 40.

Paris, S. G., & Lindauer, B. K. (1976). The role of inference in children's comprehension and memory. *Cognitive Psychology, 8*, 217-227.

Paris, S. G., Newman, R. S., & McVey, K. A. (1982). Learning the functional significance of mnemonic actions: A microgenetic study of strategy acquisition. *Journal of Experimental Child Psychology, 34*, 490-509.

Paris, S. G., & Turner, J. C. (1994). Situated motivation. In P. R. Pintrich, D. R. Brown, & C. E. Weinstein (Eds.), *Student motivation, cognition, and learning: Essays in honor of Wilbert J. McKeachie*. Hillsdale, NJ: Erlbaum.

Paris, S. G., & Winograd, P. (1990). How metacognition can promote academic learning and instruction. In B. F. Jones & L. Idol (Eds.), *Dimensions of thinking and cognitive instruction*. Hillsdale, NJ: Erlbaum.

Park, O. (1984). Example comparison strategy versus attribute identification strategy in concept learning. *American Educational Research Journal, 21*, 145-162.

Parke, R. D. (1972). Some effects of punishment on children's behavior. In W. W. Hartup (Ed.), *The young child* (Vol. 2). Washington, DC: National Association for the Education of Young Children.

Parke, R. D. (1974). Rules, roles, and resistance to deviation: Explorations in punishment, discipline, and self-control. In A. Pick (Ed.), Minnesota Symposia on Child Psychology (Vol. 8). Minneapolis: University of Minnesota Press.

Parke, R. D. (1977). Some effects of punishment on children's behavior—revisited. In E. M. Hetherington & R. D. Parke (Eds.), *Contemporary readings in child psychology*. New York: McGraw-Hill.

Parke, R. D., & Deur, J. L. (1972). Schedule of punishment and inhibition of aggression in children. *Developmental Psychology, 7*, 266-269.

Parke, R. D., & Walters, R. H. (1967). Some factors determining the efficacy of punishment for inducing response inhibition. *Monograph for the Society for Research in Child Development, 32* (Whole No. 109).

Parrish, J. M., Cataldo, M. F., Kolko, D. J., Neef, N. A., & Egel, A. L. (1986). Experimental analysis of response covariations among compliant and inappropriate behaviors. *Journal of Applied Behavior Analysis, 19*, 241-254.

Parsons, J. E., Adler, T. F., & Kaczala, C. M. (1982). Socialization of achievement attitudes and beliefs: Parental influences. *Child Development, 53*, 310-321.

Parsons, J. E., Kaczala, C. M., & Meece, J. L. (1982). Socialization of achievement attitudes and beliefs: Classroom influences. *Child Development, 53*, 322-339.

Pascarella, E. T., & Terenzini, P. T. (1991). *How college affects students: Findings and insights from twenty years of research*. San Francisco: Jossey-Bass.

Pashler, H. (1992). Attentional limitations in doing two tasks at the same time. *Current Directions in Psychological Science, 1*, 44-48.

Pavlov, I. P. (1927). *Conditioned reflexes* (G. V. Anrep, Trans.). London: Oxford University Press.

Pea, R. D. (1993). Practices of distributed intelligence and designs for education. In G. Salomon (Ed.), *Distributed cognitions: Psychological and educational considerations*. Cambridge, UK: Cambridge University Press.

Pearson, P. D., Hansen, J., & Gordon, C. (1979). The effect of background knowledge on young children's comprehension of explicit and implicit information. *Journal of Reading Behavior, 11* (3), 201-209.

Pellegrini, A. D., & Bjorklund, D. F. (1997). The role of recess in children's cognitive performance. *Educational Psychologist, 32*, 35-40.

Pellegrini, A. D., Huberty, P. D., & Jones, I. (1995). The effects of recess timing on children's playground and classroom behaviors. *American Educational Research Journal, 32*, 845-864.

Penfield, W. (1958). Some mechanisms of consciousness discovered during electrical stimulation of the brain. *Proceedings of the National Academy of Sciences, 44*, 51-66.

Penfield, W. (1959). Consciousness, memory, and man's conditioned reflexes. In K. Pribram (Ed.), *On the biology of learning*. New York: Harcourt, Brace, & World.

Penfield, W., & Roberts, L. (1959). *Speech and brain-mechanisms*. Princeton, NJ: Princeton University Press.

Pepper, J. (1981). Following students' suggestions for rewriting a computer programming textbook. *American Educational Research Journal, 18*, 259-270.

Perfetti, C. A. (1983). Reading, vocabulary, and writing: Implications for computer-based instruction. In A. C. Wilkinson (Ed.), *Classroom computers and cognitive science*. New York: Academic Press.

Perfetti, C. A., & Hogaboam, T. (1975). The relationship between single word coding and reading comprehension skill. *Journal of Educational Psychology, 67*, 461-469.

Perfetti, C. A., & Lesgold, A. M. (1979). Coding and comprehension in skilled reading and implications for reading instruction. In L. B. Resnick & P. Weaver (Eds.), *Theory and practice of early reading* (Vol. 1). Hillsdale, NJ: Erlbaum.

Perin, C. T. (1942). Behavior potentiality as a joint function of the amount of training and the degree of hunger at the time of extinction. *Journal of Experimental Psychology, 30*, 93-113.

Perin, C. T. (1943). A quantitative investigation of the delay-of-reinforcement gradient. *Journal of Experimental Psychology, 32*, 37-51.

Perkins, D. (1992). *Smart schools: From training memories to educating minds*. New York: Free Press/Macmillan.

Perkins, D. (1995). *Outsmarting IQ: The emerging science of learnable intelligence.* New York: Free Press.

Perkins, D. N., & Salomon, G. (1987). Transfer and teaching thinking. In D. N. Perkins, J. Lochhead, & J. Bishop (Eds.), *Thinking: The second international conference.* Hillsdale, NJ: Erlbaum.

Perkins, D. N., & Salomon, G. (1989). Are cognitive skills context-bound? *Educational Researcher, 18* (1), 16-25.

Perkins, D. N., & Simmons, R. (1988). Patterns of misunderstanding: An integrative model for science, math, and programming. *Review of Educational Research, 58,* 303-326.

Perone, M., & Baron, A. (1980). Reinforcement of human observing behavior by a stimulus correlated with extinction or increased effort. *Journal of the Experimental Analysis of Behavior, 34,* 239-261.

Perry, D. G., & Perry, L. C. (1983). Social learning, causal attribution, and moral internalization. In J. Bisanz, G. L. Bisanz, & R. Kail (Eds.), *Learning in children: Progress in cognitive development research.* New York: Springer-Verlag.

Perry, M. (1991). Learning and transfer: Instructional conditions and conceptual change. *Cognitive Development, 6,* 449-468.

Perry, W. G., Jr. (1968). *Forms of intellectual and ethical development in the college years.* Cambridge, MA: President and Fellows of Harvard College.

Peterson, C. (1988, August). *Explanatory style and academic performance.* Paper presented at the annual meeting of the American Psychological Association, Atlanta.

Peterson, C. (1990). Explanatory style in the classroom and on the playing field. In S. Graham & V. S. Folkes (Eds.), Attribution theory: Applications to achievement, mental health, and interpersonal conflict. Hillsdale, NJ: Erlbaum.

Peterson, C., & Barrett, L. C. (1987). Explanatory style and academic performance among university freshmen. *Journal of Personality and Social Psychology, 53,* 603-607.

Peterson, C., Colvin, D., & Lin, E. H. (1992). Explanatory style and helplessness. *Social Behavior and Personality, 20* (1), 1-14.

Peterson, C., Maier, S. F., & Seligman, M. E. P. (1993). *Learned helplessness: A theory for the age of personal control.* New York: Oxford University Press.

Peterson, L. R., & Peterson, M. J. (1959). Short-term retention of individual items. *Journal of Experimental Psychology, 58,* 193-198.

Peterson, L. R., & Peterson, M. J. (1962). Minimal paired-associate learning. *Journal of Experimental Psychology, 63,* 521-527.

Peterson, M. A. (1994). Object recognition processes can and do operate before figure-ground organization. *Current Directions in Psychological Science, 3,* 105-111.

Peterson, M. A., & Gibson, B. S. (1994). Must figure-ground organization precede object recognition? An assumption in peril. *Psychological Science, 5,* 253-259.

Peterson, P. L. (1988). Teachers' and students' cognitional knowledge for classroom teaching and learning. *Educational Researcher, 17* (5), 5-14.

Peterson, S. E. (1993). The effects of prior achievement and group outcome on attributions and affect in cooperative tasks. *Contemporary Educational Psychology, 18,* 479-485.

Petri, H. L. (1991). *Motivation: Theory, research, and applications* (3rd ed.). Belmont, CA: Wadsworth.

Pezdek, K. (1977). Cross-modality semantic integration of sentence and picture memory. *Journal of Experimental Psychology: Human Learning and Memory, 3,* 515-524.

Pezdek, K., & Banks, W. P. (Eds.). (1996). *The recovered memory/false memory debate.* San Diego: Academic Press.

Pfeiffer, K., Feinberg, G., & Gelber, S. (1987). Teaching productive problem solving attitudes. In D. Berger, K. Pezdek, & W. Banks (Eds.), *Applications in cognitive psychology: Problem solving education and computing.* Hillsdale, NJ: Erlbaum.

Pfiffner, L. J., & O'Leary, S. G. (1987). The efficacy of all-positive management as a function of the prior use of negative consequences. *Journal of Applied Behavior Analysis, 20,* 265-271.

Pfiffner, L. J., Rosén, L. A., & O'Leary, S. G. (1985). The efficacy of an all-positive approach to classroom management. *Journal of Applied Behavior Analysis, 18,* 257-261.

Phelan, P., Yu, H. C., & Davidson, A. L. (1994). Navigating the psychosocial pressures of adolescence: The voices and experiences of high school youth. *American Educational Research Journal, 31,* 415-447.

Phillips, B. N., Pitcher, G. D., Worsham, M. E., & Miller, S. C. (1980). Test anxi-

ety and the school environment. In I. G. Sarason (Ed.), *Test anxiety: Theory, research, and applications.* Hillsdale, NJ: Erlbaum.

Phillips, D. A., & Zimmerman, M. (1990). The developmental course of perceived competence and incompetence among competent children. In R. J. Sternberg & J. Kolligian (Eds.), *Competence considered.* New Haven, CT: Yale University Press.

Phillips, E. L., Phillips, E. A., Fixsen, D. L., & Wolf, M. M. (1971). Achievement place: Modification of the behaviors of predelinquent boys within a token economy. *Journal of Applied Behavior Analysis, 4,* 45-59.

Phye, G. D. (1997a). Classroom assessment: A multidimensional perspective. In G. D. Phye (Ed.), *Handbook of classroom assessment: Learning, achievement, and adjustment.* San Diego: Academic Press.

Phye. G. D. (1997b). Learning and remembering: The basis for personal knowledge construction. In G. D. Phye (Ed.), *Handbook of academic learning: Construction of knowledge.* San Diego: Academic Press.

Piaget, J. (1928). *Judgment and reasoning in the child* (M. Warden, Trans.). New York: Harcourt, Brace.

Piaget, J. (1952). *The origins of intelligence in children* (M. Cook, Trans.). New York: W. W. Norton.

Piaget, J. (1959). *The language and thought of the child* (3rd ed.) (M. Gabain, Trans.). New York: Humanities Press.

Piaget, J. (1970). Piaget's theory. In P. H. Mussen (Ed.), *Carmichael's manual of psychology.* New York: Wiley.

Piaget, J. (1971). *Psychology and epistemology: Towards a theory of knowledge* (A. Rosin, Trans.). New York: Viking.

Piaget, J. (1972). *The principles of genetic epistemology* (W. Mays, Trans.). New York: Basic Books.

Piaget, J. (1980). *Adaptation and intelligence: Organic selection and phenocopy* (S. Eames, Trans.). Chicago: University of Chicago Press.

Piaget, J., & Inhelder, B. (1969). *The psychology of the child* (H. Weaver, Trans.). New York: Basic Books.

Pianko, S. (1979). A description of the composing processes of college freshmen writers. *Research in the Teaching of English, 13,* 5-22.

Pichert, J. W., & Anderson, R. C. (1977). Taking different perspectives on a story. *Journal of Educational Psychology, 69,* 309-315.

509

Piersel, W. C. (1987). Basic skills education. In C. A. Maher & S. G. Forman (Eds.), *A behavioral approach to education of children and youth*. Hillsdale, NJ: Erlbaum.

Pigott, H. E., Fantuzzo, J. W., & Clement, P. W. (1986). The effects of reciprocal peer tutoring and group contingencies on the academic performance of elementary school children. *Journal of Applied Behavior Analysis, 19*, 93-98.

Piliavin, I. M., Piliavin, J. A., & Rodin, J. (1975). Costs, diffusion, and the stigmatized victim. *Journal of Personality and Social Psychology, 32*, 429-438.

Piliavin, J. A., Dovidio, J. F., Gaertner, S. L., & Clark, R. D., III. (1981). Responsive bystanders: The process of intervention. In J. Grzelak & V. Derlega (Eds.), *Living with other people: Theory and research on cooperation and helping*. New York: Academic Press.

Pinker, S. (1984). *Language learnability and language development*. Cambridge, MA: Harvard University Press.

Pinker, S. (1987). The bootstrapping problem in language acquisition. In B. MacWhinney (Ed.), *Mechanisms of language acquisition*. Hillsdale, NJ: Erlbaum.

Pinker, S., & Prince, A. (1988). On language and connectionism: Analysis of a parallel distributed processing model of language acquisition. *Cognition, 28*, 73-193.

Pinkston, E. M., Reese, N. M., LeBlanc, J. M., & Baer, D. M. (1973). Independent control of a preschool child's aggression and peer interaction by contingent teacher attention. *Journal of Applied Behavior Analysis, 6*, 223-224.

Pintrich, P. R., & De Groot, E. V. (1990). Motivational and self-regulated learning components of classroom academic performance. *Journal of Educational Psychology, 82*, 33-40.

Pintrich, P. R., Marx, R. W., & Boyle, R. A. (1993). Beyond cold conceptual change: The role of motivational beliefs and classroom contextual factors in the process of conceptual change. *Review of Educational Research, 63*, 167-199.

Pintrich, P. R., & Schrauben, B. (1992). Students' motivational beliefs and their cognitive engagement in academic tasks. In D. Schunk & J. Meece (Eds.), *Students' perceptions in the classroom: Causes and consequences*. Hillsdale, NJ: Erlbaum.

Pintrich, P. R., & Schunk, D. H. (1996). *Motivation in education: Theory, research, and applications*. Upper Saddle River, NJ: Merrill/Prentice Hall.

Piontkowski, D., & Calfee, R. (1979). Attention in the classroom. In G. A. Hale & M. Lewis (Eds.), *Attention and cognitive development*. New York: Plenum Press.

Plummer, S., Baer, D. M., & LeBlanc, J. M. (1977). Functional considerations in the use of procedural time out and an effective alternative. *Journal of Applied Behavior Analysis, 10*, 689-706.

Poche, C., Yoder, P., & Miltenberger, R. (1988). Teaching self-protection to children using television techniques. *Journal of Applied Behavior Analysis, 21*, 253-261.

Polya, G. (1957). *How to solve it*. Garden City, NY: Doubleday.

Pontecorvo, C. (1993). Social interaction in the acquisition of knowledge. *Educational Psychology Review, 5*, 293-310.

Poole, D. (1994). Routine testing practices and the linguistic construction of knowledge. *Cognition and Instruction, 12*, 125-150.

Popham, W. J. (1988). *Educational evaluation* (2nd ed.). Englewood Cliffs, NJ: Prentice Hall.

Popham, W. J. (1995). *Classroom assessment: What teachers need to know*. Boston: Allyn & Bacon.

Porter, A. (1989). A curriculum out of balance: The case of elementary school mathematics. *Educational Researcher, 18* (5), 9-15.

Posner, G. J., & Rudnitsky, A. N. (1986). *Course design: A guide to curriculum development for teachers* (3rd ed.). New York: Longman.

Posner, G. J., Strike, K. A., Hewson, P. W., & Gertzog, W. A. (1982). Accommodation of a scientific conception: Toward a theory of conceptual change. *Science Education, 66*, 211-227.

Posner, M. I., Goldsmith, R., & Welton, K. E., Jr. (1967). Perceived distance and the classification of distorted patterns. *Journal of Experimental Psychology, 73*, 28-38.

Posner, M. I., & Keele, S. W. (1968). On the genesis of abstract ideas. *Journal of Experimental Psychology, 77*, 353-363.

Posner, M. I., & Keele, S. W. (1970). Retention of abstract ideas. *Journal of Experimental Psychology, 83*, 304-308.

Postman, L. (1964). Short-term memory and incidental learning. In A. W. Melton (Ed.), *Categories of human learning*. New York: Academic Press.

Postman, L., & Phillips, L. (1965). Short-term temporal changes in free recall. *Quarterly Journal of Experimental Psychology, 17*, 132-138.

Postman, L., & Underwood, B. J. (1973). Critical issues in interference theory. *Memory and Cognition, 1*, 19-40.

Powell, B. M. (1990, April). *Children's perceptions of classroom goal orientation: Relationship to learning strategies and intrinsic motivation*. Paper presented at the annual meeting of the American Educational Research Association, Boston.

Powell, S., & Nelson, B. (1997). Effects of choosing academic assignments on a study with attention deficit hyperactivity disorder. *Journal of Applied Behavior Analysis, 30*, 181-183.

Prawat, R. S. (1989). Promoting access to knowledge, strategy, and disposition in students: A research synthesis. *Review of Educational Research, 59*, 1-41.

Prawat, R. S. (1992). From individual differences to learning communities—our changing focus. *Educational Leadership, 49* (7), 9-13.

Prawat, R. S. (1993). The value of ideas: Problems versus possibilities in learning. *Educational Researcher, 22* (6), 5-16.

Prawat, R. S. (1996). Constructivisms, modern and postmodern. *Educational Psychologist, 31*, 215-225.

Premack, D. (1959). Toward empirical behavior laws: I. Positive reinforcement. *Psychological Review, 66*, 219-233.

Premack, D. (1963). Rate differential reinforcement in monkey manipulation. *Journal of Experimental Analysis of Behavior, 6*, 81-89.

Prentice, N. M. (1972). The influence of live and symbolic modeling on prompting moral judgments of adolescent delinquents. *Journal of Abnormal Psychology, 80*, 157-161.

Pressey, S. L. (1926). A simple apparatus which gives tests and scores—and teaches. *School and Society, 23*, 373-376.

Pressey, S. L. (1927). A machine for automatic teaching of drill material. *School and Society, 24*, 549-552.

Pressley, M. (1982). Elaboration and memory development. *Child Development, 53*, 296-309.

Pressley, M., Borkowski, J. G., & Schneider, W. (1987). Cognitive strategies: Good strategy users coordinate metacognition and knowledge. In R. Vasta & G. Whitehurst (Eds.), *Annals of child development* (Vol. 5). New York: JAI Press.

Pressley, M., El-Dinary, P. B., Marks, M. B., Brown, R., & Stein, S. (1992). Good

510

strategy instruction is motivating and interesting. In K. A. Renninger, S. Hidi, & A. Krapp (Eds.), *The role of interest in learning and development*. Hillsdale, NJ: Erlbaum.

Pressley, M., Harris, K R., & Marks, M. B. (1992). But good strategy instructors are constructivists! *Educational Psychology Review, 4,* 3-31.

Pressley, M., Levin, J. R., & Delaney, H. D. (1982). The mnemonic keyword method. *Review of Educational Research, 52,* 61-91.

Pressley, M., Levin, J. R., & Ghatala, E. S. (1984). Memory strategy monitoring in adults and children. *Journal of Verbal Learning and Verbal Behavior, 23,* 270-288.

Pressley, M., Levin., J. R. & Ghatala, E. S. (1988). Strategy-comparison opportunities promote long-term strategy use. *Contemporary Educational Psychology, 13,* 157-168.

Pressley, M., Levin, J. R., & McCormick, C. B. (1980). Young children's learning of foreign language vocabulary: A sentence variation of the keyword method. *Contemporary Educational Psychology, 5,* 22-29.

Pressley, M., with McCormick, C. B. (1995). *Advanced educational psychology: For educators, researchers, and policymakers.* New York: HarperCollins.

Pressley, M., Ross, K. A., Levin, J. B., & Ghatala, E. S. (1984). The role of strategy utility knowledge in children's strategy decision making. *Journal of Experimental Child Psychology, 38,* 491-504.

Pressley, M., Snyder, B. L., & Cariglia-Bull, T. (1987). How can good strategy use be taught to children? Evaluation of six alternative approaches. In S. M. Cormier & J. D. Hagman (Eds.), *Transfer of learning: Contemporary research and applications.* San Diego: Academic Press.

Pressley, M., Wharton-McDonald, R., Rankin, J., El-Dinary, P. B., Brown, R., Afflerbach, P., Mistretta, J., & Yokoi, L. (1997). Elementary reading instruction. In G. D. Phye (Ed.), *Handbook of academic learning: Construction of knowledge.* San Diego: Academic Press.

Pressley, M., Woloshyn, V., Lysynchuk, L. M., Martin, V., Wood, E., & Willoughby, T. (1990). A primer of research on cognitive strategy instruction: The important issues and how to address them. *Educational Psychology Review, 2,* 1-58.

Pressley, M., Yokoi, L., Van Meter, P., Van Etten, S., & Freebern, G. (1997). Some of the reasons why preparing for exams is so hard: What can be done to make it easier? *Educational Psychology Review, 9,* 1-38.

Proctor, R. W., & Dutta, A. (1995). *Skill acquisition and human performance.* Thousand Oaks, CA: Sage.

Pulos, S. (1980, August). M *capacity as a developmental constraint on structural learning.* Paper presented at the annual meeting of the American Psychological Association, Montreal, Canada.

Pulos, S., & Linn, M. C. (1981). Generality of the controlling variables scheme in early adolescence. *Journal of Early Adolescence, 1,* 26-37.

Purdie, N., & Hattie, J. (1996). Cultural differences in the use of strategies for self-regulated learning. *American Educational Research Journal, 33,* 845-871.

Purdie, N., Hattie, J., & Douglas, G. (1996). Student conceptions of learning and their use of self-regulated learning strategies: A cross-cultural comparison. *Journal of Educational Psychology, 88,* 87-100.

Pylyshyn, Z. W. (1973). What the mind's eye tells the mind's brain: A critique of mental imagery. *Psychological Bulletin, 80,* 1-24.

Pylyshyn, Z. W. (1979). Imagery theory: Not mysterious—just wrong. *Behavioural and Brain Sciences, 2,* 561-563.

Pylyshyn, Z. W. (1981). The imagery debate: Analogue media versus tacit knowledge. *Psychological Review, 88,* 16-45.

Pylyshyn, Z. W. (1984). *Computation and cognition.* Cambridge, MA: M.I.T. Press.

Qin, Z., Johnson, D. W., & Johnson, R. T. (1995). Cooperative versus competitive efforts and problem solving. *Review of Educational Research, 65,* 129-143.

Rabinowitz, M., & Glaser, R. (1985). Cognitive structure and process in highly competent performance. In F. D. Horowitz & M. O'Brien (Eds.), *The gifted and the talented: Developmental perspectives.* Washington, DC: American Psychological Association.

Rachlin, H. (1990). Why do people gamble and keep gambling despite heavy losses? *Psychological Science, 1,* 294-297.

Rachlin, H. (1991). *Introduction to modern behaviorism* (3rd ed.). New York: W. H. Freeman.

Rachlin, H., & Herrnstein, R. J. (1969). Hedonism revisited: On the negative law of effect. In B. A. Campbell & R. M. Church (Eds.), *Punishment and aversive behavior.* New York: Appleton-Century-Crofts.

Radebaugh, M. R. (1985). Children's perceptions of their spelling strategies. *The Reading Teacher, 38,* 532-536.

Radke-Yarrow, M., Zahn-Waxler, C., & Chapman, M. (1983). Children's prosocial dispositions and behavior. In E. M. Hetherington (Ed.), *Handbook of child psychology: Vol. 4. Socialization, personality, and social development.* New York: Wiley.

Rakow, S. J. (1984). What's happening in elementary science: A national assessment. *Science and children, 21* (4), 39-40.

Rapport, M. D., & Bostow, D. E. (1976). The effects of access to special activities on performance in four categories of academic tasks with third-grade students. *Journal of Applied Behavior Analysis, 9,* 372.

Rapport, M. D., Murphy, H. A., & Bailey, J. S. (1982). Ritalin vs. response cost in the control of hyperactive children: A within-subject comparison. *Journal of Applied Behavior Analysis, 15,* 205-216.

Raudenbush, S. W., Rowan, B., & Cheong, Y. F. (1993). Higher order instructional goals in secondary schools: Class, teacher, and school influences. *American Educational Research Journal, 30,* 523-553.

Raugh, M. R., & Atkinson, R. C. (1975). A mnemonic method for learning a second language vocabulary. *Journal of Educational Psychology, 67,* 1-16.

Reber, A. S. (1993). *Implicit learning and tacit knowledge: An essay on the cognitive unconscious.* New York: Oxford University Press.

Reber, A. S., & Allen, R. (1978). Analogical and abstraction strategies in synthetic grammar learning: A functionalist interpretation. *Cognition, 6,* 189-221.

Reber, A. S., Kassin, S. M., Lewis, S., & Cantor, B. (1980). On the relationship between implicit and explicit modes in the learning of a complex rule structure. *Journal of Experimental Psychology: Human Learning and Memory, 6,* 492-502.

Redd, W. H., Morris, E. K., & Martin, J. A. (1975). Effects of positive and negative adult-child interactions on children's social preference. *Journal of Experimental Child Psychology, 19,* 153-164.

Reder, L. M. (1982). Plausibility judgment versus fact retrieval: Alternative strategies for sentence verification. *Psychological Review, 89,* 250-280.

Reder, L. M., & Ross, B. H. (1983). Integrated knowledge in different tasks: Positive and negative fan effects. *Journal of Experimental Psychology: Human Learning and Memory, 8,* 55-72.

Redfield, D. L., & Rousseau, E. W. (1981). A meta-analysis of experimental research on teacher questioning behavior. *Review of Educational Research, 51,* 237-245.

Reed, S. (1974). Structural descriptions and the limitations of visual images. *Memory and Cognition, 2,* 329-336.

Reed, S. K. (1993). A schema-based theory of transfer. In D. K. Detterman & R. J. Sternberg (Eds.), *Transfer on trial: Intelligence, cognition, and instruction.* Norwood, NJ: Ablex.

Reed, S. K., Ernst, G. W., & Banerji, R. (1974). The role of analogy in transfer between similar problem states. *Cognitive Psychology, 6,* 436-450.

Reese, H. W., & Lipsitt, L. P. (1970). *Experimental child psychology.* New York: Academic Press.

Reese, H. W., & Parnes, S. J. (1970). Programming creative behavior. *Child Development, 41,* 413-423.

Reesink, C. J. (1984). Metric munchies. *Science and Children, 21* (7), 16-17.

Reif, F., & Heller, J. I. (1982). Knowledge structure and problem solving in physics. *Educational Psychologist, 17,* 102-127.

Reimann, P., & Schult, T. J. (1996). Turning examples into cases: Acquiring knowledge structures for analogical problem solving. *Educational Psychologist, 31,* 123-132.

Reisberg, D. (Ed.). (1992). *Auditory imagery.* Hillsdale, NJ: Erlbaum.

Reisberg, D. (1997). *Cognition: Exploring the science of the mind.* New York: W. W. Norton.

Reiser, R. A., & Sullivan, H. J. (1977). Effects of self-pacing and instructor-pacing in a PSI course. *Journal of Educational Research, 71,* 8-12.

Reiter, S. N. (1994). Teaching dialogically: Its relationship to critical thinking in college students. In P. R. Pintrich, D. R. Brown, & C. E. Weinstein (Eds.), *Student motivation, cognition, and learning: Essays in honor of Wilbert J. McKeachie.* Hillsdale, NJ: Erlbaum.

Reitman, J. S. (1974). Without surreptitious rehearsal, information in short-term memory decays. *Journal of Verbal Learning and Verbal Behavior, 13,* 365-377.

Reitman, W. R. (1964). Heuristic decision procedures, open constraints, and the structure of ill-defined problems. In M. W. Shelley & G. L. Bryan (Eds.), *Human judgments and optimality.* New York: Wiley.

Reitman, W. R. (1965). *Cognition and thought: An information processing approach.* New York: Wiley.

Renkl, A., Mandl, H., & Gruber, H. (1996). Inert knowledge: Analyses and remedies. *Educational Psychologist, 31,* 115-121.

Renninger, K. A. (1992). Individual interest and development: Implications for theory and practice. In K. A. Renninger, S. Hidi, & A. Krapp (Eds.), *The role of interest in learning and development.* Hillsdale, NJ: Erlbaum.

Repp, A. C., Barton, L., & Brulle, A. (1983). A comparison of two procedures for programming the differential reinforcement of other behavior. *Journal of Applied Behavior Analysis, 16,* 435-445.

Repp, A. C., & Deitz, S. M. (1974). Reducing aggressive and self-injurious behavior of institutionalized retarded children through reinforcement of other behaviors. *Journal of Applied Behavior Analysis, 7,* 313-325.

Rescorla, R. A. (1967). Pavlovian conditioning and its proper control procedures. *Psychological Review, 74,* 71-80.

Rescorla, R. A. (1987). A Pavlovian analysis of goal-directed behavior. *American Psychologist, 42,* 119-129.

Rescorla, R. A. (1988). Pavlovian conditioning: It's not what you think it is. *American Psychologist, 43,* 151-160.

Rescorla, R. A., & Wagner, A. R. (1972). A theory of Pavlovian conditioning: Variations in the effectiveness of reinforcement and non-reinforcement. In A. H. Black & W. F. Prokasy (Eds.), *The psychology of learning and motivation* (Vol. 4). New York: Academic Press.

Resnick, L. B. (1976). Task analysis in instructional design: Some cases in mathematics. In D. Klahr (Ed.), *Cognition and instruction.* Hillsdale, NJ: Erlbaum.

Resnick, L. B. (1983). Mathematics and science learning: A new conception. *Science, 220,* 477-478.

Resnick, L. B. (1987). *Education and learning to think.* Washington, DC: National Academy Press.

Resnick, L. B. (1989). Developing mathematical knowledge. *American Psychologist, 44,* 162-169.

Resnick, L. B., Bill, V. L., Lesgold, S. B., & Leer, M. N. (1991). Thinking in arithmetic class. In B. Means, C. Chelemer, & M. S. Knapp (Eds.), *Teaching advanced skills to at-risk students.* San Francisco: Jossey-Bass.

Resnick, L. B., & Glaser, R. (1976). Problem solving and intelligence. In L. B. Resnick (Ed.), *The nature of intelligence.* Hillsdale, NJ: Erlbaum.

Resnick, L. B., & Johnson, A. (1988). Intelligent machines for intelligent people: Cognitive theory and the future of computer-assisted learning. In R. S. Nickerson & P. P. Zodhiates (Eds.), *Technology in education: Looking toward 2020.* Hillsdale, NJ: Erlbaum.

Restle, F., & Davis, J. H. (1962). Success and speed of problem solving by individuals and groups. *Psychological Review, 69,* 520-536.

Reusser, K. (1990, April). *Understanding word arithmetic problems: Linguistic and situational factors.* Paper presented at the annual meeting of the American Educational Research Association, Boston.

Reyna, V. F. (1995). Interference effects in memory and reasoning: A fuzzy-trace theory analysis. In F. N. Dempster & C. J. Brainerd (Eds.), *Interference and inhibition in cognition.* San Diego: Academic Press.

Reynolds, G. S. (1975). *A primer of operant conditioning* (rev. ed.). Glenview, IL: Scott, Foresman.

Reynolds, R. E., & Shirey, L. L. (1988). The role of attention in studying and learning. In C. E. Weinstein, E. T. Goetz, & P. A. Alexander (Eds.), *Learning and study strategies: Issues in assessment, instruction, and evaluation.* San Diego: Academic Press.

Reynolds, R. E., Sinatra, G. M., & Jetton, T. L. (1996). Views of knowledge acquisition and representation: A continuum from experience centered to mind centered. *Educational Psychologist, 31,* 93-104.

Reynolds, R. E., Taylor, M. A., Steffensen, M. S., Shirey, L. L., & Anderson, R. C. (1982). Cultural schemata and reading comprehension. *Reading Research Quarterly, 17,* 353-366.

Rice, M. S., Hauerwas, L. B., Ruggiero, J., & Carlisle, J. F. (1996, April). *Comprehension and recall of more and less imageable text by average and above average college readers.* Paper presented at the annual meeting of the American Educational Research Association, New York.

Riding, R. J., & Calvey, I. (1981). The assessment of verbal-imagery learning styles and their effect on the recall of concrete and abstract prose passages by 11-year-old children. *British Journal of Psychology, 72,* 59-64.

Riggs, J. M. (1992). Self-handicapping and achievement. In A. K. Boggiano & T. S.

Pittman (Eds.), *Achievement and motivation: A social-developmental perspective*. Cambridge, UK: Cambridge University Press.

Rimm, D. C., & Masters, J. C. (1974). *Behavior therapy: Techniques and empirical findings*. New York: Academic Press.

Rinehart, S. D., Stahl, S. A., & Erickson, L. G. (1986). Some effects of summarization training on reading and studying. *Reading Research Quarterly, 21,* 422-438.

Ringness, T. A. (1967). Identification patterns, motivation, and school achievement of bright junior high school boys. *Journal of Educational Psychology, 58,* 93-102.

Rips, L. J., Shoben, E. J., & Smith, E. E. (1973). Semantic distance and the verification of semantic relations. *Journal of Verbal Learning and Verbal Behavior, 12,* 1-20.

Ritts, V., Patterson, M. L., & Tubbs, M. E. (1992). Expectations, impressions, and judgments of physically attractive students: A review. *Review of Educational Research, 62,* 413-426.

Roberts, K. T., & Ehri, L. C. (1983). Effects of two types of letter rehearsal on word memory in skilled and less skilled beginning readers. *Contemporary Educational Psychology, 8,* 375-390.

Robinson, F. P. (1961). *Effective study*. New York: Harper & Row.

Robinson, N. M., & Robinson, H. B. (1961). A method for the study of instrumental avoidance conditioning with children. *Journal of Comparative and Physiological Psychology, 54,* 20-23.

Roediger, H. L. (1980). Memory metaphors in cognitive psychology. *Memory and Cognition, 8,* 231-246.

Roediger, H. L., III. (1990). Implicit memory: Retention without remembering. *American Psychologist, 45,* 1043-1056.

Roediger, H. L., & Crowder, R. G. (1976). A serial position effect in recall of United States presidents. *Bulletin of the Psychonomic Society, 8,* 275-278.

Rogers, C. R. (1951). *Client-centered therapy: Its current practice, implication, and theory*. Boston: Houghton Mifflin.

Rogers, C. R. (1961). *On becoming a person: A therapist's view of psychotherapy*. Boston: Houghton Mifflin.

Rogers, T. B., Kuiper, N. A., & Kirker, W. S. (1977). Self-reference and the encoding of personal information. *Journal of Personality and Social Psychology, 35,* 677-688.

Rogoff, B. (1990). *Apprenticeship in thinking: Cognitive development in social context*. New York: Oxford University Press.

Rogoff, B. (1991). Social interaction as apprenticeship in thinking: Guidance and participation in spatial planning. In L. B. Resnick, J. M. Levine, & S. D. Teasley (Eds.), *Perspectives on socially shared cognition*. Washington, DC: American Psychological Association.

Rogoff, B. (1994, April). *Developing understanding of the idea of communities of learners*. Paper presented at the annual meeting of the American Educational Research Association, New Orleans.

Rogoff, B., Matusov, E., & White, C. (1996). Models of teaching and learning: Participation in a community of learners. In D. R. Olson & N. Torrance (Eds.), *The handbook of education and human development: New models of learning, teaching, and schooling*. Cambridge, MA: Blackwell Publishers.

Rolider, A., & Van Houten, R. (1985). Movement suppression time-out for undesirable behavior in psychotic and severely developmentally delayed children. *Journal of Applied Behavior Analysis, 18,* 275-288.

Rortvedt, A. K., & Miltenberger, R. G. (1994). Analysis of a high-probability instructional sequence and time-out in the treatement of child noncompliance. *Journal of Applied Behavior Analysis, 27,* 327-330.

Rosch, E. H. (1973a). Natural categories. *Cognitive Psychology, 4,* 328-350.

Rosch, E. H. (1973b). On the internal structure of perceptual and semantic categories. In T. E. Moore (Ed.), *Cognitive development and the acquisition of language*. New York: Academic Press.

Rosch, E. H. (1977a). Classification of real-world objects: Origins and representations in cognition. In P. N. Johnson-Laird & P. C. Wason (Eds.), *Thinking: Readings in cognitive science*. Cambridge, MA: Cambridge University Press.

Rosch, E. H. (1977b). Human categorization. In N. Warren (Ed.), *Advances in cross-cultural psychology* (Vol. 1). London: Academic Press.

Rosch, E. H. (1978). Principles of categorization. In E. Rosch & B. Lloyd (Eds.), *Cognition and categorization*. Hillsdale, NJ: Erlbaum.

Rosch, E. H., & Mervis, C. B. (1975). Family resemblances: Studies in the internal structure of categories. *Cognitive Psychology, 7,* 573-605.

Rosch, E. H., Mervis, C. B., Gray, W. D., Johnson, D. M., & Boyes-Braem, P. (1976). Basic objects in natural categories. *Cognitive Psychology, 8,* 382-439.

Rosch, E. H., Simpson, C., & Miller, R. S. (1976). Structural bases of typicality effects. *Journal of Experimental Psychology: Human Perception and Performance, 2,* 491-502.

Rosenfield, I. (1988). *The invention of memory: A new view of the brain*. New York: Basic Books.

Rosenshine, B., & Meister, C. (1992). The use of scaffolds for teaching higher-level cognitive strategies. *Educational Leadership, 49* (7), 26-33.

Rosenshine, B., & Meister, C. (1994). Reciprocal teaching: A review of the research. *Review of Educational Research, 64,* 479-530.

Rosenshine, B., Meister, C., & Chapman, S. (1996). Teaching students to generate questions: A review of the intervention studies. *Review of Educational Research, 66,* 181-221.

Rosenthal, R. (1994). Interpersonal expectancy effects: A 30-year perspective. *Current Directions in Psychological Science, 3,* 176-179.

Rosenthal, R., & Jacobson, L. (1968). *Pygmalion in the classroom: Teacher expectation and pupils' intellectual development*. New York: Holt, Rinehart & Winston.

Rosenthal, T. L., Alford, G. S., & Rasp, L. M. (1972). Concept attainment, generalization, and retention through observation and verbal coding. *Journal of Experimental Child Psychology, 13,* 183-194.

Rosenthal, T. L., & Bandura, A. (1978). Psychological modeling: Theory and practice. In S. L. Garfield & A. E. Begia (Eds.), *Handbook of psychotherapy and behavior change: An empirical analysis* (2nd ed.). New York: Wiley.

Rosenthal, T. L., & Zimmerman, B. J. (1978). *Social learning and cognition*. New York: Academic Press.

Ross, B. H., & Spalding, T. L. (1994). Concepts and categories. In R. J. Sternberg (Ed.), *Handbook of perception and cognition* (Vol. 12). New York: Academic Press.

Rosser, R. (1994). *Cognitive development: Psychological and biological perspectives*. Boston: Allyn & Bacon.

Roth, K. (1990). Developing meaningful conceptual understanding in science. In B. F. Jones & L. Idol (Eds.), *Dimensions of thinking and cognitive instruction*. Hillsdale, NJ: Erlbaum.

Roth, K., & Anderson, C. (1988). Promoting conceptual change learning from science textbooks. In P. Ramsden (Ed.), *Improving learning: New perspectives*. London: Kogan Page.

Roth, W., & Bowen, G. M. (1995). Knowing and interacting: A study of culture, practices, and resources in a grade 8 open-inquiry science classroom guided by a cognitive apprenticeship metaphor. *Cognition and Instruction, 13,* 73–128.

Rouet, J.-F., Favart, M., Britt, M. A., & Perfetti, C. A. (1997). Studying and using multiple documents in history: Effects of discipline expertise. *Cognition and Instruction, 15,* 85–106.

Roughead, W. G., & Scandura, J. M. (1968). What is learned in mathematical discovery. *Journal of Educational Psychology, 59,* 283–289.

Rovee-Collier, C. (1993). The capacity for long-term memory in infancy. *Current Directions in Psychological Science, 2,* 130–135.

Rowe, M. B. (1974). Wait-time and rewards as instructional variables, their influence on language, logic, and fate control: Part one-wait time. *Journal of Research in Science Teaching, 11,* 81–94.

Rowe, M. B. (1983). Science education: A framework for decision-makers. *Daedalus, 112* (2), 123–142.

Rowe, M. B. (1987). Wait time: Slowing down may be a way of speeding up. *American Educator, 11* (1), 38–43, 47.

Royer, J. M., & Cable, G. W. (1976). Illustrations, analogies, and facilitation of transfer in prose learning. *Journal of Educational Psychology, 68,* 205–209.

Rubin, D. C. (1977). Very long-term memory for prose and verse. *Journal of Verbal Learning and Verbal Behavior, 16,* 611–621.

Rubin, D. C. (1992). Constraints on memory. In E. Winograd & U. Neisser (Eds.), *Affect and accuracy in recall: Studies of "flashbulb" memories*. Cambridge, UK: Cambridge University Press.

Ruble, D. N. (1980). A developmental perspective on theories of achievement motivation. In L. J. Fyans, Jr. (Ed.), *Achievement motivation: Recent trends in theory and research*. New York: Plenum Press.

Ruble, D. N., & Ruble, T. L. (1982). Sex stereotypes. In A. G. Miller (Ed.), *In the eye of the beholder*. New York: Praeger.

Rueda, R., & Moll, L. C. (1994). A sociocultural perspective on motivation. In H. F. O'Neil, Jr., & M. Drillings (Eds.), *Motivation: Theory and research*. Hillsdale, NJ: Erlbaum.

Rueger, D. B., & Liberman, R. P. (1984). Behavioral family therapy for delinquent substance-abusing adolescents. *Journal of Drug Abuse, 14,* 403–418.

Rumelhart, D. E. (1980). Schemata: The building blocks of cognition. In R. J. Spiro, B. C. Bruce, & W. F. Brewer (Eds.), *Theoretical issues in reading comprehension*. Hillsdale, NJ: Erlbaum.

Rumelhart, D. E., & McClelland, J. L. (1986). *Parallel distributed processing* (Vol. 1). Cambridge, MA: M.I.T. Press.

Rumelhart, D. E., & Ortony, A. (1977). The representation of knowledge in memory. In R. C. Anderson, R. J. Spiro, & W. E. Montague (Eds.), *Schooling and the acquisition of knowledge*. Hillsdale, NJ: Erlbaum.

Rundus, D. (1971). Analysis of rehearsal processes in free recall. *Journal of Experimental Psychology, 89,* 63–77.

Rundus, D., & Atkinson, R. C. (1971). Rehearsal processes in free recall: A procedure for direct observation. *Journal of Verbal Learning and Verbal Behavior, 9,* 99–105.

Rusch, F., & Close, D. (1976). Overcorrection: A procedural evaluation. *AAESPH Review, 1,* 32–45.

Rushton, J. P. (1975). Generosity in children: Immediate and long-term effects of modeling, preaching, and moral judgment. *Journal of Personality and Social Psychology, 31,* 459–466.

Rushton, J. P. (1980). *Altruism, socialization, and society*. Englewood Cliffs, NJ: Prentice Hall.

Rushton, J. P. (1982). Social learning theory and the development of prosocial behavior. In N. Eisenberg (Ed.), *The development of prosocial behavior*. New York: Academic Press.

Russ, S. W. (1993). *Affect and creativity: The role of affect and play in the creative process*. Hillsdale, NJ: Erlbaum.

Ryan, R. M. (1982). Control and information in the intrapersonal sphere: An extension of cognitive evaluation theory. *Journal of Personality and Social Psychology, 43,* 450–461.

Ryan, R. M., & Connell, J. P. (1989). Perceived locus of causality and internalization: Examining reasons for acting in two domains. *Journal of Personality and Social Psychology, 57,* 749–761.

Ryan, R. M., Connell, J. P., & Grolnick, W. S. (1992). When achievement is *not* intrinsically motivated: A theory of internalization and self-regulation in school. In A. K. Boggiano & T. S. Pittman (Eds.), *Achievement and motivation: A social-developmental perspective*. Cambridge, UK: Cambridge University Press.

Ryan, R. M., & Deci, E. L. (1996). When paradigms clash: Comments on Cameron and Pierce's claim that rewards do not undermine intrinsic motivation. *Review of Educational Research, 66,* 33–38.

Ryan, R. M., Mims, V., & Koestner, R. (1983). Relation of reward contingency and interpersonal context to intrinsic motivation: A review and test using cognitive evaluation theory. *Journal of Personality and Social Psychology, 45,* 736–750.

Sadker, M., & Sadker, D. (1985). Sexism in the schoolroom of the '80s. *Psychology Today, 19,* 54–57.

Sadoski, M., Goetz, E. T., & Fritz, J. B. (1993). Impact of concreteness on comprehensibility, interest, and memory for text: Implications for dual coding theory and text design. *Journal of Educational Psychology, 85,* 291–304.

Sadoski, M., & Quast, Z. (1990). Reader response and long-term recall for journalistic text: The roles of imagery, affect, and importance. *Reading Research Quarterly, 25,* 256–272.

Safren, M. A. (1962). Associations, sets, and the solution of word problems. *Journal of Experimental Psychology, 64,* 40–45.

Saljo, R., & Wyndham, J. (1992). Solving everyday problems in the formal setting: An empirical study of the school as context for thought. In S. Chaiklin & J. Lave (Eds.), *Understanding practice*. New York: Cambridge University Press.

Salthouse, T. A. (1991). Mediation of adult age differences in cognition by reductions in working memory and speed of processing. *Psychological Science, 2,* 179–183.

Saltz, E. (1971). *The cognitive bases of human learning*. Homewood, IL: Dorsey.

Samuel, A. L. (1963). Some studies in machine learning using the game of checkers. In E. A. Feigenbaum & J. Feldman (Eds.), *Computers and thought*. New York: McGraw-Hill.

Samuels, S. J. (1967). Attentional processes in reading: The effect of pictures in the acquisition of reading responses. *Journal of Educational Psychology, 58,* 337–342.

Samuels, S. J. (1970). Effects of pictures on learning to read, comprehension, and attitudes. *Review of Educational Research, 40,* 397–407.

Samuels, S. J., & Turnure, J. E. (1974). Attention and reading achievement in first-grade boys and girls. *Journal of Educational Psychology, 66,* 29-32.

Sarason, I. G. (1980). Introduction to the study of test anxiety. In I. G. Sarason (Ed.), *Test anxiety: Theory, research, and applications.* Hillsdale, NJ: Erlbaum.

Sarason, S. B. (1972). What research says about test anxiety in elementary school children. In A. R. Binter & S. H. Frey (Eds.), *The psychology of the elementary school child.* Chicago: Rand McNally.

Sasso, G. M., & Rude, H. A. (1987). Unprogrammed effects of training high-status peers to interact with severely handicapped children. *Journal of Applied Behavior Analysis, 20,* 35-44.

Sax, G. (1989). *Principles of educational and psychological measurement and evaluation* (3rd ed.). Belmont, CA: Wadsworth.

Saxe, G. B. (1988). Candy selling and math learning. *Educational Researcher, 17* (6), 14-21.

Scandura, J. M. (1974). Role of higher order rules in problem solving. *Journal of Experimental Psychology, 102,* 984-991.

Scardamalia, M., & Bereiter, C. (1985). Fostering the development of self-regulation in children's knowledge processing. In S. F. Chipman, J. W. Segal, & R. Glaser (Eds.), *Thinking and learning skills: Vol. 2. Research and open questions.* Hillsdale, NJ: Erlbaum.

Scevak, J. J., Moore, P. J., & Kirby, J. R. (1993). Training students to use maps to increase text recall. *Contemporary Educational Psychology, 18,* 401-413.

Schab, F. (1990). Odors and the remembrance of things past. *Journal of Experimental Psychology: Learning, Memory, and Cognition, 16,* 648-655.

Schacter, D. L. (1993). Understanding implicit memory: A cognitive neuroscience approach. In A. F. Collins, S. E. Gathercole, M. A. Conway, & P. E. Morris (Eds.), *Theories of memory.* Hove, UK: Erlbaum.

Schank, R. C. (1975). *Conceptual information processing.* New York: Elsevier.

Schank, R. C. (1979). Interestingness: Controlling inferences. *Artificial Intelligence, 12,* 273-297.

Schank, R. C., & Abelson, R. P. (1977). *Scripts, plans, goals, and understanding: An inquiry into human knowledge structures.* Hillsdale, NJ: Erlbaum.

Schank, R. C., & Abelson, R. P. (1995). Knowledge and memory: The real story. In R. S. Wyer, Jr. (Ed.), *Knowledge and memory: The real story. Advances in social cognition* (Vol. 8.) Hillsdale, NJ: Erlbaum.

Schellings, G. L. M., Van Hout-Wolters, B., & Vermunt, J. D. (1996). Individual differences in adapting to three different tasks of selecting information from texts. *Contemporary Educational Psychology, 21,* 423-446.

Schepis, M. M., Reid, D. H., & Fitzgerald, J. R. (1987). Group instruction with profoundly retarded persons: Acquisition, generalization, and maintenance of a remunerative work skill. *Journal of Applied Behavior Analysis, 20,* 97-105.

Schiefele, U. (1991). Interest, learning, and motivation. *Educational Psychologist, 26,* 299-323.

Schiefele, U. (1992). Topic interest and levels of text comprehension. In K. A. Renninger, S. Hidi, & A. Krapp (Eds.), *The role of interest in learning and development.* Hillsdale, NJ: Erlbaum.

Schiefele, U., Krapp, A., & Winteler, A. (1992). Interest as a predictor of academic achievement: A meta-analysis of research. In K. A. Renninger, S. Hidi, & A. Krapp (Eds.), *The role of interest in learning and development.* Hillsdale, NJ: Erlbaum.

Schiefele, U., & Wild, K. (1994, April). *Motivational predictors of strategy use and course grades.* Paper presented at the annual meeting of the American Educational Research Association, New Orleans.

Schliefer, M., & Douglas, V. I. (1973). Effects of training on the moral judgment of young children. *Journal of Personality and Social Psychology, 28,* 62-67.

Schliemann, A. D., & Carraher, D. W. (1993). Proportional reasoning in and out of school. In P. Light & G. Butterworth (Eds.), *Context and cognition: Ways of learning and knowing.* Hillsdale, NJ: Erlbaum.

Schloss, P. J., & Smith, M. A. (1994). *Applied behavior analysis in the classroom.* Boston: Allyn & Bacon.

Schmidt, R. A., & Bjork, R. A. (1992). New conceptualizations of practice: Common principles in three paradigms suggest new concepts for training. *Psychological Science, 3,* 207-217.

Schmidt, R. A., & Young, D. E. (1987). Transfer of movement control in motor skill learning. In S. M. Cormier & J. D. Hagman (Eds.), *Transfer of learning: Contemporary research and applications.* San Diego: Academic Press.

Schneider, W. (1993). Domain-specific knowledge and memory performance in children. *Educational Psychology Review, 5,* 257-273.

Schneider, W., & Detweiler, M. (1987). A connectionist/control architecture for working memory. In G. H. Bower (Ed.), *The psychology of learning and motivation: Advances in research and theory* (Vol. 21). Orlando: Academic Press.

Schneider, W., Körkel, J., & Weinert, F. E. (1990). Expert knowledge, general abilities, and text processing. In W. Schneider & F. E. Weinert (Eds.), *Interactions among aptitudes, strategies, and knowledge in cognitive performance.* New York: Springer-Verlag.

Schneider, W., & Shiffrin, R. M. (1977). Controlled and automatic human information processing: I. Detection, search, and attention. *Psychological Review, 84,* 1-66.

Schoenfeld, A. H. (1979). Explicit heuristic training as a variable in problem solving performance. *Journal for Research in Mathematics Education, 10,* 173-187.

Schoenfeld, A. H. (1982). Measures of problem-solving performance and problem-solving instruction. *Journal for Research in Mathematics Education, 13,* 31-49.

Schoenfeld, A. H. (1983). Episodes and executive decisions in mathematical problem solving. In R. Lesh & M. Landau (Eds.), *Acquisition of mathematics concepts and processes.* New York: Academic Press.

Schoenfeld, A. H. (1985a). *Mathematical problem solving.* San Diego: Academic Press.

Schoenfeld, A. H. (1985b). Metacognitive and epistemological issues in mathematical understanding. In E. A. Silver (Ed.), *Teaching and learning mathematical problem solving: Multiple research perspectives.* Hillsdale, NJ: Erlbaum.

Schoenfeld, A. H. (1988). When good teaching leads to bad results: The disasters of "well-taught" mathematics courses. *Educational Psychologist, 23,* 145-166.

Schoenfeld, A. H. (1992). Learning to think mathematically: Problem solving, metacognition, and sense-making in mathematics. In D. A. Grouws (Ed.), *Handbook of research on mathematics teaching and learning.* New York: Macmillan.

Schoenfeld, A. H., & Herrmann, D. J. (1982). Problem perception and knowledge structure in expert and novice mathematical problem solvers. *Journal of Experimental Psychology: Learning, Memory, and Cognition, 8,* 484–494.

Schofield, J. W. (1995). Improving intergroup relations among students. In J. A. Banks & C. A. M. Banks (Eds.), *Handbook of research on multicultural education.* New York: Macmillan.

Schofield, N. J., & Kirby, J. R. (1994). Position location on topographical maps: Effects of task factors, training, and strategies. *Cognition and Instruction, 12,* 35–60.

Scholes, R. J., & Kardash, C. M. (1996, April). *The effect of topic interest on the relationship between text-based interest and importance in text comprehension.* Paper presented at the annual meeting of the American Educational Research Association, New York.

Schommer, M. (1990). Effects of beliefs about the nature of knowledge on comprehension. *Journal of Educational Psychology, 82,* 498–504.

Schommer, M. (1994a). An emerging conceptualization of epistemological beliefs and their role in learning. In R. Garner & P. A. Alexander (Eds.), *Beliefs about text and instruction with text.* Hillsdale, NJ: Erlbaum.

Schommer, M. (1994b). Synthesizing epistemological belief research: Tentative understandings and provocative confusions. *Educational Psychology Review, 6,* 293–319.

Schommer, M. (1997). The development of epistemological beliefs among secondary students: A longitudinal study. *Journal of Educational Psychology, 89,* 37–40.

Schramm, W. (1964). *The research on programed instruction: An annotated bibliography.* Washington, DC: U.S. Government Printing Office.

Schraw, G., & Bruning, R. (1995, April). *Reader beliefs and reading comprehension.* Paper presented at the annual meeting of the American Educational Research Association, San Francisco.

Schraw, G., & Moshman, D. (1995). Metacognitive theories. *Educational Psychology Review, 7,* 351–371.

Schraw, G., Potenza, M. T., & Nebelsick-Gullet, L. (1993). Constraints on the calibration of performance. *Contemporary Educational Psychology, 18,* 455–463.

Schroth, M. L. (1992). The effects of delay of feedback on a delayed concept formation transfer task. *Contemporary Educational Psychology, 17,* 78–82.

Schultz, K., & Lochhead, J. (1991). A view from physics. In M. U. Smith (Ed.), *Toward a unified theory of problem solving: Views from the content domains.* Hillsdale, NJ: Erlbaum.

Schunk, D. H. (1981). Modeling and attributional effects on children's achievement: A self-efficacy analysis. *Journal of Educational Psychology, 73,* 93–105.

Schunk, D. H. (1982). Effects of effort attributional feedback on children's perceived self-efficacy and achievement. *Journal of Educational Psychology, 74,* 548–556.

Schunk, D. H. (1983a). Ability versus effort attributional feedback: Differential effects on self-efficacy and achievement. *Journal of Educational Psychology, 75,* 848–856.

Schunk, D. H. (1983b). Developing children's self-efficacy and skills: The roles of social comparative information and goal setting. *Contemporary Educational Psychology, 8,* 76–86.

Schunk, D. H. (1985). Participation in goal setting: Effects on self-efficacy and skills of learning disabled children. *Journal of Special Education, 19,* 307–317.

Schunk, D. H. (1987). Peer models and children's behavioral change. *Review of Educational Research, 57,* 149–174.

Schunk, D. H. (1989a). Self-efficacy and achievement behaviors. *Educational Psychology Review, 1,* 173–208.

Schunk, D. H. (1989b). Self-efficacy and cognitive skill learning. In C. Ames & R. Ames (Eds.), *Research on motivation in education: Vol. 3. Goals and cognitions.* San Diego: Academic Press.

Schunk, D. H. (1989c). Social cognitive theory and self-regulated learning. In B. J. Zimmerman & D. H. Schunk (Eds.), *Self-regulated learning and academic achievement: Theory, research, and practice.* New York: Springer-Verlag.

Schunk, D. H. (1990, April). *Socialization and the development of self-regulated learning: The role of attributions.* Paper presented at the annual meeting of the American Educational Research Association, Boston.

Schunk, D. H. (1991). Goal setting and self-evaluation: A social cognitive perspective on self-regulation. In M. Maehr & P. Pintrich (Eds.), *Advances in motivation and achievement* (Vol. 7). Greenwich, CT: JAI Press.

Schunk, D. H. (1995). Inherent details of self-regulated learning include student perceptions. *Educational Psychologist, 30,* 213–216.

Schunk, D. H. (1996a). Goal and self-evaluative influences during children's cognitive skill learning. *American Educational Research Journal, 33,* 359–382.

Schunk, D. H. (1996b). *Learning theories* (2nd ed.). Upper Saddle River, NJ: Merrill/Prentice Hall.

Schunk, D. H., & Hanson, A. R. (1985). Peer models: Influence on children's self-efficacy and achievement. *Journal of Educational Psychology, 77,* 313–322.

Schunk, D. H., Hanson, A. R., & Cox, P. D. (1987). Peer-model attributes and children's achievement behaviors. *Journal of Educational Psychology, 79,* 54–61.

Schunk, D. H., & Rice, J. (1989). Learning goals and children's reading comprehension. *Journal of Reading Behavior, 21,* 279–293.

Schunk, D. H., & Zimmerman, B. J. (Eds.). (1994). *Self-regulation of learning and performance: Issues and educational applications.* Hillsdale, NJ: Erlbaum.

Schutz, P. A. (1994). Goals as the transactive point between motivation and cognition. In P. R. Pintrich, D. R. Brown, & C. E. Weinstein (Eds.), *Student motivation, cognition, and learning: Essays in honor of Wilbert J. McKeachie.* Hillsdale, NJ: Erlbaum.

Schwartz, B., & Reisberg, D. (1991). *Learning and memory.* New York: W. W. Norton.

Schwartz, S. H. (1971). Modes of representation and problem solving: Well evolved is half solved. *Journal of Experimental Psychology, 91,* 347–350.

Schwebel, A. I., & Cherlin, D. L. (1972). Physical and social distancing in teacher-pupil relationships. *Journal of Educational Psychology, 63,* 543–550.

Scoville, W. B., & Milner, B. (1957). Loss of recent memory after bilateral hippocampal lesions. *Journal of Neurology, Neurosurgery, and Psychiatry, 20,* 11–19.

Sears, R. R., Maccoby, E. E., & Levin, H. (1957). *Patterns of child rearing.* Evanston, IL: Row Peterson.

Seddon, G. M. (1978). The properties of Bloom's taxonomy of educational objectives for the cognitive domain. *Review of Educational Research, 48,* 303–323.

Seligman, M. E. P. (1975). *Helplessness.* San Francisco: W. H. Freeman.

Seligman, M. E. P. (1991). *Learned optimism.* New York: Alfred Knopf.

Seligman, M. E. P., & Campbell, B. A. (1965). Effects of intensity and duration of punishment on extinction of an avoidance response. *Journal of Comparative and Physiological Psychology, 59,* 295-297.

Seligman, M. E. P., & Johnston, J. C. (1973). A cognitive theory of avoidance learning. In F. J. McGuigan & D. B. Lumsden (Eds.), *Contemporary approaches to conditioning and learning.* Washington, DC: V. H. Winston & Sons.

Seligman, M. E. P., & Maier, S. F. (1967). Failure to escape traumatic shock. *Journal of Experimental Psychology, 74,* 1-9.

Selkow, P. (1984). Effects of maternal employment on kindergarten and first-grade children's vocational aspirations. *Sex Roles, 11,* 677-690.

Semb, G. B., & Ellis, J. A. (1994). Knowledge taught in school: What is remembered? *Review of Educational Research, 64,* 253-286.

Semb, G. B., Ellis, J. A., & Araujo, J. (1993). Long-term memory for knowledge learned in school. *Journal of Educational Psychology, 85,* 305-316.

Sergeant, J. (1996). A theory of attention: An information processing perspective. In G. R. Lyon & N. A. Krasnegor (Eds.), *Attention, memory, and executive function.* Baltimore: Paul H. Brookes.

Shachar, H., & Sharan, S. (1994). Talking, relating, and achieving: Effects of cooperative learning and whole-class instruction. *Cognition and Instruction, 12,* 313-353.

Shaffer, D. R. (1988). *Social and personality development* (2nd ed.). Pacific Grove, CA: Brooks/Cole.

Shafto, F., & Sulzbacher, S. (1977). Comparing treatment tactics with a hyperactive preschool child: Stimulant medication and programmed teacher intervention. *Journal of Applied Behavior Analysis, 10,* 13-20.

Shapiro, K. L. (1994). The attentional blink: The brain's "eyeblink." *Current Directions in Psychological Science, 3,* 86-89.

Shapley, K. S. (1994, April). *Metacognition, motivation, and learning: A study of middle school students' use and development of self-regulated learning strategies.* Paper presented at the annual meeting of the American Educational Research Association, New Orleans.

Sheffield, F. D. (1966a). A drive-induction theory of reinforcement. In R. N. Haber (Ed.), *Current research in motivation.* New York: Holt, Rinehart & Winston.

Sheffield, F. D. (1966b). New evidence on the drive-induction theory of reinforcement. In R. N. Haber (Ed.), *Current research in motivation.* New York: Holt, Rinehart & Winston.

Sheffield, F. D., & Roby, T. B. (1950). Reward value of a non-nutritive sweet taste. *Journal of Comparative and Physiological Psychology, 43,* 471-481.

Sheffield, F. D., Roby, T. B., & Campbell, B. A. (1954). Drive reduction versus consummatory behavior as determinants of reinforcement. *Journal of Comparative and Physiological Psychology, 47,* 349-354.

Sheffield, F. D., Wulff, J. J., & Backer, R. (1951). Reward value of copulation without sex drive reduction. *Journal of Comparative and Physiological Psychology, 44,* 3-8.

Shepard, R. N. (1967). Recognition memory for words, sentences, and pictures. *Journal of Verbal Learning and Verbal Behavior, 6,* 156-163.

Shepard, R. N., & Metzler, J. (1971). Mental rotation of three-dimensional objects. *Science, 171,* 701-703.

Sheveland, D. E. (1994, April). *Motivational factors in the development of independent readers.* Paper presented at the annual meeting of the American Educational Research Association, New Orleans.

Shiffrin, R. M., & Cook, J. R. (1978). Short-term forgetting of item and order information. *Journal of Verbal Learning and Verbal Behavior, 17,* 189-218.

Shiffrin, R. M., & Schneider, W. (1977). Controlled and automatic human information processing: II. Perceptual learning, automatic attending, and a general theory. *Psychological Review, 84,* 127-190.

Shimmerlick, S. M., & Nolan, J. D. (1976). Reorganization and the recall of prose. *Journal of Educational Psychology, 68,* 779-786.

Shimoff, E., Catania, A. C., & Matthews, B. A. (1981). Uninstructed human responding: Sensitivity of low-rate performance to schedule contingencies. *Journal of the Experimental Analysis of Behavior, 36,* 207-220.

Short, P. M., & Noblit, G. W. (1985). Missing the mark in in-school suspension: An explanation and proposal. *NASSP Bulletin, 69* (484), 112-116.

Shrager, L., & Mayer, R. E. (1989). Note-taking fosters generative learning strategies in novices. *Journal of Educational Psychology, 81,* 263-264.

Shuell, T. J. (1996). Teaching and learning in a classroom context. In D. C. Berliner & R. C. Calfee (Eds.), *Handbook of educational psychology.* New York: Macmillan.

Shulman, H. G. (1971). Similarity effects in short-term memory. *Psychological Bulletin, 75,* 399-415.

Shulman, H. G. (1972). Semantic confusion errors in short-term memory. *Journal of Verbal Learning and Verbal Behavior, 11,* 221-227.

Shymansky, J. A., Hedges, L. V., & Woodworth, G. (1990). A reassessment of the effects of inquiry-based science curricula of the 60's on student performance. *Journal of Research in Science Teaching, 27,* 127-144.

Sieber, J. E., Kameya, L. I., & Paulson, F. L. (1970). Effect of memory support on the problem-solving ability of test-anxious children. *Journal of Educational Psychology, 61,* 159-168.

Siegel, S., & Andrews, J. M. (1962). Magnitude of reinforcement and choice behavior in children. *Journal of Experimental Psychology, 63,* 337-341.

Siegler, R. S. (1978). The origins of scientific reasoning. In R. S. Siegler (Ed.), *Children's thinking: What develops?* Hillsdale, NJ: Erlbaum.

Siegler, R. S. (1991). *Children's thinking* (2nd ed.). Upper Saddle River, NJ: Prentice Hall.

Siegler, R. S., & Ellis, S. (1996). Piaget on childhood. *Psychological Science, 7,* 211-215.

Signorella, M. L., & Liben, L. S. (1984). Recall and reconstruction of gender-related pictures: Effects of attitude, task difficulty, and age. *Child Development, 55,* 393-405.

Silver, E. A. (1981). Recall of mathematic problem information: Solving related problems. *Journal for Research in Mathematics Education, 12,* 54-64.

Silver, E. A. (1982). Knowledge organization and mathematical problem solving. In F. K. Lester & J. Garofalo (Eds.), *Mathematical problem solving: Issues in research.* Philadelphia: The Franklin Institute Press.

Silver, E. A., & Kenney, P. A. (1995). Sources of assessment information for instructional guidance in mathematics. In T. Romberg (Ed.), *Reform in school mathematics and authentic assessment.* Albany, NY: State University of New York Press.

Silver, E. A., Shapiro, L. J., & Deutsch, A. (1991, April). *Sense-making and the solution of division problems involving remainders: An examination of* students' solution processes and their interpretations of solutions. Paper presented at the annual meeting of the American Educational Research Association, Chicago.

Silverman, W. K., & Kearney, C. A. (1991). *Educational Psychology Review, 3,* 335-361.

Simkin, D. K., Lederer, J. P., & Seligman, M. E. P. (1983). Learned helplessness in groups. *Behaviour Research and Therapy, 21,* 613-622.

Simon, H. A. (1973). The structure of ill-structured problems. *Artificial Intelligence, 4,* 181-201.

Simon, H. A. (1974). How big is a chunk? *Science, 183,* 482-488.

Simon, H. A. (1978). Information-processing theory of human problem solving. In W. K. Estes (Ed.), *Handbook of learning and cognitive processes: Vol. 5. Human information processing.* Hillsdale, NJ: Erlbaum.

Simon, H. A. (1980). Problem solving and education. In D. T. Tuma & F. Reif (Eds.), *Problem-solving and education: Issues in teaching and research.* Hillsdale, NJ: Erlbaum.

Simon, H. A., & Hayes, J. R. (1976). Understanding complex task instructions. In D. Klahr (Ed.), *Cognition and instruction.* Hillsdale, NJ: Erlbaum.

Simons, P. R. J. (1984). Instructing with analogies. *Journal of Educational Psychology, 76,* 513-527.

Sinclair, K. E. (1971). The influence of anxiety on several measures of classroom performance. In E. Gaudry & C. D. Spielberger (Eds.), *Anxiety and educational achievement.* Sydney, Australia: Wiley.

Singley, M. K., & Anderson, J. R. (1989). *The transfer of cognitive skill.* Cambridge, MA: Harvard University Press.

Sizer, T. R. (1992). *Horace's school: Redesigning the American high school.* Boston: Houghton Mifflin.

Skiba, R., & Raison, J. (1990). Relationship between the use of timeout and academic achievement. *Exceptional Children, 57,* 36-46.

Skinner, B. F. (1938). *The behavior of organisms: An experimental analysis.* Englewood Cliffs, NJ: Prentice Hall.

Skinner, B. F. (1948a). Superstition in the pigeon. *Journal of Experimental Psychology, 38,* 168-172.

Skinner, B. F. (1948b). *Walden Two.* New York: Macmillan.

Skinner, B. F. (1953). *Science and human behavior.* New York: Macmillan.

Skinner, B. F. (1954). The science of learning and the art of teaching. *Harvard Educational Review, 24,* 86-97.

Skinner, B. F. (1957). *Verbal behavior.* New York: Appleton-Century-Crofts.

Skinner, B. F. (1958). Reinforcement today. *American Psychologist, 13,* 94-99.

Skinner, B. F. (1963). Behaviorism at fifty. *Science, 140* (3570), 951-958.

Skinner, B. F. (1966a). An operant analysis of problem solving. In B. Kleinmuntz (Ed.), *Problem solving: Research, method, and theory.* New York: Wiley.

Skinner, B. F. (1966b). What is the experimental analysis of behavior? *Journal of the Experimental Analysis of Behavior, 9,* 213-218.

Skinner, B. F. (1967). B. F. Skinner. . . An autobiography. In E. G. Boring & G. Lindzey (Eds.), *A history of psychology in autobiography* (Vol. 5). New York: Irvington.

Skinner, B. F. (1968). *The technology of teaching.* New York: Appleton-Century-Crofts.

Skinner, B. F. (1971). *Beyond freedom and dignity.* New York: Alfred Knopf.

Skinner, B. F. (1973). The free and happy student. *Phi Delta Kappan, 55,* 13-16.

Skinner, B. F. (1989). The origins of cognitive thought. *American Psychologist, 44,* 13-18.

Skinner, B. F., & Epstein, R. (1982). *Skinner for the classroom.* Champaign, IL: Research Press.

Slavin, R. E. (1983a). *Cooperative learning.* New York: Longman.

Slavin, R. E. (1983b). When does cooperative learning increase student achievement? *Psychological Bulletin, 94,* 429-445.

Slavin, R. E. (1987). Mastery learning reconsidered. *Review of Educational Research, 57,* 175-213.

Slavin, R. E. (1990a). *Cooperative learning: Theory, research, and practice.* Upper Saddle River, NJ: Prentice Hall.

Slavin, R. E. (1990b). Mastery learning reconsidered. *Review of Educational Research, 60,* 300-302.

Slusher, M. P., & Anderson, C. A. (1996). Using causal persuasive arguments to change beliefs and teach new information: The mediating role of explanation availability and evaluation bias in the acceptance of knowledge. *Journal of Educational Psychology, 88,* 110-122.

Small, M. Y., Lovett, S. B., & Scher, M. S. (1993). Pictures facilitate children's recall of unillustrated expository prose. *Journal of Educational Psychology, 85,* 520-528.

Smith, E. E. (1988). Concepts and thought. In R. J. Sternberg & E. E. Smith (Eds.), *The psychology of human thought.* New York: Cambridge University Press.

Smith, E. E., Shoben, E. J., & Rips, L. J. (1974). Structure and process in semantic memory: A feature model of semantic decisions. *Psychological Review, 81,* 214-241.

Smith, E. L. (1991). A conceptual change model of learning science. In S. M. Glynn, R. H. Yeany, & B. K. Britton (Eds.), *The psychology of learning science.* Hillsdale, NJ: Erlbaum.

Smith, K., Johnson, D. W., & Johnson, R. T. (1981). Can conflict be constructive? Controversy versus concurrence seeking in learning groups. *Journal of Educational Psychology, 73,* 651-663.

Smith, R. E., & Smoll, F. L. (1997). Coaching the coaches: Youth sports as a scientific and applied behavioral setting. *Current Directions in Psychological Science, 6* (1), 16-21.

Smith, S. M., Glenberg, A., & Bjork, R. A. (1978). Environmental context and human memory. *Memory and Cognition, 6,* 342-353.

Smoke, K. L. (1932). An objective study of concept formation. *Psychological Monographs, 42* (Whole No. 191).

Sneider, C., & Pulos, S. (1983). Children's cosmographies: Understanding the earth's shape and gravity. *Science Education, 67,* 205-221.

Snow, R. E. (1989). Aptitude-treatment interaction as a framework for research on individual differences in learning. In P. L. Ackerman, R. J. Sternberg, & R. Glaser (Eds.), *Learning and individual differences: Advances in theory and research.* New York: W. H. Freeman.

Snow, R. E. (1994). Abilities in academic tasks. In R. J. Sternberg & R. K. Wagner (Eds.), *Mind in context: Interactionist perspectives on human intelligence.* Cambridge, UK: Cambridge University Press.

Snow, R. E., Corno, L., & Jackson, D., III. (1996). Individual differences in affective and conative functions. In D. C. Berliner & R. C. Calfee (Eds.), *Handbook of educational psychology.* New York: Macmillan.

Snowman, J. (1986). Learning tactics and strategies. In G. D. Phye & T. Andre (Eds.), *Cognitive classroom learning: Understanding, thinking, and problem solving.* Orlando: Academic Press.

Snyder, M., & Swann, W. B. (1978). Behavioral confirmation in social interaction: From social perception to social reality. *Journal of Experimental Social Psychology, 14,* 148-162.

Sokal, R. R. (1977). Classification: Purposes, principles, progress, prospects. In P. N. Johnson-Laird & P. C. Wason

(Eds.), *Thinking: Readings in cognitive science*. Cambridge, UK: Cambridge University Press.

Solnick, J. V., Rincover, A., & Peterson, C. R. (1977). Some determinants of the reinforcing and punishing effects of timeout. *Journal of Applied Behavior Analysis, 10*, 415-424.

Solomon, R. L., & Wynne, L. C. (1954). Traumatic avoidance learning: Acquisition in normal dogs. *Psychological Monographs, 67* (Whole No. 354).

Sosniak, L. A., & Stodolsky, S. S. (1994). Making connections: Social studies education in an urban fourth-grade classroom. In J. Brophy (Ed.), *Advances in research on teaching: (Vol. 4). Case studies of teaching and learning in social studies*. Greenwich, CT: JAI Press.

Spandel, V. (1997). Reflections on portfolios. In G. D. Phye (Ed.), *Handbook of academic learning: Construction of knowledge*. San Diego: Academic Press.

Spaulding, C. L. (1992). *Motivation in the classroom*. New York: McGraw-Hill.

Spence, K. W. (1956). *Behavior theory and conditioning*. New Haven, CT: Yale University Press.

Sperling, G. (1960). The information available in brief visual presentations. *Psychological Monographs, 74* (Whole No. 498).

Sperling, G. (1967). Successive approximations to a model for short-term memory. *Acta Psychologia, 27*, 285-292.

Spielberger, C. D. (1966). The effects of anxiety on complex learning in academic achievement. In C. D. Spielberger (Ed.), *Anxiety and behavior*. New York: Academic Press.

Spielberger, C. D., & DeNike, L. D. (1966). Descriptive behaviorism versus cognitive theory in verbal operant conditioning. *Psychological Review, 73*, 306-326.

Spilich, G. J., Vesonder, G. T., Chiesi, H. L., & Voss, J. F. (1979). Text processing of domain-related information for individuals with high and low domain knowledge. *Journal of Verbal Learning and Verbal Behavior, 18*, 275-290.

Spires, H. A. (1990, April). *Learning from a lecture: Effects of comprehension monitoring*. Paper presented at the annual meeting of the American Educational Research Association, Boston.

Spires, H. A., Donley, J., & Penrose, A. M. (1990, April). *Prior knowledge activation: Inducing text engagement in reading to learn*. Paper presented at the annual meeting of the American Educational Research Association, Boston.

Spiro, R. J. (1977). Remembering information from text: The "state of schema" approach. In R. C. Anderson, R. J. Spiro, & W. E. Montague (Eds.), *Schooling and the acquisition of knowledge*. Hillsdale, NJ: Erlbaum.

Spiro, R. J. (1980a). Accommodative reconstruction in prose recall. *Journal of Verbal Learning and Verbal Behavior, 19*, 84-95.

Spiro, R. J. (1980b). Constructive processes in prose comprehension and recall. In R. J. Spiro, B. C. Bruce, & W. F. Brewer (Eds.), *Theoretical issues in reading comprehension*. Hillsdale, NJ: Erlbaum.

Spivey, N. N. (1997). *The constructivist metaphor: Reading, writing, and the making of meaning*. San Diego: Academic Press.

Sporer, S. (1991). Deep-deeper-deepest? Encoding strategies and the recognition of human faces. *Journal of Experimental Psychology: Learning, Memory, and Cognition, 17*, 323-333.

Stacey, K. (1992). Mathematical problem solving in groups: Are two heads better than one? *Journal of Mathematical Behavior, 11*, 261-275.

Staddon, J. E. R., & Higa, J. J. (1991). Temporal learning. In G. H. Bower (Ed.), *The psychology of learning and motivation: Advances in research and theory* (Vol. 27). San Diego: Academic Press.

Standing, L. (1973). Learning 10,000 pictures. *Quarterly Journal of Experimental Psychology, 25*, 207-222.

Standing, L., Conezio, J., & Haber, R. N. (1970). Perception and memory for pictures: Single-trial learning of 2560 visual stimuli. *Psychonomic Science, 19*, 73-74.

Stanovich, K. E., & Cunningham, A. E. (1991). Reading as constrained reasoning. In R. J. Sternberg & P. A. Frensch (Eds.), *Complex problem solving: Principles and mechanisms*. Hillsdale, NJ: Erlbaum.

Stazyk, E. H., Ashcraft, M. H., & Hamann, M. S. (1982). A network approach to mental multiplication. *Journal of Experimental Psychology: Learning, Memory, and Cognition, 8*, 320-335.

Steele, B. G., & Pollack, C. B. (1968). A psychiatric study of parents who abuse infants and small children. In R. E. Helfer & C. H. Kempe (Eds.), *The battered child*. Chicago: University of Chicago Press.

Steffensen, M. S., Joag-Dev, C., & Anderson, R. C. (1979). A cross-cultural perspective on reading comprehension. *Reading Research Quarterly, 15*, 10-29.

Stein, A. H. (1971). The effects of sex-role standards for achievement and sex-role preference on three determinants of achievement motivation. *Developmental Psychology, 4*, 219-231.

Stein, B. S. (1978). Depth of processing reexamined: The effects of the precision of encoding and test appropriateness. *Journal of Verbal Learning and Verbal Behavior, 17*, 165-174.

Stein, B. S. (1989). Memory and creativity. In J. A. Glover, R. R. Ronning, & C. R. Reynolds, (Eds.), *Handbook of creativity*. New York: Plenum Press.

Stein, B. S., & Bransford, J. D. (1979). Constraints on effective elaboration: Effects of precision and subject generation. *Journal of Verbal Learning and Verbal Behavior, 18*, 769-777.

Stein, B. S., Bransford, J. D., Franks, J. J., Owings, R. A., Vye, N. J., & McGraw, W. (1982). Differences in the precision of self-generated elaborations. *Journal of Experimental Psychology: General, 111*, 399-405.

Steinmetz, S. K. (1977). *The cycle of violence*. New York: Praeger.

Stensvold, M. S., & Wilson, J. T. (1990). The interaction of verbal ability with concept mapping in learning from a chemistry laboratory activity. *Science Education, 74*, 473-480.

Stepans, J. (1991). Developmental patterns in students' understanding of physics concepts. In S. M. Glynn, R. H. Yeany, & B. K. Britton (Eds.), *The psychology of learning science*. Hillsdale, NJ: Erlbaum.

Stephens, C. E., Pear, J. J., Wray, L. D., & Jackson, G. C. (1975). Some effects of reinforcement schedules in teaching picture names to retarded children. *Journal of Applied Behavior Analysis, 8*, 435-447.

Stepich, D. A., & Newby, T. J. (1988). Analogical instruction within the information processing paradigm: Effective means to facilitate learning. *Instructional Science, 17*, 129-144.

Sternberg, R. J. (1985). *Beyond IQ: A triarchic theory of human intelligence*. Cambridge, UK: Cambridge University Press.

Sternberg, R. J. (1996). *Cognitive psychology*. Fort Worth, TX: Harcourt Brace.

Sternberg, R. J., & Davidson, J. E. (1982). Componential analysis and componential theory. *Behavioural and Brain Sciences, 53*, 352-353.

Sternberg, R. J., & Davidson, J. E. (1983). Insight in the gifted. *Educational Psychologist, 18*, 51-57.

519

Sternberg, R. J., & Frensch, P. A. (1993). Mechanisms of transfer. In D. K. Detterman & R. J. Sternberg (Eds.), *Transfer on trial: Intelligence, cognition, and instruction.* Norwood, NJ: Ablex.

Sternberg, R. J., & Wagner, R. K. (Eds.). (1994). *Mind in context: Interactionist perspectives on human intelligence.* Cambridge, UK: Cambridge University Press.

Sternberg, S. (1966). High-speed scanning in human memory. *Science, 153,* 652-654.

Steuer, F. B., Applefield, J. M., & Smith, R. (1971). Televised aggression and the interpersonal aggression of preschool children. *Journal of Experimental Child Psychology, 11,* 442-447.

Stevens, R. J., & Slavin, R. E. (1995). The cooperative elementary school: Effects of students' achievement, attitudes, and social relations. *American Educational Research Journal, 32,* 321-351.

Stevenson, H. C., & Fantuzzo, J. W. (1986). The generality and social validity of a competency-based self-control training intervention for underachieving students. *Journal of Applied Behavior Analysis, 19,* 269-276.

Stevenson, H. W., Chen, C., & Uttal, D. H. (1990). Beliefs and achievement: A study of black, white, and Hispanic children. *Child Development, 61,* 508-523.

Stiggins, R. J. (1994). *Student-centered classroom assessment.* New York: Prentice Hall/Merrill.

Stinessen, L. (1975). Conditions which influence acquisition and application of verbal representations in problem solving. *Psychological Reports, 36,* 35-42.

Stipek, D. J. (1984). Sex differences in children's attributions for success and failure on math and spelling tests. *Sex Roles, 11,* 969-981.

Stipek, D. J. (1993). *Motivation to learn: From theory to practice* (2nd ed.). Boston: Allyn & Bacon.

Stipek, D. J. (1996). Motivation and instruction. In D. C. Berliner & R. C. Calfee (Eds.), *Handbook of educational psychology.* New York: Macmillan.

Stipek, D. J., & Gralinski, H. (1990, April). *Gender differences in children's achievement-related beliefs and emotional responses to success and failure in math.* Paper presented at the annual meeting of the American Educational Research Association, Boston.

Stipek, D. J., & Kowalski, P. S. (1989). Learned helplessness in task-orienting versus performance-orienting testing conditions. *Journal of Educational Psychology, 81,* 384-391.

Stodolsky, S. S., Salk, S., & Glaessner, B. (1991). Student views about learning math and social studies. *American Educational Research Journal, 28,* 89-116.

Stokes, T. F., & Baer, D. M. (1977). An implicit technology of generalization. *Journal of Applied Behavior Analysis, 10,* 349-367.

Strage, A., Christopoulos, J., Rohwer, W. D., Thomas, J. W., Delucchi, J. J., & Curley, R. G. (1988, April). *Grade-level differences in study activities as a function of perceived and observed course characteristics.* Paper presented at the American Educational Research Association, New Orleans.

Strauss, M. A., Gelles, R. J., & Steinmetz, S. K. (1980). *Behind closed doors: Violence in the American family.* Garden City, NY: Doubleday.

Strike, K. A., & Posner, G. J. (1992). A revisionist theory of conceptual change. In R. A. Duschl & R. J. Hamilton (Eds.), *Philosophy of science, cognitive psychology, and educational theory and practice.* New York: State University of New York Press.

Sue, S., & Chin, R. (1983). The mental health of Chinese-American children: Stressors and resources. In G. J. Powell (Ed.), *The psychosocial development of minority children.* New York: Brunner/Mazel.

Suina, J. H., & Smolkin, L. B. (1994). From natal culture to school culture to dominant society culture: Supporting transitions for Pueblo Indian students. In P. M. Greenfield & R. R. Cocking (Eds.), *Crosscultural roots of minority child development.* Hillsdale, NJ: Erlbaum.

Sulin, R. A., & Dooling, D. J. (1974). Intrusions of a thematic idea in retention of prose. *Journal of Experimental Psychology, 103,* 255-262.

Sullivan, J. S. (1989). Planning, implementing, and maintaining an effective in-school suspension program. *Clearing House, 62,* 409-410.

Sulzer-Azaroff, B. (1981). Issues and trends in behavior modification in the classroom. In S. W. Bijou & R. Ruiz (Eds.), *Behavior modification: Contributions to education.* Hillsdale, NJ: Erlbaum.

Sund, R. B. (1976). *Piaget for educators.* Columbus, OH: Merrill.

Sussman, D. M. (1981). PSI: Variations on a theme. In S. W. Bijou & R. Ruiz (Eds.), *Behavior modification: Contributions to education.* Hillsdale, NJ: Erlbaum.

Swan, K., Mitrani, M., Guerrero, F., Cheung, M., & Schoener, J. (1990, April). *Perceived locus of control and computer-based instruction.* Paper presented at the annual meeting of the American Educational Research Association, Boston.

Swanson, H. L. (1987). Information processing theory and learning disabilities: An overview. *Journal of Learning Disabilities, 20,* 3-7.

Swanson, H. L., O'Connor, J. E., & Cooney, J. B. (1990). An information processing analysis of expert and novice teachers' problem solving. *American Educational Research Journal, 27,* 533-556.

Sweller, J., & Chandler, P. (1994). Why some material is difficult to learn. *Cognition and Instruction, 12,* 185-233.

Sweller, J., & Levine, M. (1982). Effects of goal specificity on means-end analysis and learning. *Journal of Experimental Psychology: Learning, Memory, and Cognition, 8,* 463-474.

Swenson, L. C. (1980). *Theories of learning: Traditional perspectives/contemporary developments.* Belmont, CA: Wadsworth.

Tanner, B. A., & Zeiler, M. (1975). Punishment of self-injurious behavior using aromatic ammonia as the aversive stimulus. *Journal of Applied Behavior Analysis, 8,* 53-57.

Taylor, B. M. (1982). Text structure and children's comprehension and memory for expository material. *Journal of Educational Psychology, 74,* 323-340.

Taylor, J. C., & Romanczyk, R. G. (1994). Generating hypotheses about the function of student problem behavior by observing teacher behavior. *Journal of Applied Behavior Analysis, 27,* 251-265.

Taylor, M. J., & Kratochwill, T. R. (1978). Modification of preschool children's bathroom behaviors by contingent teacher attention. *Journal of School Psychology, 16,* 64-71.

Tennyson, C. L., Tennyson, R. D., & Rothen, W. (1980). Content structure and instructional control strategies as design variables in concept acquisition. *Journal of Educational Psychology, 72,* 499-505.

Tennyson, R. D., & Cocchiarella, M. J. (1986). An empirically based instructional design theory for teaching concepts. *Review of Educational Research, 56,* 40-71.

Tennyson, R. D., & Park, O. (1980). The teaching of concepts: A review of instructional design literature. *Review of Educational Research, 50,* 55-70.

Tennyson, R. D., & Tennyson, C. L. (1975). Rule acquisition design strategy variables: Degree of instance divergence, sequence, and instance analysis. *Journal of Educational Psychology, 67,* 852-859.

Tennyson, R. D., Youngers, J., & Suebsonthi, P. (1983). Concept learning by children using instructional presentation forms for prototype formation and classification-skill development. *Journal of Educational Psychology, 75,* 280-291.

Terrell, G., & Ware, R. (1961). Role of delay of reward in speed of size and form discrimination learning in childhood. *Child Development, 32,* 409-415.

Tessler, M., & Nelson, K. (1994). Making memories: The influence of joint encoding on later recall by young children. *Consciousness and Cognition, 3,* 307-326.

Thapar, A., & Greene, R. (1993). Evidence against a short-term store account of long-term recency effects. *Memory and Cognition, 21,* 329-337.

Tharp, R. G. (1989). Psychocultural variables and constants: Effects on teaching and learning in schools. *American Psychologist, 44,* 349-359.

Théberge, C. L. (1994, April). *Small-group vs. whole-class discussion: Gaining the floor in science lessons.* Paper presented at the annual meeting of the American Educational Research Association, New Orleans..

Thelen, D. (1989). Memory and American history. *Journal of American History, 75,* 1117-1129.

Thiagarajan, S. (1989). Interactive lectures: Seven more strategies. *Performance and Instruction, 28* (2), 35-37.

Thomas, E. L., & Robinson, H. A. (1972). *Improving reading in every class: A sourcebook for teachers.* Boston: Allyn & Bacon.

Thomas, J. W. (1993). Expectations and effort: Course demands, students' study practices, and academic achievement. In T. M. Tomlinson (Ed.), *Motivating students to learn: Overcoming barriers to high achievement.* Berkeley, CA: McCutchan.

Thomas, S., & Oldfather, P. (1997). Intrinsic motivations, literacy, and assessment practices: "That's my grade. That's me." *Educational Psychologist, 32,* 107-123.

Thompson, A. G., & Thompson, P. W. (1989). Affect and problem solving in an elementary school mathematics classroom. In D. B. McLeod & V. M. Adams (Eds.), *Affect and mathematical problem solving: A new perspective.* New York: Springer-Verlag.

Thompson, H., & Carr, M. (1995, April). *Brief metacognitive intervention and interest as predictors of mem-*

ory for text. Paper presented at the annual meeting of the American Educational Research Association, San Francisco.

Thompson, R., & McConnell, J. (1955). Classical conditioning in the planarian, *Dugesia dorotocephala. Journal of Comparative and Physiological Psychology, 48,* 65-68.

Thorndike, E. L. (1898). Animal intelligence: An experimental study of the associative processes in animals. *Psychological Review Monograph Supplement, 2* (8).

Thorndike, E. L. (1903). *Educational psychology.* New York: Lemcke & Buechner.

Thorndike, E. L. (1911). *Animal intelligence.* New York: Macmillan.

Thorndike, E. L. (1913). *Educational psychology: The psychology of learning* (Vol. 2). New York: Teachers College Press.

Thorndike, E. L. (1924). Mental discipline in high school studies. *Journal of Educational Psychology, 15,* 1-22; 83-98.

Thorndike, E. L. (1932a). *The fundamentals of learning.* New York: Teachers College Press.

Thorndike, E. L. (1932b). Reward and punishment in animal learning. *Comparative Psychology Monograph, 8* (39).

Thorndike, E. L. (1935). *The psychology of wants, interests, and attitudes.* New York: Appleton-Century-Crofts.

Thorndike, E. L., & Woodworth, R. S. (1901). The influence of improvement in one mental function upon the efficiency of other functions. *Psychological Review, 8,* 247-261, 384-395,553-564.

Thrailkill, N. J., & Ormrod, J. E. (1994, April). *Facilitating lecture recall: Effects of embedded imagery-evoking phrases on memory for proximal and non-proximal material.* Paper presented at the annual meeting of the American Educational Research Association, New Orleans.

Thyne, J. M. (1963). *The psychology of learning and techniques of teaching.* London: University of London Press.

Timberlake, W., & Allison, J. (1974). Response deprivation: An empirical approach to instrumental performance. *Psychological Review, 81,* 146-164.

Tirosh, D., & Graeber, A. O. (1990). Evoking cognitive conflict to explore preservice teachers' thinking about division. *Journal for Research in Mathematics Education, 21,* 98-108.

Titcomb, A. L., & Reyna, V. F. (1995). Memory interference and misinformation effects. In F. N. Dempster & C. J. Brainerd (Eds.), *Interference and inhibition in cognition.* San Diego: Academic Press.

Tobias, S. (1980). Anxiety and instruction. In I. G. Sarason (Ed.), *Test anxiety: Theory, research, and applications.* Hillsdale, NJ: Erlbaum.

Tobias, S. (1985). Test anxiety: Interference, defective skills, and cognitive capacity. *Educational Psychologist, 20,* 135-142.

Tobias, S. (1994). Interest, prior knowledge, and learning. *Review of Educational Research, 64,* 37-54.

Tobin, D., & Fox, L. H. (1980). Career interests and career education: A key to change. In L. H. Fox, L. Brody, & D. Tobin (Eds.), *Women and the mathematical mystique.* Baltimore: Johns Hopkins University Press.

Tobin, K. (1986). Student task involvement and achievement in process-oriented science activities. *Science Education, 70* (1), 61-72.

Tobin, K. (1987). The role of wait time in higher cognitive level learning. *Review of Educational Research, 57,* 69-95.

Toglia, M. P. (1996). Recovered memories: Lost and found? In K. Pezdek & W. P. Banks (Eds.), *The recovered memory/false memory debate.* San Diego: Academic Press.

Tolman, E. C. (1932). *Purposive behavior in animals and men.* New York: Century.

Tolman, E. C. (1938). The determiners of behavior at a choice point. *Psychological Review, 45,* 1-41.

Tolman, E. C. (1942). *Drives toward war.* New York: Appleton-Century.

Tolman, E. C. (1959). Principles of purposive behavior. In S. Koch (Ed.), *Psychology: A study of a science* (Vol. 2). New York: McGraw-Hill.

Tolman, E. C., & Honzik, C. H. (1930). Introduction and removal of reward, and maze performance in rats. *University of California Publications in Psychology, 4,* 257-275.

Tolman, E. C., Ritchie, B. F., & Kalish, D. (1946). Studies in spatial learning: I. Orientation and the short-cut. *Journal of Experimental Psychology, 36,* 13-24.

Torrance, E. P., & Myers, R. E. (1970). *Creative learning and teaching.* New York: Dodd, Mead & Company.

Tourniaire, F., & Pulos, S. (1985). Proportional reasoning: A review of the literature. *Educational Studies in Mathematics, 16,* 181-204.

Trachtenberg, D. (1974). Student tasks in text material. What cognitive skills do they tap? *Peabody Journal of Education, 52,* 54-57.

Trawick-Smith, J. (1997). *Early childhood development: A multicultural perspective.* Upper Saddle River, NJ: Merrill/Prentice Hall.

Treisman, A. M. (1964). Verbal cues, language, and meaning in selective attention. *American Journal of Psychology, 77,* 215-216.

Trenholme, I. A., & Baron, A. (1975). Intermediate and delayed punishment of human behavior by loss of reinforcement. *Learning and Motivation, 6,* 62-79.

Triandis, H. C. (1995). *Individualism and collectivism.* Boulder, CO: Westview Press.

Trowbridge, M. H., & Cason, H. (1932). An experimental study of Thorndike's theory of learning. *Journal of General Psychology, 7,* 245-252.

Tryon, G. S. (1980). The measurement and treatment of test anxiety. *Review of Educational Research, 50,* 343-372.

Tudge, J. (1990). Vygotsky, the zone of proximal development, and peer collaboration: Implications for classroom practice. In L. C. Moll (Ed.), *Vygotsky and education: Instructional implications and applications of sociohistorical psychology.* Cambridge, UK: Cambridge University Press.

Tudor, R. M. (1995). Isolating the effects of active responding in computer-based instruction. *Journal of Applied Behavior Analysis, 28,* 343-344.

Tulving, E. (1962). Subjective organization in free recall of "unrelated" words. *Psychological Review, 69,* 344-354.

Tulving, E. (1968). Theoretical issues in free recall. In T. R. Dixon & D. L. Horton (Eds.), *Verbal behavior and general behavior theory.* Englewood Cliffs, NJ: Prentice Hall.

Tulving, E. (1975). Ecphoric processes in recall and recognition. In J. Brown (Ed.), *Recall and recognition.* London: Wiley.

Tulving, E. (1983). *Elements of episodic memory.* Oxford, UK: Oxford University Press.

Tulving, E. (1991). Concepts of human memory. In L. R. Squire, N. M. Weinberger, G. Lynch, & J. L. McGaugh (Eds.), *Organization and locus of change.* New York: Oxford University Press.

Tulving, E. (1993). What is episodic memory? *Current Directions in Psychological Science, 2,* 67-70.

Tulving, E., & Psotka, J. (1971). Retroactive inhibition in free recall: Inaccessibility of information available in the memory store. *Journal of Experimental Psychology, 87,* 1-8.

Tulving, E., & Thomson, D. M. (1971). Retrieval processes in recognition memory: Effects of associative context. *Journal of Experimental Psychology, 87,* 116-124.

Tulving, E., & Thomson, D. M. (1973). Encoding specificity and retrieval processes in episodic memory. *Psychological Review, 80,* 352-373.

Turnbull, C. M. (1961). *The forest people.* New York: Simon & Schuster.

Turner, J. C. (1995). The influence of classroom contexts on young children's motivation for literacy. *Reading Research Quarterly, 30,* 410-441.

Turnure, J., Buium, N., & Thurlow, M. (1976). The effectiveness of interrogatives for promoting verbal elaboration productivity in young children. *Child Development, 47,* 851-855.

Turvey, M. T., & Kravetz, S. (1970). Retrieval from iconic memory with shape as the selection criterion. *Perception and Psychophysics, 8,* 171-172.

Tversky, A., & Kahneman, D. (1973). Availability: A heuristic for judging frequency and probability. *Cognitive Psychology, 5,* 207-232.

Tversky, A., & Kahneman, D. (1974). Judgment under uncertainty: Heuristics and biases. *Science, 185,* 1124-1131.

Tversky, B. (1981). Distortions in memory for maps. *Cognitive Psychology, 13,* 407-433.

Tyler, B. (1958). Expectancy for eventual success as a factor in problem solving behavior. *Journal of Educational Psychology, 49,* 166-172.

Uhl, C. N. (1973). Eliminating behavior with omission and extinction after varying amounts of training. *Animal Learning and Behavior, 1,* 237-240.

Uhl, C. N., & Garcia, E. E. (1969). Comparison of omission with extinction in response elimination in rats. *Journal of Comparative and Physiological Psychology, 69,* 554-562.

Ullmann, L. P., & Krasner, L. A. (1969). *A psychological approach to abnormal behavior.* Englewood Cliffs, NJ: Prentice Hall.

Underwood, B. J. (1948). "Spontaneous recovery" of verbal associations. *Journal of Experimental Psychology, 38,* 429-439.

Underwood, B. J. (1954). Studies of distributed practice: XII. Retention following varying degrees of original learning. *Journal of Experimental Psychology, 47,* 294-300.

Underwood, B. J. (1957). Interference and forgetting. *Psychological Review, 64,* 49-60.

Underwood, B. J. (1961). Ten years of massed practice on distributed practice. *Psychological Review, 68,* 229-247.

Underwood, B. J. (1983). *Attributes of memory.* Glenview, IL: Scott, Foresman.

Underwood, B. J., & Erlebacher, A. H. (1965). Studies of coding in verbal behavior. *Psychological Monographs, 79 (Whole No. 606).*

Underwood, B. J., Kapelak, S., & Malmi, R. (1976). The spacing effect: Additions to the theoretical and empirical puzzles. *Memory and Cognition, 4,* 391-400.

Underwood, B. J., & Schulz, R. W. (1960). *Meaningfulness and verbal learning.* Philadelphia: J. B. Lippincott.

Urdan, T. C., & Maehr, M. L. (1995). Beyond a two-goal theory of motivation and achievement: A case for social goals. *Review of Educational Research, 65,* 213-243.

van der Broek, P. (1990). Causal inferences and the comprehension of narrative text. In A. C. Graessner & G. H. Bower (Eds.), *Inferences and text comprehension. The psychology of learning and motivation: Advances in research and theory* (Vol. 25). Orlando: Academic Press.

van Dijk, T. A., & Kintsch, W. (1983). *Strategies of discourse comprehension.* New York: Academic Press.

Van Houten, R., Nau, P., MacKenzie-Keating, S., Sameoto, D., & Colavecchia, B. (1982). An analysis of some variables influencing the effectiveness of reprimands. *Journal of Applied Behavior Analysis, 15,* 65-83.

Van Meter, P., Yokoi, L., & Pressley, M. (1994). College students' theory of notetaking derived from their perceptions of notetaking. *Journal of Educational Psychology, 86,* 323-338.

Van Patten, J. R., Chao, C. I., & Reigeluth, C. M. (1986). A review of strategies for sequencing and synthesizing information. *Review of Educational Research, 56,* 437-472.

Van Rossum, E. J., & Schenk, S. M. (1984). The relationship between learning conception, study strategy, and learning outcome. *British Journal of Educational Psychology, 54,* 73-83.

VanSledright, B., & Brophy, J. (1992). Storytelling, imagination, and fanciful elaboration in children's historical reconstructions. *American Educational Research Journal, 29,* 837-859.

Vaughan, W. (1988). Formation of equivalence sets in pigeons. *Journal of Experimental Psychology: Animal Behavior Processes, 14,* 36–42.

Vaughn, B. J., & Horner, R. H. (1997). Identifying instructional tasks that occasion problem behaviors and assessing the effects of student versus teacher choice among these tasks. *Journal of Applied Behavior Analysis, 30,* 299–312.

Vernon, M. D. (1969). *Human motivation.* Cambridge, UK: Cambridge University Press.

Veroff, J., McClelland, L., & Ruhland, D. (1975). Varieties of achievement motivation. In M. T. S. Mednick, S. S. Tangri, & L. W. Hoffman (Eds.), *Women and achievement: Social and motivational analyses.* New York: Halsted.

Viken, R. J., & McFall, R. M. (1994). Paradox lost: Implications of contemporary reinforcement theory for behavior therapy. *Current Directions in Psychological Science, 3,* 121–125.

Vosniadou, S. (1991). Conceptual development in astronomy. In S. M. Glynn, R. H. Yeany, & B. K. Britton (Eds.), *The psychology of learning science.* Hillsdale, NJ: Erlbaum.

Vosniadou, S. (1994). Universal and culture-specific properties of children's mental models of the earth. In L. A. Hirschfeld & S. A. Gelman (Eds.), *Mapping the mind: Domain specificity in cognition and culture.* Cambridge, UK: Cambridge University Press.

Vosniadou, S., & Brewer, W. F. (1987). Theories of knowledge restructuring in development. *Review of Educational Research, 57,* 51–67.

Voss, J. F. (1987). Learning and transfer in subject-matter learning: A problem-solving model. *International Journal of Educational Research, 11,* 607–622.

Voss, J. F., Greene, T. R., Post, T. A., & Penner, B. D. (1983). Problem-solving skill in the social sciences. In G. H. Bower (Ed.), *The psychology of learning and motivation* (Vol. 17). New York: Academic Press.

Voss, J. F., & Schauble, L. (1992). Is interest educationally interesting? An interest-related model of learning. In K. A. Renninger, S. Hidi, & A. Krapp (Eds.), *The role of interest in learning and development.* Hillsdale, NJ: Erlbaum.

Voss, J. F., Tyler, S. W., & Yengo, L. A. (1983). Individual differences in the solving of social science problems. In R. F. Dillon & R. R. Schmeck (Eds.), *Individual differences in cognition.* New York: Academic Press.

Voss, J. F., Wolfe, C. R., Lawrence, J. A., & Engle, R. A. (1991). From representation to decision: An analysis of problem solving in international relations. In R. J. Sternberg & P. A. Frensch (Eds.), *Complex problem solving: Principles and mechanisms.* Hillsdale, NJ: Erlbaum.

Vurpillot, E., & Ball, W. A. (1979). The concept of identity and children's selective attention. In G. A. Hale & M. Lewis (Eds.), *Attention and cognitive development.* New York: Plenum Press.

Vygotsky, L. S. (1962). *Thought and language* (E. Haufmann & G. Vakar, Eds. and Trans.). Cambridge, MA: M.I.T. Press.

Vygotsky, L. S. (1978). *Mind in society: The development of higher psychological processes.* Cambridge, MA: Harvard University Press.

Vygotsky, L. S. (1987). *The collected works of L. S. Vygotsky* (R. W. Rieber & A. S. Carton, Eds.). New York: Plenum Press.

Vygotsky, L. S. (1997). *Educational psychology.* Boca Raton, FL: St. Lucie Press.

Waddill, P. J., McDaniel, M. A., & Einstein, G. O. (1988). Illustrations as adjuncts to prose: A text-appropriate processing approach. *Journal of Educational Psychology, 80,* 457–464.

Wade, S. E. (1983). A synthesis of the research for improving reading in the social studies. *Review of Educational Research, 53,* 461–497.

Wade, S. E. (1992). How interest affects learning from text. In K. A. Renninger, S. Hidi, & A. Krapp (Eds.), *The role of interest in learning and development.* Hillsdale, NJ: Erlbaum.

Wadsworth, B. J. (1989). *Piaget's theory of cognitive and affective development* (4th ed.). New York: Longman.

Wagner, A. R. (1976). Priming in STM: An information processing mechanism for self-generated or retrieval-generated depression in performance. In T. J. Tighe & R. N. Leaton (Eds.), *Habituation: Perspectives from child development and animal behavior.* Hillsdale, NJ: Erlbaum.

Wagner, A. R. (1978). Expectancies and the priming of STM. In S. H. Hulse, H. Fowler, & W. K. Honig (Eds.), *Cognitive processes in animal behavior.* Hillsdale, NJ: Erlbaum.

Wagner, A. R. (1979). Habituation and memory. In A. Dickenson & R. A. Boakes (Eds.), *Mechanisms of learning and motivation.* Hillsdale, NJ: Erlbaum.

Wagner, A. R. (1981). SOP: A model of automatic memory processing in animal behavior. In N. E. Spear & R. R. Miller (Eds.), *Information processing in animals: Memory mechanisms.* Hillsdale, NJ: Erlbaum.

Wagner, A. R., & Rescorla, R. A. (1972). Inhibition in Pavlovian conditioning: Applications of a theory. In R. A. Boakes & M. S. Halliday (Eds.), *Inhibition and learning.* New York: Academic Press.

Wagner, E. D. (1989, February). *Graphic facilitation effects: Instructional strategies to improve intentional learning outcomes.* Paper presented at the annual meeting of the Association for Educational Communications and Technology, Dallas.

Wahler, R. G., & Fox, J. J. (1981). Setting events in applied behavior analysis: Toward a conceptual and methodological expansion. *Journal of Applied Behavior Analysis, 14,* 327–338.

Walberg, H. J., & Uguroglu, M. (1980). Motivation and educational productivity: Theories, results, and implications. In L. J. Fyans, Jr. (Ed.), *Achievement motivation: Recent trends in theory and research.* New York: Plenum Press.

Walker, H. M., Mattsen, R. H., & Buckley, N. K. (1971). The functional analysis of behavior within an experimental class setting. In W. C. Becker (Ed.), *An empirical basis for change in education.* Chicago: Science Research Associates.

Walker, J. E., & Shea, T. M. (1995). *Behavior management: A practical approach for educators* (6th ed.). Englewood Cliffs, NJ: Merrill/Prentice Hall.

Wallas, G. (1926). *The art of thought.* New York: Harcourt Brace Jovanovich.

Walters, G. C., & Grusec, J. E. (1977). *Punishment.* San Francisco: W. H. Freeman.

Walters, R. H. (1964). Delay of reinforcement gradients in children's learning. *Psychonomic Science, 1,* 307–308.

Walters, R. H., & Parke, R. D. (1964). Influence of response consequences to a social model on resistance to deviation. *Journal of Experimental Child Psychology, 1,* 269–280.

Walters, R. H., Parke, R. D., & Cane, V. A. (1965). Timing of punishment and the observation of consequences to others as determinants of response inhibition. *Journal of Experimental Child Psychology, 2,* 10–30.

Walters, R. H., & Thomas, E. L. (1963). Enhancement of punitiveness by visual and audiovisual displays. *Canadian Journal of Psychology, 17,* 244-255.

Walters, R. H., Thomas, E. L., & Acker, W. (1962). Enhancement of punitive behavior by audio-visual displays. *Science, 136,* 872-873.

Walton, G. E., & Bower, T. G. R. (1993). Newborns form "prototypes" in less than 1 minute. *Psychological Science, 4,* 203-205.

Wang, M. C., & Stiles, B. (1976). An investigation of children's concept of self-responsibility for their school learning. *American Educational Research Journal, 13,* 159-179.

Ward, M. H., & Baker, B. L. (1968). Reinforcement therapy in the classroom. *Journal of Applied Behavior Analysis, 1,* 323-328.

Ward, T. B., Vela, E., & Haas, S. D. (1990). Children and adults learn family-resemblance categories analytically. *Child Development, 61,* 593-605.

Ward, T. J., Jr. (1991, April). The effects of field articulation and interestingness on text processing. In G. Schraw (Chair), *Cognitive processing and text comprehension in specific knowledge domains.* Symposium presented at the annual meeting of the American Educational Research Association, Chicago.

Wasserman, E. A. (1993). Comparative cognition: Toward a general understanding of cognition in animals. *Psychological Science, 4,* 156-161.

Wasserman, E. A., DeVolder, C. L., & Coppage, D. J. (1992). Non-similarity-based conceptualization in pigeons via secondary or mediated generalization. *Psychological Science, 3,* 374-379.

Waters, H. S. (1982). Memory development in adolescence: Relationships between metamemory, strategy use, and performance. *Journal of Experimental Child Psychology, 33,* 183-195.

Watkins, M. J., & Watkins, O. C. (1974). Processing of recency items for free-recall. *Journal of Experimental Psychology, 102,* 488-493.

Watson, J. B. (1913). Psychology as the behaviorist views it. *Psychological Review, 20,* 158-177.

Watson, J. B. (1914). *Behavior: An introduction to comparative psychology.* New York: Holt, Rinehart & Winston.

Watson, J. B. (1916). The place of a conditioned reflex in psychology. *Psychological Review, 23,* 89-116.

Watson, J. B. (1919). *Psychology from the standpoint of a behaviorist.* Philadelphia: J. B. Lippincott.

Watson, J. B. (1925). *Behaviorism.* New York: W. W. Norton.

Watson, J. B., & Rayner, R. (1920). Conditioned emotional reactions. *Journal of Experimental Psychology, 3,* 1-14.

Watts, G. H., & Anderson, R. C. (1971). Effects of three types of inserted questions on learning from prose. *Journal of Educational Psychology, 62,* 387-394.

Weaver, C. A., III, & Kelemen, W. L. (1997). Judgments of learning at delays: Shifts in response patterns or increased metamemory accuracy? *Psychological Science, 8,* 318-321.

Weaver, C. A., III, & Kintsch, W. (1991). Expository text. In R. Barr, M. L. Kamil, P. B. Mosenthal, & P. D. Pearson (Eds.), *Handbook of reading research* (Vol. 2). New York: Longman.

Webb, N. M. (1989). Peer interaction and learning in small groups. *International Journal of Educational Research, 13,* 21-39.

Webb, N. M., & Farivar, S. (1994). Promoting helping behavior in cooperative small groups in middle school mathematics. *American Educational Research Journal, 31,* 369-395.

Webb, N. M., & Palincsar, A. S. (1996). Group processes in the classroom. In D. C. Berliner & R. C. Calfee (Eds.), *Handbook of educational psychology.* New York: Macmillan.

Webber, J., Scheuermann, B., McCall, C., & Coleman, M. (1993). Research on self-monitoring as a behavior management technique in special education classrooms: A descriptive review. *Remedial and Special Education, 14* (2), 38-56.

Wegman, C. (1985). *Psychoanalysis and cognitive psychology.* London: Academic Press.

Weiner, B. (1979). A theory of motivation for some classroom experiences. *Journal of Educational Psychology, 71,* 3-25.

Weiner, B. (1980). *Human motivation.* New York: Holt, Rinehart & Winston.

Weiner, B. (1984). Principles for a theory of student motivation and their application within an attributional framework. In R. Ames & C. Ames (Eds.), *Research on motivation in education: Vol. 1. Student motivation.* Orlando: Academic Press.

Weiner, B. (1986). *An attributional theory of motivation and emotion.* New York: Springer-Verlag.

Weiner, B. (1994). Ability versus effort revisited: The moral determinants of achievement evaluation and achievement as a moral system. *Educational Psychologist, 29,* 163-172.

Weiner, B., Russell, D., & Lerman, D. (1978). Affective consequences of causal ascriptions. In J. Harvey, W. Ickes, & R. Kidd (Eds.), *New directions in attribution research* (Vol. 2). Hillsdale, NJ: Erlbaum.

Weiner, B., Russell, D., & Lerman, D. (1979). The cognition-emotion process in achievement-related contexts. *Journal of Personality and Social Psychology, 37,* 1211-1220.

Weinert, F. E., & Helmke, A. (1995). Learning from wise Mother Nature or Big Brother Instructor: The wrong choice as seen from an educational perspective. *Educational Psychologist, 30,* 135-142.

Weinraub, M., Clemens, L. P., Sockloff, A., Ethridge, T., Gracely, E., & Myers, B. (1984). The development of sex role stereotypes in the third year: Relationships to gender labeling, gender identity, sex-typed toy preference, and family characteristics. *Child Development, 55,* 1493-1503.

Weinstein, C. E. (1978). Elaboration skills as a learning strategy. In H. F. O'Neil, Jr. (Ed.), *Learning strategies.* New York: Academic Press.

Weinstein, C. E., Goetz, E. T., & Alexander, P. A. (Eds.). (1988). *Learning and study strategies: Issues in assessment, instruction, and evaluation.* San Diego: Academic Press.

Weinstein, C. E., Hagen, A. S., & Meyer, D. K. (1991, April). *Work smart. . . not hard: The effects of combining instruction in using strategies, goal using, and executive control on attributions and academic performance.* Paper presented at the annual meeting of the American Educational Research Association, Chicago.

Weinstein, C. E., & Mayer, R. E. (1986). The teaching of learning strategies. In M. C. Wittrock (Ed.), *Handbook of research on teaching* (3rd ed.). New York: Macmillan.

Weinstein, M. (1969). Achievement motivation and risk preference. *Journal of Personality and Social Psychology, 13,* 153-173.

Weisberg, R. W., DiCamillo, M., & Phillips, D. (1979). Transferring old associations to new situations: A nonautomatic process. *Journal of Verbal Learning and Verbal Behavior, 17,* 219-228.

Weiss, K. (1983). In-school suspension—time to work, not socialize. *NASSP Bulletin, 67* (464), 132-133.

Weiss, M. R., & Klint, K. A. (1987). "Show and tell" in the gymnasium: An investigation of developmental differences in modeling and verbal rehearsal of motor skills. *Research Quarterly for Exercise and Sport, 58,* 234-241.

Weisz, J. R. (1986). Understanding the developing understanding of control. In M. Perlmutter (Ed.), *Cognitive perspectives on children's social and behavioral development. Minnesota Symposia on Child Psychology* (Vol. 18). Hillsdale, NJ: Erlbaum.

Weisz, J. R., & Cameron, A. M. (1985). Individual differences in the student's sense of control. In C. Ames & R. Ames (Eds.), *Research on motivation in education: Vol. 2. The classroom milieu.* Orlando: Academic Press.

Welch, G. J. (1985). Contingency contracting with a delinquent and his family. *Journal of Behavior Therapy and Experimental Psychiatry, 16,* 253-259.

Welford, A. T. (1977). Serial reaction-times, continuity of task, single-channel effects, and age. In S. Dornic (Ed.), *Attention and performance VI.* Hillsdale, NJ: Erlbaum.

Wellman, H. M., & Gelman, S. A. (1992). Cognitive development: Foundational theories of core domains. In M. R. Rosenzweig & L. W. Porter (Eds.), *Annual review of psychology* (Vol. 43). Palo Alto, CA: Annual Reviews.

Wells, G. L., & Loftus, E. F. (Eds.). (1984). *Eyewitness testimony.* Cambridge, UK: Cambridge University Press.

Welsh, R. S. (1976). Severe parental punishment and delinquency: A developmental theory. *Journal of Clinical Child Psychology, 5,* 17-23.

Wentzel, K. .R. (1989). Adolescent classroom grades, standards for performance, and academic achievement: An interactionist perspective. *Journal of Educational Psychology, 81,* 131-142.

Wertheimer, M. (1912). Experimentelle Studien über das Sehen von Bewegung. *Zeitschrift für Psychologie, 61,* 161-265.

Wertheimer, M. (1945). *Productive thinking.* New York: Harper.

Wertheimer, M. (1959). *Productive thinking* (enl. ed.,Michael Wertheimer, Ed.). New York: Harper.

West, R. F., & Stanovich, K. E. (1991). The incidental acquisition of information from reading. *Psychological Science, 2,* 325-329.

Whimbey, A., & Lochhead, J. (1986). *Problem solving and comprehension* (4th ed.). Hillsdale, NJ: Erlbaum.

White, J. J., & Rumsey, S. (1994). Teaching for understanding in a third-grade geography lesson. In J. Brophy (Ed.), *Advances in research on teaching: Vol. 4. Case studies of teaching and learning in social studies.* Greenwich, CT: JAI Press.

White, R. (1959). Motivation reconsidered: The concept of competence. *Psychological Review, 66,* 297-333.

Whitehead, A. N. (1929). *The aims of education and other essays.* New York: Macmillan.

Whitley, B. E., Jr., & Frieze, I. H. (1985). Children's causal attributions for success and failure in achievement settings: A meta-analysis. *Journal of Educational Psychology, 77,* 608-616.

Whitlock, C. (1966). Note on reading acquisition: An extension of laboratory principles. *Journal of Experimental Child Psychology, 3,* 83-85.

Wickelgren, W. A. (1973). The long and the short of memory. *Psychological Bulletin, 80,* 425-438.

Wickelgren, W. A. (1974). *How to solve problems: Elements of a theory of problems and problem solving.* San Francisco: W. H. Freeman.

Wielkiewicz, R. M. (1986). *Behavior management in the schools: Principles and procedures.* New York: Pergamon Press.

Wigfield, A. (1994). Expectancy-value theory of achievement motivation: A developmental perspective. *Educational Psychology Review, 6,* 49-78.

Wigfield, A. (1997). Reading motivation: A domain-specific approach to motivation. *Educational Psychologist, 32,* 59-68.

Wigfield, A., & Eccles, J. (1992). The development of achievement task values: A theoretical analysis. *Developmental Review, 12,* 265-310.

Wigfield, A., Eccles, J. S., & Pintrich, P. R. (1996). Development between the ages of 11 and 25. In D. C. Berliner & R. C. Calfee (Eds.), *Handbook of educational psychology.* New York: Macmillan.

Wigfield, A., & Meece, J. L. (1988). Math anxiety in elementary and secondary school students. *Journal of Educational Psychology, 80,* 210-216.

Wiggins, G. (1989). The futility of trying to teach everything of importance. *Educational Leadership, 47* (3), 44-48,57-59.

Wilkins, A. T. (1971). Conjoint frequency, category size, and categorization time. *Journal of Verbal Learning and Verbal Behavior, 10,* 382-385.

Williams, S. B. (1938). Resistance to extinction as a function of the number of reinforcements. *Journal of Experimental Psychology, 23,* 506-522.

Wilson, J. E. (1988). Implications of learning strategy research and training: What it has to say to the practitioner. In Weinstein, C. E., Goetz, E. T., & Alexander, P. A. (Eds.), *Learning and study strategies: Issues in assessment, instruction, and evaluation.* San Diego: Academic Press.

Wilson, P. S. (1988, April). The relationship of students' definitions and example choices in geometry. In D. Tirosh (Chair), *The role of inconsistent ideas in learning mathematics.* Symposium conducted at the annual meeting of the American Educational Research Association, New Orleans.

Wilson, P. T., & Anderson, R. C. (1986). What they don't know will hurt them: The role of prior knowledge in comprehension. In J. Orasanu (Ed.), *Reading comprehension: From research to practice.* Hillsdale, NJ: Erlbaum.

Wine, J. D. (1980). Cognitive-attentional theory of test anxiety. In I. G. Sarason (Ed.), *Test anxiety: Theory, research, and applications.* Hillsdale, NJ: Erlbaum.

Winer, G. A., & Cottrell, J. E. (1996). Does anything leave the eye when we see? Extramission beliefs of children and adults. *Current Directions in Psychological Science, 5,* 137-142.

Wingfield, A., & Byrnes, D. L. (1981). *The psychology of human memory.* New York: Academic Press.

Winik, M. (1994). *Telling.* New York: Random House.

Winn, W. (1991). Learning from maps and diagrams. *Educational Psychology Review, 3,* 211-247.

Winne, P. H. (1995a). Inherent details in self-regulated learning. *Educational Psychologist, 30,* 173-187.

Winne, P. H. (1995b). Self-regulation is ubiquitous but its forms vary with knowledge. *Educational Psychologist, 30,* 223-228.

Winne, P. H., & Marx, R. W. (1989). A cognitive-processing analysis of motivation within classroom tasks. In C. Ames & R. Ames (Eds.), *Research on motivation in education: Vol. 3. Goals and cognitions.* San Diego: Academic Press.

Winograd, E., & Neisser, U. (1992). *Affect and accuracy in recall: Studies of "flashbulb" memories.* Cambridge, UK: Cambridge University Press.

Winston, P. (1973). Learning to identify toy block structures. In R. L. Solso (Ed.), *Contemporary issues in cognitive psychology: The Loyola Symposium.* Washington, DC: V. H. Winston.

Witt, J. C., Elliott, S. N., & Gresham, F. M. (Eds.). (1988). *Handbook of behavior therapy in education.* New York: Plenum Press.

Wittgenstein, L. (1958). *Philosophical investigations* (2nd ed.). Oxford, UK: Blackwell.

Wittrock, M. C. (1986). Learning science by generating new conceptions from old ideas. In L. H. T. West & A. L. Pines (Eds.), *Cognitive structure and conceptual change.* Orlando: Academic Press.

Wittrock, M. C. (1994). Generative science teaching. In P. J. Fensham, R. F. Gunstone, & R. T. White (Eds.), *The content of science: A constructivist approach to its teaching and learning.* London: Falmer Press.

Wittrock, M. C., & Alesandrini, K. (1990). Generation of summaries and analogies and analytic and holistic abilities. *American Educational Research Journal, 27,* 489-502.

Wixson, K. K. (1984). Level of importance of post-questions and children's learning from text. *American Educational Research Journal, 21,* 419-433.

Wixted, J. T., & Ebbesen, E. B. (1991). On the form of forgetting. *Psychological Science, 2,* 409-415.

Wlodkowski, R. J. (1978). *Motivation and teaching: A practical guide.* Washington, DC: National Education Association.

Wlodkowski, R. J., & Ginsberg, M. B. (1995). *Diversity and motivation: Culturally responsive teaching.* San Francisco: Jossey-Bass.

Wolf, M. M., Braukmann, C. J., & Ramp, K. A. (1987). Serious delinquent behavior as part of a significantly handicapping condition: Cures and supportive environments. *Journal of Applied Behavior Analysis, 20,* 347-359.

Wolf, T. M., & Cheyne, J. A. (1972). Persistence of effects of live behavioral, televised behavioral, and live verbal models on resistance to temptation. *Child Development, 43,* 1429-1436.

Wolfe, J. B. (1936). Effectiveness of token-rewards for chimps. *Comparative Psychology Monographs, 12* (60).

Woloshyn, V. E., Pressley, M., & Schneider, W. (1992). Elaborative-interrogation and prior-knowledge effects on learning of facts. *Journal of Educational Psychology, 84,* 115-124.

Wolpe, J. (1958). *Psychotherapy by reciprocal inhibition.* Stanford, CA: Stanford University Press.

Wolpe, J. (1969). *The practice of behavior therapy.* Oxford, UK: Pergamon.

Wolpe, J., & Plaud, J. J. (1997). Pavlov's contributions to behavior therapy: The obvious and the not so obvious. *American Psychologist, 52,* 966-972.

Wolters, C. A. (1997, March). *Self-regulated learning and college students' regulation of motivation.* Paper presented at the annual meeting of the American Educational Research Association, Chicago.

Wong, B. Y. L. (1985). Self-questioning instructional research: A review. *Review of Educational Research, 55,* 227-268.

Wood, C. J., Schau, C., & Fiedler, M. L. (1990, April). *Attribution, motivation, and self-perception: A comparative study—elementary, middle, and high school students.* Paper presented at the annual meeting of the American Educational Research Association, Boston.

Wood, D., Bruner, J. S., & Ross, G. (1976). The role of tutoring in problem-solving. *Journal of Child Psychology and Psychiatry, 17,* 89-100.

Wood, D., Wood, H., Ainsworth, S., & O'Malley, C. (1995). On becoming a tutor: Toward an ontogenetic model. *Cognition and Instruction, 13,* 565-581.

Wood, E., Willoughby, T., Reilley, S., Elliott, S., & DuCharme, M. (1994, April). *Evaluating students' acquisition of factual material when studying independently or with a partner.* Paper presented at the annual meeting of the American Educational Research Association, New Orleans.

Woodworth, R. S. (1918). *Dynamic psychology.* New York: Columbia University Press.

Wulbert, M., & Dries, R. (1977). The relative efficacy of methylphenidate (Ritalin) and behavior-modification techniques in the treatment of a hyperactive child. *Journal of Applied Behavior Analysis, 10,* 21-31.

Yager, S., Johnson, D. W., & Johnson, R. T. (1985). Oral discussion, group to individual transfer, and achievement in cooperative learning groups. *Journal of Educational Psychology, 77,* 60-66.

Yarmey, A. D. (1973). I recognize your face but I can't remember your name: Further evidence on the tip-of-the-tongue phenomenon. *Memory and Cognition, 1,* 287-290.

Yee, D. K., & Eccles, J. S. (1988). Parent perceptions and attributions for children's math achievement. *Sex Roles, 19,* 317-333.

Yell, M. L. (1993). Cognitive behavior therapy. In T. J. Zirpoli & K. J. Melloy, *Behavior management: Applications for teachers and parents.* Columbus, OH: Macmillan.

Yerkes, R. M., & Dodson, J. D. (1908). The relation of strength of stimulus to rapidity of habit-formation. *Journal of Comparative Neurology and Psychology, 18,* 459-482.

Yokoi, L. (1997, March). *The developmental context of notetaking: A qualitative examination of notetaking at the secondary level.* Paper presented at the annual meeting of the American Educational Research Association, Chicago.

Zacks, R. T., Hasher, L., & Hock, H. S. (1986). Inevitability and automaticity: A response to Fisk. *American Psychologist, 41,* 216-218.

Zahorik, J. A. (1994, April). *Making things interesting.* Paper presented at the annual meeting of the American Educational Research Association, New Orleans.

Zajonc, R. B. (1980). Feeling and thinking: Preferences need no inferences. *American Psychologist, 35,* 151-175.

Zaragoza, M. S., & Mitchell, K. J. (1996). Repeated exposure to suggestion and the creation of false memories. *Psychological Science, 7,* 294-300.

Zazdeh, L. A., Fu, K. S., Tanak, K., & Shimura, M. (Eds.). (1975). *Fuzzy sets and their applications to cognitive and decision processes.* New York: Academic Press.

Zechmeister, E. B., & Nyberg, S. E. (1982). *Human memory: An introduction to research and theory.* Monterey, CA: Brooks/Cole.

Zeiler, M. D. (1971). Eliminating behavior with reinforcement. *Journal of the Experimental Analysis of Behavior, 16,* 401-405.

Zeitz, C. M. (1994). Expert-novice differences in memory, abstraction, and reasoning in the domain of literature. *Cognition and Instruction, 12,* 277-312.

Zeller, A. F. (1950). An experimental analogue of repression: II. The effect of individual failure and success on memory measured by relearning. *Journal of Experimental Psychology, 40,* 411-422.

Zentall, T. R., Sutton, J. E., & Sherburne, L. M. (1996). True imitative learning in pigeons. *Psychological Science, 7,* 343-346.

Zhu, X., & Simon, H. A. (1987). Learning mathematics from examples and by doing. *Cognition and Instruction, 4,* 137-166.

Ziegler, S. G. (1987). Effects of stimulus cueing on the acquisition of ground-strokes by beginning tennis players. *Journal of Applied Behavior Analysis, 20,* 405-411.

Zimmerman, B. J. (1989). Models of self-regulated learning and academic achievement. In B. J. Zimmerman & D. H. Schunk (Eds.), *Self-regulated learning and academic achievement: Theory, research, and practice.* New York: Springer-Verlag.

Zimmerman, B. J. (1994, April). *From modeling to self-efficacy: A social cognitive view of students' development of motivation to self-regulate.* Paper presented at the annual meeting of the American Educational Research Association, New Orleans.

Zimmerman, B. J. (1995). Self-regulation involves more than metacognition: A social cognitive perspective. *Educational Psychologist, 30,* 217-221.

Zimmerman, B. J., & Bandura, A. (1994). Impact of self-regulatory influences on writing course attainment. *American Educational Research Journal, 31,* 845-862.

Zimmerman, B. J., Bandura, A., & Martinez-Pons, M. (1992). Self-motivation for academic attainment: The role of self-efficacy beliefs and personal goal setting. *American Educational Research Journal, 29,* 663-676.

Zimmerman, B. J., & Risemberg, R. (1997). Self-regulatory dimensions of academic learning and motivation. In G. D. Phye (Ed.), *Handbook of academic learning: Construction of knowledge.* San Diego: Academic Press.

Zirin, G. (1974). How to make a boring thing more boring. *Child Development, 45,* 232-236.

Zirpoli, T. J., & Melloy, K. J. (1993). *Behavior management: Applications for teachers and parents.* Columbus, OH: Macmillan.

Zola-Morgan, S. M., & Squire, L. R. (1990). The primate hippocampal formation: Evidence for a time-limited role in memory storage. *Science, 250,* 288-290.

Zook, K. B. (1991). Effects of analogical processes on learning and misrepresentation. *Educational Psychology Review, 3,* 41-72.

Zook, K. B., & Di Vesta, F. J. (1991). Instructional analogies and conceptual misrepresentations. *Journal of Educational Psychology, 83,* 246-252.

Zuckerman, G. (1994). A pilot study of a 10-day course in cooperative learning for beginning Russian first graders. *Elementary School Journal, 94,* 405-420.

Zuriff, G. E. (1985). *Behaviorism: A conceptual reconstruction.* New York: Columbia University Press.

Author Index

Subject Index

Abstract analog, 235
Abstract concepts, 245
Acclimation, 259
Accommodation, 156
Achievement, need for, 417–19
Acquired drives, 15, 411
Acquisition, vicarious, 122
Actions, encoding of information in terms of, 236–38
Activation, memory, 198–99
Active avoidance learning, 96
Active responding, 73
Activity reinforcers, 47
Actual developmental level, 161
Advance organizers in expository instruction, 288–89
Affect, 407
    role of, 419–26
Affiliation, need for, 416–17
Aggression, 126
Algorithms, 358–59
    combining, 371–72
Ambiguous stimulus, 207, 227
Analogies, 289, 290
    drawing, 375–76
Anxiety, 421
    common sources of, 425–26
    debilitating, 424
    effects of, 422–25
    facilitating, 424
    mathematics, 426
    state, 421–22
    test, 425–26
    trait, 422
Appeal of reinforcement, 49

Appearance, encoding of information in terms of, 234–35
Applied behavior analysis (ABA), 82
    adding cognitive component to, 88
    components of, 82–85
    effectiveness of, 88
    with large groups, 85–88
Apprenticeships, 386, 399–400
Approval, need for, 417
Arguments, 236
Articulation, 400
Associate cues, 268–69
Associationistic theories, 238
Associative bias, 30
Attention, 5, 128
    factors influencing, 182–83
    as limited capacity, 186–87
    nature of, 184–86
    role of, 181–87
Attributes, 247
Attribution retraining studies, 455–56
Attributions, 443
    changing, 454–56
    dimensions underlying people's, 443–46
    effects of, 446–49
    explanatory style, 453
    factors influencing development of, 449–53
    of others, 451–53
    theory of, 433
Authentic activities, 386, 400–401
    effectiveness of, 401–2
Authentic assessment, 314–15
Autobiographic memory, 232n
Automaticity, 274, 379–80
    development of, 274–76

547